Psychology
of
Language

Psychology of Language

ALLAN PAIVIO
University of Western Ontario

IAN BEGG
McMaster University

PRENTICE-HALL, INC., ENGLEWOOD CLIFFS, NEW JERSEY 07632

Library of Congress Cataloging in Publication Data

Paivio, Allan.
   Psychology of language.

   Bibliography: p.
   Includes index.
   1. Psycholinguistics. I. Begg, Ian,
joint author. II. Title.
P37.P35   1981   401'.9   80–21607
ISBN 0–13–735951–9

Printed in the United States of America

10 9 8 7 6 5 4 3 2 1

Editorial production and interior design by Marina Harrison
Cover design by Carol Zawislak
Manufacturing buyer: Edmund W. Leone

Acknowledgments for figures and quoted materials on page 406

Prentice-Hall International, Inc., *London*
Prentice-Hall of Australia Pty. Limited, *Sydney*
Prentice-Hall of Canada, Ltd., *Toronto*
Prentice-Hall of India Private Limited, *New Delhi*
Prentice-Hall of Japan, Inc., *Tokyo*
Prentice-Hall of Southeast Asia Pte. Ltd., *Singapore*
Whitehall Books Limited, *Wellington, New Zealand*

In memoriam, to our fathers:

AKU PAIVIO, poet, 1879–1967
JOHN ARTHUR BEGG, entomologist, 1916–1965

contents

3

LINGUISTIC APPROACHES TO THE STUDY OF LANGUAGE   27

4

PSYCHOLOGICAL APPROACHES TO THE STUDY OF LANGUAGE   56

5

THE ANALYSIS OF MEANING   75

8

LANGUAGE AND MEMORY   171

Memory Effects of Behavioral Variables   174

Effects of Linguistic Variables   179

Effects of Cognitive Variables   185

9

LANGUAGE PRODUCTION   201

preface

Our aim in this book is to provide a comprehensive introduction to the psychology of language—comprehensive in content and approach. The content ranges from such standard topics as perception, comprehension, and production of language to such specialized and currently hot research areas as metaphor, bilingualism, and the neuropsychology of language. In our broad approach, we lean toward historical and interdisciplinary concerns by emphasizing facts and issues of lasting interest to psychologists, linguists, and other students of language.

Our reading of language research over the last few decades suggested to us that several distinct perspectives have guided the work of psychologists and linguists. We describe those theoretical perspectives and then use them as frameworks to understand the facts of language behavior and why certain questions about that behavior are of particular interest. This means that the reader encounters contemporary issues in an historical context that reveals why the issues remain interesting and, where the issues are controversial, what the shooting is all about.

The emphasis on general theoretical and historical perspectives may also help the student to avoid being trapped by the latest methodological and theoretical fads. In the language sciences as in other areas of life, fads come and go, sometimes distressingly quickly. The research fashions of the 1950s became outdated in the 1960s, and the issues that were the rage of the 1960s brought yawns in the 1970s. And the beat goes on, so that we cannot predict which of the life-and-death issues of today will be used to bore future generations of students, perhaps in as little as five years from now. This is precisely why we need an historical perspective. As the fashions change, some facts and issues decline to the level of esoterica. From a viewpoint sobered by time, however, much of what remains after the shooting has died down is worthy of serious consideration. Each decade leaves a legacy of persistent problems, effective variables, and fruitful theoretical ideas. We have tried to emphasize those enduring contributions that we feel will be useful guides to the student embarking on the exciting journey into the psychology of language.

The book was designed for university students with some background in psychology, but not necessarily linguistics. It will be useful for upper-year under-

graduate students of psychology, as well as for graduate students in psychology, linguistics, or allied areas concerned with the scientific study of language.

ACKNOWLEDGMENTS

We are grateful to the many colleagues and students (or former students) who read and commented on sections of this book at various stages of its evolution. An early version was used as a mimeographed text by several graduate and undergraduate classes. Many of the students in those classes provided helpful feedback. Detailed suggestions were made by Professors Marc Marschark and Albert Katz, as well as John te Linde, Alain Desrochers, and John Mitterer. A number of colleagues with special expertise in particular areas of language study were kind enough to comment on the relevant chapters: Professors Doreen Kimura (Chapter 15), Wallace Lambert (Chapters 13 and 15), Stephen Lupker (Chapter 14), Peter Denny (Chapter 3), William Yovetich (Chapter 3), and S. Winokur (Chapter 4). We also thank Professors Charles Clifton, Dan Slobin and an anonymous reviewer who evaluated the penultimate version for Prentice-Hall. Their criticisms and suggestions, stemming from perspectives that differ from our own, helped us to improve the final version in content as well as style.

We are also indebted to the following people for their technical assistance. Early drafts were typed by Elizabeth Henderson. Later versions were typed by Bev Pitt, assisted by Wendy Tasker as well as Dianne Yaxley, Mary Jane Deary, and Sheila Campbell. The index was painstakingly prepared by Ginny Begg, who also found time to provide helpful comments as a reader. We thank all of them for the efficiency with which they met our sometimes unreasonable deadlines.

It is fitting as well that we acknowledge the financial support provided to each of us by granting agencies. Our individual and collaborative research on the language-related topics cited in this book were supported by grants A0087 and A8125 from the Natural Sciences and Engineering Research Council of Canada (formerly the National Research Council). One of us (Paivio) was also supported by a Leave Fellowship from the Social Sciences and Humanities Research Council of Canada during the last year of the writing enterprise. This book is one of the tangible outcomes of those grants.

Finally, we thank our wives, Kathleen and Ginny, as well as our children, for their patient support and encouragement over the years in which we devoted increasing amounts of time to the completion of this book.

Allan Paivio, London, Ontario

Ian Begg, Hamilton, Ontario

problems
and
perspectives

1

In this book we seek to reach a scientific understanding of the nature of language and its use by intelligent beings. The issues and approaches are psychological, since they are based on facts and theories of language behavior as studied through systematic observation and experimentation. Studying language can be fascinating as well as challenging. It is fascinating because language is a spectacular example of species-specific behavior, a crowning achievement of evolution. Although some aspects of language behavior have parallels in the behavior of other species, no other has yet achieved even the rudiments of human language on its own, let alone produced a Shakespeare. The task is challenging because no other behavior is quite so complex and difficult to unravel. We may not recognize the difficulties at the outset because we are so skilled at using our native language that we simply take it for granted. The problems become more apparent, however, when we encounter other languages that sound very different from our own as well as from each other. As inhabitants of cosmopolitan cities or as world travelers, we may be overwhelmed by the profusion of foreign languages that variously assault and caress our ears. We are struck, on the one hand, by their incomprehensibility and strangeness and, on the other, by the fact that even young children are fluent in the language of their community, using it skillfully to make their ideas and desires known.

Potential Obstacles to Scientific Language Study

Our fluency in a shared language is a mixed blessing when we approach the scientific study of language. It gives us a useful basis for beginning our study, but it might also lead to narrowness and bias in our approach. On the positive side, our linguistic intuitions may alert us to important questions. We might notice, for example, that we typically use language as a medium in which to frame and assemble messages, but the messages are usually about something not itself linguistic in nature. From the child's request for dinner to the poet's search for truth and beauty, the message refers to something outside of language, and we will understand the message only if we share that extralinguistic knowledge. It follows that an important question about language use is how extralinguistic knowledge—knowledge

of the world of concrete objects and events—relates to the language in which that knowledge can be expressed. On the negative side, our fluency and intuitions can also hinder our study of language. We may not be surprised to find that a simple act, such as raising an arm, for example, requires a complex interaction of neurological and muscular activity; yet we may not be so ready to learn that another superficially simple act, such as uttering "What's for dinner?" also requires a complex interaction, this time of linguistic and psychological activity. There is absolutely no guarantee that all useful analyses of language behavior will appeal to our intuitions. When they do not, we have no recourse but to struggle with the counterintuitive complexities if we are to get anywhere in our attempt to understand language scientifically.

A second problem created by our fluency is that many of us are truly fluent in only one language. There is a danger in presuming that any new language will be structured and used in the same way as our own. In school we learned grammar, a useful device for parsing sentences into such mundane constituents as nouns and verbs and into more esoteric gerunds and future pluperfect subjunctives. We shall see later that it is more valuable to approach a language structure with an open mind, discovering the most useful and natural categories into which the language can be partitioned, than it is to force that language into the categories and types of our own native language. The categories discovered in this fashion may even give us a better perspective from which to understand our own language.

Perspectives in the Study of Language Behavior

We have said that human language is a complex phenomenon. One day we may have a single comprehensive viewpoint that accommodates all that complexity, but to date, there is no such viewpoint. It is necessary, nonetheless, to adopt some perspective, and we have chosen three different ones, each offering a somewhat different slant on the phenomenon.

We shall describe these presently, but first, why do we need perspectives at all? The reason is that intelligent language use is too broad in scope to be understood at a glance. We shall find it necessary to divide language behavior into component skills, such as speech comprehension, and to fragment those activities into even smaller components, such as the perception of short speech segments. While focusing our study in that way, we could lose sight of the forest in the trees unless we also take a broader perspective. Each of the three perspectives that we adopt helps prevent utter fragmentation by offering a coherent global picture of language. However, the coherency of the pictures is usually at the expense of glossing over some details. Any theoretical perspective directs our attention to some aspect of the phenomenon and not to others. We have no way of knowing today which aspects of language will ultimately turn out to be the most central in a final picture.

The adoption of any particular perspective introduces some problems. Attempting to adopt several perspectives presents others. It is difficult, in particular, to adopt someone else's viewpoint when we have firm views of our own. Nonetheless, we must try to do so. Folk wisdom tells us we ought to walk a mile in someone else's shoes before judging that person. We wish to extend the same courtesy to adherents of the different viewpoints of language. Accordingly, despite the difficulties, we shall attempt to give a fair treatment to all the positions we consider. It should be understood at the same time that we (Paivio and Begg) have our own

preferences regarding viewpoints (in fact, we do not agree with each other about everything), and we shall present those views. Nevertheless, the psychology of language is complex enough to admit several competing accounts, and we believe that knowledge will advance by fair consideration of the different views, including those that we may not like. Another problem with this strategy is that the different perspectives are not equally appropriate in all contexts. Language phenomena central to one viewpoint may be ignored by another. The result is that although it seems neat and tidy to organize the presentation around three different perspectives, sometimes only one or two of the perspectives will be relevant, and there will even be cases in which none will be particularly appropriate.

We have stated that our concern is with intelligent language use by people. Our perspectives will focus on language, how it is used, and relevant cognitive processes in the user. First, from a linguistic perspective, we shall be concerned with language itself, independently of the users of the language. Second, from a behavioral perspective, we shall be concerned with language behavior as it relates to the more general class of behaviors performed by language users as well as by members of other species. Third, from a cognitive perspective, we shall be concerned with language use as it relates to other intellectual capacities and functions. Each perspective or approach offers a coherent picture of what it is we are studying. At times the perspectives will contradict each other, while at times they will merely differ. Let us briefly consider the approaches separately.

Linguistic Approaches

Linguistic approaches focus on language itself as the object of study, viewing it as an abstract system that underlies linguistic behavior. Long ago, language was approached with reverence and awe. The New Testament tells us that "In the beginning was the Word." At various stages in history, words have assumed enormous importance. For example, to know a god's name was to hold power over that god, a power to be wielded with care, since wanton or vain use of the name would weaken the god's powers. Because language was considered to be a divine object, it was important to discover its original and "correct" forms. Accordingly, language study was dominated for centuries by historical searches for the roots of language and by debates concerning the correct and proper rules for language use.

However, as linguistic knowledge advanced, students of language became less obsessed with the discovery of universal truths of creation and more concerned with determining the properties of languages as inferred from usage. Modern linguists are not so much concerned with how or why people speak as they are with the structure and nature of the linguistic knowledge that underlies what is said. Suppose a child said "We goed to them's house." To a parent, the utterance is an interesting bit of behavior to relate to the grandparents. To a linguist, the utterance provides clues to the rules of language possessed by the child: "goed" shows a grasp of the implicit rule that past tense is denoted by adding "-ed" to a verb, and "them's" shows possession is denoted by adding "-s" to a substantive.

From the linguistic perspective, language is a rather abstract entity consisting of conventions and rules. People understand each other only if their speech corresponds to the same rules. By studying many examples of speech, we attempt to determine the particular rules shared by the members of a linguistic community. The goal is to capture the rules in a grammar capable of producing all the sentences

speakers can understand but not capable of producing any nonsense, such as "Procrastination drinks quadriplexity." As we shall see later, the linguistic approach has advanced our understanding of language and has produced several valuable ways of conceptualizing the abstract language system.

Behavioral Approaches

Concern with human behavior likewise has its roots in antiquity. Folk wisdom has it that "by your deeds shall you be known," "actions speak louder than words," and "the road to Hell is paved with good intentions." In short, how we behave is what really counts. The behavioral approach shares with linguistics an early concern with codes for proper conduct, before becoming interested in the objective study of behavior as an actually occurring system. With specific reference to language behavior, the focus has taken several forms. Some behaviorists have considered speech sounds to be similar in principle to other environmental sounds and stimuli in general, and the movements in speaking to be similar in principle to other movements and responses in general. Such an approach leads naturally to studies of common properties of all learned behavior in many species and thus has led to many useful discoveries about and conceptions of language use.

Other behavioral approaches have used conceptions farther removed from sounds and movements, including dispositions (habits, behavioral tendencies) and relatively abstract classes of stimuli and responses, in addition to the less abstract, covert muscular reactions and sensory reactions. Such *mediational approaches* retain the stress on behavior but direct us also to the internal activity that underlies the observed behavior. It is evident that the abstract substrates of behavior are not necessarily at odds with the abstract structures that interest the linguist. Each approach draws inferences from behavior. However, the purpose of doing so is quite different in each case. The goal of the linguist is to develop a coherent account of language *independent* of the users of the language, and the goal of the behaviorist is to develop a coherent account of language *in terms of* its users. We shall find that one approach may be more useful than the other in some domains but that both are equally appropriate in others.

Cognitive Approaches

Modern cognitive approaches are more recent arrivals than linguistic or behavioral approaches, although thinkers have long been fascinated with the nature and functions of human intelligence. Central concepts in the cognitive approaches include mental organization, ideas, imagery, and knowledge of the world. The basic idea behind the approaches is that from our experience with the objects and events of the world, we acquire knowledge of the world. Language is both the result of acquiring that knowledge and the means by which further knowledge may be gained and shared with others. People possess many forms of knowledge, ranging from the rather concrete memory for the taste of French onion soup to a more abstract understanding of the theory of relativity. The study of language, by such an approach, is intimately tied to the knowledge of which language is a part and of the interactions between knowledge and language as it is used to *express* knowledge.

More than the other approaches, cognitive approaches stress a certain duality

of functioning. The linguistic and behavioral approaches are both relatively monistic, stressing as they do either the language itself or the general laws governing performance. The cognitive approach sets off the relatively abstract linguistic knowledge against the more concrete knowledge of the sensory and behavioral world in which the language is applied. As a result, cognitive approaches share similarities with linguistic approaches on some fronts, particularly with regard to mental representations and structures, and with behavioral approaches on other fronts, especially with regard to mediational processes and performance.

Having introduced the approaches, let us consider, in an equally brief and introductory way, some of the topics to which the approaches are applied.

Some Aspects of Language

The core areas considered throughout the book are the structure of language, the problem of meaning, and the functions of language in relation to perception, comprehension, memory, production, acquisition, and thought. These basic processes come up again in chapters dealing with figurative language, bilingualism, reading, and the relation between language and the brain.

The structure of language

Our goal in considering language structure is to develop a way of talking about language. This means that we must be able to isolate units of language and to specify the rules by which the units are combined. It seems clear from a common-sense viewpoint that a language consists of words and that a grammar consists of rules for putting words together. Words can be classed as to parts of speech, further helping to dictate correct orders for words. The word-based approach does have its uses, but it runs into four problems that are hard to overcome. First, although most of us can easily decide whether some linguistic segment is a word or is not, it is not obvious how we make those decisions. The problem is that there is not yet a definition of "word" that enables us to make the same decisions about unknown languages. Consider, for example, what would happen if we were to list our English words and then to study a new language by finding the foreign words that correspond to them. Sometimes this approach works quite well; for example, the word "dog" in English is quite equivalent to "chien" in French for most purposes. However, even an apparently simple word like "water" does not have a single equivalent in Hopi, in which there are separate labels for such occurrences as a pool of water, running water, and so on. What we express in phrases, other languages may express in wordlike units; what we express in single words, other languages may express in phrases.

A second problem is that the concept of "word" is most appropriate for written language, in which, for convenience, we use spaces between some segments. However, there are few gaps in speech, "sinceallthesoundsarestrungtogetherina continuoussequence." Speakers of foreign languages always seem to talk quickly, but that is only because we are not familiar enough with the language to identify the speech segments. Written Latin, for instance, also did not leave spaces between segments. Undeniably, there are some recurrent meaningful segments in speech, but the segments are not related in a simple way to our concept of "word."

A third problem is that our conceptions of the parts of speech are not universal, either. Our subject-verb structure may seem like the only natural way to construct a language, but that type of prejudice will obscure the many other, equally "natural" ways that language structure has evolved around the world. In fact, our subject-verb structure often leads us to statements that would seem strange to other people. For example, we say that a road "goes" to Montreal; however, no matter how long we sat on the road, we would not arrive. The fact is that roads do not really go anywhere; they just sit there. There are ways to avoid such problems, but we do not usually bother because they are not really problems to us. They are problems only to people, including children, who are new to a given language. Nevertheless, some of the consequences of our particular language structure are inappropriate for discussion of other languages, just as theirs are for ours.

The final problem is that there are many different ways to approach the analysis of language, each of which may be most efficiently conducted using different units of analysis. Units of sound are not the same as units of meaning or higher-order idea units. In a real sense, the point of view *creates* the most useful units. If we decide on a-priori grounds to use one type of unit, we might miss important regularities within and across languages.

The general point is that language structure is not a geometric entity open to a single analysis but rather exists in a dynamic form that is amenable to as many types of structural analyses as prove useful. Our investigation of the structure of language will use many definitions of structure and many types of units. Each approach is useful for some purposes but not for others. Although it is by no means an easy task, we should try to choose levels of analysis that are best for the purpose at hand.

Of the three perspectives we have chosen, the linguistic perspective is most concerned with the structure of language. Structural linguists use many different levels of analysis, with different units for each level. For example, phonemes are units at an acoustic level, and noun phrases are units at a syntactic level. At some levels, the descriptions offered by linguists may be extremely useful for psychological purposes. However, not all units and structures reached by linguistic analyses turn out to be psychologically important. For example, people do not remember the grammatical structure of sentences very well, leading to the conclusion that although some structure is necessary, it does not matter as much to a psychologist as to a linguist which particular structure is used. Conversely, some units that are useful for psychological purposes do not have ready linguistic definitions. For instance, we have seen the problems in defining "word" on linguistic grounds, but we cannot deny the importance of words in language use. One of the reasons we do experiments is to find out whether units resulting from careful linguistic analyses are psychologically "real," in the sense of having reliable effects on the behavior of language users.

The meaning of language

As difficult as they may seem, the problems with structure are nothing compared to the problems with meaning. Common sense tells us that each word has a meaning and that the meaning of a sentence is easily predictable from the combined

meanings of the words. But consider a simple case: What is the meaning of "bald"? How many hairs must a person lose to become bald? Can a man who is bald beside Peter Frampton cease being bald beside Telly Savalas? But even if we could come to a precise definition, would we understand a "bald lie" or "bald eagle"? The problem is that meaning is not nearly as precise a concept as we might think from daily use. Later on, we shall review several approaches, each offering a precise definition of "meaning," thus giving a different perspective on the whole problem of meaning.

Several points are, however, relevant to all of the approaches. One is the distinction between denotation and connotation. For example, *corpulent matron* and *fat woman* are equivalent in that they denote an adult female human whose weight exceeds the average by a noticeable amount, but they connote different emotional reactions. Linguistic approaches stress denotational meaning somewhat more than do behavioral or cognitive approaches. Along the same lines, it is useful to distinguish between dictionary meaning, in which a word is defined by a string of other words, and referential meaning, in which a word can be defined by pointing to a referent. Again, different approaches stress different types of meaning. The question of what *the* meaning is, is unanswerable as it stands; we must specify which type of meaning is of interest.

The perspectives of interest lead to quite different approaches to the problem of meaning. As mentioned above, the linguistic approaches place more emphasis on linguistic structure than do the psychological approaches. Consequently, a linguistic perspective leads us to seek structural accounts of meaning. For example, the meaning of a word can be expressed by a definition, itself a string of words. The definition could replace the word in appropriate contexts without altering the overall meaning of the sentence in question. Other structural approaches to meaning yield larger systems in which each word's meaning depends on the relation between the word and others in the system. The purpose is the same, however: namely, to describe the meaning of words or larger units in terms of the linguistic system, not in terms of the speakers and hearers. In contrast, the psychological approaches place more emphasis on the users. Behavioral approaches lead us to consider meaning from two sources. First, words are stimuli that have come to influence people's reactions, and second, words are responses that people produce in certain situations. Thus, meaning can be equated with the class of responses that people make to a given word or with the class of stimuli that leads to the production of the word. Cognitive approaches lead us to yet another conceptualization of meaning, usually in terms of knowledge of the world, and of intellectual functions. In all, then, we will not be as concerned with the question of what a word means as with what it is used to accomplish, what linguistic properties are important to that task, and what psychological processes are used in the task.

Functions of language

Language is used for many purposes, including the communication of intentions to others, thinking, solving problems, indicating facts, expressing feelings, and so on. In later chapters, we consider the role of language in many basic situations requiring perception, comprehension, memory, and so on. One thing we shall discover is that language is useful to many human concerns, and any interpretation of

the function of language will depend largely on one's point of view. From a biological viewpoint, language can be interpreted as having evolved as a behavioral capacity because it is biologically adaptive, useful in promoting the survival of humans as a species. Psychologically, language can be viewed, at least in part, as behavior that indirectly serves the biological, social, or aesthetic needs of the individual. The sociologist could ask about the role of language in promoting and maintaining social systems. A functional linguistic analysis, as we have already said, can be entirely intralinguistic, without reference to the speaker or listener, as when one inquires into the grammatical or semantic functions of the components of a sentence. Much of the structural analysis alluded to in the preceding section depends implicitly on such a conception of linguistic function—the morpheme, for example, is a functional unit of language.

No one has attempted an exhaustive taxonomy of all possible functions of language at every level of analysis, although Robinson (1972) proposed a rather comprehensive scheme, with an emphasis on the functions most relevant to social behavior. His list illustrates the diversity and range of functions that can be revealed by a careful analysis. Fourteen functions are listed, including (1) verbal behavior as a means of avoiding other problems—a kind of personal filibustering; (2) conformity to norms ("There is a time to speak and a time to keep silence"); (3) aesthetic functions, as revealed in witty conversation, poetry, rhetoric, and so on; (4) regulation of the interactions in social encounters; (5) performative utterances, such as promises, contracts, and bets, in which the utterance is, or is part of, the action; (6) self-regulation, as illustrated by Luria's (1961) studies of how key-pressing reactions are affected when a child says "Press!" or "Don't press!"; (7) regulation of others, by commands, requests, and the like; (8) expression of feeling; (9) speech as an indicator of characteristics of the speaker—for example, age, sex, occupation, and nationality; (10) definition of role relationships by such means as the rights and obligations to use particular forms of address, as in the *tu-vous* distinction in French; (11) reference—the communication of propositional knowledge; (12) language as a medium of instruction; (13) inquiry as a form of information seeking; and (14) metalanguage functions, in which language is used to talk about language (as we are doing in this book).

Obviously, there is a good deal of overlap in this list, and we could collapse some of the categories into more inclusive ones. Alternatively, we could add to the list. The roles of language as a determinant of one's mode of thinking (see chapter 11), as an aid to problem solving, or as a carrier of values and attitudes warrant separate mention in any definitive list of language functions. Such an exercise is useful when attention centers on the content of behavior, as in any analysis of social behavior, but it is less useful when one is concerned with general principles, as we are here. The general point is that language serves many different functions, all important to some purposes or interests.

The Plan of the Book

The remainder of the book will fill in some details about what has been sketched in this chapter. In chapter 2, we discuss the nature of human language and communication in general. Chapters 3 and 4 develop several different approaches to the scientific study of language and we refer the interested reader to other ap-

proaches covered in other books and in later chapters. Chapter 5 wrestles with the problem of meaning. Several approaches are relevant to language in general, although we consider them only with reference to meaning. Chapters 6 through 9 are concerned with the central functions of language, namely perception, comprehension, memory, and production. Again, the coverage is selective, with emphasis on the theories and research that fit the themes built around the three perspectives.

Chapter 10 deals with the acquisition of language. Since we could ask how any aspect of language is acquired, this chapter could easily be as long as the rest of the book, and indeed many books have been written on this topic. Consequently, we again have been selective, in line with our attempt to present broad perspectives illustrated by experimental research. By and large, the most "meat-and-potatoes" areas of consideration finish with chapter 10. In the remaining chapters, the focus changes to more specialized topics. Chapter 11 addresses the relation between language and thought from a relatively philosophical vantage point, and we attempt to give a fair hearing to Whorf's views. Chapter 12 concerns the newly blossoming area of interest in metaphors and figurative language in general; we find the area to be both valuable and fun. In chapter 13, the practical questions raised by a concern with bilingualism are raised, and these too offer general insights into the psychology of language. Chapter 14 addresses reading and other visually guided processes related to using language. Finally, in chapter 15, recent advances in the study of the biological substrates of language are reviewed. This is a fascinating area and is also useful in bringing theorizing a little closer to the "blood-and-guts" limitations of our bodies.

Two final points regarding the book will be made here. First, we place a great deal of emphasis on the results of experiments. In part, this is because we are experimental psychologists, and we make our living by doing experiments. But this is not the main reason. What exactly is an experiment? An experiment is a controlled look at nature. That is, the experimenter sets up a situation in which the structure of the task is explicit, the nature of the performance being studied is explicit, and the question being asked is precise. An experiment is simply a way of asking nature a question, and the results are answers to that question. Our emphasis on experiments reflects our belief that the best answers come from well-thought-out questions. One simply cannot do a good experiment without careful analysis of the problem. We think the experiments we review are examples of experimentation at its best, directed towards answering questions raised by theoretical interests and providing results to help refine those theoretical interests. Perhaps *you* have opinions about how language works. Try to think of experimental tests of your opinions, and you are doing what we do for a living (well, part of it).

The other point is that we consider in detail theoretical accounts that most other books do not consider. For example, Skinner's account is not detailed in most books about the psychology of language. One reason for considering some of these older approaches is that they establish an historical continuity and in so doing present a background against which some of the concepts of more current interest are well defined. But there is also a far more important reason to consider these approaches. Simply put, the older approaches are no less adequate as explanations of many facets of language than are the newer ones. The psychology of language is an area that, like almost every other human undertaking, is subject to fashions, fads, and trends. It is good to keep rethinking old problems, rephrasing old

questions—often exciting new insights result. At the same time, however, some of the insights of the older approaches become lost as the fad changes. Although there are serious problems with some of the approaches we consider, there are also considerable areas of strength. Consequently, we shall place more emphasis on the accounts of the fifties and sixties than do most of our colleagues. At the same time, we shall also present the most recent accounts. We hope that the interplay between then and now will revitalize the older accounts, place a rein on the newer ones, and lead us to general notions about the psychology of language as a timeless system.

what is language?

2

The term *Language* has many meanings in everyday usage. People speak of body language, the language of love, and the language of bees, to name a few. About the only thing the expressions have in common is that each has something to do with *communication*. Language, too, is a communication system, but it has special characteristics that set it apart from the above examples and many more. In this chapter, we shall try to arrive at a more definite view of the nature of human language by considering several ways in which the term has been used and by contrasting language with other forms of communication. Let us begin by drawing some distinctions to help guide us.

Natural versus Formal Languages

Because it is relevant to later discussions, we shall begin by drawing a distinction between natural languages, such as English, and formal languages, such as mathematics. A formal language is characterized by being completely rule determined, thus allowing a computer to be programmed to handle it. Indeed, computers perform all their functions in terms of formal languages like FORTRAN or ALGOL. Natural languages are similar to formal languages to the extent that they can be characterized in terms of formal rules (of grammar, for example), and some linguists have gone rather far in that direction, as we shall see later on. Others feel that some of the most interesting features of natural languages, such as their strong tendency to be idiomatic and metaphorical, cannot be captured by formal rules. Perhaps the truth is that natural languages have a "core" that is describable in formal terms, as well as a sizable fringe that is not. We shall see, in any case, that many of the classical theoretical debates concerning the nature of human language have centered, either explicitly or implicitly, on the question of formalism, usually embedded in the context of other issues.

Linguistic Knowledge versus Concrete Speech

Another important distinction to bear in mind is the difference between the actual speech acts produced by individual speakers and the more abstract language system shared by members of a linguistic community. The first writer to emphasize

this distinction was Marcus Terentius Varro, in about 100 B.C. (see Dinneen, 1967). At that time, intellectual circles were engaged in a vigorous debate concerning the fundamental nature of the universe in general and language in particular. One group of scholars, the *anomalists*, believed that language was not lawful but rather, conventional. In contrast, the *analogists* believed that language was inexorably lawful. Some believed that even the relation between words and the things they signify was lawful, and others believed, more moderately, that it was possible to construct grammars, or laws of speech. Varro emphasized that concrete language, as spoken by individuals, was as subject to change as clothing style. However, the abstract language, the system shared by a community, was seen as more regular and lawful than the actual speech acts of individuals. Abstract language would change as needed, since language was basically a tool for conducting the business of life, but the changes would not be as whimsical as fluctuations in the speech of individuals.

La langue versus la parole

The distinction between two sorts of language did not have much effect on linguistic science until the Swiss linguist Ferdinand de Saussure (1974 edition) popularized the distinction some two thousand years later. Saussure argued convincingly for a separation of language (*le langage*) into *la langue*, the abstract language system, and *la parole*, the actual speech acts or utterances. *La parole* is determined by *la langue* and also by characteristics of individual speakers. That is, what speakers actually say (*la parole*) depends on their general knowledge of the language system as it "exists" in their language community (*la langue*) and on their specific personality characteristics, experiences, memories, and so on. Saussure considered *la langue* to be a repository of *linguistic signs*. A sign, he said, was a two-faced psychic entity resulting from the association between an *acoustic image* and a *concept*. The acoustic image was itself an abstraction of speech sounds; for example, different speakers pronounce "dog" in somewhat different ways, but we still treat those pronunciations as equivalent. Similarly, the concept is an abstract representation of the "thing meant" by the acoustic image; people may mean different things by the word "dog," but there is some aspect of that meaning that is sufficient to distinguish the thing meant from other concepts. Saussure felt that the proper study of linguistics pertained to linguistic signs. We shall have more to say about this idea later on.

Competence versus performance

More recently, Noam Chomsky (1965), an American linguist, drew a distinction similar to *la langue* and *la parole*. Chomsky distinguished between *competence*, the abstract linguistic knowledge we must possess in order to use the language, and *performance*, the actual production or comprehension of speech. For example, suppose a child says "I goed to them's house." Since the child probably never heard anyone say "goed" or "them's," the utterance is not simply a repetition. The very fact that the child can produce such words is evidence for the existence of some knowledge of language, in this case referring to tense and possession. From such *observable events*, we can *infer* the structure of that knowledge. Moreover, Chomsky proposed that the underlying structures can be described in formal terms. We present his ideas in more detail in chapter 3.

Language as stimulus, response, and disposition

Note that the distinctions proposed by Varro, Saussure, and Chomsky all distinguish between the observable events that constitute the use of language and the inferred structures or systems that allow those events to occur. Analogous distinctions have been made by psychologists. The observable events can be classified as verbal *stimuli* or verbal *responses*. Speech sounds and printed pages are linguistic stimuli that can be analyzed in terms of their relation to the verbal or other behavior of the hearer. Similarly, verbal responses can be analyzed in terms of their articulatory properties and their relations with larger response units, such as sequences of words that people produce. Unlike most other environmental events, however, speech sounds are both stimuli *and* responses, depending only on how we choose to analyze them. In short, one person's response is another person's stimulus.

Psychologists have also been concerned with inferences from observable events. The inferences, which correspond more or less to *la langue* and competence, are usually described as *dispositions*, such as language habits, verbal mediators, or mediational processes in general. Each of these refers to a learned disposition that contributes to the production and comprehension of speech. That is, a disposition is a relatively stable psychological process that mediates the relation between verbal stimuli and verbal responses. Such dispositions can be treated as being both properties of individuals and general properties common to members of a linguistic community. Communication is possible only if dispositions are shared. Moreover, the dispositions need not be only linguistic—they may also include general knowledge of the world, expressed sometimes as images, emotions, or intuitions of various sorts.

Language as a System of Signs

Saussure believed that it was possible to develop a science of signs (semiology), that would include language as one component. Recall that *la langue* is a repository of signs, each one a psychic entity consisting of an acoustic image, or signifier, and a concept, or thing signified. In Saussure's analysis, the unit of study was not the relation between the signifier and the things signified, but the entire sign consisting of the signifier, the thing signified, and the relation between them. A given sign could be related to other signs with similar images or concepts, or the relation could be more abstract, as when two signs often occur together in speech or could occur in the same places. To illustrate Saussure's preferred approach, consider a dollar. There are three different levels of description of a dollar bill. First, we could describe its physical appearance, serial number, and so on, but such a description would tell us little of importance; to Saussure, analysis of speech sounds as signs was of this level. Second, we could describe the dollar in terms of its *conceptual value* with reference to other units in the currency system; this level of analysis is analogous to defining a sign with reference to other signs in the linguistic system. Third, we could consider the *material value* of the dollar in terms of goods and services for which it may be exchanged; similarly, each sign can be considered in terms of the circumstances to which it can refer.

More recent developments have led to some changes in the study of signs in general and of language as a system of signs. The modern usage of *sign* is quite similar to its general language usage, as in a traffic sign. Simply put, a sign is a phys-

ical signal that directs behavior to something other than itself. A bell is a sign to dogs that salivate, and the opening bars of the national anthem are a sign to those who stand. That is, each sign stands for something other than itself to some users of the sign system. In 1938, Charles Morris used the term *semiotic* for the science of signs and suggested three main areas for the study of signs. The relations among signs themselves constitute *syntactics*. The relations between signs and the things, actions, or qualities they signify constitute the area of *semantics*. The relations between signs and the users, as well as the uses, constitute *pragmatics*. Note that the sign as a physical entity is not the same as the sign as a mental entity in Saussure's approach. The closest parallel is that a single unit consisting of a sign, the thing it signifies, and the signification relation, taken all at once, constitutes Saussure's sign. It is also worth noting that syntactics, semantics, and pragmatics have different meanings in Morris's system than they do in general linguistics. However, this will not present any problems for our purposes.

Regardless of whether we conceptualize language as a system of physical signs or as physical tokens that relate to mental signs, it is obvious that the study of language has many levels. To the psychologist, the user is of considerable concern; to the linguist, the user is of less interest. As we shall contend in the discussion of meaning in later chapters, the various levels are not independent. The signification of a sign or token is itself derived from use, so that the study of semantics is actually a study of a pragmatic system. We feel that pragmatic study is more likely to reveal relations of value for our understanding of human language than either semantic or syntactic study is, precisely because pragmatics explicitly takes into account the user of the language and the factors that influence that usage. Further, the relations that characterize pragmatics will constrain the relations within semantics and, in turn, will dominate syntactics because it is the behavior of the user that ultimately defines the meaning and organization of linguistic signs.

Language as a Communication System

Implicit in the above discussion is our bias that language be studied in terms of its use. Language signs are most often used for interpersonal communication, so much so that it is hard to imagine why we would have a language for any other purpose. We shall now consider the properties of communication systems in general. By contrasting human language with other communication systems, we shall arrive at a more precise conception of how language differs from those systems.

We shall define human language within this context, as *a biological communication system that is specialized for the transmission of meaningful information between and within persons by means of linguistic signs.*

This definition (a) places language in the context of communication systems in general; (b) implies a distinction between biological and nonbiological systems; (c) implies, within biological systems, a distinction between human and animal communication; (d) suggests that we are concerned with a functional rather than a purely structural system, one that is specialized for transmitting information of a particular kind; and finally, (e) contrasts communication between individuals with intraindividual communication systems in which information is transmitted from one part to another within the person. The last point refers to the role of language in thinking, in which individuals sometimes communicate with themselves by means of inner speech.

Communication systems

First, language is a communication system. A dictionary tells us that a system is a set of interconnected things or parts. A communication system is one in which the parts are specialized for the transmission of information. Scientists concerned with communication as an engineering problem (Shannon & Weaver, 1949) envisaged such a system in the way shown schematically in Figure 2-1. The model has been used as a theory of human language, so we shall explain it in some detail.

The components of the system include an information *source* and a *destination* connected by a *channel* capable of carrying messages from one to the other. In addition, the system requires a *transmitter* to transform the message produced by the source into signals the channel can carry and a *receiver* to transform those signals into a form that the destination can accept. The signal carried by the channel is an *information code*, so that the activity of the transmitter is often referred to as *encoding* and that of the receiver as *decoding*. Note also the concept of *noise* which refers simply to the sources of error in the communication of messages. Most often it refers to disturbances in the communication channel that distort the message, but errors could also occur during encoding or decoding.

The communication model has been applied to the analysis of biological systems (physiological, psychological, social) and nonbiological systems (electrical, mechanical). Many familiar systems are complex, with some components being biological and others not. A telephone system is an obvious example, with a human

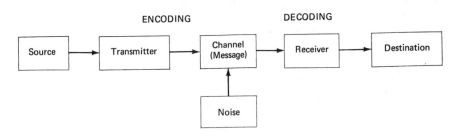

NOTE:

source—e.g., speaker

destination—e.g., hearer

channel—capable of carrying message from source to destination

transmitter—transforms message produced by source into signals that the channel can carry (encoding).

receiver—transforms signals back into form destination can receive (decoding).

information code—the form of the signal carried by channel.

noise—sources of error in the communication of messages (usually in channel, but also during encoding and decoding).

FIGURE 2-1. Components of a communication system according to the Shannon-Weaver Theory.

speaker as source and a listener as destination, together with their encoding and decoding activity. The telephone transmitter that encodes the vocal message of the speaker into electrical signals, the wire channel that carries those signals, and the receiver that decodes them back into sound waves are mechanical and nonbiological, although they are, of course, the product of human activity, so the entire system could be called biological in the general sense.

Except for the medium that carries the message, ordinary human communication is entirely biological. Moreover, each person functions at once as source, transmitter, and receiver of messages; in brief, a self-contained communicational unit. Such multiplicity of communicational functioning also occurs but is not universal among other organisms. Among electrical-mechanical systems, the computer approximates a self-contained communication unit in that it can receive, transform, and transmit messages. The message itself ultimately has a human source, however, so the analogy is only approximate.

The same information-processing terminology can be applied to any level of a complex communication system. The individual as listener is said to receive and decode a message; as speaker, he or she encodes and transmits another message. Decoding implies comprehension, and encoding refers to speech production. But between these two phases, there are thought processes that themselves encode, decode, and transmit cognitive information carried as some kind of neural code along different pathways or channels. The terms encoding and decoding may appear to be used interchangeably in much psychological literature, so a further word is in order. In most human activity, signals are changed from one code, such as sound, into another, such as thought. Thus, the decoding activity with respect to the first code is itself also encoding activity with respect to the second. The choice of whether to call the activity encoding or decoding depends on which code we wish to stress. In many cases, we shall simply refer to the activity as *coding* or *recoding*.

Nonlinguistic informational components

The coding processes within the individual need not be only linguistic. For example, if someone asks you where the hammer is, you may transform "hammer" into a mental picture or image of the object and then try to remember where you last saw it. If the memory search is successful, you must decode the memory image of the location of the hammer into a verbal code in order to answer the question. Thus, the decoding and encoding at the social level of communication entail or encompass internal encoding and decoding processes that might include both nonverbal and verbal components in a series of transformations.

Definition of information

Recall that we referred to human language as a communication system specialized for transmitting meaningful information. The term *meaningful* is crucial, for it alludes to a characteristic of language that seems to fall outside the bounds of the Shannon-Weaver communication model. An appreciation of this point requires an understanding of the special meaning of information within that model. Following a rather detailed explanation of that meaning, we shall return to the question of the psychological relevance of the approach.

Information is defined in information theory as the reduction of uncertainty.

Consider what happens when you answer the telephone: a male voice says, "Hello!" The voice is informative because it reduces your uncertainty about the identity of the caller by at least one-half—you know that it is a man rather than a woman. But considerable uncertainty remains if you cannot identify the person from his voice because the number of potential male callers and possible messages is very large. The voice says, "This is Joe's garage." Aha! More reduction of uncertainty— the call is about your car rather than about any number of other matters. But what could be wrong with it? "Your car needs a new generator." More information. "It will cost X dollars." Still more uncertainty reduction. And so on. Each item of information is informative precisely because it reveals one of a number of possible alternatives. Consider the reverse situation: you dial the number for Joe's garage, and the voice that answers says, "Good morning. Joe's garage." This is informative in that you could have dialed the wrong number or the line might have been busy, but the content of the response transmitted no further information because there was no uncertainty about where you were calling.

The account so far has used common-sense units of information. More abstractly, the analysis can apply to symbolic units of any specified size (for example, letters, words, sentences). Regardless of the size of the symbol, the amount of information in a given symbol is a function of the number of potential symbols that might occur in its place. If only one could occur, that symbol would be said to transmit no information because the receiver could expect it to occur with absolute certainty, provided that the receiver knows the statistical structure of the code being used (that is, the probabilities of the alternatives). Thus, in written English, the letter U after Q contains no information because the receiver knows that a U must follow Q. If other alternatives are possible, however, the occurrence of a given symbol informs in proportion to the number of possible alternatives.

Measurement of information

A convenient unit for measuring information is the *bit*, which is a contraction of "binary digit." A bit is the amount of information gained by reducing uncertainty in a situation by one-half. In our telephone example, the male voice reduced uncertainty about the identity of the speaker by roughly one bit if we assume that half of the potential callers are male and half are female, and ignore such additional information as the age of the caller, which might be revealed by the voice. Because of such assumptions, it is difficult to analyze many natural situations in any rigorous way. As a more precise example, consider a game in which you are asked to guess a particular letter from the first sixteen letters of the alphabet (A to P). Let us say that the letter is M. How many bits of information would we have to transmit in order to do this? More informally, how many yes-or-no questions would have to be asked? We determine this by first dividing the sixteen symbols into two halves, the first eight *versus* the second eight, eliminating one-half on the basis of the answer, then dividing the remainder into halves, and so on. Thus:

1. Is it a letter from A to H (not I to P)? No.
2. Is it a letter from M to P (not I to L)? Yes.
3. Is it a letter from O to P (not M to N)? No.
4. Is it the letter N? No. Therefore, the letter must be M.

We see, then, that four items of yes-no information are required to determine a particular symbol from fifteen possible alternatives. Note that each yes-no decision reduced uncertainty by one-half; each decision by definition equals one bit of information. Therefore, a set of sixteen alternative symbols contains four bits of information. Note that four is the power to which two must be raised in order to obtain the sixteen possibilities; $2^4 = 16$. Thus the exponent specifies the number of bits of this information. More generally, the amount of this information (the number of yes-no decisions required to reduce uncertainty to zero) in a given number of alternatives is *equal to the logarithm to the base two of that number.* In the letter example, $\log_2 16 = 4$. With eight alternatives, the amount of information is $\log_2 8 = 3$; with six alternatives, 2.58; with three alternatives, 1.58; and so on. The general equation is $H = \log_2 m$, in which H refers to amount of information and m refers to the number of equiprobable alternative symbols.

The above expression can be rephrased as the amount of information communicated by one member of the set of alternatives. With sixteen possible letters, presentation of M provides four bits of information. We can now reconsider our telephone example in this context: how informative was it for the caller to say "This is Joe's garage"? To answer this in a quantitative way we would need to know the number of alternative statements that might have been offered. Restricting the question simply to the identity of the caller, suppose that sixteen people know your telephone number and that they are equally likely to call. Then the caller is providing four bits of information when she says, "Hello! This is Mary." If only two people know your number, the same message would provide only one bit of information.

The preceding analysis used two important assumptions. First, the alternatives must be known; the measurement of information always requires knowledge of alternatives. Second, each alternative was equally likely. Since this assumption is not usually met, the amount of uncertainty, H, must be extended to cover unequal likelihoods, although the rationale is unchanged. Generally, H is defined by the formula

$$H = -\Sigma Pi(\log_2 Pi)$$

in which Pi is the probability of occurrence of unit i (one of the alternatives) and Σ refers to summation over all the alternatives. This basic statistic measures the absolute uncertainty for a set of alternatives, one of which must occur.

Variants of the equation can be used to determine *conditional uncertainty,* the information value of a symbol, x, given that it is preceded by another symbol, y. In other terms, conditional uncertainty refers to the degree to which x can be predicted from a knowledge of y. Let us again consider a common-sense example to illustrate this concept. Consider a sentence such as "A stitch in time saves nine," as opposed to "The next digit in the winning number is nine." The word "nine" conveys less information in the first example than in the second, because the preceding context makes "nine" more predictable in the first case than in the second. This is precisely the type of situation referred to by conditional uncertainty. If the amount of information provided by x is less if y has occurred than if y has not, then y reduces uncertainty about x, with the result that x is less informative than it would be otherwise. An extension of this approach allows us to measure the

average informational capacity of all of the units in a sequence. It is unnecessary for our purposes to go into further detail concerning the mathematics of information analysis. Suffice it to say that H is a variable that can be calculated for any communication system in which the number of alternative message units and their respective probabilities are known. The value of H is maximal when all alternatives are equally probable, and it is zero when only one can occur and hence is perfectly predictable.

Redundancy

The idea that symbol sequences can vary in redundancy or predictability is an extension of the concept of conditional uncertainty. A redundant message is one in which the sequence is low in information because the successive symbols are not independent. Thus the probability of occurrence of a particular symbol depends on the units that preceded it. This means that the same amount of information could be carried by a smaller number of independent units. The "qu" sequence in written English is an example: the u is completely redundant, so that the word "quiet" could be spelled "qiet" without any loss of information.

All languages are redundant, at every level of analysis. Consider the sentence, *The two boys are running.* Plurality is communicated by three features of the message: number (two), the plural morpheme -s (boys), and the plural form of the verb to be (are). The first of these would suffice, so why the redundancy? One reason is that *redundancy reduces the probability of error owing to noise.* Even if one misses one of the plural "markers," the others would indicate that the message is about more than one person.

Psychological relevance of information theory

The general concept of information as outlined above has been applied to various psycholinguistic problems, such as the determination of the statistical structure of the units or sequences of units in a language (such as letters, words, redundancy of a sequence of letters or words), the effect of the linguistic context on the perception of linguistic units, and the effect of the statistical structure (the degree to which a sequence of letters or words approximates English sequential structure) on the ease of learning a sequence of words. Such studies will be considered later in appropriate contexts. The point here is that information theory represents an approach that emphasizes the informational function of the symbols of a language and relates such information to the structural units of the language in a rigorous way.

Unfortunately, the formal rigor of information measurement does not readily generalize to some important aspects of language. As originally intended, information theory was applied within, rather than between, levels of relations. The theory is primarily syntactic, since it pertains to the probabilities of occurrence of the signs (letters and words) of the language. The same rationale can be applied to semantics and pragmatics, but measurement becomes approximate, since alternatives may be unknown. Consider a sentence such as "Harry cut himself shaving." To most of us, Harry is an adult male, shaving his face with a razor, probably in the bathroom, and he cut his face with the razor. However, Harry could have been shaving his chest, he might have been using an ax, he could have been in church, it could have

been his finger that was cut, and the cut could have been made by a broken mirror; in short, the alternatives are innumerable. The point is that sentences convey information about much more than the particular words used.

Although it may prove impossible to measure the set of alternatives possible in a linguistic communication, the conceptual basis of information theory is valuable for discussing communication. Several current conceptions of meaning, which we shall discuss in later chapters, characterize semantic knowledge as containing sets or networks of relationships or features. A message is informative to the extent that it narrows the range of interpretation. We shall have more to say on this later.

As a formal system, however, the fact remains that information theory has been less useful as an approach to the psychology of language than its early psycholinguistic proponents had hoped. The reasons for this are not entirely clear, but a major factor might be that information as defined within the theory is *semantically* empty and, therefore, psychologically irrelevant in communicational situations that require the sender or receiver to take account of qualitative semantic distinctions in the production and understanding of language. In human language, the semantic information is always *about something*. This functional characteristic of human language is crucial, and it is not captured by information theory alone. Indeed, it takes us beyond language itself to the objects and events of the nonlinguistic world and to their psychological (nonlinguistic) representations within the communicating individuals. In brief, language use depends on both *knowledge of the world* and knowledge of the language. Thus, when our telephone caller says, "This is Mary," the linguistic message carries information only if we know someone called Mary. The message is meaningful because it somehow taps into that knowledge. The general point is no less valid if the caller says, "This is Joe's garage," for the utterance at least places the unknown voice in the context of a known environmental setting. Moreover, the generalization holds even when the referent of the communication is itself linguistic, such as a statement about some feature of language, or a poem, or whatever.

The preceding discussion leads to the following generalization: *The semantic information conveyed by a linguistic utterance is always something other than itself.* Information theory cannot, in principle, quantify such information because *it defines information entirely in terms of units of the symbol system itself.* If the word is taken as a unit, its informational value is related entirely to the number of alternative words that might have occurred (along with their respective probabilities) and not to the additional psychological information that the word might arouse. Information theory has a closed symbol system; human communication does not. We shall argue in later chapters that this limitation of information theory applies to all formal theories of language.

Having placed language in the context of communication systems in general, we turn next to a comparative analysis of human language in relation to other (infrahuman) biological communication systems.

Language as a Biological Communication System

We are concerned in this section with two broad questions: What does human language share with the communication systems of other animals? And what, if anything, is unique about human language? These questions have been discussed

over a long period of time by many students of language. We shall consider only a few attempts to deal with them.

Levels of communication

Hebb and Thompson (1954; see also Hebb, Lambert, & Tucker, 1971) distinguished three levels of communication in animal behavior. The lowest level is *reflexive*, in which a particular cue reliably elicits a particular response in a member of a species, and that response reliably has signal value for other members of the species. The warning cry of the baboon and the "language of the bees" are examples of such reflexive communications. They occur as a reflexive reaction to particular cues and are unmodified by the reactions of other members of the species. Such unpurposive reflexivity is not the hallmark of language behavior. The second level is *purposive* communication, which differs from reflexive in that it is usually modified by the sender to take account of the receiver's behavior, toward some purposeful end. The begging and beckoning reactions of chimpanzees clearly have such purposes. The third level, *true language*, is also purposive, but it is characterized as well by a high degree of constructiveness and creativity lacking in the purposive and reflexive behavior of other animals. Thus, new messages can be constructed freely using old and familiar components in different arrangements for different effects ("I thirsty," "Mommy thirsty," "Mommy fix," "Daddy fix"). The salient feature of such behavior is its syntacticity (its capacity for novel patterning), so Hebb and Thompson propose to define human language as *syntactic behavior*.

Design features of human language

C. F. Hockett (1963), a linguist, presented a very thorough analysis of this issue in the context of an inquiry into *linguistic universals*, that is, characteristics of language shared by all human languages. Hockett proposed a set of *design features* of language that are common to all human languages but are not shared by all animal communication systems. Note that the latter criterion does not require a particular feature to be absent among all animals but rather that it not be present in the communication systems of all animals. We may question some aspects of Hockett's list and his arguments regarding them, but the features have been carefully considered, and it is worth going over them in some detail because they highlight important features of language and thereby advance our aim of arriving at a clear conception of the nature of language.

1. *Vocal-auditory channel.* The information transmission channel for all linguistic communications is vocal-auditory, from mouth to ear. Some animal communications, such as the chirping of the cricket, are auditory but not vocal. Others use totally different channels. For example, bees communicate information about the location and quality of a food source by means of a "dance" performed in the hive (von Frisch, 1967). A bee returns to the hive and begins the dance; other bees in the hive join in and eventually fly out to find the food. The information includes an olfactory component (the odor of pollen carried by the forager), the energy with which the dance is performed (the farther the food the slower the dance), and its general pattern and orientation (for food sources farther than fifty meters or so

from the hive, the dance includes a direction component in which the direction of the bee's movement, relative to the vertical, corresponds to the direction of the food source horizontally away from the hive in relation to the direction of the sun). The information includes kinesthetic, visual, and olfactory components but none based on sound (the precise nature of the effective cues is currently a matter of controversy, but this does not affect the present discussion. Students interested in the controversy might start with Gould's article in *Science*, 1975).

Note that Hockett intentionally excludes written language because it does not meet his criterion of human universality: spoken language is culturally universal; written language is not. We should also note that this feature excludes gestural languages, such as the sign language of the deaf. This is an important exception not mentioned by Hockett—important because sign language can function as a complete communication system with its own grammatical and semantic properties. As used by the deaf, it clearly represents a human language system, although it does not use the vocal-auditory channel and is not universal among human communities. The exception suggests that we must look beyond particular sensory-motor channels for the most fundamental universals of language. Nonetheless, the vocal-auditory channel has great generality as a design feature of language, and it will be duly emphasized in this book without ignoring important exceptions.

2. *Broadcast transmission and directional reception.* All linguistic signals are transmitted broadcast, in all directions at once, as opposed to "tight-beam" or directional transmission. Conversely, they are directionally received in that the hearer can generally locate the direction of the source. This feature is a consequence of the nature of sound, which is carried in all directions by air molecules, and of binaural hearing, in which the separation of the two ears permits the hearer to home in on the sound source. This feature has important psycholinguistic consequences when contrasted with the directional transmission and reception associated with visual stimuli, including the sign language of the deaf, since broadcast transmission to some extent frees the receiver from being locked in to the source. Simply stated, one is more free to do other things while listening to a message than while looking at one. This feature allows us to make love in the dark and still whisper sweet nothings. We shall examine this and other consequences of the vocal-auditory feature of language in some detail throughout the book.

3. *Rapid fading.* All linguistic signals are evanescent. This again is a consequence of the vocal-auditory channel, and is obviously not true of writing or tape recordings. These exceptions are, of course, technological extensions of language as a natural communication system. Some animal communications, such as a dog's scent mark on a tree on a hot day, also tend to linger on.

4. *Interchangeability.* Interchangeability has been discussed earlier. It means that the adult members of a speech community are both transmitters and receivers of linguistic signals. This is not true of all animal communicators. Among some species of crickets, for example, only the males chirp, although both sexes respond to chirping. You probably know people who would rather transmit than receive, but the fact remains that they can receive if they have to.

5. *Complete feedback.* Except in certain pathological conditions, the transmitter at the same time receives the message he or she transmits.

6. *Specialization.* Language is specialized for communicating rather than for producing any effect directly as a result of the physical energy of sound. The direct effects are usually biologically trivial. As Hockett so aptly puts it, "Even the most heated conversation does not raise the temperature of a room enough to benefit those in it" (1963, p. 10). As an infrahuman exception, Hockett points to the male stickleback (a fish) which will not court the female unless her abdomen is distended by roe. Thus, the effect of the signal correlates with its physical magnitude. This is true also of the bee's dance, in which the physical energy of the dance has direct communicational consequences. There are also some human communications in which physical energy has direct consequences, such as punching or kicking. Such communications, however, are not language.

7. *Semanticity.* "Linguistic signals function in correlating and organizing the life of a community because there are associative ties between signal elements and features in the world; in short, some linguistic forms have denotations" (Hockett, 1963, p. 10). Quite simply, words mean something beyond themselves.

8. *Arbitrariness.* Arbitrariness is essentially a corollary of the two preceding features. It means that the semantic relation is independent of any physical or geometrical resemblance between the meaningful linguistic element and its referent. The word "horse" bears no resemblance to a horse. This contrasts with *iconic* signals that do resemble what they denote. The bee's dance, for example, is directionally iconic in that the target site is woven into a directional component in the dance. Human communication also contains iconic signals. Language includes some element of onomatopoeia, in which the sound of a word resembles the referent (*buzz, cough, whippoorwill* are familiar examples). Another set of examples comes from words that begin with sn. If you pronounce sn, you will feel the n sound coming out of your nose. A disproportionate number of such words refer to nasal activity—sniffle, snuffle, snout, snooty, snot, sneeze, snore. Even snoopy means "nosey," a metaphoric extension. Although such cases are interesting, they are certainly in the minority in language. Other communications are iconic. A painting of a horse does resemble the animal. The gestural languages of the deaf include iconic signs as a major part of their communication system. Finally, nonverbal imagery is an iconic system that can mediate language behavior. It remains true, nonetheless, that language itself is generally not iconic, although its cognitive foundation includes iconic processes.

9. *Discreteness.* The possible messages of a language constitute a discrete rather than a continuous repertoire, in which discrete refers to a sudden, stepwise change rather than a gradual one. Thus, two different messages must differ by at least one discrete phonological feature. This is not true, for example, of the bee's dances, in which the speed and direction of the dance can vary in infinitely small steps. Note that the reference here is to the linguistic code itself. We shall argue later that the meaning of a message can vary continuously—a possibility acknowl-

edged by Hockett only in regard to systems with iconic semantics (such as one using pictures). Moreover, features such as relative pitch and stress can vary continuously, as can the actual responses or sounds that a speaker produces when uttering a linguistic message.

10. *Displacement.* Linguistic messages may refer to objects and events remote from the site of the communication in time or space. We can talk about what is not here and now as well as what is. Gibbon calls are never displaced from the perceptual field, but bees' dances always are. Human utterances can be freely displaced or not. This means that language and memory are intimately related (see chapter 8).

11. *Openness or productivity.* Language is a creative or productive system. New linguistic messages can be created freely and easily, so that we can say something that has never been said before and be understood. Bees do this as well, but gibbons do not. Humans do it in at least two different ways: by grammatical patterning, in which new messages are created by blending, analogizing from, or transforming old ones; or by new idioms created by assigning new meanings to linguistic elements. The first is *grammatical creativity*; the second, *semantic creativity*. For example, have you ever *really* seen a kettle boil?

12. *Tradition.* Linguistic conventions are passed on from generation to generation by teaching and learning, not by genes. Some animal communications, such as bees' dancing, are probably genetic in the main.

13. *Duality of patterning.* Duality of patterning refers to the contrast between the phonological and grammatical-lexical subsystems of a language or, more simply, its sounds and meaning. A large number of semantically functional elements, such as morphemes, can be constructed from a small number of nonmeaningful phonological elements. Such duality probably is absent among animal communication systems.

14. *Prevarication.* Linguistic messages may be false or logically meaningless. I might tell you that it is ten miles from the earth to the moon or, using a classic example of semantic anomaly, that colorless green ideas sleep furiously. We are hard put to find examples of lying or anomaly among animals. Note that this feature depends on other design features, including semanticity, displacement, and openness. A test of the validity of a message depends on meaning; a lie is possible only by displacement of the message from the immediate context; and meaningless messages can be generated only if the system is open.

15. *Reflexiveness.* Language can "reflect on itself." That is, we can communicate about communication. Bees cannot dance about dancing. More generally, we can talk about anything we can experience, including language itself. This is obviously an enormously powerful feature.

16. *Learnability.* A speaker of a language can learn another language. This feature is altogether lacking in many infrahuman systems of communication, such as bees' dancing.

Hockett elaborates on the significance of these features and extends them in interesting ways, but we need not pursue the matter. The important point is that Hockett has been able to identify many characteristics of human language that are not universally shared by the communication systems of other animals. Moreover, taken as a whole, the list of design features clearly distinguishes language from any natural infrahuman communication system known to us. That is, at most only a few of the features are combined in the system of any one species, although different species may use different subsets. Can we go beyond Hockett's analysis, however, and identify a few features that would suffice to distinguish language from the natural communication systems of animals?

For our part, if we were pressed to choose a single crucial feature, we would propose that *semanticity* is the *sine qua non* of human language: effective signals can stand for something else. Naming is undoubtedly the most straightforward and dramatic example of such semantic behavior. A child says "apple," and the parent promptly gets a reddish round object, hands it to the child, who begins to eat it. Many animals can signal need states generally or perhaps convey distinctions between such states as distress and satisfaction, but the signal is itself a component or direct expression of the distress or satisfaction rather than an unrelated piece of behavior that only indirectly *means* distress or satisfaction. Plainly stated, people can talk about distress or satisfaction without necessarily experiencing these emotions at the moment, just as we can discuss apples independent of having one present. Animals, too, can react to the not-here-and-not-now, but they do not usually emit signals that stand for the absent objects and are understood by others.

Semanticity cannot stand alone as a defining attribute, however. It depends on or subsumes several other features, including especially an open patterning of a limited number of discrete units that usually bear an arbitrary relation to the thing itself. Arbitrariness is implied by the abstract concept of semanticity, and discreteness and openness are attributes of syntacticity. These two features, *semantics and syntax*—meaning and grammatical patterning—are the indispensable core attributes of any human language.

Note that we have omitted many features that Hockett regards as crucial. For example, we have not included the vocal-auditory channel and the other features that hang on it because the gestural language used by the deaf is too important an exception to ignore; we have left out displacement because so many examples of displaced signals can be found among other animals; learnability is not mentioned because it is implicit in the meaning of semanticity and syntacticity as concepts; and so on. We do not, however, wish to take a strong stand on whether the omitted features should or should not be included in a rigorous definition of language. We have been deliberately selective only to emphasize the centrality of meaning and syntactic patterning in any definition of human language.

The preceding comparative analysis of the defining criteria of human language was concerned with natural communication systems, that is, systems that arise naturally in the course of phylogenetic and ontogenetic development. It is probably safe to conclude that only humans have naturally acquired a syntactically organized semantic language. Until recently, it was assumed also that only humans can acquire language. However, Gardner and Gardner (1969) have been able to teach a chimpanzee a gestural language that apparently meets the criteria of syntacticity and semanticity. Premack (1971) has similarly trained chimpanzees to use plastic tokens in a meaningful and productive way. Rumbaugh (1976) did so as

well, using a procedure in which a chimpanzee learned to read and construct sentences using symbols presented on a computer push panel. Finally, Patterson (1978) has succeeded in teaching a female gorilla to use a manual sign language in much the same productive way as the Gardners' chimpanzee who uses signs. These findings are challenging to psychology and linguistics, as well as to the biological sciences generally, for they point to evolutionary continuity in the very behavior that seemed to set Homo sapiens uniquely apart. These discoveries enormously increase the possibilities for the rigorous investigation of language acquisition (but see also Terrace, Petitto, Sanders, & Bever, 1979).

Summary

This chapter has attempted to sharpen our conception of language, in order to provide some guidelines for later discussions. Our concern is more with the natural languages that people use than with formal languages. However, much of natural language can be addressed formally, even if some aspects of natural language cannot. The question becomes clearer if we contrast two aspects of natural language, namely *la parole*, the actual speech acts performed by individuals, and *la langue*, the more abstract linguistic system shared by members of a language community. By observing *la parole*, we infer the nature of *la langue*, describe its rules, and generally attempt to elucidate the structures and dispositions that underlie our ability to use language.

Language can be seen as a system of signs that can be syntactically related to each other, semantically related to the things referred to, and pragmatically related to the users of the signs. Once linguistic use is highlighted, it becomes clear that a major use of language is to communicate information between its users. Language shares much with other communication systems, although linguistically transmitted information may be less readily quantifiable than other types of information. Nonetheless, the communication-information metaphor further sharpens our conception of language.

The final consideration in the chapter was to contrast human language with the communication systems of other species. There are many features of human language not universal to all biological communication, but the most important appear to be semanticity and syntax—meaning and grammatical patterning.

linguistic approaches
to the
study of language

3

The study of language is of interest to scientists from many disciplines. Psychology, anthropology, sociology, philosophy, and computer science are just a few obvious examples. In this chapter, we consider some linguistic approaches to the problem, with special emphasis on the psychological implications of those approaches.

Linguistics, like psychology, has a history scarred by numerous battles. One classic debate in both disciplines contrasts *mentalism* with *materialism*. Bloomfield (1933) polarized the debate quite crisply. Mentalists believe that language expresses some underlying, nonphysical event, such as an idea, image, thought, concept, or proposition that exists independently of and prior to its linguistic expression. We all learned in school that a sentence *expresses* a thought; this view implies that the thought *underlies* the utterance. The opposing view is materialism, which holds that separating expression and thought is unjustified dualism; thought *is* subvocal speech, accompanied by memory of the circumstances in which units of that speech were uttered in the past. It is important to note that neither mentalism nor materialism is a single view; each has had many different forms, sometimes at odds with each other. Each has virtues—materialism leads us to analyze the publicly observable side of language, and mentalism leads us to analyze the intellectual and motivational content of speech (J.J. Katz, 1964, presents a readable argument for mentalism on a much broader scale).

In the remainder of the chapter, we shall consider *structural linguistics* as an account of the material side of language and *transformational generative grammar* as a mentalistic account of language. A word of caution: linguistic theories are complex, so you should not be surprised or discouraged if you find that some of the ideas take a bit of work to get through. Also, we shall stress linguistic theories that have been influential in psychological domains, although some alternatives will be mentioned briefly later on.

STRUCTURAL LINGUISTICS

Structural linguistics presents us with a systematic way to describe the units of language and how those units combine to produce acceptable sentences. A language can be considered from several levels, each related in some way to the others. Thus

sounds combine to form syllables and words, which in turn combine to form phrases and sentences. Commonly used terms, in increasing order of size, are phone, phoneme, morpheme, word, phrase, sentence, and text. The terms correctly imply that structural linguistics has emphasized the sound system (phonology) and the grammatical structure (syntax), although syntax has been less of a concern than phonology. Before considering these emphases separately, we introduce three general points that characterize the structural approach to the study of linguistic units.

The structural linguist ignores meaning

The statement that the structural linguist ignores meaning is based on a view first expressed by Bloomfield. It is true in one important sense but not in others. It is true that the linguist does not ask *what* the meaning of a unit is; however, he or she does ask *whether* a unit is meaningful or, more importantly, whether two units *differ* in meaning. Thus a non-English-speaking linguist might ask whether the different spoken words, *ship* and *sheep,* also differ in meaning. The fact that the words do differ is more important to determining structure than is knowledge of what the terms denote.

Units are contrastive

As implied above, if two units differ in meaning, regardless of what the meanings are, the differences in sound become important as well. Thus the vowel sounds in *ship* and *sheep* are contrastive units in English but not in some other languages, such as Spanish. We shall say more about this in a later section.

Units are defined by composition and distribution

Composition refers to the *hierarchical* nature of language—the units of one level are made up of the discrete units of another level: sentences are made up of phrases, phrases of words, and so on. Distribution refers to the systematic nature of language—some units are more likely than others to occur in certain places. For example, given a frame or *paradigm* such as "I saw a ____," the blank can be filled by some units (for example, cat, hypotenuse, or dirty old man eating cheese) but not others (for example, silence, big, or water). The units that can occur in the same paradigm are in *parallel* distribution (sometimes referred to as contrastive); units that cannot are in *complementary* distribution (also called noncontrastive) with the units that can.

We will expand on the above points in the context of the discussions that follow. Let us start with the structuralist's approach to speech sounds.

Phonological Units and Structures

Phonology is concerned with the analysis of speech sounds. It draws on the science of *phonetics*, which is concerned with the analysis of the characteristics of elementary units of speech sounds (phones) more or less independent of their function as parts of more complex entities (phonemes, morphemes, and the like) in language use. The physical analysis can be based on the physical, acoustic properties or on the articulatory properties (the way they are pronounced) of the phonetic units. The articulatory approach is the more useful to the linguist or psycholinguist, and we shall examine it after a brief summary of the acoustic approach.

1. Acoustic Phonetics

Acoustic phonetics actually has as much to do with physics as with language. You may recall from high-school physics that sound occurs when air molecules vibrate. The vibrations of many molecules produce a sound wave, much like a wave in water. The wave travels through the air as molecules bump into other ones. Although complex sounds have complex waveforms, each one may be broken down into a number of simple sine waves. The advantage of doing this is that a sine wave can be uniquely described as having three characteristics, namely *intensity, frequency*, and *duration*. Duration refers to how long the wave lasts before the vibrations stop. Frequency refers to the number of vibrations or cycles each second; the higher the frequency, the higher the pitch (have you ever played a record album at 45 or 78 rpm?). Intensity refers to how violent each vibration is; more intense vibrations produce louder sounds. Simply put, sounds may be longer or shorter, higher or lower, and louder or softer.

Speech sounds, as we have seen, constitute an acoustic pattern that can vary in intensity, frequency, and duration. These characteristics can be analyzed by means of *speech spectography*, in which a spectograph converts the sound into a visual pattern (spectogram) by passing the sound through a set of filters that resonate to different frequencies. This breaks up the speech sound into ten to twenty frequency bands. The intensity at different frequency levels is recorded as blackened areas on a moving band of paper. The intensity or energy level of a particular frequency at a given point in time is represented by the degree of darkness of the graphical tracing at that point. Time is recorded along the horizontal axis. Figure 3-1 shows an example of a spectogram. The analysis of such tracings reveals differences between vowels and consonants and between different vowels. With vowels, the vocal cavity acts as a filter for some frequencies and as a *resonator* (reinforcer) for others. This is revealed in the spectogram as different peaks of intensity, in which different frequency bands show concentrations of energy (darkness). Usually two of these are prominent, as in Figure 3-1. Such concentrations of energy in a relatively narrow frequency band are called *formants*. The position and number of formants identify different vowels (but these are not the only factors). Consonants are revealed by a sudden change in the even pattern of the formants over time. The consonant pattern is particularly affected by the quality of the neighboring vowel. We shall have more to say about this later in our discussion of speech perception (chapter 6).

2. Articulatory Phonetics

Articulatory phonetics focuses on the production of speech sounds. In a phonetic description of a language, the linguist typically transcribes the sounds made by a skilled speaker, or informant, into a standard phonetic script. The most widely used script is the International Phonetic Alphabet (IPA), which is fully described in *The Principles of the International Phonetic Association* (1949). We need not consider the entire script, because not all sounds made in one language are made, or are important, in all others. Our purposes will be served by emphasizing English while providing some basis for comparison with another language. We have chosen French because of its importance in the North American context and because it is at least somewhat familiar to most readers of this text. Accordingly,

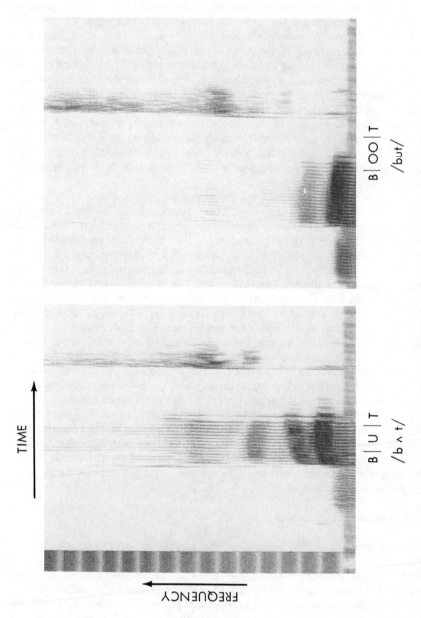

FIGURE 3-1. Speech spectrograms for the words BUT and BOOT.

Table 3-1 presents the portion of the IPA that is adequate for English and French. We shall be especially concerned with the sounds and sound differences relevant to these two languages.

Articulatory mechanisms

Speech sounds are made by modifying the flow of air from the lungs to the lips. The organs that form the channel obstruct the passage of air in various ways. The most important organs are presented in Figure 3-2, including the vocal cords, tongue, lips, upper teeth, alveolar ridge (behind the upper front teeth), palate, and velum (the fleshy part at the back of the roof of the mouth). Sound is produced when the air stream is set into vibration at some point along this vocal tract. This is usually done by the vocal cords, two bands of elastic cartilage near the top of the windpipe. When these are open, air passes unobstructed through the space between, called the glottis. When they are tightly closed, air cannot flow through the windpipe; when they are partially closed, the air stream sets them in vibration, producing a sound called *voicing*. Speech sounds with vibration are called *voiced*, and those without it are *voiceless*. Other qualitative aspects of speech sounds are affected by *closure, constriction,* or *alteration in the shape* of the vocal tract at some point. The resulting sounds are identified in terms of such features as the *degree of opening,* the *articulators involved,* and the *primary point of articulation* along the vocal tract. We shall first discuss consonants and then vowels in terms of these articulatory features.

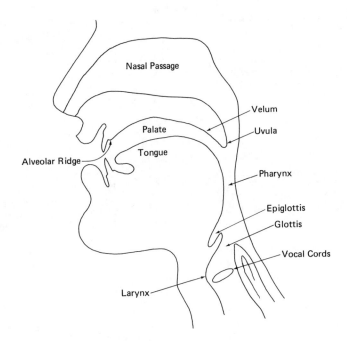

FIGURE 3-2. Speech organs.

TABLE 3-1 Phonetic Symbols (IPA) with English and French Examples

Vowels and Semi-vowels (Semi-consonants)

Symbol	Example English	Example French	Symbol	Example English	Example French
[i]		vite	[ə]*	sofa, rodent	le, petit
[i:]	eat, feel		[y]		cru, fume
[ɨ]	children		[y:]		mur, dur
[I]	it, fill		[ɸ]		feu, noeud
[e]		fée, j'ai	[ɸ:]		feutre
[ɛ]	bet, fell	fait, très	[œ]		jeune, oeuf
[ɛ:]		père, fête	[œ:]		peur, soeur
[æ]	at, add		[ɛ̃]		vin, main
[a]		chat, là	[ɛ̃:]		prince, feinte
[a:]		phare, noir	[ã]		temps, enfant
[ɑ]	follow, fall	pas, tantôt	[ã:]		danse, ample
[ɑ:]		âge, sable	[õ]		mon, plomb
[ɔ]	was, loss	donne, folle	[õ:]		nombre, honte
[ɔ:]		forte, côte	[œ̃]		un, lundi
[o]	obey	faux, dos	[œ̃:]		défunte, humble
[o:]		faute, rôle	[j]	yell	yeux, fille
[U]	wool, full	toute, foule	[w]	well	oui, noir
[u],[u:]	too, fool	cour, four	[ɥ]		huit, muet
[ʌ]	cut, cover				

Diphthongs

Symbol	Example English	Example French	Symbol	Example English	Example French
[i:j]		fille	[ɑ:j]		bâiller, rail
[eI]	fail		[ɔI]	foil	
[ɛ:j]		soleil, paye	[uU]	fool	
[aI],[aj]	aisle, file	travail, médaille	[aU]	fowl, bough	
[a:j]		ferraille	[oU]	foal, low	
			[œ:j]		oeil, fauteuil

Consonants

Symbol	Example English	Example French	Symbol	Example English	Example French
[p]	pill	peau	[tʃ]	chill	
[b]	bill	beau	[dʒ]	Jill	
[t]	till	tant	[θ]	thigh	
[d]	dill	dent	[ð]	thy	
[k]	kill	quand	[m]	mill	maître
[g]	gill	gant	[n]	nil, sin	naître
[f]	fan	fou	[ŋ]	sing	camping
[v]	van	vous	[ɲ]		oignon, vigne
[s]	seal	sel, baisser	[l]	lot, tall	lit, pelle
[z]	zeal	zèle, baiser	[r]**	rot, tar	rit, père
[ʃ]	shell	chou	[h]	hill	
[ʒ]	measure	joue			

*This is called "schwa," the neutral vowel.
**This is actually the IPA symbol for the rolling r, common to many European languages and Scottish English. The English and North American English r is symbolized ɹ, and the international variety of French uses the uvular R.

Consonants

Consonants are produced by constricting or closing the vocal tract at some point. Figure 3-3 summarizes the articulatory information for English consonants. The same consonants are relevant in French, which also adds the alveopalatal [ɲ], the gn sound in words like *campagne,* and the uvular [R]. The four major classes of consonants are *stops, affricates, fricatives,* and *resonants;* each is described separately below.

Stops are produced by closing the vocal tract by the lips (bilabial), the tongue (in the alveolar region), or the velum, each producing a different sound. At each position, the sound can be either voiced or voiceless, as illustrated by the contrasting pairs of words in the figure. You can sense the various articulatory positions by paying attention to your own articulatory organs as you pronounce pill, till, and kill—the point of closure shifts backwards; similarly, with bill, dill, and gill, the closure

		Articulatory Position						
		Bilabial	Labiodental	Dental	Alveolar	Alveopalatal	Velar	Glottal
Stops								
	V−	p (pill)			t (till)		k (kill)	
	V+	b (bill)			d (dill)		g (gill)	
Affricates								
	V−					tʃ (chump)		
	V+					dʒ (jump)		
Fricatives								
Slit	V−		f (fan)	θ (thigh)				h (hot)
	V+		v (van)	ð (thy)				
Grooved	V−				s (sue)	ʃ (asher)		
	V+				z (zoo)	ʒ (azure)		
Resonants								
Lateral	V+				l (lot)			
Nasal	V+	m (some)			n (sun)		ŋ (sung)	
Semivowels	V+	w (watt)			r (rot)	j (yacht)		

FIGURE 3-3. English consonants with some examples of minimally contrasting pairs.

also moves backwards. In actual speech, stops have an additional characteristic, *aspiration;* carefully pronounce *pill* and *spill,* noting the "p" sound in each case. There is a slight puff of air in the first case, but not in the second; in fact, if you tape-recorded *pill* and replayed it *backwards,* it would sound more like *lisp* than *lip,* and *spill* would sound like *lips.* However, the difference in aspiration is one that English speakers normally do not even hear, because it is not a functional difference in English; that is, there is no pair of words, *pill* and *p*(h)*ill,* that differs in meaning. Moreover, the aspirated *p* does not even occur in some languages, including French and Finnish. However, a complete phonetic description would include aspiration, because it is important in other languages, such as Thai.

Affricates, like stops, require a closure of the vocal tract, but the closure is followed by a release that produces turbulence. In English, the only affricates are alveopalatal, although there are many others in other languages. By pronouncing *chump* and *jump,* you can experience the voiceless and voiced quality of the affricates. Actually, affricates are complex sounds, and in some systems they are included as stops, but in others they are included with grooved fricatives because they share features of both.

Fricatives are produced by constricting the vocal tract, so that air is released with an audible hissing, scraping, or buzzing sound. These also are identified by the presence or absence of voicing, as the contrasting pairs illustrate. The various fricatives are differentiated by the place of narrowest constriction and by the shape of the channel (*slit* or *grooved*) at that point. Note that [h] is not pronounced in French and that it generally has no voiced counterpart in English (an exception is the intervocalic h, as in *aha*), although it does in other languages. Also, in several American regions, the difference between [ʃ] and [ʒ] tends to be suppressed.

Resonants are articulated by changes in the oral cavity that permit air to escape in a restricted way, through the mouth or nose, with a characteristic resonance. All the resonants are voiced, and all can be extended to be long sounds. With [l], air escapes from the sides of the mouth, with the tongue closing off the center region. The *nasals* all permit air to escape through the nose; if you have a cold, with the nasal passages plugged, a sentence such as *Mike is not singing* sounds more like *Bike is dot siggig.* The nasal [ŋ] only occurs inside or at the end of words in English, as in *bank* or *thing;* in other languages, it is a frequent beginning for words. Finally, the semivowels share many characteristics with the vowels, to be discussed shortly. The [w] and [j] sounds are particularly important in English, because they can combine with vowels to produce *diphthongs;* they are often referred to as *glides.* French adds the semivowel [ɥ], as in *lui* [lɥi].

This concludes our brief look at English and French consonants. The sounds are not the only possible ones. However, any language makes use of only a portion of the possible sounds, and that portion is quite different from language to language. This is one reason that adults retain accents when learning to speak a new language.

Vowels

In general, different vowels are produced by changing the shape of the vocal tract so that different component frequencies will be emphasized. This is primarily accomplished by the tongue in English; in French and other languages, the lips are either *rounded* or *unrounded,* and the tongue height is more finely subdivided. The

basic vowel structures of English and French are shown in Figures 3-4 and 3-5, respectively. *Tongue advancement* refers to the part of the tongue that is highest, ranging from the tip, or front, to the back. *Tongue height* refers to the height of the tongue at that point, ranging from the roof to the floor of the mouth.

The English *front* vowels are [i], [I], [ɛ], [e], and digraph [æ], as in *meat, mitt, met, mate* [meɪt], and *mat,* in decreasing order of height. These are unrounded vowels, to which French adds the rounded vowels. [y], [ɸ], and [œ], corresponding in height to their unrounded counterparts, [i], [e], and [ɛ]. Examples are shown in Figure 3-5 and Table 3-1. In actual speech, vowels differ in other qualities as well. For example, *hit, hid,* and *his* are progressively longer versions of [I], although length is not as important in English as in some other languages. Although most speakers of American English have versions of the front vowels, the *central* and *back* vowels are harder to illustrate. A relaxed pronunciation of *He just bought a gorgeous couch for the business* shows three cases of barred [ɨ] *–just* and the final vowel in *gorgeous* and *business.* In some dialects, however, [ɨ] is hard to distinguish from [I] in *hid* or *children.* The relaxed vowel, schwa [ə], occurs in *but* and twice in *butter* for many speakers, although again there are differences. It is also quite hard to locate [ɑ], as in *hot,* in some English dialects; try pronouncing *cot* and *caught*–to many speakers, the two are identical, with the tongue advancement farther back than [ɑ]. For example, *hot* and *father* both have [ɑ] sounds in the eastern United States, but both are pronounced farther back in central Canadian English. Perhaps the hardest vowels to identify in American

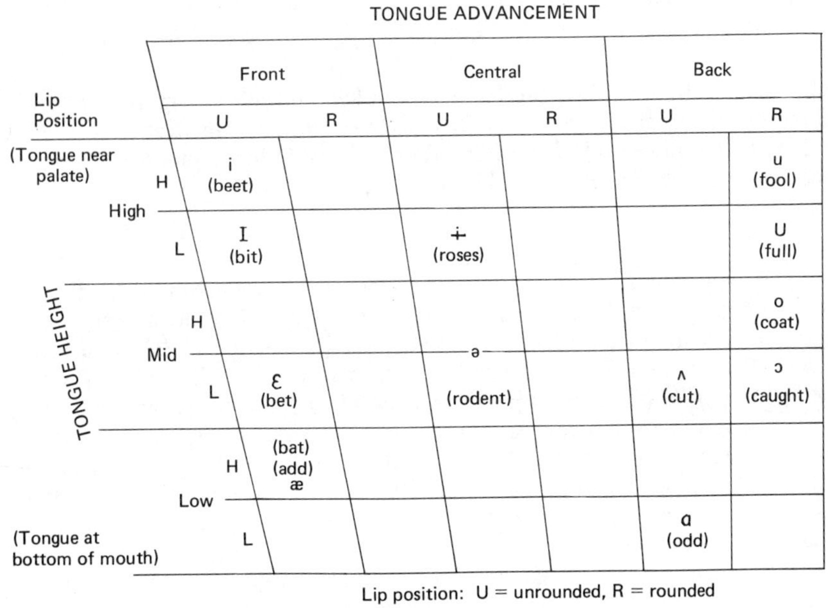

TONGUE ADVANCEMENT

		Front		Central		Back	
Lip Position		U	R	U	R	U	R
(Tongue near palate)	H	i (beet)					u (fool)
High	L	I (bit)		ɨ (roses)			U (full)
Mid	H						o (coat)
	L	ɛ (bet)		ə (rodent)		ʌ (cut)	ɔ (caught)
	H	(bat) (add) æ					
Low							
(Tongue at bottom of mouth)	L						ɑ (odd)

Lip position: U = unrounded, R = rounded

FIGURE 3-4. Basic vowel positions for English with some examples of contrasting pairs (phonemes). Note that [ɨ], [ə], and [ʌ] are all variants (allophones) of the phoneme schwa / ə /.

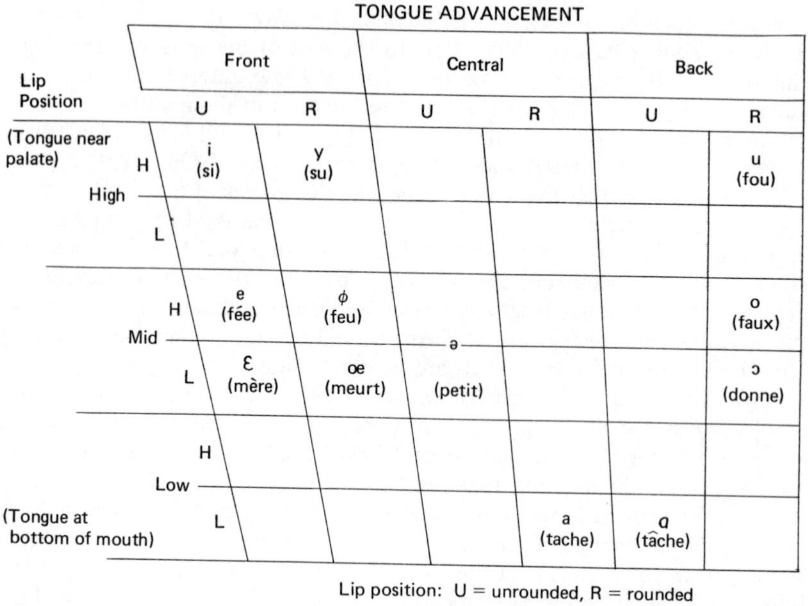

TONGUE ADVANCEMENT

Lip Position	Front		Central		Back	
	U	R	U	R	U	R
(Tongue near palate) H — High	i (si)	y (su)				u (fou)
L						
H — Mid	e (fée)	φ (feu)	ə			o (faux)
L	ɛ (mère)	œ (meurt)	(petit)			ɔ (donne)
H — Low						
(Tongue at bottom of mouth) L				a (tache)	ɑ (tâche)	

Lip position: U = unrounded, R = rounded

FIGURE 3-5. Basic vowel positions for French with examples of contrasting pairs. Note that rounding is relevant (phonemic) in French although not in English (cf. Fig. 3-4).

English are the back vowels. The [U] sound in *book* is quite common, but both the [o] and open [ɔ] sounds are rarely heard alone. In some American speech, [o] is heard with the glide [w], as in *boat* [bowt]; [o] is heard in *obey* [obeI], but other speakers pronounce it [oUbeI], and so on.

Diphthongs

The diphthongs are made by combining two vowels with each other or a vowel with a glide. All combinations are possible, but they do not all occur in English or French. Some English examples are *bait* [beIt], *bite* [baIt], *boat* [boUt], and *bout* [baUt]. French diphthongs consist primarily of vowels combined with the glide [j], as in *fille* [fi:j], *veille* [vɛ:j], *travail* [travaj]; *rail* [ra:j], and *oeil* [œ:j].

The consonants and vowels of a language are phonetically treated as discrete elements or segments. Such features as length, pitch, and stress are also relevant in most languages. In English, they are called prosodic or suprasegmental features because of the practice of describing them phonetically by means of marks (diacritics) over or beside the segmental symbols. We need not go into the details of this aspect of linguistic description here. What is important is the general point that these suprasegmentals form part of a complex bundle of phonetic characteristics that distinguish one speech sound from another. Each segment is distinct because of a particular combination of articulatory features. Whether or not such phonetic distinctions are *functionally* distinct in that they are noticed and used by a speaker of a given language is another question, to which we now turn.

3. Functional Units

The phoneme

At several points in our discussion of phonetics we suggested that particular sound distinctions may be relevant in some languages but not in others. This means that phonetic distinctions that make a difference and are readily noticed and used by the speakers of one language may not make a difference or even be noticed by the speakers of another language. A clear example is the contrast between [l] and [r]. This is a significant distinction for a speaker of English: *lamp* does not mean the same thing as *ramp*. This phonetic difference is not similarly significant in Japanese, so that a Japanese learning English as an adult might confuse the two sounds when pronoucing English words, perhaps saying "ramp" for "lamp" and vice versa.

In structural linguistics, such distinctive sound units are called phonemes. A phoneme is the smallest relevant (psychologically "real") sound unit in a language. It is an abstraction that refers to a *class* or set of phones to which the speakers of a language react as one sound. The phonetic variants of a phoneme are called *allophones*. Thus [r] and [l] are the allophones of one phoneme in Japanese and Korean, but represent different phonemes in English. The aspirated [kʰ] in *k*ill and the unaspirated [k] in s*k*ill, on the other hand, are allophones of a single phoneme, /k/ in English, although they are phonemically distinct in Hindi. (Note that the phonemic /k/ is symbolized by enclosing the consonant in slashes. This is a descriptive convention that distinguishes phonemes from the bracketed phonetic units discussed in the preceding section.) The language qualification is important: *Sounds are phonemic or nonphonemic only with reference to a particular language.*

The concept of phoneme is interesting psychologically because it implies that a speaker of a given language must have learned to pay attention to particular phonetic differences while in a sense ignoring other differences that may be equally perceptible if attention is directed to them. What phonetic characteristics determine whether or not a particular distinction is phonemic? To answer this question, let us consider how a linguist goes about a phonological analysis aimed at identifying the phonemic and nonphonemic distinctions of a sound system.

Minimal contrasts

Basically, the linguist systematically introduces minimal changes in a speech sound in a given context, as in "lamp" versus "ramp," and asks an informant whether this alters the meaning of the larger unit. Consider a series of English words like *pill, bill, till, dill;* these are identical except for the initial sound. By contrasting these in pairs, like *pill* versus *bill,* we find that each difference is significant in English. Note, too, that the difference is phonetically minimal: [p] and [b] both are bilabial stops, but the first is voiceless and the second is voiced. Similarly, *till* and *dill* are phonemically distinct because of a difference in voicing the initial alveolar stops, [t] and [d]. Again, *pill* and *till* differ only in the articulatory location of the initial voiceless stop—one is bilabial, the other, alveolar. The same procedure can be applied to other sets with consonant contrasts in the initial position (*yet, wet; pun, bun*) and in other positions (*his, hiss*), so that eventually all of the consonantal phonemes of English are identified. By vowel substitutions, as in the set *bit, bet, bat* and *but,* we can discover the vowel phonemes of English.

Parallel contrasts are found in French together with ones that do not occur in English. For example, the rounded-unrounded distinction is important in French but not in English vowels, as illustrated by the constrasting pairs, *si:su, fée:feu,* and *mère:meurt* in Figure 3–5. Again, the front-back contrast between /y/ and /u/ distinguishes such pairs as *tu:tout, du:doux,* and *nu:noue,* but the difference is irrelevant in English. The front-back contrast also distinguishes the French semivowels / ɥ / and /w/, as in *lui* /lɥi/:*Louis* /lwi/, but the former does not occur in English. The general point is that *different phonemes contrast in the same context since a minimal sound change in a given position changes the meaning of the larger unit. Furthermore, such minimal phonemic contrasts are language specific.*

Complementary distribution of allophones

Let us compare the above phonemic differences with the nonphonemic differences between the allophone members of a phoneme. Note, first, that phonemic differences associated with the initial sound segments of the words *pill, bill, dill, till, mill,* and so on cannot be predicted on the basis of some rule. The person learning English has no alternative but to learn each patterning of sounds individually. It is in that sense that /p/, /b/, /d/, and so on are distinctive in both English and French. Now contrast this with the nondistinctive difference between the /k/ in *kin* and *skin. Kin* has an aspirated [kʰ], *skin* an unaspirated [k]. There are parallel differences in the pairs, *key: ski, cool: school,* and *called: scald.* Note that /k/ is always aspirated if it is the initial sound of a word and unaspirated if it is preceded by /s/. The difference is predictable from a rule. But the rule is more general than that, since it applies also to contrasts like *pin: spin* and *top: stop.* Thus, in English, initial voiceless stops are always aspirated, but ones following /s/ are not. In French, similarly, /r/ tends to be voiced in initial and intervocalic positions but not at the end of a word. Such contrasts are in *complementary distribution* since the contrasting sounds never occur in the same phonemic context. The differences are predictable from the context, so they are redundant. This is presumably why they ordinarily go unnoticed by the native speaker and why it is meaningful to refer to them as nondistinctive differences.

Psychologically, the speaker's reactions to phonemic and nonphonemic characteristics are learned during the acquisition of language. Just as the speakers have learned to attend to relevant differences, they also have learned to ignore irrelevant differences—indeed, both kinds of learning can be regarded as two aspects of a common process that results in the formation of abstract categories like phonemes. The acoustic and articulatory distinctions between phonemes are somehow accentuated psychologically, whereas the phonetic distinctions within phonemes (that is, between the allophones of each phoneme) are minimized. How such categorization comes about is one of the important questions that students of language development have attempted to answer.

Suprasegmental phonemes

Just as minimal pairs point out significant consonantal or vocalic sounds, they also point out other features of sound that are contrastive in a language. For example, contrast présent with presént, pérmit with permít, cóntract with contráct,

and import and impórt. In each case, the pairs differ primarily in stress, with an accompanying vowel change in some instances (present). Therefore, stress is phonemic in English. Actually, careful analysis shows that three or perhaps four levels of stress can be perceived as distinguishing minimal pairs. The levels are described elsewhere in more detail (for example, Dinneen, 1967).

Three other types of suprasegmental phonemes are also necessary to distinguish all minimal contrasts. One such phoneme, *plus (or open) juncture,* is needed to distinguish *blackbird* /blækbɔrd/ from *black bird* /blæk + bɔrd/. Similarly, in normal speech, *pitch* provides meaningful information; four pitch levels are identifiably phonemic in English. Finally, in some utterances the pitch is rising, falling, or relatively constant at the end. Such changes are sometimes referred to as *terminal contour.* For example, contrast *He's my friend* with *He's my friend?* and *He's my friend (and I like him).* Phonemically, the sentences would become /²hɪz + maj + frɛnd³¹↘/, /²hɪz + maj + frɛnd³⁴↗/, and /²hɪz + maj + frɛnd³→/; the numerals represent relative pitch, the arrows terminal contour.

Our reason for pointing out the suprasegmental phonemes is simply to illustrate their importance in understanding speech. English and French writers do not *write* these phonemes, but Chinese writers do. It is probably an historical accident that we do not write such sounds, since they are just as necessary for understanding speech as the ones we choose to dignify by writing them in books.

Distinctive features

The minimal sound differences that are phonemically relevant are called distinctive differences, and the articulatory or acoustic characteristics that produce these differences are called *distinctive features.* The latter concept, introduced in 1951 by Jakobson, Fant, and Halle, has been widely adopted in phonological analysis and extended to other problems (for example, semantic analysis) that we will discuss later. It is accordingly important for the student of psycholinguistics to understand the basic idea. Distinctive phonological features are binary (plus or minus) specifications of the articulatory characteristics that are sufficient to define a particular phoneme. We have already encountered some distinctive features in our discussion of phonetic units, since most of the examples used happen to be phonemes of English. Thus, /b/, /p/, /d/, and /t/ are English consonants that can be described, respectively, as a voiced bilabial stop, a voiceless bilabial stop, a voiced alveolar stop, and a voiceless alveolar stop. These descriptions specify the features *voice, stop, bilabial,* and *alveolar.* Each of the four consonants can be described in terms of these four binary dimensions. For example, /b/ could be represented as +voice (it is voiced), +stop (it is a stop), +labial (it is bilabial), –alveolar (it is *not* alveolar); /p/ would be –voice, but otherwise the feature description would be identical to that of /b/; and so on. Such a description is typically represented as a matrix, as follows:

	p	b	t	d
voice	–	+	–	+
stop	+	+	+	+
labial	+	+	–	–
alveolar	–	–	+	+

Of course, this example is only a partial set of features, insufficient to account for all of the consonants and vowels of English, let alone the speech sounds of other languages. To distinguish consonants from vowels, for example, we need the feature *consonantal* (all consonants would have a plus on this, and all vowels, a minus). Fricatives, in general, could be distinguished from other consonants by the feature *spirant* (that is, pronounced with a constant outflow of breath). The feature list for French vowels would need to include the feature *round.* And so on. Different linguists have proposed somewhat different lists, but the basic idea remains the same.

A major advantage of the distinctive feature matrix is that it makes for *descriptive parsimony:* all of the relevant sound segments of a language can be described in terms of a relatively small number of distinctive differences, each unit consisting of a unique bundle of distinctive features. The analytic scheme also has potential psychological value. Note, for example, that some phonemes, like /p/ and /b/, differ on only one feature but that others, like /w/ and /o/, differ on many features. We could say that the former comparison has a smaller phonemic difference than the latter. Can we also infer that the smaller differences are more difficult to perceive, or learn, than the larger ones? If so, phonemic distinctive features could be said to have "psychological reality." Psychologists have in fact explored such possibilities, and their findings will be described later. The present mention of the fact indicates the potential psychological relevance of a concept that comes from structural linguistics.

We have discussed phonemes as the minimal functional units of speech sound. It is important to emphasize, however, that they do not function either linguistically or psychologically as isolated units. A phoneme has significance only in the context of larger grammatical units of language. We turn now to these larger units.

Grammatical Units

The *word* is the basic grammatical unit in the classical grammar with which we all are familiar. Words are, however, analyzable into smaller structural units. The branch of structural linguistics that deals with the composition of language is called morphology, and its unit of analysis is the *morpheme.*

Morphemes

The term morpheme refers to minimal grammatical units of a language. A morpheme is usually a sequence of phonemes, although it may be only one phoneme in length. Morphemes may be intact words like *boy, dog,* and *garden;* or meaningful parts of words, like the *tele-* in *telegraph, telephone,* and *television;* or prefixes like *un-, pre-* and *pro-,* and suffixes like *-er, -ness, -ly,* and the plural *-s.* Thus a word may consist of a number of morphemes; *unfaithfulness,* for example, is constructed from the morphemes *un-, faith, -ful,* and *-ness.* One of these (faith) can stand alone as a word; the others cannot, but all have a unitary meaning of a kind (for example, *un-* has negative valence, equivalent to *not*), and all can appear with the same meaning in other words (*faith*less, *un*necessary, care*ful,* sad*ness*). Thus the hallmark of a morpheme is that it is a *minimal meaningful unit,* one that

cannot be further subdivided without destroying or changing its grammatical meaning.

Like the phoneme, the morpheme is an abstract construct that has its specific phonetic variants, called *allomorphs.* For example, the allomorphic variants of the English plural morpheme include the [s] in *cats,* [z] in *dogs,* and [ɫz] (or [əz]) in *roses;* the idiosyncratic forms in *oxen* and *children;* and sometimes zero form, as in *sheep* and *fish,* whose singular and plural are pronounced alike. Still others replace part of a word (*man* versus *men*) or the entire word (*person* versus *people*).

Descriptive linguists classify morphemes in various ways, such as the distinction between *free* and *bound* morphemes, *full* and *empty* morphemes, and *roots* and *affixes.* Free morphemes like *cat* and *soap* can stand alone as independent words; bound morphemes like *-s, -ness,* and *un-* cannot. Full morphemes are nouns, verbs, adjectives, and adverbs that are relatively meaningful even when presented alone. Empty morphemes are forms like articles, prepositions, and conjunctions which make little semantic sense in isolation. Roots are core morphemes like *man* in unmanly; *un-* and *-ly* are affixes added to the root.

The word

It should be clear by now that morphemes are not equivalent to words, although in many cases the same form is both a word and a morpheme. Although most of us would agree quite readily that some forms are words and some are not, it has proved impossible to reach an unambiguous decision about how to define "word." Why has such a simple task proved so difficult? At a common-sense level, it is tempting to think of a word as a vocal sound that has some agreed-upon meaning. But this definition includes constructions such as *Good morning* or *Let's go for a beer* and excludes forms such as *the,* which are not meaningful in isolation. This is essentially the definition offered by Aristotle, who was quite content to refer to articles as linking particles, or generally nonsignificant speech (*syndesmos*), rather than as words. Before forming our own conclusion, let us consider some of the defining criteria that have been suggested in the past (Lyons, 1968).

Minimal free form

The most common definition of words was offered by Priscian, an influential Roman grammarian around the turn of the millennium, and was further elaborated in 1933 by Bloomfield. A form is free if it can stand alone and be meaningful, and minimal if changing part of it removes its meaning; *unhappiness* is free but not minimal, and *tele-* is minimal but not free. The major difficulty with this definition is once again that empty morphemes such as *a* are meaningless in isolation. For this reason, rather than attempting to define *word,* many linguists prefer to study *forms,* which are more easily defined.

Potential pause

One way of identifying words is through the potential pauses in speech. For example, in saying *The unfaithful woman,* we are more likely to pause before or after *unfaithful* than after *un-.* However, it is quite easy to pause after any syllable,

and in normal speech, there are usually no pauses between words—just listen to the speaker of a foreign language! Thus, pausing is not a reliable criterion.

Internal cohesion

The general notion of internal cohesion is that the word is uninterruptable, since the parts always occur together in the same order, and are mobile in that they can be moved into different positions in a sentence without destroying its meaning. However, phrases such as *the White House* are functionally equivalent to words such as *blackbird* by this definition. Thus it, too, runs into a stumbling block.

Others

In some languages, words are accented by changes in stress or pitch; however, such phonological marking is not universal. Additionally, as we saw above, attempts to define words on semantic grounds run into many of the same problems as the other suggested criteria.

What are we to conclude from all this? One possibility is that "word" is not an *intrinsic* unit in languages; although it is certainly convenient for us to use the term in talking about language, there are languages that appear not to contain words at all—some consist of syllables, some of sentences as minimal forms. Despite such problems the word is an intuitively comfortable level of analysis, and for many psychological purposes it is treated as a basic unit by speakers. Whether this is because of our familiarity with a written language, dictionaries, or whatever, the word has a fundamental place in our daily use of language, and we shall treat it as such, without ignoring larger or smaller units.

Compound words, idioms, and habitual phrases

A particular sequence of words may be used so frequently in a language that it functions as an integrated structure much like a word. One class of such structures is the compound word, of which *rainbow, insofar, textbook,* and *paperback* are familiar examples. Note that the meaning of such compounds is not necessarily predictable from each component word: *rainbow* is not the sum of rain and bow, *bigwig* does not mean a big wig, and *wallflower* is not a flower that grows on a wall. Such compounds are actually *idioms,* whose meanings are only metaphorically related to the meanings of the component words, and the person learning English has no alternative but to learn the compounds essentially as separate units. This is less true of other compounds such as *longbow, dishpan,* and *wildflower,* whose meanings are more or less predictable from their lexical components. An excellent description of such words can be found in Marchand (1967). Comparable French examples are discussed in Mitterand (1976).

The *idiomatic expression* or phrase, like the idiomatic compound word, is another type of complex structure whose meaning is metaphorical, not predictable directly from the meanings of the individual words. Some common examples are *knock down a straw man, fly the coop,* and *hit the sack.* Such idiomatic phrases create an unusually difficult problem for the language learner, not only because their meanings are idiosyncratic, but also because they are usually open to plausible although inappropriate literal interpretations. Consider the following example: A

little girl was chattering away charmingly, and her mother remarked to the girl's father, "Won't Grandpa get a kick out of that mouth!"—whereupon the girl began to sob. Asked why she was crying, she said, "I don't want Grandpa to kick me in the mouth!"—that day she learned the meaning of one English idiom. The anglophone child or adult learning French may be similarly baffled by *chercher la petite bête* ("to be overcritical") or *donner sa langue au chat* ("to give up")!

In addition to their idiosyncratic meaning, many idioms cannot be treated grammatically in the same way as analogous literal phrases. For example, *he spilled the beans* loses its idiomatic meaning if we transform it into the passive, *the beans were spilled by him*. (Try doing the same with other common idioms, such as *he flew off the handle, he got the point,* and so on.) Literal phrases are not similarly affected by such transformations (for example, *he spilled the soup* versus *the soup was spilled by him*). For a more detailed discussion of this point, see Chafe (1970).

Compound words and idioms are complex structures that become part of the common lexicon of a linguistic community. Other *habitual phrases* may do so as well, but undoubtedly all of us have in addition a large repertoire of phrases that form part of our idiolect, or personal language system. Phrases like *spot of tea, spell of weather,* and *back and forth* are common enough in English-speaking communities, but other phrases might be every bit as habitual for a given individual without being similarly so for others.

The general point is that habitually used complex structures, whether words, compounds, idioms, or common phrases, can function as linguistic units because they are understood or uttered as integrated structures with well-defined meaning. All form part of the speaker's *lexicon*, the stock of meaningful, discrete linguistic units that is drawn upon in generating larger structures such as sentences. The way the units are put together in those larger structures is crucial, and it is to that problem we now turn.

Grammatical Structure

Grammatical structure refers to productive *combinations* of units. Recall that productivity means that new messages can be created freely from old and familiar units. Given this tremendous variety, how are we to find regularities in the patterning and combinations we actually use? The general procedure is to describe the abstract basis of language in terms of its grammatical categories and syntactic rules by which members of those categories are combined.

Form classes

In elementary school, each of us learned grammatical parts of speech, ranging from nouns and verbs to articles, participles, and so on. Although such categories are useful in parsing English sentences, they are not present in all languages, nor are they the best units for analyzing the structure of English. Let us briefly illustrate a formal linguistic approach to the problem.

First, an attempt is made to classify various forms by composition, or morphology. English has a relatively small number of bound forms that are useful for this purpose. For example, a morphological definition of a *noun* is a form that can combine with the plural morpheme /-s/, the possessive morpheme /-'s/, and

their allomorphs. The bound forms (the plural and possessive morphemes in the example) are called *inflections,* and forms containing them are called *inflected forms.* By this definition, many words we typically call nouns are easily identified, such as *dog, dogs, dog's,* and *dogs', ox, oxen, ox's,* and *oxen's;* many others, such as *truth,* are not morphological nouns, although they may satisfy other criteria of nounness to a sufficient degree that most of us refer to them as nouns. Similarly, verbs are defined by entering into combinations with inflectional morphemes for past /-d/, progressive /-ing/, and the like; thus, *catch, caught, catching,* and *chase, chased, chasing* qualify as morphological verbs. *Adjectives* are identified by the inflectional morphemes for comparative /-er/ and superlative /-est/, as in *big, bigger,* and *biggest.* Finally, *adverbs* are identified by the presence of the morpheme "in the manner of the preceding form" /-ly/, as in *hotly, manly,* or *purposefully.* By this procedure, we can identify a core of the vocabulary units that are nouns, verbs, adjectives, or adverbs in a morphological sense.

Once basic forms have been identified, the next step is to generate sentence frames, or *paradigms,* including those forms. For example, we discovered that *dog* is a noun; if we delete *dog* in *My brother has a dog,* what other items can we replace *dog* with? Obviously, forms such as *headache, new house,* and *rotten temper that constantly gets him in trouble throughout the summer months* all fit. Forms in parallel distribution with nouns are called *nominals,* or *noun phrases.* Each nominal has a *head* noun and an optional addition called an *expansion.* Thus *house* is the head noun and *new* is the expansion in the nominal *new house.* In a similar fashion, we can determine *verbals* or *verb phrases* as well as *adjectival* and *adverbial* phrases. By and large, we shall use the more familiar labels of noun, verb, adjective, and adverb throughout the book, although the phrase names will be used when it is useful to do so.

Functional classes

To this point, we have discovered various form classes by composition and various constructed forms that are distributed in parallel with those members. Another property of interest is the *function* of those forms in sentences. Although we shall say much more about syntax shortly, let us note that there are three major functions. First, some forms, usually nominals, serve as *subjects* of sentences; the logical subject of a sentence is that segment that identifies the *topic* of the sentence. Second, some forms, usually verbals, serve as *predicates;* the logical predicate of a sentence is the segment that provides a *comment* about the topic. Finally, adjectivals and adverbials typically modify either the subject or predicate; in either case, the modifying form provides a comment about some other sentence component.

Syntactic structure

Grammars describe the categories of forms and also the ways those forms are ordered in correct sentences. It should be clear from our discussion of composition and distribution that the two are by no means independent. However, there are enough interesting conceptual problems to justify separate treatment.

The major structural approach to grammar is Bloomfield's *immediate constit-*

uent analysis, in which a sentence is subdivided into progressively smaller and smaller units, much as in the traditional procedure of sentence parsing. Generally the divisions are dichotomous, or binary, although they need not be. Thus a sentence is first divided into subject and predicate, then subject into article and noun, predicate into verb and object, and so on. The segments resulting from a division are the *immediate constituents* of the level that was divided. The subject and predicate are the immediate constituents of the sentence; the article and noun are the immediate constituents of the subject, and so on. The smallest units, the *ultimate constituents,* are the individual morphemes of the sentence. A constituent analysis can be represented by a system of bracketing in which the immediate constituents are enclosed with brackets. Thus the sentence *The girl hit the cat* would first be subdivided into subject (the girl) and predicate (hit the cat), subject into article (the) plus noun (girl), predicate into verb (hit) plus object (the cat), and so on. Put together, the complete constituent analysis would be represented as ((the) (girl)) ((hit) ((the) (cat))). This representation of brackets within brackets reveals the hierarchical nature of the structure of the sentence. It is revealed even more clearly by a graphical representation:

The girl hit the cat

Many sentences are ambiguous in isolation, so that alternative descriptions are possible. A frequently used example is *they are cooking apples,* which could mean either that some people are doing the cooking or that the apples are for cooking. An immediate constituent analysis would reveal the ambiguity by assigning alternative structural descriptions to the sentence, that is, (they) ((are cooking) (apples)) versus (they) ((are) (cooking apples)). Graphically these are represented as follows:

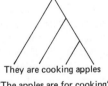

They are cooking apples
("The apples are for cooking")

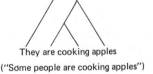

They are cooking apples
("Some people are cooking apples")

This concludes our description of the structural linguists' approach to the analysis of linguistic structures. We have seen that it is basically a compositional approach in which larger functional units are built up from small units—phonemes to morphemes to words to phrases to sentences. Later we will consider in more detail the psychological significance of such units and structures. The approaches we have considered are not the only ones, but they are among the most influential ones.

In earlier sections, we considered the distinction between linguistic performance and linguistic competence, a distinction introduced by Noam Chomsky (for example, 1957, 1965). In Chomsky's view, the goal of linguistic theory is to describe and explain competence. Actual performance would be a direct reflection of competence only in the ideal case, with a speaker-listener who knows a language perfectly and is not influenced by such irrelevant factors as the limitations of memory, attention, or other psychological factors. Because of its enormous influence on and importance to almost all later work, Chomsky's theory of competence is covered here in detail. Other, more recent accounts are covered in later chapters.

According to Chomsky, a language is an infinite set of sentences. The device that can generate such a set is a *generative grammar*. Formally defined, a generative grammar consists of *a finite set of rules operating on a finite vocabulary to generate an infinite number of acceptable grammatical sentences and no unacceptable ones.* As applied to humans, the goal of a generative grammar is to describe the linguistic competence that underlies our use of our shared language. Although it is quite easy to invent generative grammars, it becomes clear very quickly that some grammars are more limited than others. Chomsky described three generative grammars that differ in their capacity or adequacy to account for linguistic competence. The three grammars, namely, finite state, phrase structure, and transformational, are progressively more complex. Because of the importance of generative grammars to psycholinguistics, we shall analyze each one in detail.

Finite State Grammars

Finite state grammars are the simplest grammars. They generate sentences from left to right, one word at a time, with the choice of each word in the sequence limited by the earlier words. Such grammars are often referred to as sequential dependencies, Markov processes, or simply left-to-right grammars. We shall see that the general idea is related to some of the characteristics of information theory as described in chapter 2. As an example, consider how a finite state grammar could generate the sentence, *The boy runs to the store.* The initial word, *the,* would be selected from all the words that can occur at the start of a sentence. Once *the* has occurred, there is a restriction on what words can follow; most usually a noun, such as *boy,* or an adjective will follow. Note that *the* allows both singular and plural nouns, but *a* would limit the nouns to being singular. After *boy, runs* is permissible, as would be *ran,* but not *run;* other permissible words could be *and, with, from,* and so on. The grammar thus proceeds from left to right, with permissible words being generated at each stage. By the time *the boy ran to the* has been generated, the choice of the next word is limited to concrete nouns and their modifiers.

If we ignore practical considerations, we can see that such a grammar is capable of generating an infinite number of sentences simply by adding new words to the end of the string; for example, *the boy went to the store and bought some candy and then returned home and ate the candy and. . . .* However, according to Chomsky, there are sentence constructions in English that are beyond the scope of the grammar. Consider the sentence, *The glass that the woman dropped on the*

floor broke. Although *broke* follows *floor,* it is *glass* that shares a grammatical dependency with *broke,* even though they are separated by an embedded clause. Even within the clause, *woman* and *dropped* could be further separated by embedding another clause such as *that the cat frightened,* yielding *The glass that the woman that the cat frightened dropped on the floor broke.* Such self-embedding of clauses within clauses, or sentences within sentences, is beyond finite state grammars, for the simple reason that grammatical dependencies are between words that are quite far apart. Embedding is a very common property of English, as in cases such as *If S1, then S2* or *Either S3 or S4;* in either case, S1, S2, S3, or S4 can be complete sentences, requiring grammars that "remember" the history and structure of each sentence.

Phrase Structure Grammar

Finite state grammars work on a word-to-word basis, which makes them insufficient in dealing with real language. However, immediate constituent analysis, or parsing, gives some clues as to where to go next. In general, phrase structure grammars operate with the phrase as the unit in generating sentences. Rather than working with words, the grammar works with abstract entities or symbols, such as S for sentence, NP for noun phrase, VP for verb phrase, and so on. The grammar contains rules, called *rewrite rules,* that specify how to replace or rewrite some symbols with other symbols. Let us first begin informally, then become more formal. The informal account will highlight the major ideas of the grammar, but it is useful to work through some formal examples to get a feel for the way the grammar works.

Suppose we were given the following information and were asked to construct sentences on the basis of the information: A complete sentence must include a noun phrase and a verb phrase; the noun phrase contains an article and a noun; the verb phrase contains a verb and another noun phrase (which also contains an article and a noun); the article can be *a* or *the;* the noun could be *boy* or *girl;* and the verb could be *hit* or *kissed.* If we follow the instructions, we could produce *The boy hit the girl, The girl kissed the boy,* and so on. In fact, there are thirty-two sentences that could be produced, using the combinations of The (A) boy (girl) hit (kissed) the (a) girl (boy). This example illustrates an important point regarding the job a grammar must do to account for a language. That is, the grammar makes it possible to generate a particular sentence; it does not guarantee it will do so. The miniature grammar here would allow us to decide that any of the thirty-two sentences are permissible, since they obey the rules. Left on its own, however, we do not know which sentence it would produce.

The rewrite rules of a phrase structure grammar are the "could be" and "must" statements above. Thus, "a sentence must contain a noun phrase and a verb phrase" is presented as "S → NP + VP," in which → means "is rewritten as." Our entire example would be presented as follows:

1. S → NP + VP
2. NP → Det + N
3. VP → V + NP

4. Det → a, the
5. N → boy, girl
6. V → hit, kissed

The model is often represented as a branching-tree diagram with labeled nodes, known as *phrase markers* or P-markers. For example, one of the sentences produced by the above rules is shown in Figure 3-6. The branching lines that connect the symbols represent the rewrite rules, or arrows. The words at the bottom are *terminal* symbols, since the grammar stops when the string consists of words.

To this point we have informally examined an example of a phrase structure grammar. Although such an examination highlights some properties of the grammar, it does not allow general decisions about the limitations of the system. Accordingly, let us consider in more detail Chomsky's formalization of phrase structure grammars. A phrase structure grammar can be represented as a production system, $[\Sigma, F]$. Such a system contains two components, namely a starting state, Σ, and a set of rules, F; in the example above, Σ is S, since that is the starting point, and F refers to the set of all six rewrite rules. Notice in the example that the rules continue to be applied until only words appear in the string. For that reason, there are two types of symbols; *nonterminal* symbols are symbols such as NP, VP, and N, and *terminal* symbols are words in the example.

In order to understand how such a grammar works, let us consider a miniature grammar in which $\Sigma = X$, and F is a set of two rules, $X \rightarrow ab$, $X \rightarrow aXb$; a and b are terminal symbols, and X is nonterminal. In this example, we begin with X. In the next stage, X can be replaced by either ab, in which case we stop, or aXb, in which case we continue. Similarly, the X in aXb can be replaced by ab, in which case we stop with aabb, or it can be replaced with aXb, in which case the string becomes aaXbb. By continuing, we could thus produce aaabbb, and so on. In general, the grammar produces a string of a's followed by an equal number of b's.

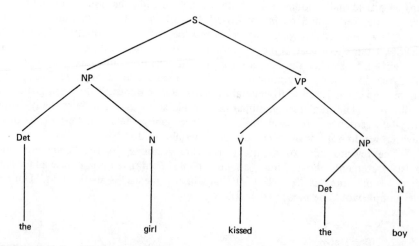

FIGURE 3-6. Phrase marker representation for the sentence *The girl kissed the boy.*

There are two points to note. First, a finite state grammar cannot do this job because the grammar must "remember" the number of a's in order to generate an equal number of b's. Second, notice that the grammar works by embedding, or adding to the middle. The property of the grammar that allows the grammar to be self-embedding is *recursion,* or the ability to use a rule on its own output, as in X → aXb; by looping back and forth across the arrow, it is possible to generate an infinite number of strings.

In general, a phrase structure grammar begins with an initial symbol, replaces that symbol with other symbols, and keeps replacing those symbols with others until the entire string consists of terminal symbols. Such a grammar is quite efficient in producing embedded sequences and is capable of generating an infinite number of sequences. Another property of natural languages that needs to be contained in a grammar is *context sensitivity.* For example, we say *the boy runs,* but *the boys run;* the verb is dependent on the plural or singular status of the subject noun. Such dependency could be produced by the following rules:

1. NP → NP sing, NP plural
2. V → runs/NP sing
3. V → run/NP plural

Again, let us work through this type of context sensitivity more concretely in another miniature grammar. We want a grammar that will generate a string of a's and b's so that every time an *a* occurs, *b* follows, and every *b* is preceded by an *a.* Let Σ = X and F = {X → aY, Y → bX, Y → b}. Step 1 gives us X, the starting symbol. X is then rewritten as aY; if Y becomes b, we will stop at ab, but if Y becomes bX, we will continue by replacing the X in abX, and so on. In this fashion we can generate ab, abab, ababab, and so on. Since Y can occur only after a, there is some degree of context sensitivity in the rule X → aY. One of the most important places for context sensitivity is with reference to verb parts. For example, we say *is walking, is running,* and so on; that is, if *is* is followed by a verb, we add *-ing* to the verb (is + Verb + ing). Often in English, several words appear between *is* and the verb to which *-ing* must be added—he *is* not *walking; is* the fat old man who pinched my sister yesterday still *walking?* And so on. In other words, the grammar must be able to embed a phrase or sentence between the *is* and the verb and still "remember" to add *-ing* to that verb.

Another point about phrase structure grammars pertains to the type of rule. Some rules are *optional;* for example, if both X → bX and X → b are possible, either one could be chosen, and it can be symbolized as X→b(X). Similarly, NP→ Det + N could be NP → Det + (Adj) + N, as in *the (fat) man.* In each case, the symbol in parentheses is optional. Other rules are *obligatory,* since they must be carried out; if Y → aX is the only rule with Y on the left, then Y must be rewritten as aX and nothing else.

As we can see, phrase structure grammars are really quite simple, but rather powerful as well. By recursion, limited context sensitivity, and optional rules, it is possible to generate an infinite number of sentences with considerable flexibility in the form of those sentences. However, the grammars become quite unwieldy in performing other important functions, to which we now turn.

Limitations of phrase structure grammars

Phrase structure grammars are cumbersome in dealing with conjunctions, auxiliary verbs, and verb voices. With regard to conjunctions, consider the following pair of sentences.

1. The scene of the movie and of the play was in Toronto.
*2. The scene of the movie and that I wrote was in Toronto.

The first example is acceptable, but the second is not. The first example joins the following two sentences:

1a. The scene of the movie was in Toronto.
1b. The scene of the play was in Toronto.

In effect, joining the two sentences takes the words between *scene* and *was* in sentence 1b and inserts them with *and* after *movie* in sentence 1a. However, try the same procedure with

2a. The scene of the movie was in Toronto.
2b. The scene that I wrote was in Toronto.

Applying the same rule produces sentence 2, which is unacceptable. Therefore, to use conjunctions properly, we must in some way *mark* the constituents to be conjoined, with reference to their own structure.

There is another problem in considering auxiliary verbs. For example, consider

3. It is heating
4. It is heated
5. It ought to have been heating
6. It ought to have been heated

Considered superficially, sentences 3 and 4 are quite similar, as are sentences 5 and 6. However, sentences 3 and 5 are related (the pronoun *it* might refer to a furnace), but sentences 4 and 6 are related in a somewhat different way (*it* could refer to a house). A useful feature of a grammar would be to point out the underlying similarity between sentences of very different form and the underlying difference between sentences of similar form, as well as to allow the production of the complicated agreements in the first place.

The final problem to consider is the relation between active and passive sentences. A pair of sentences such as *The boy chased the girl* and *The girl was chased by the boy* seem to be saying much the same thing. However, that similarity is not captured readily by a phrase structure grammar. Suppose we were to add a new rule:

$$NP1 + Vtrans + NP2 \Rightarrow NP2 + Auxiliary + Vpast2 + by + NP1$$

This rule allows us to transform the active sentence into a passive one, thereby

pointing out the similarity between the forms despite their superficial differences. Thus, active and passive sentences both are expressions of some common underlying form. The new type of rule does not rewrite constituents; it *transforms* entire strings. Just as finite state grammars work on words and phrase structure grammars work on phrases, so do transformational grammars work on entire strings. Let us now consider Chomsky's model of grammar.

Transformational Generative Grammar

In this section we shall consider Chomsky's theory as originally proposed in 1957, along with some modifications introduced in 1965. Since the modifications refer to the original version, it is useful to understand the original before broaching the more recent formulation.

The 1957 version

The earlier version of the theory consisted of three components through which a speech production proceeded in going from an initial state to speech (in an ideal speaker-hearer). The first component is a *phrase structure* component, followed in turn by a *transformational component* and a *morphophonemic component*. The phrase structure component is essentially the phrase structure grammar just discussed. In this component, the initial state (S, or sentence) is progressively rewritten until it consists of a string of terminal elements that may be identified with the morphemes of the language. The string is not yet speech, nor is it fully grammatical; the context-sensitive rules necessary for grammatical agreement have not yet been applied.

The second component, the transformational component, takes the strings produced by the phrase structure component and applies rules that add or delete morphemes or change their order. Some transformation rules are *obligatory*, since they ensure agreement among the various sentence components. Other transformations are *optional*, including such options as the passive construction, questions, and negatives. Because there are two kinds of transformations of terminal strings, two different kinds of sentences result. Sentences produced by obligatory transformations are *kernel sentences*; all other sentences can be broken down to consist of kernels and optional transformations of those kernels. Thus, transformations apply to anything, whether it is a terminal string from the phrase structure component or a transformed string from other transformations. Transformations sound rather magical and mysterious at first. However, a transformation rule is not very different from the phrase structure rules already considered. The major difference is in the unit involved: phrase structure rules operate on symbols, and transformation rules operate on strings of symbols.

To illustrate the operation of transformations, let us consider another miniature grammar. Our first example, which contained the rule $X \rightarrow a(X)b$, could generate any string of a's followed by an equal number of b's. The second example, with the rules $X \rightarrow aY$ and $Y \rightarrow b(X)$, would generate a sequence of any length beginning with a, ending with b, and alternating between them throughout. Suppose what we wanted to do was simply to produce *any string* of a's and b's, then *duplicate it*. The first part is easy; $X \rightarrow (a)(b)(X)$ will generate any such string.

In the second part, we add a new rule, K ⇒ K + K, in which K is any terminal string produced by the first rule. Quite simply, we apply the first rule until it finishes or terminates; suppose the terminal string was aaababba. Then the entire string (K) is duplicated (K + K); thus, aaababba ⇒ aaababba aaababba. The magic is gone; a transformation is simply a rule that changes one string into another. Some transformations *add*, as in the example; some transformations may leave a string unchanged except for the *deletion* of one or several morphemes; some transformations change the order of (*permute*) some symbols; and so on.

To this point, we have seen that the grammar converts a starting symbol into a finished product that is rather crude, by applying the phrase structure component. The transformational component refines and polishes the product into a form ready to be spoken. The third component, the morphophonemic component, then applies its own rules to convert the morphemes to phonemes for speech. For example, if we symbolize morphemes in normal typeface, one such rule could be walk → /wɑk/; another could be take + past → /tUk/ or hit + past → /hIt/. Note that every irregular verb requires a separate rule for becoming past. Most verbs, however, are quite regular in becoming past, as shown in the following three rules:

1. / . . . . D/ + past → / . . . . D/ + /ɨd/ (D = /t/ or /d/)
2. / . . . . V-/ + past → / . . . . V-/ + /t/
3. / . . . . V+/ + past → / . . . . V+/ + /d/

Loosely speaking, the first rule tells us to determine whether a verb ends in a /t/ or a /d/ sound, such as *flit* or *hid*; if so, the verb is made past tense by affixing an /ɨd/ sound, yielding /flItɨd/ or /kIdɨd/. All other verbs will end either in a voiceless (V-) phoneme or in a voiced (V+) phoneme. If voiceless, add /t/; thus *kiss* becomes *kissed* or /kIst/; *heap* becomes *heaped* or /hi:pt/. If voiced, add /d/; thus *fill* becomes *filled*, /flld/; and *move* becomes *moved* or /mu:vd/. Because we use the letter *d* to indicate past tense, we are often unaware of different pronunciations. However, contrasting *kidded, kissed,* and *killed* shows different pronunciations of the terminal morphophoneme.

A similar system converts nouns to plural. Again there are irregulars, such as sheep + plural → /ʃi:p/ or ox + plural → /ɑksən/. However, the regular nouns can again be handled by three rules.

1. / . . . . F+/ + plural → / . . . . F+/ + /ɨz/ (F+ is fricative)
2. / . . . . V-/ + plural → / . . . . V-/ + /s/
3. / . . . . V+/ + plural → / . . . . V+/ + /z/

The first step is to determine fricative endings, as in *rose*, which becomes *roses* or /roUzɨz/ and *buzz*, which becomes *buzzes* or /bʌzɨz/. Other nouns end either in voiced or voiceless phonemes. Voiced phonemes such as in *dog* and *kid* become /dɔgz/ and /kIdz/; voiceless phonemes such as in *riff* and *heap* become /rIfs/ and /hi:ps/. The same rules apply to other *s* endings, such as third person singular verbs (run, runs) and possessives (Tom, Tom's). Once again, because we use the letter *s* in writing, pronunciation differences may not be obvious until we focus on the sounds; contrast *boozes, boots,* and *boobs*.

Overall, the original version of Chomsky's theory contains three stages in converting an initial symbol to speech. First, a phrase structure component converts the initial symbol into other symbols, continuing until a terminal string, a rather crude string of morphemes, is produced. Second, a transformational component accepts that terminal string and applies rules to polish it; obligatory rules produce grammatical kernels, and optional rules rewrite the kernels in various ways. Third, a morphophonemic component converts the strings of morphemes into strings of phonemes ready for speech. Each component has rules and operates in an orderly fashion.

The 1965 version

Fundamentally, the revised version of the theory is much like the earlier version, with a few changes that make the system somewhat easier to conceptualize. Recall that in the version just discussed the phrase structure component was the base, generating strings of terminal symbols to be transformed. In his later work, Chomsky made the system more economical by amalgamating the base and the transformational component into a *syntactic component*. In the syntactic component, one subcomponent is the *base*, a set of rules that generates a relatively small set of strings, each with a structural description called a phrase marker, or P-marker. The strings and P-markers produced by the base are referred to as *deep structure*. The other part of the syntactic component is the *transformational subcomponent*, which, as in the earlier version, rewrites base strings in a more polished form referred to as the *surface structure*.

In overview, the syntactic component generates deep structures that are interpreted by a *semantic* component and surface structures that are interpreted by a *phonological* component. Although the distinction between deep and surface structure seems clear, there are some fine points that muddy the waters somewhat. For example, we have seen strings that consist of symbols such as S, NP, and VP, symbols such as boy and kiss, and symbols such as past and plural. Symbols such as NP are *category symbols* that clearly belong to the deep structure. However, the *lexical formatives* (boy) and *grammatical formatives* (past) are elements of the surface structure (1965, p. 143). The problem becomes one of describing precisely what elements in the deep structure underlie such formatives. According to Chomsky, it is the morphemes of the language that underlie the formatives. Chomsky points out that the morphemes are not necessarily identical to the formatives, since some morphemes may be added or deleted by transformations. Nonetheless, for most purposes, the morphemes of the deep structure correspond quite closely to the formatives of the surface structure, despite transformations of the morphemes in generating the formatives. Conceptually, each structure can be seen as a plane, with points on each plane connected to points on the other.

To summarize, the revised version of transformational generative grammar consists of three components. The basic component is syntactic. The syntactic component consists of *phrase structure rules*, a *lexicon*, and *transformational rules*, by which an initial symbol is rewritten as a terminal string of symbols, or morphemes. The deep structure, the strings generated by the phrase structure rules, is then interpreted by the semantic component, which itself consists of two parts. The *dictionary* provides semantic interpretations for lexical items, and *projection*

rules assign semantic interpretations to strings (how the dictionary and projection rules operate is described in chapter 5, in the context of meaning). Once the base strings are further transformed, they are interpreted again by the final component, the phonological component. In the phonological component, lexical formatives are represented by *distinctive feature matrices* from which speech is produced. As we can see, the system is one of rules within rules, context sensitivity, and successive refinement in generating, polishing, and editing speech.

Some psychological implications

The most contentious part of the theory, from a psychological perspective, is that the syntactic component is the most important, with semantic interpretation occurring after much of the work is done. However, this is not a theory of the way people *speak*. Rather, it is a theory of the abstract, formal structure of *la langue*, which may have nothing whatsoever to do with actual performance. As psychologists, we might wish to propose a still deeper system of intentions, wishes, ideas, or whatever, to *precede* the initial state of the grammar, and a still shallower system with tongues and lips or ears, to allow the system to meet the world. But such additions say nothing about the theory itself; in this regard it is important to note that the semantic component is not to be equated with meaning; it is instead a lexicon, an entirely intralinguistic set of substitution rules.

Because this latter point appears to be widely misunderstood, we shall dwell on it somewhat. Recall from chapter 2 that Saussure differentiated between the conceptual and material value of signs, or speech tokens. The conceptual value of a token is its relation with the other terms in its system; this is precisely a semantic definition, which specifies how a term fits and is distributed within a system. Material value is something else again, referring to things outside the linguistic system, to which the term is also related. Now here is the major point: Regardless of the structural or formal descriptions of language, it is still true that we use the language to convey messages about something *other than language*. The conceptual or formal linguistic system is *necessary* if we wish to produce understandable sentences, and it places *constraints* on what we *must* say to be understood. The system pertains to *what we say*, but not to what we say it *about*. Intuitively, it seems that we normally decide on some message, and then we speak. Consequently, the questions of meaning and intent themselves form a system, whose output is the *initial point* for a linguistic system. As a result, theories such as Chomsky's are not addressed by psychological experiments, which study the input to and output from the linguistic system, not the system itself. However, any formal system can be interpreted in many ways; the interpretations *can* be tested. Negative results pertain to the interpretations and therefore limit the domain of *applicability* of the theory (cf. Hjelmslev, 1961, p. 14), not the theory.

Other Linguistic Approaches

We have emphasized structural linguistics and transformational grammar because of the great influence each has had on linguistics and on the psychological study of language. You should be aware, however, that the linguistic story we have presented is not complete. European structuralism, for example, continues to be

active in the work of Halliday (1973) and others. There are, as well, numerous variations and offshoots of American structural and transformational approaches, some emphasizing surface structure and others deep structure, some putting their money on syntax and others on semantics. Thus, Yngve (1960) proposed a surface structure model based on the idea that sentence generation proceeds hierarchically through the various levels of phrase structure, in a left-to-right manner. The model has implications for comprehension and memory that will be discussed in later chapters. Lamb's (1966) stratification grammar, which shares some of the features of Yngve's depth model, has been psychologically exploited by Peter Reich (1970). Montague (1970) attempted to apply the logician's method of formal syntax and semantics to natural language so that syntactic rules would correspond in a one-to-one fashion with semantic rules. Barbara Partee (1975, 1976, 1977) extended Montague's grammar by adding transformational rules and suggested how the modified approach might function as a psychologically relevant model, capable of representing the speaker-hearer's perceptual view of the world as reflected in language. The sanctity of transformational rules is not assured, however, since Chomsky (1975) has begun to take a different theoretical approach to language. The eventual impact of many of these approaches on psychologists and linguists remains to be seen.

Another group of linguistic theories has already had considerable influence on the development of certain cognitive approaches to the psychology of language. Although inspired by Chomsky's work, these models generally place more emphasis on semantics and less on drawing a sharp distinction between syntax and semantics than did Chomsky. The theories come under such names as case grammars and generative semantics. We shall describe them in detail later, in the context of the topic of meaning (chapter 5) and in later chapters dealing with comprehension and memory (chapters 7 and 8).

Summary

In this chapter we have outlined various ways in which linguists approach the study of language. Structural linguistics offers procedures for classifying language in various ways, particularly with regard to distinctive or functional features discovered in minimally contrasting pairs. Most recently, generative grammars, influenced by Chomsky's transformational generative grammar, have become the most widely influential grammars. Transformations prove to be useful because they allow easy solutions to various problems with earlier grammars. Although transformational grammar has influenced much psychological research, the results of the research have provided, at best, equivocal support for the hypotheses derived from the theory. The major problem is the exclusion by the theory of knowledge of the world from the linguistic enterprise. The psychological theories in the next chapter typically place more stress on knowledge of the world, as we shall see.

psychological approaches
to the
study of language

4

In this chapter we consider the basic principles of the behavioristic and cognitive approaches to the study of language. A few accounts will be presented in detail to illustrate the major concepts of the different approaches. Other psychological and psycholinguistic approaches will be presented in later chapters, as the accounts apply to specific language phenomena. The aim of this chapter is to make you familiar with the basic concepts and terms of the different approaches.

BEHAVIORISTIC APPROACHES

Although behavioral approaches differ from each other and from the linguistic approaches we have just considered, there are many points of agreement. For instance, many behavioral approaches distinguish between *learning* and *performance* in a manner somewhat analogous to Chomsky's distinction between competence and performance. The difference is that the behavioral theorists tend to have both a theory of performance and a theory of learning, but linguistic approaches often lack a theory of performance. Behavioral theories generally consider learning as the establishment of an *association* between a class of stimuli and a class of responses. They attempt to explain the acquisition of such associations in terms of concepts and processes that apply to all behavior, not just to language. The performance theories attempt to explain the occurrence of verbal behavior in various situations. Simply put, how is language learned and how is it used? Of course, the two questions are not independent, because language is learned through use, and use depends on prior learning. Let us now consider some of the key concepts common to many behavioral approaches.

As mentioned above, learning is acquiring associations. Acquisition is analyzed by the principles of two kinds of conditioning. *Classical conditioning*, also called respondent or Pavlovian conditioning, will be discussed later. The other type of conditioning, *operant* (or instrumental) *conditioning*, refers to the acquisition of overt verbal responses by the mechanism of *reinforcement*. A reinforcer is a stimulus that strengthens the response it follows, in that the response becomes more

likely. In *discriminated* operant conditioning, verbal responses are emitted in the presence of certain stimuli, followed by some reinforcing event. Then, if a member of the stimulus class is encountered later on, the responses are more likely to be emitted. Reinforcers can be positive or negative and conditioned or unconditioned. Conditioned reinforcers acquire their reinforcing properties by being paired with unconditioned reinforcers. For example, food is an unconditioned positive reinforcer (S^R) to a hungry person, and stimuli associated with food, such as the sight of a table being set, are conditioned positive reinforcers (S^r). Positive reinforcers, which are like rewards in many respects, are stimuli whose *presentation* increases response probability. On the other hand, negative reinforcers (S^{R-} and S^{r-}) are stimuli whose *termination* increases response probability. For example, suppose your mother shouts at you, and you say "I'm sorry." If the shouting stops and if there is an increased probability that you will say "I'm sorry" in a similar state of affairs later, then the shouting is a negative reinforcer.

The meaning of the terms stimulus class and verbal behavior should also be clearly understood. First, the notion of a *class* of stimuli or responses is more abstract than it might appear at first. For example, your mother is quite different from day to day, and even from second to second the pattern of stimulus energy she emits changes substantially; yet you can recognize her in army boots or a blonde wig. Thus, your mother is a class of stimuli; similarly, cats, red lights, cars, and your dog all are classes of stimuli. Responses, too, form classes; if we were to ask you to write a capital A, you might do it differently each time—in fact, you could do it with a pencil held in your teeth or by stamping it out in the snow. Thus, response classes are much more general than movements of specific muscles. In general, references to stimuli and responses should be understood as class designations. The second point pertains to the concept *verbal behavior.* We can respond with verbal utterances when encountering either nonverbal stimuli or verbal stimuli; thus, if you hit your thumb with a hammer, you might say, "Goodness me, but that's unpleasant," and if someone says "Hello," you might respond, "What's new with you?" Also, given a verbal stimulus, you may respond verbally, as above, or nonverbally, if you smiled and shook hands. Thus, verbal behavior encompasses both *verbal responses* to verbal or nonverbal stimuli, and all responses to *verbal stimuli*. Quite simply, we must both speak and understand verbal events.

Another central concept in behavioral approaches is classical conditioning, which concerns the acquisition of certain internal or private reactions that in part constitute the psychological aspects of meaning. For example, words presumably acquire "good" and "bad" connotations by being associated with unconditioned stimuli that elicit pleasant or painful reactions. This can be illustrated by reactions to people's names. You may have known an obnoxious person, and come to dislike that person's name—if you know an obnoxious Allan or Ian (which seems unlikely to us!), those names are probably not going to be passed on to your children.

The basic processes of both classes of conditioning include, in addition to reinforcement, generalization and discrimination. Stimulus generalization means that a response that has been reinforced in one situation occurs in other situations *similar* to the original one. Also relevant is *response generalization* (often called response induction), in which responses that are similar to the specific one that was originally followed by reinforcement are also emitted. *Discrimination* is the narrowing down of stimulus generalization when the stimulus situation is too

different from the original conditioning situation and reinforcement no longer follows. Thus a young girl shows stimulus generalization when she calls all men "Daddy" and shows stimulus discrimination when the response is restricted to a particular man (presumably because the generalization is not reinforced and occasionally leads to a great deal of embarrassment). Similarly, a narrowing down on the response side is referred to as response differentiation.

Occurrence of verbal behavior is conceptualized objectively in terms of the *probability* of particular verbal responses. It is also conceptualized theoretically by some behaviorists in terms of *habit strength*, which is not directly observable but refers instead to a hypothetical *disposition* to respond in particular ways in certain situations. The probability of occurrence or habit strength of verbal responses is based partly on the reinforcement history of the individual and partly on situational cues for the response. Note especially that habit is an abstract concept that can be applied to the analysis of abstract characteristics of language behavior. For example, the concept of grammatical rule has its counterpart in the concept of *grammatical habit,* which Underwood (1965) has defined as a second-order habit. A second-order habit determines the occurrence of a class of responses at any moment but not the specific instance of the class. Thus the stimulus conditions that determine the occurrence of nouns, verbs, and so on are the controlling conditions for second-order (grammatical) habits.

Next we shall consider two general varieties of the behavioristic approach, differing in certain specific assumptions, but both based on associations between stimuli and responses. Although the theories are not as much in vogue as others discussed in the book, they help focus the discussion and illustrate some aspects of language use.

Skinner's Functional Approach to Verbal Behavior

B. F. Skinner (1957) analyzed verbal behavior in terms of the conditions that determine its occurrence. In so doing, he rejected such concepts as ideas, images, and meanings as explanatory fictions. Utterances do not "convey" meanings, or at least their effect is not thereby explained. The meaning of a word is simply its tendency to occur under certain conditions, plus its stimulus effect on the occurrence of other words. Thus, Skinner is clearly materialistic rather than mentalistic in his analysis.

The basic analytic functional unit for Skinner is the *verbal operant*, a class of verbal responses defined by the antecedent conditions that *control* their occurrence. The antecedent conditions include *deprivation conditions, aversive stimulation,* and various kinds of *discriminative stimuli.* Such conditions gain control of behavior, that is, they become causal variables as a result of the reinforcement histories associated with the behaviors that occur in their presence. The following illustration (adapted from Winokur, 1976) shows the verbal operant conditioning paradigm in a general way:

$$\underbrace{\text{ANT COND}^n \rightarrow R_v}_{} \rightarrow S^R \text{ or } S^r \rightarrow P^R v. \text{ANT COND}^n \uparrow$$

$$\text{VERBAL OPERANT}$$

The symbol R_v refers to a verbal response, and S^R (or S^r) indicates a reinforcing stimulus. The symbol $P^R v.ANT\ COND^n\uparrow$ indicates an increase in the probability (P) of R_v in the presence of the same antecedent conditions. In words, this formula is really quite simple: A verbal response that occurs in a given situation and is followed by a reinforcer becomes more likely to occur again in the same situation.

The R_v and S^R (or S^r) concepts require some clarification. In the case of R_v, what precisely is the size of the response unit? Recall from chapter 3 that linguists have specified units as small as a phoneme and higher-order units as large as a sentence. In operant analysis, the unit can vary from small to large, depending upon the controlling conditions that are present. Sometimes the conditions might produce responses as simple as the phoneme, as in the common tendency to produce rhymes and to repeat sounds in ordinary speech. Not all reach the repetitive extremes of tongue twisters like Peter Piper, but observe carefully and you will notice that most speakers will occasionally perseverate on a simple sound ("Sufferin' succotash," "Prickly pears"). At the other extreme, the response unit might consist of a long verbal chain. This usually occurs in response to such cues as "Recite the Lord's Prayer" or "Recite the Gettysburg Address."

The concept of a reinforcing stimulus is much more complex in the context of verbal behavior than in the context of lever pressing by rats. The complexity stems particularly from the social nature of verbal behavior. Thus reinforcements for verbal behavior are *mediated by other people* (the audience), who in turn are reinforced by the speaker so that they will continue to "dispense" reinforcers. The appropriate paradigm is the *interlocking verbal operant paradigm*, in which people reinforce each other's verbal responses without necessarily being aware that they are doing so. Of course, each person's verbal responses and general presence also function as discriminative stimuli for the other person. The precise nature of the interlocking paradigm varies somewhat, depending on the precise class of verbal operant in use, "class" itself being defined by the particular antecedent conditions and reinforcements associated with the particular verbal responses. We turn now to an analysis of five different classes of verbal operants, which Skinner named *mands, tacts, echoics, textuals,* and *intraverbal* operants.

The mand

The mand is a verbal operant which is under the control of *deprivation* or *aversive* stimulation and which characteristically produces appropriate reinforcement. It parallels the imperative mood of syntax and is manifested as commands, demands, and so on (note that *mand* is the root morpheme is such words, which is why Skinner selected it as the name of the class). Simply stated, commands and requests occur because the speaker wants something and because in the past such utterances have caused someone else to supply what is manded. In other words, the mand specifies its own reinforcer—it tells the reinforcement mediator (the listener) what to do. An example is the young child's request for milk. The response follows a period of milk deprivation, and it does so because in the past it has been reinforced by the milk's being provided by a parent. Thus mands require a particular kind of interaction between antecedent condition, verbal response, behavior of the reinforcement mediator, and type of reinforcement. The following inter-

locking verbal operant paradigm (patterned after Winokur, 1976) describes the interaction:

$$\text{SPEAKER} \qquad\qquad\qquad S^{AV} \text{ or } DEP^N \longrightarrow R_v \longrightarrow S^R$$

$$\begin{array}{l} \text{LISTENER} \\ \text{(REINFORCEMENT} \\ \qquad \text{MEDIATOR)} \end{array} \qquad\qquad\qquad\qquad\qquad S^D \rightarrow R$$

This conveys the idea that a speaker under an aversive or deprivation condition emits a verbal response that functions as a discriminative stimulus (S^D) for the listener, who responds by giving the specified item to the speaker (thus terminating the aversive stimulation), with the effect of further reinforcing the mand.

The mander's verbal behavior is obviously designed to get what is wanted. But why does the listener comply? Skinner's answer is that the mander and reinforcement mediator must switch roles once in a while. The mediator's compliance presumably increases the probability that the speaker will return the favor in the future. The speaker in turn must provide some immediate "promissory note," a conditioned reinforcer of some kind. Smiles, nods, and expressions of thanks can serve that function, just as money reinforces working behavior. The following extended interlocking paradigm shows what might happen in the case of a child's request for milk:

$$\text{CHILD (MANDER): } R_v \overset{\text{"Milk,}}{\underset{\text{please"}}{}} \longrightarrow S^{R.D} \longrightarrow R \overset{\text{Smile}}{\underset{\text{"Thank you, Mommy"}}{}}$$

$$\text{MOTHER (MEDIATOR): } S^D \longrightarrow R^{Give} \longrightarrow S^r$$

The symbol $S^{R.D}$ indicates that the milk given to the child acts both as an unconditional reinforcer for the manding behavior and as a discriminative stimulus for further behavior, such as smiling and saying "Thank you." Of course, the child's "Thank you" must also be explained in similar terms. You will not find it difficult to think of how this might occur: Members of the reinforcing community shape such behavior by providing appropriate prompts and rewards—"Say thank you," "Say thank you or I'll take it away and I won't give you any next time you ask," and so on. This gives you a hint of how complex the analysis of mands can become, even though the fundamental principles are simple. For a fuller analysis of the complexities, including those associated with mands based on aversive stimulation, you should consult Skinner's book or Winokur's "primer" based on it.

The tact

The controlling stimulus for a tact ordinarily is a nonverbal object or event. Tacts parallel the declarative function of syntax and are reflected in naming and what in general would be called reference in a linguistic analysis, although the meaning of tact is more general than either of these traditional concepts (Winokur, 1976, p. 43). Stimulus control is gained by generalized reinforcement through

social approval and the like when the child uses a word correctly. The stimulus object becomes the *occasion* for the occurrence of tacting. Thus the tact is a kind of *discriminated operant* that occurs when a certain stimulus is present—highly discriminated in the case of a proper name as R_v. Note that *tact* is the root morpheme in contact, which gives the idea that the verbal operant makes "contact" with the object. These features can be represented as follows: The tact is defined by the relation $S^D \to R_v$, in which S^D refers to the discriminative stimulus that functions as the controlling variable for the R_v. The role of the reinforcement mediator is illustrated by the following interlocking paradigm, which shows that the speaker's tact serves as the S^D for the mediator's response, which in turn functions as a reinforcer for the speaker; that is, it strengthens the $S^D \to R_v$ connection.

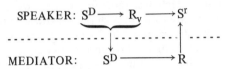

Note especially that the S^D for the mediator is not the speaker's R_v alone but rather the entire operant—the R_v together with its controlling variable. Thus a mother reinforces a child's tacting by saying "Yes, that's a kitty cat" when the child says "kitty" in an appropriate context. Of course the mother might also reinforce the child's R_v, "kitty," in the absence of the S^D, cat, but the reinforced operant in that case would not be a tact. If the child has not seen the cat for a while (deprivation), the R_v might be part of a mand, and the mother's response could serve to reinforce that mand. Or the child's R_v might be part of one of the other classes of operants described below, depending on the precise controlling conditions. This suggests that the same R_v can be part of different verbal operants, sometimes controlled by one set of conditions, sometimes by another, and sometimes by a combination. The latter situation is what Skinner calls an *impure verbal operant*. Thus if the bartender asks you "What'll ya have to drink" and you look over a row of bottles and then say "I'll have a gin—gin and tonic, please," your R_v probably is both a mand and a tact, controlled by prior deprivation and a particular S^D.

Some additional qualifications should also be noted. A given S^D could participate in different tacts by serving as a controlling variable for more than one R_v. For example, a particular structure might be called a building, edifice, church, place of worship, or house of the Lord by the same person at different times. Conversely, the same R_v can be controlled by different S^D's, as in the case of everyday labeling behavior using such terms as chair, table, car, woman, boy, or house, since each is controlled by a large class of discriminative stimuli. Such effects are examples of stimulus generalization which, according to Skinner, can extend to the point of producing metaphorical or figurative speech, as when we use "head" to refer to the "head of a cane," "head table," or "head of the parade" (more examples are presented in chapter 12, where we analyze the problem of metaphor in more detail). Of course, the generalization must be prevented from going so far that a word tacts almost anything, and this occurs because the listener tends to reinforce relatively discriminated tacts.

The echoic

The echoic refers to verbal behavior that is controlled by previously heard speech and that duplicates its form. S^D "snake" $\rightarrow$ R_v "snake" illustrates the operant in schematic form. In brief, the echoic is the imitation of speech. It may have been deliberately shaped by the reinforcing community under circumstances in which the reinforcer says, "Repeat after me . . ." as well as under a variety of more subtle circumstances in which positive consequences follow echoic behavior. For example, when asked a question we might repeat the question simply to give ourselves more time to come up with the answer.

The textual

Textual is Skinner's technical term for reading, which he defined as verbal behavior controlled by written stimuli such that the form of the behavior correlates with the form of the written material (for a more precise and technical definition, see Winokur, 1976, p. 93). The correlation is the systematic relationship between the orthography or spelling patterns of a language and the verbal responses of reading it directly; the correlation, of course, is far from perfect, so that a reader will sometimes generalize R_v's inappropriately until the generalization has been counteracted by discriminative learning. In textuals, as in tacts, the same R_v can be controlled by different stimuli as a result of stimulus generalization or independent reinforcement histories using the different stimuli. The following example illustrates some of the possibilities for one R_v (the textual S^D's are enclosed in boxes):

$$S^D \;\; \boxed{\text{CATS}} \;\; \rightarrow R_v \text{ "cats"}$$

$$S^D \;\; \boxed{\text{cats}} \;\; \rightarrow R_v \text{ "cats"}$$

$$S^D \;\; \boxed{\textit{cats}} \;\; \rightarrow R_v \text{ "cats"}$$

$$S^D \;\; \boxed{\text{KATZ}} \;\; \rightarrow R_v \text{ "cats"}$$

$$S^D \;\; \boxed{/\text{kæts}/} \;\; \rightarrow R_v \text{ "cats"}$$

We all are familiar as well with textual ambiguities, such as homographs, in which the same printed word serves as the discriminative stimulus for different R_v's. The alternative pronunciations of LEAD and READ are familiar examples. Words spelled the same but pronounced differently in two different languages illustrate the same point in the case of the bilingual speaker; for example, IMAGE elicits the R_v's [Imədʒ] or [ima:ʒ] for the English-French bilingual. Which pronunciation will occur depends, of course, on the presence of contextual stimuli which act as S^D's along with the specific textual S^D to control the R_v. Such examples show that textuals can be quite a bit more complex than we might think at the outset.

The intraverbal operant

The intraverbal operant is a verbal operant under the control of the speaker's own prior verbal behavior. An example is the word-association test in which a printed word such as "table" generally produces a response such as "chair." In this

case, the stimulus word "table" elicits a textual response (one pronounces the word covertly), and the resulting proprioceptive stimulus feedback is the cue for the response "chair." Schematically, this becomes $R_v : S^D$ "table" $\rightarrow R_v$ "chair," in which $R_v : S^D$ denotes that the S^D itself is generated by a previous response. The assumption is that something like this goes on all the time when we are speaking, so that what we have just said has a controlling influence on what we will say next. Such intraverbal responding might be in the form of verbal *chains*, in which the responses occur in a fixed order, or they might be in *clusters* in which words tend to evoke one another without any fixed ordering. Counting, saying the alphabet, habitual phrases, idioms, proverbs, and formulas, and giving dates of historical events are examples of verbal chains.

A word-association task, in which we give continuous associations to a single stimulus word, typically produces clusters of responses that are related in some way but that may occur in different sequences at different times. Thus the stimulus word "green" might first elicit the R_v's blue, yellow, red, grass, leaves, spinach, snake, envy, and so on. These thematically related clusters might be emitted in a different order on another occasion.

In general, intraverbal chains are presumably learned because reinforcement ordinarily occurs only after some extended period of verbalization, so that the sequence of responses and the sounds they produce become the stimulus conditions for the verbal response that happens to be reinforced. You might try explaining the contrasting speech habits of talkative and taciturn people in such terms.

Note that the five classes of verbal operants are controlled by three general classes of stimuli, including (a) prior deprivation, or aversive stimuli associated with manding, (b) nonverbal objects and events (tacting), and (c) other verbal stimuli (in the case of echoic, textual, and intraverbal operants). Complex combinations of these stimuli as well as other classes of controlling events are ordinarily part of verbal behavior, however, as the following analyses show.

Grammatical behavior: The autoclitic

The autoclitic is the most complex and subtle part of Skinner's analysis. Autoclitic behavior refers to words that play a grammatical role in utterances and to the way that verbal responses are ordered over time. The autoclitic can be regarded as a kind of tact for which the discriminative stimulus is one of the primary operants discussed previously (mands, tacts, intraverbal clusters; Winokur, 1976). The following illustration defines the autoclitic. Note that the upper part, S^D or $Dep^N \rightarrow R_v$, represents a primary verbal operant and that *the entire primary operant* serves as the S^D for another R_v. The latter $S^D \rightarrow R_v$ relation is the autoclitic.

$$\underbrace{S^D \text{ or } Dep^N \rightarrow R_v}$$
$$\downarrow$$
$$S^D \quad \rightarrow R_v$$

Loosely speaking, the primary operants make likely the occurrence of other verbal behaviors that comment upon the operant and also determine the order of its emission. Those "other" operants are autoclitics. Suppose that the primary operant is the tact "John is in Montreal." If the speaker says, "I hear that John is

in Montreal," we have an example of autoclitic words in which "I hear that" is a comment on a primary operant that is presumably an echoic (that is, the speaker heard someone say that John is in Montreal). If instead the speaker says, "I see by the paper that John . . ." the primary operant on which the autoclitic comments is presumably a textual. Other examples of autoclitics in this context include such comments as "John *is not* . . . ," "This reminds me . . . ," and so on. Autoclitics are thus analogous to grammatical rules and share some features with transformations.

Ordering as an autoclitic process is an alternative to using autoclitic words. That is, ordering depends upon primary operants just as the autoclitic words do. This is another way of saying that we order our verbal behavior in a certain way because we have something to say for some particular reason. Winokur illustrates the idea with an example from typing. Typing the word HITS is a different response from typing the word THIS, although each has exactly the same "primary" operants. What varies is the order, and that variation is an example of autoclitic behavior. For speech, the controlling condition for autoclitics results in our saying "The book is red" instead of "Is red book the" or some other nongrammatical arrangement.

The reinforcement of autoclitics is based on a subtle and complex combination of stimulus and response generalization. Thus, if the child is reinforced for saying "red book," this generalizes to other responses such as "green book" and "red ball." The complexities of the analysis increase as the verbal behavior becomes more complex. We cannot get into those complexities here, but we urge you to consult Skinner (1957) or the readable "primer" of verbal behavior by Winokur (1976).

The role of the audience

The audience or hearer plays a crucial role as a reinforcer (S^r) *and* as a discriminative stimulus (S^D) for verbal operants. The audience is the mediator of the social reinforcements that shape verbal behavior. The audience is also the most important element in the social context that determines what we say. More often, it serves as a *supplementary S^D* which affects either the manner of speaking (for example, loudness) or what is said. We learn to speak differently to friends than to strangers, to children than to adults, and to students than to colleagues, all because of different reinforcement histories associated with the different audiences.

Multiple causation

The preceding summary should make it clear that a Skinnerian functional analysis is not a "simple" S-R analysis in which a single response is under the control of a single stimulus. Instead, verbal operants are multiply controlled by the totality of the individual's past history and the complex of stimuli in a given situation. The controlling stimuli include the social context, the nonsocial objects and events, prior verbal behavior by others and by ourselves, and so on. An appreciation of the full range of possibilities inherent in this approach demands that we also be aware of the complexities of multiple causation.

Evaluation of Skinner's approach

The operant approach was systematically criticized by Chomsky (1959) in a way that had a great impact on psycholinguistics for a decade or more thereafter. Chomsky argued that Skinner used terms like stimulus, response, and reinforcement in a vague and imprecise way, in sharp contrast to the precision with which they are used in animal research. In the case of the tact, for example, the idea of operant strength implies that the operant "Tom" is at high strength in the presence of the person named Tom. In fact, it is not, since it is more likely to occur when Tom's friends are talking about him in his absence than when he is present. What, then, is the controlling stimulus for the tact? Thus, despite the attempt at rigor, Skinner's analysis has no advantage over traditional terminology. Chomsky also argued that evidence is lacking that verbal behavior is learned through imitation and systematic reinforcement. Chomsky's review will not be presented in detail here because he did not comment specifically on the various paradigms we have considered. However, some of the general points raised by Chomsky should be kept in mind. One general point mentioned above concerned Skinner's terminology. Chomsky maintained that the technical terms hide the implicit operation of "purposiveness," "belief," and the like. That is, the account becomes mentalistic once the materialistic terms are analyzed in detail. The second general point, concerning the absence of evidence for the system, also merits consideration. The third point concerns circularity in defining such terms as stimulus, response strength, and reinforcement. Some of these points will be considered again in later sections. We encourage you to read Chomsky's critique and also a response to it by MacCorquodale (1970), who persuasively defended Skinner's views and showed how sharply they differ from traditional views. For now, we point out that the criticisms should be kept in mind but should not be accepted uncritically.

Whatever the criticisms, much research has been motivated by Skinner's approach, particularly in the areas of language development in children and the conditioning of verbal behavior in adults as well as in children. Such studies are reviewed in chapter 10.

Mediational S-R Approaches

Various *neobehavioristic* approaches are based on the idea that verbal responses are determined not only by the specific situational stimuli but also by the inner states of the individual that mediate the relationship between stimuli and responses. This can be schematized as follows: S → Mediational Process → R. This analysis jibes with the common-sense notion that comprehension, for example, is not a direct response to speech. Instead, comprehension is private—one "gets the meaning" and may then respond overtly. Of course, Skinner's approach also makes room for private events in the form of implicit stimuli and responses, but Skinner insists that the *real* causes of verbal behavior lie in the reinforcing stimuli that have followed particular verbal responses in particular situations. The mediational theorists assign a *causal* role to the inner events, whereas Skinner does not. Let us briefly examine two general classes of mediational theory.

Nonverbal mediational theories

The traditional view was that nonverbal ideas or images were the real mediators of language behavior. Comprehension was said to occur once an image or a series of images has been aroused by a word or sentence. This traditional view has been criticized for a variety of reasons. Roger Brown (1958), for example, argued that not everyone experiences conscious images, yet they understand language, and that even concrete words are generic in meaning (they refer to classes of objects or events), but images are specific, and so on. Despite such criticisms, image theory has a certain common-sense plausibility, and it has been incorporated in a modified way into some recent cognitive approaches to language, although in that context it is not viewed as the only mediator of verbal behavior. The issue will be discussed further in the section on cognitive approaches.

Other neobehavioristic students of language (for example, Mowrer, 1960; Osgood, 1973; Staats, 1968) have proposed that the mediation process consists of internalized nonverbal responses and the *self-stimulation* that such responses produce. Osgood, for example, suggests that these miniature responses are derived from the pattern of responses originally made to objects. These responses become conditioned to verbal stimuli and then mediate appropriate (meaningful) responses to such stimuli. Thus the word "evil" elicits negative reactions originally evoked by situations in which the word was used. The affective reactions were conditioned to the word and mediate one's reactions to it. For example, we might avoid persons who are labeled evil.

The mediation process entails two kinds of learning. The first is the *acquisition of the mediational reactions* themselves. This presumably occurs through classical conditioning in which language stimuli are associated with objects and events that elicit typical patterns of emotional or motor reactions that can become conditioned to words. Second, we can learn *instrumental* (verbal or other) responses to the mediator. In the earlier example, we may learn to avoid a person whom others call "evil," without any direct unpleasant experience with that person. It is sufficient that the label (evil) elicits the unpleasant reactions.

The preceding account forms the basis of a theory of meaning proposed by Osgood, which will be discussed in chapter 5, and of a theory of the acquisition of meaning proposed by Staats, which will be discussed in chapter 10.

Verbal associationism

Verbal associationism assumes that the mediating events are verbal, consisting essentially of inner speech. Language behavior is verbal *chaining*, in which some components of the chain are unobservable (covert) verbal responses. Perception, comprehension, production, and retention of language all depend on such intraverbal associations. For example, according to the theory, a phrase or sentence is easier to perceive, understand, and remember if the associative strength between the words in the sentence is high than if it is low. This analysis refers not only to *direct associations* but also to the idea that two words may be linked by an entirely implicit association whose effect can be detected only by special experimental techniques. Meaning, according to this view, is based on the total pattern of verbal associative relations that words share with other words. This approach to meaning will be examined in some detail in chapter 5.

Cognitive approaches to language are generally like mediation theories, but with a special emphasis on the influence of nonverbal objects and events and their cognitive representations. In other terms, the interest is in the effects of *context* and *knowledge of the world* on language behavior. Both linguistic and behavioristic (mediational) approaches have generally stressed linguistic or verbal processes to the relative exclusion of nonverbal ones as a result of the influence of Watson's (1913, 1930) behaviorism. Watson rejected such mentalistic concepts as images and ideas, and substituted for them the notion of implicit verbal responses (inner speech) and other covert behaviors. As a result, neobehaviorists interested in language tended to view mediation processes similarly in behavioristic terms. Behaviorism also influenced Bloomfield's structural approach to linguistics, particularly in that he de-emphasized knowledge of the world. Cognitive approaches have reasserted the importance of nonverbal factors and have generally shown much interest in how information is represented and organized in long-term memory, which, theoretically, is the psychological repository for our knowledge of the world as well as for language. This view is central to various models of language and cognition. We shall briefly review some of the key concepts associated with two general classes of theoretical approaches to the relation between language and cognition. Later chapters will show how particular cognitive theorists have applied such theoretical ideas to the analysis of meaning, comprehension, memory, and so on.

The two approaches are based on contrasting views regarding the content and structure of knowledge. According to one view, information is stored mentally, much as in a richly illustrated encyclopedia or an audiovisual film library, with knowledge of the world represented as perceptual images of objects and events accompanied by relevant verbal descriptions and commentaries. According to the other viewpoint, the perceptual images and verbal forms are only superficial expressions of a single abstract informational base, more like the programming language used by computers than it is like pictures or words. We now shall consider each approach in more detail.

A Dual-Coding Approach

This theoretical approach corresponds more or less to the audiovisual metaphor. Its principal assumption is that language behavior is mediated by two independent but partly interconnected cognitive systems that are specialized for encoding, organizing, transforming, storing, and retrieving information. One of these (the *image system*) is specialized for dealing with information about nonverbal objects and events. The other (the *verbal system*) is specialized for dealing with linguistic information. The theory assumes that the two systems differ in the nature of the representational (cognitive) units, the way the units are organized and transformed, and in their function as mediators of performance in perceptual, memory, language, and cognitive tasks. Let us unpack this rather complex statement.

The term *system* is used to refer to a set of connected things or parts forming a complex or unitary whole. The idea is that the image system combines visual, auditory, kinesthetic, and other sensory components of nonverbal information into

integrated wholes. Thus the representational unit (image) contains information from the various sensory modalities about objects and events. We sometimes experience this knowledge in the form of conscious imagery which includes not only visual information about how things look but also information about how they sound, feel, and so on. Similarly, the verbal system deals with linguistic information in various modalities (speech, print, and so on), but its expression in consciousness is usually auditory-motor, as though we hear and feel our inner "speech" as we talk to ourselves.

Symbolic versus sensory modalities

The description of the two systems implicates an important conceptual distinction between symbolic and sensory modalities. The two systems are distinguished in terms of *symbolic* modality, that is, the verbal-nonverbal distinction. The assumption is that the universe is psychologically (cognitively) divided into verbal and nonverbal entities, that is, into words and things. Each of these symbolic categories can be represented objectively in terms of the sensory modality of the stimulus, as shown in Table 4-1. The further assumption, of course, is that the two symbolic systems include representations and processes specialized for dealing with the different classes of stimulus events in a symbolic fashion. It is important to note that we are not saying the world consists of *images* and words. Imagery is sometimes used here in a general sense meaning nonverbal, as well as in a more specific sense, usually with reference to visual imagery.

Independence and interconnectedness of systems

The independence and interconnectedness of systems are depicted graphically in Figure 4-1. Independence implies that activity can go on in one system or the other, or both in parallel (simultaneously). Thus we can imagine a scene without necessarily describing it verbally, talk about some things without necessarily experiencing imagery, or do both simultaneously as when we describe some familiar scene from memory. We can even imagine familiar things while talking about something quite different. Such common experiences are evidence of the independence of the systems. We shall see in later chapters that such ideas have been translated into experiments that demonstrate more rigorously that the two systems can function independently in cognitive tasks.

TABLE 4-1   Examples of Stimulus Input Corresponding to Orthogonal Symbolic and Sensory Modalities

Sensory Modality	Symbolic Modality	
	Verbal	Nonverbal
Visual	Printed words	Pictures or objects
Auditory	Speech sounds	Environmental sounds
Tactual	Braille	Feelable objects
Kinesthetic	Motor feedback from writing	Motor feedback from haptic exploration of objects

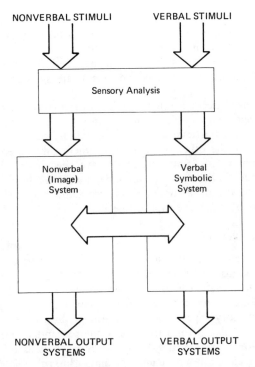

NONVERBAL STIMULI   VERBAL STIMULI

Sensory Analysis

Nonverbal
(Image)
System

Verbal
Symbolic
System

NONVERBAL OUTPUT
SYSTEMS

VERBAL OUTPUT
SYSTEMS

FIGURE 4-1. Schematic representation of verbal and nonverbal symbolic systems showing their connections with input and output mechanisms and with each other.

At the same time, a little reflection tells us that the two systems are interconnected since information can move from one system to the other. This means that we can make symbolic transformations from one kind of information to the other or, more accurately stated, that one of our symbolic systems can initiate activity in the other. For example, suppose that you are asked to imagine your living room and to describe its contents. This is possible only if there is a connection between the language system that receives and interprets the request and the memory system that contains the information about the appearance of your living room. The input is verbal, and according to the dual-coding theory, it is transformed into nonverbal imagery, which is then decoded and expressed in words. The following diagram summarizes the example schematically, with the arrows representing input from one processing stage to another and V.S. and I.S. standing for verbal and image systems, respectively:

INPUT	MEDIATING COGNITIVE EVENTS			OUTPUT
"Describe living room" ⇒	V.S. interprets instructions	→ I.S. generates living room image	→ V.S. interprets image	⇒ Description of living room

The sequence of events would be reversed if the input is a nonverbal object or picture: the perceptual information is interpreted by the image system, which then activates representations in the verbal system when one describes or comments on the nonverbal stimulus. These interconnections between the two symbolic systems and their respective information input and output are symbolized by the arrows in Figure 4-1.

The general theoretical statement also indicates that the interconnections are only *partial*. Metaphorically speaking, information can cross over only at certain points, much as in two traffic systems running side by side. There can be traffic flow on one road or the other or on both of them simultaneously; traffic can cross over, but only when connecting roads have been built. The psychological problem is to specify where such interconnections have been established, and how particular pathways are activated. Such problems will be discussed in more detail later, particularly under the topic of meaning.

Qualitative distinctions

The general statement suggests that the two systems are specialized for handling different kinds of information. The nonverbal (image) system can be viewed as an *analogue* system in the specific sense that some knowledge of the world is represented as perceptual analogues of concrete objects and events. This means that our memory representations of things, as expressed in images for example, are highly similar in form to parts of the perceptual patterns aroused by the things themselves. The verbal system, however, contains information whose units are discrete or digital in nature and are only arbitrarily related to the objects and events they signify. Note that these characteristics of the verbal system refer to the *symbolic* function of the verbal representations, their relation to nonverbal referents. Their relation to speech stimuli and responses obviously must be non-arbitrary, or we would not be able to recognize spoken words or to pronounce them ourselves. Thus a "mental word" must have characteristics that correlate directly with the acoustic and articulatory patterns of its heard or spoken counterpart. Regardless of their form, however, linguistic units appear to function as discrete, all-or-none entities in the way they relate to external, nonverbal referents.

Organization of information

The qualitative differences extend to the way units of information are organized into higher-order units in the two systems. The image system organizes information in a *synchronous* or spatial manner, so that different components of a complex thing or scene are available at once in memory. Nonverbal objects and events have these characteristics in a perceptual sense. Consider a human face: we see more or less simultaneously a head together with the hair, eyes, nose, mouth, and so on. Not all parts are equally clear, but the various components are nonetheless available at one time in the visual field. The assumption is that these characteristics apply also to our memory images of faces and other objects. Moreover, the synchronous representations would include information from other modalities, such as how things feel or sound. An important implication of this kind of organization is that it permits a high degree of *integration* or *unitization* of multicomponential information. Thus the memory representation of our living room includes a

great deal of information, all of which is more or less equally available. This means that you can respond equally well if asked what is in the center of your living room or immediately to the right as you enter it, or to the left, and so on. You cannot give out all of that information at once (this is a limitation of our response systems), but the information is nonetheless available synchronously.

In contrast, verbal information is organized *sequentially* into higher-order structures. This is a reflection of the characteristics of the auditory and motor systems used in hearing and speaking language. Linguistic units unfold sequentially over time, and the assumption is that the cognitive system that deals most directly with speech is similarly specialized for sequential processing.

The distinction between spatial and sequential organization is illustrated by the contrast between the following examples: Form an image of an upper-case block letter such as E, and from the image, count the angles or corners beginning, say, at the upper right-hand corner of the middle bar, moving counterclockwise. You should be able to do that accurately and rapidly with any letter, moving in either direction. Now compare that with saying the alphabet forward and backward. Unless you have practised the backward sequence, it will prove difficult. And even if you had learned both sequences, these sequential structures differ qualitatively from the visualized block letter that you can operate on much as you can with the printed letter itself.

Transformational distinctions

The theory assumes that both systems can transform symbolic information, and that when they do so, the changes follow the sensory and organizational characteristics of the two systems. The visual image system is capable of transformations in spatial characteristics such as size, shape, and orientation, as well as in color, motion, and so on. Thus the things that we know can be imagined as large or small, upright or tilted in space, red or green in color, and so on. Moreover, we can imagine them being rotated or otherwise moved about in our "mind's eye" (try doing some of these things with your visualized block letter E). The verbal system, on the other hand, permits us to make transformations on a *sequential* frame. We can change the order of words in a sentence, we can add or delete items from the sentence, but all of these transformations occur within the limitations of the sequential ordering of speech and of grammatical rules. Thus both systems are dynamic, capable of transforming information, but in different ways.

Concreteness-abstractness of functioning

The distinction between concreteness and abstractness of functioning is implicit in much of what has been already said. Imagery is specialized for dealing with concrete information, or concrete objects and events. The verbal system can also represent concrete information since we can name or describe things and actions, but in addition, the verbal system can be used to symbolize highly abstract concepts such as time, number, and relations, which may be relatively difficult to represent as concrete images. It should be understood, however, that this is a relative distinction and in certain respects a rather tentative one because we know that abstract information can be concretized and represented mentally as images. For example, we can think of time in terms of imaginary clocks, calendars, horizontal time lines,

characteristics of people or situations that stand for particular time periods in the past or future, and so on. Nevertheless, imagery may be less efficient for such purposes and perhaps dependent on verbal processes even when it is part of abstract thinking. This relative emphasis is presumably because verbal symbols are abstract by definition and can be used to represent any kind of conceptual information, whereas images more directly symbolize concrete objects and events. As in the case of the other theoretical assumptions, this distinction will be discussed later and more fully in specific contexts.

Common-Coding Theories

Although dual coding was likened to an audiovisual film library, other contemporary cognitive theories are more appropriately characterized in terms of a computer metaphor. That is, they assume that both verbal and nonverbal information are ultimately represented in some common abstract format, rather like computer language. According to this class of theory, verbal and nonverbal stimulus events are kept separate in the initial stages of information processing, establishing the sensory and perceptual distinctions between linguistic and nonlinguistic information. However, both classes of information are eventually stored in some common, *amodal* form. That is, the verbal-nonverbal distinction and the various kinds of sensory information are not *directly* represented in long-term memory. Instead, such information would have to be reconstructed when necessary from the abstract format by other systems under the control of some hypothetical "executive." The reconstruction might take the form of images or language. The general model is schematized in Figure 4-2.

The nature of the abstract representational units varies with the theorist, but today they tend to be expressed as semantic descriptions. The common practice has been to refer to the information unit as a *proposition* which is rather like a descriptive statement about things and the relationships between their attributes, as well as between them and other propositions. Some propositional representations that theorists have proposed look rather like the NP-VP constructions used in Chomsky's deep structure grammar. Such entities are organized into networks that constitute the long-term memory or knowledge of the individual. Often they are referred to as semantic memory networks; such structures will be described in more detail in the next chapter.

Information processing

Most cognitive theories today adopt an information-processing approach. They assume different stages or levels of information processing, beginning with a relatively superficial sensory level and proceeding through deeper perceptual levels to semantic processing using long-term memory. These approaches tend to adopt the computer as the dominant metaphor of the mind, and accordingly, the theoretical descriptions use such computer terminology as input, output, information flow, structural descriptions, control processes, storage locations, availability and access of information, and so on. Consistent with this approach, many cognitive theorists have developed computer simulations of their theories and occasionally have tested such models against actual language behavior.

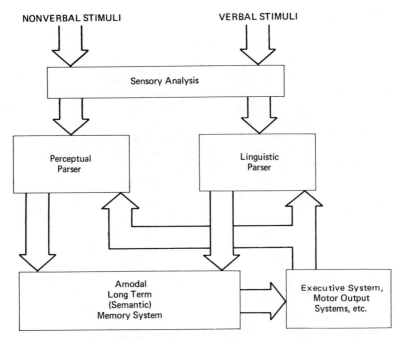

NONVERBAL STIMULI   VERBAL STIMULI

Sensory Analysis

Perceptual Parser

Linguistic Parser

Amodal Long Term (Semantic) Memory System

Executive System, Motor Output Systems, etc.

FIGURE 4-2. Schematic representation of an abstract representational model in which verbal and nonverbal events are stored in a common amodal system.

The Problem of Operational Definition and Measurement

Both linguistic and psychological approaches to language behavior are faced with the problem of translating theoretical concepts into empirical ones that can be observed and measured. In other words, the theoretical concepts must be operationally defined before they can be tested. In the case of the linguistic approaches discussed in the last chapter, we encountered operational specification in the case of concepts such as the phoneme, which is defined behaviorally by the method of minimal contrasts. Later, we shall observe how some psycholinguists have attempted to distinguish between surface and deep structure variables in order to test offshoots of Chomsky's theory. In short, any experimental tests of the theories require a performance theory relating the abstract concepts of the theory in question to overt performance.

Among psychologists, behaviorists have always been careful to provide clear measures of such concepts as associative strength and verbal habits. The problem has often been more difficult in cognitive theories. In dual-coding theory for example, how are we to differentiate the contributions of the two postulated symbolic systems? The problem is even more difficult in abstract representational theories, for how do we measure and test the effects of abstract, amodal entities? Whatever the difficulty, theories are not testable without operational definitions of their concepts, and in later chapters we will consider various ways in which this has been done in the context of specific studies.

Summary

In this chapter we have considered behavioral and cognitive approaches to language. Behavioral approaches, of which the most developed is that of Skinner, stress associations between classes of observable events as the central aspects of language. Cognitive approaches focus our attention on knowledge of the world and on cognitive processes, regardless of whether these factors are conceptualized as unimodal or dual in nature. Later chapters flesh out the sparse details we have covered here and add some more theories that share concerns with those covered here. You should keep in mind in later sections that many accounts presented in specific contexts are actually general theories.

the analysis
of meaning

5

The concept of meaning has had a stormy history, largely because it is a slippery idea that has proved difficult to define. As we pointed out earlier, the most obvious function of a language is the communication of messages between people. It is to these messages that we must turn to address the problem of meaning. A design feature of language is that verbal signals themselves do not have meaning, except through their relation with something outside of the language or through their relation with other units of the language. Consequently, communication would fail if users did not share knowledge of the world and did not share the language that is related to parts of that knowledge.

The simplest and oldest view of meaning stems from Aristotle. According to that view, knowledge of the world consists of mental copies, or images, of the things in the world and is accordingly shared by all people. A language consists of units, each of which is the label of some copy. Thus, to speak, we utter the labels of some images and to understand, we generate the images corresponding to the labels we hear. The search for meaning is accordingly a problem for the natural sciences. Once natural scientists tell us how the world is, we can describe a mental world that corresponds to it, defining meaning, and a language system that corresponds to the mental world, allowing communication.

If everything were that simple, we could end the chapter here, because there would be no issues to discuss. However, there are some serious problems with the classical view. Most notably, as we shall expand later (chapter 11), the world is not conceived in the same way by speakers of all languages, so the common meaning system called for by the theory does not exist. The theory also leads us to expect that each word has a single invariant meaning, or at most a few meanings. Unfortunately for scientists, but fortunately for poets, the shades and gradations of meaning of even the simplest words quickly become bewildering.

A useful metaphor to keep in mind as we discuss meaning is the distinction between a dictionary and an encyclopedia. A dictionary defines each word in the language in terms of other words that can replace it but an encyclopedia relates each entry to events or things outside the language. Some views of meaning have models that resemble dictionaries, some have models that resemble encyclopedias, and some strike a balance between the two.

Definition of Meaning

Instead of giving a specific, formal definition of meaning, let us consider how the concept can be approached. Most linguists and psychologists have treated the concept in one of three general ways: (a) as a property of stimuli (usually words), (b) as a property of responses, or (c) as a relationship among stimuli, responses, or both. The relational approach is the most common one, and in this context meaning has generally been viewed as a set of processes within the individual, by which we understand language. In brief, meaning is treated as a *mediator* between stimuli and responses. The theoretical problem here is to specify the nature of this mediation process. We will consider a variety of linguistic and psychological approaches to that problem after viewing it from a common-sense point of view.

The concept of meaning arises frequently in everyday conversations. Children and adults alike often ask what a word or expression means. What kinds of answers are typically given? If a child asks what "armadillo" means (or what it is), we might actually show him or her an armadillo or show a picture of one; alternatively or additionally, we might provide a verbal definition of the armadillo as a South American animal with bony armor, which burrows, sometimes rolls itself into a small ball, and so on. The former would be more common with young children, with an increasing reliance on verbal definitions as the child gets older. For adults who ask "what do you mean?" the answer is often a paraphrase or an elaboration of the original utterance. This simple example illustrates several important features of the concept of meaning, features that can be found in both scientific and common-sense usages of the term. The following are some of the key features and distinctions implied by the example:

Denotative (and referential) versus connotative defining relationships

Many common-sense definitions are expressed as a relationship between a word and something else, such as an object, a picture, or other words. One class of relationship is *denotative,* in which the word is defined by pointing to the referent object or picture, or doing so metaphorically by painting a verbal "picture" of the object. Such denotative meaning indicates a relationship between the linguistic *sign* and its *referent* or *significate.* Showing a picture of an armadillo and describing its physical attributes are examples of denotative definition. A *connotative* definition refers to more abstract implications of the word; that is, it suggests what else the word makes one think of, what it implies in addition to what it denotes or signifies. A dictionary example of the distinction is that the denotative meaning of both *slender* and *skinny* is provided by the word *thin,* but slender connotes approval and skinny connotes disapproval.

Although pointing at objects is useful in defining some words, it is inadequate as a model of meaning. In the first place, any object we point at could be named in many ways—my desk is a desk, but it is also brown, wooden, furniture, and so on. In the second place, many words can only be *illustrated,* rather than *defined,* by pointing. For example, we cannot point to a truth in the same way we can point to a cat; we can certainly point to examples that we would describe as being true, but there is no world object signified by truth.

Formal definitions versus psychological meaning

Formal definitions, like those provided by dictionaries, specify the way a word is to be used within a particular linguistic community. However, people may not know the definition (the semantic rules), so the word is meaningless to them. Knowing and not knowing imply psychological meaning, which is crucial if we are to understand the role of meaning in language performance.

Nonverbal versus verbal defining relationships

In the common-sense example, armadillo was defined either by pointing to an instance or by describing its characteristics. The former is more concrete; the latter, more abstract. The important point is that the different defining relationships implicate the basic distinction between the concrete world of objects and events and the language used to describe them. It also raises the question of how these are represented cognitively. A nonverbal denotative relation implies that associations have been established psychologically between the word and the thing. More precisely, it entails verbal and nonverbal *cognitive* representations as well as the relationship between them; otherwise we could not use the word in the presence of the thing, let along in its absence. Similarly, a verbal definition means that associations or relationships must have been established between words or concepts. The verbal-nonverbal distinction arises repeatedly in future discussions.

It should be noted that the term nonverbal need not apply only to perceptual objects. Nonverbal motor responses and emotional reactions can be the referents of words, by definition. Thus the command "Bend your arm" results in an action understandable only if we assume a relation between the phrase and a motor control system. Similarly, "I am afraid" implicates an interconnection between an emotional state and the utterance.

To summarize thus far, meaning implies relations between a target word or sentence and any of four classes of events, including perceptual objects, linguistic (verbal) responses, nonlinguistic motor responses, and emotional or affective reactions. The purpose of a theory of meaning is to conceptualize such relations in some systematic way.

Field versus atomic approaches

Linguists and psychologists alike have tended to adopt one of two general approaches in their analysis of meaning. *Field* approaches are generally based on the word as the analytic unit, and they analyze meaning in terms of relationships between words. By contrast, the *atomic* (or *componential*) approaches attempt to break down the meaning of a word or a larger linguistic unit into more elementary features or components.

LINGUISTIC APPROACHES TO MEANING

Early linguistic studies of meaning were primarily concerned with *etymology* (the origins of word meaning) and *semantic change* (changes in word meaning over time). Thus they were concerned with semantics as part of diachronic (historical)

linguistics. This interesting work has been reviewed by Ullmann (1962), who also attempted to classify and explain the major kinds of semantic change in terms of some general principles. Some of these are examined in chapter 12. Here we shall concentrate on structural and cognitive linguistic approaches to word meaning in a more synchronic sense.

Field Theories of Meaning

Early structural linguists were strongly influenced by associationistic psychology in their approach to semantics, relying on their own intuitions to infer semantic relations among sets of words. Saussure (1974, pp. 125-127) described such relations as associative families or constellations in which a particular word functions as the center or point of convergence of an indefinite number of coordinated words. Figure 5-1 shows Saussure's example of a partial constellation for the word *enseignement* ("teaching"). Saussure assumed that different kinds of associative relations could determine an associative series. Thus, for *enseignement*, one series is based on formal and semantic similarity mediated by a common radical, another by semantic similarity based on synonymy, another on a common suffix, and a fourth on sound similarity. In brief, "A word can always evoke everything that can be associated with it in one way or another" (p. 126).

Associative fields

Bally, a student of Saussure, introduced the concept of associative fields and analyzed their characteristics in greater detail (Ullmann, 1962, pp. 239-240). He viewed the associative field as a halo that surrounds a sign and merges into its lexical environment. This is illustrated in Figure 5-2 for the word *ox: ox* makes one think of closely related words like *cow,* then more remote ones like *plow,* and

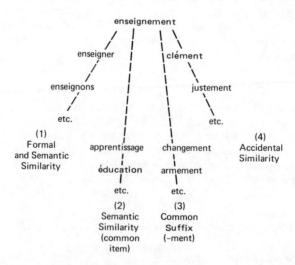

FIGURE 5-1. An associative family and the basis of each similarity relation as viewed by Saussure.

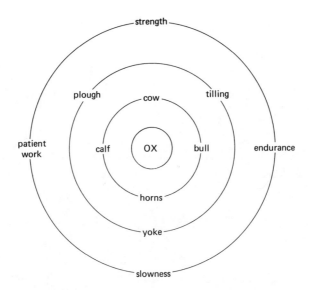

FIGURE 5-2. Associative field of the word OX according to Bally.

finally more abstract ideas of *strength,* and the like. Thus the field is an intricate network of associations based on similarity, contiguity, or other relations as revealed by subjective or linguistic methods.

Conceptual spheres and semantic fields

Trier (1934; cited in Ullmann, 1962, p. 245) developed a related theoretical approach identified by such terms as conceptual spheres and semantic fields. This idea in a sense reverses the associative field approach. The associative field implies associations between individual words radiating *out* from a central word. By contrast, the semantic field theory views language as an organized whole that can be divided up into smaller related fields and these, in turn, into smaller ones (see Figure 5-3). The word is simply the smallest unit in a total mosaic in which the significance of each element is determined by its relation to its neighbors and its position in the overall structure. Thus the influence that determines meaning moves *downward* from the whole to the part, rather than upward (or outward) as the associative field theory implies. The meaning of a word is determined by the field as a whole. You can see that this is very much a contextual or configural theory of meaning.

The semantic field theory has been used to analyze various concrete and abstract lexical groupings, such as color terms, kinship terms, and intellectual terms. The semantic field as a linguistic approach to the problem of semantic structure has been criticized because the structural picture it portrays is too neat (see Ullmann, 1962). Except in such well-defined spheres as color and kinship terms, lexical units are structured much more loosely and less systematically than the semantic field theory implies. Nonetheless, the theory has been an influential and important development in structural semantics. It succeeded even better than the associative

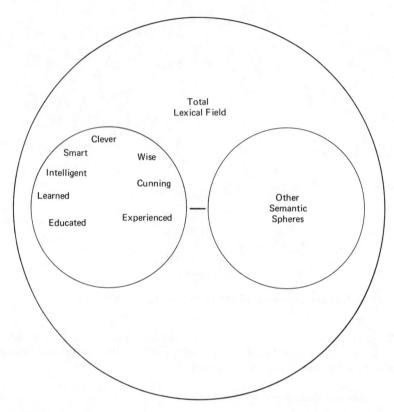

FIGURE 5-3. Semantic fields (Trier).

field theory in bringing a structural approach to that branch of linguistics; it enabled the semanticist to formulate problems that would not have been noticed in a traditional inquiry into the history of word meanings; and it provides one possible bridge between language and thought.

Componential Analysis Based on Semantic Features

A contrasting linguistic approach was based on an analysis of word meanings into semantic components or features. The general approach closely parallels the distinctive-feature approach to the analysis of linguistic sounds. Like phonological features, semantic features are conceptualized as abstract elements which are the building blocks of word meaning. No exhaustive list of semantic features has been proposed, but common examples include such noun features as animate-inanimate, common-proper, human-nonhuman, and concrete-abstract. As in phonological analysis, the descriptive terms for a feature are often designated by positive and negative signs: +animate or –animate (inanimate), +common or –common (proper), and so on. Since the features may be hierarchical, so that one subsumes another, each relevant feature need not always be stated explicitly. Thus *boy* could be

characterized as +Concrete, +Animate, +Human, +Male, and –Adult, but the first two components are redundant because +Human implies that the word is also Concrete and Animate. It simplifies matters, therefore, to identify *boy* simply as Human, Male, and not Adult.

The analysis typically uses binary (+ or –) features, as in the above examples, but sometimes there are more levels. In all componential analyses, however, semantic components are assumed to be discrete, atomistic elements of some kind. This feature distinguishes linguistic componential analyses from some psychological ones discussed in a later section, in which the components underlying meanings are treated as continuous variables.

Componential analysis of kinship terms

Componential analyses of kinship terms were introduced by anthropologists in order to solve some of the semantic problems they face in working with different linguistic groups. Alternative structural models were proposed by Wallace and Atkins (1960) and Romney and D'Andrade (1964). Wallace and Atkins found that American kinship terms could be adequately described by three semantic components, SEX, GENERATION, and LINEALITY. The binary SEX component divides all kinship terms into MALE (*grandfather, father, son, grandson, uncle, brother, nephew*) and FEMALE (*grandmother, mother, daughter, granddaughter, aunt, sister, niece*). Only cousin lacks the SEX component in English language groups, although the distinction is explicit in other languages such as French (*cousin-cousine*).

The GENERATION component has five levels, with the target person's (ego's) position as the reference level: two generations above ego (*grandfather, grandmother*), one generation above *(father, mother, uncle, aunt)*, ego's own generation (*ego, brother, sister*), one generation below (*son, daughter, nephew, niece*), and two generations below ego's (*grandson, granddaughter*). Note that three generation levels suffice to define *uncle, brother, nephew,* and their female counterparts, and *cousin* again remains undifferentiated. Obviously this is not a necessary restriction, since we can easily extend these relations to five levels by using adjectival modifiers (great-uncle, grandnephew, cousin once removed, cousin twice removed), but such semantic distinctions are less important in English and American cultures than they are in others.

Finally, LINEALITY is a three-part division into lineals (ancestors or descendants of ego), colineals (those nonlineals whose ancestors include or are included in all the ancestors of ego, such as *uncle, brother, nephew*), and ablineals (blood relatives that are neither lineals nor colineals—in this case, *cousins*). Wallace and Atkins did not claim that their model was the best representation of the relations among these terms, but they did argue that it was adequate to define and differentiate all of the terms within one paradigm.

Romney and D'Andrade offered an alternative model for which they claimed certain advantages. They retained sex and generation as relevant dimensions but added a new dimension, RECIPROCITY, to mark such contrasts as grandfather-grandson, mother-daughter, and uncle-nephew. Finally, lineality was reduced to two levels, direct and collateral, the latter subsuming the colineals and ablineals of the Wallace and Atkins model. Romney and D'Andrade also went on to compare

the two models in terms of psychological criteria and found some behavioral evidence to suggest that their analysis fits the data better than the other does. For example, their model differentiates relationships in terms of their closeness in semantic space. Thus *father* is classed as more similar to *mother* than to *daughter* and more similar to *son* than to *daughter*. The Wallace-Atkins model does not incorporate semantic distance in the same sense. Romney and D'Andrade gave high-school students a classification task in which they indicated which one of a set of three terms was least like the other two. They found that the number of times a pair of terms was classed together corresponded to predictions from their model. Other data obtained by these investigators and later by Wexler and Romney (1969; cited in Fillenbaum and Rapoport, 1971) similarly showed the Romney-D'Andrade model to be the better predictor. Fillenbaum and Rapoport (1971) also reported results in agreement with those of Romney and his associates, despite substantial differences in methods of data collection and analysis. Thus the model has psychological validity since it predicts how people will group kinship terms together in accordance with the componential features specified by the model. In general, people respond to kinship terms as if each term was made up of a bundle of distinct meanings.

Later, we shall consider whether such a componential analysis can be successfully applied to all "conceptual spheres." But first let us see how this approach has been extended to the analysis of semantics in relation to grammar and the sentence.

Semantic Components and Grammar

It is not enough for a semantic theory to account for the meanings of individual words. It must also specify how sentences are to be interpreted and what kinds of words can be combined in acceptable sentences. This can be done only by a theory that includes syntactic considerations in the semantic model. J. Katz and Fodor (1963) pioneered in formulating such a theory, and Katz and Postal (1964) subsequently combined the Katz-Fodor conception with Chomsky's (1957) theory of generative grammar. Other versions have been proposed since then (for example, Bierwisch, 1970); but the Katz-Fodor theory illustrates the general nature of such a theory, and we shall use it as our main example, concentrating on the two principal concepts in the theory, namely the *semantic dictionary* and *projection rules*.

Semantic dictionary

The dictionary consists of a lexicon together with *syntactic markers, semantic markers,* and *distinguishers.* Semantic markers (features) have the function already discussed: they are the elements in terms of which semantic relations are expressed, just as syntactic markers are the elements in terms of which grammatical relations are expressed. Thus the marker MALE represents an aspect of the conceptual similarity between such words as *man, boy, uncle, rooster,* and *bull,* distinguishing these from their FEMALE-marked counterparts, *woman, girl, aunt, hen,* and *cow.* Note that such markers express the systematic relations between words. Katz and Fodor recognized that lexical units also have idiosyncratic meaning that must be specified in a semantic description, the distinguisher.

The lexical information contained in the different classes of markers can be

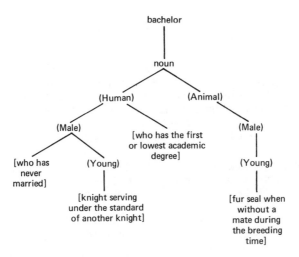

FIGURE 5-4. Dictionary entries for the word *bachelor* in terms of grammatical markers, semantic markers, and distinguishers. From Katz and Fodor (1963, p. 190).

expressed hierarchically as a tree diagram. Figure 5-4 shows such a dictionary entry for the word *bachelor*. The representation includes a syntactic marker (noun), semantic markers (human, animal, male) in parentheses, and distinguishers (who has never married) in brackets. The advantage of such a representation is that unlike an ordinary dictionary, it shows how different meanings are related in terms of the hierarchical features.

Projection rules

While the dictionary gives semantic "readings" for each lexical item, the projection rules specify which of the semantic entries for different words can be combined in order to arrive at an acceptable interpretation of a given sentence. The projection rules use the *selection restrictions* imposed by the grammar of the language. Consider the sentence, *The man hits the colorful ball.* Our grammatical knowledge tells us that *colorful* modifies *ball* rather than some other word in the sentence. However, the phrase is ambiguous in itself: *ball* could refer to a physical object or to a social activity (ballroom dancing), and *colorful* could be understood in its literal sense (abounding in color) or in its evaluative sense of picturesqueness or distinctiveness. The phrase is disambiguated by the verb *hits*, which can take only a physical entity as the object. Thus we know that colorful ball must refer to a spherical physical object and not to ballroom dancing. The grammatical context of the sentence has in effect restricted our choice of possible meanings.

The semantic theory formalizes such intuitions. The projection rules select and combine the appropriate semantic markers for each word and phrase according to grammatical information provided by a phrase-structure analysis of the sentence. (Katz and Fodor applied the rules to the surface structure of the sentence. Whether the semantic interpretation should be applied to surface structure, deep structure,

or both has been debated by linguists, but for our purposes we need not concern ourselves with this issue.) *The rules are applied progressively at each level of the phrase marker tree, beginning at the lowest level and working up the tree.* Thus the semantic information from the dictionary is assigned to the lexical items at the bottom of the tree, and the projection rules then proceed up the tree, amalgamating readings of the items in order to derive appropriate semantic interpretations for higher-order constituents, ultimately the sentence itself. Consider again the example sentence, *The man hits the colorful ball.* Its phrase structure is shown in Figure 5–5. The projection rules would operate in the following steps:

1. Amalgamate readings for *colorful* and *ball*: The projection rules apply first to those lexical items that occur together at the lowest level, namely, *colorful ball.* Thus, the possible readings for *ball* are:

   Ball[1] → Noun concrete → (Social activity) → (Large Assembly) → [For the purpose of social dancing]

   Ball[2] → Noun concrete → (Physical object) → [Having a globular shape] or [War missile]

The word *colorful* similarly has alternative meanings marked by adjective, (color), (physical object), and (social activity) on the one hand; and by adjective, (evaluative), (aesthetic object), and (social activity) on the other. Permissible semantic combinations depend on common markers for the two words. In this case, *colorful* and *ball* have (social activity) and (physical object) as common semantic markers. Thus the projection rules would retain those alternative readings up to the noun phrase (*the colorful ball*) level on the VP side of the sentence.

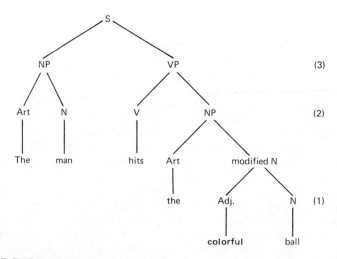

FIGURE 5–5. P-markers for the sentence *The man hits the colorful ball.* The numbers at the side refer to the sequence of application of projection rules (see text).

2. Amalgamate readings for NP and V: At the VP level, the projection rules amalgamate readings for the verb *hits* and the NP, *the colorful ball.* The verb *hits* has (physical object) but not (social activity) as a marker, which restricts the meaning of *colorful ball* in this context to the physical object sense of the phrase. The verb *hits* itself could mean either "collide with" or "strike with hand or instrument," but both of these meanings include (physical object) as a marker, so both meanings are retained at this level.

3. Amalgamate readings for VP and NP: Which of the alternative meanings is intended could be made clear at the sentence level, which combines readings from the noun phrase and verb phrase, but not in this case because the NP, *The man*, includes (physical object) as a marker, among others. Thus according to Katz and Fodor, the sentence is left with four possible amalgamations of semantic markers or interpretations: some definite (*the*) human adult male (*man*) collides with or strikes (*hits*) some definite (*the*) brightly colored (*colorful*) globular shape or war missile (*ball*). The sentence would be made completely clear by further contextual information provided by other sentences or by extralinguistic information which Katz and Fodor choose to exclude from a semantic theory (we return to this point later).

The example shows how the Katz-Fodor theory applies to a sentence. Let us be sure about what the theory has allowed us to do. First, by revealing that the sentence has more than one interpretation, the theory points out the *ambiguity* of the sentence and offers a way to characterize ambiguity. Second, because the sentence has at least one interpretation, we can conclude that the sentence is *meaningful* as opposed to *anomalous*; a sentence is anomalous if application of the projection rules does not allow a permissible amalgamation of features. Third, any other sentence having at least one reading in common with the given sentence can be seen as a *paraphrase* of the sentence. You should note that these decisions can be reached, at least in principle, entirely on linguistic grounds, without recourse to subjective decisions beyond the intuitions on which the system is founded. Consequently, the theory could be a part of a larger system including a psychological theory of how people use a semantic system to understand language.

Evaluation of the Katz-Fodor approach

The model has had considerable impact on both linguistic and psychological approaches to meaning. The idea of semantic features has been particularly appealing, and some form of it appears in several theories concerned with the understanding, retention, and production of language. Nevertheless, the theory runs into serious difficulties on a number of points (see, for example, Bolinger, 1965; Weinreich, 1966). We shall consider the objections that seem most relevant from a psychological viewpoint.

1. Arbitrariness of semantic markers. One problem is that semantic markers are arbitrary, with no principled limit to the number that might be included in the semantic representation of a word. On the basis of his or her intuitions about language, the linguist can add whatever components are necessary to distinguish one word from another. Katz and Fodor recognized this problem and accord-

ingly proposed to restrict semantic markers to general dimensions of meaning that would indicate "systematic relations" between lexical units. Whatever is idiosyncratic about a word was to be indicated by distinguishers. However, there is no clear theoretical basis for deciding between the two classes of markers, since distinguishers can be readily broken down into features that identify systematic relations between some set of words. Thus the distinguisher [who has never married] as one reading for *bachelor* presumably could be replaced by the semantic marker (unmarried) which would be applicable also to *spinster*. Where does one draw the line on such expansion? Although redundancy rules reduce the number of markers necessary in the dictionary entry for an item, theoretical or empirical grounds are needed for choosing components relevant to a semantic analysis. The necessary motivation is lacking at the moment, and it is not even clear what form it might take. Psychological procedures that have been developed for identifying semantic dimensions and structures might help resolve this particular problem empirically, but it is not the only one to be faced.

2. Discreteness of semantic markers. Another issue is the discreteness of semantic components as formulated by Katz and Fodor: markers refer to sharp, plus-or-minus dichotomies in meaning. This is appropriate for taxonomic categories like human-nonhuman and male-female, but some important connotative and denotative attributes of meaning are continuous rather than discrete. Thus the pleasantness, goodness, happiness, hardness, and length implied by a word vary by continuous degrees, and a particular value can be identified only by somehow locating the item on a predefined scale or by explicitly indicating the value of one item relative to another on a particular attribute. The first of these approaches is contained in Osgood's *semantic differential* (to be considered later under psychological approaches), which identifies the position of an item in a "multidimensional semantic space." The other approach would be to include in the lexicon *relational components* that directly indicate the relative position of two items on a dimension that could be continuous (Bierwisch, 1970; see further below). This idea is captured in ordinary language by such expressions as *Sam is taller than Bill,* which does not mean that Sam is tall and Bill is short but identifies their relative positions on a dimension of tallness. It could be argued, of course, that these examples illustrate psychological rather than linguistic attributes, but then we are faced with the problem of deciding between psychological and linguistic criteria for semantic attributes.

3. Exclusion of knowledge of the world from the theory. Bloomfield (cited in Esper, 1968, p. 199) recognized that accurate definitions of word meaning require accurate knowledge of everything in the speaker's world and that such knowledge is simply not available for most words. For this reason he saw the study of meaning as the weak point in linguistics. Katz and Fodor avoided the problem by excluding knowledge of the world from semantic theory—they sought to outline the form of a semantic dictionary rather than an encyclopedia. But is this possible, even in principle? We have already seen that they were forced to introduce distinguishers to identify the idiosyncratic meaning of a word and to resolve some instances of knowledge of the world. Thus [having globular shape] as a distinguisher

for ball rests on the referential meaning of *globular shape,* and there seems to be no way of introducing such information into a dictionary without somehow taking account of knowledge of the world. This is no less true of semantic markers. After all, where do markers like (animal), (physical object), and (female) come from if not from knowledge of the world (Bolinger, 1965)? The linguist could leave the problem of defining such elements to psychology, except that by thus attempting to avoid the problems raised by knowledge of the world, the linguist may be excluding too much from the domain of linguistic semantics. Skilled speakers routinely use knowledge of the world to make sense of sentences that would otherwise be ambiguous or anomalous. There is no ambiguity in *Our store sells alligator shoes* because our knowledge of the world tells us that alligators do not wear shoes, so it cannot mean "shoes for alligators." Should a semantic theory not include a way of representing such knowledge? The issue has not been satisfactorily resolved, although some recent semantic theories incorporate concepts that are intended to reflect aspects of such knowledge. We shall presently review some of these theories.

4. Exclusion of contextual determinants of meaning. Finally, the Katz-Fodor approach (and feature theories generally) does not give sufficient weight to the linguistic or situational context as determinants of meaning. Most obviously, the general context may determine which of several dictionary meanings associated with a particular word is appropriate. Less obvious but equally general and important is the emergence of new shades of meaning as a word is used in different contexts. This is the basis of the metaphorical usage of language. Consider, for example, the word *hit* in sentences like *The play hits it on Broadway; The boy made a hit with her; He always hits it on the nose;* and so on. None of these makes sense in terms of the two dictionary readings suggested by Katz and Fodor for the verb *hits.* One might argue in response that Katz and Fodor intended only to suggest the form that a dictionary might take rather than to write an exhaustive dictionary and that whatever is systematic in the various metaphorical senses of *hit* or *hits* could be represented by additional semantic markers and what is not could be left to distinguishers. The argument might have some force in relation to frozen metaphors in common use, although even here the situational context might be needed to make a sentence clear. The problem becomes infinitely greater when we realize that metaphors are continually arising anew and that their meanings are readily understood by the language user in poems, puns, and other examples of semantically creative language. Such problems can be avoided simply by saying that they are beyond the scope of a *linguistic* semantic theory because such a theory should concern itself with stable meanings that can be formally represented. However, this would rule out some of the most interesting features of language. Weinreich stated the point aptly: "Whether there is any point to semantic theories which are accountable only for special cases of speech—namely, humorless, prosaic, banal prose—is highly doubtful" (1971, p. 311).

In fairness to Katz and Fodor, it must be said that these problems and many others are beyond the scope of any semantic theory as currently formulated. They pioneered in the attempt to develop a formal theory, and their effort drew attention once again to such problems and to the role of semantics within a general linguistic

theory. We shall now consider some alternative linguistic approaches to semantic representation and its relation to grammar.

Alternative Linguistic Approaches to Semantics

The Katz and Fodor approach and subsequent versions (see Katz & Postal, 1964; Chomsky, 1965) were based on Chomsky's conception of linguistic theory. Other linguists have proposed modifications that range from important extensions to the basic approach (Bierwisch, 1970) to more drastic modifications of the entire model (for example, Chafe, 1970; Fillmore, 1968, 1971; Lakoff, 1971; McCawley, 1968, 1971). This area of linguistic science is in considerable turmoil at the moment, and we shall simply present some general characteristics that are emphasized by most of the theories, followed by a brief account of an approach that has particularly influenced some recent psychological semantic theories.

1. Common Characteristics

Relational components

The recent extensions have added relational components to the semantic dictionary. Relational considerations appeared in the Katz-Fodor theory as selection restrictions based on grammatical relations among words. The theories under consideration here include grammatical and other relational information directly in the lexical entries for an item. These are typically expressed in terms of predicate calculus, which allows for the representation of word units and the relation between them. Thus, a noun-verb-noun structure is a *proposition* in which the nouns are *arguments* and the verb specifies the predicate *relation* between the arguments. This can take an abstract form such as *X hit Y,* in which X and Y are the arguments and hit is the relation.

Bierwisch (1970) pointed out that many words cannot be adequately defined without introducing such relational components into the semantic dictionary. This is the case, for example, with dimensional adjectives such as *long, high,* and *wide* (as opposed to *short, low,* and *narrow*), which must be defined in terms of relational components that express that something is long, high, and so forth, in relation to some implicit norm. Thus, the sentence *This table is high* implies that the table is *higher than* the expected height for tables. Thus the meaning of *high* includes at least two relational components which can be symbolically stated as Y Height of X and Y Greater Z, in which Z is a norm for *high.* Such components function as selection restrictions since a qualified object must have the required property as one of its defining features. Thus, according to Bierwisch, *The cigarette is high* is semantically anomalous because one does not normally talk about the height of cigarettes.

The same argument applies to certain nouns, such as *father, mother,* and *friend.* For example, the semantic representation of *father* might include the relational component, X Parent of Y, and Male X, and *son* includes its inverse, X Child of Y, and Male X, and so on for other related terms from the kinship group.

Presuppositions

Several recent approaches explicitly include presuppositions among the features that should be included in the semantic representation of an item. A presupposition is not necessarily a part of the specific meaning but refers instead to the conditions that must be satisfied before an item can be used appropriately in a sentence. For example, the verb *blame* presupposes that the subject of a sentence is human, and it would be inappropriate to use the word in a sentence in which this presupposition is violated. This feature is particularly interesting psychologically because the semantic information in presuppositions depends upon knowledge of the world in addition to linguistic intuitions.

Relations between semantics and syntax

The most general departure from the theory proposed by Katz and Fodor is the treatment of the relation between semantics and syntax. Recall that Chomsky's model treats these as separate components, with syntax as the central generative component and the semantic component as purely interpretive, operating on the output of the syntactic (deep structure) component to indicate what the sentence means. The alternative approaches give more weight to semantic considerations and eliminate any sharp distinction between semantics and syntax. Thus the theories deal with the two components together rather than separately, so that the semantic component is mapped directly onto surface structure by transformational rules, as we shall see in the following example.

2. Fillmore's Case Grammar

Fillmore (1968, 1971) accepted the concept of deep structure but argued that *case relations* rather than phrase markers are the basis of deep structures. These case relations (described below) have syntactic and semantic significance. This can be illustrated by referring to Fillmore's conception of sentence structure.

According to Fillmore, a sentence has a *modality* component and a *propositional* component, expressed as S → M + P. Modality (M) includes such sense attributes as tense and mood. The proposition (P) is a relational description that includes a verb and at least one *case category*, which refers to the *role* of arguments (nouns) in sentences. These roles are determined by the relation to the verb, hence the term, case relations. The types of cases include concepts like Agent (A), Experiencer (E), Instrument (I), and so on. Table 5-1 presents Fillmore's (1971) list of cases, together with their definitions.

As an overview of the application of such concepts, consider the sentence *John broke the toy with a hammer*. This might be derived from a deep structure like the one shown in Figure 5-6. The modality component indicates that the sentence is in the past tense. The propositional component is everything under the P node. The case labels identify John as Agent (A), the toy as Object (O), and a hammer as Instrument (I). Prepositions (K) accompany every noun in the deep structure (they may be empty, ϕ, as in the case of O in the example) and may be deleted when that structure is transformed into a surface structure, which is done by conventional transformational rules and also by special ones related to preposi-

TABLE 5-1   Fillmore's (1971) List of Cases

Agent (A)—the instigator of the event.
  (e.g., *John* hit the ball.)

Experiencer (E)—the entity which receives or accepts or experiences or undergoes the effect of an action.
  (e.g., *Joan* received the gift from John.)

Object (O)—the entity that moves or changes or whose position or existence is in consideration.
  (e.g., John hit the *ball* out of the park.)

Instrument (I)—the stimulus or immediate cause of an event.
  (e.g., John hit the ball with the *bat.*)

Source (S)—the place from which something moves.
  (e.g., John hit the ball out of the *park.*)

Goal (G)—the place to which something moves.
  (e.g., John hit the ball into the *street.*)

Counter-Agent (C)—the force or resistances against which the action is carried out.
  (e.g., John hit 3 home runs against *the Expo's.*)

Result (R)—the entity that comes into existence as a result of the action.
  (e.g., Joe built a *house*).

---

tion selection. This example should make it clear that both semantic and grammatical distinctions are incorporated directly into deep structures. That is, the structural description includes grammatical categories such as V, K, and NP, as well as the relational semantic information specified by the case categories. Let us

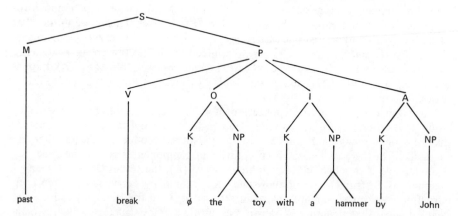

FIGURE 5-6. Fillmore's case grammar representation for the sentence *John broke the toy with a hammer* (see text).

examine in more detail some of the key points in this overview as well as other features proposed by Fillmore.

The distinction between semantic roles and grammatical functions of arguments

The distinction between semantic roles and grammatical functions of arguments can be appreciated by comparing the two kinds of information in sentences. Consider first the sentence *John gave Joan the gift.* John is the *Agent* but also the grammatical *Subject;* Joan is the *Experiencer* but also the *Indirect Object* (that is, the underlying prepositional phrase is *gave the gift to Joan*). Contrast this with the sentence *Joan received the gift from John.* Joan is still the Experiencer but now the grammatical *Subject,* and John is still the Agent but also now the grammatical *Object.* Thus the semantic roles of the arguments remain invariant in the two sentences, although their grammatical function changes.

Case structure of verbs

According to Fillmore, the semantic information about verbs should include reference to the number and kind of cases they can take. Consider the verbs *ascend, lift,* and *rise.* These can be represented schematically as follows:

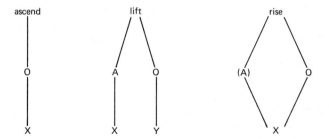

The descriptions show that *ascend* is associated with one argument from the case category, Object, and that *lift* requires Agentive and Objective case arguments. That is, *ascend* is used only in connection with an object that moves upward (*the kite ascended*), but *lift* conceptually requires both an Agent and an Object (*the man lifted the rock*). The representation for *rise* illustrates that a single argument can have different case functions; that is, *rise* takes one argument which might serve only as an Object (*the kite rose*) or simultaneously as both Agent and Object (*John rose*). Other verbs require three or more arguments. *Rob* and *steal,* for example, require arguments to represent the culprit, the loser, and the loot; and the verbs *buy* and *sell* require four arguments representing the one who receives the goods or services, the one who provides them, the goods or services themselves, and the sum of money that changes hands.

These examples illustrate that there may be a one-to-many relation between a verb and the roles its associated arguments can take. Furthermore, the argument is sometimes implicit in the meaning of the verb itself, so that it is left out of the surface sentence containing the verb—*dine,* for example, is conceptually the same as *eat dinner,* but it does not ordinarily take a direct object. In other instances, a case

role may or may not be specified. This is true of verbs like *blame* or *hit:* one can say *The boy hit the dog with a stick* or be indefinite about the instrument used and simply say *The boy hit the dog.* According to Fillmore, this kind of information should be included in the lexical entries for predicate verbs.

Elementary components (features)

The lexical information for verbs should also include certain elementary, biologically given notions regarding time, space, movement, and so on. The following are examples of such features:

1. Momentary versus continuative. Continuative verbs refer to activities that change in time (*sleep*), whereas others refer to momentary acts that do not change over time (*wake up*).

2. Surface contact verbs. Such verbs as *hit, touch, knock,* and *strike* have in common the notion of surface contact, which may be momentary (*hit*) or continuative (*touch*).

3. Attributes of motion. Verbs such as *leap, jump,* and *slide* may be described by associating them with such attributes of motion as direction and speed. For example, *leap* implies both horizontal and vertical direction, whereas *jump* implies only vertical movement. *Dart* and *amble* differ on speed. *Slide* and *leap* differ in that *slide* indicates surface contact whereas *leap* does not.

4. Achievement. Such verbs as *find* and *look for* have a built-in reference to the outcome of an activity.

5. Intentionality. Some verbs differ on an intentional-versus-nonintentional dimension. For example, *John means X by Y* indicates intent, whereas *John understands X by Y* does not.

Other features. Other features proposed by Fillmore include *presuppositions* and *evaluative features.* As explained earlier, presuppositions are conditions that must be assumed before a sentence can be used appropriately to give commands, make assertions, and so on. Thus, *Please open the door* presupposes that the receiver knows what door and that the door is closed. Such properties should be included in the lexical entry for the verb *open.* Evaluative features apply to arguments. For example, such nouns as *pilot* and *pianist* include as part of their definition the evaluative idea that the Agent is skillful in the activity. Other proposed semantic components would specify the prepositions that are appropriately used with each verb and case relation, and which arguments normally serve as subject and predicate.

A summary of Fillmore's semantic features

We conclude this section with an example of Fillmore's lexical entries, showing the kinds of information that might be included as semantic components. The example lists these for the verb *accuse.*

Accuse:	+Performative, +Locutionary, +Momentary
arguments:	x, y, z
cases:	Source + Agent, Goal, Object
prepositions:	by, ϕ, of
normal subject:	x
direct object:	y
presuppositions:	x and y are human
	z is an activity
	x judges [z is 'bad']
meaning:	x indicates [y caused z]
zero for indefinite:	x
zero for definite:	z

The list means that *accuse* is a verb that refers to a momentary speech (locutionary) act that can be described in the first person singular (thus it is performative; *I accuse*); it takes three argument classes as Source and Agent (accuser), Goal (accused), and Object (accusation); it can take the prepositions *by* or *of,* or the prepositions may be omitted (ϕ); the Source-Agent argument (the accuser) is the normal subject, and the Goal argument (the accused) is the direct object in the grammatical sense; and so on in regard to presuppositions, meaning, and what elements can be omitted in indefinite and definite expressions using the verb. Thus the sentence *Joe accuses Jim of stealing* has Joe, Jim, and stealing as the arguments x, y, and z. In the indefinite version, *Jim was accused of stealing,* x (Joe) is omitted; whereas in the definite version, *Joe accuses Jim,* z (stealing) is omitted.

Such lexical entries provide the semantic information from which sentences using the verb *accuse* can be generated by applying certain transformational rules.

Psychological Reality of Linguistic Semantic Theories

Although the theories of Katz and Fodor, and Fillmore, are entirely linguistic, they suggest interesting psychological questions about whether the concepts of the theories have a counterpart in human behavior. Such psychological implications have been investigated in numerous studies. For example, Miller (1969) studied categorization of words by having people sort words into groups on the basis of similarity or closeness of meaning. The data were analyzed in terms of the number of people who put different words into the same class. The results showed that nouns in particular resulted in hierarchical clusters that corresponded to the kinds of features that linguists have identified. For example, objects and nonobjects (that is, concrete and abstract words) were grouped separately; the object words were divided into living and nonliving, the living into human and nonhuman, and so on. The data suggest that the judges sorted the words as though they had semantic features in mind.

Fillenbaum and Rapoport (1971) used a procedure in which subjects were also required to construct "trees" or hierarchical structures on the basis of closeness of meaning. This was done for words from different semantic domains, such as kinship terms and color names. The results were that different domains produced different semantic structures, so that different sets of features are required to de-

scribe different domains. We shall return to their data in more detail in the context of language and memory (chapter 8). The important point in the present context is that such procedures can be used to provide a psychological basis for defining semantic features.

The concepts of Fillmore's case grammar have also been studied. For example, Shafto (1973) investigated the psychological reality of the Agent, Experiencer, Instrument, and Object cases, using a procedure designed to reveal whether subjects could treat these categories as concepts. The materials were sentences containing the different case relations. The following are examples of each of the four types:

(A) The *lioness* snarled fiercely.
(B) The *editor* was shocked by the novel.
(I) The rat died from the *poison.*
(O) The *trunk* was in the attic.

Case was defined generally for the subjects as the relation between the underlined word and the rest of the sentence. No definition was given for specific cases, since the purpose of the study was to discover whether cases would be conceptually distinguished by the subjects without such definitions. They were presented with 120 sentences, 30 for each case. The subjects were asked to classify these into four categories (simply labeled A, B, C, D). The subjects went through a series of trials in which the experimenter told them after each trial whether or not they were correct. In terms of the mean number of correct identifications over trials, concept learning was best for the Agent case, followed by Experiencer. The Instrument and Object cases were not learned very well. Thus Agent and Experiencer are clearer psychologically, but Instrument and Object, though grammatically justified, are more difficult psychologically.

Healy and Levitt (1978) went a step farther and compared case grammar concepts with deep structure concepts. They found that their participants learned the case concept Experiencer more quickly than the concept deep-structure subject. Fillmore's case grammar was similarly favored over Chomsky's standard theory in two other experiments that used a recognition memory procedure. Again, such data illustrate the kinds of procedures necessary to determine whether linguistic semantic concepts have psychological reality. Thus far we have seen that such concepts have some predictive validity.

BEHAVIORAL PSYCHOLOGICAL APPROACHES TO THE STUDY OF MEANING

Behavioral approaches identify meaning with the pattern of responses that have become associated, through learning, with a stimulus. The stimuli may be linguistic or not (objects, too, have meaning in this sense), and the responses may be verbal or nonverbal. We consider first the nonverbal-response approach.

Meaning as Nonverbal Conditioned Responses

J. B. Watson, the father of American behaviorism, defined meaning as the reactions conditioned to a word or other stimulus. Exhaust these, he asserted, and you have exhausted all the possible meanings of the given word. The responses may

be overt or covert. The covert responses occur first as overt than as implicit responses to the objects themselves; then, by classical conditioning, they transfer to words and constitute their meaning.

The most explicit, general, and productive theory of this kind was developed by C. E. Osgood. He calls it the *representational mediation process theory of meaning*. Osgood derived the theory originally from Hull's learning theory and in particular from his concept of the *fractional anticipatory goal response*, symbolized as r_g. The r_g was interpreted as a response, such as salivation, which becomes conditioned to stimuli associated with a goal object such as food and then generalizes progressively to stimuli along the path leading to the goal. The r_g together with the self-stimulation (s_g) arising from it, guides an animal to a goal by providing a consistent mediator for a chain of responses occurring, for example, at different points in a maze. This can be illustrated schematically as follows:

$$S_1 \rightarrow (r_g\text{-}s_g) \rightarrow R_1 - S_2 \rightarrow (r_g\text{-}s_g) \rightarrow R_2 \ldots . S_G \rightarrow (r_g\text{-}s_g) \rightarrow R_G$$

In this example, one can view the mediator, $r_g\text{-}s_g$, as giving to the different overt stimuli and responses a common meaning—it "stands for" the goal.

Osgood generalized the theory to the analysis of meaning, translating the symbol r_g into r_m, which stands for mediational or meaning response. Osgood describes the process as follows:

> A stimulus pattern $\boxed{S}$ which is not the same physical event as the thing signified (S) will become a sign of the significate when it becomes conditioned to a mediation process, this process (a) being some distinctive representation of the total behavior (R_T) produced by the significate and (b) serving to mediate overt behaviors (R_X) to the sign which are appropriate to ("take account of") the significate (Osgood, and McGuiggen 1973).

This process can be diagrammatically represented as in the following figure:

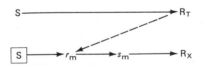

As an example, S might be a lemon, and R_T would be the salivation response to the lemon. $\boxed{S}$ might represent the word "lemon," and r_m would represent the conditioned salivary response to the word, together with the self-stimulation (s_m) arising from the salivation. The overt response, R_X, might be some appropriate comment, such as saying that lemons are sour. The following points regarding Osgood's theory should be particularly noted:

1. Meaning is equated with responses. According to Osgood, meaning is derived historically from *behaviors* to things. Thus objects like faces, bottles, and pets have distinct meanings because of our distinctive patterns of behavior toward them, rather than because of differences in appearance per se. This means that such behavioristic concepts as habit strength and generalization can be applied to the analysis of meaning.

2. Things as well as words have meaning. Osgood emphasized the meaning of things as well as words. An apple becomes meaningful because of the handling, biting, chewing, and tasting responses we make to the object. A fractional portion of the *pattern* of responses becomes conditioned to the sight of apples and to pictures of apples. Thus the perceived object is a *perceptual sign* by virtue of the r_m's that have been conditioned to it. Similarly, the pattern becomes conditioned to the word *apple*, which then functions as a *linguistic sign.*

3. The representational mediation process is componential. Osgood emphasizes that r_m is not a single response, but a pattern composed of multiple components. Thus Osgood uses the subscript upper-case M to symbolize the total representational mediation process elicited by a sign ($S \rightarrow r_M - s_M$) and the lower-case m to symbolize the mediational components ($M = r_{m1}, r_{m2}$, and so forth) into which M can be analyzed. Like the distinctive features in phonology and the semantic features of the linguists, r_M *is a simultaneous, distinctive bundle of fractional responses (r_m components) evoked by a particular sign.* These component r_m's may be peripheral, autonomic, or purely cortical reactions.

Like phonological (or semantic) features, the component r_m's are bipolar in character (presumably because of the opposite nature of such reactions as approach and withdrawal with respect to biologically significant goals). Unlike phonological or semantic features, however, r_m's can vary continuously in strength, rather than being discrete all-or-none conceptual entities, since they are essentially internal responses.

The componential analysis means that a relatively small number of independent r_m components, combined in diverse, simultaneous patterns, can differentiate the meanings of a very large number of distinctive total r_M's.

4. The theoretical construct allows analysis of similarities and differences in the meaning of linguistic signs. Synonyms like *happy* and *joyful* share many r_m's, but unrelated items like *happy* and *adore* do not.

5. The r_m is an abstract entity. Note, finally, that the component r_m's are abstracted from the total pattern of R's evoked by an object. Moreover, the same abstracted components can occur in different combinations as reactions to different signs. Thus, like the phoneme, Osgood's r_m is very much an abstract entity.

The Semantic Differential

How might we measure the particular pattern of distinctive r_m's that comprise the meaning of a given concept, according to Osgood? Osgood and his coworkers devised the *semantic differential* for this purpose. The semantic differential is a series of rating scales in which the end points are defined by bipolar (antonymous) adjectives like *good-bad* and *strong-weak*. The reasoning behind this procedure was that the polar opposites reflect antagonistic reactions to objects, which become highly generalized internal r_m's that constitute the meaning of the adjectives themselves.

Factor analyses of large numbers of such scales have consistently revealed that they tend to group together into three groups of factors, called *Evaluative*

(defined by such scales as good-bad, pleasant-unpleasant, and the like), *Potency* (strong-weak, hard-soft, and the like), and *Activity* (fast-slow, active-passive, and the like). Moreover, these three factors have emerged in more than twenty-five different linguistic communities around the world. Note in this connection that these factors do not represent denotative dimensions but refer instead to connotative or *affective* reactions. Osgood has reasoned that the three general dimensions are so universal because of the importance of emotion in human affairs.

Next, we shall consider some of the ways in which the semantic differential has been applied to the study of meaning and language.

Meaning as a location in semantic space

The meaning of a concept can be defined by its location in multidimensional semantic space. The space could include any number of dimensions, but in keeping with the importance of the Evaluative, Potency, and Activity factors, a three-dimensional space consisting of these factors would exhaust much of the connotative meaning, according to Osgood. The location of an item along each dimension is indicated by the factor loading on that dimension. Thus the concept *coward* might be rated as quite bad, very weak, and slightly active. The meanings of different concepts can be compared in terms of their locations in the semantic space. This is illustrated in Figure 5-7 for the concepts *coward, hero,* and *traitor.* The figure represents the factor score of each item for the Potency dimension on the

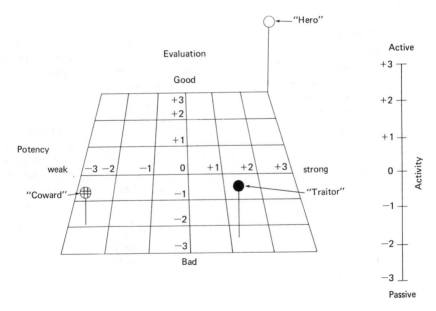

FIGURE 5–7. Representation of the meanings of the words *hero, coward,* and *traitor* in three-dimensional semantic space. Note that the score on the ACTIVITY dimension is represented by the height above or below the horizontal plane.

horizontal axis, the Evaluative dimension on the vertical axis, and Activity on a dimension at right angles to the plane corresponding to the two other factors. In the diagram, Activity is indicated by the lengths of the locational markers, which should be interpreted as rising above the page. The locations convey the idea that the concepts are very different in meaning, with hero as very good, very strong, and very active, and traitor as very bad, slightly strong, and quite active. Traitor, however, is closer to the meaning of coward than to hero.

The degree of the connotative similarity of concepts is precisely expressed by a correlation coefficient, the index of *semantic distance* (D). The index D describes the relation between the semantic profiles of two concepts by the average difference between the rating scores for a pair of words over all semantic differential scales and subjects (the precise formula is described by Osgood, Suci, & Tannenbaum, 1957, p. 91).

You might expect that synonyms would have very similar profiles, unrelated words would not, and antonyms might be highly negatively correlated. The facts are not quite so simple. It turns out that synonyms do indeed yield highly similar semantic profiles, but highly similar profiles do not necessarily imply synonymity. *Nurse/sincere* and *hero/success*, for example, are pairs with nearly identical scores on the three factors, but they would hardly be considered synonyms. Similarly, words that differ widely in their semantic profiles are not necessarily seen as antonyms. These factors probably reflect an inherent limitation of the semantic differential—it reveals the connotative similarity of words like *nurse* and *sincere* without revealing their denotative differences.

Individual differences

The preceding discussion refers to similarities and differences in the average semantic differential ratings given to different words. The semantic differential can also be used to measure similarities and differences in how different people interpret concepts. An interesting example is a bilingual study by Lambert, Havelka, and Crosby (1958). The subjects were two groups of French-English bilinguals who had learned their languages in different ways. One group, the *compound* bilinguals, had learned both French and English in the same setting; another group, the *coordinate* bilinguals, had learned the languages in separate contexts (in different countries, for example). The subjects rated a series of French and English translation-equivalents, such as *house* and *maison*, on the semantic differential. The outcome was that the semantic profiles for equivalent terms in the two languages were more similar for the *compound* than for the *coordinate* group. Similar acquisition contexts apparently resulted in semantically similar language systems, whereas separate acquisition contexts produced somewhat different meaning systems.

Another example is the analysis of a case of multiple personality. The case became widely known through a book and movie entitled *Three Faces of Eve*. Eve was a woman undergoing psychiatric treatment for a multiple personality which manifested itself in three distinct personalities. A form of the semantic differential was administered to Eve in each of her different personalities. The responses were analyzed by Osgood and Luria (1954) *blindly*, without knowledge of which personality corresponded to which profile. The analysis revealed different patterns of semantic distances for the different personalities, which were interpretable in

ways consistent with the psychiatric descriptions made independently by Thigpen and Cleckley (1954), the psychiatrists in the case. Osgood, Luria, Jeans, and Smith (1976) recently reported a similar application of the semantic differential to another case of multiple personality.

Word combinations

Osgood and Tannenbaum (1955) extended the semantic differential approach to the analysis of words in grammatical contexts. Their guiding principle was the *congruity hypothesis*, which is essentially a theory of the contextual modification of meaning. It was originally used to predict attitude change and semantic fusion for word combinations like *breezy husband* and *sincere prostitute* (Osgood et al., 1957, pp. 275-284). The hypothesis predicts the semantic ratings of such phrases from the ratings of the word components. This is done individually for each factor, using a formula in which individual word ratings of +3 and 0 (neutral) on a factor yield a predicted value of +3 when the words are combined; +2 and -2 yield 0; +2 and +2 yield +2; +2 and -1 yield +1; and so on. Note that the predicted values are not simply the average of the individual ratings. Instead, the word with the higher score carries more weight in the semantic fusion. Also, when the two ratings have the same sign, the model predicts compromise rather than intensification: two "goods" simply remain good when combined. The predictions from the model have generally been quite successful, but there are some important exceptions that are discussed below.

Evaluation of Osgood's Approach

It is a compliment to Osgood's theoretical and methodological contributions to the study of semantics that both have been subjected to vigorous criticism as well as praise. We shall briefly review some of the more important objections and indicate what modifications, if any, might be introduced as a result.

Evaluation of meaning as r_m

The implicit response as the basis of Osgood's theory can be questioned. Can meaning be reduced, even historically, to responses? Should it not be based in part on *perceptions* of things? Osgood's answer, typical of neobehaviorists, hinges on a definition of response that is general enough to accommodate any organismic reaction, including the cortical activity to which r_m is ultimately reduced in his approach. Osgood is quite clear nevertheless in his theoretical claim that semantic distinctions originate in *behaviors* to things rather than simply in differences in perceptions of things. This preference is not entailed by the neobehavioristic learning theory that Osgood espouses, because other neobehaviorists have identified meaning with learned perceptual reactions, or images, conceptualized as *conditioned sensations* (Mowrer, 1960; Sheffield, 1961; Staats, 1961). According to this view, sensory responses evoked by an object become conditioned to contiguous verbal stimuli. Such conditioned images represent the denotative meaning of signs and can serve as mediators in Osgood's sense. Thus we can respond appropriately when asked "Where are the scissors?" because "scissors" arouses a memory image. Osgood's reply to such a commentary would be that such images occur but that they

are generated by feedback from the representational meaning system rather than directly by the words. We shall return to this point later.

Another criticism is that the r_m concept is redundant in that the only feature that differentiates the mediation model from simple stimulus-response theories is the nonobservability of r_m. The two classes of theory are otherwise formally identical because mediation theories must assume that the mediating response is in a one-to-one correspondence with the observable response originally made to the referent object. Thus the postulated mediating response yields no predictive advantage over simple S-R theories (Fodor, 1965). The simplest reply is that r_m's might occur even if they are theoretically redundant. The more telling rejoinder, however, is that Osgood's theory deals with *classes* of stimuli and responses and that the analysis therefore entails a many-to-one rather than a one-to-one correspondence between external and internal events. The many-to-one relation is that of observable *instances* to a prototype of the *class*, as represented by r_m. As Osgood (1971) stated the argument, the component r_m's are indeed derived historically from overt reactions (R_T's) to the things signified and therefore bear direct, part-to-whole relations to the R_T's, but the unique *pattern* of r_m's to a *sign* do not. Because the total r_M is made up of different r_m features, no particular R_T can be substituted for them. Thus, his two-stage mediation theory cannot be reduced to a one-stage S-R theory.

Criticisms of the semantic differential

The semantic differential technique has also been the target of various criticisms. One objection is that the factors that emerge depend entirely on what concepts and semantic differential scales are included in the analysis. Osgood has necessarily used a limited number of both, so the resulting factor space is also limited. As Carroll (1964) pointed out, if Osgood had used not only the red-green scale, but also pink-turquoise, orange–pale green, strawberry red–moss green, and had asked his subjects to rate the concepts *cheek, grass, forest, tulips,* and *glowing coals*, his semantic space would have a red-green dimension. Similarly, a general denotative dimension can emerge under appropriate conditions. Osgood and his co-workers themselves suggested that the tangible-intangible and substantial-insubstantial scales might reflect a separate dimension, but none of the studies included enough relevant scales to permit it to emerge as a strong dimension. Such a dimension did show up, however, in a study (Paivio, 1968) as an imagery-concreteness factor, defined by such intercorrelated scales as high imagery–low imagery, concrete-abstract, and tangible-intangible (see also DiVesta & Walls, 1970; Frincke, 1968). These examples point up a limitation of the semantic differential technique, but they also indicate that the method could be modified and extended to reveal dimensions other than the affective ones originally identified by Osgood.

A related problem is that of *scale-concept interaction*. This is a special case of context effects, in which the concepts being rated can determine the interpretation of the scale adjectives themselves. For example, although masculine-feminine and strong-weak correlate highly and therefore are assumed to measure the same dimension (potency), they could behave quite differently when applied to different concepts. Thus Winston Churchill would be rated as strong and masculine, whereas Eleanor Roosevelt might be rated as strong and feminine. The counterargument

could be made that this fact merely reflects the nature of meaning: meaning is contextually determined in part, and the semantic differential reflects that fact. Such instability, however, makes it difficult to apply the same scales consistently to different concepts without special analyses designed to reveal the nature of the interactions. There seems to be no easy way to handle this problem, so it remains a weakness of the semantic differential.

The final criticism we shall mention leads directly to the next section on verbal associative approaches to meaning. The semantic differential has been criticized on the grounds that it measures verbal associative relatedness rather than nonverbal meaning (Bousfield, 1961). The essence of the argument is that the polar adjectives in the scales are themselves part of the associative hierarchy of the concept being rated. If the association with one of the polar terms is strong, the rating will be polarized toward that term. Thus the word *evil* will be rated at the bad end of the good-bad scale because *evil* elicits *bad* as a fairly strong associate. When the association with both polar terms is weak or equal, the rating will occupy a neutral position on the scale. Osgood (1961) concedes the role of verbal chaining but insists that it is not the only mechanism; nonverbal processes also mediate verbal behavior, because pairs of words can be strong associates of each other without being highly related according to a semantic differential analysis or vice versa. For example, *joy* is rated on semantic differential scales as extremely *kind, savory, successful, good, important, colorful,* and *beautiful* but only *good* appears among associations to *joy* (Osgood, 1961, p. 99). Staats and Staats (1959) also distinguished word meaning, in Osgood's sense, from the word's verbal associates, although the two measures are correlated. This correlation was interpreted as a result of word-word contiguities in experience, which strengthen the connections between the word and its associates and also result in the meaning of the associate becoming conditioned to the word. Accordingly, the associates tend to have the same semantic differential meaning as the words. Thus both Osgood and Staats have proposed compromises that may have resolved the controversy.

Verbal Associative Approaches to Meaning

Verbal associative approaches are less popular today than they used to be, for reasons that we shall discuss at the end of the section. Verbal associationism nevertheless remains plausible as an explanatory approach to many aspects of language behavior that implicate meaning, when interpreted in modern terms (for example, Hayes-Roth & Hayes-Roth, 1977; Kiss, 1973). Moreover, verbal associative variables have powerful effects in such tasks as memory and production (see chapters 8 and 9), so that proponents of other approaches at the very least need to take account of such variables by controlling them in experiments. For these reasons, as well as the historical importance of associationism, we shall discuss the basic concepts and procedures in some detail. Whereas Osgood's theory stresses nonverbal reactions as the basis of meaning, the associative definitions and theories place their emphasis on the pattern of verbal associates that a word elicits. These approaches represent the combined influence of early word-association research, the rote-learning tradition that began with Ebbinghaus, and Watson's behaviorism.

The experimental study of word associations began with Sir Francis Galton (1883), who was concerned with the association of ideas. He looked at seventy-five

words individually, starting a stopwatch the moment he saw each word and stopping it as soon as two different associated ideas had occurred. He observed that different types of words gave rise to different types of associations: some elicited purely *verbal associations* most frequently, and others were as likely to arouse *visual images* as verbal associations. Still others frequently aroused some kind of "nascent sense of muscular action," or *histrionic* association.

Later researchers emphasized especially the nature of verbal associations. Galton's test of association of ideas became a word-association test, probably because words appear to be the most objective of the three types of reactions. One need only analyze the discrete words produced by the subject. This would have been particularly appealing to behavioristic investigators, who could apply the S-R analysis directly to verbal stimuli and verbal responses. For decades this was the dominant emphasis of association research, and only recently has there been a rediscovery of the frequency and importance of images as associative reactions to words. But more about that later.

1. Characteristics of Verbal Associations

The earliest systematic studies concerned the nature and speed of associations given by subjects who were instructed to respond as quickly as possible to each word with one other word. This is the *discrete free association* technique. We will first examine three basic characteristics of such associations that were investigated in the earlier research (for a thorough review, see Woodworth & Schlosberg, 1954), namely, *commonality, latency,* and *classificatory* type.

Commonality

Commonality is the frequency with which an association is given to a word by a group of people. In a normative study, Kent and Rosanoff (1910) obtained discrete free associations for about 250 words from 1,000 subjects. They found that certain words are given by many subjects as responses, but others are given rarely. Moreover, this frequency distribution often has a characteristic shape: a few associations appear frequently in the group's responses, but a large number of different associations are produced by a few subjects. Consider, for example, the responses to the stimulus word *needle* in the Kent-Rosanoff norms: *thread* was given as a response by 160 subjects, *pin* (or pins) by 158, *sharp* by 152, *sew(s)* by 135, and *sewing* by 107. Then there was a rapid drop in frequency for the responses *steel* (53), *point* (40), *instrument* (26), and so on. At the other extreme, 31 different responses (for example, *blood, broken, camel, crocheting, cut*) were given by only 1 subject each. The frequent responses like *thread* have high commonality; infrequent ones like *blood* have low commonality. The most frequent response (in this example, *thread*) is sometimes called the *primary* response.

There is some evidence that the frequency distribution of associations conforms to Zipf's law. Zipf (1935, 1945) was concerned with the frequency of occurrence of different words in ordinary language use, rather than with associative frequencies. He related the frequency of different words to the rank order of their frequency, as illustrated in Figure 5-8. Note that the abscissa is divided according to the rank order of the words: Rank 1 is the most frequent word, Rank 2 the

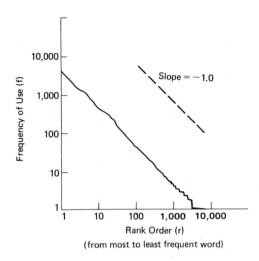

FIGURE 5-8. Zipf's standard curve for English words. The frequency of occurrence of different words from American newspapers is plotted against the rank of the words when ordered with respect to frequency of occurrence (both on logarithmic scales). After Zipf (1935).

second most frequent, and so on, for all the words from a text. The ordinate shows the frequency with which each word occurs in the text. Obviously the two sets of scores will be related, since the most frequently occurring words have been assigned to Rank 1, and less frequently occurring words have been assigned to progressively higher ranks. Interestingly, however, when both sets of scores are plotted on logarithmic scales, the result is a straight line. This relation has been observed in different studies. The steepness of the line varies, depending on the sample—a flatter curve results, for example, if the speaker uses rare words more often and frequent words less often than is usual—but a linear logarithmic relation nonetheless emerges. Expressed in a different way, the product of frequency and rank is an empirical constant (fr=C), hence the term Zipf's law.

Perhaps not surprisingly, the same logarithmic relation holds between the frequency of an associative response and its rank order of frequency (it is interesting, incidentally, that this was first demonstrated in 1936 by Skinner). Thus ordinary language usage and word association responses appear to obey similar laws. This is important because it is indirect evidence that the word-association test taps at least one aspect of natural language behavior. More direct evidence will be offered in later chapters. For the moment, we will note just one study of a quantitative relationship which was provided by Howes (1957). He determined how often certain words occurred as associative responses in the Kent-Rosanoff norms, and the frequencies with which the same words occurred in ordinary language usage according to the Thorndike-Lorge (1944) word-frequency count. He found that the two measures were highly correlated. Howes concluded that verbal behavior in the association experiment is statistically equivalent to "natural" verbal behavior. We shall encounter numerous examples later in which association norms are indeed predictive of verbal behavior in a variety of situations.

Associative latency

Early studies of association also revealed an interesting relation between the frequency of an association and its latency or reaction time. Thumb and Marbe (1901) found that frequent associations generally occur more quickly than less frequent associations. This negative correlation between associative commonality and latency, known as Marbe's law, has been firmly established (see Woodworth & Schlosberg, 1954, p. 61; Laffal, 1955). It is theoretically interesting in the present context because it can be interpreted in behavioristic terms as reflecting the relation between response probability and response latency, which have been traditionally viewed as alternative measures of S-R habit strength. It also fits generally with predictions from information theory: infrequent associative responses have greater conditional uncertainty than frequent ones, and increased uncertainty results in longer reaction time.

Types of associations

The third general feature of associations is their qualitative nature. There have been numerous attempts to classify associations. We have already noted that Galton identified visual, verbal, and histrionic associations. The Würzburg psychologists, Mayer and Orth, also classified associations into those with and without images (Deese, 1965, p. 23). This distinction did not influence much association research, although we shall see later that its psychological implication may be quite profound. The more common classificatory systems have distinguished such types of association as synonyms (swift-fast), contrasts or antonyms (fast-slow), subordinates (animal-cat), superordinates (hammer-tool), coordinates (dog-cat), completions (sharp-needle), assonant or rhyming associations (pin-tin), and various personal or egocentric associations (lonesome-never).

Some investigators have grouped the various associative types into a smaller number of psychologically useful categories. Woodworth (1938), for example, proposed four general categories, consisting of (1) definitions, (2) completion and predication, (3) coordinates and contrasts, and (4) valuations and personal associations. Another linguistically based distinction between *syntagmatic* and *paradigmatic* associations appears often in psycholinguistic literature. Syntagmatic associations are ones that could follow each other in a sentence, for example, hole-deep, chair-sit. This category corresponds to completion and predication in Woodworth's scheme. Paradigmatic associations are from the same grammatical class, hence could replace each other in a sentence (table-chair, run-walk, in-out). The category subsumes most of the associations listed under coordinates, subordinates, superordinates, synonyms, and antonyms in more exhaustive classification schemes. The syntagmatic-paradigmatic distinction is also useful in developmental psycholinguistic research (see chapter 10) and in studies of aphasia (chapter 15). Other classification distinctions find a place in various psycholinguistic studies, and they will be mentioned in those contexts. By and large, however, the traditional classification schemes have not been theoretically useful, perhaps because they are a conceptual hodgepdoge derived from psychological, logical, linguistic, and philosophical ideas (Deese, 1965, p. 22). Associative verbal behavior nonetheless remains important in

psycholinguistic investigations, and the search for a theoretically useful conceptualization of such associations is worthwhile.

2. Relevance to Meaning

What is the relevance of all this to the problem of meaning? Both the quantitative and qualitative aspects of associative behavior have been related directly to the concept of meaning—the quantitative aspects being expressed in studies of *meaningfulness*, the qualitative aspects in studies of semantic (associative) *relations* among words. We shall now consider each aspect in turn.

Meaningfulness

Meaningfulness became important following Ebbinghaus's pioneering study of memory in 1885. Ebbinghaus explicitly invented the nonsense syllable to control the effect of prior associative habits on the formation of new associations between verbal units. This approach implicitly related meaningfulness to associations: nonsense words like XOP and TIV are nonsensical because they arouse associations with difficulty if at all. The relation was made explicit when it became apparent that nonsense syllables are not devoid of meaning, and various investigators attempted to measure their association value. Glaze (1928) first defined association value as the percentage of subjects who gave an association to a syllable within a given time interval. Similar or modified methods were subsequently developed by others (for example, Hull, 1933; Kreuger, 1934; G. Mandler, 1956; Witmer, 1935). These methods essentially define meaningfulness in terms of the two quantitative features of the word associations discussed earlier, namely, probability and reaction time. Thus Glaze measured the probability of an association (percentage of subjects) in a brief time interval. In a direct study of the implied relation, R. C. Johnson (1964) obtained a high correlation between the average associative reaction times and the association values for eighty items—the higher the association value, the faster the associative response.

Noble (1952) extended the basic approach to real words. In his approach, each word is repeated many times on a page, and subjects are asked to respond with as many different written associations as they can within a given time interval (one minute in his original study). Meaningfulness (m) is then defined as the average number of associations given to an item.

Underlying Noble's m index is his general definition of meaning as a relation between stimulus and response, analogous to Hull's (1943) habit-strength construct. A particular R to a given S represents an S-R habit which can be regarded as defining one particular meaning of the stimulus, S. Other responses define other meanings, and all of the responses taken together define the overall meaningfulness of the stimulus. Also, Noble's approach reflects Watson's original behavioral definition of meaning in terms of the responses evoked by a stimulus. Noble simply emphasized verbal associations and the quantitative aspect (intensity or amount) of meaning they define.

We shall have many occasions to consider these verbal associative measures

of meaningfulness and to compare their effects with other measures of intensity of meaning in various psycholinguistic tasks.

Meaning as associative structure

We are concerned here with interword associations between two or more words, thereby yielding a relational or structural definition of meaning. The simplest instance is the two-word relationship already discussed: A and B form an associative structure if they are associates of each other. Larger structures contain not only more items but also the possibility of indirect (mediated) relations among items—A and B may not be directly related as associates but might share an association with C. For example, *soldier* frequently elicits *sailor*, which in turn elicits *navy* as a strong associate, but *soldier* rarely elicits *navy*. The latter two words are linked only indirectly by the common associate, *sailor*. Because of their direct and indirect associations, *soldier, sailor,* and *navy* form an associative network or structure.

It is possible to quantify such interword relations in terms of all of the common (direct and mediated) associative responses within a set of items—their *associative overlap*, so to speak. Various indices of this kind have been described and analyzed by Marshall and Cofer (1963). In general, these measures assume what Bousfield in particular has emphasized (for example, Bousfield, Whitmarsh, & Berkowitz, 1960), namely, that the first response to a stimulus word is a *representational response*. When we hear or read the stimulus word *soft*, for example, we say "soft" to ourselves. This assumption is convenient because it permits us to count direct associative responses as part of an associative overlap score. For example, *soft* and *loud* do not have any associations in common, but they do elicit each other as associates. Accordingly, "soft" can be counted as a response to *soft* as well as to *loud*, and vice versa for the response "loud."

Deese (1965) has presented the most detailed and thorough analyses of such associative structures. He uses the term *associative meaning* to refer to the distribution of responses obtained in the free-association test. It is assumed to be a subset of the set *meaning*, which itself is defined by the hypothetical distribution of all of the associative responses (verbal and other responses, including images) aroused by a linguistic form. Deese claimed that "associative meaning is the largest subset that it is possible to obtain empirically by any single technique" (p. 43). He especially emphasized the relations between associations because, for him, meaning is a *relational concept*: it refers to the relations between words or between words and nonlinguistic events. Associative meaning of a word is accordingly specified by the distribution of responses both alone and as related to other stimuli.

Deese developed a measure called the index of *interitem associative strength*. The procedure is to set up a matrix in which the same words serve as column headings (stimuli) and as row headings (responses), along with any other common responses that did not serve as stimuli. Each cell of the matrix shows the number of times that a particular word occurs as a response to a particular stimulus. The index is based on the sum of all of the entries in the matrix. Table 5–2 shows the results of Deese's (1962) analysis of nineteen stimulus words and the frequencies of the same words as responses (twenty-three other words also occurred as responses, but we have omitted these in order to simplify matters). The associations were obtained

TABLE 5-2 Frequencies of Associates in Common to Nineteen Words Highly Related in Associative Meaning

	Responses	Stimulus Words 1	2	3	4	5	6	7	8	9	10	11	12	13	14	15	16	17	18	19
Responses using the stimulus words	1 Fly	50	15	12	10	9	4		2	1						1				
	2 Bird	4	50	25			4	1	1	9						2				
	3 Wings		4	50	2		5													
	4 Moth				50	2	7	8	1											
	5 Insect	3			1	50	6	3												
	6 Butterfly						50	8												
	7 Cocoon						2	50												
	8 Bug	4				24			50	1										
	9 Bees					1		2	2	50	2									
	10 Flower						2			2	50	10	1	2		1		1	2	
	11 Garden										6	50								
	12 Sunshine												50	2	1					
	13 Spring													50	3					
	14 Summer				2					1		1	1		50					
	15 Nature													1		50				
	16 Sky	1											1				50	6		
	17 Blue	1	1								2		1				40	50	2	8
	18 Yellow						3				2		4					1	50	
	19 Color				1													6	5	50

(From Deese, 1962.)

from fifty university students. Note that this number (fifty) is the frequency of the unobserved but assumed representational response in the diagonal cells corresponding to the intersections of the nineteen stimuli and their occurrence as responses.

An overall index of associative strength derived from the data of Table 5-2 quantifies the degree to which the nineteen stimulus words are associatively interrelated, on the average. The index can be used to predict other verbal behavior. For example, Deese (1961) calculated the interword associative index for eighteen different lists of words. Other groups of subjects were asked to recall each list after one presentation. Deese found a high correlation (.89) between measures—the more interrelated the words in a list, the better the recall.

By themselves, however, such associative indices and their quantitative relations to other behaviors tell us nothing about the nature of the associative relations or about their specific relevance to the concept of meaning. To obtain such information we can look for common characteristics in a group of associatively related words and for features that link such clusters in larger associative structures. A casual inspection of Table 5-2 suggests, for example, that *wings, bird,* and *fly* are associatively related. The stimulus word *bees* also seems to be related to this cluster through the responses *bird* and *fly*, but it is related as well to *flower, bug,* and *summer*. Thus *bees* enters into two different and intuitively meaningful associative contexts. Such intuitions were confirmed by factor-analytic procedures. Thus, an analysis of the common associations among the nineteen words divided the words initially into independent animate and nonanimate clusters. The animate cluster included words like *moth, insect, bird,* and *butterfly*; the nonanimate group included *yellow, flower, color, sunshine,* and *garden*. A third factorial grouping

contained only animate words, which were further split, with *wings, bird, fly, bees*, and *nature* at one pole and *moth, insect, bug, cocoon,* and *butterfly* at the other. A fourth factor similarly divided nonanimate words into a bipolar set composed of *yellow, blue, color,* and *sky* on the one hand, and *flower, summer, sunshine, garden,* and *spring* on the other. Note that these clusters are not easily described in terms of the traditional schemes for classifying associations. Most of the clusters are, however, intuitively sensible: animate and nonanimate words in general and then more specific clusters of insects, colors, and "sunny nature" words.

The factor-analytic results have been psychologically validated in several objective ways (Deese, 1965, pp. 79–83). Subjects asked to sort the words into two piles produce the animate and nonanimate clusters revealed by the factor analysis. Another study showed that both the ease of learning a set of words and the pattern and distribution of errors during learning are strongly affected by the way in which the factor clusters are arranged within a list. It is quite impressive that the free-association technique reveals associative structures that are sensible and that predict successfully other objective behaviors. It provides a systematic approach to the identification of psychologically relevant semantic features. Moreover, computer technology has made it feasible to analyze associative relations among large numbers of words, so that the method can be applied in a realistic way to natural language behavior (see Kiss, 1975).

Associative structure and grammatical structure

Deese (1965, chap. 5) also explored the relations among associative distributions, associative meaning, and grammatical class. Grammatical classes, according to Deese, have larger and more diffuse structures than do semantic associations. No sharp line can be drawn between grammar and meaning, but meaning is more influenced by relations in the natural world, which fall outside the scope of the verbal associative approach.

Deese analyzed the associative relations among words of various form classes primarily in terms of the paradigmatic-syntagmatic distinction described earlier. He found that form classes differ systematically in the degree to which they yield associations of the two types. The associations to nouns are primarily paradigmatic; that is, nouns predominantly yield other nouns as associates: *action* yields *life, movement,* and *motion* as common associates. At the other extreme, adverbs are overwhelmingly syntagmatic in their associations; that is, the associates are words that occupy different positions within phrases or sentences. Thus the adverb *amazingly* yields *right, new, accurate,* and so on. Verbs and adjectives fall in between, yielding about equal proportions of paradigmatic and syntagmatic associations.

The associative structures of nouns and adjectives led Deese to propose two basic laws of association. The fundamental relational scheme for nouns is *grouping*. Some groupings are well-defined, such as instances of the concept animal, but other groupings do not have simple names (for example, *bees-flowers*). The basic associative scheme for adjectives, on the other hand, is *contrast*. Familiar adjectives often yield contrasts or antonyms as associates, for example, *alone-together, active-passive, alive-dead, back-front, bad-good, big-little,* and *black-white*. Such contrast pairs accounted for about 29 percent of the 278 common adjectives sampled by

Deese. A noteworthy exception is color names, which do not show the contrast property nor do they obey other grammatical rules characteristic of adjectives (for example, color names cannot be negated by *not* or by a prefix so as to yield a polar opposite, as many other adjectives can—*not bad* means mildly *good; not red* has no similar implication). Deese's explanation is that color names are in some essential respects more like nouns than like adjectives—they are words that describe multidimensional rather than unidimensional relations. Other exceptions to the contrast pattern also seem to be words that are ambiguous in regard to their adjectival status (Deese, 1965, p. 137).

Deese (1965) generalized these two fundamental characteristics, contrast and grouping, into associative laws: "(1) Elements are associatively related when they may be contrasted in some unique and unambiguous way, and (2) . . . when they may be grouped because they can be described by two or more characteristics in common" (p. 165). These structures develop partly through experience with perceptual objects and social usage requiring verbal elements, and new relations constantly arise as the social and nonsocial context changes. This observation is important because it makes it clear that associative meaning is not fixed. Instead, the underlying associative structures are modified by new experiences, and associative reactions can vary as the situational context changes.

Extensions and implications of association research

The simple association task has been modified and extended in various ways. One extension is the use of continuous rather than discrete associations. These provide a larger associative sample than discrete associations do and permit us to study the nature of associative relations both within and between individuals (see Marshall & Cofer, 1963). Research on such comparisons has shown, for example, that responses emitted frequently by a group tend to be emitted early by an individual (for example, Garskof & Houston, 1963; Laffal, 1965).

Other variations include contextual constraints on verbal association, such as sentence completion; priming of associations by the presentation of an associative context for a stimulus (for example, presenting the words *devil, fearful,* and *sinister* along with the critical word *dark*; see Cofer, 1967); controlled association instructions, such as asking for a particular class of associates (such as adjectives as responses to nouns); and the "cloze" procedure in which words are systematically deleted from passages of discourse and the subject's task is to fill in the blanks.

Sorting or classification is another association technique in which subjects sort words into piles on the basis of some common feature such as meaning or similarity. The procedure is associative in the general sense that subjects judge the degree of relationship between words. You will recall Deese's findings that the first two factors emerging from a factor analysis of association data are reproduced reliably when subjects sort the words into two piles. Of course, the techniques are sufficiently different so that such correlations would not be uniformly expected. Miller (1967) has used a particular classification technique with some success to reveal semantically based structures. The most extensive and elaborate comparison of systematic classification and other procedures to study how sets of words are related to each other in the individual's "subjective lexicon" has been presented by Fillenbaum and Rapoport (1971).

The relation between verbal association and Osgood's semantic differential should also be clear by now. In the latter, a person in effect judges the associative strength between a concept and the polar adjectives of each scale. This is not free association, of course, and the ratings need not nor do they always correlate highly with associative strength as measured by word-association norms (Osgood, 1961). Nonetheless, common processes are undoubtedly used. We should also note that Deese's studies support the appropriateness of using adjectival antonyms as polar terms since contrast seems basic to adjectives, and there are a very large number of more-or-less independent adjectival dimensions that can be used to describe things.

3. Evaluation of the Verbal Association Approach

Verbal association is an objective and reliable approach to the study of meaning. It can be used as a measure of meaningfulness in terms of association value or *m*. The number of different associations to a given word provides an estimate of sequential dependency between the word and ones that might follow, thereby relating the association technique to information theory. The associative clusters derived from factor analyses of associative overlap data reveal some important semantic characteristics of linguistic concepts, including synonymity, antonymity, and membership in common conceptual categories. They also suggest basic ways in which information might be structured in long-term memory, as for example, with contrast and grouping. All of these are positive features of the verbal associative approach to meaning.

On the negative side, this approach is subject to the kinds of criticisms that Chomsky directed at S-R theories in general (see chapter 3). In particular, extensions of the free-association technique imply that natural language can be characterized as a finite-state chain—a view that was most categorically rejected by Chomsky. But even more serious is the general restriction of the associative approach to *verbal* associations, because the technique is not designed to reveal extralinguistic determinants of verbal associations. Thus the verbal associative approach provides only a partial account of meaning.

COGNITIVE PSYCHOLOGICAL APPROACHES TO MEANING

Recent cognitive psychological approaches to the problem of meaning fall into two general categories. One group, if not extensions of linguistic approaches, at least reflect a strong influence by them. The second type are more psychological in their historical derivation and in the concepts that they emphasize. Both groups nonetheless differ from linguistic and behavioral approaches by emphasizing cognitive processes and world knowledge.

The linguistically oriented approaches use linguistic semantic concepts such as features, propositions, and case categories, along with syntactic constructs. They also add knowledge of the world to the language analysis. Moreover, they aim to provide testable performance models of the cognitive structures underlying language behavior. These models of long-term or semantic memory also share the assumption, discussed earlier in the context of cognitive approaches to language,

that perceptual information and linguistic information are ultimately represented in the same conceptual format. Thus, linguistic semantic information and knowledge of the world are represented by the same abstract theoretical entities and processes in semantic memory, generally conceptualized as descriptive propositions and procedures.

Hierarchical Network Models

A computer simulation approach presented by Quillian (1968) and Collins and Quillian (1969) bears a general resemblance to the original associative field theories of meaning, in which every word was defined in terms of other units in the network, as in a dictionary. Collins and Quillian proposed a model in which concepts are hierarchically related in semantic memory. Semantic features or properties appropriate to a particular level are stored along with the concept. Figure 5-9 shows such a hierarchy for two branches of the *animal* tree. The most general concept level, animals, is associated with such properties as having skin; at the next level, birds are accompanied in semantic memory by such features as having wings; and at the most specific level, such exemplars as canaries are associated with specific semantic properties relevant to each type (for example, can sing).

This model has specific implications in regard to reaction time for answering such questions as *Are canaries animals? Are birds animals? Do birds have wings?* and *Do birds have skin?* Specifically, the prediction was that reaction times would increase as the distance between the two key terms in the question increased, according to their hierarchical location. Such predictions were strongly supported in initial

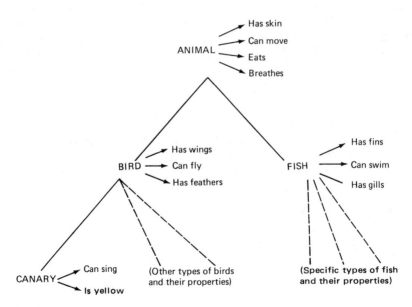

FIGURE 5-9. Example of part of a hierarchical memory structure according to Collins and Quillian (1969).

tests of the model, but later studies showed that the effects could be largely attributed to uncontrolled factors such as differences in associative frequencies between items at different levels in the formal hierarchy. A later version of the model, referred to as "spreading activation theory" (Collins & Loftus, 1975) improved some of the questionable features of the earlier model.

Different versions of the network approach to semantic memory have been presented by others (for example, J. R. Anderson, 1976; J. R. Anderson & Bower, 1973; Kintsch, 1974; Norman & Rumelhart, 1975; Rumelhart, Lindsay, & Norman, 1972; Schank, 1972). We shall not review in detail here the concepts and assumptions, but we shall discuss in later chapters some of the psycholinguistic research that these models have generated. A general point that should be noted is that these theories generally resemble linguistic approaches to semantics in that concepts are defined in terms of their relationship to other abstract descriptions, rather like words or propositional statements. Thus the whole network resembles a dictionary in which words are defined in terms of other words, whose definitions in turn are to be found elsewhere in the dictionary. Finally, most of the models use the computer as their dominant metaphor, and some have even been simulated as computer programs.

Procedural Semantics

The computer metaphor that describes the structure of a network can also be applied to describe the processes or procedures by which either networks or propositions are built. In a sense, the meaning of such a procedure to a computer can be described in terms of the operations the computer is instructed to carry out. As Johnson-Laird (1977) points out, a computer compiles a given input sentence by translating it into a program in some machine language; this compiled form is a meaning of the sentence. A procedural semantic model requires a lexicon of the type we have seen previously, and a compiler. In short, such a model includes some basic knowledge, probably in propositional form, and some powerful procedures that accept propositions as arguments and convert them to specific procedures, the meanings of the sentences. The procedural approach seems promising and has led to some important advances in the conceptualization of meaning (see Johnson-Laird's 1977 overview). However, the approach is in a state of flux at the moment. You might read Fodor's (1978) rather scathing review of it, Johnson-Laird's (1978) reply to Fodor, and Fodor's (1979) last (?) word. At this moment, let us just say that the approach has promise. Perhaps in a few years a stronger statement can be made.

A Referential-Contextual Approach to Meaning

Olson (1970) proposed a cognitive theory of meaning that directly emphasizes knowledge of the world and contextual factors as determinants of semantic interpretations. According to Olson, a word does not have a fixed meaning based on a fixed set of semantic features. Instead, meaning is based on knowledge of the referents of words and especially the context in which they are used.

We shall consider two important points concerning this approach. First is the assertion that *semantic decisions are determined by the speaker's knowledge*

of the intended referent, not by syntactic or semantic selection restrictions. Consider what happens in pronoun selection using the following pairs of sentences:

A. (1) I bought the apple and I ate the apple.
   (2) I bought the apple and I ate *it*.
B. (1) The man killed the man.
   (2) The man killed *himself*.

The second form of each sentence may occur if the second noun phrase is *identical* to the first one. However, identity is not in the lexical entry itself, for if that were the case, one would get a substitution of *it* in A_1 even if the apple is another one. The identity is in the referent instead—"apple" must refer to the same intended object. The same is true of the reflexive form in B; what ensures the identity of the two noun phrases *the man* is reference to the same person. Even such identity is not enough, however, because one referent may have many names. Consider the sentence *Mr. Carter was told that the President would be invited.* Substitution of a pronoun may not be appropriate in this case. The resolution of such problems depends on a theory of the relationships between words and their referents.

The second important point regarding Olson's formulation concerns such a theory. Specifically, Olson proposed that *semantic decisions such as the choice of a word are made so as to differentiate an intended referent from some perceived or inferred set of alternatives.* The point is best illustrated by referring to one of Olson's experiments concerning communication between two people. The speaker sees a gold star placed under a small wooden block and is required to tell the listener where the gold star is. The star is always placed under the same block (a small, round, white one), but one of four different alternatives is also present. One alternative is a small, round, *black* block. Another is a small, *square*, white one. A third condition has three alternative blocks. In the fourth condition, the speaker is shown no alternatives. Instead, he or she sees the star being put under the same block and is told that the listener has a large number of alternatives present but that the star is under the object that is identical to the one presented. Note that this condition uses inferred alternatives only.

The crucial result is that what the speaker says varies with the conditions. The essential form of these utterances is shown in Figure 5-10. Thus, for the first case, the speaker says "It's under the *white* one"; for the second case, "It's under the *round* one"; and for the third case, "It's under the *round, white* one." In the fourth case, in which there are no physical alternatives, the speaker generates an utterance that would distinguish the object from a large set of *inferred alternatives*. In general, the descriptive utterance selects labels and descriptions sufficient to distinguish the intended referent from the perceived or inferred alternatives, with some redundancy added. In terms of information theory, the statements are phrased so as to reduce uncertainty. Finally, an utterance does not exhaust the potential features of perceived or inferred referents. New possibilities can always be found, depending on the particular context of the referent object.

Olson's theoretical contribution has had considerable influence on cognitive approaches to language (for example, R. C. Anderson & Ortony, 1975), as we shall see in later contexts.

	Event	Alternative	Utterance
Case 1	○	●	It's under the white one
Case 2	○	□	It's under the round one
Case 3	○	□ ● ■	It's under the round white one
Case 4	○		It's under the round, white wooden block that's about 1" across

FIGURE 5-10. The relation between the form of the utterance and the intended referent in the experiment by D. R. Olson (1970).

A Dual-Coding Approach to Meaning

Olson's theory and other cognitive approaches to meaning emphasize the importance of nonverbal context. The basis for such an analysis is clear when the nonverbal context and the referent are present, but what about when such a context is absent? The answer has been in terms of knowledge of the world, or, as Olson stated it, the inferred context. But how is such knowledge represented in its absence?

An old answer was that knowledge of the world and word meaning is represented as imagery. This view has been repeatedly criticized over the centuries. Roger Brown (1958) summarized the major objections as follows: First, images cannot account for abstraction, because imaginal representations must be specific, whereas meaning is general. This is so even in the case of specific terms such as *dog*: the concept refers to a class of animals, not to a specific instance. A second criticism is that an image explanation seems to rely on consciousness. However, many people do not report conscious images as responses to language. Finally, according to Brown, images are fixed and static, but meaning is dynamic and variable.

Whatever the force of such arguments at one time, they can be answered and rejected on the basis of contemporary approaches to imagery. In such approaches, images can be abstract to some degree because they may lack detail, and even specific images can symbolize or "stand for" abstract ideas. A specific dog or the image of one may represent dogs in general or even animals in general for particular individuals (R. C. Anderson & McGaw, 1973; Rosch, 1975a,b,c).

The apparent dependency of an imagery explanation on consciousness can be handled by distinguishing between an imagery *system*, which somehow retrieves or generates conscious images as well as other external manifestations, and the conscious imagery itself. The system can function without necessarily producing conscious imagery, although such images can occur if necessary. That is, the theory refers to imaginal competence, rather than to the performance of an imaginal act.

Third, the evidence is that imagery is variable and dynamic rather than fixed and static. This point has already been discussed in connection with the dual-coding approach to cognition in terms of the dynamic transformability of images. In the present context, we conceive of imagery as a hierarchy of imaginal

responses to words or larger linguistic segments. A large number of images could occur, with some being more probable than others. Which ones do occur depend on (a) past experience (that is, the long-term memory information stored in the imagery system), (b) the immediately preceding situational context, and (c) the verbal and nonverbal context in which the verbal response actually occurs.

Finally, we do not claim that imagery is all of meaning. Meaning is a broader concept than that. Even if we restrict the definition to those reactions that occur to stimuli, it must be broad enough to encompass verbal, affective, and nonverbal motor reactions along with the inner perceptual ones that characterize imagery.

We now turn to a dual-coding approach that emphasizes imagery and verbal associative reactions as the basis of meaning. Emotional and motor components are also included because imagery, for example, includes motor components as part of the reaction. The essentials of this approach were originally spelled out by Paivio (1971b, chap. 3). The theory concerns the component processes in the imaginal and verbal systems, their structures and interrelations, and their relations with language and nonverbal objects and events. Three "levels" or kinds of processes are related to the concept of meaning. These are theoretical processes, but they are also linked explicitly to particular empirical indicators or defining operations. The three are referred to as *representational, referential,* and *associative* levels of symbolic representation or, in the present context, meaning. The different levels and the relations among them are illustrated in Figure 5-11. Let us consider each in turn.

Representational meaning

Representational meaning refers to the availability, in long-term memory, of representations corresponding to things and to linguistic units. These hypothetical units can be described simply as verbal and imaginal representations, but for our purposes we shall refer to them as *logogens* and *imagens*. The term logogen is borrowed from Morton (1969), who introduced the term to refer to the cognitive representations activated when one perceives a word. Thus the term refers to the hypothetical cognitive process that gives birth to (*generates*) a word (*logos*) percept. Morton's analysis of word-recognition data in terms of the logogen concept will be reviewed in the next chapter. The term imagen is logically comparable to the logogen but refers instead to the representational units that give birth to consciously experienced images as well as to other external manifestations, such as drawing. We assume also that imagens are activated when one perceives and interprets pictures or perceptual scenes. These terms distinguish between the underlying symbolic representations and their manifestations in consciousness or behavior.

The assumption that imagens are activated when we imagine nonverbal objects and events and when we perceive such events is an assumption of isomorphism (formal similarity), already discussed earlier in connection with dual-coding theory. Imagens are analogue representations that preserve the perceptual form and modality of objects as perceived or imagined. Logogens similarly correspond to processes aroused by linguistic units (for convenience, words are taken as the basic units). Thus logogens are *phonemic* (auditory-motor), although they must also be connected to visual word-representations in the case of people who are able to read.

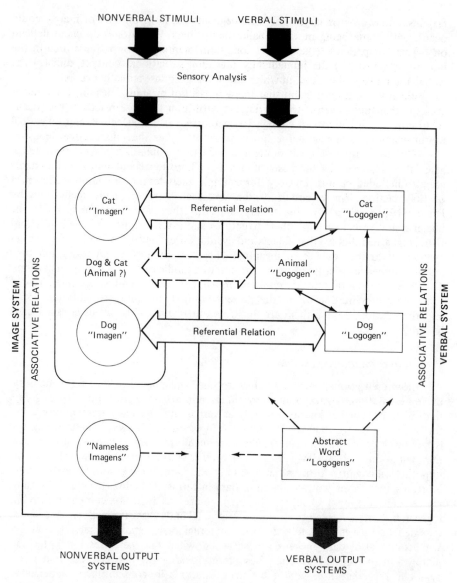

FIGURE 5–11. Schematization of representational, referential, and associative levels of meaning.

Psychological meaning at the representational level corresponds to *familiarity*, which is assumed to be related to the availability of a corresponding representation (imagen or logogen). Thus, appropriate measures of representational meaning would include frequency counts of words, familiarity ratings of words or pictures, and so on.

Representational meaning does not ordinarily exist in isolation, although it could be approximated in the laboratory by manipulating the frequency of exposure of items. Usually, however, special procedures are required to separate representational from other levels of meaning.

Referential meaning

Referential meaning corresponds to reference or denotation in traditional theories of meaning. It implies a connection between imaginal and verbal representations, that is, between imagens and logogens. Such a connection is necessary because things can be named, the referents of words can be imagined, and images can be translated into words and vice versa entirely at the cognitive level. Thus, given a word such as "cottage," we can imagine a house of a particular kind, then label or describe it to ourselves. Psychological meaning at the referential level corresponds to the concreteness or imagery value of words and to the nameability of things or pictures. For example, the imagery value of words has been measured as the average ratings on a scale extending from low imagery to high imagery. Table 5-3 shows the imagery values for some relatively concrete and abstract words. A related measure is the time interval between the presentation of a word and the point at which a subject begins to draw a picture. The imagery ratings and reaction times are highly negatively correlated; that is, high imagery ratings are associated with short reaction times, as shown in Figure 5-12. Analogous measures have been obtained for the nameability of pictures in terms of the average reaction time for giving a label. The logic behind such measures is quite apparent: the ratings and the reaction-time measures are rather direct indications of the degree to which a nonverbal representation is available as a referential reaction to the word, and vice versa in naming reaction times to pictures. The higher the imagery ratings of words and the faster the reaction times to words or pictures, the more direct the referential relation is between imagen and logogen.

TABLE 5-3 Imagery Values for a Selected Set of Nouns and Adjectives

Nouns				
assumption 1.91	issue 3.00	hatred 3.97	basin 4.97	ladies 5.97
instance 2.00	necessity 3.00	period 4.00	cross 4.97	vaccination 5.97
unreality 2.10	routine 3.00	anxiety 4.03	death 5.00	hand 6.00
factor 2.13	instinct 3.03	madness 4.03	emergency 5.00	mermaid 6.00
soul 2.13	rumour 3.03	mischief 4.03	lotion 5.03	bear 6.03

Adjectives				
noisy 1.38	complete 3.00	aggressive 3.97	sharp 4.97	round 5.41
significant 1.97	deliberate 3.00	gentle 3.97	colourful 5.00	married 5.91
unfair 2.00	modest 3.00	sarcastic 4.00	intimate 5.00	muscular 5.94
apparent 2.03	presentable 3.00	energetic 4.03	loving 5.00	yellow 5.97
tentative 2.03	persistent 3.03	valuable 4.03	weeping 5.03	bronze 6.17

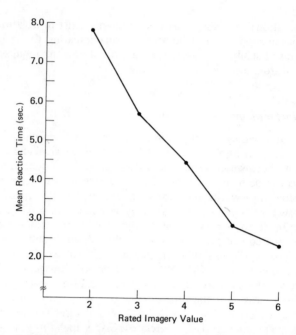

FIGURE 5-12. Relation between the rated image-arousing value of words and the reaction time to begin drawings of referent objects corresponding to the words.

Associative meaning

Associative meaning refers to associations or higher-order structures within each system. These are composed of intraverbal associations on the one hand and compound images on the other. The intraverbal associations presumably reflect connections between logogens corresponding to different words, and the compound images reflect associations between different imagens. Because of such connections, a word can arouse another word as an associative reaction, and objects or pictures can arouse a stream of associative imagery. Logogens are organized into associative networks, perhaps in the hierarchical fashion suggested in Figure 5-11 in regard to the concepts *cat, dog,* and *animal.*

The imaginal associative structures are also hierarchical but typically take the form of nested sets. A clear example is the perceptual structure of a face. The structure has a head containing eyes, nose, ears, mouth, and so on. The eye in turn includes an eyeball, iris, and pupil. Similarly, all other parts can be analyzed into smaller components, all of which are simultaneously available in the perceptual structure that we call a face. The structure is synchronous in that the information at different levels of the hierarchy is simultaneously available for perception or imagination, although not all parts are equally clear because of the limitations of our perceptual span.

Standardized measures of associative meaning are available for verbal associations, as we saw earlier. Comparable procedures that would reveal the structure of

imaginal associations are only beginning to be developed. Such procedures should be capable of revealing the synchronous nature of compound images. One implication, for example, is that the arousal of one component of an imaginal structure should redintegrate some portion of the rest of the compound. Thus, if one is asked to imagine the shape of the province of Manitoba as it appears on a map, one is likely to visualize at least a portion of the central region of Canada; asked to visualize a *nose*, one is likely to imagine part of the rest of the face; and so on. The best evidence that this may be the case comes from an experiment by Bower and Glass (1976). Their subjects studied a series of line drawings of nonsense figures, and then they tried to draw them from memory. On some trials, they were shown a fragment of each figure as a recall cue. The fragments were good or bad in terms of whether they comprised a natural subunit in the original drawing. The good cues were highly effective in cuing memory for the whole pattern, their "redintegrative power" being more than five times that of the bad ones. The results make it plausible to assume that there might be similar redintegrative effects in regard to our images of familiar complex structures.

Note that the preceding analysis implies that representational meaning merges into associative meaning. Words can become associatively concatenated into higher-order units such as compound words or habitual phrases. Elementary imagens similarly become organized into compound ones, such as the components of a face that can be imagined individually or together as an intact face. To the extent that this occurs, it also has implications for referential relations. Thus, as illustrated in Figure 5-11, a direct, referential connection might be established between the logogen for *animal* and some kind of compound imagen that incorporates perceptual information from different animals into its structure. Or, as suggested earlier, a specific imagen (for example, of a dog) may become the cognitive referent or prototype for the word animal. Such possibilities will be discussed further in chapter 11, particularly in connection with recent work by Rosch (1975a,b,c).

Implications of the dual-coding approach

The dual-coding approach has implications for virtually all aspects of language behavior. For example, since referential and associative reactions to words can occur only after a logogen has been activated, empirical variables related to these higher levels of meaning should be irrelevant to immediate perception. Only representational meaning as measured by indices of familiarity should be important. All levels of meaning, however, should be important to comprehension, memory, and production tasks. In regard to language development, the theory has implications for the acquisition of vocabulary and even grammar. For example, concrete words should be acquired earlier than abstract words and meaningful language learning should depend on the availability of meaningful referents. Most generally, the theory implies axiomatically that thinking cannot be equated with language alone. Nonverbal processes are used together with their interaction with the language system through referential interconnections. We conclude this chapter with a summary of a study that directly compared dual-coding approaches to the other approaches to meaning, as discussed in earlier sections. The study illustrates the contrasting theoretical features and implications of the three models in a very specific way.

Dual Coding Compared with Verbal and Abstract Representational Models

Synonymy was identified in earlier discussions as one of the key problems that must be handled by theories of semantics and meaning. J. Clark (1978) analyzed the different ways in which the problem is interpreted according to verbal representational, conceptual (abstract) representational, and imagery-verbal (dual-coding) theories. The main contrasting features are schematized in Figure 5–13. The three models concern what happens when a word and its synonym are interpreted, in which interpretation activates mental representations corresponding to the synonyms. The three models all assume that these mental representations are organized into an associative-relational network. The verbal model states that the mind codes information in some verbal form, as in the verbal-associative approach to meaning discussed earlier. The conceptual model assumes that the units of semantic memory consist of abstract entities corresponding to ideas or concepts. That is, the representations are neither wordlike nor thinglike, but something quite amodal. The associative, relational network consists of relations among such abstract entities. This is the common characteristic of the abstract representational approaches to meaning discussed earlier. The third model is dual coding, which includes both verbal and imaginal codes.

According to the verbal model, synonyms maintain separate semantic representations, as shown in Figure 5–13 by the parallel lines that enter the associative-relational network. Thus the synonyms *boy* and *lad* are represented separately in long-term memory, but they are related through their association with each other and the associations they share with other representations. The conceptual model states that synonyms share a semantic representation. This means that words like *boy* and *lad* remain separated only at a superficial level and enter into an association with a common conceptual element. The meaning identity of the synonyms *is* that common conceptual representation. Note that neither the verbal nor the conceptual model differentiates between different types of words. For example, concrete synonyms (*boy-lad*) and abstract synonyms (*mistake-error*) are represented in exactly the same general way.

The verbal-imaginal model, according to Clark, combines the verbal and conceptual hypotheses. All classes of verbal material, concrete and abstract, main-

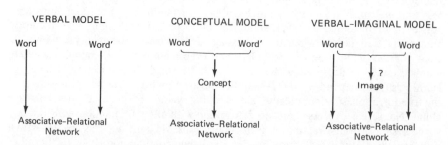

FIGURE 5–13. The structure of semantic similarity for three models of semantic memory according to Clark (1978).

tain distinctive verbal representation prior to their input into the associative-relational network. However, concrete synonyms also converge on a common referential representation, or image. Thus, the verbal-imaginal model is like the verbal model for abstract synonyms and like the conceptual model for concrete ones. The dual-coding model differs from the conceptual model since the common imaginal representation for synonyms such as *boy* and *lad* retains some perceptual character-istics of the referent object rather than being completely abstract, as is the case with conceptual representations.

Clark's study was quite elaborate, but the above account presents the main testable features of the different models. Clark included free-recall and association experiments, which generally provided more support for the dual-coding model than for the other two. For example, in one of the association experiments, the stimulus words consisted of concrete synonym pairs like *avenue-street* and *revolver-pistol*, as well as abstract ones like *freedom-liberty* and *reply-answer*. The concrete and abstract synonyms were equally synonymous, as judged by other subjects' ratings. The participants in the association experiment produced verbal associates for one member of each synonym pair, with different groups of subjects receiving the other member. The measure of interest was the degree of associative overlap between synonyms, that is, the common associations given by the different subjects to the synonymous words.

What exactly are the predictions generated by the different models in regard to associative overlap? The verbal and conceptual models are similar in that they do not predict any systematic differences between concrete and abstract synonyms, since the same mechanisms apply to each class of words. The difference between the two approaches, according to Clark, is that they predict different levels of over-lap generally. The conceptual model predicts a relatively high level of associative overlap because the test taps associative relations among conceptual representations in semantic memory. Since synonyms share a conceptual representation and since it is these common representations that enter into associative relations with other concepts, the subjects should tend to produce many common associations. The verbal model predicts a lower level of associative overlap because the synonyms have sepa-rate verbal representations in semantic memory, and each will enter into its own rela-tionships with other representations. The imaginal-verbal model shares predictions with both of the other models. It predicts a relatively high level of associative overlap for concrete synonyms because they share an imaginal representation. Overlap should be low for abstract words because they do not converge on a common referential image. The predictions from the three models are shown graphically in Figure 5–14.

The results were most consistent with the dual-coding model because the associative overlap score was significantly higher for concrete synonyms than for abstract ones. The proportion of related responses was .35 for concrete and .23 for abstract synonyms. Similar results were obtained when subjects produced associa-tions to both members of synonym pairs. In that case, the proportions of related responses were .45 and .32 for concrete and abstract sets, respectively. Despite the support for the imagery-verbal model, Clark cautiously points out that other inter-pretations are possible and that the problem needs further research to tease apart these alternatives. For our purposes, the study illustrates how one might go about distinguishing experimentally between different theoretical approaches to meaning.

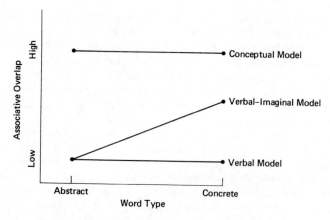

FIGURE 5-14. Levels of associative overlap predicted from the three models of semantic memory compared by Clark (1978).

Summary

In this chapter a wide-ranging view of meaning has been presented. Linguistic approaches range from field to componential approaches, with most effort in the latter. More recent approaches, such as Fillmore's case grammar, have a decidedly psychological flavor. Within the psychological approaches, the behavioristic theories of Osgood and Deese, reflecting both nonverbal and verbal biases, stress stimuli and responses. In contrast, cognitive theories stress knowledge of the world in some form or other.

language
and perception

6

Our aim in this chapter is to consider the relation between language and perception as very broadly conceived. In the first section we ask how we perceive language in general and speech in particular. Then we shall discuss the units of perception, with particular emphasis on word perception and identification. Finally, we consider the perception of more complex stimuli. As you can see, we shall ask not only how we go about perceiving language but also how language affects other aspects of perception. Many of the studies we shall review concern general theoretical issues of the sort we have been emphasizing throughout the book, with perceptual tasks used to investigate the claims of the theories. We should point out that our review is selective, motivated by our hope to address the key issues, and that some of the questions raised will not be satisfactorily answered. Hopefully, by using perception as a vehicle for studying language, and language as a vehicle for studying perception, our aim of understanding language use will be advanced.

Speech Perception

How do we perceive speech? Speech perception occurs so easily and rapidly that we seldom pause to think about the enormous complexity of how we do it. Before we consider the problem more formally, here are some basic facts about speech. For example, it has been estimated that the ordinary speech rate is about twelve phonemes per second. Therefore, whatever discrimination and classification there are must be very rapid indeed. In addition, have you ever noticed that foreigners speaking their native tongue seem to talk too fast, as do professors when they lecture? A major reason for this feeling is that when people speak normally, the stream of noise is continuous, *without* pauses between words. This means that the *hearer* must *impose* segmentation and classification on speech signals (Marler, 1975; Studdert-Kennedy, 1975), and of course this cannot be done without knowing what the segments and classes are. How are we to explain our easy perception of most speech? Here we discuss one particular theory of speech perception and

some of the evidence for it. Our selection is motivated by the fact that it has been the most influential theory proposed so far.

Motor theory of speech perception

The motor theory was advocated by A. Liberman and his colleagues at the Haskins Laboratory in New Haven, Connecticut (see the review by Liberman, Cooper, Shankweiler, & Studdert-Kennedy, 1967). The theory proposes that we discriminate speech sounds, or categorize them, based on feedback from speech articulation to speech perception. That is, we tend to categorize speech we *hear* in terms of speech we *produce*; perception thus has a motor component. The idea is that listeners covertly evoke *idealized articulations* for the possible interpretation of speech sounds. If the generated representation matches the input, recognition has occurred. This view contrasts with the more obvious and traditional view that speech perception is directly based on the acoustic signal, that we hear differences in sound simply because the sounds are different. Note that dogs can respond to speech, such as their names, babies can differentiate between phonemes before they can speak, and some mutes can hear speech perfectly well; these observations indicate that it is possible to hear and perceive without articulating. The motor theory posits that normal perception makes use of articulatory mechanisms, not that it *must* do so for all perception. Loosely speaking, the accuracy of speech perception depends on the hearer's ability to "imitate" the speech subvocally, or to repeat the sounds internally. The theory is consistent with quite a lot of evidence, only some of which we consider here.

Categorical perception

Perhaps the most important implication of the motor theory is that speech perception is categorical. That is, speech stimuli are responded to in absolute terms, even though the stimuli themselves may vary continuously in some graded way (see Studdert-Kennedy, 1975). The expectation is especially strong for stop consonants, since these consonants are produced discretely rather than continuously (Stevens, 1972). As the argument goes, the acoustic signal may vary continuously in very small gradations, but since articulation is discrete, the signals should be perceived as discrete categories. In perhaps the best-known test of this hypothesis, Liberman and his co-workers presented subjects with fourteen speech sounds. The speech was generated synthetically by a machine, thus allowing the sounds to differ from each other in small steps. Sounds at one of the ends of the dimension sounded like /b/, more middle sounds were like /d/, and sounds at the other end were like /g/. You may recall from chapter 3 that the three stop consonants all are voiced, differing in that /b/ is bilabial, /d/ is alveolar, and /g/ is velar; the acoustic dimension was equivalent to moving the articulatory position farther back. In one part of the experiment, people were presented with the stimuli and asked to identify each one as /b/, /d/, or /g/. If perception was continuous, we would expect some sounds to be ambiguous; thus a sound halfway between /b/ and /d/ should be responded to as a blend, or at least inconsistently. However, the results showed no such thing. Perception was in three sharply divided categories, with no gradual transition in between: subjects heard only /b/, /d/, or /g/.

In a second part of the experiment, the stimuli were presented in pairs, and the subjects were asked to state whether they noticed a difference. The results can be interpreted with reference to the following diagram, which shows the phoneme boundaries according to the results of the first part of the experiment.

Acoustic variable ⟶

Stimuli: 1 2 3 4 | 5 6 7 8 | 9 10 11 12 13 14

Perceived as: /b/ | /d/ | /g/

The essential finding was that discrimination was more acute at the perceived phoneme boundaries than in the middle of a phoneme category. That is, subjects perceived essentially no change between 1 and 4, then an abrupt change between 4 and 5, and again no change between 5 and 8, and so on.

This phenomenon appeared not to be true for vowels or for nonspeech sounds (but see the critique at the end of this section). This is evidence, therefore, that the speech perception mechanism for consonants is categorical, like the articulatory mechanisms for the production of distinct phonemes. *Acoustically similar stimuli, which are produced by different patterns of articulation, lead to different perceptions.*

A second finding is essentially the reverse of the above, showing that *acoustically different stimuli, which are produced by similar patterns of articulation, lead to similar perceptions.* The evidence emerges from a spectrographic analysis of a given consonant followed by different vowels. Figure 6-1 presents an example of the results for the consonant /g/. Note that the second formant shows an invariant point of departure at about 3000 Hertz (this is the basis of the consonant /g/) for the vowels /i/ to /a/, followed by a sudden change in the acoustic picture between /a/ and /ɔ/. That is, the point of departure for /g/ drops to a much lower frequency when it is followed by /ɔ/, /o/, and /u/. The listener, however, still reports a /g/! That is, spectrographically the /g/ sounds are different but perceptually and in terms of articulation the series is continuous, with an initial /g/ before each vowel. Try producing the sounds yourself and asking whether the /g/ sounds the same to you.

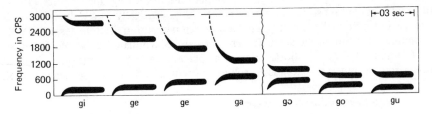

FIGURE 6-1. Spectrographic patterns that produce /g/ before various vowels. The dashed line is an extrapolation to the /g/ "locus." Based on Figure 3 in Liberman (1957).

Perception influences articulation

The final piece of supporting evidence to be mentioned here entails delayed speech feedback. This is a procedure in which a subject's speech is recorded and then fed back through earphones after a slight delay. The result is that a delay of about 180 msec produces artificial stammering. This is further evidence of a close relation between perception and articulation. It is particularly hard to speak while listening to what you said a moment ago. There is no problem, however, if the speaking and hearing are simultaneous, as they are under ordinary circumstances.

Evaluation of the motor theory

The motor theory of speech perception has been criticized on a number of grounds. One criticism is that speech perception and comprehension do not appear to depend on the ability to produce speech. Linguists distinguish numerous phonemes in unfamiliar languages, even though they cannot produce them. Eimas, Siqueland, Jusczyk, and Vigorito (1971) found that infants can learn to respond differentially to different phonemes at ages as young as four months, long before they can produce the sounds. Lenneberg (1967) has described cases of children who demonstrate good speech comprehension despite being unable to speak because of a pathological deficit, and Marler (1975) summarizes speech perception in other species whose members do not speak. These examples supplement the common observation that perception and understanding precede production in speech development. It could be argued, however, that even without overt speech production, the mechanisms could still be present in the form of a motor plan or program for the production of speech, presumably in the speech motor cortex.

Physiological evidence of phoneme production (P. F. MacNeilage & L. A. MacNeilage, 1973) is also troublesome for the theory. The motor theory requires some invariance in motor patterns for phoneme production. This is because the theory assumes that speech perception is based on specific patterns of articulatory activity used in producing specific phonemes. The evidence, however, reveals considerable variation in the motor pattern used in producing a particular phoneme, depending to a considerable degree on what phoneme follows or precedes.

Finally, there is quite a lot of evidence that the perception of nonspeech sounds can also be categorical. This has been demonstrated, for example, in the perception of pitch by musicians with relative and absolute pitch (W. Siegel, J. A. Siegel, Harris, & Sopo, 1974). Along similar lines, Cutting and Rosner (1974) find that a graded musical stimulus is perceived categorically as a "pluck" when it is short, but a "bow" when it is long, again with perception discrete despite almost continuous variation in the acoustic signal (see also Macmillan, Kaplan, & Creelman, 1977; Pisoni, 1977). In short, categorical perception is by no means unique to speech sounds and even extends to sounds we would have trouble producing at all.

Alternatives to the motor theory

Despite these problems, the motor theory has been extremely productive in generating research and has accounted for many of the basic phenomena in speech perception. No completely satisfactory alternative has yet emerged, but attempts are under way. These generally emphasize the importance of a primary auditory

analysis, based on the acoustic properties of the stimulus, with perhaps an additional role attributed to motor processes at a later stage of perceptual processing (see the reviews by Massaro, 1975; Paap, 1975; Studdert-Kennedy, 1974). Some theorists, like Cutting and Eimas (1975) argue that discrete phonetic feature detectors, rather than production processes, account for the categorical nature of perception. Palermo (1975) goes one step farther, suggesting that categorical perception results from innate perceptual mechanisms and that speech production develops from perception—just the reverse of the motor theory. Along a different line, Neisser (1967) has outlined an "analysis-by-synthesis" account, in which the perceptual system forms hypotheses about what the stimulus might be, then matches the incoming information to the hypothesis in order to test it. Although each account can explain why perception should be categorical without reference to the motor-speech system, you can appreciate that the problem has not been solved yet. It remains one of the most interesting and important theoretical problems in the psychology of language. However, we shall leave that problem and turn to specific perceptual phenomena, beginning with a brief discussion of perceptual units.

Perceptual Units

The problem of the size of the psychological unit of language was discussed in chapters 3 and 4. It was concluded that the unit could be as small as a phoneme or as large as a familiar poem, depending on what the task requires. The question in the present context is, what is the smallest unit that can be identified as a speech sound?

The phoneme

The motor theory basically assumes that the minimal unit is the phoneme. This seems not to be the case, however, because consonants are not perceived as speech sounds unless accompanied by vowels. That is, presentation of the early part of the acoustic pattern of a sound such as /di/ produces a nonspeech sound. As successive parts are added, the perception changes suddenly to /di/. The phoneme /d/ is never heard alone. Another argument against the phoneme as the perceptual unit is that phonemes are produced so quickly in ordinary speech that our perceptual apparatus would have to make about twelve decisions per second if identification required a phoneme-by-phoneme analysis. Various kinds of evidence suggest that we can make such sequential decisions only at a rate of about four per second.

The syllable

For the above reasons and others, the consonant-vowel sequence has been proposed as the minimal unit necessary for speech perception (for example, Kimura & King, 1971, reported in Kimura, 1973; Massaro, 1975, pp. 137–140). Syllables occur in speech at a rate of four or five per second, and they seem to be the smallest units that can be distinguished from nonspeech sounds. Thus there is good reason to accept the syllable as the smallest functional unit, at least in the first stages of speech processing. Indeed, Studdert-Kennedy (1975) suggests that the syllable is the building block of perception.

The word

The syllable may have a primary role in speech perception, but the word has more often been treated as the unit in more general studies of language perception, particularly those using visual stimuli. In fact, Osgood and Hoosain (1974) reported a series of experiments that consistently showed that visually presented words were easier to recognize than small units such as morphemes and that word-like nominal compounds (*stumbling block*) were easier than ordinary noun phrases (*copper block*) or nonsense compounds (*sympathy block*). They concluded that the word has special salience in the perception of language. Their results and conclusion justify the attention that the word has received in studies of perceptual recognition. We now turn to a detailed discussion of that problem, usually with reference to visually perceived language (see further in chapter 14).

Word Recognition

There is much research literature on the perceptual identification of words. We can touch on only some of the highlights that are particularly relevant to the theoretical approaches we have been emphasizing. Thus this section will concentrate on the effects of behavioral, linguistic, and cognitive variables. Two situations will be considered: first, perception without explicit context for each word and then perception with contextual information provided.

1. Recognition without Context

Recognition without context refers to the absence of context other than a list of successively presented items, or the context provided by individual differences in personality and other factors. Most of the studies have concerned the effects of various word attributes: frequency, structural attributes, meaningfulness, pronounceability, concreteness, and emotional connotations.

a. Frequency of usage

Numerous studies have shown that common words are easier to recognize than rare words, both when presented visually and when presented auditorily. In visual tasks, words are exposed by means of a tachistoscope (an apparatus that permits a stimulus to be flashed for a measured period of time, which may be as brief as a few milliseconds and which can be increased by very small amounts until the stimulus can be recognized). Response measures include the exposure duration at which a word is recognized and the percentage of correct identifications at some fixed duration. The auditory task often presents words in a background of noise, and the response measure is the *signal-to-noise ratio* at which a word is recognized, or the percentage of correct recognitions at some constant ratio. Another procedure, less often investigated, measures the *reaction time* for word recognition—the time between the moment a word is exposed and the moment the person identifies it.

Although common and rare words differ on other characteristics besides frequency, the frequency effect seems to be generally independent of such correlates. Perhaps the strongest evidence that frequency per se is effective came from a study by Solomon and Postman (1952), which showed that experimental variations

in word frequency affect recognition accuracy. In the study, nonsense words such as *nansoma* and *zabulon* were shown one, two, five, ten, or twenty-five times, and the subjects pronounced the items as they appeared. The words were then presented individually for tachistoscopic recognition, with the result that the subjects found it easier to recognize words that they had seen often prior to the recognition test than words they had seen less often.

Theoretical interpretation of the frequency effect

Most current theories of the frequency effect are *response bias* theories. That is, they assume that recognition responses are somehow biased in favor of common words. Perhaps the most blatant form of response bias was demonstrated in a study by Goldiamond and Hawkins (1958). Their subjects pronounced nonsense words such as *miv, wux, tud,* and *zof* one, two, five, ten, or twenty-five times. In the second phase, the participants were told that the words would be presented tachistoscopically and that they were to report what words they saw. In fact, no words were actually presented, but the subjects' responses were scored as though words had been shown. The results showed that the subjects were more "accurate" in identifying words that had been more frequently experienced in the first phase, because they responded more often with such words. The point is that such biased responding would artifactually increase the accuracy of recognition of common words in the ordinary recognition experiment.

Response bias is, however, open to a number of different interpretations. Broadbent (1967) describes four versions: (1) One is *pure guessing*, according to which a subject just guesses when he or she cannot make out a word, and the guesses are more likely to be common than rare words. (2) Another is *sophisticated guessing*, which states that some words are ruled out on the basis of partial information, such as recognizing some of the letters, and the subject then guesses from the remaining "pool" in a probabilistic fashion. (3) The *observing response* version states that the subject somehow adjusts his or her sense organs or central mechanisms so as to maximize the effects of the expected stimulus. This version has sometimes been called perceptual tuning, selective sensitization, or simply expectancy. (4) Finally, *criterion bias* is a version based on signal detection theory (also called decision theory). This view asserts that the subject is biased to accept a smaller amount of evidence before deciding in favor of a probable (common) word rather than an improbable (rare) one. The last interpretation is the one favored by Broadbent, but others have recently argued in favor of other alternatives.

Morton (1969) proposed a criterion-bias model of word recognition. It is called the logogen model, in which logogen refers to a hypothetical cognitive representation corresponding to words, as discussed in the preceding chapter, but in this case with a more specific meaning. The term logogen was coined by Morton from the Greek words *logos* ("word") and *genus* ("birth"). A logogen is a hypothetical device that accepts information relevant to a particular word, and when enough information has accumulated, it is capable of generating the word response. That is, the response becomes available; the subject may or may not respond overtly, depending on task requirements. The logogen is a representation that can vary in its level of excitation or strength. According to Morton, it can accept auditory, visual, or semantic information. One might think of it as a kind of *counter* for

incoming sensory information—as information comes in, the counter accumulates it, and when the count rises above a *threshold* value, the corresponding response is made available.

The model is illustrated in Figure 6–2. Note that in addition to components for the analysis of auditory and visual word information, the model includes a *context system* from which information about semantic attributes of words can influence word recognition. The output of the logogen system goes into an output buffer which determines whether an overt response will be emitted or whether the output information is fed back into the logogen system by means of implicit rehearsal. The flow diagram shows that activation of a logogen depends on information about the auditory or visual structure of the word, as well as contextual stimuli.

The word frequency effect is explained by this model in terms of the *response threshold*: logogens corresponding to words of high frequency in a language have lower thresholds than do low-frequency words. That is, for high-frequency words, less information is needed for the logogen to make the response available. This interpretation is illustrated in Figure 6–3. The diagram represents the level of excitation in a logogen in terms of a probability distribution for different levels of excitation. The curve on the left shows the normal state of the logogen, and the broken-lined curve on the right shows the distribution resulting from the combined effect of a word stimulus and contextual cues. The vertical lines represent the thresholds of response availability for high-, medium-, and low-frequency words. High-frequency words have the lowest thresholds; hence the logogen will make the response available with less added information from the stimulus and context. It is as though a counter starts off at a higher value for high-frequency than for low-frequency words. We shall refer to this model again later, in relation to the effect of context on word recognition.

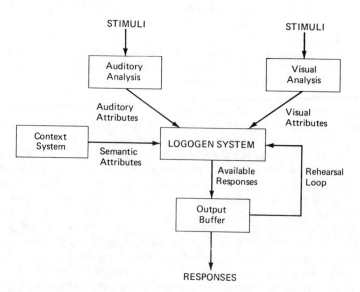

FIGURE 6–2. Flow diagram for the Logogen Model. From Morton (1969).

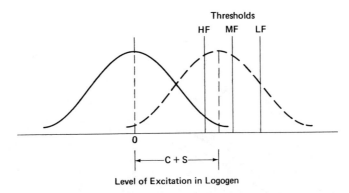

Thresholds
HF   MF   LF

0

|←——C + S——→|

Level of Excitation in Logogen

FIGURE 6-3. Effects of stimulus and context on the state of a logogen: O = original state (mean of distribution); S = effect of stimulus; C = effect of context. HF, MF, LF refer to levels of word frequency. HF has lower threshold, hence logogen will make response available with less stimulus information. Adapted from Morton (1969).

b. *Structural attributes*

The effects of structural attributes such as length, pronounceability, and phoneme structure are not completely clear because it is difficult to test the effects of one variable while holding all others constant. Nonetheless, their effects are important considerations, and they have been introduced as variables in a sophisticated guessing model by Rumelhart and Siple (1974).

The *statistical structure of letter sequences* was studied by Miller, Bruner, and Postman (1954). They constructed pseudowords that varied in the degree to which their sequential structure approximated that of English words. Four degrees of approximation were used. Zero-order words were eight-letter sequences for which the letters were selected at random from the alphabet. Examples are *yrulpzoc* and *ozhapmtj*. First-order approximations (*stanugop, vtyehulo*) were selected according to the relative frequency of occurrence of the letters in written English. Second-order approximations (*wallyoff, therares*) reflected the relative frequency of pairs of letters. Finally, fourth-order approximations (*ricaning, vernalit*) were based on the relative frequency of sequences of four letters. The pseudowords were presented one at a time tachistoscopically, and the subjects attempted to write down, in their correct order, the letters they saw. The exposure duration was increased over six trials. The results are plotted in Figure 6-4, where it can be seen that more letters can be perceived as the letter sequences become more familiar and more predictable from one's knowledge of English. In a sense, of course, this can be viewed as another demonstration of the effect of frequency, defined in terms of the length of the familiar sequence in a nonsense word.

Word length is an obvious variable in that one might expect shorter words to be easier to recognize than longer ones. It turns out that this is not necessarily so. Often longer words are easier to perceive, perhaps because they contain more redundant information, or are easier to guess because they have fewer alternatives in long-term memory than do shorter words. This is true particularly of auditory

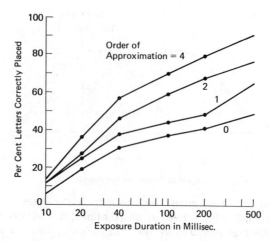

FIGURE 6–4. Percentage of letters recognized in their correct positions with eight-letter pseudowords constructed at four orders of approximation to the statistical structure of English. (After Miller, Bruner, & Postman, 1954.)

recognition. For visual thresholds, shorter words are usually easier to perceive than longer ones, but even here there are exceptions.

Pronounceability is another relevant variable. Its effects were studied by Gibson, Bishop, Schiff, and Smith (1964), who compared meaningful trigrams like IBM and FBI with pronounceable but meaningless ones like MIB and BIF. They found that the *pronounceable* trigrams had lower recognition thresholds than the meaningful but unpronounceable ones. This finding is consistent with a response-availability interpretation: the logogens corresponding to more pronounceable words have lower activation thresholds than do less pronounceable items.

Finally, several structural attributes are related to word frequency, thereby confounding its effects. Landauer and Streeter (1973) found that common words and rare words differed as a group on such structural characteristics as the distribution of phonemes. For example, /n/, /l/, /t/, and /ɚ/ (the terminal "er" sound in words like further) are more characteristic of common than rare words, whereas /z/, /p/, /g/, and /æ/ are more characteristic of rare than common words. These investigators also showed that with common, monosyllabic words, those with "common word phonemes" (like FLOOR) were more intelligible in terms of the signal-to-noise ratio than were words with "rare word phonemes" (like JUDGE). They point out that this effect and the other correlates of frequency do not rule out frequency as an effective determinant of perceptual recognition but they do complicate the interpretations.

Correlational studies using word attributes are in fact plagued by this problem. When investigating the effect of some word attribute, we can never be absolutely sure that all other relevant attributes have been controlled. That is why experimental manipulation of a single variable (holding all others constant) is so important when it can be achieved.

c. Semantic and associative attributes

Many studies were conducted in the late 1940s through the 1950s and early 1960s on the effect of the *pleasantness* of word meaning on perception. Other meaning attributes such as meaningfulness and concreteness have also been investigated. All of these variables pertain to features that are defined by reactions aroused by the word rather than by attributes intrinsic to the word itself, as with frequency and structural attributes. Thus, if the semantic variables have an effect on the recognition of a word, it is theoretically puzzling, for *how can an associative attribute, which depends on word recognition for its arousal, affect perception of the word itself?* Stated another way, does the word not have to be recognized before we know what it means?

The earliest research (see the review by Erdelyi, 1974) was concerned with the effect of emotional or affective meaning on word recognition. For example, studies compared taboo words (that is, "dirty" words—you can think of your own examples) with emotionally neutral ones, or words related to a person's dominant interests or values as compared with words unrelated to such values. Some studies showed more difficult recognition for taboo than for neutral words. This was interpreted in terms of the concept of *perceptual defense*, which was defined as a perceptual mechanism that is sensitive to meaning and somehow "defends" against the conscious recognition of a word if it is anxiety arousing. Much of the evidence for perceptual defense was later explained in terms of two variables that we have already considered, namely, word frequency and response bias. Frequency was implicated because taboo words turned out to be less common than neutral ones. Nonetheless, with frequency controlled, recognition thresholds were still higher for taboo words. Response bias in this context refers to response *suppression*: the average subject is simply embarrassed to say such words in front of an experimenter. The effect of response bias was clearly demonstrated by Zajonc (1962). His experiment consisted of two phases relevant to our discussion. In the first phase, his subjects learned a list of paired associates in which one type of pair consisted of a taboo word and a neutral word, for example, *apple-raped* and *vomit-broom*. Learning was continued until all of the associations were fully mastered. In the next phase, visual recognition thresholds were determined, but the participants were asked to respond either with the word that was actually flashed or with its learned associate that was not actually presented tachistoscopically. The important result was that recognition thresholds were determined by what the participant had to *say*, rather than by what was *shown*. Thus, if the presented word was neutral (*apple*) but the subject had to report its taboo associate (*raped*), the "threshold" was higher than if the subject was shown *raped* and had to indicate recognition by saying *apple*.

Semantic subception is another phenomenon related to the perception of affectively loaded words. It refers to perception without awareness as indicated, for example, by physiological reactions occurring to words with strong emotional tone even when they are flashed so briefly that the subject is unable to report them. The phenomenon has received popular attention because of attempts to exploit it in the marketplace under the label of subliminal advertising. Thus it is important to evaluate the validity of the idea for practical as well as theoretical reasons. An experimental demonstration was first provided by Lazarus and McCleary (1951).

They created affectively negative and neutral stimuli by associating five nonsense syllables with shock during a training period and presenting five others without shock an equal number of times. Enough trials were conducted so that the shocked syllables became unpleasant to the subjects. Following this training, recognition thresholds were measured along with recording of the galvanic skin response (GSR, a measure of autonomic arousal). The crucial result was that on trials when the participant's recognition response was incorrect, there was a higher GSR to the previously shocked syllables than to the neutral ones. The findings supported the idea of subception defined as autonomic discrimination without awareness.

Subsequently, however, Eriksen (1958) showed that the subception effect is partly an artifact resulting from differences in how the verbal identifying response and the GSR are scored. In verbal identification, the participant had to identify each syllable exactly in order to obtain a correct score. Since there were ten different stimuli, there was a *10 percent* chance of being correct simply by guessing. The GSR, however, could indicate only whether the syllable was a traumatic or a neutral one. Thus an increase in GSR to a stimulus could be correct by chance *50 percent* of the time. The verbal report would be comparable to the GSR only if subjects were asked to report whether or not a given stimulus was one that had been previously shocked, rather than having to identify the specific stimulus. When this is done or when the appropriate baseline for guessing is otherwise used to analyze the data, the threshold of a GSR response is not lower than the threshold for verbal identification. Nonetheless, the GSR response did have a better-than-chance accuracy in these experiments when the verbal response was wrong. Eriksen explained such effects in terms of the partial independence of the GSR and the verbal report as response systems. This means that sometimes one response may be correct and sometimes the other. This explanation leaves the phenomenon of subception intact but removes the necessity of discussing it in terms of the distinction between conscious and unconscious functions, unless we simply define that distinction in terms of verbal and autonomic response systems.

Another affective dimension relevant to perception is *personal values or interests.* Postman, Bruner, and McGinnies (1948) used a questionnaire called the Study of Values (Allport, Vernon, & Lindzey, 1951) to measure six different values, namely, *theoretical, economic, aesthetic, social, political,* and *religious.* A score was obtained for each subject on each of these values or interests. The same subjects were then shown, by means of a tachistoscope, six words that were meaningfully related to each of the value areas. Examples of the words are shown in Table 6-1. The results showed that the participants recognized words related to their dominant values more easily than words related to lower-ranking values. Thus, a person

TABLE 6-1   Examples of Value-Related Words

Value Area					
Theoretical	Economic	Aesthetic	Social	Political	Religious
theory	useful	beauty	loving	govern	worship
science	income	artist	helpful	citizen	prayer
verify	wealthy	poetry	sociable	politics	sacred

scoring high on the religious value and low on the theoretical value was likely to recognize words with religious connotations more easily than words with scientific or theoretical connotations, whereas the reverse was true for persons higher in theoretical than in religious values.

The effect of value holds also in an auditory perception situation called the "cocktail party" phenomenon. Paivio and Steeves (1967) constructed two prose passages, one of which had a religious theme and the other a theoretical or scientific one. Examples of sentences from the religious passage are: In times of trouble, religion is a consolation. Pious persons take refuge in this. Their faithfulness also aids them. Examples of the theoretical passage are: We wish to verify this matter. Measurements must be made carefully. Analytic procedures must be used. The two passages were recorded separately, then the two recordings were played simultaneously and rerecorded on another tape sounding much like two conversations going on simultaneously at a cocktail party. The cocktail-party tape was played to subjects who wrote down what they heard following each one-minute segment. They also completed the Study of Values so that their scores on the religious and theoretical values could be compared with their reports of what they heard from the tape. The result was that persons who had higher theoretical than religious values reported more theoretical words, whereas those who scored higher on the religious value reported more of the religious material. Thus, speech perception, like visual word recognition, is influenced by the personal values of the subjects interacting with the value-related semantic content of the linguistic material.

The early visual recognition findings were first interpreted in terms of the concept of *selective sensitization*, according to which values somehow tune or bias the perceptual apparatus so that it responds selectively to value-related words. As in the case of perceptual defense, however, it could be that individuals use and are exposed to words related to their personal values more frequently than to less related ones. However, later studies (Johnson, Thomson, & Frincke, 1960) demonstrated that word frequency and affective value can independently influence perceptual recognition of words. That is, high-frequency words such as *think* and *sweet* are easier to recognize than less frequent ones such as *vision* and *agile*, although the words at different frequency levels are matched on rated goodness. Conversely, with frequency matched, "good" words (*glisten, prosper*) are easier to recognize than "bad" ones (*corrupt, hinder*). Perhaps a concept such as selective sensitization may be needed to explain the data, although the tendency today would be to interpret such sensitization in terms of a decision-theoretical model. In fact, a theory proposed by Bruner and Postman (see Allport, 1955, chap. 15) had some of the characteristics of Morton's logogen theory. Bruner and Postman referred to theirs as hypothesis-set theory or (later) expectancy theory. The hypothesis, a mediating mechanism corresponding to stimulus information, could be weak or strong. If the stimulus information is congruent with the hypothesis, the subject accepts it and responds accordingly; if the hypothesis is strong, it takes little congruent information to confirm it, and much incongruent information to disconfirm it. Thus it was a kind of response-threshold model which could be restated to mean that value-related logogens have relatively low thresholds.

The observation that frequency and values of words are correlated is itself an intriguing problem. Across many languages, rated goodness and frequency of occurrence are positively correlated. The immediate explanations are twofold. The first

explanation has been called the Pollyanna hypothesis—we prefer to talk about pleasant things, such as love and beauty, rather than unpleasant things, such as snot and disease. Thus, frequency and goodness are correlated because we talk mostly about good things. The second explanation, the mere-exposure hypothesis, turns out to be a better one. By this hypothesis, the more often we encounter a word, the more pleasant it becomes. In fact, if nonsense syllables or faces are presented to subjects in an experiment, the more frequently they are presented, the more pleasant or good they are rated as being (Johnson et al., 1960; Zajonc, 1968). Thus frequency might be directly responsible for both recognition and value.

The dual-coding approach in terms of levels of meaning suggests yet another way to analyze the effects of semantic and associative attributes. A study by Paivio and O'Neill (1970) compared the effects of word frequency, meaningfulness, and imagery-concreteness on visual recognition. Frequency is relevant to the representational level of meaning: according to the analysis discussed in chapter 5, the availability of a word representation (logogen) depends primarily on the frequency of experience with the verbal unit. Word imagery (and concreteness) is defined by the availability of a nonverbal image to the word; hence it is an index of referential meaning. This is a kind of nonverbal associative reaction that *depends on* prior word recognition for its arousal; therefore it should have no effect on the perceptual recognition of the word itself. Meaningfulness, as defined by the number of word associates elicited by a stimulus word, is an index of verbal associative relations. Such associations, too, should have no effect on recognition because the stimulus word itself must be perceived before its verbal associates can be aroused.

The results generally confirmed these expectations. Frequency had its usual positive effect on recognition. Word imagery had no effect, and meaningfulness had little effect independent of familiarity. Similar results were obtained in an auditory recognition experiment. Thus we conclude that representational meaning (familiarity) is most strongly related to ease of recognition.

Conclusions

What is the present status of the relationship between semantic attributes and perceptual recognition? A few studies still support phenomena such as perceptual defense (Worthington, 1964) and semantic subception (Wickens, 1972). That is, some results suggest that emotional information about a perceptually degraded word seems to be communicated even when subjects are unable to *report* the word accurately. These remain theoretically puzzling at the present time. Perhaps the most promising approach to their interpretation is provided by contemporary information-processing approaches, as discussed by Erdelyi (1974). He suggests that perceptual defense and vigilance are special instances of selectivity in cognitive processing. Selectivity is brought into play through various mechanisms which operate at different points in the information-processing sequence. No single site is likely to provide a complete explanation of any substantial selective phenomenon. The loci of selectivity for the visual modality include the following: (a) selective looking strategies (orienting movements of the eyes and head—in common-sense terms, people often avoid looking at unpleasant stimuli); (b) selection in peripheral receptor systems, such as changes in pupil diameter, that alter the perceiver's sensitivity to the stimulus; (c) selective reporting strategies (this is the component that

response-bias theories emphasized); and (d) selective encoding into short-term and long-term memory, which determines whether or not a stimulus is remembered at the time of the recognition test. The point is that perceptual recognition is no longer viewed as a kind of simple perceptual phenomenon but rather as a complex process with many stages, including peripheral and central selective mechanisms.

2. Contextual Effects on Word Recognition

This section primarily concerns the effects of other words, presented along with a target word, on the perception of the target. The general finding is that associatively or semantically related words facilitate perception of the target more than unrelated words do. Several examples of such effects follow.

Auditory recognition and sentence contexts

Miller, Heise, and Lichten (1951) found that the intelligibility of spoken words heard against background noise was better when the words were in sentences, as compared to when they were alone. They explained these results in information-theoretic terms: the sentence context reduces uncertainty, that is, the number of possible alternatives for a given word.

Visual recognition thresholds

Rouse and Verinis (1962) gave their subjects one word to fixate (for example, *river*); then a second word (for example, *stream* or *month*) was flashed. The results showed that recognition thresholds for associated test words were lower than for nonassociated words. Thus, with *river* as the fixated context, thresholds were lower for *stream* than for *month*, but not when the context was unrelated to *stream*.

Tulving and Gold (1963) presented as contexts strings of words that were either congruous or incongruous with the subsequent target word. For example, *The actress received praise for being an outstanding* . . . is congruous for *performer* but not for *collision*. Tachistoscopic duration thresholds were measured for target words as a function of the length and congruence of the context. The results showed that the length of the context was unimportant but that congruence was crucial. The correlation between the visual duration threshold for the target and the congruity with the context was -.93; that is, the higher the congruity of the context, the briefer the duration at which the target word was recognized. The correlation between the thresholds and the length of the context was only -.35.

Such results can be interpreted in terms of the general effect of context on the availability of a response or, in terms of Morton's theory, on the level of the count in relevant logogens as a result of semantic information from the context system.

Backward masking

A related effect that requires slightly different interpretation was obtained by Jacobson (1973). It was in part a backward-masking effect. A stimulus is "masked" (becomes more difficult to recognize) if it is followed shortly by another stimulus.

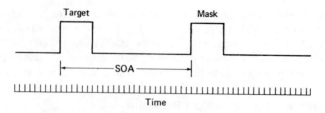

FIGURE 6-5. Schematization of the critical stimulus onset asynchrony (SOA), which is the time that mask onset must be delayed in order for the preceding target word to be read correctly.

The critical *stimulus-onset asynchrony* (the mask delay necessary for the target word to be read correctly—see Figure 6-5) varied somewhat with the nature of the mask. Jacobson used words as target stimuli and masks, with the two being either associates or nonassociates (for example, *square-circle* versus *square-sheep*). He first presented the target word, then the mask word after 10 msec. The subject tried to identify the target; if he or she was unable to do so, the stimulus-onset asynchrony was increased by 10 msec, and so on, until recognition was achieved.

The results, presented in Figure 6-6, showed that the stimulus-onset asynchrony for effective masking was longer for nonassociated than for associated masks. Stated another way, the target word is more readily reported when it is masked by an *associated word* than by a *nonassociated word*. Other conditions in the study permitted Jacobson to rule out guessing as the explanation and also showed that the effect is due to *facilitation* by an associated mask, rather than *interference* by a nonassociated mask. Moreover, he obtained facilitation *cross-modally*, with the associate or nonassociate presented auditorily. In another experiment, Jacobson found that reading was faster when the target word was preceded by an associate than by a nonassociate.

How are these findings to be interpreted? Jacobson used a "lattice-overlap" theory. The neuronal substrate of a word concept is a neuronal lattice, as in Hebb's (1949) cell assembly theory. Related words share neuronal units so that more related words have greater lattice overlap (see Figure 6-7). Consequently, activa-

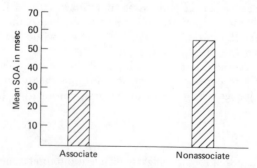

FIGURE 6-6. Mean critical SOA when target is masked by an associated and an unassociated word. Based on data in Jacobson (1973).

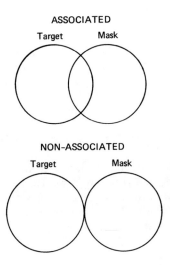

ASSOCIATED

Target   Mask

NON-ASSOCIATED

Target   Mask

FIGURE 6-7. Schematic representation of Jacobson's "lattice-overlap" theory of the neuronal substrates of associated and non-associated words, which is used to interpret the effects of backward masking.

tion of the lattice by a word will stimulate the lattice of an associate. In the masking situation, a word should be less fully masked by an associated than by a nonassociated mask because the associated mask will restimulate much of the target's lattice. Note that the overlapping-lattice idea is similar to the assumptions of many theories of semantic memory, in which memory structure is viewed as a network in which semantically or associatively related words are closer together in the network than are less related ones (see chapter 5).

Reaction time for visual word recognition

Our final example is from research by David E. Meyer and his colleagues on contextual effects on reaction time for word recognition (see Meyer, Schvaneveldt, & Ruddy, 1975). The subject is successively presented with two words. He or she classifies each as a word or a nonword. The words may be semantically associated (*bread-butter, nurse-doctor*), unassociated (*nurse-butter, bread-doctor*), or one or both could be nonwords (*wine-plame, soam-glove, nist-barue*). The typical result is that the second word is classified as a word faster when the first word is an associate than when it is not. This, too, demonstrates a *semantic context effect*, which seems to be present at an early stage of visual word recognition (reflecting encoding rather than retrieval). The suggestion that the effect occurs during encoding has been supported by various findings; for example, the context effect was stronger when the words were perceptually degraded. Thus semantic context was particularly effective when stimulus recognition (at an early stage of processing) was difficult, suggesting that recognition and semantic context effects occurred at the same (early) stage. Regardless of their locus, however, Meyer interprets such effects generally in terms of lexical or semantic memory, in which the structures

of associated words are close together, so that excitation can spread from one to another.

Note that in terms of the dual-coding theory, the context effects seem to be based on the verbal associative system. The question arises whether similar priming or masking effects on word perception would occur if the contextual stimuli were nonverbal. We would expect so, although tests of the idea have apparently not been reported.

Grammatical and Semantic Variables in Sentence Perception

The studies considered in this section use more complex stimuli than the word-perception studies do and accordingly require more complex interpretations. In particular, we might ask again about the psychological reality of various linguistic units, as those units influence the perception process. The following examples illustrate the different tasks that have been used:

Perception through noise

Miller and Isard (1963) tried to separate the effects of syntactic and semantic features of spoken sentences on their intelligibility when presented in white noise. To achieve this end, they used three groups of sentences. One consisted of normal grammatical sentences, such as *Colorless cellophane packages crackle loudly*. A second consisted of grammatical but semantically anomalous sentences, such as *Colorless yellow ideas sleep furiously*. The third consisted of ungrammatical scrambled strings of words, such as *Sleep roses dangerously young colorless*. As shown in Figure 6-8, the normal sentences were easiest to hear in terms of the percentage of correctly reported strings, the anomalous sentences were next, and the ungrammatical strings were the most difficult. Since the normal and anomalous sentences

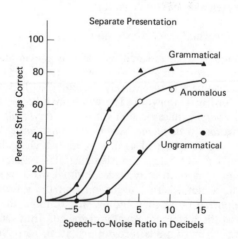

FIGURE 6–8. Percent strings heard correctly as a function of speech-to-noise ratios and type of word sequence. From Miller and Isard (1963, Figure 3, p. 223).

both are grammatical, one could argue that the perceptual difference between them represents a semantic effect. Similarly, since both the anomalous and ungrammatical sentences violate semantic rules, the obtained perceptual difference is apparently due to grammatical factors. Miller and Isard suggested that the subjects used both syntactic and semantic rules in the task. It is not sure, however, that semantics and syntax were clearly teased apart by their procedure, since the anomalous sentences seem more meaningful in an odd sense than do the ungrammatical strings.

Rosenberg and Jarvella (1970) conducted a similar study in which they held syntax constant by using only meaningful sentences, all of which had the same grammatical structure. However, half of the sentences were *semantically well integrated* in that they contained words that were associatively related (*The actor played the part*), whereas the others were semantically poorly integrated in that the words were not associatively related to each other (*The lawyer named the road*). The semantic-integration variable is discussed in more detail in chapter 8. For present purposes, note that it is a kind of semantic or associative variable, which was varied independently of syntax. Subjects were required to shadow (immediately repeat) sentences presented with or without background noise. The main result of interest here was that shadowing under the noise condition was much better for semantically well integrated rather than poorly integrated sentences. The authors suggested that subjects used the semantic information provided by the perceived words to reconstruct words that were unintelligible.

Other studies, using different methods, have also been concerned with the problem of distinguishing the effects of semantic and grammatical variables and in addition have attempted to distinguish between surface structure and deep structure in the case of the grammatical variables.

Click migration

Fodor and Bever (1965) initiated a series of studies designed to reveal perceptual effects of phrase structure. Their subjects listened to tape-recorded sentences, each of which had an auditory "click" superimposed at some point. The clicks in different sentences were positioned around the major constituent break according to a phrase-structure analysis. For example, compare *His hope of marrying Anna was unreasonable* with *In her hope of marrying Anna was unreasonable.* In the first sentence, the major break is between *Anna* and *was,* but in the second, the break is between *marrying* and *Anna.* One question of interest is where one would report a click superimposed over *Anna.* The click was located at the major break in one copy of the sentence, and clicks were placed progressively farther from the break in other copies. The participants wrote down each sentence immediately after it was presented and then indicated by a slash where they thought the click had occurred. The majority of errors were in the direction of the major constituent break, as though the clicks were "attracted" toward such boundaries. This outcome was consistent with the hypothesis that errors in click locations would be systematically related to the structural descriptions of the sentences. Fodor and Bever derived the expectation from the more general theoretical position that the *perception* of sentences is an active process which includes a structural analysis of the sentence, rather than a passive response to acoustic cues. In brief,

their basic notion was that the underlying clause is a unit in speech perception, and because it is a unit, it should resist interruption by an external event such as a click.

Since then, however, the interpretation of the phenomenon has become more complicated. It is not clear whether the effect is due to a deep structure analysis, a surface structure analysis, or a semantic analysis, or simply is an artifact of uncontrolled factors that have nothing to do with syntax.

a. Deep structure versus surface structure

Deep structure and surface structure have been manipulated separately in several studies. Some studies suggest that the clicks are perceptually attracted to the boundary between the underlying clauses even when the boundaries seem to be unmarked in the surface structure. Bever, Lackner, and Kirk (1969) compared noun-phrase and verb-phrase complements. With a noun-phrase complement, such as in the sentence *The corrupt police cannot bear criminals to confess very quickly*, the underlying clause is treated like a noun phrase. A click located at *criminals* was often reported as having occurred between *bear* and *criminals*, which is the boundary between the underlying clauses. (This can be tested by paraphrasing the sentence in the form *What the police cannot bear/is for criminals to confess very quickly*.) Conversely, a superficially similar verb-phrase complement, like *The corrupt police cannot force criminals to confess very quickly*, did not have the same effect. In this case criminals is the object of *force* and the subject of *confess* in the deep structure (note that the sentence cannot be paraphrased as *What the police cannot force is for . . .*). The essential point is that Bever and his associates claimed that there is no surface structure break between the main verb and the following noun phrase and that the clicks migrated to the boundary between the underlying clauses.

Conversely, however, Chapin, Smith, and Abrahamson (1972) found that clicks placed midway between a major surface boundary and a *subsequent* underlying clause boundary were attracted to the *surface* boundary, but there was no consistent effect when the underlying clause boundary *preceded* the surface boundary.

b. Artifacts

Several experiments have shown that the click-migration phenomenon is influenced by nonlinguistic artifacts. For example, Reber and Anderson (1970) found that clicks, even nonexistent "subliminal" ones, migrated toward the middle of a sentence, a random string of words, and even strings made up of bursts of white noise! Feldmar (1969) and others have found that the click displacement effect does not occur when subjects make their judgments immediately after they hear the sentence. With a delay, however, the original effect was observed. Thus the phenomenon is apparently related to memory and response factors, rather than to factors operating at the initial stages of perceptual processing.

There is no resolution of such inconsistencies up to this time. We must conclude that the click-migration phenomenon is more complex than it was originally assumed to be and that it is sensitive to many factors other than linguistic structure.

Phoneme monitoring

Donald J. Foss (1970) devised phoneme monitoring to study the effect of linguistic variables on the perception of phonemes. In the basic task, a subject listens to sentences and is required to perform two tasks, first, to comprehend the sentence and, second, to press a button whenever he or she hears a particular phoneme, such as a word starting with a /b/ as in *book*. Foss assumed that both tasks are carried out by the same perceptual processor. The crucial implication is that to the extent that one decision is difficult, the other should take longer. This was supported by several experiments that showed that the reaction time for identifying a phoneme was longer when the sentence or part of it was more difficult to understand. For example, responses were slower when a target phoneme followed a rare adjective than when it followed a common one. Other experiments showed that responses are slower when the syntax is more complex (Foss & Lynch, 1969). For example, self-embedded sentences like *The rioter that the whisky the store sold intoxicated broke the window* are more complex and resulted in slower phoneme monitoring than right-branching sentences like *The store sold the whisky that intoxicated the rioter that broke the window*. Moreover, phoneme detection is faster when the sentence contains relative pronouns than when it does not. Thus *The car that the man whom the dog bit drove crashed* is easier than *The car the man the dog bit. . . .* It has also been found that phoneme monitoring is slower for ambiguous than for nonambiguous sentences (see further in Newman & Dell, 1978).

Finally, Morton and Long (1976) demonstrated that the transition probability of the word containing a target phoneme affects the reaction time for identifying the phoneme. Consider, for example, the sentence *At the sink she washed a plate, thinking of the time when she was younger* as compared to *At the sink she washed a pan, thinking of the time when she was younger*. The sentences are identical except for the words *plate* and *pan*; *plate* has a higher transition probability (is more predictable as a missing word in the target sentence) than *pan*. In the phoneme-monitoring task, it turned out that the subjects responded faster to the same initial phoneme target (/p/ in the example sentence) when it occurred in *plate* than in *pan*. Morton and Long have concluded that transition probability is a potent factor that could have affected the results of earlier studies of phoneme monitoring.

Thus phoneme monitoring promises to be a useful technique for psycholinguistic research, such as the determination of effective syntactic, semantic, and contextual variables in sentences that require different levels of processing.

Rapid serial visual presentation (RSVP)

RSVP is a method introduced by K. I. Forster (1970). The basic procedure is to project the words of a sentence one after the other on the same spot on a screen, at a rapid rate (for example, sixteen per second). Immediately after the presentation of a sentence, the subject writes it down from memory.

The RSVP technique is quite sensitive to certain syntactic and semantic variables, although not to some others. This was shown in a study by Forster and Ryder (1971), who varied the *syntactic complexity* and *semanticity* of sentences. The former compared one-clause and two-clause sentences, and the semanticity variable

compared normal, bizarre, and anomalous sentences. Examples of each are as follows:

Simple (one clause)

Normal: Five girls waded into the large pool.
Bizarre: Three bugs jumped over the moldy meat.
Anomalous: Four banjos slept about the empty watch.

Complex (two clauses)

Normal: The dress that Pam wore looked ugly.
Bizarre: The aunt that Jim ate tasted foul.
Anomalous: The hero that Alan tore seemed fresh.

The results in terms of the average number of words reported for each of the conditions are shown in Table 6-2. Note that both syntactic complexity and semantic variation had significant effects. That is, normal sentences exceeded the bizarre, which in turn were reported more accurately than the anomalous. Within each semantic type, simple sentences were easier to report than complex. This suggests that syntactic and semantic perceptual processing go on independently. These observations and other analyses suggested to Forster and Ryder that syntactic processing precedes semantic processing. The conclusion is consistent with the hypothesis held by Fodor and Garrett, among others, that perception includes hypothesis testing. The initial perceptual hypothesis is concerned with the syntactic structure; once the structure has been established, semantic interpretation begins. Findings from other studies, however, suggested that semantic effects precede syntactic ones, contrary to the Forster and Ryder study. Thus different interpretations of perceptual processing are supported by different studies. Yet another view, proposed by Bever (1970), is that both syntactic and semantic processing go on at the same time, in parallel.

We can now express the same general conclusions concerning the various techniques we have considered, namely click migration, phoneme monitoring, and RSVP. All apparently are sensitive to syntactic factors, but it is not always clear whether they reflect surface or deep structure variables. They also clearly reflect semantic influences, but the results leave open the question of which comes first, semantics or syntax, or whether both go on in parallel. Such uncertainty suggests that a clear separation between semantics and syntax may not be possible, and such a conclusion would favor those cognitive linguistic and psychological approaches that try to deal with semantics and syntax without drawing a sharp distinction.

TABLE 6-2   Mean Number of Words Reported Following RSVP of Sentences Varying in Syntactic Complexity and Semanticity

	Normal	Bizarre	Anomalous
Simple	4.20	3.21	2.80
Complex	3.79	2.81	2.66

Effects of Language on Perception of Nonverbal Stimuli

Several related theories assume that linguistic processes influence perception in general. The classical version of such an approach is the Sapir-Whorf hypothesis of linguistic relativity, which will be discussed in more detail in chapter 11. Other versions include verbal-coding theory (Bruner, 1957; Haber, 1966) and the verbal-loop hypothesis (Glanzer & Clark, 1963). The following discussion illustrates such approaches:

The verbal-loop hypothesis

Glanzer and Clark proposed that subjects faced with a perceptual task encode the information verbally and then translate the verbal information into a final response. The "length" of this verbal loop is therefore critical: the shorter the verbalization required by the perceptual task, the more accurate the performance. The hypothesis has been supported by studies that showed the predicted relation. The support is not invariable, however; for example, training subjects in verbal encoding of binary numbers actually impaired the accuracy with which such numbers were reported after brief tachistoscopic exposure. The verbal-encoding effect presumably depends on how much time the observer has to encode the perceptual material.

Haber's verbal-encoding hypothesis

Haber argued that the perceptual processing of briefly presented visual stimuli requires encoding the stimulus as a memory trace after the stimulus terminates, because the immediate perceptual trace left by the stimulus fades rapidly. Haber also suggested that the encoding is usually verbal, although he acknowledged other modes. The encoding effects depend on the speed of encoding and its resistance to errors during the interval before the subject reports the stimulus.

The following study illustrates the application of such ideas to perceptual phenomena (see the review by Haber, 1966). The task entailed tachistoscopic recognition of stimuli that varied in number, color, and shape. For example, the array might consist of one red triangle on the left and three blue stars on the right, as in the following illustration:

Harris and Haber (1963) previously observed that subjects used different encoding strategies for such stimuli. One was an *objects code*, in which the subject separated the stimuli into objects. Thus, for the above illustration, the subject might report "one red triangle," "three blue stars." The other strategy used a *dimensions code*, in which the stimulus was separated into three dimensions. Thus the subject might say "Red, blue; triangle, star; one, three." Note that such a strategy requires shifting

back and forth between the configuration on the left and the one on the right. Harris and Haber emphasized the linguistic distinction between these two coding strategies. The *dimensions code* can be varied without disturbing the strategy; that is, it does not matter which dimension is reported first. The *objects code*, by contrast, has its order fixed by the rules of English syntax so that we say, for example, "One red triangle" rather than "Red one triangle." Harris and Haber investigated the implications of their reasoning by training subjects to use one strategy or the other and also by varying the order in which the attributes were to be reported. Subjects who had been trained to use the dimensions code should do better on the first-reported dimension than on later ones, whereas objects coders should not show the differential accuracy because the syntactic constraints associated with objects coding would prevent them from giving special treatment to the emphasized dimension. This is precisely what they found. In addition, objects coders were generally more accurate and completed their encoding of stimuli faster than dimensions coders.

Dual coding provides an alternative interpretation of the above findings. The essence of the argument is that training in objects coding encourages the observer to pay attention to the stimuli as concrete, integrated objects and, accordingly, to encode and store them as images. Dimensions coding, on the other hand, encourages the person to attend to the abstract properties of the objects and to translate the stimuli into sequential verbal form. Objects coding generally results in more accurate reporting because the stimulus is stored in memory as two integrated units from which relevant information can be decoded quickly when required, whereas coding by dimensions slows up the encoding process, which is verbal. In the latter case, moreover, the order of verbal coding is important because the information is sequentially organized.

On the Distinctions among Perception, Comprehension, and Memory

The studies considered in this chapter were generally not "pure" perceptual studies if indeed there is such a phenomenon (see the discussion of Erdelyi's (1974) information-processing approach to perception). The closest approximation may be experiments requiring simultaneous or immediately successive comparisons of stimuli as being the same or different, since little or no memory is necessary. Most of the studies of this kind have found no effect even of the familiarity of stimulus material, let alone higher-order meaning. Thus the word-familiarity effects on perceptual recognition, the associative or semantic priming effects, and the effects of sentence syntax or semantics on verbal behavior all are effects of long-term memory factors on identification or immediate memory for some stimulus event. Thus perception and memory (both long-term and short-term) are clearly involved.

Similarly, comprehension is part of most of the studies. For example, Foss's phoneme-monitoring task requires the subject to understand the sentences. Detection of a phoneme may not always require understanding the word in which it occurs, but sometimes it may. In any case, the research discussed in this chapter is also relevant to the problem of comprehension. Conversely, comprehension certainly implicates perception and memory, as we shall see in the next chapter.

Summary

In this chapter, we have considered various phenomena and theories of relevance to the perception of language. According to the motor theory of speech perception, articulation of speech sounds is important to normal speech perception. Although the theory encounters some problems, it directs us toward interesting phenomena, such as the categorical nature of consonant perception. Perception has its own units, which are not identical to the units in all other cases. Of particular importance are the perception of words out of context, in which factors such as frequency and semantic attributes play an integral role, and the perception of words in context, on which associated words exert an influence. At more comlex levels, associative, grammatical, and semantic factors are very important to the perception of speech, as shown in a variety of interesting tasks. Finally, it is useful to bear in mind that perception is not as distinct from such processes as comprehension and memory as one first might think.

comprehension

7

What is comprehension? At a general level, the answer is obvious: we understand or comprehend a message when we get the meaning. However, as we saw in chapter 5, there are many different ideas about what meaning is. Each different view of meaning leads naturally to a different view of comprehension. For instance, if meaning is seen as collections of abstract features, then comprehension is a matter of abstracting features from a message and combining those features in some way to construct an overall meaning. On the other hand, if meaning is seen as being variable depending on the context, then comprehension is a matter of narrowing down a global impression by ruling out alternative interpretations until a particular interpretation remains. At this general level, it seems to us that the conception of comprehension to be favored is largely dictated by the idea of meaning we prefer. Since each conception of meaning is reasonable in some areas of interest, comprehension will sometimes be best seen as a building up of information and other times as a narrowing down of information. In this chapter, we are concerned with comprehension at a more concrete level. That is, we consider experimental analyses of comprehension, with an eye towards finding out what makes understanding easier or harder, and deeper or more superficial.

Even if we restrict our interest to an experimental analysis of comprehension, there are some general problems to be faced. One problem is that in most naturally occurring examples, understanding can be expressed in many ways. We may indicate our understanding of a message by saying "I see," we may nod our heads, we may proceed to carry out a command, or we may just sit there, leaving comprehension entirely implicit. Another problem is that comprehension may be more or less complete. A superficial understanding is enough for some purposes, but others may require richer, more penetrating interpretations. However, the only way we can study comprehension is to require people to make some response indicating at least some degree of comprehension. We shall consider many different responses. As in the areas we have already discussed, the measures of comprehension and the variables studied are meaningful only in the context of some theoretical framework. Let us review the three basic frameworks to see how each one frames the issues of interest.

THEORETICAL APPROACHES

Behavioral Approaches

The different theoretical orientations that we have been considering conceptualize the process of comprehension in quite different ways. Most behaviorally oriented theorists have had little to say about the process, perhaps because of its covert nature. However, behaviorists could interpret comprehension in terms of learned reactions to verbal stimuli as a function of response availability, associative variables such as sequential probabilities, reinforcement history, and so forth. In a Skinnerian analysis, for example, comprehension would be reflected primarily in echoic and intraverbal responses. As Winokur puts it, "Understanding . . . is our ability to echo and use our echoic R_V's to discriminate stimuli for our intraverbal behavior which leads ultimately to our reinforcement" (1976, pp. 145-146). However, we will leave it to interested readers to explore such possibilities, because neither this nor other behavioristic viewpoints have directly led to much research.

Linguistic Approaches

The main common assumption of linguistic approaches is that sentence comprehension is more difficult if sentences are more complex. Superficially, this seems obvious. However, the advantage of the approaches is that each provides some way of assessing complexity independent of comprehension. To illustrate the measurement of complexity, let us consider a simple surface structure model, suggested by Yngve (1960); most recent accounts are more complex, but this simple one illustrates the general point. In this model, a sentence is more complex if its words are more deeply embedded, with *depth* defined by phrase structure. Consider the sentence *The strong young boy ran quickly*. The listener, upon hearing *the*, expects (a) a completion of the noun phrase and (b) some kind of predicate; *the* thus has a depth of 2. For the same reasons, both *strong* and *young* have depths of 2. *Boy* has a depth of 1 because only the predicate is expected; *ran* also has a depth of 1 because the intonation of the speaker indicates there is more to come; finally, *quickly* has a depth of 0. The total depth of the sentence, adding up the individual words, is 8. The most usual way to measure depth is by drawing a phrase structure tree, as illustrated in Figure 7-1, counting the total number of *left* branches leading from S to the words. The result is, of course, the same as above.

The psychological hypothesis states that the greater the depth of a sentence, the more difficult it is to understand, remember, and produce. Note that this hypothesis says nothing about the nature of the encodings or expectations; that is, it is silent with respect to the ultimate basis of comprehension. Nonetheless, it has led to predictions about the effects of grammatical variables, and these will be examined later.

Most linguistic approaches have included a deep structure hypothesis, generally inspired by Chomsky's (1957) theory. According to Chomsky:

> To understand a sentence it is necessary (though not, of course, sufficient) to reconstruct its representation at each level, including the transformational level where the kernel sentences underlying a given sentence can be thought

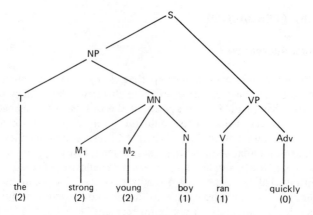

FIGURE 7-1. Yngve's measure of surface-structure complexity. Complexity = *depth* to which words are embedded in a sentence. Word depth = number of left branches leading to a word in a phrase-structure tree (the number is shown below each word in the example). Sentence depth = sum of depth scores for words.

of, in a sense, as the "elementary content elements" out of which this sentence is constructed. (1957, pp. 107–108)

The basic assumption is that people understand complex sentences by decoding them into their underlying kernels. Thus the ease of understanding sentences is partly a function of their *transformational complexity*, that is, the number and nature of the transformations that separate a sentence from its underlying structure. In other words, the process of understanding is the *inverse* of production or generation.

The general implication of the hypothesis is the same as that of the surface structure model, but complexity is defined differently. According to the transformational generative grammar of the 1960s, the order of derivational complexity is from kernel, to negative, to passive, to passive-negative, in increasing order of difficulty. The increasingly complex transformations from the different types of sentences are illustrated by the following examples:

The girl kisses the boy (K)
The girl does not kiss the boy (K + NEG.)
The boy is kissed by the girl (K + PERM. + BY)
The boy is not kissed by the girl (K + PERM. + NEG. + BY)

What is the basis of comprehension according to the deep structure approach? Although there is a syntactic contribution to the process of comprehension, understanding ultimately depends on the *semantic interpretation* of the output of the deep structure analysis. Thus, a complete linguistic theory of comprehension must say something about the role of the semantic component in interpretation. From linguistic semantics it is but a short step to psychology, in which the problem of

comprehension merges with the problem of meaning. In other words, comprehension implies "getting the meaning" of what is said.

Cognitive Approaches

The cognitive approaches differ from the preceding ones in that they emphasize knowledge of the world and the reference that language makes to that knowledge. They also emphasize general cognitive processes related to perception and memory, and context. The general point is that understanding occurs when the phrase or sentence arouses some kind of cognitive representation—in short, *meaning*. Thus, the central theoretical issues concern the representations comprising meaning and the processes by which that meaning results. Although the representations are seen variously as linguistic entities, nonlinguistic entities, or both, the general feature of the cognitive approaches is that meaning is equated with what is aroused and that comprehension is equated with the arousal of meaning.

RESEARCH EVIDENCE

This section covers some of the most common research approaches to comprehension, with examples and attempts to relate the findings to the different theoretical positions discussed above.

Transformational Reaction Time

George Miller (1962) measured reaction times as a way of testing the transformational-complexity hypothesis. The straightforward deduction from the hypothesis is that the time it takes to transform a given sentence should be related directly to the number of steps and the complexity associated with the transformations. For example, it should take longer to change a kernel sentence into a passive than into a negative form. Miller presented subjects with two columns of sentences containing transformations of each other. For example, one column contained affirmative-passive and the other negative-passive sentences. All kernel sentences used *Jane, Joe,* or *John* as the first word, *liked* or *warned* as the second, and *the small boy, the old woman,* or *the young man* as the final phrase. Each column contained eighteen sentences in all (you yourself might generate the eighteen sentences from the components; does this remind you of the rewrite rules in chapter 3?).

Each subject found which sentence in the right-hand column matched the first sentence on the left, then the second, continuing for up to one minute. The measures were the number of correct sentences and the time taken. Using both kinds of data, the investigator could estimate transformation times for each of the six kinds of transformations that result from matching the four types of sentences two at a time. The predictions are easily grasped by considering the following diagram, in which the lines joining the labeled corners represent the transformational distances. Thus, one transformational step separates any adjacent pair, and two steps separate all others. The predictions then are that transformation time should be longer from K to PN than from K to N or P, and longer from P to N than

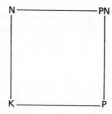

from P to PN or K. In addition, however, the transformational generative grammar of that period stated that passive sentences are more complex than negative ones, relative to kernels (the negative needs only to add the negative morpheme, but the passives require permutations of the subject and predicate and the addition of *by*). Of course, PN sentences would be still more complex.

The results are presented in Table 7-1, which shows the estimated transformation times for four one-step transformations and two two-step transformations. The model was roughly supported: two-step transformations took more time than one-step ones. Moreover, the results were in the predicted order, namely, K, N, P, and PN, in increasing order of sentence complexity and transformation time.

The above experimental approach is not used very often today because it has become clear that comprehension depends on much more than syntactic complexity. It depends also on semantic processing and context, that is, the situation in which the sentence is used. This problem has been studied using the true-false verification task, which continues to be a popular paradigm.

Sentence Verification

Miller's lead was followed by other researchers who measured how long it takes to decide whether a sentence is true or false with respect to a referent situation, which is usually a picture, although other sentences have also been used as the referents.

In some of the earliest experiments, Gough (1965, 1966) used sentences like *The boy hit the girl* (active), *The boy did not hit the girl* (negative), *The girl was hit by the boy* (passive), and *The girl was not hit by the boy* (passive-negative)

TABLE 7-1 Estimated Transformation Times in Seconds for Kernel (K), Passive (P), Negative (N), and Passive-Negative (PN) Sentences

Test Condition		Transformation Time
One-step	K:N	1.1
	P:PN	1.2
	K:P	1.5
	PN:N	1.8
Two-step	K:PN	2.7
	N:P	3.5

(From Miller, 1962.)

TABLE 7-2 Mean Verification Time in Seconds Collapsing over True and False Responses for Four Types of Sentences

	Affirmative	Negative
Active	0.99	1.29
Passive	1.11	1.36

(From Gough, 1965.)

along with pictures that showed a boy hitting a girl or showed some other event. The subject's task was to indicate whether the sentence was true or false by pressing a labeled key. Verification time was measured from the moment the sentence was presented to the key press. Gough (1965) found that verification time increased from active to passive to negative to passive-negative, as seen in Table 7-2. This ordering is consistent with the transformational decoding hypothesis, except that the negative should be simpler and therefore faster than the passive, according to the hypothesis. Thus the data suggested that negative sentences are generally harder to understand than affirmative sentences.

Qualification of effects of negation

Research by Wason (1965) showed that negative statements are not always harder to understand than are affirmative statements. He had demonstrated in a series of earlier studies that the combined reaction time for true and false affirmative sentences is less than the combined time for true and false negative sentences. Wason's 1965 study showed that this effect is qualified by the situational context. Specifically, he argued that *plausible denial* is easier to understand than implausible denial, in which plausibility depends on how unusual the particular stimulus being referred to is, relative to the other stimuli in the situation. For example, if a train is usually late, it is plausible to say "The train was not late this morning." To appreciate this point, you might ask yourself when you would use a negative sentence. You likely use negatives to rule out something your listener might believe. You might say "This coffee is not bitter" to people who might think coffee is bitter, but you probably would not say "This candy is not bitter," because it would not have occurred to anyone in the first place. Similarly, it would be unusual for a politician to say "I am not a crook" if there was no question about his or her honesty.

Wason's hypothesis about plausible denial was confirmed by a study in which people were shown a series of eight circles, of which seven were colored red and one was blue, or seven were blue and one red. An affirmative or positive sentence stem was shown to the subject—for example, "Circle 7 is . . ." or "Circle 7 is not. . . ." The subject indicated affirmation or denial by pressing one of two keys corresponding to the colors. The response was timed. The results, summarized in Table 7-3, supported Wason's hypothesis: negative sentences were generally verified more slowly than affirmative ones, but the difference was smaller (.36 sec) if the target item was unique than if it was similar to six others (.60 sec). Thus Wason demonstrated that the difficulty of understanding negative statements is not purely a

TABLE 7-3 Mean Response Times in Seconds for Completion of Affirmative (A) and Negative (N) Sentence Stems under Dissimilar (D) and Similar (S) Contextual Conditions

Condition		Response Time
DA	Circle No. 7 is . . . *red* (rest are blue)	1.60
DN[a]	Circle No. 7 is not . . . *blue* (rest are blue)	1.96
SA	Circle No. 7 is . . . *red* (so are 6 others)	1.93
SN[b]	Circle No. 7 is not . . . *blue* (only 1 other is blue)	2.53

(From Wason, 1965.)
[a]Plausible denial
[b]Implausible denial

syntactic matter but is influenced by the situational context and general cognitive factors, such as what the subject is thinking about at the time.

Qualifications of active-passive differences

Recall that the early versions of transformational generative grammar suggested that passive sentences are more complex than active ones. This was supported by the comprehension studies showing that passive sentences take longer to verify than active ones. Subsequent research has shown, however, that this finding, too, is qualified by contextual factors. Slobin (1966b) measured verification time for reversible sentences such as *The boy is being hit by the girl*, in which the subject and object can be interchanged, and nonreversible ones like *The boy is raking the leaves*, in which the subject and object cannot be interchanged without creating an anomalous sentence. Slobin found that active reversible sentences were verified more quickly than passives, but verification time did not differ for active and passive nonreversible sentences. Why the difference? The answer seems to be that in nonreversible sentences, it is easy to determine which noun is the logical subject, so that passives do not result in any special problem. With reversible sentences, however, it is more difficult to determine which noun is the logical subject, so that passives are more difficult. Note, however, that this is a semantic rather than a syntactic effect since it is based on the kind of semantic relation that can exist between the logical (underlying) subject and object. Slobin analyzed this in terms of selection restrictions based on the semantic features of verbs, nouns, and their case relations according to linguistic analysis. Such restrictions in many ways parallel the kinds of events that can occur between objects described by the language, that is, knowledge of the world. For example, boy and girl are both "potent" in that either can serve as agents of action, whereas this is not true of leaves.

Another factor affecting the active-passive difference in comprehension time is the *focus* of the sentence, that is, whether the receiver's attention is centered on the subject or the object. Olson and Filby (1972) investigated this problem by showing subjects a picture that created a focus, prior to sentence verification. They reasoned that an active sentence, such as *The car hit the truck*, would be more easily verified if the subject coded the preceding picture in terms of the actor

(*car hit truck*), but a passive sentence such as *The truck is hit by the car* would be easiest if the subject focused on the receiver of the action (*truck hit by car*). This was done by showing the subjects two pictures in succession and asking them to look at the second picture in terms of the first, as if to find out what happened to the object shown in the first (for example, the car or truck). Examples are shown in Figure 7-2. The hypothesis was confirmed in three experiments: passive sentences were processed more quickly than active ones when the subject's attention was focused on the receiver, or the grammatical subject of the passive.

One important general conclusion from the research on active-passive differences, like that of Wason's research on affirmative-negative differences, is that comprehension time for sentences with different syntax depends on the context in which the sentence is presented. Context is established by the situation to which the sentence refers or by other sentences in the larger linguistic context. In brief, no account that characterizes complexity on entirely linguistic grounds can be complete. We must consider the cognitive environment of the receiver to understand the comprehension process.

Theoretical Analysis of Verification

Most theoretical interpretations of sentence verification have been cognitive, in that they stress information processing, but they have been linguistically oriented, in that some linguistic notions govern the variables studied. Although there are differences in detail, the models generally include three ordered stages, namely *encoding* of the sentence and the situation to which the sentence refers, *comparison* of the two encodings, and *response output* based on the results of the comparison.

Stage 1, encoding, is the process of translating the stimulus displays into internal representations. Because the sentence to be verified with reference to a picture and the picture itself are different kinds of information, it is usually assumed that both sources of information are encoded into some common format in order to be compared. For example, both the sentence and the picture could be encoded into basic propositions, each of which is represented as "true" (for example, Chase & Clark, 1972; see also Clark, 1976). Thus a statement such as *The car hit the truck*, or an equivalent picture, might be represented as *true (car hit truck)*.

Stage 2, comparison, is the process by which the two encodings are compared.

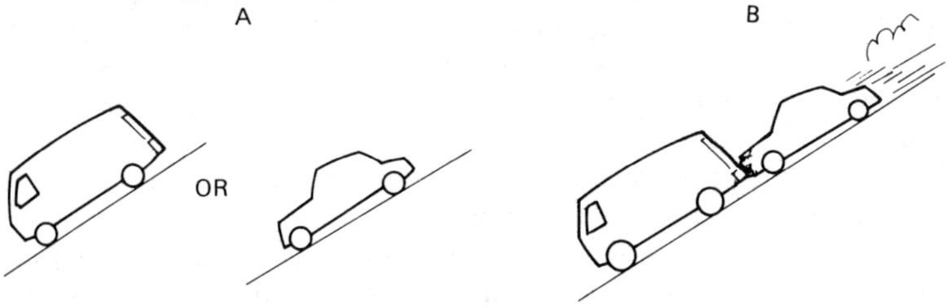

FIGURE 7-2. Pictures used to produce focus on the subject or object of a sentence (A), and the picture subsequently used in the sentence verification task (B). Redrawn from Olson and Filby (1972).

By Chase's and Clark's account, comparison is a series of match-mismatch operations. If the encodings do not match, the "truth index" of the sentence is changed to "false." For example, if the picture shown was a car being hit by a truck, the encoding would be *true (truck hit car)*, which does not match the above proposition, *true (car hit truck)*; accordingly, the sentence encoding becomes *false (car hit truck)*. The truth index would then remain "false" if no new data arrived or would change to "true" if there is another mismatch. By the end of comparison, the truth index will be either "true" or "false."

Stage 3, response output, simply means that the subject responds with the final value of the truth index.

Different information-processing theories differ in terms of their emphasis on deep structure, surface structure, or semantic representations, particularly as regards encoding. Clark and others have favored a deep structure representation in which active and passive sentences such as *The car hit the truck* and *The truck was hit by the car* both are represented in terms of the underlying, logical relations, namely, *Car hit truck*. The implication of this account is that the individual words are processed in the same order for both actives and passives. Thus, in the above example, *car* would be processed first, then *hit*, and finally *truck*, despite the differences in the surface form of the sentences.

Olson and Filby (1972), in contrast, favored a representation based on the surface order of elements, namely, grammatical subject, then verb, and then grammatical object. Thus the representations for the active and passive examples given above would be *car hit truck* and *truck hit by car*, respectively. By their account, comparisons are made in the surface structure order: the participant first compares the grammatical subjects, then the verbs, and then the objects if necessary, responding "false" if there is a mismatch. Their approach was favored over Clark's deep structure interpretation because of their results, which were described earlier. Thus the focus of the sentence or picture was manipulated by preceding the comparison task with a picture that drew the subject's attention to the actor or the receiver of the action. Verification time was affected by this manipulation so that passives were verified faster than actives when the subject's attention was on the receiver of the action, indicating that the grammatical subject was the first item encoded. The reverse was true when the focus was on the actor. In both cases, therefore, verification time depended on the match between the surface ordering of the elements of the sentence and the subject's interpretation of the picture.

As if the matter were not complex enough, an experiment by Glucksberg, Trabasso, and Wald (1973) supported yet another form of the model. The entire study is too complex to discuss in detail here, but we shall consider some relevant points. It was assumed that sentences are represented as a list of propositions with *case relational* information (recall the discussion in chapter 5). When the sentences precede the pictures, their assumption was that only the sentence is fully encoded into propositions. Moreover, the propositional elements are assumed to be represented in the order verb, noun, noun. Thus *Car hit truck* becomes *Hit (car, truck)*. This results in predictions that differ from those of Clark and of Olson and Filby. Clark assumed that in the sentence *Truck hit by car*, the deep structure subject *car* is processed first; Olson and Filby assumed that the surface structure subject *truck* is processed first; and Glucksberg and his colleagues assumed that the verb *hit* is processed first. Thus, following the sentence, the picture is searched for the

relevant evidence concerning the verb, then the first noun, then the second noun. The search ends at any point at which a labeled event or object is not found. This implies that the subject can say "false" quickly if the action specified by the verb is *not* found in the picture. If it is found (that is, if the picture shows the action specified by the verb), the subject looks for the first noun, and so on.

The data generally supported aspects of Glucksberg's model. The study used subject-verb-object sentences and corresponding pictures. The subject, verb, or object could be false, that is, absent from the picture. The latencies for false sentences showed that verb mismatches were fastest, then grammatical subject, and finally grammatical object, supporting the idea of an ordered search beginning with the verb. More generally, they emphasized the importance of *context, task demands,* and *semantic factors* to comprehension. Thus the trend in the series of studies we have reviewed has been toward increasingly cognitive interpretations which stress nonlinguistic processes in addition to purely linguistic ones. Despite this agreement, we still do not know the precise conditions that will dispose a person to attend first to the verb or the logical subject or the grammatical subject.

Imagery in Comparison Tasks

The studies discussed up to this point have generally emphasized abstract representations, such as propositions and semantic features. Olson and Filby emphasized a transformed surface structure, and some others (for example, Morris, Rankine, & Reber, 1968) suggested that many of the findings could be accounted for equally well by a surface structure model such as Yngve's. Many of the studies mentioned that imagery may have been used in the comparison task, but this possibility was not systematically investigated in them. This was done, however, in the following studies.

Skehan (1970) carried out a verification experiment in which sentences were matched against referent sentences rather than pictures. The referent sentences were high, medium, or low in their imagery value but did not differ on rated meaningfulness. The following are examples of the three types of referent sentences:

High imagery: The bird is eating the insect.
Medium imagery: The professor is fascinating the pupil.
Low imagery: The speech is supporting the opinion.

The referent sentences were grammatical kernels. They were judged against comparison sentences that were grammatical transformations of the referents and that were either true or false with respect to the referent. The following are examples of a high-imagery referent sentence and the five types of transformations that Skehan used:

The animal is chasing the cat. (Referent kernel)
The cat is chasing the animal. (False kernel)
The cat is being chased by the animal. (True passive)
The animal is being chased by the cat. (False passive)
The animal is not chasing the cat. (False negative)
The cat is not chasing the animal. (True negative)

Skehan presented a referent sentence until the subject indicated that the sentence was understood. Then a comparison sentence followed, and the subject pressed a key to indicate whether it was true or false with respect to the first sentence. The major result was that verification time was significantly faster for high- and medium-imagery sentences (means = 2.21 and 2.24 seconds, respectively) than for low-imagery sentences (2.58 seconds). The imagery effect was present in true and false sentences in each type of grammatical transformation. Skehan had expected imagery to be helpful to comparisons of true passives because a person could visualize the relationship and compare this with the visualized meaning of the referent kernel sentence. Negative sentences, on the other hand, are indefinite in regard to the actual situation—they state what is *not* rather than what is. Accordingly, Skehan expected that it would be difficult to visualize their meaning and that therefore the imagery level of their constituent words should not affect verification time. As it turned out, however, imagery enhanced the speed of comprehension even for negative sentences.

The direct implications of the results are that people can somehow code or tag imagined situations as negative and that such images facilitate comparative judgments. On the other hand, the results could simply be due to some other variable. Although the imagery hypothesis seems best at the moment, the problem needs further investigation in regard to both potential artifacts and the "negative imagery" hypothesis.

There is clearer evidence of the role of nonverbal imagery from studies using both pictures and verbal material. Rosenfeld (1967) tested three hypotheses regarding same-different comparisons of descriptions and pictures. The pictures were figures that varied in number, color, and shape, such as two red triangles or three blue circles. The corresponding descriptions were exactly as stated: *two red triangles, three blue circles,* and so on. In the task, two stimuli were presented successively, and the subject indicated whether they were conceptually the same or different. All possible combinations of pictures and descriptions were presented (picture-picture, picture-description, description-picture, and description-description), and the two stimuli either followed each other immediately or had a 2.5-second delay between them. The delay condition is the only one we will consider here because in that condition, the subject has had time to transform the first stimulus into a verbal, imaginal, or abstract form before the second stimulus appears, provided he or she knows what form it will be presented in. Such knowledge was assured because the second stimulus was always either a picture or a description throughout a given experimental session. Thus the subject was able to develop an expectancy of the form of the stimulus.

Rosenfeld made predictions from three hypotheses. One was an *abstract entity hypothesis,* based on Osgood's theory of meaning as a representational mediation process. Note, however, that the same reasoning can be applied to any theory that assumes that pictures and descriptions are represented in common form. This would include all propositional theories that state that words and pictures are translated into a third, common entity for purposes of comparison. What prediction would follow from such a theory? Given enough time to make the translation, there should be no difference between the different combinations of pictures and descriptions.

The second theoretical possibility was the *verbal encoding hypothesis,*

according to which both pictures and descriptions are translated into (implicit) verbal descriptions. Since words are usually read faster than pictures are named, it follows that comparisons will be faster with descriptions than with pictures as the second stimuli. Thus the reaction times for the description-description or picture-description conditions would be faster than those for picture-picture or description-picture conditions.

The third viewpoint was the *imagery decoding hypothesis*, which states that pictures and descriptions are compared as nonverbal images, so that descriptions must be translated into images for purposes of comparison. Thus the prediction is exactly the opposite of that for the verbal hypothesis; namely, picture-picture and description-picture should be compared faster than description-description or picture-description comparisons.

The results are presented in Table 7-4. It can be seen that the observations were consistent only with the imagery hypothesis: the comparisons were made most quickly when the second stimulus was a picture, regardless of the form of the first stimulus. Similar results have been reported by Seymour (1973a, b), but he also obtained other results which suggested a theoretical need for some kind of abstract (perhaps propositional) representation. Such a representation would not necessarily exclude imaginal or verbal coding but perhaps would serve as an additional semantic code. Glushko and Cooper (1978) also support a type of spatial representation, although they report considerable influence of the exact type of task used.

A dual-coding interpretation

Dual-coding theory provides another theoretical possibility. Perhaps pictures and descriptions can be compared in either imaginal or verbal form, depending on task demands. This viewpoint has been supported by simple comparison tasks using artificial faces and names (B. Tversky, 1969) and by a visual search task using pictures and words (Paivio & Begg, 1974). Let us consider the latter in some detail. Paivio and Begg used the same combination of picture-word conditions that Rosenfeld did. The subjects in three experiments were presented with either a picture or a word as a target item. Then they were shown an array of twenty-five pictures or words, and their task was to search as quickly as possible through the array to find the target item. In two experiments, the pictures were line drawings of familiar objects, and the words were their printed labels. The search times in both experi-

TABLE 7-4   Same-Different Comparison Times in Milliseconds as a Function of Modality of the First and Second Stimulus with a 2.5 Sec Delay between Stimuli

Second Stimulus	First Stimulus	
	Picture	Description
Picture	656	675
Description	828	811

(From Rosenfeld, 1967.)

ments were consistently faster when the array consisted of pictures than when it consisted of words, regardless of whether the target item they were looking for had been presented as a picture or as a word. The search through an array of pictures was also faster with pictures than with words as targets, but the mode of the target item had no consistent effect when the search array was made up of words. These results agree with either dual coding or a strong imagery theory like the one proposed by Rosenfeld. That is, subjects may have translated both pictures and words into a picturelike representation in order to make the comparison, or they may have translated in either direction, depending on the precise conditions of the task.

Dual-coding theory predicted a different pattern of results in a third experiment, which used photographs of the faces of famous people and their printed names as stimuli. The reasoning was as follows: Faces, like names, are highly specific and may require detailed inspection in order to be correctly identified. If equally careful fixation is required in both cases, the array effect (that is, picture superiority) obtained in the previous experiments should not occur with faces as stimuli. However, the face-face comparison should still be faster than the name-face comparison because, given the name of a familiar person, one cannot predict exactly what view of the face will be presented. Such variable encoding would not be expected in naming faces. The results were exactly as predicted: the search times for the name-face condition were significantly slower than those in the remaining conditions, which did not differ from each other.

Taken together, the results of all three experiments suggested that items such as pictures and words, which are cognitively represented both verbally and as nonverbal images, can be searched and compared in either mode. The mode actually used by the subject depends on the expected mode of the comparison stimulus. In the search experiments, such expectations were determined by the contextual information provided by the mode of the search array as a whole. In other experiments, such as Rosenfeld's (1967) and Tversky's (1969), the expectations were controlled by the mode of the comparison stimuli encountered on previous trials. In general, the results have been consistent with dual coding. However, results have also been obtained that are not readily explained entirely in terms of two modality-specific cognitive representations of the kind assumed by dual-coding theory. What may be needed, instead, is a combination of dual coding and some abstract semantic code. The studies that are most compelling in regard to such a compromise are somewhat peripheral to the main problem of this chapter, namely comprehension; therefore we shall postpone their consideration until later (chapter 8).

Comprehension Reaction Time

What appears to be the simplest way to measure ease of comprehension is to ask subjects to press a button as soon as they understand a word or sentence. It turns out not to be so simple in practice, since the reaction time depends on precisely what instructions the subjects are given and their interpretation of what constitutes comprehension. Such variables affect the subject's response criterion, that is, the level of understanding at which it is appropriate to respond. Such factors have not been examined carefully in most of the research in the area, but we shall nonetheless consider several studies that have used some variant of the

comprehension reaction-time procedure and that allow tentative comparisons of behavioral, grammatical, and semantic variables in relation to comprehension.

Effects of meaningfulness and grammaticalness

Danks (1969) measured subjects' reaction time to understand sentences that varied in grammaticalness, meaningfulness, word frequency, interword associative strength, and so on. He found that comprehension time was primarily affected by meaningfulness and grammaticalness, with little or no effect from other variables.

Grammaticality itself is not as simple as it first may seem. Levelt, Van Gent, Haans, and Meijers (1977) argued that grammaticality is not simply either present or absent in any given piece of language. Rather, depending on the number and seriousness of the rules that are violated, sentences range from ungrammatical, through levels of semigrammaticality, up to fully grammatical sentences. Further, people are unreliable in their judgments of grammaticality, so that it is unclear how much value we should attribute to experiments in which the grammaticality of sentences is varied. Levelt and his associates find, in addition, that high-imagery compounds are judged to be more grammatical than abstract ones and that the judgments are made more rapidly for the high-imagery compounds. Thus much more work is needed before we can draw conclusions about the influence of grammaticality itself on comprehension.

Comprehension versus imagery reaction times

In the early part of the century, before the concept of imagery became unpopular with the advent of behaviorism, some investigators were concerned with the question of which comes first as a response to words, image or meaning. Words were presented one at a time, and the subject responded when he or she "had an image" or when he or she "had the meaning" of the word. Moore (1915), who introduced the method, found that meaning reaction times generally occurred faster than imagery. Subsequently, however, Tolman (1917) found that the relative speed of reaction depended on the subject: some subjects were faster under the meaning instruction, and others were faster under imagery.

Paivio and Begg (1971) extended the comparison to sentences. In one experiment, they presented concrete sentences like *The rich physician carried a black umbrella*, or abstract sentences like *The national election indicated a secure future*, and asked the participants to press a key either when they understood the sentence or had generated an image for it. What would be expected theoretically? Dual-coding theory suggests that imagery is an important component of the meaning of concrete language in that the imagery aroused by a sentence can be used as a context for determining what the sentence is about. It is less likely to provide such a context for abstract language. It follows that the ease of comprehension should be closely related to ease of image arousal in concrete sentences. The relation should be less close with abstract sentences because their meaning is tied more closely to the intraverbal context of the sentence itself and to verbal associations aroused by the sentence. Two predictions arise from these suggestions: first, there should be a larger difference between mean comprehension and imagery reaction times in abstract sentences than in concrete sentences; second, there should be a higher

correlation between comprehension and imagery reaction times across concrete sentences than across abstract sentences.

Both predictions were confirmed. Figure 7-3 shows the mean latencies for comprehension and imagery for the two types of sentences. Imagery reaction time was generally slower than comprehension time for both types of sentences, but the difference was significant only for the abstract sentences. Note, moreover, that images were generated more slowly for abstract than for concrete sentences, but the difference was smaller for comprehension reaction time. In regard to the correlation between comprehension and image reaction time across sentences, the correlation coefficient (Pearson's r) was .71 for concrete sentences and .60 for abstract sentences. The former was significantly higher than the latter, as predicted. The overall correlation for both concrete and abstract sentences, however, was a substantially higher .81, indicating that a common process is used in both the imagery and the comprehension task. This was confirmed in a second experiment, in which the overall correlation was .83.

The second experiment used only relatively concrete sentences, which varied in the complexity of both their surface structure and their deep structure. The experiment revealed effects of both kinds of grammatical variables on imagery and comprehension reaction time, slower processing being associated with the more complex sentences. The most salient aspect of the second experiment was that this time the image latencies were generally faster than comprehension latencies. Thus, as in the relationship between meaning and image reactions to individual words, comprehension does not necessarily precede imagery in the case of sentences. Just what determines the relative promptness of the two kinds of reactions is not yet

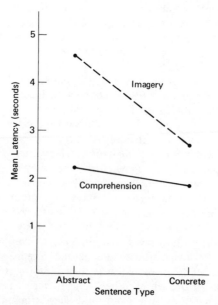

FIGURE 7-3. Mean imagery and comprehension reaction times for concrete and abstract sentences. From Paivio and Begg (1971).

known, but such factors as the grammatical and semantic complexity of the sentences obviously must be relevant. As mentioned earlier, subjects may also have different criteria for what constitutes fulfillment of the two kinds of tasks. For example, they may begin to form images for the first part of the sentence rather than waiting until the sentence is completed, whereas comprehension may not be adequate for a response until after the entire sentence has been read.

The results in any case are consistent with dual-coding theory in that imagery appears to be important to comprehending sentences, so that pictureable material is easier to understand than nonpictureable material. The thoughtful student can readily see some of the implications of this for such matters as the appreciation of literature. One reason that Shakespeare is so appealing, for example, may be the fact that his plays are unusually high in literary imagery (Spurgeon, 1935).

Modality-specific interference effects on comprehension time

The dual-coding theory received more support from an experiment by Klee and Eysenck (1973), which examined the comprehension of abstract and concrete sentences. The participants in the experiment were presented with sentences that were meaningful or anomalous, and they had to decide which was which. Note that the decision requires the subject to process the sentence for meaning; that is, one cannot decide whether or not a sentence is meaningful without first applying some kind of "test" of meaningfulness. The following are examples of the four types of sentences:

Concrete-meaningful: The veteran soldier rode the lame horse.

Concrete-anomalous: The large army beat the wild pearl.

Abstract-meaningful: The wrong attitude caused a major loss.

Abstract-anomalous: The mere knowledge brought the true hour.

The degree to which imagery and verbal processes were necessary to the task was tested using an interference task based on ones previously used by Brooks (1967, 1968). Brooks's findings suggested that visual imagery is disrupted more by concurrent visual activity, such as reading, than by auditory-verbal activity, such as listening. Conversely, verbal processing was disrupted more by auditory-verbal than by visual activity.

Klee and Eysenck used this idea in their comprehension task as follows: A sentence was read to the subject under either visual or verbal interference conditions. The visual interference consisted of presenting a visual stimulus between each pair of spoken words. The visual stimulus was a five-by-five matrix with three of its squares blacked out. The subject was required to decide whether or not the sentence was meaningful, to press a key to indicate the decision and also to recall the matrix patterns by blacking in three squares in each of six empty matrices that were given after each sentence. In the verbal interference condition, subjects heard a spoken digit between each pair of words, for a total of six digits for each sentence. After the meaningfulness decision, the subject was required to recall the six digits. In summary, the sequence was: (1) a spoken concrete or abstract sentence was presented in alternation with visual or verbal interfering stimuli; (2) the subject indicated whether or not the sentence was meaningful; and finally, (3) the subject recalled the interfering stimuli.

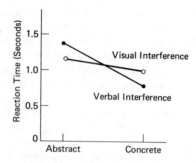

FIGURE 7-4. Mean comprehension latencies for concrete and abstract sentences under visual and verbal interference conditions. Based on data in Klee and Eysenck (1973).

The mean comprehension latencies, averaged over meaningful and anomalous sentences, are presented in Figure 7-4. The data reveal a significant interaction consistent with the dual-coding hypothesis: the comprehension latencies were longer with visual than verbal interference for concrete sentences, but these latencies were longer with verbal than visual interference for abstract sentences. These are the results that were expected from the idea that visual imagery is used in comprehending concrete sentences and that the processing of the visual matrices interferes with image formation.

What subjects attend to during processing of high- and low-imagery language

An experiment by Marschark (1978; see also 1979) used a unique reaction-time procedure for studying differences in how subjects process high- and low-imagery language. The basic procedure was introduced earlier by Aaronson and Scarborough (1976). They exposed printed sentences to subjects one word at a time, letting the subject control the rate at which the words appeared. This allowed the experimenters to measure how much time was spent processing each word. Variation in such word-by-word times could then be related to experimental conditions and to syntactic and semantic variables within sentences. Aaronson and Scarborough asked their participants either to remember the sentences verbatim or simply to try to understand them. The results suggested that the two tasks induced different perceptual coding strategies. Subjects in the comprehension condition generally processed the sentences faster than those in the verbatim recall condition. Moreover, relative to the recall subjects, the comprehension subjects paused longer at important content words, such as nouns, and more briefly at words occurring at phrase boundaries. This suggested that comprehension induced a set to attend to semantic factors and that verbatim recall induced a set to attend to syntax.

Marschark used Aaronson's procedure to study word-by-word processing latencies of prose passages differing in their rated imagery value. The passages were presented auditorily rather than visually, with subjects controlling the rate at which they heard each word. The passages were carefully constructed so that each high-imagery paragraph was matched with a low-imagery paragraph in its

syntactic structure, conceptual structure, comprehensibility, number of sentences, and number of words per sentence. The results showed striking differences in the processing patterns for the two types of passages, with high-imagery passages generally faster than low-imagery passages. Moreover, the high-imagery pattern seems to be semantically based, since subjects spent relatively more time processing semantic than syntactic aspects of the material, but the reverse was true for low-imagery material. The results of a strategy questionnaire completed after the experiment supported a dual-coding interpretation of the different processing patterns. Subjects given the high-imagery passages reported forming visual images for phrases more often than did those who had heard the low-imagery passages. Conversely, the latter subjects reported more rote rehearsal of phrases. Thus high-imagery material apparently caused subjects to attend to and visualize semantic information in the passages, whereas low-imagery material encouraged the use of a sequential, syntactically based strategy. These conclusions are consistent with those that emerged from some of the earlier studies discussed above, which used less microscopic procedures.

A second experiment by Marschark established a conceptual link with Aaronson's findings. Briefly, he compared the effects of comprehension and recall instructions on the processing of high- and low-imagery passages. The results suggested that low-imagery materials were processed in a sequential, syntactically based manner under both instructional sets. This was also the strategy for high-imagery material under verbatim recall instructions. Under comprehension instructions, however, the processing of high-imagery material again appeared to be semantically based, that is, tied to the major content words of the passages. Thus abstract, low-imagery language seems to be both understood and remembered largely in terms of its sequential, syntactic patterning. Concrete, high-imagery material is apparently understood largely by visualizing the major semantic units of a passage, whereas it might be remembered in a verbal sequential manner if the instructions induced such a mental set. We shall see in the next chapter that without such a verbal set, imagery is usually effective in memory tasks using concrete material.

Schematic World Knowledge and Comprehension of Narrative Text

Much of the discussion up to this point has emphasized the relation between world knowledge and language comprehension, with imagery being viewed as one form in which the knowledge is stored. Recently, many psychologists have used the idea that knowledge is represented in the form of abstract memory structures, variously referred to as schemata, scripts, and frames (for example, R. C. Anderson, 1978; Bower & Black, 1977; Kintsch & van Dijk, 1978; Minsky, 1975; Schank & Abelson, 1975). Such concepts are metaphorical labels for our general knowledge of classes of objects, events, situations, and activities. That knowledge can be viewed as a general framework or a set of slots that can be filled in with the appropriate details supplied by a particular story or message. Understanding a message requires fitting its words into a framework that corresponds to a possible structure in the perceptual world. In simple terms, the linguistic information is made to fit into what we know about the real world. The resulting mental construction, sometimes experienced as an image, is a *particularization* or *instantiation* of the general knowledge—one of many possible specific "scenarios" that might have been constructed.

We now shall review a few research examples to illustrate how contextual information can be manipulated so that subjects reading a given text will interpret it in quite different ways. In terms of the schema concept, subjects are induced to construct different schemata from the same narrative by being asked to read it from different viewpoints. One series of experiments by Richard Anderson and his co-workers at the University of Illinois (see Anderson, 1978) used a story that described a home. The home is owned by a well-to-do family. It has attractive features, such as spacious grounds, a tall hedge, and a fireplace, as well as some defects, including a musty basement and a leaky roof. The family has many valuable possessions such as silverware, a coin collection, and a color television set. Readers were asked to read the story from the viewpoint of a *burglar* or a *prospective home buyer*. The results showed that the different perspectives determined the rated significance of different idea units in the narrative as well as what was learned and recalled from it. A coin collection is obviously important to a burglar but not to a home buyer, but the opposite is true of a musty basement or a leaky roof. The ratings of the importance of the different items by one group of subjects predicted what was remembered by the other subjects given the same perspective. These findings and other evidence suggested that a schema affects how a story is understood or encoded, perhaps by directing attention to items that are significant in light of the schema. The schema can later affect what is remembered through its effect on search and retrieval processes.

Gordon Bower and his co-workers at Stanford have reported analogous findings. In one experiment (Owens, Dafoe & Bower, 1977), subjects were induced to identify with one of two characters in a story. Identification was controlled by the first page of a story, which introduced half the subjects to the driver of a motor boat, and the other half to a water skier. This was followed by a story, identical for all subjects, of a water-skiing scene in which there were various spills, mistakes, and misunderstandings involving the skier and the driver. The story was deliberately vague in places so that the readers' perspectives could influence their interpretations of the events. Several kinds of results demonstrated that there were such effects. A recognition-memory test showed that recognition errors were related to the reader's perspective. For example, a sentence in the story stated that the skier "reached for the handle (of the tow rope), but it escaped him." The subjects identifying with the skier and the driver incorrectly endorsed different versions of this statement during the recognition test, reflecting their differing perspectives. Those who identified with the skier relatively more often rated as correct a text item that stated that the skier "reached for the handle, but the boat hadn't come close enough for him to catch it." That is, they attributed the skier's failure to the situation. Conversely, those who identified with the driver more often endorsed an item that stated that the skier "wasn't fast enough" to catch the handle.

In a second test, subjects rated the ability of the two story characters in their respective activities. Subjects who identified with the skier rated his ability higher than that of the driver. The reverse was true for those who identified with the driver. Finally, the participants were asked to describe their mental images while reading the story. They reported that they imagined the water scene and placed themselves with the character they identified with. Their descriptions revealed a spatial perspective consistent with this idea. Thus, subjects who identified with the skier visualized the scene as though it were through his eyes and the skier's

actions as if they themselves were performing them. Conversely, they were outside observers of the driver's actions. The authors concluded that the differences in visualized perspectives could account for the actor-observer effects in the memory test and in the ability ratings.

Another experiment (Black, Turner, & Bower, 1979) studied the influence of having the reader adopt a specific vantage point when imagining an event described in a sequence of sentences. The following is a paraphrase of the metaphor they used to illustrate their theory:

> Imagine you are a cameraman filming a movie and that each sentence is like an instruction in a movie script telling you where to set up your camera to film a given event or situation. Let us suppose that you can shoot two successive events more quickly if you can maintain the same vantage point on them; but if the script requires you to shift your reference point, then it takes time for you to pack up your gear and move your camera to a new vantage point in order to film the next event. (p. 189)

The reference, of course, is to our "mental camera," and the time to change the reference point is a prediction about comprehension time given different "scripts."

The experiment used verbs such as *come* and *go* in compound sentences. The first half of the sentence introduced the main character and his or her location, and the second half described an event from either the same or a different vantage point. For example, the sentence, "Terry finished working in the yard" was followed either by the phrase "and *went* into the house" or the phrase "and *came* into the house." The former has a consistent vantage point (that is, you stay in the imagined setting and watch the actor move away from you into the house). The "*came* into the house" sentence requires you to change your vantage point (you have to move your mental camera into the house). Accordingly, it should take longer to understand the phrase with the change in vantage point than the one that keeps it the same. This is exactly what the experiment showed: reading time for the second half of the sentence was longer on the average for the changed than for the consistent vantage point version. A second experiment replicated the results and showed in addition that the changed sentences were rated harder to understand than the consistent sentences. Moreover, a recall test showed that people were very likely to transform the changed vantage point sentences during recall into sentences with the same vantage point.

The studies in this section suggest that subjects use their general memory structures as frameworks or schemata for constructing a detailed interpretation of a message. The framework adopted depends on contextual information which, for the experiments described here, was deliberately provided by the experimenters. Some of the experiments provided evidence that the interpretation was associated with mental images that were consistent with the framework. The results of these studies also are generally consonant with a dual-coding approach to the relation between language and knowledge of the world, but the idea of abstract, schematic knowledge structures implies something more. Those additional implications, whatever their nature, have not yet been studied in comprehension tasks, but parallel issues have been explored in relation to memory. This is the topic of the next chapter.

Implications of a Message

One of the most important areas of research to emerge in recent years addresses the distinction between the information directly conveyed by a message and less direct, but sensible implications that follow from the message. For example, if you were to hear "Harry cut himself shaving," you might infer that the razor did the cutting. In most cases, it does not matter that implications are drawn. However, in cases tried in court or in cases of misleading advertising, it has become important to distinguish between what was specifically encoded in the message and what further conclusions were reached by the hearer. It is useful to distinguish between logical and pragmatic implications. A *logical implication* must follow from a statement. For example, if you *forced* a child to eat spinach, it follows that the child *did eat* the spinach. Similarly, if Pete is a bachelor, it follows that he is not married. On the other hand, a *pragmatic implication* is one that does not *necessarily* follow, as in the above example of a razor. Again, you might say "Vera was easily able to pass the course." Most hearers would infer that Vera did pass the course, although it is possible that your intended message was, "Vera was easily able to pass the course, but failed because she did not attend the lectures or read the text."

Our concern here is with understanding what was said, the question being whether pragmatic implications form part of that understanding, although they were not actually stated. For example, Bartlett (1932) noted that a statement like "That Indian had been hit" was recalled as "He had been wounded by an arrow." Similarly, Schweller, Brewer, and Dahl (1976) found that in remembering "The housewife spoke to the manager about the increased meat prices," subjects were more likely to recall "spoke to" as "complained" than in control sentences, such as "The housewife spoke to the manager about the upcoming baseball game." Harris and Monaco (1978), in a review of the area, note that subjects are usually better at rejecting implications immediately after hearing the original sentences than sometime later, suggesting that memory becomes less precise over longer intervals. Further, the effect on memory remains even if subjects are specifically instructed *not* to draw inferences in simulated court cases. Although the results involve memory tasks, the clear implication is that people remember their initial interpretations, or in other words, comprehension includes reading between the lines.

Although this area is not yet as well developed as other areas concerning comprehension and memory for language, it is enormously important. For example, Black (1951) points out that witnesses in court are liable for perjury if they *assert* or *logically imply* a falsehood, but not if the falsehood is a pragmatic, but invited inference. For instance, if a prosecutor says, "Did you steal the car?" the person who did steal the car would commit perjury by saying "I did not steal the car" or by saying "I was unable to steal the car," which *logically* implies the car was not stolen. However, "I had no reason to steal the car" only *pragmatically* implies that the car was not stolen, as can be seen by adding "but I did it anyway." Research evidence shows, however, that simulated jury members treat the different answers all as denying the theft in their subsequent decisions and "remember" the "fact" of denial (Harris, Teske, & Ginns, 1975; cited in Harris & Monaco, 1978).

Another way in which inferences may be invited is by the use of leading questions, and sometimes the lead may be as subtle as using "the" instead of "a."

For example, Loftus and Zanni (1975) showed people a film of an automobile accident and later asked either (a) "Did you see the broken headlight?" or (b) "Did you see a broken headlight?" The group given "the" used fewer "Don't know" responses and made more false recognitions than the "a" group! Harris and Monaco (1978) also point to the use of character witnesses in court as attempts to invite inferences that the accused did not commit the crime, although their testimony really has nothing to do specifically with the *crime.*

A familiar case involving advertising has been considered by the United States courts regarding a mouthwash (which tastes bad but does the job). One commercial is worded very carefully, saying that the mouthwash does not really prevent colds, but the implication that it does is so strong that most listeners conclude that it *was* specifically stated. We shall leave the area now, because the research, though provocative, is still at an early stage. Clearly, however, it is important to know what people think is in each message. As regards the theoretical question of comprehension, the research does cast doubt on views that assume comprehension is just a building up of the details from separate words.

General Conclusions

Our review of the research evidence suggests that associative, linguistic, and cognitive processes are used in comprehension. The evolution of scientific thought in the area has shown an increasing emphasis on the importance of semantic and contextual factors, including nonverbal ones such as imagery and the concrete situational context of the message. Moreover, it is increasingly recognized that comprehension operates at different levels, from a relatively superficial grasp of the meaning of a message to a deep and detailed understanding (cf. Mistler-Lachman, 1975). Thus, comprehension is a complex business, which may require unconscious processing or conscious consideration of different kinds of factors: some are linguistic, and some are not, and some concern relatively superficial characteristics of the stimuli, whereas others tap resources "deeper" in the long-term memory of the individual. Linguistic processes presumably operate to transform the verbal string if necessary, prior to the arousal of semantic information, which might be propositional or imaginal in form. Finally, it must be acknowledged that our scientific understanding of the nature of comprehension is itself still relatively superficial and primitive. We have been able to identify some of the effective attributes of language, of the situational context, and of processes within the individual. A detailed theoretical interpretation of how such factors operate to result in the "click of comprehension" is yet to be written.

Summary

In this chapter we have considered language comprehension, focusing on experimental investigations that address linguistic and cognitive approaches to language. Such techniques as transformational reaction-time studies, sentence verification, and other comparisons provide useful data in this regard. Comprehension and its related events involve meaning, grammar, and especially knowledge of the world. That knowledge has been variously conceptualized as schemata, themes,

frames, images, and other cognitive events. Comprehension is not simply an extraction of meaning from stimuli but, rather, depends on the activity of an active comprehender, who sometimes distorts messages to fit expected themes and reads more into messages than was in fact present. Although comprehension is undeniably a complex business, it does seem clear that each account of comprehension clarifies some aspects of that business. It would be an error at this stage of our knowledge to rule out any of the reasonable accounts we have reviewed.

language
and memory

8

Language and memory are intimately related. Recall from chapter 2 that language often refers to events not occurring in the here and now. In fact, if everything language was used for was always present, there would be no need for a language. This suggests the intriguing idea that language may actually have *originated* as a means for tapping the memories of people for social communication. If we were concerned only with the present, pointing would be the easiest way to draw attention to particular events. It is possible that visual language, such as cave paintings, was an early attempt to draw attention to absent, but thought about, events. Perhaps our ancestors were adept at tracing outlines in sand or mud before speech developed. At any rate, it would take a time machine to find out. Be that as it may, spoken language is a particularly flexible means of tapping memories, cuing or prompting the listener to attend to memories of past events. In short, language is a very handy mnemonic system, in addition to its other virtues.

The mnemonic purpose of language is highlighted by the oral tradition of preliterate societies, in which language was used to communicate and preserve culturally valued information. This use of language shows up in linguistic rituals, poetry, and in a variety of other linguistic aspects of folklore. Traditionally, special groups of individuals within a society, including bards and poets, were entrusted with the preservation and transmission of culturally valued information. Such individuals used devices like rhyme and rhythm and a variety of language-related memory techniques in order to make the communicated information easier to remember.

This chapter is concerned mainly with contemporary research on and theories of memory *for* language, although we will also touch on how language can influence memory for nonlinguistic events. We shall begin with a discussion of an important distinction between semantic and episodic memory.

Episodic versus Semantic Memory

Tulving (1972) drew a useful distinction between *episodic* and *semantic* memory. Episodic memory refers to memories of specific events that occurred in a particular place at a particular time. Thus, your recollection of the breakfast that

you had this morning along with whatever events and conversations that may have accompanied it all are part of episodic memory. So too, at least in part, is your memory of what Professor Smith said in a lecture yesterday. Most laboratory memory tasks assess episodic memory. A subject is presented with a list of words or sentences and is required to remember those items. If the material is familiar, one obviously is not learning it for the first time. Rather, the materials are an episode in one's experience, and the memory of that experience can be conveniently described as episodic memory.

Semantic memory, in contrast, refers to our general knowledge without specification of the time and place in which it was originally learned. We know that the earth is round, that knives are sharp, that bananas are yellow, and that oceans are salty; we also know the alphabet, how to spell "democracy," and that a sentence consists of a subject and a predicate. Similarly, we demonstrate daily that we can remember thousands of words and idiomatic expressions, but we would be hard put to say when and where we first learned them. Semantic memory refers to all such general knowledge. It is not quite equivalent to the concept of long-term memory or permanent memory. Most of us can recall some of the details surrounding a frightening experience in childhood. We may not remember exactly when or where it occurred, but it is nonetheless a specific event that occurred in a particular time and place. Thus, by definition, it is episodic memory rather than semantic memory, even though the event took place a long time ago and is a part of our permanent memories.

We have already considered semantic memory in our discussions of grammatical knowledge and meaning. The emphasis in this chapter is on episodic memory because most of the studies use tasks in which subjects are required to remember linguistic material presented to them by the experimenter. However, the semantic-episodic distinction is not quite that neat because often we will be concerned with the contribution of semantic information to performance in an episodic task. These influences include semantic attributes of individual words or sentences, as well as the way that linguistic and nonlinguistic information is organized or structured in semantic memory.

Memory Tasks

Memory tasks originally were developed in experimental psychology, and only very recently have they been applied explicitly to psychological studies of language. The array of different memory tasks has become bewildering, but for our purposes, it is adequate to consider three basic types. First, there is *item* memory. For example, after hearing a list of words, you could receive a *free recall* test in which you simply write down as many words as you can remember, in any order, or you could be tested for *recognition* with questions such as "was *dog* one of the words in the list?" Second, there is *order* memory. Your memory for a telephone number is a case of remembering not only the digits but also their order. Order memory could be assessed by, for example, *serial recall*, in which people try to recall words in the presented order, or *serial reconstruction*, in which the words are given and people try to put them in the presented order. Third, there is *associative* memory. In this, you could be presented with a list of noun pairs, such as *railroad-mother*, then later be tested by being presented with one item, say, *mother*, and being asked to supply the missing member. The basic tasks we shall consider

are often more complex than the simple illustrations but are nonetheless variants of them. The major complications are the types of material used in the tasks, the procedures governing its presentation, and the measures calculated to determine what was remembered. We now turn to such considerations.

Theoretical and Empirical Variables in Overview

Many of the concepts relevant to behavioral, linguistic, and cognitive approaches have been studied in memory experiments. In this section, we shall briefly remind you of some of those concepts and point out how they are translated into variables in the experiments to be presented shortly.

Behavioral variables

Behaviorists are mainly concerned with the learning of associations between responses and stimuli, and the variables used reflect this. For example, some responses are more available than others, with respect to both their probability and ease of production. Probability is measured by, for example, frequency of occurrence in the language, while ease of production is assessed by measures like pronounceability.

The concern with associations makes it important to know how strongly associated the stimuli and responses are before any experiment is carried out; several sets of norms (for example, Battig & Montague, 1969; Palermo & Jenkins, 1964) allow careful selection. An alternative approach is to select items that are not initially associated and to have subjects learn associations in the course of the experiment, with more trials reflecting greater associative strength.

Another facet of the approach is the number of different responses that can occur with a particular verbal stimulus, rather than the strength of any particular one. Again, we could select material with different numbers of likely responses or build up associations experimentally. Such considerations of associative variety may call to mind the earlier discussion of information theory.

Linguistic variables

Since the concerns of linguistic approaches are different from those of behavioral approaches, different variables are often used, most often with reference to the theoretical constructs of surface and deep structure. Surface variables include word length, phrase structure, and surface structure complexity (recall Yngve's depth measure). Deep structure variables include the complexity of the transformations, the number of "deep" propositions that underlie given surface structures, and the complexity of single lexical items, as in *runner* versus *run*. The variables can be studied by comparing memory for materials that differ in any of the above ways or by having people process material in theoretically different ways.

Cognitive variables

Cognitive approaches are more likely than the other approaches to address knowledge of the world, organization, imagery, and the like. Again, the experiments can be conducted by selecting materials that differ in theoretically specified ways or by having people perform theoretically relevant tasks.

Effects at the Word Level

The experimental study of memory for words and nonsense words was introduced by Ebbinghaus before the end of the last century. The initial emphasis was on the study of rote memory, with frequency (or practice) as the major independent variable but with various measures of meaningfulness assuming increasing importance as time went on. Here we will summarize only a few of the findings and conclusions that are particularly relevant to later discussions of larger units.

Response availability

Frequency of usage as measured by word-frequency counts appears to be the simplest measure of response availability, but its effects on memory are far from simple. In fact, different tasks have obtained contradictory effects. Frequency generally aids memory performance in free recall, and familiarity also has a positive effect among responses in paired-associates learning. However, the effect is generally negative in recognition memory: rare words are easier to recognize than common words (McCormack, 1972). The recognition effect is not well understood as yet, but the most general explanation is in terms of interference theory. Thus, common words are used in more contexts, so that they are more likely to occur as associative reactions to other common words than to rare words on the recognition test, thereby interfering with correct recognition. Finally, repetition and rehearsal generally increase our memory for words.

Word meaningfulness has also been viewed as a measure of response strength. Ease of remembering generally increases with meaningfulness. For example, words or nonsense words that evoke many associations are easier to remember in most tasks than words that are less meaningful. Memory performance also increases with the ease of pronouncing the word. These conclusions are true mainly when the range of materials extends from relatively meaningless nonsense syllables (XEH, POJ) or disyllables (GOJEY, NEGLAN, TAROP) to meaningful words. The effect is much smaller, if it occurs at all, when meaningfulness and pronounceability are varied entirely within the range of real words. We shall return to this point later, when we consider the effects of other nonbehavioral attributes of words in the section on cognitive approaches.

Associative Strength Variables

Direct interitem associative strength

Although it seems obvious that paired-associates learning would be better when the stimulus and response members are strongly associated to begin with than when they are not, the effect is neither strong nor reliable. Children learn pairs such as *loud-soft*, which have high associative strength according to association norms, more readily than pairs like *loud-high*, which are lower in associative strength. The effect has also been found in adults, but primarily when the words are relatively unfamiliar. The reasons for the subtlety of the effect are not well known, and this rather elementary problem deserves more research.

Mediated associations

Mediated associations were discussed in chapter 5 in the context of associative structures. Thus, mediated associations are demonstrated by such structures as A → B → C, in which C does not occur as a direct response to A, but the two are indirectly linked by the common element, B. Many studies have demonstrated that common associates of this kind can be helpful in paired-associates learning. For example, Russell and Storms (1955) demonstrated this using stimulus material constructed from associative chains, such as *soldier-sailor-navy*. That is, according to the norms, *soldier* frequently elicits *sailor* as a response, *sailor* elicits *navy*, but *soldier* rarely elicits *navy*. Subjects learned two lists of pairs. The first list consisted of pairs like *ZUG-soldier* (symbolized as the A-B list). Then they learned a second list such as *ZUG-navy* (A-D). Note that although the subjects were not directly exposed to any pairs with *sailor*, the assumption was that the learning of the *ZUG-navy* association would be facilitated by the implicit occurrence of the mediating response "sailor." This expectation was supported by the finding that *ZUG-navy* was easier to learn than control pairs, in which *ZUG* was paired with words comparable to *navy* in such characteristics as familiarity but not linked to *soldier* by any mediating association.

Clustering in free recall

There also is evidence that direct and mediated associations form the basis of the organization of what is remembered. Such organization is reflected in a phenomenon called *clustering*, in which associated items tend to be recalled successively even when they were not *presented* successively to the subject. For example, Jenkins and Russell (1952) presented subjects with a list of forty-eight words consisting of twenty-four pairs, such as *table-chair*, which were strongly associated according to association norms. However, the associated words were distributed randomly through the list. Clustering was demonstrated in that the associated pairs, although separated during presentation, tended to be recalled together. Such clustering is also predicted by associative overlap scores, that is, the degree to which pairs of words in a list share associations that need not appear in the list.

Units Larger than the Word

In phrases, sentences, or longer sequences, the associative approach emphasizes word-to-word associations. These can also be expressed in terms of the information-theoretic approach, as sequential dependencies. The important assumption here is that sequences get "chunked" into higher-order integrated associative structures. This approach is best illustrated by the work of Miller and Selfridge (1950) on the effects of *order of approximation to English* on memory. The variable was defined conceptually in terms of information theory, much as in the research on the effects of letter sequences on perception, discussed in chapter 6. In the present instance, order of approximation refers to sequential dependencies in a sequence of words. We shall see later that this measure is confounded with grammatical and semantic variables, but we shall ignore that for the moment.

Miller and Selfridge constructed passages ten to fifty words long, which varied over eight steps of approximation to English. The least English-like sequences were

referred to as zero-order approximations, the next as first-order approximations, and so on up to seventh-order approximations, and ending with normal English text. Zero-order approximations were generated by drawing words randomly from the Thorndike-Lorge word count (the same end would be achieved by drawing them randomly from a dictionary). First-order approximations reflect the frequencies of occurrence of individual words, so that the passages included more common than rare words (this was actually achieved by scrambling words from higher-order sequences). Second-order approximations were constructed by presenting a subject with a common word such as *they, he, it,* or *the,* with instructions to use it in a sentence. Thus, if the given word was *they,* the subject might come up with *They went to the store.* The second subject would then be given the word that followed *they* (which, in this example, would be *went*). And so on, with each subject getting only one word. This procedure generated sequences such as *Come with sugar . . . The head and in frontal attack on an English writer that . . .* and the like.

Third-order approximations were created by giving a subject two associated words as the context, with instructions to produce a sentence. The next subject was given the second and third word from the first subject's sentence, and so on. The fourth- to seventh-order approximations were similarly created by increasing the length of the context: fourth-order approximations had a three-word context, fifth-order approximations a four-word context, and so on. As the order of approximation increased, passages became more like English text. For example, a fifty-word, fifth-order approximation reads as follows: *House to ask for is to earn our living by working towards a goal for his team in old New York was a wonderful place wasn't it even pleasant to talk about and laugh hard when he tells lies he should not tell me the reason why you are is evident.*

The passages were read aloud to the participants, who then wrote down the words they remembered in as nearly the correct order as possible. The total numbers of words recalled are shown in Figure 8-1. Note that there was little improvement beyond the fifth order of approximation. Miller and Selfridge interpreted this in terms of short-range associations, or short *chunks,* which are present to about the same extent in higher-level associations. The concept of chunking, which Miller (1956) developed more fully in a later paper, is very important because it became a key term in much of the later research. The basic idea is that a chunk functions as a unit in memory, so that we can remember about the same number of chunks regardless of how many lower-order units are used in their construction.

The implications of the chunking idea were tested by Tulving and Patkau (1962), who repeated the Miller and Selfridge experiment and also measured the length of chunks, defined by uninterrupted sequences of words in the subject's recall that corresponded to the same sequences in the original list. Tulving and Patkau found that the number of words in the recalled chunks increased as the order of approximation to English increased, but the number of recalled chunks remained constant at about 6. This result was quite consistent with Miller's (1956) original idea of unitization through chunking, together with his estimate of 7 ± 2 as the limit of memory span. Tulving's and Patkau's study suggested that this span does indeed remain constant but that the size of the unit increases as the passages more closely approximate English.

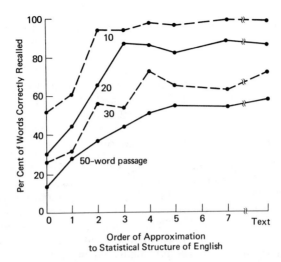

FIGURE 8-1. Accuracy of recall is plotted as a function of the order of approximation to English sentence structure. For all lengths of passages from ten to fifty words the recall was more accurate for high than for low orders of approximation. (From Miller and Selfridge, 1950).

Order of approximation and grammatical structure

Coleman (1965b) had subjects rank word strings according to their grammaticality. He found that strings that approximated English were rated as more grammatical and meaningful than lower-order approximations. Thus the effects of different variables are confounded when order of approximation is varied, and it is difficult to determine which is the causal variable. The contributions of the different factors have been clarified in some other studies. Salzinger, Portnoy, and Feldman (1962) investigated the problem using the cloze procedure. They deleted words from fifty-word passages and asked subjects to guess the missing words (note that this is a semantic rather than an episodic memory task). The results showed that the proportion of "correct" words (ones corresponding to the words that were deleted) increased from zero to the seventh order, while the proportion of words from the same grammatical category as the deleted one increased up to the third order. This was interpreted to mean that the improvement in memory with increasing approximation to English was due primarily to syntactic structure between the first and second order, about equally to syntax and meaning between the second and third, and primarily to meaning beyond the third order. This conclusion was supported by Tejirian (1968), who tested for the recall of passages ranging from the first to the sixth order and of comparable passages in which the words from particular grammatical categories were randomly altered so that semantic structure varied while syntactic structure remained constant. Recall was apparently related to syntactic structure up to the third order but depended on semantic structure alone for increases beyond the third-order approximation. Further analyses

supported Tulving and Patkau in that subjects formed larger chunks as the order of approximation increased.

The general conclusion from the research on the effects of order of approximation is that associative, syntactic, and semantic variables all contribute to the memory effect. Syntactic factors seem to operate alone up to the third order, and both syntax and meaning come in at higher levels. Finally, the effect on memory seems to operate through the mechanism of chunking.

Conditional probability (associative variety)

The effect of conditional probability was studied by Kusyszyn and Paivio (1966). They varied the number of possible noun responses to adjectives and vice versa. Simply stated, some adjectives such as *good* can modify many more nouns than ones like *sour*. Similarly, nouns vary in the number of adjectives that can modify them in a meaningful way. We could expect from information theory that it would be easier to learn pairs when there are relatively few alternative responses to the stimulus (high conditional probability) than when there are many (low conditional probability). To test this hypothesis, association norms first were obtained from subjects. This was done by giving one group a series of adjectives and asking them to write down the first noun that came to mind, and by giving another group a list of nouns and asking them to respond with an adjective to each noun. Adjective-noun and noun-adjective pairs that differed in the number of alternative associations produced by the subjects were selected. Lists of the pairs were presented to other subjects for one paired-associates trial. As can be seen in Table 8-1, the results supported the prediction from information theory: for both adjective-noun and noun-adjective pairs, recall was higher for pairs with high conditional probability than for pairs with low conditional probability.

The effects of sequential associative dependencies have also been extensively investigated by Rosenberg and his associates. The research used normative sentences obtained by Rosenberg and Koen (1968). Subjects were given sentence frames such as "The dog _____ the _____" and "The author _____ the _____." The subjects' task was to fill in the blank spaces in each sentence with the verb and the noun most frequently associated with the subject of the sentence. The responses were scored in terms of the frequency with which they were given as associates. Sentences whose verb and object noun were given frequently have high sequential dependencies. For example, *The dog bit the mailman* and *The author wrote the book* have high sequential dependencies, but *The dog*

TABLE 8-1   Mean Paired-Associates Recall of Noun-Adjective (N-A) and Adjective-Noun (A-N) Pairs of High and Low Transitional Probability (TP)

TP	N-A Order	A-N Order
High	10.09	8.78
Low	9.39	7.38

(From Kusyszyn & Paivio, 1966.)

loved the child and *The author read the review* have lower sequential dependencies. It seems clear that sentences with high sequential dependency have components that "go together" in a highly meaningful way. Thus writing books is very much a defining characteristic of authors, but reading reviews is less so.

Rosenberg's analysis emphasizes both cognitive and linguistic factors, so we shall consider it again in later sections, together with the relevant results. In the present context, we simply note that the procedure measures sequential dependencies and that this variable clearly affects memory for sentences. For example, Rosenberg (1969) showed better recall of complete sentences and their component words for the highly dependent than for less dependent sentences.

This completes our illustrations of the effect of behavioral variables. Measures of response availability and of associative strength or dependency obviously can have strong effects on memory for language. In the following sections we shall see, however, that associative variables are not the only effective ones and that sometimes the associative variables are confounded with other effective factors, as we have already noted in connection with the studies on approximations to English.

EFFECTS OF LINGUISTIC VARIABLES

Effects at the Word Level

There has been relatively little research on linguistic variables at the level of words as units. Word classes have been studied in some experiments, with the results that *content* words are generally easier to remember than *function* words, and within content words, nouns are generally the best, although this depends on the concreteness of the words. Some researchers have investigated lexical complexity, comparing simple entries, which are presumably stored as units in one's mental lexicon, with items supposedly derived from such words by transformations. Kintsch (1972) found effects of lexical complexity in paired-associates learning, with nonderived words producing better learning than derived ones. In subsequent research by Richardson (1975), however, complexity turned out to have no effect when other variables were carefully controlled (but see Holyoak, Glass, & Mah, 1976).

Units Larger than the Word: Surface Structure Variables

Surface structure and transition-error probability (TEP)

The surface-structure and TEP approach was introduced by Neal F. Johnson (1965). His analysis was based on the concept of chunking, as in the Miller and Selfridge experiments, in which chunking refers to the unitization of sequences of items into higher-order chunks. Johnson proposed specifically that subjects may chunk memory material into phrase units on the basis of their knowledge of grammar. To test this idea, he had subjects learn pairs like *8–The tall boy saved the dying woman.* The recalled sentences were scored for the conditional probability that the words in the sentence were wrong, given that the immediately preceding word was correct. This is the definition of transition-error probability. Johnson reasoned that these TEPs would reveal functional subunits related to grammatical

structure as interpreted by an immediate constituent analysis. Specifically, *TEP was expected to be higher at the boundaries of phrase units than within units.*

The results were generally as expected, as can be seen in Figure 8-2, which shows the mean TEPs for each word boundary for the sentence, *The tall boy saved the dying woman.* The TEP was highest at the major phrase boundary—between the subject and the predicate (in the example, between *boy* and *saved*). Note also that the pattern of TEPs within phrases appears to reflect the constituent structure of the entire sentence. Thus the TEP is higher between the verb and the predicate noun phrase than it is between the words within that noun phrase; it is also higher between the article and modified noun than between the adjective and noun. Similar results were obtained in several experiments.

Johnson interpreted his results in terms of a left-to-right decoding model rather like Yngve's depth hypothesis. The idea is that the subject retrieves a sentence from memory by going through a series of *decoding operations*, starting at the top of a phrase structure tree. Higher-order units are decoded into lower-order units until a response is generated. Thus a sentence is first decoded into subject and predicate. The individual stores the predicate in short-term memory and then decodes the subject into an article plus modified noun, and so on, until the terminal element is reached, permitting the generation of a response. Then the most recently stored encoding unit is taken from immediate memory and decoded in the same manner. Thus, after the subject of the sentence has been completely decoded, the individual goes back to the predicate and attempts to decode that. The pattern of errors is explained by the idea that the higher the level of the unit in the phrase structure tree, the more operations are necessary to decode it, and hence, the greater is the probability of failing to generate the response item contained within the unit. This would explain why most errors are between the subject and the predicate: having decoded the subject, the individual must now go to a level far up in the hierarchy, so that there is a good chance that the information necessary to begin to decode at that level will have been forgotten. To summarize Johnson's

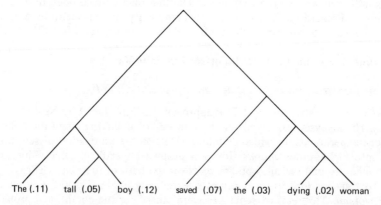

FIGURE 8-2. Constituent structure and the pattern of transition error probabilities (shown in parentheses) for a two-phrase sentence. Based on Johnson (1965).

hypothesis, the probability that an encoding unit would begin to be decoded should be inversely related to the number of operations needed to complete the task, according to a phrase structure analysis.

Johnson's analysis of memory for sentences assumes that chunking is based on grammatical units. An alternative hypothesis is that the chunking is based on interword associative habits. Johnson considered but rejected this as a sufficient explanation. Rosenberg (1968) specifically tested the alternatives by contrasting phrase structure units with strong or weak interword associations. For example, the sentence *The old king ruled wisely* has a strong association between its subject and predicate phrases; that is, between the words *king* and *ruled*. Conversely, the sentence *The poor king dined gravely* has weak associations between its constituents.

Rosenberg found that for sentences with low associations between words, the pattern of TEPs was like those obtained by Johnson, supporting the phrase-unit hypothesis. In the high-association sentences, however, the TEP decreased at the phrase boundary, suggesting that such sentences were recoded into units that transcend the phrase boundary. Rosenberg concluded that words are recoded into the largest chunk possible on the basis of syntactic and associative-semantic structure. His results showed, too, that associative-semantic relations were more important than phrase structure in that the high-association sentences were recalled better than the low-association ones.

Grammatical nonsense material and recall

Other investigators have tried to isolate the "pure" effect of syntactic structure on recall by using nonsensical word strings that contain grammatical morphemes, or do not. Epstein (1961, 1962) used Alice-in-Wonderland sentences like *A vapy koobs desaked the citar molently um glox nerfs.* Note that the sentence contains two function words and has grammatical tags like *ed* added to the nonsensical stems. In other sentences the grammatical tags were omitted or the items were randomized. The results showed that the grammatical strings were easier to learn than the ungrammatical ones.

Other similar studies have yielded variable results, however, some being positive and others negative in regard to the effect of grammatical structure as such. One general conclusion from these studies is that syntax helps memory with wordlike nonsense items, as was the case in Epstein's studies, or when real words are used. Syntax is less likely to help if the nonsense items are not wordlike, consisting, for example, of low-association-value nonsense syllables (for example, Dunne, 1968).

Marks and Miller (1964) investigated the problem by analyzing free recall of meaningful grammatical sentences, semantically anomalous word strings (created by scrambling the content words of the meaningful sentences but keeping them in their correct grammatical positions), anagram strings (formed by scrambling the order of normal sentences so that syntax is destroyed), and finally, word lists created by scrambling the words in the anomalous sentences. The following are examples of the four kinds of sentences:

Meaningful: Rapid flashes augur violent storms.
Anomalous: Rapid bouquets deter sudden neighbors.

> *Anagrams:* Rapid augur violent flashes storms.
> *Word lists:* Rapid deter sudden bouquets neighbors.

It turned out that the meaningful sentences were the easiest to learn, the word lists were the most difficult, and the other two conditions were intermediate. These results are not surprising from most theoretical points of view, but they become more interesting when considered in conjunction with the types of errors made in learning. Semantic errors (intrusions of words from one string into another) were most frequent in the anomalous sentences and word strings, both of which violated semantic rules. The "errors" presumably resulted from a tendency on the part of the subject to make the strings more meaningful. Syntactic errors (such as the omission or incorrect addition of prefixes and suffixes, and inversions of words within strings) occurred most often in anagram strings and word lists, both of which violated syntactic rules. The results suggest that both semantic and syntactic factors influenced recall.

A similar conclusion emerged from a study by Coleman (1965b), who used a generative grammar to produce nonsense sentences with four levels of grammaticality. He found that the ease of learning correlated with this variable, with the most grammatical sentences being the easiest to learn. Coleman also observed, however, that the highest-level strings were "almost meaningful" in that they included strings such as *They pushed back the homes first.* This observation again illustrates the difficulty of teasing apart grammaticality and semanticity when real words are involved.

Grammaticality also tends to be confounded with the strength of interword associations within sentences, although it is somewhat easier to distinguish these two variables than it is to separate either from meaning. Rosenberg (1966) compared the effects of syntactic and associative relations on sentence recall by using grammatical versus ungrammatical word order as one variable and high, moderate, and low associative strength between words as the other. The results showed that recall was aided both by grammatical order and by high interword associative strength. Further, there were more syntactic errors in the recall of ungrammatical rather than grammatical sentences, and there were more intrusion errors in the recall of sentences of low or moderate interword associative strength rather than ones of high strength. These patterns parallel the distributions of syntactic and semantic errors observed by Marks and Miller (1964).

The general conclusion that seems to be justified by the studies considered in this section is that grammaticality can facilitate learning independently of interword associations and semanticity. However, the effect of grammaticality per se may be relatively small compared to that of meaning (cf. Johnson, 1968).

Units Larger than the Word: Deep Structure Variables

The transformational decoding hypothesis

The transformational decoding hypothesis, as originally proposed by Miller (1962), states that a subject remembers a nonkernel sentence by transforming it into a kernel, then stores the kernel along with a grammatical tag or transformational rule. The passive sentence, *The girl was hit by the boy* would accordingly be stored as *The boy hit the girl* + PASSIVE. The prediction from this theory is

that memory for sentences is determined by *transformational complexity*, that is, the number and kind of transformations that separate the sentence from its kernel. The early evidence seemed to support the hypothesis. For example, Mehler (1963) found that prompted recall was higher for simple-affirmative-active-declarative sentences than for passives or other transformations. Moreover, errors produced responses that appeared to be nearer in form to the kernel than were the correct responses.

Savin and Perchonok (1965) had the ingenious idea that the amount of "memory space" required for storing a sentence in immediate memory could be estimated from the amount of material that could be recalled in addition to the sentence. If kernels take up less memory capacity than their transformations, more additional material should be recalled after the kernel. To test this hypothesis, they presented their subjects with a sentence and eight unrelated words and required them to recall the sentence and as many of the words as possible. For example, *The girl hit the boy* might be followed by the words *house, truth, star,* and so on. The passive transformation would be *The boy was hit by the girl,* again followed by a series of individual words. The results were consistent with the hypothesis since more additional words were recalled after kernels than after transformed sentences, given that the sentence had been correctly recalled.

Savin's and Perchonok's paradigm remains an interesting one, but their findings and interpretations have not been supported in subsequent studies that controlled for various confounding factors. For example, Glucksberg and Danks (1969) attributed some of the effect to the delay between the presentation of the word list and the recall of those words. The more complex the sentence (in transformational terms), the longer it took to recall it, and accordingly, the longer the delay before the subject could attempt to recall the additional words. Sentence length and other variables have also been shown to be effective (Boakes & Lodwick, 1971; Matthews, 1968).

Other findings have also gone against the transformational model while at the same time revealing the importance of nonsyntactic semantic variables (for example, Begg, 1971; Bregman & Strasberg, 1968; Slobin, 1968). For example, Bregman and Strasberg found evidence suggesting that subjects reconstructed the syntactic form of the sentence from other aspects of their memories, including semantic characteristics such as truth value, salience of the surface subject of the sentence, and action imagery. They argued for a theory of sentence memory that distinguishes between the *transmission code* (the sentence form) and the *semantic message* (the idea or the meaning). The transmission code is generally forgotten once it has done its job and the semantic message has been decoded. Others have expressed essentially the same idea, which we shall examine in more detail in a later section dealing with cognitive approaches to memory. At this point, we simply conclude that the transformational complexity hypothesis of sentence memory has not received consistent support from the many studies on the problem.

Deep structure complexity

It is alternatively possible to consider the complexity of the underlying structure of a sentence, according to the theory of transformational grammar, rather than the complexity of the transformational rules linking those structures to surface structures. We shall introduce this linguistic approach here and come back to it

later in order to compare it with certain cognitive alternatives. One series of experiments on the problem was carried out by Rohrman (1968). He compared subject nominalizations like *growling lions* with object nominalizations like *raising flowers*. The deep structure trees for the two types are shown in Figure 8-3. The important point to note is that the object nominalizations are more complex in deep structure than are the subject nominalizations, because they include a dummy pronominal element (PRO) essential to the meaning of the nominalization. The implication is that some agent raises flowers, but this has been deleted in the surface structure. Rohrman's experiments showed that subject nominalizations were easier to recall than object nominalizations and that this effect was not attributable to meaningfulness or the number of transformations. Later, however, we shall see that subject nominalizations tend, on the average, to be higher in imagery value than object nominalizations and that the recall difference disappears when imagery value is controlled.

Deep structure variables were also investigated by Blumenthal in two experiments. Blumenthal (1967) compared prompted recall of sentences like *Gloves were made by tailors* and *Gloves were made by hand*. The recall cues in each case were the final nouns—*tailors* and *hand* in the examples. Note that *tailor* is the logical subject of the entire sentence, which is a full passive. The active counterpart would be *Tailors make gloves*. In the second sentence, *hand* is an adverbial modifier; specifically, a manner adverbial that modifies the verb *made* by answering the question *made how?* The sentence itself is a truncated passive in which the agent is replaced by the manner adverbial. The implied underlying sense is captured by two statements: *Someone makes gloves; They are made by hand.* Blumenthal's hypothesis was that the logical subjects would be more effective prompts because they are more inclusively implicated in the sentence as a whole at the deep structure level. This expectation was confirmed by the results of the experiment.

Blumenthal and Boakes (1967) reported a conceptually similar study of free recall and prompted recall for sentence types such as *John is eager to please* and *John is easy to please*. In the cued-recall condition, the prompts were either the nouns or the adjectival modifiers. The role of each type of prompt differs in the two types of sentences. In the first example, *John* is the subject of the predication,

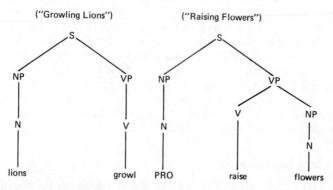

FIGURE 8-3. Deep structures of subject nominalizations (e.g., growling lions) and object nominalizations (e.g., raising flowers).

to please, and *eager* modifies the noun, *John*. In the second example, *John* is the object of the predication and *easy* modifies the entire sentence. The predictions were that prompted recall would be higher with logical subjects than with logical objects as prompts, so that *John is eager* sentences would be superior to *John is easy*. The reverse was expected with the modifiers as prompts. The predictions were tested by first having the subjects freely recall the sentences and then giving them a prompted recall test with either the noun or the adjective as the prompt. The crucial data were the increases from free recall to prompted recall. The results were exactly as predicted: logical subjects were better than logical objects as cues, and sentence modifiers were better than noun modifiers. Wanner (1974) reported comparable findings for different types of verbs.

The Blumenthal and Boakes findings have not been directly refuted to date, although Healy and Levitt (1978) suggested that the Blumenthal studies were not conclusive because they confounded deep-structure syntactic and semantic relations. Healy and Levitt varied the two independently in a recognition memory task (see our earlier description in chapter 5) and found that semantic case relations were learned more easily than syntactic deep-structure relations. It remains to be seen whether similar results would be obtained using the prompted recall task employed by Blumenthal and Boakes. We shall see later that their findings have been directly qualified in terms of the imagery level of the sentences. Those studies will be considered in the context of the cognitive approaches, which we examine next. As in the present section, we shall again draw attention frequently to the importance and difficulty of teasing apart the effects of confounded variables.

EFFECTS OF COGNITIVE VARIABLES

Cognitive approaches to memory have generally emphasized the influence of semantic variables, contextual factors, and nonverbal cognitive processes such as imagery and knowledge of the world. As before, we will first consider effects at the word level and then units larger than the word. The concern at each level is with relevant item attributes and experimental manipulations, as well as individual difference factors when these are available.

Effects at the Word Level

Word attributes

Consider, first, the effects of semantic and other attributes of words. A strong generalization is justified by the available research evidence: the image-evoking value of words is the best predictor of performance in most verbal learning and memory tasks. Imagery has been compared with associative meaningfulness, frequency, and a large number of other attributes in paired-associates learning, free recall, recognition memory, and so on. High-imagery words are easier to remember than low-imagery words even when other variables are controlled, and the effects of other semantic attributes are generally weak or nonexistent when imagery is controlled. In one study (Paivio, 1968), for example, over twenty characteristics of words were correlated with paired-associates learning and free-recall scores for the

same items. Only a few of the attributes significantly predicted the memory scores: the highest correlation was between rated imagery values and recall scores. The other predictors of memory performance, in decreasing order of predictive power, were ratings of the vividness of imagery, a reaction-time measure of the speed with which the word arouses images, and ratings of concreteness and tangibility. In fact, a factor-analytic study showed that all of these variables correlated highly with each other, constituting what was called in the study an imagery-concreteness factor. Since that time, comparisons have been made with further attributes, such as lexical complexity, the number of dictionary definitions that a word has, pronounceability, and so on. Thus far, the above generalization remains intact.

The conclusion must be qualified, however, by three important factors related to the type of task. First, item imagery does not appear to be effective in sequential memory tasks, such as immediate memory span (for example, Paivio & Csapo, 1969; for a more recent discussion of this problem, see Snodgrass, Burns, & Pirone, 1978). The second qualification is that the imagery value of words seems not to be as effective in very-short-term memory tasks as it is in tasks that presumably depend more on long-term or semantic memory. Thus, the effects of the imagery variable seem to be present in long-term memory processes and memory for items, but not short-term memory, especially if it includes memory for the sequential order of unrelated items. The importance of long-term memory, such as referential meaning, was demonstrated by Begg and Clark (1975), who showed that words that differ in image-arousing capacity differ in recall only if the context in which they appear makes that difference salient. For example, high-imagery words, such as *record*, are generally better remembered than low-imagery words, such as *miss*; however, if each word is placed in a concrete context, such as *play a record* or *pretty young miss*, as opposed to a more abstract context, such as *set a record* or *hit and miss*, it is the imagery value of the context, rather than the word alone, that is associated with recall (for a general discussion of ambiguity, see Kess & Hoppe, 1978, 1979).

The third important qualification is the locus of the word-imagery effect in associative memory tasks. It turns out that word recall is affected more by the imagery value of the stimulus than of the response. The possibility that this might be so was first investigated in the context of a phenomenon that is particularly interesting psycholinguistically. Numerous studies showed that it is easier to learn associations between nouns and relevant adjectives when the noun precedes rather than follows the adjectives. For example, it is easier to learn pairs like *valley-deep* than pairs like *deep-valley*. This is interesting in itself because it is contrary to what would be expected on the basis of associative and grammatical habits for speakers of English, since adjectives normally precede nouns in English syntax. The effect was originally interpreted in terms of the metaphorical hypothesis that nouns function as effective *conceptual pegs* from which their modifying adjectives can be hung and subsequently retrieved (Lambert & Paivio, 1956). This was later extended to the idea that the effectiveness of nouns as conceptual pegs is related to their concreteness or image-arousing value (Paivio, 1963).

Subsequent experiments extended the hypothesis to noun-noun pairs and convincingly demonstrated that the imagery effect is stronger on the stimulus side of pairs. For example, pairs like *frog-table* are generally much easier to learn than ones like *soul-table* when the first word of each pair serves as the retrieval cue

during recall. That is, the high-imagery word *frog* is a stronger retrieval cue than the low-imagery word *soul*. The difference is much less striking when the two words are compared as responses (for example, *table-frog* versus *table-soul*). We should point out that what counts is which word is used as the retrieval cue during the recall trial. Thus, whether the pair is *table-soul* or *soul-table*, recall is better when *table* rather than *soul* is presented as the cue for recall. These and other facts have shown that the imagery effect in associative recall is essentially a *retrieval* phenomenon— high-imagery stimuli are potent retrieval cues for associated information. You can find a fuller discussion of these findings and their history in reviews by Paivio (1969, 1971b). For a more recent study of the conceptual peg hypothesis, see R. C. Anderson, Goetz, Pichert, and Halff (1977).

Interpretation of the imagery effects

The results concerning imagery have been interpreted in terms of two features of the dual-coding theory discussed in chapter 4, namely, imagery organization (integration) and dual coding per se. The first implies that imagery permits the learner to integrate two or more items into an organized unit. This translates into terms already familiar to you from earlier discussions in this chapter: imagery is assumed to be a chunking mechanism. Thus a pair such as *monkey-bicycle* might be recoded as a unitized, imaginary "scene" of a monkey riding a bicycle. On the recall trial *monkey* redintegrates the entire image, from which one can retrieve *bicycle*. This interpretation is related to the conceptual peg hypothesis in that the hypothesis assumes that the imagery value of both members of a pair determines how easy it is to *form* an integrated image during the study trial, and that the imagery value of the stimulus term or retrieval cue becomes especially important during recall because it determines how readily the mediating image will be redintegrated. A high-imagery stimulus ensures *access* to the integrated image.

Several varieties of related evidence support the integration hypothesis. One kind of evidence uses pictures as memory aids or mediators in paired-associates learning. Participants in such an experiment are presented with word pairs along with a picture depicting the stimulus and response items. On recall trials, the stimulus words are presented without the pictures, and the subject attempts to recall the appropriate responses. Such cued recall is generally helped by the prior presentation of pictures during the learning trial. The crucial point, however, is that the facilitation is higher when the picture depicts the referents of the stimulus and response items in some kind of integrated or compound form than when the two things are simply presented side by side as separate elements (see Epstein, Rock, & Zuckerman, 1960; Wollen, Weber, & Lowry, 1972). The implication is that the compound pictures are retained as images that mediate recall during the test trial. The imagery interpretation is strongly supported by the further finding that merely *instructing* subjects to form an integrated or compound image, in which the two items are interacting, results in much better learning than when subjects are told to visualize the two items as separate entities (for example, Begg, 1973; Bower, 1970; Rowe & Paivio, 1971). However, we must clarify what is learned. Imagery is a highly effective means for combining information, and almost all studies do find increased organization or association after imaginal integration, as opposed to various control groups. On the other hand, increased organization does not neces-

sarily mean that more items are recalled. In this regard, Begg (1978) found that material remembered as a few large memory images produces recall of a few long chunks, and material remembered as many small images produces recall of more but smaller chunks. The procedures do not result in different *amounts* recalled in free recall, but they do differ appropriately in any associative task, since once a memory unit is accessed through an appropriate retrieval cue, its contents are available for use.

The following example is even more relevant to students of language behavior. Begg (1972) investigated the recall of meaningful phrases such as *white horse* and *basic theory*. Note that the former is concrete and easily visualized. Accordingly, the hypothesis was that the two words would be remembered essentially as one unit because they would be recoded in memory as an integrated image. The prediction follows that the memorizer should be able to remember as many *phrase units* from a list containing such phrases as *separate words* from a word list. This was not expected for abstract phrases such as *basic theory*, because such phrases cannot be readily recoded as images. They should therefore be remembered essentially as two separate words. These predictions were tested by presenting subjects with lists of phrases or word lists made up of the adjectives and nouns from the phrases. For the phrases, subjects were sometimes asked to recall only the adjectives or nouns; in other cases they were asked to recall the entire phrase; and in yet another condition they were presented with one word from each phrase as a retrieval cue and were asked to recall the other member of each pair. For the word lists, subjects were simply required to free recall as many of the words as possible.

The results of Begg's study were completely as expected. Figure 8-4 summarizes the major findings. Note that for concrete material, recall was virtually identical for word free recall, partial phrase recall, and whole phrase recall. Note, too, that this is expressed in terms of proportionate recall. Since the phrase lists contained twice as many words as the word lists, this means that subjects recalled twice as many words from the phrases as from the word lists. For abstract phrases, recall was generally much lower (a typical finding), but the important point is that the proportionate recall of phrases was about half of what it was in the free recall of word lists. Finally, note that presenting one word as a retrieval cue enhanced

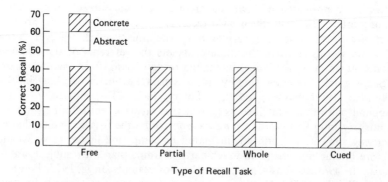

FIGURE 8-4. Percentage of items recalled from concrete and abstract adjective-noun phrases under different recall conditions. Based on Begg (1972).

the recall of the response words only for concrete phrases, which can easily be interpreted in terms of the imagery integration hypothesis: because imagery permits chunking or integration of the phrase information, the presentation of one of the components of the chunk redintegrates the memory for the entire compound, thereby enhancing recall. There apparently was no such unitization for abstract phrases, and cuing was not helpful. Notice, too, that this cuing effect relates to the conceptual peg hypothesis described earlier.

In a manner quite analogous to imagery's capacity to organize information, Rohwer (1973) has found that children learn pairs of nouns more easily if the nouns are linked by a verb (*the giant hears the boat*) rather than a conjunction (*the giant and the boat*). Although previous theories analyzed the effect in linguistic terms, it is possible to account for the effect entirely on the basis of cognitive principles, specifically, organization. By that account, pairs linked by a verb can be remembered as one unit in memory more easily than pairs linked by a conjunction. If this is true, the advantage of verbs should disappear either if the children are given an alternative means of linking the nouns presented with conjunctions or if the organizational advantage of verbs is interfered with. Begg and Young (1977) found that for children in the sixth grade or higher, interactive imagery instructions result in the recall of the conjunction-linked pairs increasing to the level of the verb-linked pairs, but instructions to visualize the members of the pairs separately reduces the recall of the verb-linked pairs to the level of those linked by conjunctions. Further, pairs linked by joining prepositions (in, on) are better remembered than pairs linked by less explicitly joining prepositions (by, near), indicating further that the effect is due to cognitive rather than linguistic differences.

The second theoretical interpretation of the effect of imagery on memory pertains to dual coding per se. The idea is that generating images of words results in two memory traces, one for the word itself and the other for its referent object. To the extent that this is true, it should increase the probability of recalling the item. Simply stated, two codes are better than one because if one is forgotten, the target memory could be retrieved from the other. If the two codes are fully interdependent, however, there could not be such facilitation because memory for one code would be entirely dependent on memory for the other. The superiority of pictures to words in many experiments would be similarly explained by the same principle: subjects are more likely to name familiar pictures implicitly than they are to visualize words. The hypothesis has been supported for both pictures and words in a series of experiments in which, for example, pictures and words were shown to have additive effects on recall (Paivio, 1975a). In addition, however, the evidence suggested that the contribution of pictures to recall performance was much greater than that of words, suggesting that the qualitative difference between the two codes is also important. The safe conclusion at the present time is that both principles are operative: the imaginal and verbal memory traces aroused by pictures or words contribute additively to recall in some tasks, and in addition, the image code contributes more than the verbal code to their additive effect.

To summarize, the research in this area leaves many questions unanswered, but so far the results strongly support the idea of functionally independent but interconnected memory systems. One is specialized for encoding, storing, organizing, and retrieving information regarding objects and events. Up to some limit, the information appears to be organized synchronously or in a spatially parallel fashion,

permitting easy integration of units into higher-order chunks and facilitating retrieval by any component of the complex. The verbal system deals with word units organized into higher-order sequential structures. This implies less efficient chunking and retrieval by component information. The dual-coding theory, of which these are some of the key assumptions, will be compared with alternative theories in the next sections in the context of experiments using larger units.

Units Larger than the Word

Much research has been carried out in recent years on the effects of semantic variables and context on memory for phrases and sentences. Some of the research has been on the effects of various semantic factors on the amount recalled, and other research has sought to identify mechanisms in the unitization or chunking of the complex linguistic information in memory. The following is a sampling of some of the salient findings:

1. Effects of Semantic Variables on Amount Recalled

Imagery-concreteness

As in word units, phrases or sentences that are concrete and high in imagery value are generally much easier to remember than otherwise-comparable abstract strings in recognition memory, free recall, and cued recall. The study by Begg (1972), discussed above, is one example of this effect at the phrase level. The mnemonic power of imagery value is interesting in its own right but especially so when considered in relation to linguistic variables. For example, it was once observed fairly consistently that the subjects of sentences are generally easier to recall than their objects. It turns out that this result is at least partly due to the fact that sentence subjects are found to be higher in imagery value on the average than are sentence objects. C. James (1972) found no recall difference when the imagery value of the two components was controlled. On the other hand, variation in the imagery of either subject or object nouns affected the amount recalled.

Imagery versus deep structure

Another series of studies compared imagery to deep structure variables. You will recall our discussion of Rohrman's research in the section on linguistic approaches to memory. Rohrman found that subject nominalizations, such as *growling lions*, were better recalled than object nominalizations, such as *raising flowers*. He interpreted this effect in terms of the idea that subject nominalizations are simpler in their deep structure than are object nominalizations. Paivio (1971a) observed, however, that Rohrman's subject nominalizations were higher in average imagery value than his object nominalizations. Paivio compared the contributions of the two variables in several experiments, with the result that nominalization type had no consistent effect when imagery level was controlled, whereas high-imagery nominalizations of both types were recalled better than their low-imagery counterparts. These conclusions were essentially confirmed by Richardson (1975).

Danks and Sorce (1973) further compared imagery and deep structure using full passive and agent-replaced passive sentences such as those employed

earlier by Blumenthal (1967). The following are examples of the four types of sentences:

High-imagery full passive: *Grades were issued by professors.*
High-imagery agent-replaced passive: *The grades were issued by letter.*
Low-imagery full passives: *The game was played by substitutes.*
Low-imagery agent-replaced passives: *The game was played by permission.*

People were required to recall lists of such sentences given the object noun of the prepositional phrase as a recall cue. Thus, in the examples, the prompts were *professors, letter, substitutes,* and *permission.* The results, presented in Figure 8–5, showed that imagery and deep structure interacted; object recall was better for high- than for low-imagery truncated (agent-replaced) passives, but imagery had no effect with full passives; and full passives were better recalled than agent-replaced passives when the sentences were low, but not when they were high in imagery value. These results are consistent with a dual-coding approach in that they demonstrate effects of both nonverbal imagery and a linguistic structural variable which presumably is related to characteristics of the verbal system. It is particularly interesting that the linguistic variable showed up when imagery was relatively unavailable as a memory code.

Imagery versus comprehensibility

In the last chapter we reviewed evidence indicating that concrete language is usually easier to understand than abstract language. This fact has led some researchers to suggest that the memory effects of concreteness may be due to differences in comprehensibility rather than imagery. That is, concrete sentences may be easier to remember than abstract ones simply because they are easier to understand, not because they are easier to visualize (for example, Johnson, Bransford, Nyberg, & Cleary, 1972; Bransford & McCarrell, 1974). That suggestion has not been supported by recent studies in which comprehensibility and imagery have been compared.

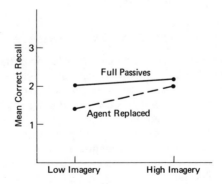

FIGURE 8–5. Effects of sentence imagery and deep structure on prompted recall. Based on data in Danks and Sorce (1973).

Kuiper and Paivio (1977) carefully matched the rated comprehensibility of concrete and abstract sentences. A separate experimental group was then presented a matched set and was asked to rate them on comprehensibility, after which the subjects were given an unexpected recognition-memory test with a set of sentences that included the ones originally rated on comprehensibility, as well as paraphrases of those sentences and new unrelated distractors. The results showed that even with comprehensibility equated, concrete sentences exceeded abstract ones in correct identification and in correct rejection of completely new ones. There also were interesting differences in the pattern of errors (false recognition for the two types of sentences), which will be discussed in a later section.

Marschark and Paivio (1977) obtained better cued recall for concrete than for abstract sentences in three experiments. In two of these, the concrete sentences exceeded the abstract ones in rated comprehensibility and imagery value. However, correlational analyses showed that imagery correlated significantly with recall even when comprehensibility was held constant statistically, but comprehensibility was unrelated to recall when imagery was similarly controlled.

As a final example, O'Neill and Paivio (1978) obtained recall scores and ratings of imagery, comprehensibility, and sensibleness for normal concrete and abstract sentences, as well as anomalous sentences that were constructed by arbitrarily substituting content words from one sentence to another. Two findings are relevant here. First, the substitutions produced rating decrements for both concrete and abstract sentences, but the effect was greater for concrete ones. This difference was especially marked in comprehensibility and sensibleness, which were higher for concrete than abstract normal sentences, but this was completely *reversed* when the sentences were highly anomalous. There was not such a reversal in regard to imagery ratings, which remained consistently higher for concrete than abstract sentences even when they were highly anomalous. The second and more relevant point is that recall was superior for the concrete material under all conditions of substitution. Thus, even when the ratings were reversed, so that concrete sentences were rated *less* comprehensible than abstract ones, they were easier to remember.

The conclusion from the studies reviewed in this section is clear: differences in comprehensibility, at least as measured by ratings, cannot account for the higher memorability of concrete as compared to abstract sentences. Imagery value, however, remains a potent predictor of memory.

Sequential-associative dependencies versus imagery

Recall that the section on behavioral variables described research by Rosenberg (1969), showing that sentences with high interword sequential dependencies (*The author wrote the book*) were easier to remember than ones with low sequential dependencies (*The author read the review*). Rosenberg described such sentences as being semantically well integrated or semantically poorly integrated and attributed the difference in recall to the differences in propositional relations. Recently, however, Rosenberg (1977) found that semantic integration was confounded with imageability. That is, semantically well integrated sentences were generally higher in their rated imagery value than were poorly integrated sentences. He found, moreover, that imageability correlated significantly with free-recall scores for semantically well integrated sentences in three separate experiments. Conversely, with imagery

held constant at a moderate level, several experiments failed to show a significant difference between well and poorly integrated sentences in free recall, but recall was much higher for the semantically well integrated sentences when the subject nouns were used as prompts. These results suggest that semantic integration and imagery interact in interesting ways, which remain to be fully explained. We address the general issue again in a section on the abstraction and integration of linguistic ideas.

A final point in regard to the general effects of imagery variables is that, as in the case of words, recall of larger linguistic units is enhanced by instructing subjects to generate images for the material. It has also been observed that such instructions can sometimes increase certain types of errors. For example, Anderson and Hidde (1971) had people rate either the pronounceability or the image-evoking value of sentences, then unexpectedly asked them to recall the verb and object of each, given the subject as a retrieval cue. The procedure presumably caused the participants to pronounce or visualize the material. Those who rated imagery recalled over three times as many words as those who rated pronounceability. In addition, when there were errors, they tended to be predominantly synonym intrusions in the case of the imagery group but not the pronunciation group. These results suggest that imagery aided recall through some kind of reconstructive process, which sometimes resulted in decoding errors. Pronunciation subjects, however, recalled verbatim and therefore avoided synonym errors but made more omission errors because they had not stored the sentence in a meaningful way.

2. Evidence for Semantic-Integrative Processes in Memory

In this section we are again concerned with the general idea of chunking, but with an emphasis on *semantic codes*, which, though separate from the wording of a passage, have the function of organizing and integrating large amounts of verbal information. Thus we are presumably dealing with some kind of semantic memory representation, which contributes to performance in episodic memory tasks by transforming the linguistic events into a more condensed form.

Thematic organization

A possible nonverbal basis for such unitization was suggested by a series of studies on the role of thematic organization in memory (Lachman & Dooling, 1968; Pompi & Lachman, 1967). Lachman and his associates proposed that the theme or gist of connected discourse generates "surrogate processes" reflecting the essential idea of a passage and that such processes can be used in the regeneration of the passage. They found support for this view in that prose passages presented in a normal, thematically organized manner were retained better than the same material presented so that the words were in a random order. Moreover, the subjects made more thematically related errors in remembering the connected discourse. Pompi and Lachman suggested that imagery may be one form in which the discourse theme is stored. Yuille and Paivio (1969) tested this hypothesis by varying the imagery level and the level of organization of passages. They found better recall for thematically organized than for randomly organized material when the passages were high in imagery value, but not when they were medium or low in imagery.

These results were confirmed by Philipchalk (1972) for both immediate and delayed recall. The findings suggest that the essential idea communicated by the thematically organized material may be in the form of organized imagery that somehow captures the theme as a whole. Alternatively, the facilitation may result from a series of images representing specific details. The function of thematic organization in either case would be to facilitate the generation of imagery that provides a meaningful, organized, referential context for the linguistic message.

Memory for meaning versus memory for wording

Similar findings and theoretical issues have arisen in connection with a series of studies on the difference between memory for meaning and memory for the wording of linguistic material. The research shows that we remember the gist of what was said better than we remember how it was said. This was empirically demonstrated in the early part of this century, but most of the studies on the problem have appeared within the last dozen years. Sachs (1967) compared recognition memory for syntactic and semantic information following the comprehension of linguistic material. Her subjects listened to recorded passages of connected discourse. Then one sentence was played back in a form that was either identical to the way it was originally heard in the passage, or in a changed form. If the sentence was changed, the change was either semantic or syntactic. Semantic changes were reversal of the subject and object of the sentence, negation, or substitution of a different word. Syntactic changes were changes from active to passive or vice versa, as well as grammatical changes that did not alter the meaning. Subjects were asked to say whether the sentence was "changed" or "identical." Different amounts of interpolated material were also inserted between the original presentation and the occurrence of the test sentence, permitting an assessment of forgetting over time. The essential result for our purposes was that semantic changes were correctly identified much more often than syntactic changes. This means that the subjects must have remembered the meaning of the passages much better than their exact wording.

Sachs used only concrete sentences in her studies. Begg and Paivio (1969) repeated the experiment, including both abstract and concrete sentences in the design. They reasoned that a concrete sentence, such as *The girl kissed the fat boy*, can be imaginally represented as an action picture in which the meaning of the entire sentence is summarized as one organized unit, or complex image. The information contained in the abstract material, on the other hand, remains more closely linked to the sequentially organized verbal units themselves and can be summarized as an imagined unit only with difficulty. It follows that the most effectively coded, stored, and retrieved aspects of concrete sentences will be those related to the sentence as a whole unit, such as its meaning. In abstract sentences, however, the specific words will be relatively better retained. The following are examples of the concrete test sentences used to evaluate the hypothesis:

The loving mother served an excellent family.
The vicious hound chased the wild animal.
The cheerful artist entertained a lovely damsel.
The rolling hillside surrounded a muddy valley.

Examples of abstract sentences are:

The absolute faith aroused an enduring interest.
The dull description constituted a boring chapter.
The passive majority defeated a listless opposition.
The final decision nullified a prior commitment.

Semantic changes were reversals of the subject and object of each sentence. Thus the first of the above examples became *The loving family served an excellent mother*. Lexical changes were synonym substitutions that preserved the essential meaning of the sentence, for example, *The loving mother served an excellent household*. It was expected that semantic changes would be recognized better than lexical changes in the case of concrete material, replicating Sachs's finding. Conversely, lexical changes should be better recognized than semantic changes in the case of abstract material. Figure 8-6 shows a striking interaction that precisely confirmed both predictions.

The above findings suggested that the idea that sentence meaning is better retained than its wording needs to be qualified by the nature of the verbal material used. It is correct for concrete sentences but not for abstract sentences. This conclusion, however, has been controversial. For example, Johnson and her associates (1972) suggested that the results obtained by Begg and Paivio, like concrete-abstract memory differences generally, reflect the difficulty of comprehending abstract as compared to concrete sentences. Other studies, too, have indicated that the crucial interaction depends on the particular conditions of the experiment (for example, Pezdek & Royer, 1974). Still others have provided confirmation of Begg's and Paivio's results for conditions in which some of the more important confounding factors have been strictly controlled. For example, in addition to the generally

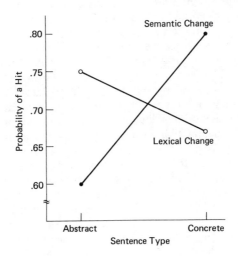

FIGURE 8-6. Correct recognition of semantic and lexical changes in abstract and concrete sentences. From Begg and Paivio (1969).

better recognition of concrete rather than abstract sentences already discussed earlier, Kuiper and Paivio (1977) found that concrete synonyms were incorrectly identified as having been in the list originally rated on comprehensibility more often than abstract synonyms. These results are consistent with Begg and Paivio (1969) in showing that exact wording was less accurately retained in concrete than in abstract sentences, presumably because the meaning of the concrete sentences tended to be stored as images that can be appropriately described by both the synonymous sentences and the original ones.

Integration of linguistic ideas

The final series of studies that we will consider has been concerned specifically with demonstrating abstraction and integration of linguistic ideas and with interpreting the mechanisms responsible for such effects. The inspiration for some of this research came from studies of the genesis of abstract ideas using perceptual stimuli. Posner and Keele (1968) showed subjects visual patterns that varied in shape, and then they tested them for their recognition memory. The test patterns included prototypical patterns that would have been central in the initial series (a kind of average of the shapes) but that had not been presented during the original series. Other new distractor items were equally similar in shape to the original exemplars but were not similarly prototypical of the entire series. The crucial result was that the new prototype was mistakenly identified as having been previously presented more often than was the case for the other new distractors. This suggests that the subjects had abstracted the prototypical representation from the instances stored in memory.

Bransford and Franks (1971) extended the idea to language. Specifically, they presented subjects with sentences that expressed a series of simple ideas, then presented a series of recognition test sentences that included both the original simple ones and some that expressed complex combinations of the simple ideas, which had never been presented together in the same sentence during acquisition. Consider the complex sentence *The ants in the kitchen ate the sweet jelly which was on the table*. This sentence was not presented, but ones like the following were presented: *The ants were in the kitchen* (a one-idea sentence); *The ants in the kitchen ate the jelly* (two ideas); *The ants ate the sweet jelly* (two ideas); *The ants ate the sweet jelly which was on the table* (three ideas); and so on. The test sentences included these and other old sentences as well as various new combinations of the ideas in the old, including the four-idea sentence presented above. The important result was that in addition to correct recognition of old sentences, the subjects incorrectly recognized new sentences as having occurred previously. Moreover, their confidence that they had heard a sentence previously increased with its complexity. This effect was most dramatic for the four-idea sentences: although they had never heard these sentences during acquisition, they were more confident that they had heard the four-idea sentences than any others. The evidence strongly suggested that memory in this case was a constructive process in which the participants integrated ideas from simple sentences into a more complex representation that somehow incorporated all of the separate ideas.

The main findings have been frequently obtained in other experiments, including one that demonstrated similar constructive memory effects for low-

imagery sentences. As might be expected, however, the later research has also raised controversial issues, particularly in regard to the interpretation of the effects. The resolution of the effects in regard to Bransford's and Franks's paradigm is important, but we shall not try to resolve it here. Instead, we will consider a final series of studies that have been concerned with the same basic problem using somewhat different procedures. Bransford's and Franks's approach and imagery theories both assume that linguistic ideas are integrated into holistic representations. These representations presumably have *emergent properties* that are different from and go beyond the linguistic information itself. They could be said to have Gestalt properties in that sentence memory is more than the sum of the associations between individual parts of the sentence.

Anderson and Bower (1972, 1973) proposed an alternative theory of human associative memory (HAM) that does not assume any holistic representation with Gestalt properties. Instead, HAM assumes that sentence memory is nothing more than the sum of the individual associations between parts. That is, it consists of the stored associations between words as these are represented in long-term memory. To understand the implications of the contrasting views, consider the sentence, *The child hit the landlord.* According to HAM, the sentence is a network of relations connecting *child, hit,* and *landlord.* In a memory task, each association is thought to be stored independently of the other, so that sentence memory as a whole is simply the sum of the separate associations. The prediction from any theory that assumes holistic representations would be that memory should be greater than the sum of the individual parts. The alternatives were tested by Anderson and Bower using a "crossover" sentence memory experiment. Subjects learned a list containing pairs of sentences of the following kind:

1. *The child hit the landlord.*
2. *The minister praised the landlord.*

The memory test was cued recall of the object of each sentence given one or another of the following cues:

Subject cue alone: *The child . . . the* _____
Verb alone: *The . . . hit the* _____
Subject + Verb from the same sentence: *The child hit the* _____
Subject + Verb crossed over: *The child praised the* _____

Note that the last cue condition includes the subject (the child) from sentence 1 and the verb (praised) from sentence 2. What are the predictions for this experiment? Any reasonable theory would predict that cuing with the subject plus predicate from the same sentence would result in better recall than when only the subject or verb is given as the cue. The important theoretical question concerns the last two conditions. Configural theory should predict that cuing with the subject and verb from the same sentence would result in higher recall than when they are from different sentences. The HAM model predicted, counterintuitively, that the reverse would be true because the cues in the crossed-over version are independent and could have additive effects. This is precisely what Anderson and Bower found.

However, other experiments have used similar procedures to obtain strong evidence of integrated, holistic representations. For example, R. C. Anderson and Ortony (1975) used a recall test in which each sentence was cued with a word judged to be closely related to the meaning of the sentence as a whole, or with a word related only to the subject or predicate. Consider the following set of four sentences:

A. *Nurses are often beautiful.*
B. *Nurses have to be licensed.*
C. *Landscapes are often beautiful.*
D. *Taverns have to be licensed.*

The words *actress* and *doctor* were the sentence and control cues for different subjects. When the cue was *actress*, Sentence A was the target sentence (actress is related to the meaning of Sentence A as a whole); Sentence B was the subject control sentence (actress is somewhat related to nurses); Sentence C was the predicate control sentence (actress is meaningfully related to beautiful); and Sentence D was a "double control" in which neither constituent bears any meaningful relation to the word actress. When the cue was *doctor*, Sentence B was the target, Sentence A the subject control, Sentence D the predicate control, and Sentence C the double control.

Anderson and Ortony (1975) used this design to contrast their own predictions with those arising from J. R. Anderson's and Bower's HAM theory. The latter states essentially that the probability that a certain cue will allow retrieval of a target sentence, t, should equal the probability that there exists an intact path from the cue to any constituent of the target sentence. In this case, those constituents are the subject, s, and predicate, p. Anderson and Ortony argued that under the conditions of their experiment, HAM's prediction is that $t = s + p$. Their own view was that the senses of the individual words interact in the process of constructing a meaning for the utterance as a whole. Thus they claim that "the whole is greater than the sum of the parts" and predicted that $t > s + p$.

The results were scored in various ways, and in each analysis t was significantly higher than $s + p$, indicating that memory performance was based on the construction of a holistic mental representation. Anderson and Ortony suggested that this constructive process depends heavily on knowledge of the world and analysis of the context in which a sentence occurs, and that current semantic feature theories and associative or semantic network theories cannot handle the results.

The above study had a rather complicated, although effective, design. A simpler design that established the same point was used by Foss and Harwood (1975, Experiment 2). They presented their subjects with sentences like *The child hit the landlord.* Then one person received the subject, *child*, as a recall cue for the sentence, and another received the verb *hit*. A third group of participants received the subject and verb, *child, hit*. In each case, the participants attempted to recall the object, *landlord*. The simple prediction from HAM (or any model that assumes independence of sentence components in memory) under these conditions would be that the probability of recalling the object, given the subject and verb as the cue, would be equal to the sum of the probabilities of recalling the object, given the subject and verb separately as cues. The results showed that the probability of

recalling the object, given both the subject and verb as cues, was .396, which is significantly higher than the sum of the probabilities (.245), given the subject (.146) and the verb (.099) as cues. Further, this difference was found for the great majority of the individual subjects. Thus the results supported the prediction from an integrational or configural model rather than from HAM.

As a final example, Marschark and Paivio (1977) extended the designs used by Anderson and Ortony and by Foss and Harwood to the recall of both abstract and concrete sentences. Recall that Begg and Paivio (1969) found evidence that subjects tended to retain the meaning of concrete sentences as a whole, perhaps in the form of imagery, but apparently stored abstract sentences more nearly in their verbal form. The general theoretical position and the results of that study suggest that evidence of holistic recall can be obtained only for concrete sentences. On the other hand, Franks and Bransford (1972) found evidence that both abstract and concrete sentences are processed in some integrative manner. The results obtained by Marschark and Paivio in three different experiments consistently supported the integration hypothesis for both types of sentences. At the same time, however, the overall level of recall was higher for concrete than for abstract sentences. Thus, concrete sentences were easier to recall than abstract sentences, but when there was recall, it tended to be integrative to the same degree in each case.

The results obtained by Marschark and Paivio seem to pose a theoretical puzzle. On the one hand, we have considerable evidence that concrete and abstract materials are processed differently. The differences can be accounted for by a dual-coding theory which assumes that two qualitatively different representational systems are used in sentence memory and that these are implicated to different degrees in concrete and abstract material. On the other hand, we have evidence that concrete and abstract sentences are processed alike, in an integrative manner that appears to be inconsistent with dual coding. Since the imagery system is presumably less accessible to abstract than to concrete material, there should not have been equivalent integration for the two types of material. Of course, dual-coding theory could explain all of the findings if it could be shown that imagery was present whenever recall was integrative, even for abstract sentences. However, the subjects in one of the experiments, when questioned about their mnemonic strategies, reported using imagery for recall if they were in the concrete sentence condition and verbal strategies if they were in the abstract condition. Although dual-coding theory does not hinge on conscious imagery as evidence that the imagery system functions in task performance, the subjects' reports cannot be ignored unless other strong evidence were available in support of the imagery hypothesis.

A further theoretical possibility might be to modify dual-coding theory by adding a common (abstract) level of representation to the two modality-specific (that is, imaginal and verbal) representational systems (cf. Potter, 1979; Potter, Valian, & Faulconer, 1977). The latter two would suffice to explain such facts as concrete-abstract differences in level of recall. The common code would be added to account for the commonalities in the semantic processing of concrete and abstract sentences. The problem with such a compromise, however, is that the theoretical nature of the common representational system is quite obscure at present. Such concepts as holistic semantic descriptions, abstract representations, and holistic ideas that have been suggested by various researchers are simply labels

for the empirical findings themselves. They remain unsatisfactory as *explanations* until they have been defined in terms of theoretical mechanisms or empirical procedures that are independent of the observed data. While awaiting such a theoretical insight, we can conclude only that some common representational mechanism (code, process, or the like) must be postulated to account for the similar patterns of recall for concrete and abstract sentences, while insisting that different mechanisms, such as those assumed in dual-coding theory, must be retained to explain the differences.

Summary

The chapter has examined episodic memory in a variety of tasks, considering many variables of relevance to the three general approaches. Behavioral accounts direct us to such factors as the availability and response strength of single words and to the statistical structure of larger units. Linguistic accounts highlight surface and deep structure, transformational complexity, and the like. Cognitive accounts focus on various subjectively defined word attributes, such as image-arousing capacity, and on meaningful properties of entire messages. Memory is a complex business, and almost all studied variables have some effect. However, some variables turn out to be effective because of other, more basic ones. The most basic variable discovered to date is imagery. Imagery processes are especially useful in integrating separate units of presented information into a single memory unit, which can be variously described as an image, theme, meaning, schema, and so on. Regardless of the preferred language, it is clear that for concrete material the whole is greater than the sum of its parts. With more abstract material, results are usually consistent with sequentially structured memory traces, but there are important exceptions. That is, abstract material in some circumstances appears to be well integrated, for reasons that are not yet clear.

language production

9

We deal next with the analysis of speech production. The process of production is in a sense the reverse of comprehension, although this does not mean that entirely different mechanisms are used. Obviously production requires both episodic and semantic memory, particularly if memory is measured by verbal recall. Nonetheless, production and memory tasks are not entirely equivalent because the attention is on different variables. Production tasks emphasize word choice and the fluency of speech as measured in various ways. We shall again distinguish between linguistic, behavioral, and cognitive variables and approaches, at least to the extent that is permitted by the sparse literature on the subject.

Theoretical Orientations

Generative grammars by definition appear to be relevant to the problem of language production. The rewrite rules of phrase-structure grammar, for example, specify how a starting symbol is to be rewritten to produce acceptable sentences. It is very important to keep in mind, however, that Chomsky's approach is a theory of linguistic *competence*, not *performance*. The theory does describe a mechanism that could generate grammatical sentences from a finite set of symbols using formal rules, and speakers do perform in a way that suggests some knowledge of grammatical rules, but their performance also depends heavily upon other psychological factors such as their perception of the situational context, memory, and motivation. Thus linguistic competence models are bound to be limited explanations of the language productions of real speakers in real situations, and further, the theories were never developed with that aim in mind.

Behavioral theories are also directly relevant to language production. Skinner's operant approach, for example, is basically *about* production, that is, verbal behavior. The variables that affect production are the controlling variables for verbal operants. The operants show themselves as verbal responses that vary both in type and in measurable characteristics such as rate and other indexes of response strength. Creativity, the production of novel combinations of verbal responses, is a result of multiple causation, with many variables operating simultaneously on the speaker.

Speakers do not choose their words or the manner of producing them; verbal behavior is determined by the verbal reinforcement history and the situation of the moment, including already-generated speech. You can fill in the details by referring to the descriptions of the Skinnerian and other behavioral approaches in chapter 4.

Like the behavioral theories, cognitive approaches to language production emphasize the situational context, but unlike Skinner at least, they stress the importance of cognitive processes related to semantic memory, knowledge of the world, and imagery.

Linguistic and Associative Variables in Production

Much psycholinguistic research has examined the relation between linguistic variables and speech hesitations, including silent pauses, filled pauses such as "ahs," and various other speech nonfluencies.

Goldman-Eisler (1958) first showed that hesitations often precede a sudden increase of information (estimated in terms of the accuracy with which judges could guess the next words in a sentence, given another part of the sentence as a context). That is, subjects hesitated at points of uncertainty in the message. Tannenbaum, Williams, and Hillier (1965) also found that words after hesitations tended to be less predictable than words in fluent speech. In common-sense terms, such hesitations reflect points at which subjects paused to think about what to say next. These points did not coincide consistently with linguistic structure, although structure appeared to be one important factor. Maclay and Osgood (1959) similarly observed that hesitations coincided with points of uncertainty and that these were related to both phrase boundaries and lexical choices within boundaries. Filled pauses ("ums" and "ahs") tended to coincide with phrase boundaries, but silent pauses fell within phrases. Maclay and Osgood viewed the data as supporting two levels of organization in language and coding, namely, a lexical or semantic level and a grammatical or structural one. Boomer (1965) found that the number of hesitations was much higher in the position following the first word of a phrase unit than in other locations, when the phrase unit was defined in terms of stress patterns in speech. Martin (1967) found that the relation of hesitations to semantic and syntactic variables depended on the speech task. Some subjects described pictures, and others listened to those descriptions and then tried to reproduce them. The describers hesitated relatively more often before content words (indicating greater uncertainty in the lexical choice), and the reproducers hesitated relatively more often at sentence breaks.

Rochester and Gill (1973) studied filled pauses and other speech disruptions in monologues and dialogues. One interesting finding was that noun-phrase complements (*The fact that the woman was aggressive threatened the professors*) were more likely to be disrupted than sentences containing relative clauses (*The book that was written by Millet was lauded by all*). The investigators suggested that this finding may reflect either syntactic or semantic factors. For example, the transformations required may be more intricate in complement than in relative-clause constructions. Alternatively, complement constructions may be more difficult because they introduce a new concept, whereas relative clauses simply extend an already-developed concept. Another interesting finding was that dialogue sentences

were less likely to be disrupted than monologue sentences, and the patterning of disruptions was also relatively less affected by syntactic variables in the case of the dialogues. The dialogue-monologue differences indicate the importance of the situational context to speech production.

The above studies suggest that hesitations in speech are related to syntactic, semantic, and pragmatic factors, but the prediction of such phenomena is as yet quite uncertain, perhaps because their occurrence is related to emotional and motivational factors as well as to linguistic and cognitive ones (see Brenner, Feldstein, & Jaffe, 1965; Lay & Paivio, 1969; Mahl & Schulze, 1964; Reynolds & Paivio, 1968; Siegman & Pope, 1965).

Other studies using different behavioral measures have found both positive and negative evidence of the role of syntactic structure in generating sentences. Consistent with the early transformational view that kernel sentences are less complex than their transformations, Singh, Brokaw, and Black (1967) found that the oral reading of kernels was less disrupted by an interfering noise than were the transformations. On the other hand, Clark (1965), using such measures as the diversity of words that subjects used in generating sentences, found evidence that people did not generate passive sentences simply by transforming active ones. Instead, they apparently generated the sentences sequentially from left to right. Such studies reinforce the conclusion from the research on sentence comprehension and memory, namely that the transformational model does not yield psychological predictions that are consistently supported.

Some support for the idea that abstract grammatical categories may mediate sentence generation was obtained by Pylyshyn and Feldmar (1968). Words such as *cross*, which can be used as either nouns or verbs, were paired with nonsense words to which were added suitable noun endings (-ness, -ility) or verb endings (-ivate, -ilize). For example, *cross* would have been paired with DAXINESS for some subjects and with DAXIVATE for others. A test administered after the paired-associates learning of such pairs showed that the ambiguous words were used in sentences predominantly as words of the same part of speech as the associated nonsense word. That is, a word such as *cross* was relatively more likely to be used as a noun after having been associated with DAXINESS and as a verb after being associated with DAXIVATE. Although the experiment only considered individual words, Pylyshyn and Feldmar suggested that the idea might be applicable to larger grammatical units such as phrases. Thus the abstract symbols of generative grammars (NP, VP, and the like) might be viewed as functioning psychologically as mediators of language behavior.

The effects of verbal associations on speech production have also been demonstrated in a number of studies. One study was on pause patterns in free recall. When subjects recall a word list orally, they tend to speak the words in bursts. The words within bursts are often associatively related in some way. For example, a burst might include a series of words that are associated according to associative norms, category membership, and so on (for example, Pollio, Richards, & Lucas, 1969). This suggests that production mechanisms either include or are linked to structures organized along associative and semantic lines, since the results are analogous to the earlier results concerning statistical uncertainty.

Other evidence comes from sentence-production tasks. Prentice (1968) found that in a sentence-completion task, word associates were put into the same

sentence more often than nonassociates. Rosenberg (1967) asked subjects to write stories that included groups of associatively related or associatively unrelated nouns. Complex sentences produced by the subjects were analyzed into basic propositions. For example, the sentence *A needle, thread, and pin are helpful if you want to do sewing* would be reduced to four propositions: *A needle is helpful. A thread is helpful. A pin is helpful. You want to do some sewing.* The results showed that associatively related nouns that occurred in the same complex sentence were relatively more likely to appear as identical constituents in the same underlying sentences (that is, the related words were amenable to paradigmatic replacement), but that the unrelated nouns occurred relatively more often in different underlying sentences. These studies, like those reviewed earlier in connection with comprehension and memory, suggest that syntax and associative habits are related in a way that cannot be ignored in any theoretical account of linguistic structure.

Speech Errors

The conclusion that pauses in speech are thinking pauses suggests that speakers plan ahead in ordering their speech. This raises the question of how far ahead of the mouth the mind is. One major source of evidence comes from errors in speech, a topic that has recently received a growing amount of attention (see Fromkin, 1971, 1973; Garrett, 1975, 1976). For example, a statement attributed to Spooner (see further below) by Espy (1971, p. 230) is "it is kisstomary to cuss the bride," instead of "it is customary to kiss the bride." Exchanging *kiss* and *cuss* implies that the speech plan was several syllables ahead of the words actually spoken, since *kiss* appeared in speech several syllables before its intended place. The errors we shall consider allow several conclusions about the nature of speech production. We shall first present an overview of the conclusions, then discuss a few types of fairly common errors.

Overview

In order that the speech errors will not seem like interesting but isolated bits of verbal behavior, we shall outline a general context in which to view them and draw some general conclusions supported by the errors. First, there are some facts to be kept in mind by anyone constructing a model of speech production. For example, if words or fragments of words are interchanged, as they often are, we conclude that the later word was available mentally at the same time as the earlier one, with some selection occurring during the act of speaking. On the basis of evidence of this sort, several theorists have suggested stage theories of speech production. Garrett's (1975, 1976) theory is typical, so we shall summarize it briefly.

Garrett proposed that speakers first decide on a message, then decide on a syntactic outline (basically slots to put words in), then select content words (such as nouns, verbs, adjectives, and adverbs), then select affixes and function words, and finally produce speech. As you will see shortly, this outline is generally consistent with the errors produced in speech. For example, if *words* are interchanged with each other, the distance between them is usually longer than the distance between interchanged *sounds*, implying that words are available earlier than precise

pronunciations. Similarly, interchanges usually are nouns for nouns, and so on, suggesting that form-class decisions are made relatively early.

McNeill (1979) is critical of the stage approach, however. He notes that in a true stage theory, each stage would need to finish before the next one can start. Thus the meaning would be decided on before syntax, which in turn would be settled before sound, for the sentence to be uttered. He argues that the stages are not independent but rather, are interdependent, with activity going on at many levels, and concludes that speech is produced as it is organized.

Regardless of the particular view favored, it is clear that the mind is ahead of the mouth in many ways. Consequently, speech planning should be conceived as being flexible in terms of how far ahead it goes and what unit is considered. As with other areas we have discussed, speech production is a complex business (see Danks, 1977), especially in spontaneous speech between people, an area recently investigated by Duncan and Fiske (1977).

Classification of errors

As you might guess, there are several different classifications of speech errors. The classification adopted here is a blend of Fromkin's (1971) and Garrett's (1975) classifications, and most examples are chosen from their presentations.

1. Exchanges. There is an exchange if two linguistic units are interchanged with each other. Exchanges occur at several different levels of production. The most widely known errors are *Spoonerisms* (also called oonerspisms), in which words and parts of words are exchanged. Thus "dear old queen" becomes "queer old dean" and "bite your tongue" becomes "tight your bung." Sometimes whole morphemes are exchanged (kisstomary to cuss the bride); sometimes only syllables are exchanged; and sometimes the exchange affects a very basic feature such as voicing (clear blue sky becomes glear plue sky). Exchanges can occur over several syllables, as in the above examples, or they can be closer together (store close becomes clore stose). Some occur within words (aminal, revelant). Thus exchanges seem to be on many different linguistic levels. Let us comment generally on exchanges and what they tell us.

First, Garrett (1975) observed that if words are exchanged, they are usually some distance apart and are the same part of speech, but if sounds are exchanged, they tend to be close together and are between different parts of speech. Thus it appears that the speech plan for words is earlier in the planning sequence than the plan for sounds. Second, because there are so many different types of exchanges, it seems that the speech plan is quite versatile, capable of incorporating information from many levels. Thus the picture is one in which speech is organized on many levels, and further, some of the units of speech that will appear later in the speech stream are cognitively available earlier on, even to the extent of interfering or competing with the intended units (see Baars & Motley, 1976; MacKay, 1970).

2. Shifts. Shifts occur if a fragment of one word appears somewhere else in the speech sequence. Some shifts are *anticipations*, as when "take my bike" comes out as "bake my bike," with the *b-* coming earlier than intended. Some other

shifts are *perseverations*, the reverse of anticipations, as in "take my tike," with reference to the preceding example. Still others simply move a single fragment, as in "he get its done" instead of "he gets it done." You can probably think of cases in which you have done the same thing. As a personal example, one of the authors (Paivio) recently asked for "smoyked oysters." As with exchanges, shifts tell us that speech is not simply a word-at-a-time plodding activity but rather, the mind skips ahead, sometimes well in advance of the mouth.

3. Others. Although there are many other types of errors, we shall mention them just briefly for your interest, because they do not add much to the general conclusions. *Malapropisms* are often used as humor, as when Archie Bunker refers to a "groinocologist," but also occur whenever any of us uses an incorrect word in place of a correct one. Most such errors resemble the right word in its stress pattern and number of syllables. Some even seem like improvements, like "civil serpents" or "pipsquirt," but others simply reflect a lack of knowledge of correct words, as when "deprecate" is used for "depreciate," "flagrant" for "fragrant," "relegate" for "delegate," and so on. *Haplologies* refer to the dropping out of part of a word or phrase, as when "probably" is pronounced "probly," "quarter to four" is reduced to "quarta four," and so on. Many simply reflect laziness, but others reflect more fundamental processes. *Blends* occur if two words are crunched together, as when "detest" and "destiny" become "detestiny," or "semantics" and "syntax" becomes "semantax" (actually, this one is intentional; see Ross, 1975). Again, you have probably done this yourself, perhaps as a child (did you ever say "butcept," or anything similar?). Finally, there are temporary *semantic accidents*, as when we say "love" for "hate," "open" for "close," and generally use a related word by mistake.

Cognitive Factors in Language Generation

This section discusses the effect of semantic factors—particularly knowledge of the world, imagery, and situational context—on fluency and lexical choice in speech. We begin with effects related to knowledge of the world and imagery.

Common-sense observations suggest that spontaneous descriptive speech is often mediated by nonverbal memories of the concrete objects and events being described. The general point has been made repeatedly in other chapters, but as a reminder of what is meant in the present context, you might try describing the inside of your house—the rooms, doorways, windows, furniture, and so on—to someone and noting the nature of your thoughts while doing so. It is very likely that imagery is prominent in generating the description. Let us review some studies that touch on this general problem.

Goldman-Eisler (1961), whose research was introduced earlier, reported an experiment in which individuals were shown humorous *New Yorker* cartoons, which are noted for their subtle point or moral. When the subject had "got the point," he or she was required to describe the contents of the story depicted by the cartoons and then to formulate concisely the general point, meaning, or moral of the story. The relevant feature of this procedure is that it varies the abstractness of the verbal task, namely in the descriptions of concrete events on the

one hand and in the generalizations abstracted from them on the other. The major finding was that there were more pauses during the generalizations than during the descriptions. In other words, concrete speech was less hesitant and more fluent than abstract speech.

Goldman-Eisler's findings were repeated and extended by Lay and Paivio (1969). The speech tasks they required their subjects to perform had three levels of difficulty, including self-descriptions (name, sex, age, and so on), cartoon descriptions, and interpretation and evaluation of pairs of proverbs, such as "You cannot make a silk purse out of a sow's ear" and "Where there is a will, there is a way." These were regarded as increasing in generality and abstractness from the self-descriptions to the proverb task. The results showed that hesitations in speech were least frequent in the self-descriptions, intermediate in the cartoon descriptions, and highest in the proverb task. Thus, speech generation became more hesitant and less fluent as the verbal task became more abstract. Precise interpretation of the results is difficult, however, because abstractness was confounded with other variables. For one thing, self-descriptions required relatively automatic speech, that is, overlearned intraverbal sequences, which implicate strong associative habits; for another, the cartoon task differed qualitatively from the others in that cartoons are nonverbal stimuli.

Reynolds and Paivio (1968) studied the effects of abstractness-concreteness, among other variables, on speech generation using only words as stimuli. Their subjects were shown, one at a time, five concrete and five abstract nouns, which they defined orally. Analysis of the definitions showed that the concrete words, relative to the abstract ones, elicited longer definitions, with faster initiation of the definitions, fewer unfilled pauses, and fewer nonfluencies of other types. In brief, the concrete words generated more fluent speech than did the abstract words.

Reynolds's and Paivio's findings were generally congruent with an earlier finding that concrete words evoke faster associative reactions than do abstract ones (Paivio, 1966), especially under imagery instructions as compared with verbal associative instructions. Thus, the differences observed by Reynolds and Paivio in the definition task are more like results in the reaction-time task with imagery instructions than they are with verbal associative instructions. Although this suggestion needs to be tested further with new experiments, the data from the different studies are consistent with the interpretation that concrete words generated more fluent definitions because they evoked nonverbal images that played a part in mediating the verbal output. The results parallel those obtained with the descriptions of cartoons as compared with the more abstract interpretation and proverb tasks in the Goldman-Eisler and the Lay and Paivio experiments.

Reynolds and Paivio also provided information about the role of verbal associative processes in the definition task. Subjects were identified as high or low on associative productivity according to the average number of written associations they gave to stimulus words in a preliminary test. The results of the definition experiment showed that the definitions given by the high-associative-productivity participants contained more words, had faster starting latencies, and were more fluent than those of the low-productivity subjects. The definitions given by the high-productivity subjects were also judged to be better definitions of the concepts. These differences are particularly interesting because the two groups were originally distinguished on the basis of a *written* association test, whereas the experi-

mental task used *oral* production of natural, grammatical speech. Thus the results apparently reflect the influence of individual differences on rather general verbal productive skills.

A dual-coding interpretation

The above findings generally can be interpreted within the framework of dual-coding theory. The concrete descriptive tasks and definitions can be viewed as having a high degree of referential exchange between the verbal and image systems. Cartoons directly activate the image system, but concrete words do so indirectly. In either case, the descriptions or definitions presumably are based on perceptual or perceptual-memory information, which activates relevant descriptive terms in the verbal system. The relative fluency and, to some extent, the grammatical ordering may be a result of the simultaneous availability of complex images relevant to the tasks. The more abstract interpretations and definitions presumably use the verbal system to a relatively greater degree. To the extent that this is so, the fluency of verbal output would depend on the availability and length of sequentially organized verbal chunks in long-term memory (as measured, for example, by associative fluency tests). The greater hesitancy of speech during the more abstract task suggests that those mediating chunks are generally smaller than in the case of descriptions.

Further information on the role of imagery in sentence production was obtained in a series of experiments by A. Segal (1976; see Paivio, 1975b). The relevant studies presented subjects with sets of two, three, or four unrelated concrete words, abstract words, or pictures, with instructions to make up sentences using the given set of items. Thus, a participant might be given the words *house, apple,* and *pencil.* Sentence generation was somewhat faster with concrete than with abstract words when three or four words had to be combined in the sentence. This finding suggested that the image system plays a positive role in planning and generating descriptive sentences about concrete objects and events, just as we have argued above.

The plausibility of such an interpretation was examined by comparing pictures and words as stimuli. The theoretical arguments and expectations went as follows: If we assume that sentences describing the arrangements of concrete objects are generated entirely by a linguistic mechanism of some kind, then sentences should be generated faster for words than for pictures because words have more direct access to the linguistic system. A second possibility is that the cognitive representation is in some kind of abstract format that is neither pictorial nor verbal (see the earlier discussions of such theories in connection with comprehension and memory). If so, the encoding time should be essentially the same for the two kinds of stimuli except for any initial difference in the time it takes to identify the individual items perceptually. The third hypothesis is the dual-coding one, according to which a concrete sentence describes perceptual information after it has been represented and organized in the imagery system. It follows that pictures would have the advantage over words even in sentence generation, particularly when there are many items, and it is accordingly difficult to organize them meaningfully.

The test of these alternatives compared concrete words with line drawings of the corresponding objects. Subjects were shown two, three, or four items of either type and were asked to construct meaningful sentences using the items. When they

had the sentence in mind, they pressed a key and then wrote down the sentence. The resulting reaction times to the point at which writing began are plotted in Figure 9-1. The illustration shows that generation latencies did not differ with only two items, but latencies were faster for pictures than words when three or four items were presented. These results suggest that the pictures activated the processes necessary for generating a descriptive sentence more directly or efficiently than did words. This is consistent with the above suggestion that a significant part of the informational substrate for descriptive sentences is to be found in the imagery system. McNeill's (1979) notion of sensory-motor ideas (see chapter 10) is also consistent with the interpretation.

Cognitive effects on lexical choice

In chapter 5 we discussed Olson's (1970) cognitive theory of meaning, according to which the choice of what words to use depends primarily on the speaker's knowledge of the intended referent. Semantic decisions of this kind are made in order to distinguish an intended referent from some perceived or inferred set of alternatives. This means that the choice of words in language production is determined largely by the situational context.

Osgood (1971) investigated how the form and content of utterances are influenced by such nonlinguistic situational variables. The study, with the provocative title "Where Do Sentences Come From?" concerned descriptive sentences produced under naturalistic conditions. The subjects were shown a series of demonstrations using a variety of objects (balls of different colors and sizes, plates, tubes, poker chips, and so on). The content and sequence of the demonstrations were

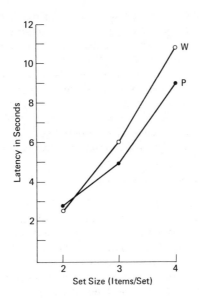

FIGURE 9-1. Reaction times for generating sentences from sets of 2, 3, and 4 pictures (P) or words (W).

designed with "psycholinguistic malice aforethought," that is, to induce certain presuppositions, to provide for both implicit contrasts over time and explicit contrasts over space, and so forth. Osgood's basic idea was that the demonstrations could create cognitive presuppositions in much the same way as previously heard or spoken sentences do. He contended that such nonlinguistic antecedents can "drive" the form and content of descriptive sentences.

For each demonstration, the subjects were told to describe the perceptual event or events in a single sentence that a hypothetical six-year-old "just outside the door and not able to see what is happening" could understand. Some of the demonstrations were designed to study the effect of preceding contexts on the use of indefinite and definite articles. Osgood reasoned that novel items would trigger an identifying tendency that would be reflected in the speaker's use of the indefinite article, "a." When that same item had been seen successively over different scenes, the speaker presumably would become familiar with the object and would show this by an increase in the use of the definite article "the." Such effects did occur. Determiners shifted abruptly from the indefinite *a* to definite *the* when there was an immediate reappearance of an object, and tended to shift back toward *a* as a function of delays in the reappearance of the object over demonstrations.

Other demonstrations were designed to induce shifts from the use of object names to pronouns. Such pronominalization required that the entities enter into more than one action or state or relation within the same demonstration. Examples of sentences describing such situations are *The man bounced the ball and it hit the plate* and *A ball is on a tube which is standing on a plate.* Each complex sentence shows the shift to a pronoun in the second half. Still other demonstrations influenced the richness of adjectival qualification in noun phrases and other aspects of description.

Some of Osgood's hypotheses were not confirmed. For example, demonstrations designed to induce the use of passive constructions or center embeddings did not have significant effects, perhaps because such constructions (particularly center embeddings) are rare in ordinary descriptive speech.

The important general conclusion from Osgood's study is that lexical choices with grammatical functions cannot be predicted entirely on the basis of a syntactic theory. Instead, certain constructions are strongly influenced by the temporal sequence of events and the spatial relations among objects in the situation in which descriptive speech occurs. The productive choices, in other words, are determined partly by pragmatic and general cognitive factors.

Cognitive effects on syntactic order

Languages differ in their syntactic rules, which manifest themselves as sequential grammatical habits. For example, nouns and their modifiers are typically expressed in the adjective-noun order in English, but noun-adjective sequences are more common in French. Again, although passive and active constructions are appropriate in English, the passive voice is not used very often (for example, Svartvic, 1966). There are numerous language-specific syntactic regularities or preferences of this kind. However, except when the sequence is completely fixed, the preferred order can be modified by cognitive factors.

The sequential ordering of adjectives is one illustration of such flexibility.

The sequential order of adjectives is generally constrained in English as in other languages (Martin, 1969; Danks & Glucksberg, 1971). Thus adjectives referring to size generally precede adjectives describing color. These in turn precede adjectives that refer to place or origin. For example, people prefer to say *The large red Turkish truck* rather than *The Turkish red large truck,* and find the latter peculiar. The fact that many different languages show the same sequential preferences suggests that semantic or pragmatic factors may be operating. Martin (1969) and Danks and Glucksberg (1971) found that adjective order in fact correlates with certain semantic properties of adjectives (ses also Richards, 1977). However, Danks and Glucksberg (1971) suggest that the semantic effect may be a more general case of a pragmatic communication rule, which states that the more informative adjectives generally come first. This effect can be seen in instances in which the usual ordering of adjectives is reversed. For example, we normally say *The large red car.* If we see two cars, one large and red and the other large and blue, however, we might prefer to say *The red large car* in order to emphasize the property that distinguishes the two, in this case color rather than size.

Osgood and Bock (1975) investigated specific hypotheses or principles in the ordering of elements in sentence production. These are *naturalness, vividness,* and *motivation of speaker.* The assumption underlying the principle of naturalness is one already familiar to us from earlier discussions, namely, that comprehension and production of sentences depend on cognitive structures that derive from perceptually based experiences. In action relations, for example, the actors and their actions are perceptually more salient than the recipients, so that the natural linguistic order will be ACTOR-ACTION-RECIPIENT.

The vividness principle states that meaning components that include more polarized (extreme) semantic codings, particularly on the dominant affective features of evaluation, potency, and activity, will tend to be processed more quickly; hence, the constituents in which they are expressed will tend to appear earlier in sentence production.

Speaker motivation refers particularly to individual differences in the degree of motivation or concern that is attributed to a meaning component by a speaker. The more motivation attributed to a meaning component, the earlier the constituent expressing the component is likely to come in the utterance.

The authors provide some supporting evidence for each of the three principles. The vividness principle is most relevant to the present context, so we shall summarize their research evidence for its significance in sentence production. Osgood and Bock used optional transformations as their testing ground so that vividness could have an effect on which grammatical option would be chosen. To achieve this end, they constructed complex, two-clause sentences that varied in clause type but whose clauses would admit operational transformation. The vividness of the constituents was varied by interchanging words having either high or low affective intensity as determined by judges' ratings. Thus *fairy tale* and *orphans* were judged to be higher in vividness than *story* and *children,* respectively. Examples of cases in which these components occur as direct and indirect objects in different combinations of high and low vividness are *The nurse told a fairy tale to the children* (high-low) and *The nurse told a story to the orphans* (low-high).

In one part of the experiment, subjects were required to construct sentences using clause pairs and a conjoiner (*and, but, although,* and the like). The prediction

was that the more vivid constituents within the clauses should tend to precede the less vivid, even when subjects had to invert the input sequence in order to construct such a sentence. The prediction tended to be confirmed in that more inversion shifts in the constituent orderings occurred for low-high than for high-low clauses.

The above results are open to a slightly different interpretation. The vividness hypothesis is similar to the conceptual peg hypothesis of imagery effects in associative learning (Paivio, 1963). Recall that this hypothesis states that high-imagery stimuli are better retrieval cues for low-imagery associates than vice versa. Perhaps there is a similar effect in a sentence-production task, such as the one used by Osgood and Bock. That is, subjects may tend to place the more vivid clause constituent before the less vivid one because it is a good conceptual peg for planning the sentence. The hypothesis is similar to Osgood's and Bock's except that they differentiate between vividness and imagery. They cite a sentence recall study by James, Thompson, and Baldwin (1973), in which subjects were more likely to shift from active to passive when the surface-structure object was higher in imagery value than was the surface subject. Osgood and Bock suggest that this effect may be a memory effect and that without the mediation of memory, imagery may not correlate well with their notion of vividness. The word *car*, for example, is high in imagery value but not particularly vivid, whereas the reverse is true for *atrocity*. This is undoubtedly correct, since imagery value is essentially uncorrelated with the connotative dimensions of the semantic differential (Paivio, 1968), but imagery may still have played a role in the production-inversion effects observed by Osgood and Bock. It would be simple and interesting to test this idea by comparing the effects of the imagery and vividness of the constituents in that experiment.

Summary

Language production has been studied in terms of variables that affect the fluency and selective content of the verbal output. Fluency is measured by how much is said or written in a given period of time and by the temporal patterning of pauses and nonfluencies of various kinds. Selective effects show up in the words chosen and in the sequence in which the words are emitted. The research to date has indicated that fluency and selection are related to syntactic and semantic variables but that they are also affected strongly by pragmatic factors implicating complex relations between the speaker and the verbal and nonverbal context in which speaking takes place. In brief, what is said and how fluently it is said depend on the speaker's grammatical, associative, and cognitive abilities as well as on the demands and restrictions imposed by the communicational situation.

In addition to summarizing, we should inject a note of caution. Speech production is not a well-studied area yet, so most conclusions should be held tentatively and not generalized too far. For example, overextending Osgood's and Bock's (1975) work would lead us to expect all languages to be produced in subject-verb-object order, which is not true. Similarly, overextending the dual-coding approach might make you think it is impossible to speak about abstract things; it is not—hard maybe, but not impossible. Future research is sorely needed.

language acquisition

10

This chapter extends our application of the behavioral, linguistic, and cognitive approaches to the problem of acquiring language, especially vocabulary, meaning, and grammar. The acquisition of phonology is equally important, but we shall have less to say about it partly because less psychological research has been done in this area than in the others. The interested student can find more extensive treatment of phonological and other aspects of language development in other sources (for example, E. V. Clark, 1977; Dale, 1976). Before turning to the theoretical approaches, we shall present a descriptive overview of the course of language development and some of the issues that arise from such observations.

DESCRIPTIVE OVERVIEW OF LANGUAGE DEVELOPMENT

Naturalistic observation and experimental methods have been used to arrive at a developmental picture of language. Many students of language have observed and described the speech of their children, beginning with the earliest sounds and continuing over a period of some years. Initially rather informal and unsystematic, such studies later became increasingly systematic in that the observers made careful note of the situational context in which the recorded utterances occurred. Some researchers added control procedures in which the child is placed in a particular situation, perhaps interacting with the mother in specified ways or playing with other children. These controlled observational studies become experiments if the experimenter systematically manipulates the stimulus conditions that elicit speech or other behaviors that permit the observer to assess the child's language comprehension. Experimenters have also used artificial language materials consisting of nonsense words, perhaps combined with real words and grammatical morphemes from the child's native language.

It would be ideal if the descriptive picture that emerges from such observations could be purely factual, uninfluenced by any theoretical preconceptions, but that is impossible. In order to describe anything as complex as language, we must be able to identify the relevant units of the phenomenon and to classify them

in some way. How we classify or categorize depends on our theoretical assumptions. For historical reasons, language development is usually described in terms of the units and categories of linguistic theory (for example, E. V. Clark, 1977). Thus we refer to the sequence of acquisition of phonemes, morphemes, word classes, types of phrases and sentences, and the like. Transformational grammar and its offshoots lead researchers to describe acquisition in terms of linguistic competence, underlying structures, types of transformations, and case grammar categories. We should recognize, however, that such concepts are more inferential than descriptive—we do not *observe* underlying structures, we *infer* them from language behavior in a particular situation, and we do so only if our theoretical approach is based on such concepts. Some psychological approaches suggest entirely different descriptive models. For example, we could adopt the functional categories of Skinner's approach to verbal behavior and describe the course of language development in terms of the emergence of mands, tacts, echoics, and so on. We shall follow convention, however, and cast our description primarily in the mold of various linguistic categories.

The Developmental Sequence

It has been suggested that infants produce vocal sounds appropriate to all human languages (for example, Osgood, 1953). This may be an exaggeration for any given child, but it is true that infants start out with a large repertoire of articulatory patterns. The initial repertoire gradually changes so that some sounds (phonemes or potential phonemes) decrease in frequency and others increase in frequency. Descriptively, we observe *selection* and *emphasis* in the vocal patterns, which become increasingly like the speech sounds produced by the adults in the child's language community. The understanding of the mechanisms and processes responsible for these changes is a very fundamental issue confronting students of language development.

The following summarizes the typical background sequence (for more complete descriptions, see any text on language development; for example, E. V. Clark, 1977; Dale, 1976; DiVesta, 1974): During the infant period, from birth to about six months, the child produces a variety of sounds, such as cries, grunts, shrieks, chuckling, and cooing. This is followed by the *babbling period*, extending from about six to nine months, during which the child begins to produce sound sequences that vary across situations and are often repetitive. These patterns sometimes resemble words (for example, "mamama"), and they become increasingly wordlike as the period progresses. This trend continues so that at about nine months, the infant produces strings of utterances with adultlike patterns of stress and intonation, sometimes in an imitative manner. Such imitation becomes characteristic of the child's utterances at about nine to twelve months, the *echolalic period*.

Words usually begin to emerge between one and two years of age. This phase is sometimes called the *holophrastic period* because the child uses single words as though they were phrases or sentences that express complex ideas. For example, "ball" may mean that the child wants the ball or wants someone to look at it, depending on the context. At this stage, children appear to understand more than they can say, although vocabulary size begins to increase rapidly toward the end of the holophrastic period, from an average of about twenty words at eighteen

months to three hundred words at twenty-four months. The acceleration in word development increases after two years, so that at age three, vocabulary size is nearly one thousand words and perhaps more, because single words are used with varying intonations. At the same time, the child begins to combine words into short utterances that differ from adult speech in ways described more fully below.

The *sentence period* begins at about three years, when the child begins to use sentences that have grammatical features corresponding to adult language. The grammar is incomplete, however, often lacking function words and grammatical inflections. The resulting speech is sometimes called *telegraphic speech* because it resembles telegrams in which nonessential words are omitted in the interests of economy.

From three to five years, the child produces sentences of all types. Many of these are incomplete in terms of adult grammars, and some sentences are not understandable. The variety, length, and complexity of the sentences continue to increase from five years to maturity, and vocabulary growth may continue to old age. We now turn to a more detailed description of some of the notable aspects of language development.

Length of utterances

Roger Brown (for example, 1973) of Harvard University has described the quantitative development of language during the early years as measured by the *mean length of utterance* (MLU). The MLU reflects the average length of a recorded sample of utterances. It is calculated by the number of morphemes rather than by words, so that the measure will reflect the rate of increase in the use of such inflectional markers as the plural *-s* and the past tense *-ed*. Brown and his students applied the measure to the speech of three children (Adam, Eve, and Sarah) whom they studied longitudinally. The MLU revealed the different rates of the children's development. For example, Eve attained an MLU of 4.0 at about twenty-six months, but the other two children reached that level only at forty-two months. Brown found it convenient to express development as MLU "stages" that reflect important changes in performance. Thus Stage I, when the MLU ranges between 1.0 and 2.0 morphemes, is characterized by the occurrence of the first multiword utterances. Stages II, III, and IV add increments of 1.5 to the MLU and are associated with utterances of increasing complexity.

Characteristics of one-word utterances

The first words of the infant are generally concrete nouns, like the names of people or pets and general object names like *milk, cup,* and *cat*. Adjectives and verbs that name familiar actions are also acquired early, with abstract words and function words generally emerging after the infant has a concrete vocabulary. As already noted, single words seem to function essentially like phrases or sentences with different meanings, which is why such utterances are called holophrastic speech. You should be aware that this label goes beyond simple description—we observe only a spoken word and the situation in which it occurs. Because the situation varies, we infer that the infants are using the word in somewhat different ways. Investigators try to make some theoretical sense out of that variety by systematically classifying and interpreting the various occurrences on the basis of

clues provided by the context. This approach has been called the *method of rich interpretation* (Bloom, 1970). We shall see later that the interpretations can be quite controversial.

Two-word utterances

Somewhere between eighteen months and two years of age, the child begins to use two-word utterances. These utterances have been classified in different ways. Braine (1963) used a simple grammar called *pivot grammar*, in which the two words are divided into *pivot* and *open* classes according to certain criteria. Pivots are a small class of words that occur often and the open class is large but such words occur less often. Thus, in the utterance *want ball, want milk*, and *want shoe, want* is a pivot, and *ball, milk*, and *shoe* are open class words. Other criteria are that pivot words have fixed positions (a given pivot tends to occur only in the first position, as with *want* in the above examples, or only in the second position, as with *on* in examples like *blanket on* or *take on*), and can occur only in combination with open class words. Open class words, in contrast, can stand alone or combine with each other in any order. Thus the grammar generates the following permissible sequences: P_1+O, O+P_2, O+O, and O, in which P_1 and P_2 are pivot words that can occur in first and second positions and O refers to open class words.

We shall examine evidence for pivot grammar in the section on linguistic approaches. Suffice it to say now that it is difficult to divide words reliably into pivot and open classes on the basis of any of the suggested criteria, and the scheme does not account adequately for two-word utterances (for example, Bloom, 1970; Bowerman, 1973). Consequently, other classification schemes have been suggested. Brown (1970) proposed a description using the *structural meanings* (semantic relations) of two-word phrases of MLU Stage I children. The scheme is summarized in Table 10-1.

TABLE 10-1 Structural Meanings in Two-word Utterances

Structural Meaning	Form	Example
1. Nomination (naming)	that + noun	that car
2. Notice	hi + noun	hi spoon
3. Recurrence	{ more / another } + noun	more milk
4. Nonexistence (negation)	{ all gone / no more } + noun	all gone kitty
5. Attribution	adjective + noun	pretty boat
6. Possession	{ noun / pronoun } + noun	baby book
7. Location	{ noun / verb } + noun	baby room / walk street
8. Agent-Action	noun + verb	Eve read
9. Agent-Object	noun + noun	Mommy sock
10. Action-Object	verb + noun	pull hat

Adapted from R. Brown (1970) and other sources.

Note that pivot grammar and the structural meaning scheme are linguistic approaches since they can be expressed as generative grammars. The approaches illustrate again how description is influenced by theoretical concepts. You can readily appreciate the general point by trying to apply other conceptual models to children's two-word utterances. For example, according to Skinner's functional categories, *want milk* as a response to an adult asking "More milk?" would be at least partly an echoic. The precise descriptive label would depend on knowledge of the antecedent conditions and the present situation. For example, the occurrence of "more milk" might also mean that the child is still thirsty, in which case the utterance is partly a mand. Which descriptive scheme is most useful depends on how well they account for the child's language and fit into the general theoretical approach adopted by the researchers.

Two-word utterances show the productive use of language more clearly than do single words. For example, the consistent occurrence of certain kinds of words in the same position (*allgone kitty, allgone Daddy*) suggests that the child is well on the way to acquiring word classes, with specific class members being selected in a creative way according to varying circumstances. The inferred productivity or creativity of such word combinations is supported by several kinds of evidence, including their variability and the fact that many are unlike the combinations that are spoken by adults in the child's environment.

Development of syntax

The idea that young children acquire grammatical rules is also inferential. What we actually observe is that the child uses the word order, inflections, and other grammatical morphemes that characterize adult language. We say that rules have been acquired when the child consistently combines words in sequences that can be described by grammatical rules. The importance of word order in English is already apparent with two-word utterances, as indicated by the contrast between noun-verb order in agent-action relationships and verb-noun order in action-object relationships. Order becomes increasingly important with longer strings. For example, subject-predicate relations are indicated by order, as in the distinction between *John chased the dog* and *The dog chased John*. Children must learn those distinctions if they are to produce sensible utterances or understand what is said to them.

Children also must learn to use articles, prepositions, and inflections that indicate different syntactic and semantic roles of words. English inflections include modifications of pronouns (*they* versus *them*), noun plurality (*girl* versus *girls, child* versus *children*), possession (*Mommy's*), verb tense (*lift* versus *lifted*), and verb number (she *runs* versus they *run*). Some other languages make even greater use of inflections. For example, Finnish nouns take sixteen different case endings that correspond to the functions of prepositions in English, as well as having inflections for plurality, number, tense, possession, and questions. Russian is also a highly inflected language.

English-speaking children rely mainly on word order for indicating syntactic structure, and they rarely depart from the word order normally used to express semantic relations. For example, when they ask for a book to be read, they are more likely to say *read book* than *book read*. This is not necessarily so in highly inflected languages. For example, Bowerman (1973) found that one of two Finnish

children that she studied used the subject-verb-object (SVO) order most frequently but that the other child used SVO and SOV about equally often.

English-speaking children begin to use inflections toward the end of Stage I (MLU 2.0), and the process of learning is a long one, extending beyond the stage at which the MLU reaches 4.0. It is particularly interesting that although the three children studied by Brown (1973) began to use particular inflections and other grammatical morphemes at different ages, they acquired the morphemes in almost the same order. For example, the present progressive *-ing* was acquired first, followed by the prepositions *on* and *in*, the plural *-s*, the past irregular, the possessive *-'s* and so on. In other words, there is a striking regularity in the order of acquiring inflections. The order appears to be partly, but not entirely, predictable from indices of the grammatical and semantic complexity of the different morphemes (Brown, 1973).

Although comparisons with other languages are difficult, it seems to be the case that regularity of acquisition is also the rule in other languages. For example, in Russian (see Dale, 1976; Slobin, 1966a), plurals are generally learned early, followed by cases, persons of the verb, possessive and progressive, and finally, gender (Russian has three types of grammatical gender markers, masculine, feminine, and neuter, which apply to nouns as well as to their modifiers). A generalization that seems to apply to various languages is that suffixes are acquired earlier than prefixes or prepositions that refer to comparable meanings (Dale, 1976, p. 46).

The development of inflections includes one of the most interesting and common features of syntactic acquisition, namely, the *overgeneralization* or *overregularization* of inflectional rules. For example, strong verbs like *do, come,* and *go* have irregular past tense inflections (*did, came,* and *went*). These verbs occur in parental speech much more often than regular verbs, and presumably as a consequence, children use the irregular tense forms correctly before they learn the past tense of regular verbs like *walked* and *washed*. After some months of exposure to the regular forms, the child begins to use them with all verbs. Thus the irregular verbs that had previously been used correctly now become *doed, comed,* and *goed.* The correct forms are dropped for a time, or both the correct and incorrect forms may occur in the child's speech. The same phenomenon occurs with the plural (*mice* becomes *mouses, geese* becomes *gooses*) and other inflections. Once children have learned regular inflections that apply to many words, they overgeneralize the rule to all instances. As would be expected, overgeneralization is very common in highly inflected languages such as Russian. The phenomenon is interesting because it poses a problem for theories of language acquisition. In particular, why would a child who has already learned the irregular inflections of strong verbs suddenly seem to "unlearn" these forms and replace them by the regular inflections of weak verbs, once the latter have been mastered to some degree? No good answer is available at this time.

Negations and questions

The development of negative utterances and questions is interesting because they are semantically and syntactically more complex than simple descriptions. For example, according to the design features of language discussed in chapter 2, both involve displacement in that they refer to states of affairs differing in some way from the current concrete situation—an absent referent (*no hot, where Daddy go?*),

missing information (*what dat?*), and so on. Syntactically, they undergo various transformations, such as the addition of appropriate morphemes (*no, not;* the wh- words *who, what, where, when, why*; auxiliaries like *do, can*, and *will*) and modifications of word order (*Mommy doing that* versus *what Mommy doing?*). The situations that call for the use of negations and questions can be very complex, requiring the child simultaneously to take account of what someone else says, the existing situation, and perhaps the child's or someone else's prior behavior in that situation or some other one. Consider, for example, what the child must grasp in order to answer such a simple question as "Did you eat the cookie that was here?"

Negations and questions develop largely, though not entirely, in parallel. During Stage I the earliest negations are one-word or two-word utterances that appear to express the semantic functions of *nonexistence* of some object (*allgone milk*), *rejection* of someone else's proposal (*no meat*), and *denial* of the truth of what someone else has said (*no Daddy hungry* in response to "Daddy's hungry") (Bloom, 1970). The negative element generally is at the beginning of such utterances. Later, between Stages II and III, the utterances are more complete and the negative generally is between the subject and the verb (*He not little, he not big*). Auxiliary verbs also occur in some utterances (*I don't want some soup*), although Bellugi (1967; cited in Foss & Hakes, 1978, p. 256) has suggested that children at this stage are not really using auxiliary verbs. The evidence for this inference is that the auxiliary verbs *do* and *can* generally occur only in negative utterances and not in affirmative ones (*don't* and *can't* occur, but *do* and *can* do not) and that they occur in inappropriate contexts. Thus *don't* and *can't* appear to be alternative ways of saying no.

Both negative and positive utterances containing true auxiliaries begin to appear rather quickly and in great variety during Stage IV. These consist of such adultlike utterances as *This doesn't work, I'm not a turtle*, and *That will make me happy*. There still are errors, especially in the more complex negative forms, but the negation of simple sentences appears to be fairly complete at this stage which, for different children, ranges from two years to about three and a half years of age.

Questions are similarly rather restricted in variety during Stage I, with yes/no questions generally indicated by rising intonation (*see hold?* and *Mommy eggnog?*) and wh- questions by a few more-or-less fixed forms (*What dat? Where Daddy going?*). Stages II and III include apparent auxiliaries in positive questions (*Who is it?*) and negative ones (*You can't fix it?*). Stage IV shows the same striking development of use of auxiliaries in questions as in negations but primarily so in the case of yes/no questions. In wh- questions, auxiliary verbs are often absent, and when they do occur they are generally not inverted with the subject of the utterance. Thus one hears *What he can ride in?* rather than *What can he ride in?* This lag may reflect the greater linguistic complexity of wh- questions than of yes/no questions and negative sentences.

Comprehension versus Production

It is generally assumed language comprehension precedes production, since children are able to respond appropriately to some questions and assertions before they are able to speak. For example, if a parent says "Where's kitty?" the child might behave as though looking for the cat. The interesting question, however, is

whether the child must be able to understand each aspect of language, such as a particular syntactic form, before being able to produce it. The question has proved to be surprisingly difficult to answer, largely because of the difficulties in defining comprehension and production. The problem of defining these concepts, already discussed generally in earlier chapters, is accentuated in young children who have little or no speech. Comprehension may have to be inferred entirely from nonverbal responses, which reflect much more than the child's understanding of a particular utterance. Production, too, depends upon the cues used to elicit speech. For example, imitation, answering questions, and naming or describing objects all are examples of production, but the eliciting stimuli are quite different, and the processes governing production might differ accordingly. When such factors are taken into account, it turns out that comprehension does not always precede production.

Fraser, Bellugi, and Brown (1963) conducted the first systematic experiment on the problem with children between thirty-seven and forty-three months old. The experimenters used a test designed to measure imitation, comprehension, and production skills. This ICP test consisted of presenting a child with a pair of sentences that contrasted on a particular grammatical feature. For example, *The girl is cooking* and *The girl is not cooking* contrast on the affirmative-negative feature. Other sentences differed on features such as singular versus plural and subject versus object. A total of ten different contrasts were tested. These are listed in Table 10-2 along with example sentences. A matching picture was prepared for each sentence. Thus, for the above example, one picture showed a girl cooking, and the other depicted the girl doing something else.

The imitation task used only sentences. The experimenter read each sentence of a pair aloud and asked the child to repeat it. In the comprehension test, the experimenter showed two pictures and recited the corresponding pair of sentences. Then the experimenter read one of the sentences and asked the child to point to the appropriate picture. Then the other sentence was read, and the child again pointed to the appropriate picture. In the production task, the experimenter read the sentences aloud and then pointed to one of the pictures and asked the child to name it.

The comprehension task was scored simply for correct pointing. The imitation and production tasks were scored correct if the child uttered the correct syntactic elements. The results, shown in Table 10-2, indicated that the imitation task was clearly the easiest and that the production task was the most difficult. Comprehension scores exceeded production scores on nine of the ten contrasts, and imitation exceeded production on all ten. The order of difficulty was replicated by Lovell and Dixon (1967) with a wider age-range of children and also with retarded children, so that it appears to be quite reliable.

However, the appropriateness of the original procedure has been questioned. Baird (1972) pointed out that chance factors could affect the results. The child has a 50-percent chance of being correct in the comprehension task, which requires choosing one of two pictures. The exact probability of being correct in the production task is uncertain, but it is much lower. Other problems were pointed out by Fernald (1972). Irrelevant responses were counted as errors even if they correctly described some aspect of the picture. Should not such responses receive some credit for production? The scoring was also more strict in the production than in the comprehension task. For example, in the contrast between the present progres-

TABLE 10-2 Examples and Results from the Imitation-Comprehension-Production Test

Contrasts in Order of Increasing Difficulty	Number Correct (out of 24)			
	I	C	P	Total
I Affirmative-Negative The boy is sitting/The boy is not sitting	18	17	12	47
II Singular-Plural of Third-Person Possessive Pronoun Her dog/Their dog	23	15	8	46
III Subject-Object in the Active Voice The boat pulls the duck/The duck pulls the boat	19	16	11	46
IV Present Progressive-Future Tense The girl is drinking/The girl will drink	20	16	6	42
V Singular-Plural Marked by *Is* and *Are* The sheep is jumping/The sheep are jumping	20	12	7	39
VI Present Progressive-Past Tense The paint is spilling/The paint spilled	17	13	6	36
VII Mass Noun-Count Noun Some string/A string	12	13	1	26
VIII Singular-Plural, Marked by Inflections The girl stands/The girls stand	14	7	1	22
IX Subject-Object in the Passive-Voice The girl is fed by the boy/The boy is fed by the girl	12	7	2	21
X Indirect Object-Direct Object The mummy shows the bear the bunny/The mummy shows the bunny the bear	11	5	3	19

(From Fraser, Bellugi, & Brown, 1963.)

sive tense and the future tense, the child was required to mark the verb appropriately and also to use the correct auxiliary (for example, *is drinking* versus *will drink*), but comprehension could be based on either element because the marking for the grammatical contrast is redundant. A third problem is that the contrasting responses (for example, *The deer is running* versus *The deer are running*) to some picture pairs were not really independent since some children consistently chose the same picture for both sentences, and others consistently alternated in their choices. Fernald proposed ways of correcting for such scoring biases and replicated Fraser's, Bellugi's, and Brown's experiment using both scoring schemes. He obtained the original pattern of results with the original scoring scheme but found no significant difference between comprehension and production when he used his revised scoring system.

We presented the above studies in some detail to illustrate some of the difficulties in research designed to answer the apparently simple question of the developmental priority of comprehension and production. It remains clear that children understand some grammatical constructions, such as passives, before they can produce them. In other cases, comprehension and production may begin at about the same time. In still others, production seems to precede comprehension. For example, de Villiers and de Villiers (1973) asked young children to act out sentences using dolls. The sentences were reversible active or passive sentences such as *Make the dog bite the cat* and *Make the boat be bumped by the train*. The experimenters observed frequent comprehension errors for both actives and passives, particularly among the youngest children, although all the children used the appropriate word order at least 95 percent of the time in spontaneous speech. The diverse findings and procedural arguments in the literature on comprehension and production show that both skills are complex. The child's performance in either depends on some combination of the ability to deal with words and word combinations and the ability to take account of the nonlinguistic context in which language must be produced or understood. In brief, comprehension and production depend on the development of linguistic, semantic, and pragmatic skills.

We now shall review the theoretical approaches to the various classes of phenomena and issues that have been summarized in this section. The different approaches have concentrated on different developmental problems, and this is reflected in our selective coverage. We shall begin with the behavioral approach because it has historical priority in the analysis of language acquisition. Contemporary linguistic approaches began largely as negative reactions to some of the main behavioral assumptions, such as the role of reinforcement in development. Cognitive approaches evolved from the aftermath, marked by an emphasis on the importance of semantic and nonlinguistic contextual factors in language acquisition.

BEHAVIORAL APPROACHES TO LANGUAGE ACQUISITION

Behaviorists have had much to say about the development of language, as would be expected from their emphasis on the importance of learning as a basic psychological process. The salient principles of learning, according to behaviorists, are classical conditioning, operant conditioning, stimulus and response generalization, extinction, reinforcement, and various motivational variables. One of the earliest systematic applications of learning principles was F. H. Allport's (1924) *circular reflex theory*, which was based on the concepts of imitation, classical conditioning, and stimulus generalization. The idea was that the infant first learns to repeat vocal sounds over and over again during the "lalling" stage. This is characterized by the "circular reflex," in which the infant's vocal response produces a vocal sound that is itself the stimulus for a further response, and so on, in an R→S→R→S . . . chain. The next step is generalization to the parents' vocalization; that is, the infant responds to the parents' vocal sounds by *imitation*. There are a number of problems with this analysis. In particular, it is difficult to see how classical conditioning alone can account for the extraordinary degree of elaboration and restructuring of simple vocal responses that must occur if lalling is to evolve into speech. In any case, classical conditioning was not used by later theorists to explain verbal *behavior,*

although it has been retained as a partial explanation of the development of *meaning*. We shall consider the analysis of meaning after examining the operant conditioning approach to language development.

Skinner's Operant Conditioning Analysis

With Skinner, the emphasis changed from classical to instrumental, or *operant* conditioning. The concepts and principles have been discussed earlier (chapter 4). Recall that verbal behavior is assumed to be reinforced by the language community. More specifically, particular vocal sounds are reinforced, and others are extinguished through lack of reinforcement. The consequence is that verbal behavior comes under the control of particular stimulus conditions. Different reinforcement contingencies and controlling variables are present in the case of mands, tacts, echoics, textuals, autoclitics, and intraverbals, in the manner outlined in the earlier discussion. The assumptions have not been systematically investigated in regard to each class of operant, but there is evidence for the general principle of operant conditioning and in particular for the concept of reinforcement. Our review deals primarily with reinforcement because the whole operant approach hangs on the assumption that verbal behavior is shaped through reinforcement. The evidence must demonstrate, therefore, that reinforcement of verbal behavior is effective.

Reinforcement of vocalization

There is some support for the idea that reinforcement will increase the general frequency of vocalization. Rheingold, Gewirtz, and Ross (1959) investigated the problem with three-month-old infants. The study had baseline, conditioning, and extinction phases, each conducted over a two-day period. In the baseline stage, the experimenter leaned over the infant with an expressionless face. During the conditioning period, the experimenter reinforced vocalizations by simultaneously smiling, clucking, and touching the infant's abdomen, all in a brief period of about one second. The extinction phase was a return to the baseline condition. As can be seen in Figure 10-1, conditioning raised the rate of vocalization above the baseline level, and extinction lowered it until it once again approached the baseline level. Other experiments have similarly demonstrated that the general level of verbal responding increases with reinforcement.

Reinforcement of word responses

Much more evidence is available from the results of laboratory studies of the reinforcement of specific verbal responses with older children and with adults. Apparently the earliest experiment on the problem was an unpublished dissertation by Kay W. Estes in 1945 (cited in Winokur, 1976, pp. 47–48). The subjects were five-year-old children. The reinforcing event was the movement of the single hand of a cuckoo clock. When the hand moved, a bell rang, and when the hand moved to twelve o'clock, a door on the clock opened and a toy animal made from pipe cleaners was pushed out. Once the hand's movement had been paired with the appearance of the toy, the movement was an effective reinforcer. The following situation was used to demonstrate such reinforcing effects. Estes got the children to talk by showing them a series of pictures of people, animals, or colored-ink

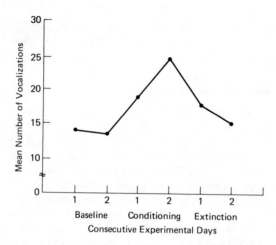

FIGURE 10-1. Mean number of vocalizations on consecutive experimental days. Based on Rheingold, Gewirtz, and Ross (1959)

blots. Each child was asked, for example, "What is the man saying?" If the child's response included the word "please," the clock hand was advanced. The results showed that the frequencies of all kinds of verbal responses increased as a result of the experimental procedure. However, the increase was proportionately greater for responses that seemed to belong to mands, and the increase was particularly great for the response "please." In a second experiment the frequency of the response "want" was similarly increased by the reinforcement procedure.

Many subsequent studies similarly showed positive effects of reinforcement on the verbal behavior of adults (for a summary, see Holz & Azrin, 1966). In a typical procedure, the experimenter instructs the subject to utter a list of nouns and then reinforces the occurrence of certain classes of nouns, such as plurals, by saying "Mm'hm," "Good," and so on, immediately after the desired response has occurred (for example, Greenspoon, 1955). This usually results in an increase in the frequency of the response class. An important point to note in connection with such studies is that they demonstrated the reinforcement of *classes* of words. Thus, reinforcement of animal names, plurals, action words, and so on resulted in increased production of words belonging to those classes, not just increased repetitions of the specific words that had been followed by reinforcement.

Reinforcement of grammatical responses

The operant verbal conditioning experiments discussed above generally were designed to modify the frequencies of classes of responses already in the subject's repertoire. Operant methods have also been used successfully to teach children new grammatical constructions. The most successful studies have combined reinforcement methods with modeling of the correct verbal response by the experimenter. For example, Guess, Sailor, Rutherford, and Baer (1968) taught a nonverbal, mentally retarded girl to use singular and plural morphemes productively using a multistage procedure in which she first was trained to imitate vocal stimuli and

then was reinforced for correctly labeling single objects, then pairs of objects (using a plural response), and finally, random sequences of single objects and pairs of objects. Correct responses were reinforced with praise and food, and the experimenter modeled correct labeling whenever the child made an error. The child learned to use the plural morpheme correctly to label pairs and novel sets of three objects, thereby demonstrating that she had acquired a generalized grammatical rule. Zimmerman and Rosenthal (1974) have provided a general review of such studies.

Critique

The operant conditioning approach has been criticized on empirical and rational grounds. One of the empirical problems is that relatively few experimental studies have been done with infants and that these have typically dealt with general effects on vocalization. Most of the evidence for more specific effects comes from experiments with older children and adults, who already have a considerable verbal repertoire. The question is whether such evidence is relevant to the shaping of verbal behavior among preverbal infants.

Another criticism applies to the experiments with older children and adults. Estes reported that most of her subjects could not describe how to "make the clock work." Similarly, in the earlier studies with adults, the subjects said that they were unaware of the relationship between the response class and the reinforcement. Later, however, more careful questioning of the subjects (for example, Spielberger & Levin, 1962) revealed that conditioning occurred mainly among subjects who were aware of the relevant relationships. Thus it appeared that the increased responding was not an automatic effect of reinforcement but was a result of cognitive factors.

The behavioristically inclined researchers remained unperturbed by such evidence. It can be argued, in the first place, that the cognitive argument is simply irrelevant to language acquisition. Knowing that a child is aware that someone is providing milk because he or she said "Milk" is of no theoretical consequence because the contingencies of reinforcement are still there. Indeed, the phenomenon of awareness itself could be regarded as a conditioned response (perhaps a verbal one). A second counterargument is that several studies have obtained conditioning of verbal responses even when awareness has been carefully controlled. For example, Dixon and Oakes (1965) used an interference procedure to reduce awareness. Their conditioning task, often used by researchers in the area, was a sequence of trials in which the subjects were presented with a verb and six alternative pronouns. The subjects' task was to construct a sentence using the verb and one of the pronouns. They were reinforced by the experimenter's saying "Good" if they used either "I" or "we" in the sentence. The novel part of the experiment was that between conditioning trials, the subjects were given a color-naming task. This procedure interfered with "awareness" but not with conditioning. That is, "I" and "we" responses increased in frequency, although the subjects were completely unable to report the relationship between their responses and the experimenter's reinforcing response. Several other studies have yielded similar results (for example, Konečni & Slamecka, 1972). Thus the conditioning interpretation of the results remains reasonable, although it is also clear that cognitive variables can influence how subjects respond in such tasks.

Showing that verbal behavior can be reinforced is one thing. Showing that parents actually go about carefully shaping their child's verbal behavior is another. The common observation that parents get excited when a child first utters something that sounds like *momma* or *dada* is certainly relevant, but how far can we generalize from such anecdotes? For instance, do parents try to reinforce grammatically correct responding? The available evidence suggests that they do not. Brown, Cazden, and Bellugi (1968), for example, found essentially no relationship between the grammatical correctness of the child's utterances and parental approval or disapproval. Instead, approval or disapproval depended on whether or not the utterance corresponded to reality. If the parents are mainly concerned with meaning and if meaning is not completely independent of syntax in normal communication, reinforcement of meaning might result in some incidental reinforcement of syntax as well. Still, parental reinforcement of speech appears to be far less frequent and less systematic than would be expected on the basis of the operant conditioning approach. The problem clearly calls for more detailed observations of and experiments on the verbal interactions of parents and their children.

The main criticism on the rational side has been Chomsky's argument that the operant approach is relevant only to S-R chains, which have the properties of finite state grammars. Recall from chapter 3 that Chomsky demonstrated logically that finite grammars cannot account for such constructions as center embeddings (or at least are very awkward accounts). Hence he rejected finite grammars as models of human languages and with them, behavioristic explanations. The general counterargument has been that Chomsky greatly underestimated the richness and explanatory potential of behavioristic approaches, including Skinner's operant approach (MacCorquodale, 1970), and especially the more complex neobehavioristic approaches of Osgood, Staats, and others, which emphasize the entire stimulus situation associated with verbal responses and their reinforcement consequences, rather than the verbal S-R chains alone. In addition, the neobehavioristic approaches have stressed the role of classical conditioning of meaning responses, which then play a mediational role in verbal behavior. We turn now to classical conditioning of meaning.

Classical Conditioning of Meaning

Arthur Staats and Charles Osgood are among the psychologists who have used classical conditioning to explain the acquisition of word meaning—both connotative and denotative meaning. Connotative meaning presumably includes affective or emotional responses, and denotative meaning is assumed to include sensory or perceptual responses such as images.

Evidence of first-order conditioning of meaning

Staats, Staats, and Crawford (1962) presented subjects with lists of words and told them to learn the lists. Among the words was the conditioned stimulus (CS) word, LARGE. The unconditioned stimulus (UCS) was a noxious stimulus (either a loud noise or a mild electric shock). The two noxious stimuli were not used at the same time; instead, they were paired at different times with the word. The experimenters measured the GSR (recall that this is a measure of physiological

reactions thought to be correlated with emotional arousal) and the evaluative meaning of the word LARGE before and after conditioning. The results indicated that the GSR became conditioned to LARGE and that LARGE was rated more unpleasant on a pleasant-unpleasant scale than were the control words. Moreover, the magnitude of the GSR correlated with the unpleasantness rating of the word— the more unpleasant the word LARGE was for a given subject, the higher the GSR. The "real life" implications of such findings are obvious. Perhaps this is how words first begin to acquire affective meaning. The following sections extend the story.

Evidence for language conditioning of meaning

Language conditioning of meaning refers to second-order conditioning, which was first demonstrated by Staats and Staats (1957). They visually presented six nonsense syllables to their subjects. One second after each syllable appeared, the experimenter spoke aloud a meaningful word. In order to conceal the purpose of this procedure, subjects were told to remember both the syllable and the word. The critical part of the design was that two syllables were always paired with evaluative (emotional) words, which differed on each trial. Moreover, one syllable was consistently paired with positive words and the other with negative words. For example, XEH may have been paired with positive words like *beauty, win, gift, sweet,* and *honest.* Conversely, YOF might have been paired with such negative words as *thief, bitter, ugly,* and *sad.* Eighteen words of each category were used, so that there were eighteen conditioning trials for each conditioned stimulus. Different UCS words were used on each trial to prevent the subject from simply learning specific associations, as in paired-associates learning. Presumably the only consistent association was between the critical nonsense syllables and the evaluative meaning of the different words with which they were paired.

Following the conditioning phase, the subjects rated the two critical syllables and the four control syllables on a pleasant-unpleasant rating scale. The results showed that the critical syllables differed appropriately in their ratings. In the above example, this means that XEH would have been rated more pleasant than YOF. They also found similar results for activity and potency dimensions. The general conclusion was that connotative or affective meaning could be acquired by classical conditioning using language.

Generalization of conditioned meaning

Staats, Staats, and Heard (1959a) used a similar procedure to demonstrate generalization of the conditioning effect to synonyms. For example, if the words *rock* and *carpet* were paired with "good" or "bad" UCS words, they were rated appropriately as pleasant or unpleasant, but so too were the words *stone* and *rug,* although they had not been present in the conditioning phase. This suggests that the conditioning effect generalized from the original CS words to their synonyms.

Paivio (1964) extended the Staats procedure to test for generalization of language conditioning of meaning to referents of the language. The CS's were color names among which were the critical ones, RED and BLUE, which were paired with "good" or "bad" UCS words. Rather than rating synonyms, however, the subjects rated the pleasantness of patches of color on test trials. The results showed generalization of the conditioning effect since the red and blue patches were rated

more or less pleasant, depending on whether their names had been associated with "good" or "bad" words.

Conditioning of denotative meaning

Staats, Staats, and Heard (1959b) extended the procedure by pairing the CS syllables with UCS words having a common *denotative* component of meaning. One class of UCS words referred to relatively round objects (for example, *coil, globe, hub, barrel, bulb, target, wheel,* and *marbles*). Another referred to angular objects (*square, box, roof, triangle, steeple, diamond*). Following eighteen conditioning trials, subjects rated two critical syllables on an angular-round scale. They found that the syllable paired with "angular" UCS words was rated more angular than the syllable that had been paired with "round" UCS words. The authors interpreted these results as evidence for second-order classical conditioning of sensory images to words. The UCS words have a common component in the images that they arouse. This common component becomes conditioned to the nonsense words. The more general implication, of course, is that this is partly how concrete words acquire their capacity to evoke sensory imagery. That is, concrete words come to arouse images both because they are directly paired with perceptual stimuli, and because they are paired with words that already arouse images.

Such a view has been independently proposed by Sheffield (1961) and Mowrer (1960), as well as by Staats. The general implications for language can be summarized by a couple of quotations from these people. Sheffield's analysis of first-order classical conditioning of sensory responses ran as follows:

> If a set of n sensory responses, R_{s1}, R_{s2}, R_{s3}, . . . R_{sn}, are elicited by different aspects of a given stimulus *object*, they will become conditioned to each other in the course of exploration of the object . . . Thus an object like an orange is smelled, touched, hefted, peeled, tasted, etc., giving rise to a succession of distinctive sensory responses which become conditioned to each other as cues. In the great variety of experience provided when a child becomes familiar with an orange, practically every stimulus aspect has sometimes preceded, sometimes followed, and sometimes occurred simultaneously with every other aspect, giving rise to a conditioned (perceptual) response pattern which is unique for oranges as objects and which can be elicited in relatively complete form by only one unique aspect of the orange. . . . This "cross-conditioning" mechanism accounts for the "filling-in" property of perceptual behavior in which a fragment of a total stimulus-pattern "redintegrates" the whole. (1961, pp. 16–17)

With respect to language conditioning of conditioned sensory responses, Staats points out:

> Words . . . may be combined in ways that yield a composite sensory response that has no real counterpart in experience . . . no one has ever experienced referents for GOD, DEVILS, FLYING SAUCERS, and many other current terms. Yet for many people these words elicit vivid sensory responses. Good examples may be drawn from history. For example, in the Middle Ages people accepted as real the existence of various forms of witches, hobgoblins,

elves, dragons, spirits, and so on . . . there are, of course, no such actual stimulus objects, so man's sensory responses to this and other such words may have been acquired through language conditioning. (1968, p. 50)

Of course, many of these fictitious entities also have been experienced as pictures, so that language conditioning would not be the sole mechanism in operation.

Evaluation of the conditioning approach to meaning

Like the operant approach, classical conditioning of meaning has been criticized on the grounds that awareness is involved and that the "real" explanation lies in cognitive mechanisms. Although Staats and his collaborators reported conditioning without subjects' reporting awareness, this has not been so in other studies (for example, Hare, 1964; Paivio, 1964). Consequently, cognitive interpretations have been suggested to the effect, for example, that the subject approaches the experiment as a problem-solving task.

In addition, it has been difficult to demonstrate experimentally that words acquire imagery value by being paired with objects. Philipchalk (1971), for example, paired nonsense syllables with pictures over a series of trials. Then, in a transfer task, the syllables were used as stimulus items in paired-associates learning. Since high-imagery stimulus items are known to produce better learning than low-imagery stimuli (see chapter 8), it was expected that there would be similar effects with the conditioned nonsense syllables. This in fact occurred in one experiment, but subsequent studies failed to replicate the finding. However, positive effects have been obtained by others (for example, Lohr, 1976).

Even without strong evidence of such conditioning, it has been assumed by linguists and psycholinguists that reference results from word-object contiguities in experience. Recent research does support the idea (Begg, 1976), with the qualification that the precise nature of the associative experience can have profound effects on the meaningful functions acquired by stimuli. Specifically, Begg used nonsense syllables either as *cues* for imagery during acquisition or as *responses* to pictures or meaningful words. In the former conditions, the syllables presumably acquired an "evocative" function, and in the latter they acquired an "expressive" function. The syllables were then used in a transfer task in which they served as cues or as responses for meaningful words or were simply freely recalled. The results showed that the syllables that had acquired image-evoking functions were particularly effective as cues in the cued-recall task but that the syllables that had acquired expressive functions were relatively more effective in free recall.

Begg concluded from the above research:

> Vocal sounds serve as functional tokens in communication. A token which expresses a mental state of the speaker also evokes a mental reaction in the hearer. Each function can be acquired separately, and has particular value in some range of circumstances. In tasks which require the production of a token in the absence of cues, expressive function and differentiation of the physical properties of the token are most important. In contrast, in situations in which a token evokes mental reactions, the nature of the symbolic information evoked is particularly important. (p. 185)

Behavioral Analyses of the Acquisition of Grammar

We have already considered one behavioral approach to the acquisition of grammar, namely, Skinner's concept of the autoclitic (chapter 3). Earlier in this chapter we also cited evidence that children can learn novel grammatical structures through operant procedures. Here, we shall review two mediational approaches to grammar acquisition.

Contextual generalization theory

M. Braine (1963) proposed a theory of the acquisition of grammar in terms of pivot grammar. Recall from our description of pivot grammar that one of the defining criteria for pivot class words is fixed position, with some pivots presumably preceding and others following open class words. Position assumes general theoretical importance in the concept of contextual generalization which was defined as follows: "When a subject who has experienced sentences in which a segment (morpheme, word, or phrase) occurs in a certain position and context, later tends to place this segment in the same position in other contexts, the context of the segment will be said to have generalized and the subject to have shown contextual generalization" (p. 323).

On the basis of this hypothesis and experimental evidence, Braine formulated a theory of how grammatical structure is learned. It includes three propositions:

1. What is learned is the location of units or expressions in utterances.
2. Such units can form a hierarchy in which larger units contain shorter units as parts, the location that is learned being the location of a unit within the next-larger unit, up to the sentence. Thus, one learns the location of letters (or phonemes) and syllables within words, words within phrases, and phrases within sentences.
3. Braine assumes that the learning is a case of perceptual learning: the learner becomes familiar with the sounds or expressions in the positions in which they occur. Thus, this would qualify as S-S learning more than S-R learning.

Braine tested his hypothesis with miniature artificial languages, in which nonsense words were embedded in grammatical structure during learning and subjects were then tested for generalization to new productions that had not been specifically taught. The experiments used relatively simple phrase-structure grammars, initially with only the two positions or classes that characterized pivot grammar.

One of Braine's experiments contained the following phrase-structure language:

$$S \rightarrow A + P$$
$$A \rightarrow (KIV, JUF, FOJ)$$
$$P \rightarrow (BEW, MUB, YAG)$$

Initial learning was of the first two words of each class, which generates four possible sentences. The method entailed sentence completion problems such as KIV_____ (JUF, BEW) or (KIV, MUB)_____ BEW. The child's task was to choose one of the two alternative nonsense words shown in parentheses. Eight such prob-

lems were used. In the generalization tests, new A or P words were introduced, with the alternatives being words that had been used in initial learning. Examples are FOJ_____ (KIV, BEW), (MUB, KIV)_____ YAG, and so on.

The results showed that initial learning was quite rapid. The generalization tests showed that, in 78 percent of the problems, the children filled the vacant positions with the word that had occupied this position in initial learning.

A second experiment in the same study was similar, but A and P classes were extended to include phrase constituents as well as words. Thus:

$$S \rightarrow A + P$$
$$A \rightarrow (KIV, GED JUF, GED FOJ)$$
$$P \rightarrow (BEW POW, MUB, YAG)$$

The results were similar to the results of Experiment I. Thus generalization occurred regardless of whether the positional elements were words or two-word phrases. The above experiments were with children four to five years of age. Later experiments (for example, Braine, 1966) showed that nine-year-old children could learn much more complex grammars in the same way.

Limitations of contextual generalization

Braine's theory was criticized particularly by transformationists, whose main objection was that contextual generalization (positional learning) is based on surface structure, whereas grammatical relations are found in the deep structure of sentences. For example, the deep structure relations are the same in actives and passives, such as *The girl kissed the boy* and *The boy was kissed by the girl*. Braine has conceded that positional learning cannot provide the basis for learning such grammatical identity. Similarly, the theory could account for simple conjunctive contrasts such as *Boys and girls* versus *Girls and boys*, but not sentences where restrictions on word order are important, like *Boys hit girls* as compared to *Girls hit boys*. Braine concluded that contextual generalization may apply only to simple-active-affirmative-declarative sentences (kernels), in which surface order and underlying structure are similar. However, syntactic learning includes, among other things, learning just *where* underlying and superficial structures *are* the same, and the theory does not explain this. Moreover, contextual generalization was concerned with positional learning, but not with learning the classes of words that go into the positions. The latter was the focal problem for another behavioral approach to the learning of grammar.

A mediational account of learning word classes

Jenkins and Palermo (1964) proposed a theory of word-class learning based on mediation theory. They assumed that initial learning occurs by imitation and reinforcement. Children first learn a small vocabulary of content words with clearly observable correlates; that is, they learn to label salient features of the environment. They then begin to attach words to other words in sequences, and ordering or structuring begins. When single-word utterances occur in similar stimulus conditions, the child forms *classes* of words through mediational processes asso-

ciated with stimulus and response equivalence paradigms. The following illustrates the paradigms:

Stimulus Equivalence	*Response Equivalence*
Learn A-B	Learn B-A
Learn C-B	Learn B-C
Test A-C	Test A-C

The letters A, B, and C refer to the stimulus and response members of the pairs. In an experimental version of the stimulus equivalence paradigm, the subject first learns a series of A-B pairs to some level of mastery and then a series of C-B pairs in which the responses of the previous list are paired with new stimuli. Finally the subject learns an A-C list constructed by pairing the stimuli from the first two lists. The critical question is whether A-C learning will be aided by each member of the pair having been previously associated with the same B item, which might serve as an implicit mediator in the sequence A-(B)-C. Numerous studies have shown that such A-C pairs are learned more easily than comparable pairs that had not been associated with a common B term. This is true also of the response equivalence paradigm as well as other mediation paradigms that we will not consider here.

How do the mediation paradigms apply to language learning in the child and in particular to learning word classes? Consider the situation in which a child obtains a ball on a shelf, sometimes by saying "ball" and sometimes by saying "want." Paradigmatically, the object (ball) corresponds to the common B element, and the verbal responses "want" and "ball" correspond to the A and C units, respectively, in a response equivalence paradigm:

Object (ball)–"want" (B-A)
Object (ball)–"ball" (B-C)

The presence of both responses in this situation leads to an increase in the association between them, so that the child begins to say "want ball" (A-C) without having had any directly reinforced learning experience with the verbal sequence, *want ball*. The same process would result in learning other constructions such as *want milk, want truck, want Mommy, want Daddy*, and so on.

The example shows how one word can come to elicit another through their shared association with a perceptual object—"want ball" is a syntamatic association. But note, too, that different object names are associated with *want*: "want milk," "want truck," and so on. The object names acquire equivalence in the same way that they elicit or are elicited by a common associate. The process generalizes further with other common contexts. For example, the child might similarly learn "like ball," "like milk," and "like truck." Now "want" and "like" develop something like class equivalence through their common associations with object names, and the equivalence of the names generalizes further because each shares associations with the two different stimulus words, *want* and *like*.

The developmental sequence of such association learning becomes clear when we consider how the model predicts the syntagmatic-paradigmatic shift in children's word associations. Recall that syntagmatic associations are normally

sequential in sentences, such as *deep-hole*. Paradigmatic associations belong to the same form class or, more accurately, normally occur in the same position in a sentence frame, such as *deep-shallow*.

The mediational account runs as follows (Jenkins, 1965, p. 88): the child repeatedly encounters two different words, X and Y, in the same verbal contexts, ABCXD and ABCYD. The result is that C first comes to elicit X and Y, and both X and Y elicit D. These are syntagmatic associations. Next, if the sequences are repeated often enough and if other contexts are available in which X and Y play similar roles, they should, according to the mediational model, come to elicit one another as paradigmatic associates. To the extent that X and Y have acquired the capacity to do so, they could be regarded as members of the same class.

This analysis is consistent with children's word associations. Children show relatively more syntagmatic associations than do adults. That is, children are more likely to provide such associations as *deep-hole* or *dark-room*, and adults are more likely to give *deep-shallow* or *dark-light* as associates. This shift to paradigmatic associations comes at around age seven to eight years. The shift presumably is a result of experience with words in a variety of contexts. In fact, there is considerable evidence that contextual variety is an important determining factor in the development of paradigmatic responding and that this in turn is related to the ability to use various parts of speech correctly in analyzing and constructing sentences (Kiss, 1973, p. 18). The variables related to the syntagmatic-paradigmatic shift turn out to be rather complex, however, and it now seems unlikely that mediation theory can provide a full explanation of the phenomenon (Nelson, 1977).

Evaluation of mediational S-R theory

It is generally conceded even by transformational theorists, who are critical of S-R theories, that mediational learning could perhaps explain some aspects of language learning. Those critics, however, deny that the model can explain the acquisition of phrase structure and transformations. Their principal objection is one that we have already encountered, namely the argument that mediation paradigms are simply an extension of the simple S-R model and are therefore limited to finite state languages. The mediational model implies that the learner must explicitly encounter all of the relevant word-word associations that he or she can understand and use. The number is less than would be required by a single-stage S-R model, but an enormous number would still be necessary—more than could be accommodated in a lifetime, according to some writers. For this reason, among others, the mediational model was rejected even by Jenkins and Palermo.

A cognitive extension of mediation theory

G. Kiss (1973) has argued that the model was abandoned prematurely, at least as a theory of word-class acquisition. If this can be substantiated, it is an important claim because word-class acquisition is necessary for any later grammatical learning. Kiss accordingly proposed an extension of mediation theory that is based not only on explicit S-R associations but also on *internal representations* corresponding to words, associative links between them, and word classes.

According to Kiss, an internal representation is a symbolic entity constructed

by the individual and stored in memory. The representation is a result of stimulation in the form of word input, but it also can be constructed entirely by internal processing. An associative link is a symbolic entity that links two internal representations so that, given one, the other can be retrieved. Thus the associative link is a retrieval mechanism that can vary in strength. All of this is tantamount to saying that for every S-R association, there is an internal representation corresponding to the S and the R as well as the associative link symbolized by the hyphen.

Word-class learning requires the construction of a *network of internal representations* that reflects the frequency distribution of words and sequences of words to which the learner is exposed. Thus, when a word representation is activated, the activity spreads along the links to other representations, the magnitude of the activation reaching them depending on the strength of the links.

Kiss's model also includes a classification mechanism. One component computes the similarity between words in terms of their "distribution vectors," essentially in terms of their associative relatedness or overlap as described in chapter 5. In other terms, this is a grouping process in which a program establishes associative links between the words and their verbal contexts. Thus the program builds a word-to-word transition network for the input corpus. A second component constructs a separate internal representation for the word groups that are similar to each other; that is, *representations are formed for word classes*. Note that this feature of the model introduces an element that is not part of the behavioral vocabulary, so Kiss parts company at this point with S-R or S-R mediational theories. The theory remains a member of that generic class in its emphasis on associative links, but it has become a cognitive-associative theory.

The theory was tested by computer simulation in which the input was a vocabulary of words from different form classes (nouns, verbs, adjectives, and so on) selected from tape recordings of seven mothers talking to their children. The program did generate classes, as can be seen in Figure 10-2, which plots the resulting organizational structure for the input vocabulary. Thus, there is a clear-cut organization of nouns into a densely interconnected network. Adjectives are organized, too, into a network with themselves, but also with nouns. Verbs also are organized, but more loosely than nouns or adjectives. And so on. Thus the output from the simulation program contained grammatically appropriate classes and exhibited some of the characteristics of young children's word-class systems. For example, nouns have been found to constitute a class early in linguistic development, generally before verbs, adjectives, adverbs, and prepositions. Thus, although Kiss's model has not been tested experimentally with children, it does provide a reasonable account of form-class development.

LINGUISTIC APPROACHES TO LANGUAGE ACQUISITION

Until the 1960s, linguistic theories had little influence on studies of language development. What influence there was came largely from traditional views of grammar and was restricted largely to vocabulary development (for example, see the summary by McCarthy, 1954), including form-class differences. For example, as indicated in our introductory review of the developmental sequence, the earliest vocabulary items are the names of things, followed later by more abstract nouns

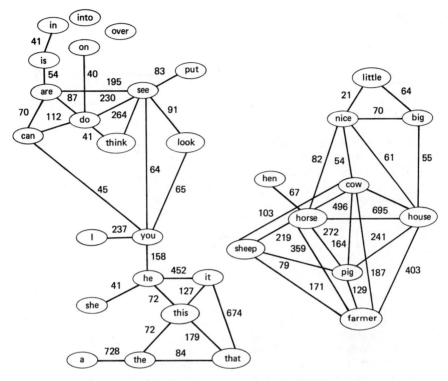

FIGURE 10-2. Organizational structure of input vocabulary in Kiss's study. The numbers show the strengths of connections. From Kiss (1973).

and other form classes. In addition, there were some normative studies done on the development of grammar, so that something is known about the average age at which children begin to show different grammatical skills. The strong influence from linguistics came in the early 1960s from an idea suggested by Chomsky (formulated originally along with G. Miller). Psycholinguistic studies of language development tended to center on that idea throughout most of that decade, and it continues to this day to guide the research of some developmental psycholinguists. We shall turn now to a review of the approach and some of the research it inspired.

The Language Acquisition Device (LAD)

The basic problem, as Chomsky saw it, was to conceptualize a mechanism or device that could infer a grammar from a limited set of utterances. Chomsky referred to such a mechanism as a *language acquisition device*, or LAD. LAD is a hypothetical device that develops a grammatical system by receiving a corpus of speech and passing it through the intellectual equipment that the child brings to bear on the problem of language learning. This idea was taken up seriously by David McNeill (1970), who also devised some ingenious ways to test it. Let us examine McNeill's formulation of the model in some detail. The following is a

schematic representation of the hypothesis:

Corpus → LAD → Grammatical Competence

This conveys the idea that language acquisition begins with a corpus of speech that passes through the child's LAD and comes out as grammatical competence. What is the internal structure of LAD? That is, what are its assumed characteristics? The following is a list of the most important ones:

1. It has a rational or *innate* basis as opposed to an empirical one. That is, it is a theory of children's inborn capacities.

2. It is essentially syntactic in that it is not dependent on semantic input, although such input could have a motivating influence and speed up acquisition.

3. It deals with syntactic *universals*—features common to all languages.

4. These syntactic universals can be described in part by Chomsky's theory of grammar, particularly the *grammatical relations* characteristic of the *deep structure* of sentences. These include the subject and predicate of the sentence, the modifier and head (noun) of the noun phrase, and the main verb and object of the verb phrase. Note that these are relational concepts. That is, they refer to the function of a unit in a higher-level unit. The subject, for example, is meaningful only in relation to the sentence—it is the subject *of* the sentence. (This relational view is explicit in Chomsky's definitions of these concepts: the subject is that NP immediately dominated by S; the predicate is the VP directly dominated by S; and the object is the NP dominated by the predicate VP.)

5. The internal structure of LAD does not contain information required to produce appropriate linguistic transformations and surface structures directly. These vary from language to language and are presumably learned. LAD may contain universal transformational *types* (permutation, deletion, addition—perhaps a half dozen in all), but the child learning a language must discover the transformations of the particular language.

6. LAD reflects at least in part a *specific linguistic capacity,* as compared to a *universal cognitive ability*. The former was described by McNeill in terms of *strong linguistic universals*, which reflect a specific linguistic ability, and *weak linguistic universals*, which are the reflections in language of a universal cognitive ability (general intellectual ability).

7. Finally, the range of LAD'S hypotheses about possible grammars is extremely limited.

What are the implications of this theory? The main one that McNeill emphasized was that "children begin speaking underlying structure directly" (1970, p. 72). The reference here is to children in general—early language structure should be the same across different languages and cultures, and this universality should be describable as basic grammatical relations without the use of transformations.

Two general kinds of evidence are possible in regard to such a nativistic view. The first is lack of support for alternative theories, especially the empiricist theories which assume that the earliest language depends entirely on experience. Learning theory would be a prime example. The second is evidence that the linguistic universals appear very early in the child's speech. We have already considered the first

one to some extent, namely, the relative lack of firm support for such empiricist principles as reinforcement and imitation. We will return to this point later when we consider criticisms of the LAD model. McNeill also presented evidence of the second kind, bearing on the points that basic grammatical relations appear early, that these are linguistic universals, and that their appearance is not predictable from the specific language to which the child is exposed.

One category of evidence is holophrastic speech. Recall from our earlier discussion that this refers to single-word utterances that appear to function like complete sentences. McNeill particularly emphasized that holophrastic speech is a limited kind of grammatical speech in that it is intended to express relations. The relations are not explicit, obviously, but must be inferred by the adult (McNeill, 1970, pp. 23-25). Holophrastic speech is first used to assert properties. For example, one child said "Ha" (hot) when something hot was before her; then it was applied to an empty coffee cup and a turned-off stove. The last two instances assert a property rather than simply being labels, according to McNeill. Other inferred grammatical relations appeared to be object of verb, as when the word "door" seemed to be used to mean "close the door"; object of preposition, as when "eye" indicated "water is in my eye"; and subject of sentence, as in the apparent use of "baby" to indicate that "The baby fell down." All of this was produced before the child combined any words. This was taken as suggestive evidence that even one-word utterances express basic grammatical relations. That is, adults see *possible* grammatical relations in such utterances, ones that they would express by relational statements. There is no direct evidence that the child who uses such words really understands anything about syntax (Bloom, 1973).

McNeill carried out a more thorough analysis of the speech of one of the three children in the studies of linguistic development by Roger Brown and his colleagues. This child, Adam, appeared to have three grammatical classes in his vocabulary at the age of twenty-eight months. These were nouns, verbs, and modifiers. These could yield nine possible two-word combinations and twenty-seven possible three-word combinations. However, only four of the two-word and eight of the three-word combinations correspond to basic grammatical relations. The rest do not. The striking observation was that there were none of the inadmissible but possible combinations in Adam's speech. All those present were consistent with grammatical relations. The following are illustrations of such combinations:

N + V(subject-predicate)—for example, *Adam run*
N + N(subject-predicate)—for example, *Adam ball*
V + N + N(verb object and modifier head)—for example, *Change Adam diaper*

There were no expressions such as *Come eat food* (V + V + N), although adults often use such sentences. According to McNeill's theory, this is because the two verbs in such utterances come from separate underlying structures, for example, *Adam come*; *Adam eat food*. The adult surface structure is a transformation from such underlying structures, and Adam did not yet have transformations. The evidence for this point is generally positive. For example, Bowerman (1973) summarized her own work with two Finnish children and with American, Luo, and Samoan children. She concluded that their early speech generally can be described by base grammar without transformations.

Critique of LAD

We shall now examine critically two basic and general assumptions of the Chomsky-McNeill hypothesis, one pertaining to the assumption of innateness and the other, to the adequacy of the linguistic model as an approach to the study of language development. First, although children's speech can be generated by the base structure rules without transformations, this does not mean that the ability to do so is innate. Could such constructions have been acquired through experience? Some evidence suggests that they could, and that the operation of general cognitive ability (in McNeill's terms, weak linguistic universals) determines what the child selects from his or her linguistic input.

Bowerman, for example, has argued that most of children's early constructions are like the parental utterances they frequently hear. Her evidence for this came from comparing different kinds of constructions by Finnish children and their mothers—subject-verb, verb-subject, verb-object, object-verb, and so on. She found a close correspondence between the relative frequencies with which mother and child produced the various word orders. She concluded, therefore, that it is hard to imagine how this correspondence could come about unless the children were relying heavily upon linguistic input as an "observation base for inference" at least in the matter of word order (1973, p. 165).

In regard to general cognitive factors, many writers have pointed to universals in experience as the basis for the development of semantics and grammar. The point is that children everywhere are exposed to similar conditions early in their lives and that language inevitably builds on this experience. We shall return to this point later, in the section on cognitive approaches to language development.

The second general point in our critique of LAD is that current syntactic theories generally, including base grammars, can be questioned as approaches to the study of language development. One reason for objecting to such theories is that they do not adequately describe (generate) children's language. This assertion is supported particularly well by the work of Bowerman (1973), so we shall review it in some detail. Bowerman evaluated pivot grammar, transformational generative grammar, and Fillmore's case grammar specifically in regard to the question of whether they could theoretically generate the speech of the Finnish children she studied.

Recall from our introductory summary that pivot grammar is a simple grammar that divides the words in two-word utterances into *pivot* and *open* classes according to certain criteria. However, Bowerman found it impossible to divide words into the two categories on the basis of any of the suggested criteria of relative frequency, position restrictions, or types of combinations. She found instead that most words occur in many different constructions, that open words occur frequently, and that pivots sometimes occur alone. In the second place, Bowerman noted that the grammar generally cannot express as much information about sentence structure as children seem to have. The last point agrees with Bloom (1970), who concluded that even when pivot grammar seems appropriate, it fails to capture the richness of the child's linguistic system.

Bowerman found transformational grammar to be better than pivot grammar in that it enables an observer to represent a child's early linguistic knowledge, that is, to write a grammar that will generate the observed utterances. However, trans-

formational grammar contains a number of questionable assumptions such as the subject-predicate division and phrase-structure analysis generally. These are assigned gratuitously to children's utterances; they are imposed on their speech; and they may not be necessary at all. Children may be able to produce combinations of words without having the same implicit understanding of phrase structure that adults have. Bowerman specifically questioned the idea of a deep structure constituent that functions as the sentence subject (NP dominated by S). The grammatical concept of the sentence subject may be more abstract and powerful than is needed to represent the child's early utterances. According to transformational grammar, the concept of the deep structure subject is needed because there are transformations (such as those that produce passive sentences) that treat nouns the same way in relation to a number of different verbs even if the nouns have different semantic functions in the different sentences. Consider the following examples:

1. The stick was broken by *John*.
2. Mary is seen by *John*.
3. The door was opened by the *key*.

In the first sentence, *John* is the deep structure subject (*John* broke the stick), whose semantic function could be described (in case grammar terminology) as Agent. In the second, *John* is the deep structure subject (*John* sees Mary) and functions as Experiencer. In the third, *key* is the deep structure subject (the *key* opened the door) and has the role of Instrument. Thus the deep structure nouns have different semantic functions, but at the surface structure level all can serve as the object of the preposition *by*, and all can be transformed in the same way, so that deep and surface structures differ. Such facts seem to justify the need for the concept of the deep structure subject.

But what if a language lacked syntactic operations that treated noun arguments the same way across different verbs and that would cause deep and surface structures to differ? Would we then need the syntactic abstraction of the deep structure subject? The early language of children in fact appears to lack such operations. That is, they can be generated mostly by the base component. Most constructions follow a simple declarative pattern. *Thus no transformations are needed that require reference to a sentence constituent with the abstract syntactic function of the deep structure subject because the deep and surface structure subjects are always identical.* Therefore, only position can serve as a basis for the abstraction of "subject." If a child says *Ball hit* and *Apple eat*, it has been customary to assume that the child has reversed the adult verb-object order—some agent *hit* the *ball* or *eats* the *apple*. Thus we conclude that *ball* and *apple* are "really" deep structure objects for the child, too. But what if the child mistakenly treats those nouns as subjects by analogy with sentences like *The toy broke* and *The door opened*, in which the noun can occur as the deep structure subject when it is not accompanied by an agent? (If accompanied by an agent, the noun is the deep structure object; for example, *The toy was broken by John* becomes *John broke the toy* in deep structure). The point is that the child at first may not recognize the distinction between verb classes and assumes that all objects acted upon (for example, ball, apple, toy, and door) can be subjects in agentless sentences. Bower-

man concludes that we cannot be sure that this is so but that it is possible. The general point again is that we cannot be sure that we should interpret a child's grammatical competence in terms of adult grammars.

Bowerman found case grammar to be better than transformational generative grammar as a representation of child language because it insists on the grammatical significance of semantic concepts. At the same time, it rejects those assumptions of transformational grammar that seem inappropriate for children's speech, for example, the basic division between subject and predicate. Nonetheless, Bowerman did not find case grammar to be entirely satisfactory because some of the cases suggested by Fillmore seem to be more abstract than the categories that children actually work with. Bowerman concluded generally that an optimal grammar for the developing linguistic competence of children should be (a) completely flexible in assigning constituent structure and (b) flexible with regard to the concepts and categories thought to be functional in the child's competence. These may be primarily semantic in nature in the earliest two- and three-word utterances, much as Brown (1970) assumed when he described two-word phrases in terms of structural meanings (see Table 10-1 in this chapter).

Our conclusion is that currently there is no general acceptance of LAD as originally formulated by Chomsky and McNeill. There is no strong evidence that it is an innate capacity, and transformational grammar has been widely rejected as the most appropriate grammar for generating children's language. During the last decade there has been an increasing emphasis generally on semantic considerations and other factors to be discussed under cognitive approaches to language acquisition. This negative conclusion does not mean that the problem posed by Chomsky has been solved; namely, what kind of device is it that can infer a grammar from a limited language input? For a time it seemed that the problem was simply abandoned (Levelt, 1974).

However, the general philosophy underlying Chomsky's hypothesis continues to be influential, and researchers are trying to redefine the issues he raised (for example, see Pinker, 1979). The argument runs somewhat as follows: Abandonment of transformational grammar or any other current grammar does not mean that LAD should be abandoned. It simply means that the internal structure of LAD needs to be rethought in contemporary linguistic terms. There is no way to disprove the role of innate factors in development, and every theory in fact assumes such factors. For example, learning theorists assume innate capacities in relation to the effectiveness of primary reinforcers, the formation of associations on the basis of contiguity, stimulus generalization, and so on (see our later discussion of the analysis of language development by Hebb, Lambert, & Tucker, 1971). The important question, however, is how to characterize in precise terms the innate mechanisms necessary to acquire a particular kind of skill or knowledge and also the environmental events that interact critically with those mechanisms. The goal is to conceptualize adequately those devices within the child that are tuned to language and account for the induction of a grammar from linguistic input. Everyone agrees that a particular native language is experientially based. The proponents of LAD would like to be able to characterize the means by which this experience is converted into internalized general patterns governing speech production and comprehension. Cognitive psychologists have the same general aim, although, as we shall see below,

they conceptualize it in different ways and emphasize relatively more the role of semantic factors and nonverbal input than do the proponents of LAD.

In all, perhaps the biggest problem with most of the linguistic approaches stems from their attempt to produce a model that would allow a grammar to be inferred from encounters with a finite number of grammatical sentences. However, as Pinker (1979) points out, this approach simply cannot work, because there are an infinite number of grammars possible for any finite number of strings. Perhaps, instead, what children learn is to express *meaning* in sentences; there is almost always nonlinguistic information present to help them understand and produce language, and to provide clues to grammatical structure.

COGNITIVE APPROACHES TO LANGUAGE ACQUISITION

This section emphasizes three features, including (a) the importance of nonlinguistic factors to acquiring semantic and syntactic "competence"; (b) the importance of meaning to acquiring both language and syntax; and (c) the idea that these factors are based largely on experience.

Cognitive Universals in Language Development

We consider first Piaget's views on language development. He did not write much specifically on that problem because he was interested more generally in intellectual development and saw language as only part of that development. He did, however, make some statements about language in the context of such cognitive universals, and other members of the Geneva group have expanded on his views. We draw especially on the writings of Sinclair-deZwart (1973).

The general point is that language develops on a basis of sensory-motor cognitive structures or schemes. These structures are acquired through the child's action upon and interaction with people and things. The sequence is roughly as follows:

1. The first period is the *sensory-motor stage*, up to about one and a half years of age, during which the child develops action patterns by acting on the environment. These action patterns eventually become organized mental structures. Simultaneously and in close connection with this action structure, the infant builds a personal world of permanent objects (*object permanence*). Behaviorally, this means that the child no longer acts as though objects cease to exist when they disappear from view. Rather, the child knows that he or she can find them again by using the appropriate action structure.
2. The next period, *representational intelligence*, begins toward the end of the second year (the end of the sensory-motor period), after the action structures have been internalized. Symbolic representation has several forms, including *symbolic play, imitation, mental images*, and *drawing*.
3. *Language* is the extension of the representational level after symbols become socialized. Linguistic structures build on the general cognitive structures established during the first two years.

Implications

Piaget (1949) suggested that the first holophrastic utterances express action patterns that mainly refer to the child itself. For example, a girl of one and one half years is reported to have said Grandpapa (Panana) whenever she wanted somebody (not necessarily the grandfather) to do what her grandfather used to do with her. Later these action-based utterances are supplemented by descriptions of past events or properties of objects and persons.

Sinclair-deZwart followed up these ideas with case categories and subject-verb-object structures. At first, the child presumably singles out a short combination of speech sounds, assuming that these express an action pattern, and will use the same series (in better and better phonetic approximation to adult speech patterns) whenever a recurrence of the action pattern is perceived. The action pattern is related to the child, and in it agent, action, and eventual patient (the recipient of the action) are intertwined. In a second phase, the child expresses the result of an action done by somebody else (a subject-verb construction), then differentiates his or her own action from the object, and subsequently differentiates himself or herself as agent from other persons or objects as agents. This gives rise to the first grammatical functions of subject-predicate and object-action, resulting in a subject-verb-object structure (or Agent + Action + Patient), which is established through the verb as the focal element.

Sinclair-deZwart presented some preliminary results of a study in which children aged two years, ten months or older were presented three-word sequences of verbs and two nouns in different combinations (VNN, NVN, NNV). For example, the children were presented with one of the possible combinations of the words *push, boy,* and *girl* and were asked to guess what the experimenter meant by showing the action with toys. The interpretations of the youngest children were not in terms of adult grammar. For instance, *boy-push-girl* was interpreted by two-thirds of the children with the verb *push* used in the intransitive sense. Thus the child might make the toy boy and girl walk on the table, saying "they are walking" or "they go ahead," apparently meaning something like *they push on*. Note that there is no subject-verb-object (or agent-action-patient) structure in this interpretation. Rather, it appears to have a subject-verb or agent-action construction. Sinclair-deZwart accepts this as evidence that the action patterns determine the child's interpretation. That is, the child interprets the event as his or her own or others' actions without reference to the object, or as a verb-object (or object-verb) pattern with no subject because the child assumes himself or herself as the subject. Only later are the two patterns combined into a complete subject-verb-object structure.

Edwards (1973) presented an even more extensive theoretical elaboration combining Piaget's approach with case grammar in a model of language acquisition. Edwards's theory is concerned with "the interface between universal semantic relations and universal sensory-motor cognitions, which meet in the content and process of language acquisition at the beginning of syntax" (p. 398). The universal semantic relations are expressed as a basic set of clause types, cases in Fillmore's sense, and so on, and the universal sensory-motor cognition refers to knowledge of the states of affairs, relations, and interactions between persons and objects. As in the work of Sinclair-deZwart, there is as yet too little evidence for this particular approach to know how successful or influential it will be, although Edwards has

provided some supporting data based on observations of the language behavior of his own child. More generally, however, the general idea of a relationship between universal cognitive structures and linguistic structures is clearly becoming a dominating idea in contemporary research on the development of language.

Semantics in Language Development

Macnamara (1972) wrote an article on the cognitive basis of language learning that is representative of the reaction to the Chomsky-McNeill approach to the problem. Macnamara's main point was that "infants learn their language by first determining, independent of language, the meaning which a speaker intends to convey to them, and by then working out the relationship between the meaning and the language . . . the infant uses meaning as a clue to language rather than language as a clue to meaning" (1972, p. 1). The following discussion expands on the important components of this statement.

Meaning and linguistic code are distinct

Macnamara deliberately left the definition of meaning rather general. He suggested that meaning refers to all that a person can express or designate by means of a linguistic code. The linguistic code is separate, consisting of a set of formatives and syntactic devices, the main function of which is to relate meaning to the phonological system of the language. The two are usually experienced together, however, rather than separately.

Meaning is used as a clue to the linguistic code

When infants begin to learn language, their thought is more advanced than their language. Macnamara cited two kinds of evidence. First, Piaget and others have adduced evidence that the development of thought is at first independent of language and only later becomes intimately related to it. Second, he referred to studies of cognition, affect, and language in the deaf (for example, Furth, 1966) which show that the congenitally deaf are severely retarded in language development but nonetheless reveal all the essentials of human thought processes and feelings (see our discussion of these findings in chapter 11).

Implications and evidence for vocabulary development

On the basis of his general approach, Macnamara suggested that vocabulary learning follows a particular order. Specifically, the hypothesis is that the child first learns *names for entities*, then *names for their variable states and actions*, and finally, *names for more permanent attributes, such as color*. He cited observational evidence for this sequence. First, the infant can distinguish from the rest of the physical environment an object that the parent draws to his or her attention and names. The word is apparently taken as a name for the object as a whole rather than as a subset of its properties, position, weight, and the like (see Nelson, 1974). The nature of the child's errors suggests such a strategy. For example, he or she may refer to the kitchen stove as "hot" as though it is the object's name. This

presumably results from the parent's having told the infant not to touch the stove, saying "it's hot!"

The names for varying states, conditions, and activities are also learned early. Daddy can be variously *gone, sitting down*, and so on. Toys can be broken. One can open or close a book. These differ from attributes such as redness in that redness is usually a permanent attribute of the object. According to Macnamara, small children have a tendency to attend to varying states and activities rather than to unvarying attributes. However, the child will not learn the names for states or activities until he or she has firmly grasped the names for at least some entities that exemplify such states and activities. Thus the earliest words are proper names of brothers, sisters, pets, and the like. In brief, as we have already noted, the child learns concrete words early.

Implications and evidence for syntax

In regard to syntax, Macnamara suggested that the task of the child is to detect the structures of syntax and to relate them to meaning. This is somehow done by using meaning to discover at least certain syntactic structures of basic importance. For example, the infant cannot distinguish *The boy struck the girl* and *The girl struck the boy* from pairs like *My hair is black* and *I have black hair*, in which the last two are stylistic variants but the former are not, without independent access to meaning. Meaning is presumably determined through observing what is happening when the sentences are spoken. Note how this analysis agrees with Chomsky's LAD in suggesting that the child's basic task is to infer syntactic structure from perceptual input. They differ in that Chomsky hypothesized that LAD is essentially a syntactic device that can infer grammar from language input alone without relying on semantic input, and Macnamara suggests that syntax is discovered *through* meaning.

How does the infant use meaning as a clue to certain syntactic devices? First, according to Macnamara, this probably comes about through prior learning of *vocabulary*, especially nouns, verbs, and adjectives. Children initially may consider the main lexical items in sentences that they hear, determine referents for these items, and then use their knowledge of the referents to decide what the semantic structure intended by the speaker must be. Second, children note the regularities in the language they hear in regard to word order and the like. As evidence, Macnamara cites the observation that children's holophrastic expressions express a variety of meanings without the help of syntax (see our earlier section on holophrastic speech). Although not cited by Macnamara, Bowerman's (1973) finding of a strong relationship between the frequencies of different grammatical structures used by mother and child is relevant here.

Implications for phonological development

Finally, Macnamara proposed that children use meaning as a key to the sound system of a language. For example, the physical properties of the named objects serve as clues to the phonological units employed in naming them. Learning the sound system is easier when variation in meaning is accompanied by variation in sound. Thus, *ship* and *sheep* are easily distinguishable to English speakers because

of the correlated difference in meaning. Spanish speakers have difficulty noticing the change, however, because in Spanish the distinction in sound is of no importance. Note the relevance of this point to the discussion of phonemes in chapter 3: phonemically different sound patterns also have different meanings—*pin-pan, bat-cat*, and the like; allophones by definition are not phonemically distinct and therefore are not easily distinguished.

To summarize the above discussion, Macnamara, like Piaget, proposed that children develop nonlinguistic cognitive processes before they learn their linguistic signals. He assumed further that these processes are primarily learned: the child does not have a complete set of cognitive structures when he or she begins to learn language, but their developmental onset precedes that of language. Let us now focus directly on the role of experience in language development.

Experiential Universals in Language Development

Hebb, Lambert, and Tucker (1971) opposed Chomsky's and McNeill's nativistic viewpoint with an empiricist position based on perceptual learning. They suggested that the concepts of heredity and innate ideas do not *explain* universal grammar; instead, they remove the problem from psychological consideration. Hebb and his colleagues do accept the idea that certain capacities are genetically given, so that language is species-specific. These hereditary factors include an innate capacity for (a) auditory analysis and (b) dealing simultaneously with verbal and nonverbal representational processes (ideas, mediators). Also given are certain general capacities such as those for perceptual learning, generalization, and abstraction.

Experiential universals

Hebb and his colleagues argued that in addition to the hereditary endowment, the child is born into a language-filled environment with both verbal and non-linguistic uniformities. All children, in all cultures, will be exposed to (a) the sound of the human voice; (b) sensations from their own throats at the same time as they hear their own voices; (c) the sight of their own hands when they move them; (d) an older female who provides early care, with accompanying facial expressions, intonations, and so on; (e) sleeping in enclosed spaces; and (f) the differences between living and nonliving, human and nonhuman, and male and female. Given these facts, how can we argue that an orderly, predictable development in children's speech means that learning is not involved?

Modes of human learning

Hebb, Lambert, and Tucker emphasized the importance of *perceptual learning*, without reinforcement, and S-S (stimulus-stimulus) associations rather than only S-R learning. As evidence of perceptual S-S learning they cited the phenomenon of *sensory preconditioning*: an animal is repeatedly exposed, for example, to a sound followed by a light. The light is conditioned to an avoidance response, then the animal is tested with the sound as a stimulus. Although the sound had never been conditioned to the response, the animal now makes the avoidance response to the sound. In this way, different perceptual features of the same object become associated.

Implications for language

Hebb and his colleagues assumed that these types of learning underlie various language phenomena. The acquisition of vocabulary is a combination of perceptual and S-S learning; for example, the spoken word "doggie" is associated with the sight of the dog. Imitation, which plays a part in overt motor speech, itself depends on prior perceptual learning. Various syntactic forms, such as plurals and negatives, build on a nonverbal perceptual base. For example, the plural /z/ is associated with two or more *things* (fingers, toes, dogs); negative expressions are associated with the *absence* of things, *prohibition* of actions, and the like. The distinction between active and passive sentences is based on particular sequences of ideas, part perceptions, or images. These observations suggested to Hebb and his colleagues that *nounness* is primary—the child finds empirical criteria for nounness in things. As evidence for this suggestion, they referred to the finding that the noun-adjective word order is easier to learn than the adjective-noun word order (recall our earlier discussion of the conceptual peg hypothesis).

The views of Hebb and his colleagues resemble those of Piaget, Macnamara, and others in their emphasis on cognitive factors in language development. Piaget, however, stresses more the derivation of cognitive structures from behavior toward things, and Hebb stresses S-S learning. Nonetheless, perceptual learning to Hebb certainly includes motor activity, which has always been crucial to his neuro-psychological ("cell assembly") theory of behavior and thought.

How might the proponents of a nativistic approach respond to Hebb, Lambert, and Tucker? As we noted at the end of the section on linguistic approaches, they would simply assert that everyone agrees that learning is part of language development (how else could different languages arise?) and that it remains important to determine whether in language there is order and predictability that cannot be traced to any commonality of experience and that is specific to language.

Dual Coding and Language Development

The dual-coding approach has much in common with all of the preceding approaches, with the difference that we propose specific concepts for different kinds of cognitive representations and refer explicitly to concreteness-abstractness in the developmental sequence. The following quotation summarizes the general dual-coding approach to language acquisition as originally proposed by Paivio (1971b):

> The major implication of the . . . analysis for language acquisition is that linguistic competence and linguistic performance are dependent initially upon a substrate of imagery. Through exposure to concrete objects and events, the infant develops a storehouse of images that represent his knowledge of the world. Language builds upon this foundation and remains interlocked with it, although it also develops a partly autonomous structure of its own. Although speculative, these general assumptions would probably arouse little controversy if limited only to discrete objects and their names. An infant indicates by his behavior that he recognizes objects before he responds to their names, thereby showing that he has stored some kind of representation against which the perceptual information is matched. Later he can

respond appropriately to the name of an object even in its absence (e.g., he may begin to look for it), indicating the emergence of a word-image relationship. Serious objections might be raised, however, if such an analysis were to be extended to grammatical word sequences, for surely it is too much to suggest that syntax is in any sense built upon a foundation of imagery. Yet this is precisely what is suggested.

The argument is as follows. The developing infant is not exposed merely to static objects but to objects in relation to other objects, and action sequences involving such objects. The events and relations are lawful, i.e., they tend to repeat themselves in certain essential respects—people enter a room through the same door in the same way repeatedly, a bottle is picked up in a predictable way, and so on. In brief, there is a kind of syntax to the observed events, which becomes incorporated into the representational imagery as well. This syntax is elaborated and enriched by the addition of an action component derived from the child's own actions, which have their own patterning or grammar. The child also learns names for the events and relations as well as the objects involved in them, which we interpret theoretically to mean that associations have developed between the mental representations of the objects, actions, etc., and their descriptive names. This basic stage becomes greatly elaborated as function words are acquired and as intraverbal associative networks expand through usage. Eventually, abstract verbal skills are attained whereby verbal behavior and verbal understanding are possible at a *relatively* autonomous intraverbal level, i.e., free of dependence not only upon a concrete situational context but to some extent from imagery as well. (pp. 437–438)

The approach includes a number of points related to the dual-coding model as discussed in chapter 5.

Development of nonverbal cognitive representations (imagens)

It is assumed that the earliest learning is the development of representations corresponding to objects and events. These become organized into higher-order representational structures, capable of generating consciously experienced imagery. The relevant evidence, discussed earlier, is the primacy of concrete objects in infant perception (T. G. R. Bower, 1966; Gibson, 1969). The infant recognizes objects long before the onset of language and can look for missing objects; these facts indicate that the infant possesses nonverbal memory representations for concrete objects.

Development of verbal representations (logogens)

The development of verbal representations (logogens) refers to the mental representations corresponding to linguistic units. Here, too, there is evidence of the influence of concrete objects because of the primacy of concrete nouns in language development. The earliest speech consists of one-word utterances including proper names of people and animals and concrete object names at some middle level of generality, such as *chair* and *doggie* (Anglin, 1977; Rosch, Mervis, Gray, Johnston, & Boyes-Braem, 1976). From this basic object level, the vocabulary acquires both more specific terms (lounge, spaniel) and more general and abstract ones (furniture, animal).

Development of referential meaning

The interconnections between the verbal and nonverbal representational systems, implying referential meaning, develop concurrently with the verbal representations of concrete objects. That is, thing-names are ordinarily learned in the context of the referent situations.

Development of associative structures

From their developmental onset, nonverbal and verbal representations become progressively organized into larger and larger structures, in both the synchronous and the sequential sense. Imagens are grouped into larger integrated units and spatially related structures. Verbal units are chunked into larger sequential structures—words into phrases, idiomatic expressions, and even larger structures such as proverbs, poems, and songs.

Development of syntax

The dual-coding approach to syntax is generally similar to the positions of Piaget and Hebb. The basic new assumption is that syntax is based initially on a nonverbal cognitive base. As the above quotation indicates, there are systematic and predictable relations among the attributes of things, the relations of things to other things, and the behavior of the child toward those things. These relations become incorporated into the functional and structural characteristics of the imagery system. The relations expressed by the grammar of a language in the first instance come from that nonlinguistic structure. Later, the learning of syntax can proceed further in a manner that is at least partly independent of the perceptual events and imagery. The mechanism in that case may be very much like the cognitive mediational approach that Kiss (1973) proposed for the learning of grammatical class.

Aspects of this approach are supported by experiments carried out by Moeser and Bregman (1972, 1973), which examined the learning of miniature language systems under conditions in which perceptual referents were provided or were absent. Earlier studies of the problem had sometimes found that syntax was not acquired better when a miniature artificial language was presented along with pictorial referents than when the word sequences were presented repeatedly without referents (Miller & Norman, 1964). The absence of an effect may have been due to the use of very simple grammars, such as $S \rightarrow A + B$. In addition, when reference has aided learning, there was no strong evidence that the manner of learning was affected. Such findings led Chomsky (1965, p. 33) to argue that semantic reference may facilitate performance in syntax-learning experiments but not the manner in which the acquisition of syntax proceeds. That is, reference does not determine which hypotheses are selected by the learner—LAD may be put into operation in the child by situational information, but its manner of functioning is not affected.

Quite different evidence emerged from Moeser's and Bregman's experiments, which used more complex languages. In general, this series of experiments compared a words-only condition, in which instances of the miniature language were presented without any accompanying pictures, with conditions in which the lan-

guage instances were accompanied by pictures variously related to the language. The most relevant of these is the *syntax correlation* condition, in which the syntactic constraints of the language were also mirrored in the logical constraints of the pictures. The studies clearly showed superior learning of syntax under the syntax correlation condition. The 1973 experiment included conditions particularly relevant to the dual-coding approach, and so we shall review it in some detail.

The study concentrated on the influences of the semantic referent and imagery at a late stage of learning. Thus it is relevant to the hypothesis suggested above, that verbal skills eventually free themselves from dependence on concrete images and that this is the basis of the difference between concrete and abstract language.

The subjects in the study learned a miniature artificial language with a phrase structure described by the following rewrite rules:

$$S \longrightarrow AP + BP$$
$$AP \longrightarrow (D) + A$$
$$BP \longrightarrow \begin{cases} B_1 + (CP) \\ B_2 + CP + (CP) \end{cases}$$
$$CP \longrightarrow (D) + C$$

The words used in the language were twenty-nine nonsense syllables of which different numbers were assigned to the four classes, A, B, C, and D. The subjects learned the syntax of strings of these words, which were constructed to be grammatically correct sentences according to the phrase structure grammar. Three subjects in the words-only condition saw only a series of such strings. The three subjects in the semantic referent condition saw the same series of sentences presented along with a picture that the sentence described. The information in the pictures consisted of perceptual attributes related to the class membership of the words in the sentences. Thus, Class A words referred to colored rectangles; Class B_1 words referred to changes in the orientation or shape of the rectangles; Class C items referred to nonrectangular forms; and so on. The words and referents used in the artificial language are shown in Figure 10-3. A specific example of a correct sentence would be MIR FET CAS LIM. The corresponding picture would be a tilted red rectangle with a double-lined border, followed by a triangle.

The subjects in each condition were presented with eighty different sentences varying in length, repeated 40 times for a total of 3,200 instances of correct sentences. After each eighty-sentence trial, the subjects were tested with twenty-one pairs of alternative sentences from which they were to choose the correct one in each pair. These interspersed trials were designed to test the various rules of the phrase structure grammar.

Two more tests followed initial learning. In one, the subjects were tested for learning of the syntax class of a word given only a verbal context. This test contained new words representing new instances of the word classes, so that the new word appeared in the sentence position with the same privilege of occurrence as an already-learned word. The subject was shown sample sentences containing the new word and then was asked to pick out the correct sentence from a test set. The second test was one of visual imagery which referred only to the prior context-

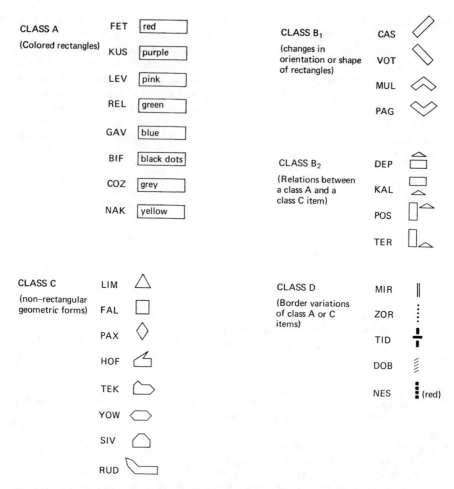

FIGURE 10–3. The "words" of the miniature artificial language and their pictorial referents. Based on Moeser and Bregman (1973).

learning phase. The question was whether visual imagery was present while the syntactic classes of the new words were being used. The subject was asked to draw the referent (for example, draw a BUK), followed by the question "Did you have this picture in mind while doing Question 1 (the context-learning phase), or did you just make it up now?"

The results of the initial learning phase showed that there was essentially no learning of syntax in the words-only condition but excellent learning in the syntax-correlation condition. The average test scores for the two groups were 55.3 and 91.3 correct; 52.5 is the score possible by guessing, and 105 is the maximum score possible.

Acquisition by context in the second phase showed that the subjects in the syntax-correlation condition did very well, with two of the three subjects achieving

perfect scores and the third having difficulty with two of the five new words. The subjects in the words-only condition again performed only at a chance level. The visual imagery test showed that the subjects did not necessarily have the picture in mind or show the ability to draw the correct picture corresponding to the context-learning test.

The authors concluded that semantic referents and imagery are necessary for initial learning of syntax. After the syntax had been learned by the mediation of pictures, the syntactic class membership of new words could be learned in a purely verbal context, without reference to pictures and sometimes without imagery. "Thus it appears that much of early syntax learning must be mediated through an understanding of the reference field, while later learning may be built directly upon the already existing syntactic framework" (Moeser & Bregman, 1973, p. 91).

These conclusions are generally consistent with cognitive approaches that assume that sensory-motor experience and semantic factors are primary in language development. This view seems to be the dominant one in contemporary developmental psycholinguistics, having been adopted even by David McNeill (1979). In a sharp departure from his earlier syntactically based and nativistic approach in which LAD was the central concept, McNeill has proposed a theory that incorporates some Piagetian assumptions and some features of recent network models of mental representations.

The most relevant point in the present context is McNeill's basic assumption that organized speech output is programmed or controlled by concrete *sensory-motor* ideas, which presumably emerge initially from action schemes based on the child's coordinated actions in concrete situations. These sensory-motor representations are the basis of both functional units called *syntagmata*, which control meaningful speech output units, and *conceptual structures*, which are organized meaning structures composed of different sensory-motor ideas. Thus, sensory-motor ideas are simultaneously part of action and part of meaning. Moreover, by a process of *semiotic extension*, the sensory-motor ideas extend to meanings that are abstract rather than directly sensory-motor.

McNeill's analysis has much in common with the dual-coding approach outlined above, but the two views differ sharply in at least one respect. Whereas dual-coding theory assumes separate but interconnected representations for nonlinguistic and linguistic sensory-motor information, McNeill appears to combine sensory-motor meaning and speech output systems into one representational unit, the sensory-motor idea. Thus his model shares a basic assumption with other common-coding approaches to language and cognition, and like them differs from the dual-coding approach. The difference is overridden, however, by the general agreement that language development is founded on the prior emergence of nonlinguistic cognitive representations, which are themselves based on perception and action in the world of concrete objects and events.

We have now concluded our detailed review of issues and approaches in this important area of language study. As a parting note, we draw attention to one other, highly promising area for studying language acquisition, which comes from computer programs assembled to understand language, to build grammars, and so on. Kiss's computer simulation model of how grammatical classes might be acquired is an example of such models, as applied to a specific problem. Despite their promise, we have not included other, more general models here, for two reasons. First,

in order to understand the models in any deep sense, one would need to have a fairly good background in computer science, artificial intelligence, or the like. Second, the models do not as yet have enough experimental support to allow a firm choice of which ones to include. Generally, the models now available include semantic and referential information and so are much more cognitive than the earliest models. We urge you to read Pinker's (1979) very thorough review and to follow up some of his references. Pinker presents a well-reasoned discussion of what the models should be able to accomplish, with a critique of several existing ones.

Conclusions and Summary

The study of language acquisition has undergone rapid and drastic changes over the last couple of decades—from a descriptive cataloguing of developmental changes in children's speech patterns, to operant and classical conditioning approaches to verbal behavior, to the linguistic nativism of LAD, and most recently, to cognitive psychological approaches in which nonlinguistic experience and non-linguistic representations are dominant. None of these approaches needs to be rejected entirely. We still require better and more detailed descriptive information about language development. The behavioristic emphasis on language as behavior, which is determined by experiential variables and processes such as reinforcement, generalization, and discrimination, remains relevant. At the same time, language *is* species-specific and is therefore influenced by hereditary mechanisms peculiar to humans, with other higher primates perhaps following close behind in the evolutionary ascent toward meaningful communication. We conclude with our bias, that all of these approaches converge on language behavior as a specific skill founded on more general cognitive abilities, which in turn come from the infant's exposure to a world of concrete objects and events, and his or her own actions toward them. Linguistic skills build on this foundation and remain at least partly interlocked with it. We further explore this interrelation between language and nonlinguistic cognition in the next chapter.

language and thought

11

The relation between language and thought is one of the most fascinating areas of language study. The topic has occupied a central place in the writings of our greatest thinkers for over two thousand years. Because so much careful thought has paved the way for psychological investigation, this chapter approaches the issues as much from the standpoint of philosophy as from the standpoint of psychology. The central question is this: How does language relate to the way we think about our world? Do all people in the world have basically the same ideas about the nature of reality, with different languages just being different ways of labeling and expressing those ideas? Or does each language subtly influence the way its speakers think about the world? Let us begin by considering the traditional view, that differences between languages are not associated with different conceptions of reality.

The Copy Theory

The copy theory originated in the writings of Aristotle. He wrote:

> Words are spoken symbols or signs of affections or impressions of the soul . . . speech is not the same for all races of men. But the mental affections themselves, of which the words are primarily signs, are the same for all of mankind, as are also the objects of which those affections are representations or likenesses, images, copies. (Dinneen, 1967, p. 80)

The major strength of the theory is that it appeals so much to common sense. It seems self-evident that the world is made up of objects that are the same for everyone, no matter what words they use to talk about them. It was not until the eighteenth century that philosophers began to question the theory. We shall find some serious problems with the theory when we scrutinize it carefully.

One problem is the fundamental assumption that the world consists of objects. Although few would debate the existence of trees, grass, sand, water, sun, moon, animals, and rocks, equally few would contend that the psychological universe is exhausted by such a concrete list. Are there "things" corresponding to

beauty, truth, justice, love, and gravity? Certainly each term suggests a concept, but the concept is not something to be directly seen or heard. This is true also of *categories* of objects. A case could be made for the naturalness of categories corresponding to experiences that most people are likely to share, such as animal, vegetable or mineral, edible or inedible, floating object or sinking object, and the like. However, it would be silly to pretend that experience leads us all to the same categories of lucky or unlucky things, things possessed by good or evil spirits, things suitable for wedding presents, deeds that are sinful, professors who deserve tenure, and so on.

The crucial point is that although we all encounter the same types of physical energy from the world outside, psychology is not physics. Many of the concepts and categories that we use daily have very little to do with physical energy but come instead from the traditions of our society, passed on largely by the language we share. Even for something as basic as size, perception does not simply follow physics. For example, it is not obvious to the eye that the sun is far bigger than the moon or that some stars are much bigger than the sun. Indeed, even educated adults in ancient Greece believed the stars were little things on a domed sky. They were not being foolish, since big things far away are impossible to distinguish from little things closer up unless there is some physical or psychological context to effect the judgment. Much of that context is transmitted linguistically from generation to generation. Thus, the concepts and categories expressed in language are not simply labels for mental events that themselves merely copy the energy of physics.

All of this does not mean that the relation between physical energy and psychological concepts is totally arbitrary. For example, the perception of color is much the same for people whose languages describe colors quite differently (this topic will be discussed later); such linguistic differences are apparently superficial (Rosch, 1975a, b, c). Rosch also suggests that many other natural concepts, such as dog, tree, man, and woman are labeled in most languages. Thus there is some correspondence between physical reality and our conceptual world, but that correspondence is far less precise than the copy theory would lead us to expect.

The central point regarding the copy theory is that not all mental concepts have objective sensory counterparts. The notion that concepts are copies of real objects arises from Aristotle's basic *tabula rasa* conception that the newborn infant is a blank tablet on which experience writes itself, creating a view of the world parallel to the real world. That basic conception may be correct in that each experience changes the infant and thereby alters the manner in which later experiences are interpreted. However, linguistic and cultural traditions are also learned, and they provide a guide to the interpretation of events. Thus the infant is receptive but is hardly passive about it.

To be fair to Aristotle, we must remember two things about the times in which he was writing. First, he himself was the victim of cultural and linguistic influences. He was a Greek chauvinist; the world consisted of Greeks and barbarians, which literally means "babblers." It is not surprising, therefore, that his views were based on only one language, making it natural to think all others must be like Greek. Second, his views were based more on single words than on complete statements, perhaps because he had been rather successful in classifying his language at the word level. To be sure, languages are much more similar at the level of words that serve as labels for natural objects than at more abstract or syntactic levels, but language is more than a system of labels.

All in all, the copy theory is a rather crude dual-coding theory, which assumes a nonverbal system of thought and a verbal linguistic system that is parallel to it. Our own opinion is somewhat less extreme, since we assume only that there are *some* points of contact. In the following section, we consider an alternative to copy theory.

Linguistic Relativity

An alternative to the idea that language merely reflects thought is the notion that language influences thought. This theory is most strongly associated with Benjamin Whorf, whose studies of North American native languages convinced him that the speakers of the different languages actually perceive the world in different ways:

> We dissect nature along lines laid down by our native languages. The categories and types that we isolate from the world of phenomena we do not find there because they stare every observer in the face; on the contrary, the world is presented in a kaleidoscopic flux of impressions that has to be organized by our minds—and this means largely by the linguistic systems in our minds. We cut nature up, organize it into concepts, and ascribe significances as we do, largely because we are parties to an agreement to organize it this way—an agreement that holds throughout our speech community and is codified in the patterns of our language. The agreement is, of course, an implicit and unstated one, BUT ITS TERMS ARE ABSOLUTELY OBLIGATORY: we cannot talk at all except by subscribing to the organization and classification which the agreement decrees. . . . We are thus introduced to a new principle of relativity, which holds that all observers are not led by the same physical evidence to the same picture of the universe, unless their linguistic backgrounds are similar, or can in some way be calibrated. (Whorf, 1956; pp. 213–214)

Whorf's theory is thus completely at odds with the copy theory. The key concepts bring to mind our earlier discussion of obligatory and optional aspects of language. Since obligatory aspects must be encoded in speech, and since what is obligatory in one language may be optional in another, it follows that speakers of different languages differ in what environmental events they *must* attend to in order to speak. For example, number is an obligatory contributor to the English use of nouns; any noun must be either singular or plural. However, in Chinese, the speaker may mark nouns to indicate *single, dual, plural,* or *number is irrelevant.* Therefore, speakers of English must attend to number, but speakers of Chinese need not. Another case is the first person plural, *we.* In English, *we* refers to the speaker and the person spoken to (you and I), or the speaker and some other party (he and I). In other languages, *we* is several different words, one for each case, even including *we* meaning myself now and at some other time. (English speakers also use *we* when they mean *I,* but this practice has been disparaged by, for example, Mark Twain, who wrote that "only presidents, editors, and people with tapeworms have the right to use the editorial we.") Thus, speakers of languages with more finely divided pronouns must attend to aspects of the situation that speakers of English could ignore.

There are many examples of linguistic differences in what information must be encoded in speech, several of which will be mentioned here. Latin distinguishes

between the paternal uncle (*patruus*) and the maternal uncle (*avunculus*), and Chinese has different terms for all varieties of cousins; we can, of course, convey this information in English, but the point is that we do not have to do so. Some Eskimo languages have a variety of personal pronouns, which indicate the location of the speaker relative to the person being spoken to (left, right, front, back) and the direction in which the speaker is facing (north, or whatever); in order to use such pronouns, the speaker must note environmental factors that most of us would ignore (what direction are you facing now? If you had to think about it, you did not automatically notice it). Finally, in English we can tell our spouses we were late because we were sitting up with a sick "friend," but some languages have separate words for male and female friends, requiring a different battery of excuses.

The general point is not that speakers of different languages are incapable of perceiving the world or talking about it, since "a language is so constructed that no matter what any speaker of it may desire to communicate, no matter how original or bizarre his idea or fancy, the language is prepared to do his work" (Sapir, 1949, p. 153). Rather, it is only necessary to attend to the parts of the environment that must be encoded in speech. We should therefore expect different perceptions of the same nominal event by speakers of different languages in many circumstances, but we should also anticipate substantial similarity in many others.

Linguistic Evidence

In this section, we consider in more detail the evidence for this linguistic-relativity hypothesis. One reason for the popularity of the topic is "the suggestion that all one's life one has been tricked, all unaware, by the structure of language into a certain way of perceiving reality, with the implication that awareness of this trickery will enable one to see the world with fresh insight" (Carroll, 1956, p. 27). Let us be quite clear about what the hypothesis does and does not state. The hypothesis states that language influences the way we *conceive* reality, not the way our sensory cells work. As Whorf wrote: "the apprehension of space is given in substantially the same form by experience irrespective of language . . . but the concept of space will vary somewhat with language" (1956, p. 158), and "visual perception is basically the same for all normal persons past infancy and conforms to definite laws" (p. 163).

The hypothesis does not state that speakers of some languages are incapable of describing things that other language speakers could describe with ease. As Whorf says:

> The Hopi language is capable of accounting for and describing correctly, in a pragmatic or operational sense, all observable phenomena in the universe. . . . Just as it is possible to have any number of geometries other than the Euclidean which give an equally perfect account of space configurations, so it is possible to have descriptions of the universe, all equally valid, that do not contain our familiar contrasts of time and space. (p. 58)

Let us consider how SAE (standard average European) languages contrast with Hopi in how they treat space and time. In SAE, we apply plurality and cardinal numbers to both real and imaginary things. Thus, we say "ten dogs" in reference

to real, spatially perceptual, countable objects; but we also say "ten days," metaphorically treating "day" as a thing. In Hopi, "day" cannot be pluralized, nor can a cardinal number be used; instead, an ordinal number, as in "the tenth day" is used. Thus we tend to treat nonspatial events as if they were objects. This tendency carries over to our use of mass nouns, such as "water," "sand," or "meat." Statements using mass nouns, for example, "a stick of wood, a bottle of beer, a cup of coffee," obey a binomial formula containing a formless item and a form; that is, there is some substance, water, that appears in a form, glass. In Hopi, however, *single* terms refer to "glass of water" and "pool of water." We, as English speakers, extend the binomial formula to include time, as in "a moment of time" and "an hour of time." We treat "summer, September, Monday, and morning" as forms for the substance of time. When we say "it is morning," what does *it* refer to? The speaker of Hopi says something more like "morning now."

The reason SAE languages lead their speakers to objectify abstractions, according to Whorf, is that the languages require a subject-predicate structure. This distinction is not entirely drawn from nature—"the light flashed" refers to a single event that occurred, not to a thing that did something. In other words, "we are constantly reading into nature fictional acting entities, simply because our verbs must have substantives in front of them" (Whorf, 1956, p. 243). What is the *it* in "it is raining"?

Whorf also maintained that SAE languages extend the objectification of time into our verb tenses, namely, past, present and future. The underlying conception is of static space and flowing time, giving rise to a psychological past, present, and future. In contrast, the Hopi contrast manifest, objective, sensory events with subjective, nonsensory events. For example, events that the speaker saw or is seeing are asserted in a *reportive* tense, irrespective of past or present time, but events that the speaker thinks are likely to have occurred, to be occurring, or to occur later are asserted in an *expective* tense. (A third tense, the *nomic,* asserts general truths.) The clear distinction between subjective and objective is retained in Kwakiutl, in which abstract "nouns" are normally preceded by personal pronouns. Thus in English we talk of "the truth," and in other languages we talk of "my belief or opinion."

The tendency of SAE languages to make abstractions more objective also shows up in our use of sensory terms. We talk of "hard" courses, "sharp" wits, "noisy" data, "bright" students, and so on; in these cases, the metaphoric use is apparent. But "educate" derives from "lead out," "comprehend" from "grasp," "communicate" from "share," "compose" from "pull together," "true" from "straight," and "simple" from "without folds." The sense of metaphor has gone, and we feel as if we are speaking abstractly. Moreover, once these terms enter the language, they may influence our conception of reality.

Whorf also argued that some of the categories we perceive as being in the world stem from linguistic categories. Languages contain both overt and covert categories. A category is *overt* if there is a formal mark present in all sentences using the category; in English, "plural" is overt, marked by inflections in the verb, noun, pronoun, and so on. A category is *covert* if it is formally marked in some constructions but not all. For example, "Helen is thirsty" contains no mark to distinguish the gender of the referent; we must remember the names that correspond to sexes. However, "Helen wants her bottle" includes a formal mark (her) that must occur in the context of a female name. We can say "the baby wants its

bottle" but not "Helen wants its bottle," at least if we want the statements to mean the same thing. If a dog is named George, "he" needs food; if a car is named Betsy, "she" needs gas. Thus gender is a covert category in English, requiring that we make note of sex in order to speak. In German, French, and Latin, gender is formally marked for all nouns, but the gender is not related to sex in quite the same way as it is in English. To quote Whorf again:

> As outward marks become few, the class tends to crystalize around an idea—to become more dependent on whatever synthesizing principle there may be in the meanings of its members. It may even be true that many abstract ideas arise in this way; some rather formal and not very meaningful linguistic group, marked by some overt feature, may happen to coincide very roughly with some concatenation of phenomena in such a way as to suggest a rationalization of this parallelism. (p. 80)

It might be interesting to determine whether English speakers have different ideas about femininity and masculinity than speakers of other languages.

Psychological Research

Although the linguistic-relativity hypothesis is not really amenable to experimental test, it has served a heuristic function in motivating a closer analysis of the relation between language and thought. What makes the hypothesis difficult to test is Whorf's tendency to qualify his conclusions. As Whorf pointed out repeatedly, salient physical correlations between events, particularly with regard to color and shape, will be reflected in the language. However, he denied that the presence of a word or concept necessarily implies that there must be a corresponding physical correlation. Logically, all that is required to support his view is one case in which a linguistic concept does not correspond to any physical commonality among instances of the concept. What characteristic is possessed by all professors who are "acceptable for tenure" but not possessed by anything else? On what physical basis can we decide whether a thing is "possessed by evil spirits," "guilty as charged," "good art," or "a drug"? Investigators have nonetheless found it useful to frame psychological hypotheses, inspired by their reading of Whorf, and to test those hypotheses.

Fishman (1960), a social psychologist, outlined four levels at which the relativity hypothesis could be examined. Two levels require determining the semantic or lexical units in a language to see whether easily coded concepts are reflected first in the culture and second in the behavior of individuals. The hypothesis seems to be supported at both levels. Thus, Eskimo languages contain words for precisely discriminated varieties of snow, and it is culturally important for the people who speak those languages to be able to communicate those distinctions accurately and readily; in contrast, to English speakers, the similarities among the different kinds of snow are seemingly more important than the differences (although children are concerned with whether the snow is "good packing," and skiers care about "powder"); Aztec is even further from snow, containing only a general term for cold. At the level of the behavior of individuals, we shall show in a later section that more easily coded events are more easily remembered. Thus there is some reason to believe that the types of words present in the lexical-semantic struc-

ture of a language are related to culture and behavior in nontrivial ways. The other two levels outlined by Fishman (1960) compare the linguistic structure and syntax of a language to the same two types of data as above, namely cultural and individual behavior. Here the results are less clear, because there is as yet little evidence that such structural features as subject-predicate constructions and covert classes, as discussed previously, have correlates in cultural and individual behavior. It is easy to present a good case for the existence of such correlates, but difficult to conceive of good ways to collect firm data one way or the other.

More recently, Miller and McNeill (1969) distinguished three levels of hypotheses regarding the influence of language on behavior, namely strong, weak, and weakest. The strong form asserts that thought derives from language and that accordingly, the influence of language pervades nonlinguistic behavior. The weak form asserts that language affects perception; if perceptual difficulties arise because of ambiguity, linguistic principles guide perception and, therefore, the behavior that results from it. The weakest form asserts that language affects memory; since we remember what is encoded about events and since linguistic encoding is pervasive, aspects of events that are readily encoded linguistically will be better retained than aspects that are less readily encoded.

Most research findings have been unclear with respect to the strong and weak forms, but the weakest form is supported by numerous investigations, usually of memory for color. Brown and Lenneberg (1954) used twenty-four color chips of equal intensity and brightness, but of different hue, and asked English speakers to name each chip. Codability was defined on the basis of the time taken to name the chip, the agreement on its name, and the length of the name itself. For example, a chip called "red" quickly by most people is highly codable; a chip called "bluish green" by some people but "greenish blue" by others, with a long latency to name it, is less highly codable. Different subjects were then presented with chips to remember, later recognizing those chips from among chips not previously presented. The results were that with as little as a seven-second delay between presentation and test, recognition favored the more codable chips. In a later investigation, Lenneberg and Roberts (1956) found that Zuni speakers made more errors in recognizing yellows and oranges than English speakers did, with bilinguals in between; this is interesting because in Zuni, there is one word for yellows and oranges, but in English we use separate words.

One explanation of the effect of codability on retention is encoding variability or, in information-theoretic terms, coding uncertainty. If one person were to label a particular hue "sunset pink" on one occasion, that label might not be used by other people or even by the same person on other occasions. Nor is it clear that given the label, the person could mentally regenerate the named color for matching purposes. On the other hand, some labels, such as "red," are applied reliably and can lead to the generation of appropriate referents. In line with this account, Lantz and Stefflre (1964; see also Stefflre, Vales, & Morley, 1966) found that codability was not as good a predictor of recognition as was communication accuracy; thus colors that subjects could communicate well (in that another subject could pick the appropriate color from alternatives, based only on the verbal description) were particularly well remembered when used as stimuli in another task. In a sense, the "direct" measures of codability were not as good conceptual definitions as the superficially indirect measures derived from communication.

Despite the early support for the hypothesis, it has become increasingly clear

that mental categories, although they are not merely reflective of physical distinctions, are not arbitrarily related to those distinctions. This point has been tellingly and elegantly demonstrated by Eleanor Rosch, both within the English language and by cross-cultural comparisons between English and Dani speakers. Rosch (1975a, b, c) asks why, if the world is infinitely and arbitrarily categorizeable, there is so much similarity among people in how that categorization is accomplished. For example, Berlin and Kay (1969) found that speakers of twenty different languages substantially agreed in their choice of the best examples of colors corresponding to basic color names (RED, BLUE, GREEN, YELLOW, and the like) in their language. Berlin and Kay referred to these salient regions in the color space as color-name focal points.

Rosch went on to show that eight chromatic focal colors were psychologically salient even for the Dani people of West Irian who have essentially a two-term color language. She found in a recognition-memory experiment that the Dani recognized focal colors better than nonfocal ones, although the focal colors were not more linguistically codable than in-between colors for the Dani. Rosch then showed that the Dani learned new color names in a paired-associates task more easily when the names were paired with focal colors, according to Berlin's and Kay's best-example clusters, than when they were paired with nonfocal colors. The data supported the conclusion that the perceptually salient colors functioned as "natural prototypes" for the learning of color names. Other experiments by Rosch used geometric forms, facial expressions of emotion, and a series of semantic categories as stimuli. Her evidence suggested that some forms, expressions, and category exemplars are better perceptual representations of the categories than are other exemplars. For example, a robin is generally viewed as a highly representative bird, but a turkey is not. Thus categories, whether linguistic or perceptual, seem to be organized around key prototypes, or best examples, rather than being discrete, all-or-none classes as linguistic definitions suggest. This aspect of category structure is reflected in various behaviors in addition to the learning and judgmental data. For example, the time taken to decide whether a beast is a dog depends on how different that beast is from a "typical" dog.

Rosch's work seems to demonstrate just the opposite of linguistic relativity, namely, that it is the human perceptual system that determines linguistic categories rather than the other way around. In short, much of the mental world mirrors or reflects the nature of the external world, and most important differences in the real world have mental correlates reflected in language. Again, however, consider our logical caveat; even if *every* aspect of the world had a mental correlate, this would not imply that every mental concept has a "real" correlate. Rosch's work is valuable in purging us of the notion that the relation between the world and our view of it is totally arbitrary, but it would be inappropriate to draw the conclusion that the world view is no more than a reflection of reality. After all, you cannot find truth, love, beauty, justice, or religion under a rock.

Roger Brown (1976), in a memorial to Eric Lenneberg, reviewed the two decades of research on memory for colors and concluded that the similarities among cultures regarding which colors are best remembered are far more impressive than the differences, despite considerable variation in how those colors are described in the different languages. In short, language is an insignificant factor in memory for color. However, recall that Whorf himself did not expect to find differ-

ences in simple perception parallel to differences in language. Perhaps, as Schonbach (1977) concluded, the color tasks are just too simple to have any bearing on the linguistic issues. Brown (1977) also expressed his belief "that in other cognitive domains, the Whorfian hypothesis may prove to be more nearly correct" (p. 187). Let us therefore go to a more complex level.

It is easy to find other cases in which more codable sensory attributes are perceived and remembered better than less codable ones, and further, the notion of codability is not restricted to linguistic codes. One class of evidence comes from verbal memory research carried out with people who have sensory deficits, such as those who have been blind or deaf from birth. Words such as *thunder* are high in auditory imagery but low in visual imagery, and *lightning* and *rainbow* have high visual imagery but low auditory imagery. The interesting finding (Paivio & Okovita, 1970) is that blind people show better memory for words of high auditory imagery than words that are low in such imagery, but they do not similarly benefit from visual imagery value. Conversely, the memory performance of sighted people is more affected by visual than by auditory imagery of words. It is also the case that deaf people who are skilled in sign language remember words that are easy to sign better than ones that are difficult to sign (Conlin & Paivio, 1975). Thus, codability is an important factor in retention, and some types of codability are linguistically determined, whereas others are derived from nonlinguistic perceptual experience and overt articulatory behavior.

One of the difficulties in studying linguistic codability and memory effects is that it is not clear which causes which. It might be that some things are easily remembered because they are codable, or it could be that easily remembered things become more codable. For example, there is abundant evidence that concrete words are more memorable than abstract words (see chapter 8). It is also the case that concrete words are more codable than abstract words, since people agree more on the meaning of concrete words than on the meaning of abstract ones, and the concrete words are less easily confused with each other than are the abstract ones. Moreover, concrete words are more successfully communicated from person to person than are abstract ones (Begg, Upfold, & Wilton, 1978). It seems to us that both of the possible causal sequences are reasonable. The relation between memory and language is an interdependency, with remembered sensory information providing anchor points between the nonverbal and verbal worlds of thought; nonverbal codability, assessed by how far removed the percepts are from the anchors, and verbal codability, equivalently defined, are only partially correlated, with the degree of correlation declining as we move farther from the anchors. Highly codable events are the most likely to be easily encoded both verbally and perceptually; such events are the dogs, trucks, and books that we encounter. However, the subtle nuances of perfume and the subtle linguistic distinctions embodied by words like *truth, beauty,* and *justice* are less codable.

Symbolic Comparisons and Language

In the preceding sections, our major focus was on the influence of language on thought and perception. One of the major points to arise was that the two enterprises exert a mutual influence on each other. The striking notion was this: when we think that we are being objective, dealing with real perceptual categories, we

might actually be subtly guided and swayed by the language we learned in childhood. The immediately preceding sections suggest that there is another side to the same notion: when we think we are engaged in purely verbal activity, we might covertly be using remembered perceptual information. Perhaps the clearest evidence of this latter influence comes from studies using a symbolic-comparison paradigm. We shall turn now to a review of those studies.

The earliest studies go back many decades (for example, Dashiell, 1937), but the systematic contemporary research began with an experiment by Robert Moyer (1973). Moyer presented his subjects with pairs of animal names and asked them to choose the animal that was larger in "real life." The pairs were constructed using the names of seven animals ranked according to size, so that some pairs differed greatly (BEE-COW), and others differed less (SHEEP-HORSE). The interesting result was that the time to choose the larger one varied inversely with the size difference—the larger the difference, the faster the choice. In fact, the relation was logarithmic, similar to the psychophysical function observed when people directly compare stimuli that differ on some perceptual dimension, such as size or length. The important point about Moyer's study is that it used a kind of memory psychophysics, in which the critical attribute is varied symbolically rather than perceptually. Moyer and Bayer (1976) appropriately referred to that function as the *symbolic distance effect:* the greater the distance between stimuli on a symbolic dimension, the faster subjects can decide which one has more (or less) of the symbolic attribute.

Note that the stimuli in the example are words and that the symbolic distance effect shows that the relation between the words and thought is systematic rather than arbitrary. Comparing mental size is a simple act of thought, representative of what we often do when we "weigh things in our minds" before making a behavioral choice. The words that evoke the mental act are arbitrarily related to the things they name (the word *bee* is not smaller than the word *cow*), but the semantic relation is not arbitrary because the words activate mental representations that somehow preserve the size relations that exist in the perceptual world. The nature of those mental representations is a matter of lively debate at the moment, with the chief alternatives being image based and other perceptual analogue models on the one hand, and versions of abstract, propositional models on the other. The theories, issues, and evidence are reviewed in detail elsewhere (Banks, 1977; Moyer & Dumais, 1978; Paivio, 1978a, b). We shall emphasize only the points most relevant to this chapter.

Note, first of all, that the facts compel us to distinguish between language and thought. A linguistic approach to thought could account for the symbolic distance effect only on some kind of associative frequency basis. For example, we often call large animals "big" and small animals "small." Given *elephant-mouse,* we quickly choose elephant as the larger because the word "big" is strongly associated with the word *elephant.* When the difference is smaller, the associative reactions are also less distinct, and reaction times are slower. If this analysis were true, we would still have a nonarbitrary relation between language and thought, although linguistic units do have an arbitrary structural relation to the "real life" entities. The nonarbitrariness lies in the associative reactions that we make to perceptual and linguistic entities alike. However, other evidence rules out a purely verbal explanation. Paivio (1975c) selected pairs in some experiments so that the differences in asso-

ciative habits would be minimized. The symbolic distance effect appeared nonetheless. Another experiment compared pictured objects that differed in real-life size but not in depicted size. Thus the pictures were just as symbolic as words in that they did not directly represent the perceptual size information. Nonetheless, according to dual-coding theory, comparisons should be faster with pictures than with words because pictures have a more direct access to the nonverbal image system that contains the information about the perceptual attributes of things. The verbal theory would make the reverse prediction, since words are read faster than pictures are named. The result was that size comparisons were faster with pictures than with words, which is consistent with dual coding. Several other findings were similarly consistent with the general conclusion that language and thought cannot be equated. Language certainly plays a part in thinking, but it does so by both interfering with and activating memory representations that bear a nonarbitrary, perceptual relation to real-world objects.

The symbolic distance effect and various other findings relevant to the present issues have been obtained with mental comparisons on many other dimensions, both concrete and abstract. For example, the inverse relation between comparison time and symbolic distance has been found from comparisons of shape (which is rounder, a *toaster* or a *book*?), brightness (which is darker, a *cucumber* or a *lime*?), hue (is a *peach* closer to yellow or orange?), pleasantness (which is more pleasant, a *butterfly* or a *baseball*?) and value (which costs more, a *house* or a *ship*?) (Paivio, 1978b). Other studies have found the effect for the time dimension (Holyoak & Walker,1976), animal intelligence (Banks & Flora, 1977), and ferocity (Kerst & Howard, 1977). Such findings permit us to extend the generality of our conclusion about the nonarbitrary relation between thought and language to verbal statements about perceptual, affective, and even more abstract attributes of objects and events. Of course, no one ever doubted that language and knowledge of the world are related. The point is that the symbolic comparison studies reveal just how systematic and fine grained the relation is and that it is probably mediated by separate representational systems for language and world knowledge.

It is particularly interesting that thinking may remain intimately linked to concrete objects even in the case of abstract attributes. Consider, for example, pleasantness and value. Paivio (1978b) found that the greater the difference in the rated pleasantness or value of two concepts, the faster subjects choose the more pleasant or valuable member of the pair. In addition, however, the choice reaction times were generally faster with pictures than with words as items. This suggests that the attributes are linked more closely to the perceptual memory representations of things than they are to their names or, in dual-coding terms, to imagens rather than logogens. The image interpretation was further supported by the finding that subjects with high-imagery ability, as measured by spatial ability tests, were faster than low-imagery subjects on both pleasantness and value comparisons. The same significant relation did not hold for verbal ability as measured by association tests. These findings make sense generally when we realize that pleasantness and value are, after all, properties of things, not of words. Therefore, to evaluate the relative pleasantness or value of named objects, we must first think about those things. We are able to think about them quickly if we have relatively direct access to their memory representations (for example, through pictorial stimuli) and if we are good at manipulating perceptual information mentally.

The picture is complicated by findings associated with some dimensions, such as color and hue, but a full consideration of such issues would be irrelevant here. The point is that even for rather abstract thought, the stuff of thought may have a nonverbal, continuously variable, concrete base—one that is systematically related to linguistic units across groups of subjects. Note that this generalization is compatible with that of Rosch (1975a, b, c) for color terms and other general concepts. These are represented so that specific instances serve as good prototypes for a general class of stimuli (for example, the color *red* or the concept *animal*). The symbolic comparison research establishes a similar point even with respect to certain abstract attributes. Of course, what is valuable or pleasant would differ for different cultures, but it appears likely that language would incorporate those dimensions in a similar systematic way, as in the symbolic comparison studies in Canada and the United States. Nonarbitrariness is established by the symbolic distance effects, that is, the negative relation between comparison time and the difference between symbolic stimuli on a given attribute. The priority of nonverbal experience and cognition is suggested by the faster comparisons with pictures rather than words and by the fact that imagery ability predicted reaction times better than did verbal abilities.

Concluding Views on the Relation between Language and Thought

Up to this point we have discussed issues and research concerning language and thought without explicitly defining thought and how it might be related to language in the light of that definition. We conclude by attempting to provide a perspective on the global problem.

Until quite recently it was not uncommon to find theorists who went to the extreme of equating human thinking with language; that is, thought *is* language. Few would accept the strong version of this approach today, but it might still be tempting to equate "higher-order" reasoning and problem solving with language. The view is easily dispelled, however, by such facts as the ability of linguistically deficient, deaf individuals to perform well on cognitive tasks. In fact, when experiential differences are controlled, deaf people seem to perform as well as hearing subjects on cognitive tasks other than ones dependent on language (see Furth, 1966; Paivio, 1971b, chap. 14). Thus, even a weaker version of the linguistic dominance view of thinking seems not to be justified.

Other approaches place language and thought under labels that reflect the general theoretical assumptions of those approaches. For example, behaviorists equate thinking with behavior in general. People thinking are people behaving, and the behavior can be verbal or nonverbal, overt or covert (Skinner, 1957). Cognitive psychologists whose theories are guided by a computer metaphor equate language and thought with abstract conceptual structures and processes of the kind discussed in chapters 4 and 5. Both the behavioral and cognitive approaches implicitly view thought as a conceptual hierarchy in which thought is a higher-order category label that includes language and other lower-order concepts. For the behaviorist the relation is one of whole to part: thinking is behavior; behavior may be verbal or nonverbal. For the common-conceptual-entity cognitive psychologist, thinking is the activity of a conceptual network, which is a system of abstract entities, relations, and processes separate from modality-specific linguistic and nonlinguistic

information. Behavioral and cognitive views alike place language and thought at different levels of generality. They differ in at least one basic assumption: the behavioral view does not necessarily imply that verbal and nonverbal thinking would be correlated, but the uniprocess cognitive view does.

The dual-coding approach resembles the above accounts in certain respects and differs from them in others. It is consistent with the hierarchical view that thinking is a general term, which cannot be equated with the more specific concept of language. Thinking can go on in the form of verbal behavior, but it can also go on in terms of nonverbal cognitive activity that may be reflected in overt nonverbal behavior or conscious imagery. Moreover, the verbal and nonverbal processes are viewed as independent although capable of influencing each other through their interconnections. This is essentially a restatement of the theoretical assumptions described in chapters 4 and 5. The implications have already been discussed in relation to problems of comprehension, memory, and so on. Those discussions are relevant because memory, for example, is clearly one aspect of thinking. Let us briefly consider some additional implications, addressed quite explicitly to the question of the relation between language and thought.

Some problem-solving tasks are clearly nonverbal in that it is difficult to imagine how they might be done in a purely verbal way. One such task is block visualization, which was introduced as an approach to the study of imagery in the early part of this century and later transformed into a quantifiable cognitive-ability test by Guilford (1967). The following example illustrates the problem: a three-inch cube, painted blue, is cut up into twenty-seven one-inch cubes by making two parallel cuts along each of the three dimensions. How many of the inch cubes have paint on three faces? How many on two faces? How many have no paint on them? The task uses verbal processes in that one must be able to understand the description. However, the problem solving itself seems to be carried out nonverbally, by performing mental operations on an image. Subjects invariably report that this is how they solve the problem. In addition, performance on the task correlates with other measures of spatial ability, specifically, the ability to manipulate or transform figural information mentally (Guilford, 1967; Paivio, 1978c). That is, people who do well on such ability tests also do well on the cube-visualization problem, whereas the reverse holds for people who are poor in spatial ability. Verbal abilities, on the other hand, do not correlate with performance on the cube-visualization problem. These facts agree in showing that the latter requires predominantly nonverbal thinking.

The general independence of verbal and nonverbal modes of thinking is supported by the observation that verbal and nonverbal cognitive-ability tests are factorially independent (Guilford, 1967). More specifically, various imagery-ability tests are factorially independent of verbal-ability tests (for example, see Ernest, 1977; Paivio, 1971b, pp. 495–497). Thus, although nonverbal and verbal processes obviously must cooperate in the performance of many intellectual tasks, the cognitive systems are statistically independent. Further evidence for such independence comes from neuropsychological studies, to be reviewed in chapter 15.

The general conclusion is that some tasks require predominantly nonverbal thought processes, others require verbal processes, and still others require both to varying degrees. Thinking can go on linguistically, nonlinguistically, or both, with either system eliciting cooperative activity in the other. Such a view helps to make

sense of some apparent conflicts in the literature. A notable case included a debate on the processes required in solving linear syllogisms, such as the following three-term series problem:

Tom is taller than Sam.
John is shorter than Sam.
Who is tallest?

The issues concern the representation of the relevant information (in this case, relative height) and what happens when the form of the premises is altered. Thus, the above example might be presented in the form: Sam is shorter than Tom; Sam is taller than John. Who is tallest (or shortest)? Two contrasting types of theories have been proposed to handle the problem, one based on the concept of spatial imagery and the other on abstract linguistic processes (propositions).

Image theory

Somewhat different image-based approaches were proposed by DeSoto, London, and Handel (1965) and by Huttenlocher (1968). What makes the image approach particularly interesting is that it was applied to problems more abstract than the relative-height example. Thus, DeSoto and his associates proposed that the subject forms a unitary visual representation that contains the premises—a visual image of a vertical or horizontal array on which the items of the premises are located. Comparatives such as *better* and *worse* are represented vertically, with *better* at the top and *worse* toward the bottom. *Wider* and *narrower* are represented on a horizontal array. DeSoto and his associates assumed that the subjects prefer to "construct" vertical arrays from the top down and horizontal arrays from left to right. The difficulty of the problem then depends on how the problem is stated. Specifically, a premise is easier to represent in the array if its first term occurs at one end of the array rather than in the middle.

One prediction from the image model is that a premise is easier to interpret when items can be put into a vertical array working downward rather than in some other order. This was supported, for example, by the finding that A is better than B, B is better than C was easier to solve than B is better than C, A is better than B. Other findings were similarly consistent with the model.

Huttenlocher (1968) presented a similar model, with a greater emphasis on the role of grammatical variables, such as subject-object relations. Thus, the construction of a spatial image is easiest when the first item is the grammatical subject of the sentence. The theory was derived first from research on children's comprehension of sentences such as *The red truck is pushing the green truck.* Comprehension was measured by the time it took the child to place one toy truck relative to another, which was fixed in place. The statements were presented in an active form, as above, or in a passive form (*The green truck is pushed by the red truck*). Among other things, it was found that for active statements, it was easier to place the truck that was the grammatical subject than the one that was the grammatical object. For passive sentences, conversely, it was easier to place the truck when it was the logical subject but the grammatical object. Thus, in both of the example sentences the red truck was easier to place than the green one. The task was the

most difficult when the to-be-placed truck was the logical object but the grammatical subject (the green truck), as in the sentence *The green truck is pushed by the red truck.*

Huttenlocher analysed the task as follows: The child first performs a grammatical analysis to identify the logical subject, which is more difficult for passive statements. Then the child brings the statement and situation into correspondence by means of transformational imagery. For example, when the mobile truck is the logical object, as in the case of the green truck in *The green truck is pushed by the red truck,* the child coordinates logical subject and perceived actor by imagining that the fixed truck (the *red* one in this instance) is mobile.

Huttenlocher extended the model to the solution of three-term series problems by adults. The subject is presented problems such as A_1 is leading A_2; B is leading A_1; who is first (or last)? These are stated in active or passive form. The results were generally comparable to those with children, so that, for example, the problems took the longest to solve, with the most errors, when B was the grammatical subject-logical object in passive premises (B is led by A, or B is trailed by A). Huttenlocher interpreted this to mean that the subject imagines A_1, A_2, and B as real objects to be arranged in space. This is done by creating a correspondence between the perceived actor and the logical subject in order to understand where B goes.

Linguistic theory

Clark (1969) presented an abstract linguistic analysis of deductive reasoning, based on processes that presumably operate at a deep structure (propositional) level. These processes are essentially the same as those used in comprehension, according to Clark (see chapter 7). The analysis was based on three principles. The first asserts the *primacy of functional relations.* Basic functional relations, such as subject-predicate, are more available from memory than are other kinds of information. Thus *John is worse than Pete* contains (implicitly) the functional relation *John is bad* as well as a comparison, *more than.* According to this principle, the participant realized that John and Pete both are bad more readily than the information that John is more bad.

The second is the *principle of lexical marking,* which states that unmarked adjectives, such as *long* and *good,* are easier to understand and remember than marked ones, such as *short* and *bad.* The prediction that follows is that "better" and "isn't as good as," both with *good* in their deep structures, will be more easily understood and retrieved than "worse" and "isn't as bad as" propositions, which have *bad* in their underlying structures.

Finally, the *principle of congruency (of premise and question)* states that the listeners can retrieve from memory only information that is congruent at the deep level to the information they are searching for. The implication is that an answer will be retrieved more quickly when propositions and questions are congruent in their base strings than when they are not. Thus, *If John is better than Pete, then who is best?* is easier than *If John is better than Pete, then who is worst?*

Clark's theory was quite successful in predicting differences in the time required to solve syllogistic reasoning problems—better in some cases than the image-based theories of DeSoto and his associates or of Huttenlocher. This was so especially in the case of negatives, such as *John isn't as bad as Pete.* The contrasting

models and findings resulted in a series of exchanges between their authors (see Clark, 1972; Huttenlocher & Higgins, 1972), which did not resolve the issues.

A resolution was suggested by Johnson-Laird (1972). He proposed that the subject changes strategies with increasing experience with the task. The individual initially may use an image-based procedure, perhaps supplemented by some principle of "natural order" (for example, A better than B better than C). Subsequently, as a result of practice, he or she may develop a procedure more analogous to Clark's linguistic model. Such a proposal has precedent. For example, Paivio and Yuille (1969) found that subjects will change mediation strategies over trials in paired-associates learning, the nature of the change depending on the type of material being learned. Moreover, subjects apparently preferred imagery strategies with concrete-word pairs, and verbal (or rote repetition) strategies with abstract pairs. These findings were consistent with the expectations from dual-coding theory. Extended to the deductive reasoning task, dual coding implies that both imaginal and verbal processes can be involved, with the latter assuming relatively greater importance as the task becomes more abstract. Moreover, different subjects might prefer different strategies, depending on their cognitive abilities and their habitual modes of thinking (cf. Hunt, 1978, pp. 121-124). Specific supporting evidence remains sparse, but what exists is consistent with the suggestion that thinking can go on linguistically, nonlinguistically, or both, depending on the nature of the task, the subject's experience with the task, and individual differences that predispose subjects to favor one cognitive mode or the other.

Our conclusion with respect to the theme of the chapter is that language and thought are related in several ways. In part, language *is* thought, but the converse is not necessarily true, since some thinking goes on nonlinguistically. Nonlinguistic thinking often spills over into conscious imagery, and it may go on autonomously or initiate supplementary, cooperative verbal activity. Conversely, linguistic (or verbal) thinking can engage nonverbal (for example, imagistic) processes in the interests of task performance. To the extent that the last possibility occurs reliably and in similar ways among different individuals in a given linguistic community, we have something analogous to linguistic determinism. Thus each of the different views concerning the relation between language and thought contains a kernel of truth. But only a kernel.

Summary

This chapter has been quite different in approach from the others, in that more philosophical and argumentative statements were made than usual. The ancient copy theory of Aristotle was criticized in detail because that theory, we believe, is implicitly accepted by almost everyone but is usually not difficult to undermine. In contrast, the relativity theory of Whorf is less intuitive but in its broadest form is difficult to disagree with. The theory may or may not be useful at more detailed levels. However, the emphasis on linguistic coding is well placed, judging by many modern results, although the results have not previously been framed as being relevant to Whorf. On balance, it is unjustified to conclude that thought, language, or reality completely dominates the others. Rather, some aspects of thought are dominated by language, and others are dominated by the perceptual properties of concrete objects and events.

figurative language

12

In this chapter we shall talk about figurative language in general, with particular attention to the kind of figurative language called metaphor. In fact, metaphor is such an important example of figurative language that all types of figurative expressions are often referred to as metaphoric language. Accordingly, we shall consider metaphor in both its specific and general senses.

Figurative or metaphoric language was once thought to be a rather special form of language that contrasts sharply with literal language, and as a result, metaphor has been both damned and praised by philosophers and linguists. From the negative side, metaphor is regarded as a low form of expression because metaphors are imprecise and distort "real" meaning. From the positive side, metaphor is regarded as the ultimate in creative and poetic expression. However, a more balanced view is that metaphoric expressions pervade all language, even the most literal. It has even been claimed that existing languages consist mainly of expressions that were once metaphoric. The origins of such frozen metaphors presumably lie in concrete things, qualities, or actions. These experiences are labeled, and the labels become more general and abstract through metaphoric extension and transfer. Interestingly, this process can be illustrated by the term metaphor itself, which comes originally from the Greek *metaphora* meaning "transfer." *Metaphora* itself derives from *meta* ("over") and *pherein* ("carry"), quite directly suggesting the idea that meaning is carried over or transferred from one linguistic unit to another. Several other examples will be examined shortly.

Until quite recently, the study of metaphor was the exclusive province of philosophers and writers. Aristotle presented a rather detailed analysis of the subject, and this philosophical tradition has continued up to the present day as reflected, for example, in the thoughtful treatments of metaphor by Black (1962; 1979) and Turbayne (1971). Many students of poetry and prose also have presented detailed literary analyses. For example, Spurgeon's (1935) work on *Shakespeare's Imagery* is an impressive study of figurative language in literature. In contrast, the area has been so neglected by psychologists that many recent textbooks in psycholinguistics do not even contain the term, metaphor, in their indexes. Skinner is an interesting exception, since he presented a penetrating and extensive

treatment of the topic in his book *Verbal Behavior* (1957). We shall examine his approach later, along with other precursors of the lively interest that is now beginning to flicker among psycholinguists and cognitive psychologists.

Earlier, in chapter 2, we discussed the design features of language. The feature for considering metaphor is the *creative* or *productive* aspect of language, especially with regard to semantic creativity. The role of metaphor in such creativity has been viewed as a major force in the shifts in the meanings of words (for example, Sturtevant, 1917). Metaphor also underlies the creative use of language that we admire in poetry and other forms of writing. Although historical change in word meaning is a much more global instance of the influence of metaphor than is poetry, historical changes ultimately depend on productive creations by individuals, which accumulate and gradually spread until there is a completely new meaning whose metaphorical roots are unknown to most speakers. That is, except in dictionaries, the original metaphorical sense has disappeared.

The process described above is related to the distinction between *frozen* or *dead* metaphors and *living* metaphors. Frozen metaphors were discussed in chapter 3 under idioms as units of language. Among the numerous examples are *mouth* of a river, *foot* of a mountain, and *grasp* an idea. Each key word has a different meaning in its metaphorical context than in its literal usage, and the meanings may become so separate that one needs to be reminded of the relation between grasping an idea and grasping a tool. On the other hand, in such living metaphors as *pumping* someone for information, *exploding* in anger, or calling a car a *lemon,* the literal sense of the words is at least dimly felt. The metaphoric uses are not yet distinct meanings and are usually listed in dictionaries as *figurative* or *metaphorical.* Psychologists are especially interested in newly created metaphors. They are not yet part of the general idiomatic language, but someone has given birth to a metaphor when referring to skyscrapers as "trees in the jungle of the city." Below we shall consider in detail the novel metaphorical expression that "metaphor is a solar eclipse."

Definitions of Some Figurative Constructions

Students of figurative language have identified various kinds of figurative expressions that differ from each other in subtle ways. We shall briefly examine a few of the more common ones (for a more extensive discussion, see Ullmann, 1962). The term metaphor, in its technical definition, refers to a comparison between two things, based on a *similarity of senses.* This also defines *simile* which, you will recall from your school grammar, differs from metaphor in the explicit use of the comparative "like" or "as." Thus, "he has a face like stone" is a simile, but "his face is stone" and "he has a stone face" are metaphors. The distinction has some psychological significance, but we shall not be concerned with it here.

I. A. Richards (1936) described the principle terms of the metaphor as *tenor, vehicle,* and *ground.* The tenor is the subject or topic of the metaphor, the thing being talked about ("face" in the above example). The vehicle is the predicate of the metaphorical expression, the thing to which the tenor is being compared ("stone" in the example). The ground is what the tenor and vehicle have in common (in our example, hardness or roughness). The logic is implicit in the meanings of the different terms. Tenor refers to the general meaning or drift (from the Latin *tenor,* originally meaning "a holding on" and yielding *tenere,* "hold"; cf. the

French *tenir*). Thus the idea is that the vehicle carried a common meaning (ground) over to the tenor or, more correctly, that a common ground *connects* the tenor and vehicle. We shall adopt Richards's terminology in our discussion, with the difference that we shall use *topic* in preference to tenor.

Note that the above analysis applies to metaphorical words and expressions. For example, the word "muscle" comes from the Latin word *musculus* meaning "little mouse." The term was used in both senses, muscle and mouse, presumably because the action of a muscle looked like a little mouse running up and down under the skin. Thus *muscle* is the topic, *little mouse* is the vehicle, and the imagined similarity between the two is the ground. Explicitly stated, the comparison would be that a muscle is like a little mouse under the skin. What we have, instead, is a "condensed comparison" (Ullmann, 1962, p. 213).

Another type of figurative expression is *metonymy,* literally meaning "change of name." The basis for metonymy is sensory contiguity between associated words. For example, we might say "The prime minister's office issued a report," although *offices* do not literally issue reports; rather, people do. We might also say "the university reports a deficit," or "he owns a Rembrandt." The French word *cuisse,* "thigh," comes from the Latin *coxa,* "hip," which is a contiguous part of the body. In English, we say that a host sets a "good table," which fades over the course of time to "board" (literally table, meaning "regular meals"). Consider as well "the kettle is boiling."

Another common figure of speech is *synecdoche,* in which an object is named by its parts or qualities, or vice versa. We speak of laborers as "hands," and a sword or its user as a "blade." Similarly, we speak of "redcoats," "redcaps," and "redbreasts." Synecdoche is clearly a force for transforming general concepts into more concrete ideas. Again some examples have faded, as in the term "youth" for a young person. It is not always clear whether a particular usage is metonymy or synecdoche, as in "chair" for professorship.

Our final example is the *proverb,* defined by the dictionary as a short saying expressing a general truth, accepted and used for a long time. Some proverbs, such as "a stitch in time saves nine," are obviously metaphorical. Others are not as metaphorical in the strict sense, although they do contain some extended, figurative meaning. Thus "all that glitters is not gold" does not imply a transfer of meaning from one term to another, but the entire expression is applied in a nonliteral manner to a variety of situations. Again, this is consistent with our more general usage of metaphor to refer to all varieties of figurative language.

Common Types of Metaphors

Ullmann describes four of the most common types of metaphors. *Anthropomorphic metaphors* describe inanimate objects or abstract situations in terms of body parts. *Brow* of a hill, *mouth* of a river, *heart* of the matter, *sinews* of war, and *bottleneck* are familiar examples. *Animal metaphors* compare persons with animals that typify particular characteristics—*dog, cat, mouse, rat, sheep, goat, ass, pig, tiger;* or *catty, dogged, sheepish;* to *ape* someone, to *parrot* someone; and so on. A third group is based on *concrete to abstract* shifts. The word *light,* for example, has yielded *enlighten, leading lights,* to *throw light on a subject, to put in a favorable light, to be in the spotlight* (or *limelight*), and so on. Finally, *synesthetic meta-*

phors transpose one sense modality to another. More generally, synesthetic experiences are perceptual transpositions, such as seeing colors when one hears music. Synesthetic metaphors indicate sensory meaning rather than actual perceptual shifts. The following are familiar examples: a *warm* (or *cold*) voice or personality, *piercing* sounds, *loud* colors, *sweet* voices or odors, and so on. This type is particularly interesting because it is the basis of Osgood's work on meaning (chapter 5). The semantic differential is a metaphorical use of rating scales, primarily in the synesthetic sense. Rating the concept *mother* on a *hard-soft* scale is an obvious example.

All of the above types of metaphors are common bases for meaning change over time. We turn now to a detailed discussion of that topic and other functions of metaphor in language behavior.

Functions of Metaphor

The functions of metaphor have been analyzed in relation to both *la langue* and *la parole,* that is, to language both as a general system and as individual verbal behavior. In the former, metaphor is part of the historical development of language, specifically in relation to the origins of word meaning (etymology) and the changes in meaning over time. The origins and changes are, of course, based on the metaphorical verbal behavior of individuals, but the cumulative effects become institutionalized in the behavior of entire linguistic communities and enshrined in dictionaries. Let us look at a few examples of metaphor in meaning change before turning to its function in individual language behavior.

The English word *pupil* seems to have two distinct meanings, one being a synonym for student, the other referring to part of the eye. In fact, the two meanings are etymologically related through metaphorical extensions. The "student" meaning stems from the Latin *pupillus* and *pupilla,* meaning "ward," which in turn comes from *pupus,* "boy," and *pupa,* "girl." The second meaning (pupil of the eye) also comes from *pupilla,* originally meaning "little doll" (the diminutive of *pupa,* "girl," "doll"), which was applied to the reflection of a person in another's eye! This would qualify as a rather unusual example of metonymy.

The word *contemplate* is a good example of a concrete-to-abstract shift, also based on metonymy. It stems from the Latin *con,* "with," and *templum,* "temple." The sense is captured by the idea that a temple is a place where one *contempl*ates, but the origin of temple is also directly relevant to the abstract meaning. A *templum* was originally a restricted area for the taking of auguries (predictions and rites interpreting the positions of the intestines of animals, and so on). Thus, *contemplate* is an abstraction from a particular kind of ritualistic behavior in a concrete setting.

A famous example of metaphorically based meaning change is the French word *tête* ("head"). Originally, the French word for head was *chef* (from the Latin *caput*), and *tête* meant "earthenware pot" (from the Latin *testa,* "pot, jug, shell"). The change came about gradually, with *tête* being used jokingly as a comparison, *chef-tête*—"head like a pot." or "jughead." Eventually the usage became metaphorical, "head is a pot," until finally *tête* replaced *chef* as the word for head. At the same time, chef underwent a metaphorical change so that it is now used in a social context to refer to the head of a company, kitchen, and the like ("le chef d'une

compagnie, de la cuisine"), paralleling the use of "chief" in English. Today, many other French words have the same humorous, metaphorical function as *tête* once had: *poire* ("pear"), *citrouille* ("pumpkin"), *citron* ("lemon") and even *cruche* ("jug") are used to refer to the head. Suppose that the French increasingly used *cruche* in that sense until eventually it replaced *tête:* that would duplicate what actually happened in the shift from chef to *tête!*

Such examples of the role of metaphor in the origins and evolution of word meaning, innumerable and interesting though they be, do not explain the creation of the metaphorical expressions themselves. Why do they arise at all in communication? The reasons must be pragmatic, referring to the verbal behavior of individuals in communicational contexts in which metaphor must serve some essential functions. Ortony (1975, 1979) has discussed the problem in terms of a general assumption and three hypotheses related to it. The general assumption is that metaphor fulfills the necessary communication function of conveying continuous experiential information—the flow of perceptual events over space and time—using a discrete symbol system. The three hypotheses pertain to how metaphor fulfills this general function. One hypothesis is that metaphor provides a compact way of representing the subset of the cognitive and perceptual features salient to the metaphor. It allows large "chunks" of information to be converted or transferred from the vehicle to the topic. The second is the inexpressibility hypothesis, which states that a metaphor enables us to talk about experiences that cannot be described literally. The third hypothesis is that, perhaps through imagery, metaphor provides a vivid and therefore memorable and emotion-arousing representation of perceived experience. The hypotheses obviously implicate psychological processes that are themselves in need of description and explanation. The rest of the chapter is devoted to that general issue.

PSYCHOLOGICAL APPROACHES TO METAPHOR

Our discussion in the balance of the chapter draws on a review presented elsewhere (Paivio, 1979). An important point to bear in mind is that psychologists interested in metaphor seek to explain metaphorical *behavior.* Such behavior includes comprehension and retention as well as production of metaphors and implicates both motivational and cognitive factors. We have already discussed the general motivational question of why speakers use metaphors. What is the effect of metaphorical expressions on the listener? The effect centers on the effects of the incongruity and novelty of metaphors. C. Anderson (1964) discussed the effects of metaphorical novelty in terms of Berlyne's (1960) theory of arousal: the incongruity of metaphor induces a psychological state of arousal (excitement, drive) which the person seeks to reduce by means of a "conceptual resolution" of the disparate elements. The motivational basis of metaphorical expression has been of particular interest to psychoanalysts as well as students of poetry (see Billow, 1977). Such views have received almost no direct research attention by psychologists. Moreover, they have not clarified the problem of the comprehension of metaphor, so we will not pursue them further.

The comprehension of metaphor is basically a cognitive problem that focuses on the following question: *How does a novel conceptual entity, a new unitary*

meaning, arise from apparently disparate parts? The question as stated entails the concepts of *similarity, relation,* and *integration,* as well as the idea of *novelty.* Similarity and relation are implied in definitions of metaphor. According to one definition, linguistic metaphor is "the application of a word or expression that properly belongs to one context to express meaning in a different context because of some real or implied similarity in the reference involved" (C. Anderson, 1964, p. 53). The basis of similarity, or ground, may lie in shared attributes of some kind, as in referring to a submissive person as a "sheep." Or it may be relational similarity, as in the so-called proportional metaphor in which four or more elements of a sentence are related proportionately (Billow, 1977, p. 82). The expression, "Put a tiger in your tank," could be analyzed as a proportionate metaphor implying that a certain gasoline is to a car what power is to a tiger.

The concepts of similarity and relation are particularly interesting because both are old and thorny conceptual problems in psychology. Similarity has always been prominent in the analysis of generalization, transfer of training, and forgetting in tasks ranging from motor performance to paired-associates learning of nonsense syllables (see, for example, Osgood, 1953). The basis of similarity, however, continues to be a theoretical puzzle. An operational definition seems straightforward in the case of formal similarity, which can be defined as the number of identical elements shared by two stimuli, although the concept of identical elements itself was highly controversial in early psychological debates on the transfer of training (the effect of practice on one task on another task that is related to the first in some way).

Consider, for example, the difficulties we would encounter if we wanted to test the idea that studying Latin helps us to learn modern languages and that the degree of this positive transfer depends on how similar the languages are to Latin in terms of common elements. How would we identify those common elements? Would we consider units of sound (acoustic features)? Units of pronunciation (articulatory features)? Of grammar? All of these together? As already indicated in chapter 5, the analysis of similarity in meaning is even more difficult, particularly in regard to the nature of the common elements. Psychologists found it necessary to invoke such concepts as functional equivalence, response similarity, and mediated similarity, all of which also led to conceptual problems in their own right. These problems are further accentuated in the case of metaphor, which involves a particularly subtle form of semantic similarity. Those problems have rarely been raised, let alone solved, in that context. Osgood (1953) represents a notable exception to this generalization, for he was an early contributor to both the theoretical interpretation of mediated similarity (see chapter 5) and metaphor. More recently, A. Tversky (1977) has proposed a feature-matching approach to similarity that solves some of the classical problems, generates novel predictions, and has some testable implications for metaphor that we will touch on later. For the moment, however, we should recognize that similarity is not as easy to deal with as it may first seem.

The concept of relation has been historically prominent in perceptual psychology, particularly in the context of the transposition problem (Reese, 1968), in which the question was whether an organism will respond to relations (for example, choosing the smaller of two circles) as compared to absolute stimulus quantities (choosing a circle of a particular size, regardless of the size of the other).

Gestalt psychologists championed the view that relational responding usually predominates. The Gestalt view is particularly relevant to the assumption that the comprehension of metaphor involves a special kind of relational perception or response (cf. Verbrugge & McCarrell, 1977).

The concept of relation is also implicated in the third key term, integration, because relational perception is often interpreted as the perception of a new entity, distinct from the related elements considered separately. This conceptualization extends directly to metaphor, in which, according to Billow (1977), "the two (or more) ideas of the metaphor work together to produce a new concept for which there may be no other expression" (p. 82).

All of these concepts—similarity, relation, and integration—are implicated in the various psychological approaches to the study of metaphor, although as we shall see, the concepts are not always defined the same way in the different approaches. Let us now consider several of those approaches.

Behavioral Approaches

Skinner (1957) avoids mediational and cognitive terminology in his analysis of metaphorical behavior. Nonetheless, close examination suggests that he, like most others, assumes mediational responses. The Skinnerian interpretation is based on the idea that verbal responses generalize to properties of stimuli that were present with the salient discriminative stimuli when the responses were originally reinforced. The following examples show how some common figurative expressions may have arisen by such a mechanism (Winokur, 1976, pp. 57-61): The verbal response "eye" would be reinforced in the presence of a stimulus cluster that includes in addition to an eye, a "person," and also such properties as "recessed," "oval," "near the top," "part," "surrounded by flesh," and "contains fluid." Later, some of the parts occur as parts of another whole, and the verbal response will also tend to occur. A needle, for example, would include the parts "recessed," "oval," "near top," and "part," hence the metaphorical verbal response, "eye of needle." This approach implies quite a different interpretation of the novelty of metaphorical behavior than is the case in more traditional analyses. The response is not *created* by the speaker; it is simply *controlled* by stimuli through the mechanism of generalization. The analysis apparently does not depend on any elaborate mediating processes unless we seek explanations for generalization itself and inquire into the nature of the identity of the "parts" in two very dissimilar wholes. Other examples more obviously call for mediational constructs. For example, Skinner's analysis of "Juliet is the sun," explicitly invokes a common mediating reaction. Thus, "the metaphorical extension might have been mediated by, say, an emotional response which both the sun and Juliet evoked in [Romeo]" (1957, p. 97). A similar example can be noted in the recent songs, "You Light up My Life" and "You Are the Sunshine of My Life." (Does anyone remember "You Are My Sunshine"?)

Verbal associative interpretations of metaphor differ from Skinner's in that they attribute the similarity relation between the key terms entirely to common verbal associations. The common associations may vary in their remoteness, that is, their position in the hierarchy of associations to the key terms. Presumably, more remote common associates would take longer to "find," making for more difficult metaphors. The influence of contextual factors can be similarly analyzed in terms

of the concept of associative priming, which refers to the modifying effect of contextual stimuli on the associations most likely to occur to individual words.

The associative model has often been applied to anecdotal data or literary examples, but direct research studies of metaphor from this viewpoint are relatively scarce. Koen (1965) obtained experimental evidence for the model in a situation in which subjects selected either a *metaphor* or a *literal word* to complete a sentence such as "The sandpiper ran along the beach leaving a row of tiny STITCHES/MARKS in the sand." They were instructed to choose the word (*stitches* or *marks*) most closely related to the group of ideas suggested by four cue words which, according to associative norms, were most often associated with the metaphorical word, the literal word, or equally often with each. The results showed that the metaphor was greatly preferred to the literal word when cued by its frequent associates, but not otherwise.

The third behavioral approach we shall consider is Osgood's mediational theory. You will recall that the theory emphasizes the mediational function of fractional responses (r_m-s_m), which combine in different ways to yield abstract mental entities. Osgood (1953, 1963) was probably the first psychologist to apply such a theory systematically to the analysis of metaphor. In fact, his theoretical work began with the analysis of synesthesia, the basis of one class of metaphorical constructions (recall that synesthesia refers to activity in a seemingly indirect sensory modality). For Osgood, the basis of similarity in synesthesia and metaphor is in the common affective reactions aroused by sensory stimuli and by words. Evaluation, potency, and activity are the primary components of these affective reactions. Osgood proposed that:

> the highly generalized nature of the affective reaction system—the fact that it is independent of any particular sensory modality and yet participates with all of them—is at once the reason why Evaluation, Potency, and Activity appear as dominant factors and the psychological basis for metaphor and synesthesia. It is because such diverse sensory experiences as a *white* circle (rather than black), a *straight* line (rather than crooked), a *rising* melody (rather than a falling one), a *sweet* taste (rather than a sour one), a *caressing* touch (rather than an irritating scratch)—it is because all these diverse experiences can share a common affective meaning that one easily and lawfully translates from one sensory modality into another in synesthesia and metaphor. (1963, pp. 246-247)

The common affective reactions are abstract in that they are independent of "particular sensory modality" and in that the affective reactions themselves are assumed to be abstractions of reactions originally aroused by things. Specifically, Osgood views the representational process as a bundle of responselike components that simultaneously differentiate among classes of meaning.

Systematic studies of metaphorical behavior have not yet followed from Osgood's theory, but the research on the semantic differential itself extensively but indirectly supports the relevance of the model. As we have already noted, when individuals use scales such as *fast-slow, hard-soft,* and *weak-strong* to rate such diverse concepts as MOTHER and DEMOCRACY, they obviously must do so in a metaphorical way. Moreover, the emergence of stable factors indicates that individuals within a culture agree in their metaphorical interpretations of the bipolar terms in the rating scales. Such agreement is necessary if the model is to be relevant

to the comprehension of metaphorical expressions, which must allow common interpretations if they are to be used for communicative purposes. Indeed, there is considerable cultural generality in the metaphorical application of a nonverbal visual form of the semantic differential (Osgood, 1963, pp. 247–248). These observations suggest that it would be profitable to study metaphor comprehension more directly using the semantic-differential approach. For example, how would the semantic-differential ratings of STONE and FACE differ if they were presented alone, as opposed to being presented in the metaphor "he has a stone face"?

Cognitive Approaches

Cognitive theorists approach the psychology of metaphor primarily as a problem of semantic memory (for example, Kintsch, 1972). This is implicit in the idea that metaphor is a problem of meaning, which is based on long-term memory information associated with the terms of the metaphor. Comprehension and generation of metaphorical expressions accordingly are based on the retrieval of such information from long-term memory. The organizational structure of the information is crucial to the analysis of metaphor because that structure will determine what attributes of the topic and vehicle will be likely to mediate the metaphorical relationship. Different theories assume different mediators. We have already seen that verbal associative theory assumes that the relation is mediated by the structure of verbal associations and that Osgood views it as being based on r_m components. We shall now see that imagery-based theories stress the structural similarities in perceptual memories but that other cognitive theories stress overlap in abstract semantic representations, which may be organized into networks or hierarchies. Each class of theory asserts or implies that the comprehension of a metaphor depends on a structural match of the information activated by the linguistic metaphor or on the construction of a new, relational entity from such information.

But comprehension also requires *episodic memory* which, you will recall from chapter 8, refers to memories of specific, dated events. For metaphor comprehension, one's episodic memory for the metaphorical expression and the linguistic context in which it was uttered must be taken into account along with extralinguistic factors. The linguistic context includes the ongoing topic of conversation. The extralinguistic context includes the general communicative setting and the persons in the exchange. All of these situational stimuli will determine precisely what semantic information is relevant to interpreting the metaphor. In brief, the metaphorical expression and the situation provide the *retrieval context* that guides the search through long-term memory. Since the linguistic aspects of the retrieval context are episodic events that fade rapidly, their influence will depend on their memorability, which in turn depends on such long-term memory characteristics as their concreteness or meaningfulness.

The preceding account provides a general framework for the analysis of metaphor in terms of mediation processes, long-term memory information, retrieval cues, and the like. We shall turn now to more specific analyses of such processes in relation to metaphorical behavior, particularly comprehension. Three approaches are considered, one based on perceptual processes and imagery, another on abstract representations, and a third on the dual-coding approach that combines imagery and verbal processes.

Perceptual experience and imagery

Metaphor has been traditionally analyzed in terms of perceptual imagery of a rather abstract nature. Suzanne Langer, for example, wrote that "metaphor is our most striking evidence of *abstractive seeing,* of the power of the human mind to use presentational symbols" (1948 reprint, p. 14). Conversely, the symbolic function of images is revealed in "their tendency to become metaphorical . . . they are . . . our readiest instruments for abstracting concepts from the tumbling stream of impressions" (p. 117). These symbolic images are not composed only of "fantasies." They derive from experience, but the original perception of the experience is "promptly and spontaneously abstracted, and used symbolically to represent a whole kind of actual happening" (p. 118). Further abstraction of this literal generality under appropriate circumstances results in a metaphorical fantasy, a figurative meaning.

Langer finds the origin of metaphorical thinking not in language but in the nature of perception itself, in "abstractive seeing." Her account is in striking agreement with Arnheim's (1969) analysis of visual perception as an abstractive process. Particularly relevant is an experiment in which observers were asked to describe their impressions of two paintings of quite different styles, shown side by side. One painting was then replaced by another, and the effects of this new combination on the perception of the remaining picture were noted. Arnheim reports that these changes had strong effects, often leading to distortions in the perception of a picture. The experiments were actually "designed to illustrate the psychological mechanism on which metaphors are based in literature. There, the pairing of two images throws into relief a common quality and thereby accomplishes a perceptual abstraction without relinquishing the context from which the singled out quality draws its life" (p. 62). The confrontation of the two images "presses for relation" which produces changes in the related items—changes in keeping with the structure of the context. Even single pictures can be vehicles for such perceptual abstractions, as Kennedy (1976) has demonstrated, particularly in regard to movement indicators in static pictures. Postural cues, lines of motion, and the like are essentially pictorial metaphors that elicit sensations or images of movement.

Other psychologists have also emphasized the perceptual basis of metaphor without necessarily referring explicitly to imagery. Roger Brown suggested that metaphorical extensions of the vocabulary of sensations, as when words like *warm, cold, heavy,* and *dull* are applied to personality and social manners, may be based on "correlations of sense data in the non-linguistic world" (1958, p. 154). Asch (1958) referred to functional similarities between the referents of metaphors and corresponding functional literal terms. We have already noted how Osgood (1953) related metaphor to the intersensory experience of synesthesia, a form of imagery. Finally, Werner and Kaplan (1963) reported that subjects who were required to express relational statements in terms of lines or images often did so in an abstract, metaphorical way. Such interpretations do not in themselves *explain* how the perceptual processes and images achieve their abstract functions or how they become linked to language, but they do emphasize the primacy of such processes in the origins of metaphor.

Despite the traditional emphasis on the relation of metaphor to perception and imagery, only a few studies have directly investigated the effects of relevant

variables on the comprehension of metaphor. Billow (1975) studied, among other things, the effect of pictorial accompaniment on children's comprehension of similarity metaphors. For example, "The branch of the tree was her pony" was accompanied by a picture of a girl riding on the branch of a tree. Billow's results suggested that pictures facilitated comprehension, although the effect was not large (about 10 percent above the level of comprehension observed when the metaphors were initially presented without any pictures). Moreover, the pictures also produced interference in that 26 percent of the changes in interpretation when the pictures were presented were from an initially correct to an incorrect interpretation. Billow concluded that "the results emphasized the linguistic nature of the metaphor task and the relatively minor input supplied by pictorial accompaniment" (p. 421). However, the results do not justify the conclusion that *imagery* played only a minor role in the task. The metaphors were originally "chosen for their relative concreteness. The compared objects were tangible and shared an attribute referring to tangible qualities or familiar actions or functions" (p. 416). Thus the metaphorical sentences themselves were high in image-evoking value, and the pictures presumably added little relevant imagery and sometimes contributed irrelevant detail that led to erroneous interpretations.

The effectiveness of the imagery value of metaphorical expressions was demonstrated in an experiment by Honeck, Riechmann, and Hoffman (1975). The subjects were presented with high- or low-imagery proverbs accompanied by interpretations either conceptually related to the proverbs or unrelated to them. The interpretations subsequently served as cues for the recall of the proverbs. The results showed that related interpretations were more effective cues than were unrelated ones, but only for high-imagery proverbs. The results suggest that imagery is somehow part of the comprehension and recall of some metaphors, but its function is not clear from the research, and the authors in fact proposed an interpretation in terms of an abstract, possibly imagery-free conceptual base (this class of hypothesis is discussed below in more detail). Their preference was partly motivated by an unpublished experiment which showed that subjects recognized interpretations of proverbs better after instructions to encode them for their intended meaning than after instructions to visualize their literal meanings. However, metaphorical imagery may be quite different from literal imagery in that it appears to be of a symbolic or abstract nature. We shall return to this point later on.

Abstract, conceptual representations and metaphor

Others have suggested a variety of different abstract representational approaches to the analysis of metaphor. Malgady and Johnson (1976) proposed a model in which metaphor processing is described in terms of cognitive features (similar to semantic features, as discussed in chapter 5). Such features are inferred from association data, most particularly adjectival, descriptive associations to nouns (cf. Johnson, 1970). This aspect renders it operationally similar to the verbal associative approach, but the features are theoretically viewed as units more elementary and abstract than words. In this general respect, although not in its details, the conceptual approach is similar to that of Osgood. Malgady's and Johnson's experiment measured similarity of constituents, as well as goodness and interpretability of metaphors using noun pairs initially chosen to be high or low in

rated similarity. The pair members were modified by adjectives associatively related to (a) both nouns together (*soft hair is shiny silk*), (b) each noun separately (*long hair is elegant silk*), (c) the opposite (nonadjacent) noun in the pair (*elegant hair is long silk*), or (d) neither noun (*distant hair is fatal silk*). A fifth condition related two unmodified nouns (*hair is silk*). It was found that constituent similarity, goodness, and interpretability all were related to the pattern of modification. Metaphors in which the adjectives were associated with both nouns were generally highest in constituent similarity, goodness, and interpretability. The three variables were moderately intercorrelated when the individual nouns were initially high in similarity, but interpretability was essentially uncorrelated with constituent similarity and metaphorical goodness when the nouns were low in similarity.

Malgady and Johnson suggested that in metaphor interpretation, the constituents are encoded into a single feature representation. The degree of similarity of the constituent nouns and the adjectival modifiers will influence the integrity of the whole. Similar but "deviant" constituents, such as the noun pairs in their experiment, will be synthesized into a well-organized whole that is readily interpreted and viewed as a good metaphor. Dissimilar noun constituents usually result in a fragmented representation that is difficult to interpret.

It is an intriguing idea that the separate, feature-defined meanings of the constituents are assumed to form a single representation with a qualitatively distinct meaning. The problem remains, however, of further specifying the psychological nature of the elementary features and, more particularly, of the new integrated representation that presumably results from their combination. Given their definition as controlled associations, the features could be interpreted in verbal associative terms unless independent evidence suggests otherwise.

There is reason to believe that descriptive associations are related to several different processes. A. Katz (1978) factor-analyzed a variety of measures obtained on concept instances, including the descriptive associative norms published by Underwood and Richardson (1956). The associations were sense impression words, whose frequency defined the dominance level of the instance with respect to a given sensory attribute. Thus, *globe* has a higher dominance level than *pearl* with respect to the attribute ROUND because round was a more frequent response to globe. These sensory associations are a subset of features in Malgady's and Johnson's sense. Katz found that dominance level correlated substantially with several different measures, including image salience (the degree to which an attribute, for example, *round,* is a salient aspect of the image aroused by the instance, for example, *pearl*), the rank of the attribute in the verbal associative hierarchy, and the judged goodness of the instance as an example of a sense-impression category. Subsequent experiments showed that each of the three factors related to dominance level independently predicted the ease of concept discovery. These results suggest that the elementary cognitive features and integrated representations in the metaphor research could be similarly broken down into different components, including verbal associative and imaginal reactions, and each might be part of metaphor comprehension. In regard to imagery, it is interesting that Johnson (1977) himself has recently stressed the perceptual basis of metaphor processing, without necessarily implying that the perceptual process "spills over" into conscious imagery.

The ultimate nature of the abstract representational process is similarly unspecified in other current theories of metaphor processing—unavoidably so, given

the present state of scientific knowledge in the area. We have already referred to the conceptual-base hypothesis proposed by Honeck and his co-workers. They left the characteristics of the conceptual base relatively undefined except for the assertion that it is abstract and perhaps imagery free. This view is similar to ones proposed by a number of psychologists (for example, Brewer, 1975; R. C. Anderson & Ortony, 1975) in regard to the semantic processing of sentences in general (cf. chapters 7 and 8). Verbrugge and McCarrell (1977) stressed the perceptual origins and relational nature of the common abstract representations that emerge in metaphor processing. The support for such representations came from a series of experiments in which the recall of metaphors was prompted by the topic, vehicle, or ground of the metaphor. Thus, for the metaphor *Billboards are warts on the landscape,* the prompts were *billboards, warts,* or the (implicit) ground (are ugly protrusions on the surface). The grounds from a different list served as irrelevant prompts. The results of one experiment showed that the topic, vehicle, and relevant ground all were effective prompts, in that they produced recall levels that far exceeded the levels obtained with the irrelevant prompts. The interesting result, of course, is the high recall with grounds as prompts, since they contained no words that appeared in the related sentences.

Verbrugge and McCarrell concluded that, in metaphor processing, one recognizes an abstract resemblance, or abstract relation, between the vehicle and topic domains, which is more than the sum of the attributes of each constituent. However, the precise nature of this abstract perceptual relation and how it arises from the separate parts remain to be specified, as do the abstract representational mechanisms postulated by Malgady and Johnson (1976) and Honeck and his associates (1975). We note once again how comparable this theoretical situation is to the one that prevails in recent approaches to sentence memory (cf. chapter 8).

A dual-coding approach

The preceding views all have merit, but each theoretical process is incomplete and insufficient in itself. Here we discuss, as a final alternative, the dual-coding approach which combines the imagery and verbal associative views in that both processes are assumed to cooperate in metaphor processing as in language and thought generally. We believe that the analysis highlights salient processes not similarly emphasized by other approaches to metaphoric language and that the ideas suggest experimental tests that would increase our factual knowledge. Recall that the two symbolic systems are assumed to be able to function independently as well as cooperatively and to differ qualitatively in the nature of the information they handle and generate. The imagery system presumably constructs synchronously organized, integrated informational structures analogous to the structure of the perceptual world. Thus imaginal representations (not necessarily consciously experienced) are assumed to have just those properties that would account for the integrated representation that appears to emerge when a metaphor is understood. The verbal system organizes discrete linguistic units into higher-order sequential structures. Taken together, these assumptions imply that the two systems can contribute independently yet cooperatively to metaphor comprehension. They provide the cognitive mechanisms for conveying continuous experiential information using a discrete symbol system—the communication function that Ortony (1975) con-

siders so essential to metaphor. We shall now consider five specific ways in which these processes might contribute to metaphor comprehension and production.

1. Dual coding enhances the probability of finding a common ground in long-term memory. Having two independent but interconnected sources of information in long-term memory increases the probability of finding a connection between topic and vehicle. A relevant verbal associative connection might be found in verbal memory, or some similarity might be found in the imaginal referents of the topic and vehicle, or both processes might contribute somehow to the construction of an integrated symbolic image or a reasonable verbal interpretation that could constitute the ground of the metaphor.

The additive effects of the two systems show up in memory experiments and other tasks (see chapters 7 and 8). For example, verbal recall is increased if subjects are encouraged to generate mental images of the objects or events suggested by the verbal material. It is particularly important to note here that such techniques are most effective when they are used in associative tasks requiring the mental construction of a link connecting two unrelated terms. In fact, participants in certain memory experiments spontaneously construct imaginal mediators that are metaphorically related to the memorized items. Some experiments have required subjects to learn pairs of abstract nouns using images. Such image-mediated learning is understandable only as the instantiation of the abstract information. Occasionally this seems to occur in the form of an image that symbolizes both members of a pair. For example, one subject reported "boy scout" as the imaginal mediator for the pair *chance-deed* (Paivio & Yuille, 1969). The image in this case is clearly metaphoric, symbolizing in a single representation a complex idea that incorporates the meaning of both terms: a boy scout is someone who takes the *chance* to do a good *deed.* The example is relevant here because the metaphorical connection was constructed by the subject in a manner analogous to the discovery of a common ground between the vehicle and topic of a novel metaphor. The discovery presumably involved dual coding in that the image had to be generated from verbal cues.

Another study illustrates more directly the discovery of a common mediator. It was a concept-learning task (A. Katz & Paivio, 1975). Subjects learned pairs in which nonsense words were associated with instances of several concepts. The subjects' task was to learn the concepts represented by the nonsense words. Although the specific instances did not differ in imagery value, the to-be-learned concepts themselves were either high or low in imagery value. Thus *a four-footed animal* is relatively high in imagery, but *an optical instrument* is relatively low in imagery value. In addition, some individuals were instructed to use visual imagery to learn the pairs, but others were not. The results showed that the high-imagery value of the conceptual categories and the imagery instructions facilitated concept acquisition. This outcome suggested that the addition of high-imagery conditions increased the probability that concept learning would be mediated by either imaginal or verbal representations, or by both. The study is important to metaphor interpretation because such interpretation is analogous to concept discovery. The subject must discover what the vehicle and topic have in common in a conceptual sense. The experiment demonstrated that verbal conditions that encourage image arousal also facilitate concept discovery. The hypothesis remains to be tested more directly in experiments on metaphor interpretation.

There is considerable evidence too that imagery contributes to the comprehensibility of sentences (see chapter 7). The general assumption is that imagery provides an additional (subjective) situational context for the interpretation of a sentence. It is reasonable to suppose that imagery contributes similarly to the comprehension of metaphorical expressions. Note, however, that the context would be inappropriate if it draws attention to its literal aspects. This possibility was mentioned earlier in connection with Honeck's research on proverb recall. There is suggestive evidence from a study in which subjects rated normal and anomalous sentences for comprehensibility (O'Neill & Paivio, 1978). Anomalous sentences were constructed by interchanging nouns from different sentences (examples are given in our earlier review of the study, chapter 8). The pertinent result was that anomalous sentences were rated as less sensible than normal ones, but the manipulation had little effect on imagery ratings. That is, subjects could visualize sentences even when they make no sense. Something similar might occur in novel metaphorical expressions that initially seem somewhat anomalous—if they contain highly concrete terms, one might easily visualize those terms without arriving at an appropriate metaphorical understanding. On the other hand, if the situation draws attention to nonliteral possibilities, concrete terms might prompt figurative interpretations of both anomalous sentences and metaphors. Pollio and Burns (1977), for example, found that subjects could interpret anomalous sentences under instructions to do so and that many of the interpretations were metaphorical in nature. However, the precise conditions under which anomalous sentences and novel metaphors do or do not lead to appropriate interpretations are unclear at this time, and the nature of figurative interpretation itself remains obscure. These problems will be clarified as we obtain more information about the interactive effects of such variables as sentence concreteness, instructions to interpret literally or figuratively, and the like, on metaphor interpretation.

The discussion now turns to the qualitative differences that might result in different contributions by the two systems.

2. Integrated images make for efficient information storage. The hypothesis that integrated images make for efficient storage of information is based on the assumption that imaginal information in long-term memory is organized synchronously into large integrated chunks (cf. chapters 5 and 8). The idea, you may recall, goes back to the British associationists, who distinguished between simultaneous and successive associations. Simultaneous associations are especially characteristic of visual perception and imagery, although they can be multimodal as well. Think of the sun and you simultaneously think of the sky. Imagine your home and you have available, more or less at once, its components and contents—windows, doors, rooms, furniture, colors, and so on. Integration also implies redintegration, so that access to part of the structure tends to redintegrate the whole. This means that large amounts of information become quickly available if the information is stored in the form of integrated images.

To appreciate the implications of this analysis for metaphor, consider the vehicle in the expression *a metaphor is a solar eclipse.* The term "solar eclipse" will tend to arouse a compound image that includes the blackened center together with the glowing ring that surrounds it. Both components, obscurity and light, will then be simultaneously available to arouse further relevant associations. These

may be further imagery, or the component information may be described verbally, and the descriptions in turn may evoke further verbal associations or imagery; and so on, in a continuous exchange until a reasonable interpretation is achieved. (We shall return to the interpretation of this particular metaphor shortly. In the meantime, how would you interpret the expression?)

3. Imagery ensures processing flexibility. The synchronous nature of images also promotes efficient memory search because such information can be processed in a way that is flexible and relatively free from sequential constraints. If we ask you how many windows there are in your house, you will probably arrive at the answer by imagining your house from different positions and counting the windows from the image. You could do so by working around the house in either direction, inside or out. By contrast, the processing of organized verbal information in long-term memory is sequentially constrained to a high degree. We can recite the alphabet forward more quickly than backward, and backward recitation of a poem would be painfully slow.

The idea of flexible processing applies also to the generation of novel, integrated images from unrelated words. Consider once again the experiment by A. Segal (already summarized in chapter 9). Segal presented his subjects with sets of two, three, or four nouns and required them to generate either meaningful images, which they drew, or sentences, which they wrote. Segal measured reaction time from the point of exposure of the words to the moment when the subject pressed a key to indicate completion of the task. The interesting result was that the image generation time increased only slightly as the number of items increased but that the sentence generation time increased sharply with set size. This was predicted from the idea of differences in sequential constraints: things can be put together in various ways in a meaningful image, but words do not enjoy the same freedom in sentences.

The flexibility of image processing implies a special advantage in creative discovery and invention, specifically in that it makes for speed and efficiency in the search for relevant information and for the construction of novel combinations from component information. The implication for metaphor comprehension is that imagery can increase the efficiency of the search for relevant information and for the generation of a novel, integrated representation that would constitute the common ground for vehicle and topic.

4. Topic and vehicle are retrieval cues for relevant information. Relevance requires a guided search through long-term memory, which is initiated by appropriate retrieval cues. This function is served by the metaphorical expression itself together with contextual information. We propose that the vehicle and topic are the key terms and that the former is usually prepotent because, by definition, its properties are to be "conveyed" to the topic. Moreover, the concreteness of the vehicle should be crucial because a concrete term provides rapid access to information-rich images.

You will recognize that the idea originates with paired-associates learning tasks in which the concreteness or image-evoking value of the stimuli and responses are systematically varied. Typically, recall accuracy depends particularly on the concreteness of the item presented as the retrieval cue: pictures or concrete nouns

are good reminders for their associates; abstract nouns are not. This effect was metaphorically expressed as the "conceptual peg" hypothesis: concrete nouns and pictures are effective pegs for the storage and retrieval of associated information.

In the case of metaphor comprehension, we extend the idea to the retrieval of relevant information from long-term memory. The vehicle serves as an efficient conceptual peg for metaphor comprehension since it promotes retrieval of images and verbal information that intersect with information aroused by the topic. Retrieval of integrated images will be particularly useful for reasons already discussed: they are information rich and permit flexible processing.

There is no direct experimental evidence for the hypothesis as a whole, although aspects of it are supported by recent experimental findings and some informal observations. The experimental findings bear on the asymmetry of the topic and vehicle. Verbrugge and McCarrell (1977) found that the vehicle was generally superior to the topic as a retrieval cue for the entire metaphor. This supports the special salience of the vehicle in episodic memory for the metaphorical expression, but it does not necessarily follow that the vehicle is also prepotent in retrieval of information from semantic memory or other aspects of the comprehension process. Moreover, Verbrugge's and McCarrell's study was not intended to provide any evidence for the role of imagery in their task.

A. Tversky's (1977) demonstration that similarity relations are not symmetrical is also relevant to the present hypothesis. Specifically, he found systematic asymmetries in comparative tasks (*A* is like *B*). The direction of the asymmetry was determined by the relative salience (for example, judged prominence, figural goodness, prototypicality) of the two stimuli, so that similarity was greater when the less salient stimulus was compared to the more salient one than vice versa. For example, it seems more natural for a European to say that Canadians are like Americans than to say that Americans resemble Canadians because, for most Europeans, Americans are more salient than Canadians. The application to metaphor and simile is obvious: such expressions should be more acceptable when the more salient noun serves as the vehicle than when it serves as the topic. Moreover, Tversky suggested that the interpretation of similes and metaphors is "scanning the feature space and selecting the features of the referent that are applicable to the subject" (1977, p. 349). The relevant point in the present context is not the feature model per se, but Tversky's emphasis on the priority of the vehicle (that is, the referent) in the interpretation process. That aspect seems consonant with the present hypothesis, although Tversky's analysis is open to alternative interpretations (for example, Harwood & Verbrugge, 1977; Ortony, 1979).

Some informal observations bear more directly on those features of the hypothesis. One of the authors asked a number of colleagues and graduate students to interpret the "meta-metaphor" introduced briefly above. The complete expression stated that *for the student of language and thought, metaphor is a solar eclipse*. The participants were then asked to describe how they arrived at their interpretation. Most agreed at least partly with the interpretation that originally motivated its construction; namely, the idea that in a metaphor, as in an eclipse, something is obscured. In addition, several respondents gave interpretations completely in agreement with the author's, saying, for example, that both metaphor and eclipse enlighten while they obscure and that they cover up the real thing so that you can see it better, or that they block out the central stuff so that you can see the subtle stuff around it better.

What would be expected from their introspective reports on the manner of arriving at an interpretation? The hypothesis that the vehicle functions as a conceptual peg suggests that it should have been processed before the topic, and as an image. This seemed to be generally the case. One person spontaneously reported that the statement did not make any sense until he visualized an eclipsed sun (the vehicle in the metaphor). Another said that he first visualized a partial eclipse and then a full one. A third said that he certainly visualized "that thing with all the fuzzy stuff around it." And so on. There was one exception who said that he first thought of what metaphor might be to the student of language, then what an eclipse means to the student of astronomy, and then what the two have in common. He may have visualized, he said, but it did not seem salient. It is interesting that this respondent is also the only one whose interpretation did not include the idea of something being covered up or obscured. He referred instead to "exotic events from which one can learn something." This certainly is an appropriate interpretation, although not the most common one for this group of respondents. His interpretation and his introspections are consistent with the conclusion that he used the topic rather than the vehicle as his conceptual peg, whereas the others apparently were drawn to use the vehicle in that role.

The theoretical analysis has some obvious testable implications. For example, metaphors could be constructed so that the concreteness of the topic and the vehicle are independently varied. Concreteness of either term should facilitate interpretation (as measured, for example, by its speed and appropriateness), but concreteness of the vehicle should have the greater effect. Moreover, the interpretation should more often be initiated by the vehicle than by the topic, although this may be modified by the relative concreteness level of the two terms.

5. Verbal processes keep search and retrieval on track. We have suggested that imagery specifically contributes to the speed of reaching into long-term memory and to the speed and flexibility of the search for information that would provide the basis for a relevant interpretation of a metaphor. We propose, finally, that relevance itself is largely governed by the verbal system. The sequential nature of verbal processes contributes to an orderly, logical sequence in the flow of ideas. In brief, the verbal system keeps the search process "on track" in regard to the goal of discovering a relevant relational idea. Thus, in our thematic metaphor, the image of a solar eclipse could lead to flights of fantasy bearing no relevance to the meaning of metaphor to a student of language. It is our episodic memory for the verbal concepts themselves that keeps us from being blinded by the glare of the solar image and thereby stumbling aimlessly through our memory storehouse.

Summary

We have reviewed some psychological research findings and theories concerning the way we understand, produce, and remember metaphors. Various mechanisms have been emphasized by different theorists, including generalization of verbal responses, perceptual processes and imagery, verbal associations, abstract conceptual representations, and dual (verbal and imaginal) coding reactions to contextual stimuli and (in the case of comprehension) to the key words in the metaphorical expression. The theoretical ideas are for the most part highly speculative because

relevant research is still sparse. Moreover, the basic problem of comprehension itself is only poorly understood (cf. chapter 7). We have expressed the hope that the study of metaphor might lead to a better conceptualization of comprehension in general. This implies that "ordinary language" and metaphor are continuous phenomena, employing common cognitive and linguistic processes. Research might prove otherwise, but in any case, without it we shall never know. Much of the psychological research on metaphor to date has not been directed at really fundamental problems in the area. Such work might require the systematic development of a large pool of novel metaphors that vary in type, difficulty, concreteness, and whatever other dimensions may seem relevant. It may demand systematic extensions of some of the traditional paradigms that have been developed in verbal memory and language research. It would require detailed factual information on precisely how people respond to novel metaphorical expressions and under what conditions they produce them. A few possibilities were suggested in connection with the role of the vehicle and topic as retrieval cues, but such informal approaches need to be translated into systematic observational studies and experiments before real progress can be made in this fascinating area of language research.

bilingualism

13

Bilingualism is an important practical and theoretical problem. Its practical importance stems from the fact that many of the world's citizens speak more than one language. They do so because they live in countries that are made up of diverse linguistic groups or that border on countries with different languages. India is an extreme example of linguistic diversity, with its fourteen major languages and many minor ones. Switzerland illustrates linguistic border diversity, with France, Germany, and Italy as its neighbors. Even in North America, often noted as an example of the monolingual norm, there are enormous numbers of bilinguals or multilinguals. Several million people in Canada speak French and English, and large numbers of others speak various other languages, usually along with English. Although the United States does not have a similar bilingual language policy, millions of people speak at least one other language in addition to English. Whatever its origins, bilingualism poses important social problems, ranging from language-based social conflicts to the practical problem of providing educational opportunities in more than one language. The social problems in turn raise theoretical questions about second-language acquisition and the social psychology of bilingualism. In addition, the mere fact of possessing two or more language repertoires poses interesting puzzles regarding the nature of the underlying memory systems, thought processes, productive efficiency, and the like.

We cannot hope to deal fully with all aspects of the psychology of bilingualism in one chapter, so we have selected a few key issues to emphasize. Following an overview of theoretical approaches, we shall consider in turn the problems of measuring bilingualism, bilingual memory and performance, cognitive correlates and consequences of bilingualism, second-language acquisition in childhood, and finally, second-language acquisition in older children and adults.

Theoretical Approaches

The approaches that we have traced throughout the book are directly applicable to the language behavior of the bilingual, much as if they were applied to two monolinguals speaking different languages. Thus a structural linguistic

approach would emphasize surface structure differences in languages at each level of analysis, phonological, morphological, and grammatical. A transformational approach, as shown by McNeill's approach to language acquisition (chapter 10), would emphasize linguistic universals in basic grammatical relations. The approach would then stress differences in the transformational rules appropriate to the bilingual's different languages and in different deep and surface structures that result from the transformations. In addition, the interpretive rules of the semantic and phonological components would differ in many specific respects for the different languages.

Skinner's verbal operant approach would simply assume two complete verbal response repertoires, each controlled by the same general classes of antecedent conditions that apply to verbal operants in general. Echoics, textuals, and intra-verbals are obvious examples, since the discriminative stimuli result from behaviors in one language or the other and the verbal responses of the bilingual follow suit. The language of the tact would depend on these other classes of discriminative stimuli, and all classes of operants would depend particularly on the general influence of the audience as a controlling condition for the emitted language. Other behaviorists (the neobehaviorists) would stress differences in language habits and in the mediation processes that determine the nature of verbal behavior in the two languages. In Osgood's theory, for example, one can ask about similarities and differences in the representational mediation processes that underlie each language. Osgood's theory assumes, in addition, that connotative meaning is universal in regard to the dimensions of evaluation, potency, and activity.

Cognitive theories would emphasize the role of contextual factors, knowledge of the world, and general cognitive processes in the language behavior of the bilingual. In regard to cognitive processes, a problem of current interest is the nature of the long-term (semantic) memory systems that subserve the different languages. Is there one semantic memory system or a separate one for each language? If one, is it abstract, amodal (propositional), and rule governed, or more perceptual and imaginal in nature?

The last points hint at some of the special problems associated with bilingualism, which require particular theoretical mechanisms. One stems from the bilingual's capacity to switch languages with little or no interference. This does not pose any unique problem for behaviorists, who would simply handle it as changed stimulus conditions that evoke different verbal habits or mediation processes. Some cognitive psycholinguists, however, postulate special switching mechanisms that operate on language input and production. Such issues will be examined later in detail.

Measurement of Bilingualism

What exactly is a bilingual? Some define a bilingual as one who has equal ability in two languages. Others apply the label to anyone who has even a smattering of knowledge of a second language. Still others refer to degrees of bilingualism, perhaps crudely differentiated as dominant and less dominant (or strong and weak) languages or more finely differentiated by some measure of linguistic ability. The differentiated approach seems most reasonable and is the one we adopt here. A second aspect of the question turns on qualitative distinctions: are there different

types of bilinguals, resulting perhaps from different learning histories and contexts? We shall briefly address that question as well.

Subjective ratings and objective performance tests have been used to measure degree of bilingualism. These have been reviewed in detail by various authors (for example, Fishman & Cooper, 1969; Macnamara, 1969). The rating approach may simply require a global self-rating of the degree of proficiency in the different languages, or it may require more specific self-ratings on a variety of language skills—reading, writing, listening, and speaking. Other self-ratings require the person to indicate the degree to which each language is heard or used in various situations. Another procedure is to sample language behavior in various situations and to determine the extent to which the speaker uses each language (Mackey, 1965). Finally, various performance tests have been devised to measure bilingual fluency, flexibility, and dominance. Which of the above procedures is best depends partly on what aspect of bilingual skill is to be predicted, but some methods are more generally valid than others. We offer a sampling of some representative studies that have considered the predictive power of one or more tests.

Macnamara (1969) included two kinds of subjective ratings in a study with sixth-grade pupils in Montreal. One approach used a language background questionnaire, on which subjects estimate how often each of their languages is used at home. This was included among a number of other measures in an attempt to predict scores on fifteen tests of bilingual (English-French) ability. The questionnaire contributed to the prediction of ten of the test scores, but in no case was it the best predictor. As a second measure, subjects rated their speaking, listening, writing, and reading skills in each language. These ratings were much better predictors of ability than was the language background questionnaire.

Fishman and Cooper (1969) obtained various subjective and objective measures of proficiency in and frequency of usage of Spanish and English among Spanish—English bilinguals in New York, using a language census and a psycholinguistic interview and testing session. The criterion bilingualism scores to be predicted were based on phonological ratings made by two linguists. It turned out that the census scores were generally the best predictors of ability, with language most often used at home being the best single one. Note that these findings contrast somewhat with those of Macnamara, who found that the language background questionnaire was less powerful as a predictor of criterion measures of second-language proficiency than were the self-ratings of language skills. However, Macnamara did conclude that ratings of language use are likely to be influenced by social pressures to exaggerate or understate the use of a particular language, so that the validity of language background questionnaires is likely to vary from country to country.

Reaction time is among the objective tests that have been used to measure bilingual fluency. For example, Lambert (1955) required French-English bilinguals to press a key with a specific finger in response to a series of instructions like "Left, one," meaning, "Press the key with the first finger of the left hand," or to press on the basis of the color of the key ("Left, red" or "Gauche, rouge"). There were clear differences in the speed of responding to the two languages, depending on the subject's experience with them. English-speaking undergraduate students of French were slower in responding to French than to English instructions; graduate students

of French showed a smaller difference favoring English; and the French natives (who had lived about seven years in an English-speaking country) showed either no difference or small differences favoring French.

Other fluency measures include speed of naming pictures in both languages (Ervin, 1961), word production in both, and speed of reading in both. The last of these seems to correlate particularly well with language skill (Macnamara, 1969). Flexibility tests require subjects to give meanings or synonyms for words in both languages. As you can see, dominance could be measured by any test that provides a score in both languages of the bilingual. Tests specifically designed for this purpose may require the subjects to pronounce and interpret ambiguous verbal stimuli—words that are spelled the same but differ in pronunciation and perhaps meaning in the two languages (for example, *cane* for French-English bilinguals). As mentioned above, a variety of such tests can be useful, depending on the specific purposes of the study.

Lambert, Havelka, and Gardner (1959) conducted an extensive experimental study which included seven different measures of bilingual behavior. One was the bilingual fluency or balance measure used in the Lambert (1955) study described above. The others were word-recognition threshold; facility in word completion in both languages, given word beginnings such as "vi"; facility in word detection (finding English or French words in a series of letters like DANSONODEND); reading speed; response set to respond in one language to ambiguous words (the flexibility test described above); and facility in translation. All of the tests except translation correlated significantly with bilingual fluency. Moreover, the analysis showed that all of the measures were moderately intercorrelated and could be interpreted as measuring a single dimension. As a general conclusion, it seems that most measures of bilingualism can predict proficiency in the two languages to some degree.

The qualitative distinction that has received the most attention is that between *compound* and *coordinate* bilinguals. The compounds have learned their two languages in the same acquisition context, such as English and French being spoken by both parents in the home, and the coordinates have learned their languages in separated contexts, perhaps in different countries. This difference was presumed to affect meanings in the two languages, so that compounds attribute identical meanings to words and expressions in each language, but coordinates interpret the translation equivalents somewhat differently in each language. In chapter 5, we described a semantic-differential study (Lambert et al., 1958) that supported the distinction, and other results have also been consistent with it. Other studies, however, have failed to find evidence that the two types differ in any interesting ways, raising doubts about the validity and usefulness of the distinction (Diller, 1970; Lambert, 1969). Nonetheless, there is a sense in which it remains interesting, and we shall return to the issue later.

Performance Correlates and Consequences of Bilingualism

In this section we shall deal first with the general intellectual consequences of bilingualism, followed by a consideration of possible specific behavioral correlates in such areas as memory.

Bilingualism and intelligence

Do bilingual individuals pay an intellectual price for their ability to speak two languages, or can they have their bilingual cake without suffering a loss in some other domain? The prevailing view for many decades was that bilingualism is associated with a general intellectual deficit relative to monolingualism. This view was supported by studies in which bilingual children in various communities in Europe and America were, on the average, inferior to monolinguals in their performance in school subjects and in tests of intelligence. The first major challenge to this conclusion came from the work of Peal and Lambert (1962) with French-English bilinguals in Montreal. They controlled important variables more effectively than the earlier work did, particularly differences in social class and educational opportunities. They found no intellectual deficit among their bilinguals. On the contrary, the bilinguals scored better than the monolingual children on both verbal and nonverbal tests of intelligence. Moreover, the bilinguals appeared to have a more *diversified intellectual structure* and more *flexibility of thought,* according to scores on specific cognitive tests. The latter conclusion has been supported in subsequent studies (see Lambert, 1977) in other settings. Specifically, bilinguals have sometimes shown an advantage in measures of cognitive flexibility, creativity, and divergent thinking as measured by tests that stress variety and quantity of output (for example, word fluency, associative fluency, and so on; for a description of such tests, see Guilford, 1967).

Other studies also fail to show intellectual deficits. This was the case, for example, in an experimental immersion French program begun in St. Lambert, Quebec, in 1965. Relative to controls in standard English and French school systems, the immersion school children showed no cognitive or intellectual confusion as a result of complete immersion in their nonnative language (Lambert & Tucker, 1972). We shall later consider the effects of that program on bilingual competence itself. The main point here is that the study and other recent research suggest that bilingual competence is not won at the price of general intellectual loss. If anything, bilingualism may be associated with a gain in cognitive flexibility and creativity, although a definite conclusion of that kind must await further research.

Bilingual memory

The memory problem that has received the most attention is the degree to which the two languages of the bilingual are separated in memory. One view states that there are two independent memory stores that only contact each other via translation. Another holds that bilingual memory is a single system that taps into two lexical systems by a code-switching mechanism of some kind. The two extreme views make sense only if they are interpreted in terms of semantic memory, since it seems obvious that the bilingual speech systems must be capable of functioning independently. Given that proviso, we shall briefly review the evidence on the issue (for a more detailed overview, see McCormack, 1976, 1977).

Kolers (1963, 1966a, b) found several kinds of support for the independence hypothesis. For example, he found that the word associations of bilingual subjects for translation equivalents in the two languages differed more than would be expected if the associations were mediated by one memory store. Interestingly, however, Kolers also found that common associations occurred somewhat more

frequently for concrete nouns, such as *table* and its German equivalent *Tisch,* than for abstract nouns (*freedom-Freiheit*) or affective terms (*pain-Schmerz*). Kolers suggested that this might be because the referents of concrete terms are likely to be more similar than those of the other classes of words. Nonetheless, he maintained that bilingual independence in memory was the rule. That view was further supported by memory data, such as recall from lists containing words in both languages. For one thing, bilinguals are able to remember the language in which a word was presented at a far higher level than would be expected on a chance basis (for example, Kolers, 1965; Lambert, Ignatow, & Krauthamer, 1968; Saegert, Hamayan, & Ahmar, 1975). This finding has been treated as inconsistent with the single-store hypothesis because that would lead one to expect poor memory for the language of input. Alternatively, however, one can argue that subjects are able to encode or "tag" the items by input language, although semantic attributes are stored in a single memory system (Rose, Rose, King, & Perez, 1975). The results of a variety of studies, particularly ones that provide evidence on how information is organized in bilingual memory, are consistent with the one-store hypothesis, and McCormack (1977) concluded that the view "makes most sense" in predictive power and parsimony. Thus the issue is not resolved.

Note that the one-store hypothesis is consistent with cognitive theories that assume a single conceptual format for all knowledge (see chapters 4 and 5). Dual coding provides a different approach to the bilingual memory problem, however. Consider an unpublished experiment by Paivio in collaboration with W. E. Lambert and Andrew Yackley. French-English bilinguals were presented with a list containing equal numbers of easily named pictures, French words, and English words. The words in each case were concrete nouns. The participants were shown these items one at a time and were required to write down the English name of each picture, translate each French word into English, and simply copy each English word. Following this task, they were unexpectedly asked to recall the English words they had written. What would be predicted from the two memory theories we have been considering? If the concepts that correspond to the two languages are in one memory store, recall should be the same whether the word was presented in English or in French. However, if the languages are independent, recall should be higher for the translation condition because both codes are activated during the task, and recall could be mediated by either one. That is, the subjects might remember the presented French word, the English word they wrote down, or both. They would also remember the language in which they wrote the items (which was always English), so that they could retrieve (reconstruct) the required response from either French or English item memories. The results were completely consistent with the independence view in that recall in the translation condition was twice as high as recall under the monolingual coding condition.

The story does not end there, however. Consider the implications of the picture condition. Unitary semantic memory theories, such as the propositional models discussed in chapter 5, would predict equivalent recall for both pictures and words because storage in each case is in one conceptual format. Although one could argue that memory processing is "deeper" (Craik & Lockhart, 1972) in the picture and bilingual coding conditions than in the English coding condition and that recall therefore might be higher in the first two than in the last, there is no reason to suppose that the picture coding and translation conditions would differ. However,

recall in the picture condition was the highest of all (51 percent), exceeding the translation condition (34 percent) as much as the latter exceeded recall following monolingual coding (17 percent). Thus the contribution of pictures to recall appeared to be independent of and stronger than that of words in either language.

The results are consistent with the following dual-coding interpretation. The bilingual has verbal representations (logogens) corresponding to words in each language. These are organized into separate but interconnected associative structures as a result of experience with the two languages. In addition, each subsystem has referential connections with the imagery system (which may be different for the two languages, depending on whether the linguistic acquisition contexts differed). Representations in each of the subsystems are activated by the coding task, and each class of representational activity leaves a memory trace. The monolingual coding condition activated primarily English logogens. Bilingual coding activated both French and English logogens. This effectively constituted dual *verbal* coding, enhancing recall probability relative to the monolingual coding condition. The picture-naming condition activated imagens in the image system and corresponding logogens in the English verbal system, constituting cross-modal dual coding. The superior recall in the picture condition as compared to bilingual coding is consistent with the idea that mental images are easier to remember than mental words. As an aside, that idea has been independently supported in prior research. In fact, the results of a series of picture-word memory experiments were consistent with the conclusion that "an image is worth two mental words" (Paivio & Csapo, 1973, p. 194). The results under discussion here support the same empirical generalization. To paraphrase an old saying, however, one finding does not a generalization make, so the basic results need to be systematically replicated before a quantitative dual-coding interpretation can be entertained with confidence.

Consider, finally, how dual-coding theory might resolve the one-store versus the two-store controversy regarding bilingual memory. The two-store view applies to verbal representational systems, in agreement with others who assume independence at the lexical level. The one-store view corresponds to image coding of words in either language; that is, each can have access to the same imagens (at least in the case of compound bilinguals—see further below), much as in the case of synonym processing in Clark's (1978) image-verbal model discussed in chapter 5. Given Clark's synonym results, one can easily come up with predictions for comparable bilingual tasks using concrete and abstract words in memory and association tasks.

A relevant experiment was reported by Saegert and Young (1975). They studied translation errors in the learning of bilingual paired-associates. Subjects rarely make translation errors in verbal memory tasks, but Saegert and Young succeeded in increasing such errors by pairing Spanish and English translation equivalents with different stimuli in the same list. Thus the bilingual subjects had to learn which concept went with each stimulus as well as the language in which the concept was expressed. In addition, half of the pairs were concrete, and half were abstract nouns. Consistent with the dual-coding view, Saegert and Young reasoned that concrete items would be more likely than abstract items to be conceptualized in a nonlinguistic form and that this would result in more translation errors for the concrete items. The results came out exactly as predicted: there were more errors with the experimental pairs than with the control pairs in which the responses

appeared in the list in only one language, and there were more translation errors for concrete than for abstract pairs. Saegert and Young concluded that

> the subjects relied on a natural tendency to process concrete responses as images or concepts and therefore became easily confused as to which of their two language codes was appropriate for a given stimulus. Processing of the abstract words, however, was less likely to take place independently of the verbal representation since abstract words are generally less amenable to imaginal or "supralinguistic" conceptualization. (p. 6 of reprint)

The support for dual-coding theory has been less clear in other studies. Winograd, Cohen, and Barresi (1976) inferred from the theory that bilingual speakers should show poorer memory for the language in which concrete words appeared than for the language in which abstract words appeared. Their reasoning was that subjects could rely partly on an image code for the concrete but not the abstract words, and to the extent that they do so, memory for the input language would be relatively poorer for the concrete words. In fact, they found the opposite in two memory experiments. Two comments are in order. First, dual coding does not imply that reliance on the image code would *necessarily* detract from memory for the verbal code. The theory in fact assumes that verbal and imaginal codes are independent and that their effects would therefore be additive unless special conditions are introduced to restrict attention to the image. The second point is that Winograd and his colleagues suggested two image-based interpretations. One suggestion was the "cultural imagery" hypothesis, according to which bilinguals have somewhat different images associated with translation equivalents in their two languages. If this is true, then the images themselves would contain clues to the language of the concrete words from which they were generated. The second possibility was that the images associated with concrete words may function as particularly effective retrieval cues for the phonological and other features of the words themselves, thereby enhancing memory for language. We shall see later that a comparable hypothesis seems to be necessary to explain the powerful effects of image-based mnemonic techniques on second-language learning.

Mägiste (1977) investigated memory for concrete and abstract sentences among two groups of bilinguals. One group was balanced in German and Swedish, and the other was dominant in German (according to self-ratings and the time to name pictures in each language). The sentences were presented visually, sometimes accompanied by background noise. The results showed the usual superior memory for concrete sentences, and balanced bilinguals were more nearly equal in recall of sentences in either language than were the dominant bilinguals (cf. Nott & Lambert, 1968). The interesting new results were that the other effects depended on both concreteness and the presence or absence of background noise. The inferior recall for abstract sentences was especially marked for the German-dominant group when the sentences were in their weaker language. Moreover, background noise interfered with recall, but this was most true for abstract Swedish sentences, especially for the dominant bilinguals. These results suggest that recall of abstract sentences is a sensitive measure of bilingual balance and dominance. It is not clear why noise should have been more detrimental to memory for abstract than for concrete sentences. Perhaps it was because the abstract sentences were somewhat more difficult to

comprehend than the concrete ones, and noise interfered differentially with verbal encoding rather than memory.

In summarizing the bilingual memory problems we have selected for discussion, the results show that the bilingual's two verbal codes are separate, capable of functioning independently with little interference. At the semantic or conceptual level, however, the two languages appear to share an underlying system to a substantial degree. There is evidence that this commonality applies more to concrete than to abstract material, which is consistent with the dual-coding idea that what is shared is knowledge of the world as expressed in imagery. That view is relevant also to the compound-coordinate problem. As mentioned earlier, the general consensus now appears to be that the distinction is not useful as a descriptive or predictive statement about *linguistic* codes acquired separately or together. However, it might still be a valid distinction with respect to the *experiential contexts* of language acquisition (Diller, 1970) and, therefore, the culture-specific differences in the nature of imagery and affective reactions aroused by the bilinguals' two languages (Bugelski, 1977; Lambert et al., 1958; Winograd et al., 1976).

Bilingual language production

Bilingual production has been studied primarily by means of reading aloud, naming, and association tasks. Interest has centered particularly on code switching, differences in the content of associations, and conditions that might create productive interference between the bilingual's two languages. The research on code switching has often contrasted production with comprehension. For example, Kolers (1966b) required French-English bilinguals to read aloud and comprehend unilingual texts in each language, as well as mixed-language passages. The following are examples of three types of materials:

> His horse, followed by two hounds, made the earth resound under its even tread.
>
> Son cheval, suivi de deux bassets, en marchant d'un pas égal faisait résonner la terre.
>
> His horse, followed de deux bassets, faisait la terre résonner under its even tread.

Kolers found that the participants took 20 percent to 40 percent longer to read mixed texts than unilingual ones, without a comparable difference on comprehension tests. The production data enabled Kolers to calculate a phonological code-switching time of about .3 to .5 seconds for different subjects. The estimates were longer (about 1.3 seconds) when subjects freely generated mixed (as compared to unilingual) speech or summarized the text they had read. Kolers concluded that code switching inhibits production but not comprehension, perhaps because production requires the subject to switch phonological rules, but comprehension depends on the meanings of the words and not on their linguistic form.

Other studies have supported Kolers's conclusion regarding code switching in production, but the results for comprehension are mixed. Macnamara (1967) required bilingual subjects to say as many words as they could in a given time period, speaking all the words in one language, or switching back and forth between

languages from word to word. More words were spoken under the unilingual than under the language-switching conditions. Dalrymple-Alford and Aamiry (1967) presented subjects with two-word signals (left or right and one of three color names) that indicated which of six keys was to be pressed. The signals were either unilingual or mixed Arabic and English. In general, there was no difference between the unilingual and mixed conditions. Thus a language-switching requirement apparently had no effect on comprehension. These two sets of results are consistent with Kolers's conclusions. Other studies, however, have demonstrated switching effects on comprehension. Macnamara and Kushnir (1971) presented subjects with unilingual or linguistically mixed statements to which they responded true or false. The relevant results were that subjects responded faster to unilingual than to mixed material and that three switches required more time than two.

Taylor (1971) modified Macnamara's procedure by permitting some bilingual subjects to switch languages freely in a continuous association task, but requiring others to switch at fixed rates. Consistent with the conclusion from prior studies, the fewest associations were produced under a rapid switching condition. In the free switching conditions, however, performance was as good as in unilingual association, apparently because subjects tended to switch at natural boundaries, that is, between associative clusters (recall the discussion of "associative bursts" in chapter 9). Finally, analyses of conditional probabilities in the free switching condition revealed that subjects were more likely to continue associating in English or French than to switch from one to the other. Taylor interpreted this to mean that associative links were stronger within than between languages.

Wakefield, Bradley, Lee Yom, and Doughtie (1975) presented bilingual subjects with split-language sentences in which the location of the change was varied. Sometimes the switch was between major constituents and sometimes within one of the constituents. Consider the sentence (*The number of persons who have taken up parachuting as a sport*) (*is definitely increasing*), in which the parentheses indicate the two major constituents. The two types of switches are indicated by the slashes in the following English-Spanish sentences:

(*The number of persons who have taken up parachuting as a sport*)/(*esta definitivamente aumentando.*)

(*The number of persons who have taken up / el deporte del paracaidasu*) (*esta definitivamente aumentando.*)

The results of several experiments showed that the times for true-false judgments were longer for the second type of sentence, in which the language change occurred within a constituent, than for the former. The authors conclude that the major constituents of sentences function as perceptual units, much as others have concluded from different data (see chapter 6). The main point in the present context is that the study demonstrated that switching effects at input are related to grammatical structure.

We conclude that language switching takes time in both comprehension and production and that such effects are evidence that a bilingual's two languages are separate and functionally independent, at least to some degree.

Next we consider what the content of the word associations of bilinguals might reveal about the organization of their two languages. The general procedure is

to have bilinguals give discrete associations to a series of stimulus words in one language at one testing session and in the other language at another session. The resulting associations are compared with normative data for monolinguals of each linguistic group (for example, the Kent-Rosanoff norms; chapter 5). The general finding has been that bilinguals generate different kinds of associations in their two languages and that the differences correspond to those of the respective monolingual comparison groups. Lambert and Moore (1966), for example, compared Canadian English-French bilinguals with Canadian monolinguals in each language, American English speakers, and European French speakers. The relevant finding was that the bilinguals responded in either the English (Canadian or American) or French fashion, depending on the language response. In particular, the English responses showed more uniformity or stereotyping, and the French responses showed greater diversity of associations.

Shugar and Gepner-Wiecko (1971) similarly found that Polish-English bilinguals responded differently to equivalent words in their two languages, in a manner that corresponded to monolingual norms in each language. The striking difference in the study was that the English associative responses were overwhelmingly paradigmatic rather than syntagmatic (84 percent versus 16 percent), but the Polish associations were about as often paradigmatic as syntagmatic (55 percent versus 46 percent). The authors referred to Polish-English differences in grammatical structure, concluding that grammatical rules have a selective effect on the association process. This implies that persons who acquire a second language inevitably develop a verbal associative structure that differs from that of their native language.

To this point, then, we have evidence that bilinguals not only have two separate and at least partly independent linguistic systems but that the two systems also differ in their organizational structure in ways predictable to some extent from grammatical differences in the two languages. Note that these conclusions differ from those suggested earlier in regard to the compound-coordinate distinction. The conclusion in that case was that separate (coordinate) systems result from non-linguistic experiential differences and may be linked to differences in the content and structure of the imagery system. Now we are suggesting that bilinguals are bound to develop distinct intraverbal associative structure as a result of linguistic experience in the two languages. Both conclusions are quite consistent with dual-coding theory, which assumes that the organizational characteristics and content of nonverbal and verbal symbolic systems arise from nonverbal and verbal associative experiences. Differences in these experiences will result in differences in the symbolic systems.

Our final examples of production effects involve nonverbal as well as verbal stimuli. The Stroop Test is a task in which subjects are presented with color names printed in incongruent colors, such as the word RED printed in green ink, and say the name of the ink color (green, in the example). This typically produces interference in that it takes longer to name colors under the incongruent condition than when the colors and names are congruent or when the two classes of stimuli are unrelated (for example, rows of colored asterisks). The relevant question in the present context is whether the same effect would occur when a bilingual subject is required to name the colors in a language other than that of the printed color name. Thus a French-English bilingual would say "vert" given the word RED printed in

green. The theory of independent language systems controlled by an "on-off" switch suggests that no interference should occur, since the irrelevant language could be switched off. Complete dependence, on the other hand, implies that the interference would be just as great across languages as within them.

The results of a number of studies are more consistent with the dependency than with the independence hypothesis. Preston and Lambert (1969), for example, found substantial interference in the bilingual Stroop Test, although the effect was slightly smaller in the cross-language task than in the within-language one except when the orthography of the color names was similar in the two languages (for example, German *blau* and *braun,* corresponding to *blue* and *brown*). There were similar findings in other studies. Dalrymple-Alford (1968) included a condition in which English color names were congruent with the print color, and the subject had to respond with the Arabic translation. This produced somewhat less interference than in the incongruent color-color name condition. Hamers and Lambert (1972) obtained Stroop-like effects using auditory stimuli which consisted of the words "high" and "low" (or "haute" and "basse") being spoken in a voice of either high or low pitch. Response times to decide whether the voice was high or low were longer in the incongruent condition (for example, the word "high" spoken in a low voice) than in the congruent one (for example, "high" spoken in a high voice). This occurred under interlingual and intralingual response conditions and also when the response was nonverbal (pressing the upper or lower of two response keys to indicate whether the voice pitch was high or low). Again, the interference was slightly less under interlingual (cross-language) conditions.

The above results are generally puzzling because they indicate that bilinguals apparently cannot "turn off" the semantic effects of the incongruent word in one language while responding in the other, although further experimental conditions included in Hamers's and Lambert's study seemed to indicate that the problem was not one of response conflict.

The interpretation problem is compounded by the findings of other studies with different designs. B. Tversky (1974) conducted a same-different comparison task similar to those described in the context of comprehension in chapter 7. Bilingual subjects were presented with two successive stimuli, namely geometric forms or their printed names. Two different representations were used for each form, either outline or filled drawings, and the names could appear in either Hebrew or English. The response was to be "same" as long as the successive stimuli had the same meaning, regardless of form. On some trials, subjects knew whether the second stimulus would be a picture or a word; on others they did not. The results showed that knowing that the second stimulus would be a picture speeded up comparison time for pictures as compared to words, but knowing that the second stimulus would be a word had no comparable effect. Tversky concluded that the mental representations of pictures are broad enough to include two different pictorial representations but that the mental representations of words seem to be language specific. Stated differently, two different pictures of the same form could be compared directly, but words in different languages could not. The latter finding contrasts with the Stroop studies, which seemed to show automatic and direct effects of one language on another.

A learning study by Dornic (1977) is also relevant to the above issues. It was done under incidental learning conditions in which subjects performed a task

requiring the active use of one language while being incidentally exposed to information not requiring attention. This information could be in the same or the other language. The results showed that under certain conditions, bilinguals remembered much more of the incidental information when its language was congruent with that used in the primary task than when it was not. These results, too, seem to contrast with those from the Stroop experiments in that processing in one language was greatly reduced when the other was intensively used in a task, much as though a language-switching mechanism had been turned off.

We cannot resolve the empirical discrepancies in the research on the language-switching hypothesis in relation to language production and other tasks, and we conclude the section with just one additional observation. The Stroop task always uses compound stimuli with different responses associated with different components. Thus the print color of a word evokes one response, and the printed word evokes another. When responding to the color, the observer cannot avoid seeing the word. From a Skinnerian viewpoint, the situation itself contains controlling stimuli for different responses, so conflict is bound to result. This is true even in the bilingual case, in which the reading and translation responses compete with the color-naming response. The bilingual observer may not confuse the languages, but lexical selection would still be a problem, though somewhat reduced relative to the monolingual case. The task simply does not permit one language to be turned off completely because controlling stimuli for the other language are present in the form of the colored-word pattern itself. The other tasks described above have not used similar compound stimuli containing incongruent components, which may be why they yielded clearer evidence of a switching mechanism.

Second-Language Acquisition

Our discussion of second-language acquisition focuses on selected issues that have particularly attracted the attention of both researchers and educators. The following questions identify the key issues: Do young children learn a second language faster and better than adults? Does second-language acquisition differ qualitatively from first-language learning? Do the two languages interact, so that bilinguals speak their languages differently from the way monolinguals do? What kinds of psychological (motivational and cognitive) factors influence the learning rate? Finally, what second-language teaching techniques are particularly effective? The questions are not entirely independent, but we shall discuss them separately. Readers interested in a more detailed coverage can consult the reviews on which we have leaned for aspects of our summary (McLaughlin, 1977, 1978; Smythe, Stennett, & Gardner, 1975).

Are children better language learners than adults?

One of the most popular pieces of folklore concerning second-language acquisition is that children up to a certain age are veritable linguistic sponges, capable of absorbing two or more languages quickly, efficiently, and painlessly. By comparison, so the story goes, adult learning is slow and painful and rarely results in a level of proficiency equivalent to that achieved by a child. One of the most influential proponents of such a view was the famous Canadian neurologist, Wilder

Penfield, who often cited cases (including his own children) that supported such a conclusion. Thus, "A child who hears three languages instead of one, early enough, learns the units of all three without added effort and without confusion. I have watched this experiment in my home, as many others must have done" (Penfield & Roberts, 1959, p. 254). By contrast, when "new languages are taken up for the first time in the second decade of life, it is difficult, though not impossible, to achieve a good result. It is difficult because it is unphysiological" (p. 255).

Penfield's physiological hypothesis was that the brain of the child up to the age of about twelve years is plastic but that the brain of the adult is "stiff and rigid" as far as language learning is concerned. This is a version of the "critical period hypothesis" of language learning in general, which arose from studies of the effects of certain brain injuries, sustained at different ages, on language behavior (the literature is summarized in Lenneberg, 1967). The general finding is that the younger the person is at the time of the injury, the more complete is the recovery from aphasia (speech loss), presumably because the language functions are rapidly relearned by the uninjured parts of the child's "plastic" brain. Penfield simply extended the hypothesis to foreign-language learning in children and adults.

Let us examine the hypothesis and the known behavioral facts, putting aside the neuropsychological arguments and the additional complications they create. The first point is that it is extremely difficult to obtain comparable data on second-language learning of children and adults. The learning conditions differ in every way imaginable. Adults are rarely immersed totally in the new language in the same way and to the same extent as are children. Adults in a new linguistic community may attend language-learning classes, but at other times they will actively seek out friends who speak their native language, persist in speaking and reading it in the home, and so on. Children are literally forced to use the new language a good part of the day in school and among neighborhood friends. Adults are also likely to be more inhibited in speaking the new language because it is frustrating and embarrassing to speak as a child when we know and can say so much more in our native language. It is less so for a child who knows and expects less and is in any case more concerned with communicating wants and desires in any way possible than with the niceties of "proper" speech. You can easily add to the ways in which the conditions of second-language learning would differ among children and adults. The point is that comparisons of learning rate and ultimate proficiency are unjustifiable unless acquisition conditions are equated.

Such comparability has been approximated only in experimental studies, in which it is possible to control acquisition conditions. These experiments are restricted to limited aspects of language skill, and the evidence that has accumulated to this point is not enough to warrant sweeping generalizations. Nonetheless, much of the existing evidence goes against the anecdotal, "rigid brain" hypothesis of language learning: *it turns out that adults often surpass children as second-language learners in almost every sphere of language skill* (McLaughlin, 1978; Smythe et al., 1975).

The following examples support the above statement: Asher and Price (1967) compared English-speaking students in grades 2, 4, 8, and college in their acquisition of comprehension of Russian. The subjects heard Russian commands to stand, sit, walk, stop, turn, and so on. The series of commands was repeated ten times in random order. Periodic retention tests were given, and new training

sessions were introduced with increasingly complex sentences. In this study, adults were significantly better than children on the measures of retention. Other studies similarly show that older children perform better than younger ones on tests of various second-language skills acquired in the classroom (McLaughlin, 1978, p. 70). If we consider the miniature artificial languages used in experimental studies (see chapter 10) as analogous to foreign languages, we have more evidence favoring adults, since they surpass children in learning such languages (Braine, 1971). Children seem to be superior to adult learners only in the area of pronunciation—the younger the children are when they enter a foreign country, the more likely they are to acquire a nearly native accent (Asher, 1969). However, even this generalization is challenged by two experimental studies in which it was found that older students were superior to younger ones in learning to pronounce unfamiliar phonological units or sequences (Kuusinen & Salin, 1971; Olson & Samuels, 1973). Moreover, some adults do learn to speak a second language with an accent that is fully comparable to that of native speakers (Neufeld, in press), thereby casting further doubt on any strong form of the rigid-brain hypothesis.

We do not yet understand why adults and children differ in the rate at which various language skills are acquired. About all that can be said is that adults bring their mature knowledge of study methods, learning strategies, and knowledge of linguistic rules to the second-language learning task and surpass children in areas to which these are relevant.

Are there qualitative differences between first- and second-language acquisition?

It has often been said that the way a second language is acquired is qualitatively different from the way a first language is acquired. The language habits and rules already known presumably interfere with or otherwise influence second-language learning. This view seems to be supported by the observation that adults find it difficult to learn pronunciation, grammatical morphemes (for example, noun gender), and so on in the second language but that children learning a first language apparently learn such skills easily (Brown, 1973). Others (for example, Ervin-Tripp, 1974; Macnamara, 1973) have argued that these differences are caused by differences in the conditions under which the first and second languages are learned and also by differences in knowledge of learning strategies—points already considered above—rather than to qualitative differences in the acquisition process. If the input conditions were the same, so the argument goes, the basic processes would be the same.

The few controlled studies of the problem favor the view that the processes are more alike than different. Cook (1973) compared twenty foreign adults learning English with twenty-four English-speaking children (about two to four years of age) on an imitation test designed to measure linguistic ability. Subjects were shown a series of pictures accompanied by spoken sentences describing their content. The subjects repeated the sentences and occasionally answered comprehension questions. The sentences tested various syntactic features. In general, the results showed that adults and children made the same kinds of mistakes. Both groups did poorly in imitating relative-clause sentences, such as *This is the man that drives the bus*, often omitting *that* or replacing it with *what* and other substitutes. Children even

made mistakes thought to be characteristic of foreigners, such as omitting the "s" from third-person singular verbs. A second experiment compared adults with different amounts of English instruction, who were asked to identify the agent in sentences like *The wolf is happy to bite* and *The duck is hard to bite.* Those with the least instruction in English were "primitive rule users" who consistently regarded the grammatical subject as the agent of the action. Those with the most instruction gave completely correct answers to all sentences. The "intermediates," who gave mixed answers, sometimes primitive, sometimes correct, were also intermediate in amount of instruction. Cook notes that children go through a similar process.

D'Anglejan and Tucker (1975) obtained results similar to Cook's with adults learning English as a second language. These subjects were found to process complex English sentence structures without relying on the syntax of their native language. The data from beginners and advanced learners indicated, moreover, that the developmental pattern for the acquisition of the grammatical structures paralleled the developmental sequence observed among children learning their first language (C. Chomsky, 1969). Such studies point to common processes in the acquisition of languages, whether first or second.

Cook (1977) later proposed the modified conclusion that second-language acquisition is like first-language acquisition if the target skill involves only language-related processes. Conversely, if the learning depends on general cognitive processes that are independent of language, first- and second-language learning will be less similar. Of course, this raises the sticky problem, recognized by Cook, of distinguishing between linguistic and nonlinguistic processing in language skills. We have already discussed that problem in the context of the relation between language and thought (chapter 11), and we need not pursue it here, particularly since there are no relevant data in the area of second-language acquisition.

Recall that the proponents of the qualitative-difference hypothesis have generally relied on the concept of interference to explain such differences. We have seen that the evidence does not support the idea of qualitative differences. Consistent with that conclusion, the empirical evidence reveals that interlinguistic interference is less predominant than the anecdotal evidence has suggested. Errors that seem to reflect transfer or generalization from the first language do occur, particularly during early stages of second-language acquisition (Taylor, 1976). However, such errors are less frequent in later stages, and at no point do they represent the majority of errors. In fact, McLaughlin (1978, p. 67) concluded that only about a third of the errors reported in a number of studies (for example, Ervin-Tripp, 1970; George, 1972; Richards, 1971) were attributable to first-language structures. The remaining two-thirds could be described as incorrect generalization of the rules of the second language before they are mastered, morphological and syntactic simplifications typical of first-language learners, or unique errors.

We conclude that several common notions about second-language acquisition are not supported by the available facts. Most important, there is little evidence in favor of the critical-period hypothesis as applied to the ability to acquire a second language. If anything, the evidence suggests that the critical period for most second-language skills begins well after age twelve. The one exception may be pronunciation, in which young children seem to be favored over adults, although we have seen that even this generalization can be challenged. In addition, we find little evidence that the acquisition processes differ for first and second languages. The

similarities are more impressive than the differences when the usual differences in acquisition conditions are controlled. Finally, although some errors made by second-language learners can be attributed to interference or to some kind of transfer from the first language, most errors seem to be unrelated to the first—the more so as language learning progresses.

Cognitive and Motivational Factors in Second-Language Acquisition

This section deals with individual differences correlated with second-language acquisition. Everyone knows that some people are more successful than others at learning foreign languages. The differences are due in large part to differences in opportunity. For example, a late friend of one of the authors spoke a dozen languages fluently. He learned four languages as a child because he was exposed to different ones in the home, the broader community, and school. As an adult, through choice and circumstance, he lived in many other European countries long enough to learn eight more. He maintained his fluency in all of them in North America because his business interests kept him in contact with people in the different countries. His linguistic prowess seems understandable in light of environmental conditions. He also showed a lively interest in languages, but this may have been a result of his success rather than a cause of it. Even when opportunities are equated, however, some people seem to have unusually high aptitude and motivation to learn a new language, whereas others do not.

There is considerable research on both classes of individual-difference variables. Our discussion highlights two of the more important contributions to the area. J. B. Carroll (see Carroll, 1974; Carroll & Sapon, 1959) developed a Modern Language Aptitude Test (MLAT) battery to predict achievement levels in foreign-language instructional programs. The battery includes tests of phonetic coding ability, grammatical sensitivity, memory ability, and inductive learning ability. Numerous studies have shown that overall scores on the test correlate well with school grades and other indices of achievement in foreign-language learning. A specific example is given below, following the description of motivational variables.

The importance of motivation is illustrated by the work of Gardner and Lambert (for example, 1959, 1972), which emphasized the role of specific language-related attitudes and motives. These factors encompassed the learner's reactions to both the target language and the speakers of that language. Originally, Gardner and Lambert distinguished between *integrative* and *instrumental* motives. The integrative motive referred to the degree to which the individual wanted to learn the target language because of a desire to get close to or become a member of the target group. Thus individuals scoring high on the integrative motive indicate that they study the target language "to learn more about the group," "to be able to think and act like the group," and so on. Instrumental orientation, on the other hand, referred to interests based on the utility of learning the new language, as indicated by endorsement of such statements as "it will make me a better educated person" or "it will be useful in my job."

The initial research showed that scores on the two variables successfully predicted second-language achievement in several linguistic communities, including anglophones learning French in Canadian settings, native residents of the Philippines learning English, and so on. Generally, the higher the individuals' integrative motive,

the better they learned the second language. The instrumental motive was less predictive of success in the initial studies, although in later ones it sometimes emerged as a relevant predictor, particularly in settings in which the second language had special economic and practical significance. Further, correlational analyses revealed that motivational factors were independent of aptitude measures, with both factors equally related to achievement (Gardner & Lambert, 1959).

As so often happens when research on a particular problem is pursued with variations in procedures and tests, the motivational picture became more complex in later research. For example, a major study by Gardner and Smythe at the University of Western Ontario, using twenty-nine samples of English-speaking teenage students from various regions across Canada, showed that the integrative motive did not predict French achievement in some samples. However, a combined attitudinal-motivational index that included the integrative motive was a successful predictor. Similarly, Clément (1977) did not find that the learning of English as a second language among Quebec and Ontario francophones was well predicted by a specific integrative motive, although, again, English achievement was correlated with a general motivational-attitudinal factor. These studies by Gardner and his co-workers also extended the earlier research by Gardner and Lambert (1959) in showing that motivational and aptitude measures comprise independent factors and that they are equally important to second-language achievement. For example, in Gardner's and Smythe's study, the groups of teenage students completed both the MLAT and the motivational-attitudinal tests. The average correlation between a composite Attitude-Motivation Index and French grades was .37. The average correlation between the MLAT and French grades was .42. The motivational and cognitive tests were essentially uncorrelated, which means that the two were independent and equally effective as predictors of achievement in French. Thus, combining both as predictors yielded a substantial multiple correlation of .52 with French grades.

The results mentioned above should not be surprising because language is a social phenomenon and therefore susceptible to complex social influences. Especially in the case of teenagers and adults, our attitudes toward the second language and its speakers would be expected to affect the amount of effort and time we put into studying that language and also the amount of contact with the target group. Skill in the target language in turn would improve partly because of this effort and contact, as well as relevant abilities. The recent research is beginning to give us a detailed understanding of the specific nature of these two classes of individual differences and their relation to second-language acquisition.

Instructional Techniques

We turn, finally, to a consideration of the technology of foreign-language teaching. The problem has engaged the attention of teachers and scholars for several millennia (Kelly, 1969), and most of the questions and approaches that are of interest today were considered in one way or another long ago. What have changed are the technology of education, the theoretical models, and the research techniques for evaluating different approaches.

Why the historical interest in foreign-language instruction? Two of the most obvious and important reasons are conquest and enterprise. The Roman

conquests, for example, made it necessary for the Roman occupants of their new dominions to learn the languages of the conquered peoples, some of whom also had to learn Latin. Comparable pressures to learn a second language came about more recently on a large scale as British colonial power spread around the world. Entrepreneurs throughout the ages have also had to learn foreign languages to allow communication with merchants in other countries. These and other reasons (for example, religion) explain the extraordinary degree of bilingualism (or multi-lingualism) in countries such as India.

Foreign-language instruction has always occupied an important position in the educational systems of all countries, and teachers and scholars have developed their pet instructional techniques in that context. The following are some of the persistent issues and methods: Should one follow the direct method of teaching, in which the learner is exposed only to the foreign language and relevant situa-tional contexts, without ever attempting to translate? Some teachers have main-tained that position, but others have assumed that translation is sometimes a useful, supplementary short cut. The issue persists, without definite evidence to support an extreme view as yet. Should one teach language by drill and repetition, with a view toward habit formation, or by reasoned learning, with a view toward a thor-ough understanding of language concepts? This old issue has been expressed in the contemporary theoretical context as a contrast between "audiolingual habit theory" and "cognitive-code learning theory" (Carroll, 1965). The issue remains unresolved in any hard, empirical sense. Among the persistent methods we have pattern practice, which first appeared in the sixteenth century and continues to be emphasized today in texts and language laboratory exercises. Another is the use of visual aids, which goes as far back as the ancient Chinese and their use of pictures in teaching. We cannot deal with all of the relevant issues and methods in detail, so we have selected a few instructional approaches for emphasis. These are immersion programs, the language laboratory, and the use of mnemonic aids.

Second-Language Immersion Programs

Most of us have gone through the traditional classroom approach to foreign languages, in which students receive at most a few hours of exposure each week to lessons and drills on vocabulary and grammar. This approach is particularly typical in North America. The usual results are also familiar. High school graduates end up with a fair grasp of the syntax of the target language and some ability to read it, but their communicational skills are likely to be feeble at best. Such results have been documented in empirical studies (d'Anglejan, 1978; McLaughlin, 1978, pp. 155–156). In the early 1960s, a group of anglophone parents in St. Lambert, a community near Montreal, sought a more effective means whereby their children could become fluently bilingual in French and English—something that the parents themselves had not achieved through the typical school systems. They asked Wallace Lambert of McGill University, a leading researcher in bilingualism, to help with the planning and evaluation. Lambert agreed to do so provided that the program was set up as a true experiment, with appropriate control groups and rigorous tests of its effects. The community consented, and the total immersion experiment began in 1965, with dramatic consequences. The full details for the first

five years can be found in a book by Lambert and Tucker (1972). Here, we sketch out only the main outlines of the program and its results.

In the immersion program, the children were instructed entirely in French in kindergarten and first grade, with English introduced as a classroom subject in second grade. Thus French was the language of instruction, as in the French-Canadian school system of Montreal. The teachers were francophones, and they spoke only French to the children even in kindergarten. The St. Lambert program made language instruction incidental to educational content. The immersion program was continued throughout the elementary school years, with more English instruction in the later grades. The study continued with follow-up experimental groups in subsequent years.

The effects of the program were evaluated periodically by a battery of tests that measured various French and English language skills, mathematical concepts, and cognitive flexibility. These tests were administered to the immersion children and to French and English monolingual control groups in standard monolingual schools. The results were as follows: At the end of first grade the immersion children scored below the monolingual English controls on tests of English word knowledge and reading skill (the immersion children had had no instruction in English up to this point). These children were equivalent to the controls in most other aspects of English skill, such as comprehension, expression, enunciation, rhythm, and intonation.

It was also not surprising that the immersion children were inferior at the end of first grade to the French-speaking controls on almost all French language tests, although they were generally comparable on tests of word discrimination, sentence comprehension, and word order. Finally, they did just as well as the controls on arithmetic tests in both languages—this despite the fact that immersion children had learned their arithmetic entirely in French.

The differences diminished by the end of second grade. The English language skills of the immersion groups were now comparable to those of the English controls in everything but spelling. Their French still lagged behind that of the French control groups, especially in grammar, but they performed as well as the latter in overall expression, enunciation, liaison, rhythm, and intonation.

In later years, the immersion children continued to perform at the same high level in English and arithmetic. They also reached a high level of ability in French, far exceeding that of children in standard foreign-language programs, although falling short of the French control groups. Finally, as already noted in our earlier discussion of the intellectual consequences of bilingualism, the immersion children scored higher than the control groups on tests of cognitive flexibility. Thus the results of the immersion program were overwhelmingly positive. The children attained a high level of ability in French, their second language, without any detrimental effect on their first language or arithmetic and with a possible gain in certain cognitive skills, specifically, cognitive flexibility.

The St. Lambert program itself included replications of the experiment, and in addition, it served as a model for similar programs in other areas of Canada and the United States. The results have generally been comparable to those of the original project. This was so, for example, in a large study with over one thousand English-speaking children in the Ottawa region, who were immersed in French in

kindergarten and succeeding grades (Barik & Swain, 1974, 1976, 1978). The St. Lambert procedure was essentially followed in the Culver City Spanish immersion program in the United States (Cohen, 1974), in which anglophone children were exposed exclusively to Spanish from kindergarten on. Here too, the results were consistent with those obtained in the original St. Lambert project.

The above programs used total immersion. Other approaches to bilingual education have used some form of partial immersion or mixed-language instruction. The results of these studies, summarized by McLaughlin (1978), are varied but generally inferior in one way or another to the St. Lambert results. They range from no positive benefits in one mixed-language program to some benefits in certain partial immersion programs, in which the children eventually surpass monolingual controls in their skill in the second language but with some (perhaps temporary) detriment to first-language skills.

The total immersion program clearly seems to have the edge as far as second-language education is concerned, at least when carried out in cultural-linguistic contexts comparable to those in the original St. Lambert project. The last point is an important caveat, for the results may be quite different under other circumstances. For example, ethnic minority students in the United States do not do well in schools in which they receive all of their instruction in English, which is a second language to them. Why should this be so when their situation seems, at least superficially, to be comparable to that of the English-speaking children in the St. Lambert project? The general answer is that the conditions are not comparable. The ethnic children are typically in classes with native speakers of English who are bound to have a linguistic advantage. This could create differences in self-confidence and in academic achievement, with circular effects. In the St. Lambert program, in contrast, all children started off at the same level, from scratch.

Whatever the reasons for the different results, Lambert and Tucker (1972) recognized that total immersion was not the ideal solution for all communities or nations. The program should be guided by such considerations as the relative prestige of the language in question. If Language A is the more prestigious, the children for whom it is the first language should first be schooled in Language B until they are able to read and write it and then be exposed to A. Ethnic minority groups whose first language is B should have a program that permits them to consolidate their competence in that language before or concurrent with exposure to A. Thus they might learn to read and write Language B before beginning instruction in A, or have a completely bilingual program with, say, half of each school day spent in total immersion in each language. The chosen method should be designed to avoid what Lambert has termed "subtractive bilingualism," in which the first (ethnic) language of minority-group children is gradually replaced by the more dominant and prestigious national language. More detail on such ideas can be found in a comprehensive review of the effects of immersion programs by Cummins (1978), as well as in Lambert's and Tucker's book.

In closing this section, we draw attention to the remarkable contribution of the St. Lambert project as a psycholinguistic experiment. It represents one of the clearest examples of the practical educational benefits that can arise when a well-controlled experimental study is done on a complex problem in a real-life social setting. The results of the experiment proved to be replicable, and they provide a solid informational base against which various bilingual programs can be evaluated.

They also encouraged the development of similar programs in other communities. The experiment did not solve all of the problems associated with bilingual education, but it helped to pinpoint the nature of those problems, and it provided a model for further experiments designed to resolve them.

The Language Laboratory

The language laboratory was introduced in the 1920s and developed during the Second World War as a means of teaching members of the United States armed forces the languages of the peoples with whom they were at war. The invention of magnetic tapes made it possible to incorporate the method on a large scale into language-teaching programs in universities and secondary schools. The system permits a group of students to be exposed individually to tape-recorded language programs designed to develop comprehension and production skills. The students can listen to skilled speakers, repeat what they said, and then listen to the original message and their own attempted reproduction. The feedback permits the student to correct faults of pronunciation and grammar. In some modern systems, the student's reproduction is fed into a computer programmed to pass only a restricted range of phonological approximations to each sound. If the student's imitation is too far off the mark, the machine returns to the last point at which the imitation was tolerable. Other taped programs provide limited practice in language production by requiring a given phrase or sentence to be transformed in some way, such as a simple affirmative sentence into a passive, future, or negative form. All of this can be controlled from a master console, with all students getting the same program but responding individually, or each booth might have an individual cassette with the student controlling the onset and replays. In either case, the exercises can be monitored by a language teacher who can "plug in" to individual students and provide help when needed.

The programs themselves have been constructed on the basis of principles suggested by the linguistic and psychological theories in vogue at a given point in time. The earlier programs used structural paradigms motivated by structural linguistics, together with the stimulus-response-reinforcement principle derived from behavioristic psychology. More recently, Noam Chomsky's influence can be seen in the extensive use of transformation exercises.

How effective has the language laboratory proved to be? The question is difficult to answer definitively because there are surprising few well-controlled experimental studies of the problem. The available results have not been particularly encouraging. For example, Lambert (1971) concluded from his review of two large-scale studies that the language laboratory contributed very little, if anything, to the development of foreign-language skills, beyond that achieved through the "old-fashioned, grammar translation approach." Kelly also concluded that "once the language laboratory left the hands of careful experimenters, too much was asked of it and it seemed not to live up to its promise" (1969, p. 247).

This does not mean that it is time to abandon the language laboratory. It means, rather, that foreign-language teachers see the approach as less of a panacea than they originally did. It is still a useful adjunct to other, more traditional methods. In addition, it should be clear that the area remains in need of systematic research—all the more so because technological advancements are creating rapid

changes in what can be done in the language laboratory, particularly through the use of audiovisual systems. We mentioned that visual aids have long been used in the context of foreign-language instruction. In the modern era these take the form of film strips, slides, and most recently, closed-circuit television. The latter provides a particularly flexible way of providing video-tape exercises for learning basic grammatical patterns as well as referent objects and situations corresponding to recorded spoken material. Some modern instructional techniques, such as the *voix et image* (1958) approach to teaching French as a second language, systematically use pictorial accompaniments to language. However, such applications of modern technology will be of maximum benefit only when they are based on careful research. To date, such research is sparse, and the best controlled studies have dealt primarily with the effects of simple pictures on vocabulary learning. The results are encouraging in that foreign words are learned faster when pictures rather than native-language words serve as stimuli (for example, Kellogg & Howe, 1971; Webber, 1978; Wimer & Lambert, 1959). However, the surface has hardly been scratched in regard to the experimental study of more complex visual materials and language skills, the transfer of such learning to language use in naturalistic situations, and so on. The thoughtful student can readily see how some of the theoretical ideas discussed in this book might be used to guide such research. For example, the audiovisual approach could be evaluated and perhaps modified on the basis of research guided by dual-coding theory. This has not been done in relation to the language laboratory as yet, but related ideas have been applied to the use of mnemonic techniques in second-language acquisition. Our final section deals with that topic.

Mnemonic Techniques in Second-Language Acquisition

Our discussion of memory in chapter 8 touched on the strong effect that imagery can have on memory for language. For example, constructing an interactive mental image that connects the referents of a pair of words greatly increases the associative recall of the words. Such techniques are ancient, and professional mnemonists have long been advocating their use in foreign-language learning, among other things. One of the most famous of these was Gregor von Feinaigle, who lectured on the "art of memory" early in the nineteenth century (see Paivio, 1971b, chap. 6). A modern mnemonist, Harry Lorayne (1974), continues the tradition, specifically proposing an image-based system in which one learns foreign words by associating them with pictureable English words that sound like the foreign words. However, the experimental study of such techniques in relation to second-language learning has only recently begun.

Richard Atkinson and Michael Raugh (1975; see Atkinson, 1975) have reported a series of studies on the problem employing what they refer to as the "keyword technique." This technique uses a specific word in the familiar language to establish both an acoustic link and an imaginal link between a foreign word and its translation equivalent in the native language. Consider, for example, the French word *couteau* /kuto/ and its English translation, knife. To learn *couteau*, select an English keyword that sounds like some part of the French word and is easy to visualize. The word "toe" would be appropriate because it sounds like the last syllable in *couteau* and because you can easily imagine a knife cutting someone's

toe. The word *couteau* will subsequently prompt recall of "toe" because they sound alike. The word "toe" will remind you of the image, which can then be decoded as "knife."

Experimental studies have shown that the keyword technique facilitates the learning of foreign-language vocabularies among university students (Atkinson, 1975) and elementary school children (Pressley, 1977). As a specific illustration, consider Atkinson's and Raugh's (1975) experiment using a Russian vocabulary of 120 words. These were learned in sets of 40 on successive days. Subjects in the keyword condition were trained in the keyword technique. For them, a computer-controlled system presented the Russian words through headphones while at the same time visually displaying the English translation and keyword. Examples of the materials are: *zvonok* ("bell")–keyword, "oak"; *zdanie* ("building")–keyword, "dawn"; and *strana* ("country")–keyword, "strawman." For the first set, the student might imagine an oak in a belfry or an oak growing under a giant bell jar, and so on. The procedure was identical for the control subjects, except that the keywords and related instructions were omitted. On test trials, subjects were presented auditorily with Russian words one at a time, and they attempted to type the translation of each. Figure 13-1 shows the results of three study-test trials on each of the three days. Note that the keyword group received superior scores in every case.

The facilitative effect of the keyword method on comprehension (as measured by the translation test) has been shown in a number of other studies. In addition, Atkinson and his co-workers have provided answers to various questions about the technique (see Atkinson, 1975). They found that results with inexperienced subjects are best if the experimenter provides the keywords rather than having the subjects generate them, but it is better if the subject rather than the

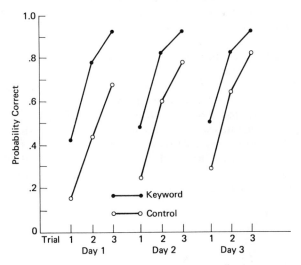

FIGURE 13-1. Probability of a correct translation response over test trials and days for keyword and control subjects. Adapted from Figure 1 in Atkinson and Raugh (1975).

experimenter generates the imagery link. Atkinson also reported that imagery instructions yielded better results in their research than instructions asking subjects to generate a meaningful sentence connecting the two words. However, this was not the case in a study by Nightingale (1976), which showed no difference between imagery and verbal mediation variants of the keyword method when applied to a Finnish vocabulary.

The keyword method as described above was designed to aid foreign vocabulary comprehension. What about the production of vocabulary? Atkinson expressed some concern that the technique might interfere with pronunciation. This does not appear to be the case, according to an applied study by Gail Singer (1978), provided that the keywords are chosen so as not to be misleading. For example, the French word *păntalon* /pătalɔ̃/ means "pants," which would be inappropriate as a keyword for English-speaking subjects because of the difference in pronunciation of the first vowel in the two words. Singer suggests that a word like "pontiac" would be preferable. A second production problem is the recall of the foreign word. Atkinson (1975) cited one study in which keyword and control subjects were brought to the same performance criterion in translating Spanish words into English. Then they were tested on "backward associations," that is, from English to Spanish. The keyword subjects scored 19 percent above the control subjects. However, the recall advantage has not been observed in other studies (Pressley, Levin, Hall, Miller, & Berry, 1980; Willerman & Melvin, 1979). Thus the keyword technique clearly benefits comprehension but not necessarily production when these effects are tested by the translation method.

We turn now to a different imagery-based mnemonic technique, explicitly designed to promote productive recall of second-language vocabulary. It adapts (Paivio, 1978c; Paivio & Desrochers, 1979) an old method, called the "hook" technique. The adaptation relies on a cued-recall procedure to increase the availability of the unfamiliar words as meaningful *responses* to associative cues presented in the second language itself, without necessarily relying on translation. To clarify the point, we first describe the hook technique as applied to English words.

The standard procedure uses an ordered series of mnemonic peg words to which new vocabulary items are "hooked" by means of images. The pegs and related images can be generated mentally to serve as retrieval cues for the new words. The pegs are pictureable words that translate into numbers by means of a consonant-number code based on visual or acoustic similarity. (The similarity relation is intended to facilitate learning of the hook system itself, although the system probably would serve its mnemonic purpose just as well even if the number-word relation were arbitrary, once the relations have been learned.) Be that as it may, the following is a recent version of the system (Lorayne, 1974), which differs from earlier ones only in the letters assigned to certain numbers:

1	2	3	4	5	6	7	8	9	0
t,d	n	m	r	l	j,[ʃ]	k,hard c	f,v	p,b	z,s

The rationale is that *t* or *d* stands for the numeral 1 because each has one down stroke; *n* stands for 2 because it has two "legs"; *m* has three legs; *r* occurs in the name for the numeral 4 in many languages; *l* stands for 5 because capital *L* is the Roman numeral for 50; *j* resembles 6; *k* resembles 7; script *f* resembles 8; *p* re-

sembles 9; and z is the first sound in zero. The sounds [ʃ], hard c, v, b, and s are acoustic variants of the basic letters, useful for generating appropriate words corresponding to numbers. These words are selected so that they contain only the relevant consonant sounds (vowels are discounted). The following are examples of possible English "hooks" (with the relevant letters in italics): 1-*t*ea, 2-*N*oah, 3-e*m*u, 4-*r*ing, 5-oi*l*, 6-*sh*oe, 7-*k*ey, 8-*f*an, 9-a*p*e, 10-*t*oe*s*, 20-*n*o*s*e, 32-*m*a*n*, 73-*c*o*m*b, 99-*p*i*p*e, and 100-*d*i*s*ea*s*e. Finally, appropriate referent images are learned for each, for example, a tea pot for 1, a bearded Noah for 2, and so on. The system is rehearsed until the associations are overlearned, and it is easy to retrieve any mnemonic image given the number. The pegs can then be used to remember new words by constructing images linking each word to a mnemonic peg, as in the other imagery mnemonic techniques described in chapter 8. Experimental studies (for example, Foth, 1973) have shown that the hook technique facilitates learning and recall of word lists in the native language.

The application of the hook technique to second-language learning differs from the above only in that the pegs are themselves words from the second language. Thus one of the authors (Paivio, 1978c) found that a French version was highly effective in his own study of French words and phrases. For example, a single study-test trial with a 100-item vocabulary list, in which the words ranged from unfamiliar to slightly familiar, typically yielded recall test scores of 90 or more correct. Paivio and Desrochers (1979) investigated the technique experimentally, comparing the hook technique with a rote-rehearsal control condition. The subjects were English-speaking students who had some knowledge of French through formal courses. Some of the items to be recalled were essentially unfamiliar, and others were familiar to some degree. This allowed Paivio and Desrochers to determine whether the hook method is as effective at an early stage of vocabulary acquisition, when the words are meaningless, as it is at a later stage, when the items are more familiar. As well, half of the words were concrete and half were abstract. The question was whether the hook technique would be relatively more effective with the concrete, high-imagery words, as Foth (1973) found in the case of native-language words. The study used 96 words in all, examples of which are shown in Table 13-1. Finally, in addition to the recall test, subjects were given a translation test before and (unexpectedly) after the experiment, so that comparisons could be made with the keyword comprehension results reported by Atkinson and his colleagues.

All participants first learned the French hook system, consisting of ninety-six numbers and related peg words. Some examples are shown in Table 13-2. At this stage, no reference was made to imagery. The subjects returned later for the actual experiment and were first tested on their knowledge of the hook system. Half the subjects were then told about the role of imagery and how to use it, after which they were given one study-test trial with twenty-four vocabulary items. The other half were instructed to use the hook technique to remember the same twenty-four items without being told about imagery. In each condition, the participants were presented with the items one at a time, accompanied by numbers (one to twenty-four) and the English translations of the French words. After the first trial, the subjects switched conditions so that the rote association group were instructed on the use of imagery and the imagery group were told to learn the next list of twenty-four words without using imagery. The alternating conditions

Low Familiarity	Medium Familiarity	High Familiarity
	Concrete	
arrosoir (watering can)	ceinture (belt)	bonbon (candy)
brume (fog)	cimetière (cemetery)	chambre (room)
cygne (swan)	écrivain (writer)	jardin (garden)
maille (stitch in netting)	matelot (sailor)	mari (husband)
seau (bucket)	soie (silk)	porte (door)
	Abstract	
attente (waiting)	accord (agreement)	année (year)
congé (holiday)	bonheur (happiness)	besoin (need)
impôt (income tax)	durée (duration)	heure (hour)
perte (loss)	règne (reign)	pays (country)
tort (wrong)	somme (sum)	samedi (Saturday)

were applied to four lists of twenty-four words, so that each subject finally learned two lists with and two without the use of imagery. All subjects returned one day after the experiment to do a second translation test.

The overall recall results for each trial are shown in Figure 13-2. Note that the imagery condition was far superior to the rote association condition on all trials. In fact, the recall under the imagery condition was about three times higher than under the rote condition. Finally, the translation tests showed that the increase in correct translations for initially unfamiliar words was twice as great under the imagery as under the rote condition. Thus the hook technique facilitated both recall and translation-defined comprehension of second-language vocabulary.

How does the hook technique compare with the keyword method? Comparisons of results from different experiments suggest that the two were about equally effective in augmenting comprehension. However, the recall results cannot

TABLE 13-2   Examples of French Mnemonic Peg-Words and Translations
with the Critical (Pronounced) Consonants Italicized.

1. *th*é (tea)	11. *têt*e (head)
2. *n*oeud (knot)	20. *n*oce (wedding)
3. *m*ât (mast)	31. *mit*e (mite, moth)
4. *r*oi (king)	42. *r*eine (queen)
5. *l*oi (law)	48. *r*êve (dream)
6. *ch*ou (cabbage)	53. *l*ame (blade)
7. *c*amp (camp)	64. *ch*ar (tank, chariot)
8. *f*eu (fire)	75. *cl*é (key)
9. *p*ain (bread)	86. *fich*e (index card)
10. *t*asse (cup)	95. *p*oi*l* (hair, fur)

(From Paivio & Desrochers, 1979.)

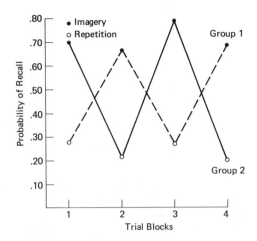

FIGURE 13-2. Probability of recall under imagery and repetition instructions for four blocks of items, with the imagery condition occurring on blocks 2 and 4 for Group 1 and on blocks 1 and 3 for Group 2. From Paivio and Desrochers (1979).

be compared directly because the different studies did not use comparable tests. Keyword recall effects had been tested only by a "backward" translation test, that is, recall of the foreign word given the English equivalent as the cue. Recall under the hook mnemonic was cued only by a number—the subjects themselves had to retrieve the French word via the number-pegword-image chain. A fair comparison of the two techniques must await further experiments, in which their effects are tested under identical conditions.

We consider, finally, some of the useful features and potential extensions of the hook mnemonic as an aid to second-language learning. One of the puzzling aspects of the technique is that it seems difficult and forbidding to second-language learners. One of us (Paivio) has described it to dozens of friends who were actively learning a foreign language. Not one of them (including Begg) ever asked to be shown how to use it, even after they were presented with evidence of its effectiveness. The same was true in regard to the keyword technique. Apparently rote rehearsal and translation techniques are so engrained in our educational system that students find it difficult to try a new approach, despite its demonstrated value. In any event, in addition to its effectiveness, the hook technique is a convenient rehearsal method because it requires no apparatus or even a written vocabulary list once the items have been pegged in memory. One can rehearse mentally while walking to work and so on, thereby taking advantage of idle moments. Secondly, it provides a naturalistic context for language use in that one generates a referent situation for each word mentally during the study trial and then actively retrieves the word from the imagined context during recall. The procedure in effect provides a means of generating pictorial aids for language learning entirely within one's own head, a kind of private *voix et image* program in which the visual referents are

constructed on the basis of knowledge of the world. Finally, the method can have motivational value. Rote study is dull. Imagery mnemonics in general can make language learning interesting because they make the language meaningful and because the results can make each trial rewarding.

The keyword and hook techniques have been described in relation to vocabulary learning, which is their most obvious domain of application. This is enough to make them worthwhile because people need a sufficient foreign vocabulary to permit communication in a wide range of situations (cf. Richards, 1974). However, knowledge of words without knowing how to put them together into grammatical phrases and sentences is also insufficient for communication. Can mnemonic techniques be of any value in that regard, at least as supplements to rote learning? Research on the problem has only begun, but the answer is likely to be yes, at least up to some level of complexity. One of us (Paivio) has applied the hook technique effectively to the study of useful French phrases and idioms. Desrochers (1980) has completed an experiment in which the technique was successfully applied to learning French noun gender, simply by asking subjects to include a gender "tag" (for example, by generating a picture of a man or woman) to the mnemonic image. There still must be extensions to more complex structures and tests of the extent to which imagery-based language study transfers to language use in naturalistic situations.

The techniques described in this last section should not be viewed as panaceas that will solve all the problems of second-language learning and replace traditional methods. They do, however, promise to be useful supplements in language teaching. There is a more general lesson here for the student of language. As Atkinson concluded with respect to the keyword technique, "the research illustrates the steps necessary to take an idea that emerged in the confines of an experimental psychologist's laboratory and develop it to a point at which it can be used in a practical teaching situation" (1975, p. 828). The comment applies equally to the hook technique, since the research is guided by ideas stemming from dual-coding theory and the empirical procedures related to it. These add to the practical potential demonstrated by other research reviewed earlier, particularly that concerned with attitudinal and motivational factors in second-language acquisition and with the experimental approach to immersion programs. These are genuine examples of the interface between research methods and theory on the one hand and educational application on the other.

Summary

This chapter has examined issues and evidence of relevance to bilingualism. Given some appropriate measure of bilingualism, it appears that having a second language does not reduce intellectual capacity. It also seems that the two languages are represented as two verbal codes capable of independent, but interconnected, activity. Because of this (at least partial) independence, switching from language to language requires time in both comprehension and production. Research on the learning of a second language serves to dispel, or at least to question, some widely held ideas. For example, children are no better than adults at the task, except perhaps in pronunciation. In fact, the similarities between the groups outweigh the dif-

ences; the appealing notion of a critical period is therefore probably wrong. One major factor in second-language learning appears to be motivation, for example. Finally, we reviewed rather concrete approaches to second-language learning. Immersion has proved to be extremely effective in certain settings, but the language laboratory has not yet lived up to its early promise as an instructional aid. Mnemonic techniques seem to be promising for some aspects of second-language learning, but it is not yet clear how well they will apply to real-world situations.

visual languages
and reading

14

Many studies that we have considered throughout the book are relevant to the theme of this chapter in that they used verbal responses to printed language and other visual stimuli. The nature of visual symbolic systems and reading were, however, taken for granted in the earlier discussions. Here, we shall deal with these as scientific problems in their own right. As with the other topics, our approach must be selective, restricted to issues relevant to psychologists interested in language and, more specifically, to the theoretical viewpoints that we have been emphasizing. We shall examine first the implications of the different approaches for the analysis of visual symbol systems and the reading process.

Linguistic and Psychological Approaches

Linguists appropriately view writing as secondary to language, since writing is a relatively recent invention, fully dependent on speech. This was already evident in the emphasis in chapter 2 on the auditory-vocal channel as a design feature of language. For that reason, modern structural and transformational linguists have not given much attention to reading and writing as phenomena related to language. The topic, however, continues to intrigue historical and comparative linguists (for example, Anttila, 1972), primarily because writing provides evidence of language change over time, including changes in phonology. Such evidence depends on phonetic symbol systems such as alphabetic writing, since these, in contrast to pictographs, are linguistically iconic. That is, the written symbols directly represent spoken language by a system of pronunciation rules. The rules vary from one language to another, but in each case the relationship is direct, spelling irregularities notwithstanding. Thus comparison of present with past spelling conventions, and also knowledge of present pronunciation (supplemented by knowledge of historical events), allows the historical linguist to make inferences about changes in pronunciation over time. For example, Chaucer did not rhyme *ea* spellings with *ee* spellings, as in *clean* and *green,* suggesting that those sounds were different at that time (Wardhaugh, 1972, p. 158).

Although linguists have concentrated on writing as an historical record of

language, psychologists have concentrated on reading as a behavioral and cognitive activity. We have already considered (chapter 4) Skinner's analysis of reading in terms of the *textual*, a verbal operant in which the controlling variable is writing or printing. Other behaviorists (for example, Osgood) might analyze reading as a set of habits, perhaps emphasizing the mediating processes aroused when we read with understanding, as distinct from simply pronouncing printed words. Finally, cognitive psychologists have generally treated reading in terms of information-processing stages, extending from the initial discrimination of visual patterns to the final constructive processing of long-term memory information aroused by those visual patterns. We shall touch on each of these approaches when relevant, but our emphasis will be on cognitive approaches because much of the research in recent years has been generated by them.

Visual Symbol Systems

Here we shall briefly review the history and nature of writing systems and other visual symbol systems, such as the sign language of the deaf, which cannot be classified as writing although it must be read. A detailed coverage of writing can be found in Gelb (1952), and useful summaries appear in various texts (for example, Gibson & Levin, 1975; Anttila, 1972).

Writing systems evolved from iconic picture writing (*pictography* or *ideography*) through the representation of meanings by pictures (*semasiography*) to more-or-less pure *phonography*, in which the written symbols stand only for sounds. Thus it evolved from bigger holistic units to arrangements of smaller ones. Picture writing has no direct connection with language, since the pictures are intended to represent things and events in the real world rather than linguistic units. Semasiography is the symbolic use of pictures, as when meanings such as "day" and "bright" are represented by a picture of the sun. True phonographic writing begins when the graphic signs are connected directly to sound. When the units are holistic elements such as words, we have *logography;* when the sign represents a syllable, we have *syllabic writing;* when the signs stand for individual sound units, we have *alphabetic writing.*

True writing in the form of a logographic system was begun by the Sumerians around 3100 B.C. Syllabaries developed later in Semitic countries and China. The first alphabet was developed by the Greeks around 900 B.C. The many alphabets around the world, including the Roman alphabet we use, followed the principles (though not the form) established in Greek writing. We should note that most modern writing systems are not purely phonographic. For example, the signs for numbers do not stand for any particular sound—2 can be read as *two, deux, zwei, kaksi,* and so on. Moreover, English is partly logographic in that the same sounds can be represented by different spellings (*right, write; pain, pane,* and so on).

Chinese, Japanese, and Korean mix pictographs or ideographs and phonographic representations of one kind or another. Chinese characters include direct iconic representation of objects such as the sun, ideographs such as a pointer above or below a line to indicate up or down, compound ideographs such as three trees to represent "forest," and phonetic units, such as radicals representing semantic features. Japanese borrowed the Chinese writing system and added syllabic writing. In Japanese the characters of Chinese origin are called *kanji.* The two syllabaries are

hiragana and *katakana,* the former being used for grammatical suffixes and the latter for loan words, such as scientific terms. Newspapers and books generally use a combination of *kanji* and the syllabaries. Examples of the different symbols are shown in Figure 14-1.

Two other visual symbol systems that will be relevant to later discussions are Blissymbolics and Sign Language. Blissymbols were developed by C. K. Bliss (1965) as an aid to international communication. They did not catch on in that sense but eventually were applied to the teaching of linguistic skills to children who have difficulty learning conventional language (Archer, 1977; McNaughton, 1975; see Silverman, 1980). Bliss was inspired by Chinese writing, and accordingly his system is a simplified logography containing both relatively concrete iconic symbols (for example ✉ for *letter*) and abstract, noniconic ones (for example, > for *but*). As in Chinese, the symbols are used productively. For example, the Chinese character for *peace,* 安, derives from *woman,* 女, and *roof,* 宀; in short, one woman under one roof was considered peaceful. Blissymbolics similarly combines *man* 人 and *protection* ⌃ to yield *father* ⥮ (cf. *mother,* ⥮). Figure 14-2 presents some other examples.

The manual communication systems of the deaf include Signed English and American Sign Language (Ameslan) as the two main systems. Signed English is more formal in that it follows the syntax of oral English, and Ameslan is more of a natural or "colloquial" system, constituting the deaf child's first language. Ameslan also adds formal elements, particularly in the form of finger spelling. Our description concentrates on Ameslan. In one striking respect it parallels written Japanese in that it includes an iconic level that parallels ideograms and logograms, and a conventional level that includes sound-related elements analogous to syllables. The

CHARACTERS	日	木	東	耳	門	聞
	Sun	Tree	East	Bar	Gate	Hear
	口	言	五	語	子	好
	Mouth	Say	Five	Language	Child	Love
HIRAGANA	は	き	ぬ	つ	わ	よ
KATAKANA	ハ	キ	メ	ツ	ワ	ヨ
	[ha]	[kɪ]	[mi]	[tsʊ]	[wa]	[jɔ]

FIGURE 14-1. Examples of Japanese characters and two types of syllabaries. Note the result of combining simple characters: *east* is the *sun* behind a *tree, hear* is an *ear* between *gates, say* is a *mouth* plus *lines, language* is what many *(five) mouths* say, *love* (or *goodness*) is a *mother* (see text) with a *child.* Selected from Walsh (1969).

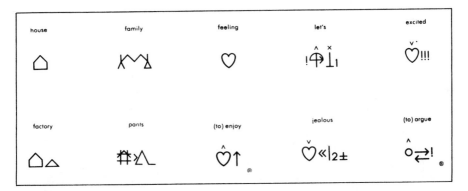

FIGURE 14-2. Examples of Blissymbols.

iconic level includes (a) *pantomimic signs,* such as the execution of a knocking action that represents itself, (b) *imitative signs* that single out for imitation some feature of the whole meaning, and (c) *indicative signs,* which point toward the referent (for example, to indicate me or you). Conventional signs include signs for the letters of the alphabet, which may be used to spell out the words or simply to spell out the initial letter of a word (for example, color names, days of the week), and name signs, designating individual persons. Examples of the different types of signs are shown in Figure 14-3.

General Psychological Implications of Visual Languages

The various iconic and phonographic symbol systems implicate psychological processes that are similar in some respects and distinct in others. All require some kind of discriminative processing at the initial perceptual level; that is, visual pattern recognition is necessary. However, this initial stage must be quickly followed by meaningful processing that may differ in some crucial respects for the two extreme classes of stimuli. Purely iconic pictographs might be processed relatively directly for meaning without mediation by linguistic coding. That is, such stimuli need not be named, and even if they are, the name can vary in different contexts and for different readers. Phonographic writing does not allow the same degree of leeway. A printed English word, for example, must be coded as a *particular* word, in a particular way. At present, there is some theoretical controversy over the nature of the identifying (meaningful) linguistic response. One view is that the reader goes directly from the visual processing of the printed word to meaning. The other view is that the visual processing is followed by a phonemic coding stage, even if only at the cortical level. It has also been proposed that the alternative processes are both necessary skills in effective reading (Mitterer, 1980). The theoretical uncertainty also does not alter the general point that printed words are read with little uncertainty in comparison with the alternatives permitted by pictographs.

Whether by reason of response uncertainty or some other processing variable, holistic signs and printed words differ in the speed with which they can be named. This is true in comparisons between pictures and words even when the pictures depict familiar and easily named objects, and even when they are geometrical forms

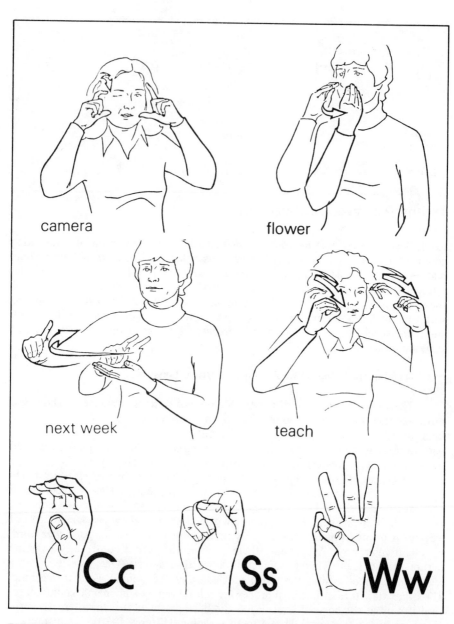

camera

flower

next week

teach

Cc

Ss

Ww

FIGURE 14–3. Examples of Ameslan signs and finger-spelled letters. From O'Rourke, 1978.

with only one label, such as a square or circle (Fraisse, 1968). Moreover, individual letters are named faster than comparable geometric forms. For example, people usually label a circle faster if it occurs in the context of other individually presented letters and is called "oh" than if it occurs in a set of geometric forms and is called a circle (Fraisse, 1967). Thus, visual stimuli that are conventionally phonographic (that is, are identified as "standing for" linguistic sounds) are named faster than signs that directly represent nonlinguistic entities.

Conversely, as suggested by the above discussion, there is evidence that iconic stimuli are processed for meaning more directly than are phonographic patterns. The statement seems obvious and relatively trivial in the case of meaning as reference, since the iconic stimulus resembles its referent but a printed word does not. However, the generalization seems to hold even at a more abstract level. For example, such category decisions as classifying a stimulus as living or nonliving are faster with pictures than with words (Byrne, 1974).

The extent to which the above distinctions apply to different kinds of ideographic and phonographic stimuli remains to be determined. Our examples simply make the point that different writing systems can implicate quite different psychological processes. We turn now to a more detailed examination of such processes, in the context of the relevant theoretical issues and research.

Perceptual Discrimination of Visual Symbols

We must learn to discriminate visual symbols perceptually before we can understand their meaning. In the case of phonographic writing, such discrimination is usually indicated by the ability to pronounce the syllables and words of the language. This ability can be quite independent of reading for understanding, as we know by the fact that many people can "read" text in a foreign language well enough to be understood by a native speaker without being able themselves to understand what they have read. Such meaningless reading can even occur with familiar print. A parent may read a story aloud to a child so often that the reading becomes automatic and mindless—we might read an entire page while thinking about something else. The adequacy of such reading as a perceptual-motor skill is shown by the fact that the child may listen to the story with rapt attention, comment on it, ask pertinent questions, and so on. And who of us has not experienced the same phenomenon entirely at a personal level, when we read a passage silently and then have to go back and reread it because our thoughts wandered away from the text? This kind of divided attention is a puzzling psychological phenomenon in its own right, and we mention it here only to illustrate the independence of reading as a perceptual-motor skill and reading for meaning. In the following sections, we shall consider some of the important processes that occur during reading.

Discriminating linguistic from nonlinguistic symbols

The identification of any perceptual pattern requires that it be distinguished from other patterns. In phonetic reading, a whole class of patterns is distinguished from others. For example, we readily distinguish a printed word from a picture, even when the response to the word (for example, *house*) is the same as the dom-

inant verbal response to the picture (for example, a picture of a house). This discrimination occurs even at the level of letters as units. Not only do we distinguish A from H, we also distinguish each of these from ⌂ by saying that the first two symbols are letters and the last is a picture of a house. This is so although all their configurations are made up of lines arranged in similar ways. The discrimination between the two classes of stimuli is so fundamental that it apparently uses anatomically distinct neural mechanisms: letters are identified better by the side of the brain (usually the left) that is specialized for speech processing than by the nonspeech (right) side, whereas the reverse is true for some nonlinguistic patterns. The pertinent neuropsychological evidence will be reviewed in more detail in chapter 15. Here we shall discuss the behavioral evidence for the distinction and the variables that affect it.

Lavine (1972; cited in Gibson & Levin, 1975) studied the development of the ability to distinguish writing from iconic (pictorial) representations. Her subjects were children between three and six and a half years of age who had not been taught to read. Lavine showed the children a review of graphic displays and asked them to classify the displays as writing or pictures and to identify each one. To obtain information about factors associated with the development of the discriminative skill, Lavine studied children of different ages and cultural backgrounds, and varied characteristics of the stimulus displays thought to be important for historical and psychological reasons. The stimulus variables were iconicity (pictorial representativeness), multiplicity of units, variety of units, linearity, and graphic characteristics of particular writing systems (Roman alphabet, cursive writing, and the like). These variables were contrasted in separate displays and also combined in various ways, as illustrated in Figure 14-4. The displays were presented on cards that the children could handle and sort into two receptacles. Their verbal responses were also recorded verbatim for later analysis.

The following results were some of the salient ones for a group of children from a middle-class area in Ithaca, New York: The ability to name three single letters increased systematically with age, so that two of the letters were correctly named by 27 percent of the three-year-olds, 47 percent of the four-to five-year-olds, and 67 percent of the five- to six-year-olds. Comparison of iconic with noniconic

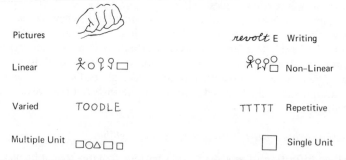

FIGURE 14-4. Examples of materials used in displays that contrast features and nonfeatures of writing as characterized by Lavine (1972). Based on Gibson and Levin (1975, Figure 8-3).

displays showed that the iconic displays were always given object labels and were never called writing. The samples of true writing were labeled in some way as writing by 86 percent, 90 percent, and 96 percent of the children in the three (youngest to oldest) age groups. Thus, even by the age of three years, most children were able to distinguish between patterns that depict objects and those that contain letters. This was true even for children who had not yet learned to read.

What variables determined the child's ability to categorize a pattern as writing? Nonrepetitiveness or variety of units was an influential factor, especially for older children. Multiple-unit displays were classified as writing more often than single-unit displays, but the two older groups of children did not indicate this difference when the stimuli were actual letters. They relied instead on perceptual features of the letters rather than on more global features of the pattern. Gibson and Levin concluded that the children had learned the contrastive features used for writing, and such global characteristics as varieties of elements and multiple units, but the most salient criteria seemed to be the component feature contrasts. Moreover, "the children did not learn individual shapes first and then later induce the component-features. It would seem that the features must be abstracted first, followed by the differentiation of individual letters as unique shapes" (1975, p. 238). Thus Gibson and Levin decided that the child learns to perceive letters by building up specific feature information about particular letters, rather than by beginning with the general shape and then learning to focus on specific features. These two contrasting possibilities represent a general controversy in the literature on letter perception, which we shall consider in more detail following the present topic.

Another interesting aspect of Lavine's study is that the children learned to identify writing without formal instruction, apparently as a result of having plenty of pictorial and written materials around to look at. The importance of mere exposure was indicated by Lavine's results for children in a rural Mexican village in which reading matter and print were scarce. These children were much less knowledgeable about writing than were the Ithaca groups described above.

Note, finally, that the children's ability to distinguish writing from pictorial symbols reflects dual coding entirely at the visual level. The example illustrates one of the assumptions of dual-coding theory that was discussed in chapter 4, namely, the independence of sensory and symbolic modalities. In this instance, the stimulus patterns in question all were visual; yet the children were able to separate them into two distinct categories, one corresponding to linguistic symbols, the other to non-linguistic ones.

Visual information processing during reading

We turn now to the nature of visual information processing that goes on during reading. We have already mentioned two contrasting views of letter perception: one is a kind of bottom-up process in which specific feature information builds up until the "list" of features is sufficient to identify a letter, and the other is a top-down process beginning with the perception of the global shape of a letter and proceeding to more specific details. Note that these alternatives at the level of letter perception are equally applicable to larger units. At the word level, for example, we can ask whether the perception of the word is based on the cumulative analysis of individual letters or on the analysis of the general shape of the whole word. Much

of the recent research has been on letter perception, so we shall emphasize that aspect in our presentation as well, drawing particularly on recent studies of the problem (for example, Lupker, 1979; Oden, 1979).

The *feature-accumulation* approach appears in models that are generally expressed in propositional language. These models specify a set of visual features sufficient to describe all letters in much the same way as phonetic features are used to describe spoken sounds in componential feature approaches to phonology (see chapter 3). The visual features correspond to the horizontal, vertical, diagonal, and curved lines of letters. Two letters might be distinguished by as little as one feature. For example, E and F have precisely the same feature list except that E has one more horizontal line segment. Some models (for example, Rumelhart & Siple, 1974) rely entirely on such features, but others (such as Gibson, 1969) assume that relational information is used along with the basic features. For the latter, therefore, characteristics such as angles and symmetry would be described as the relation between lines. These relational features are logically secondary to the basic line features because a feature like an angle could not exist without the lines. In any case, according to the feature-accumulation approach, a given letter is identified by trying to match a given stimulus against the feature list or propositional feature description of that letter in long-term memory.

The other class of model is the *global-to-local* model, which assumes that the person first notices the general shape of the letter much as if it had been presented out of focus. The information would include such aspects as the height-to-width ratio of the letter, whether it has an ascending or descending line, and so on. In some instances, depending on the set of potential stimuli, this global information may be enough for the stimulus to be identified. If not, the perceptual processing would consider more local aspects of the stimulus, such as the location of gaps and the arrangement of inner parts. You may note that this type of model, as is the case with most models stressing *discriminative* processing, is a conceptual extension of information theory as discussed in chapter 2.

Lupker (1979) tested the alternatives using a backward masking paradigm (see chapter 6) in which letters or letter features were presented, followed by a visual masking stimulus at one of several different interstimulus intervals. This procedure permitted Lupker to generate confusion matrices composed of the correct and incorrect responses given to each stimulus at each interstimulus interval. The basic stimulus set consisted of the upper-case letters L, T, V, and X, the four line features of which they are composed (|, —, /, \), and four two-feature, nonletter characters created by juxtaposing the two features in each of the letters. These permitted a test of predictions from the feature-accumulation model. The basic idea is that featural information builds up over time, so that different errors should appear at different times. When processing is terminated early by the mask, no features should have been acquired, and the errors should be random guesses. With more processing time, the basic line features should become available, allowing identification of single features but not the two-feature letters and nonletter characters. Errors at this point should be in one of the line features contained in the stimulus (for example, the subject might report only the vertical or horizontal line when a T was presented). Complete information about the two-feature stimuli should become available still later. These differences would show up generally as different masking functions, with accurate identification beginning at shorter inter-

stimulus intervals and rising more sharply with increasing intervals for the single features than for the two-feature stimuli.

Different predictions arise from the global-to-local model. Because the model assumes that the subject initially perceives a large array of perceptual information (such as the global shape of the stimulus), errors should seldom result from the perception of a stimulus smaller than the one presented. Thus, contrary to the prediction from the feature-accumulation models, single features would seldom be erroneously reported. Second, when processing is terminated early by the mask, subjects should often give a response appropriate to the largest stimulus in the set (for example, the X in the above set of four letters). In addition, specific confusions should depend on the similarities in the global shapes or general outlines of the stimuli. A test of those predictions required precise information about the global shapes of the stimuli. Such information was obtained by photographing de-focused images of the stimuli and then tracing their fuzzy outlines. The relationships among these outlines (e.g., ⊤ , ⨯ , Ɩ , ⊢), corresponding to the stimuli (T, X, I, ⊢ , etc.) were used to make the predictions from the global-to-local model.

The results showed that few, if any, of the predictions made by the feature-accumulation models were upheld. Instead, results were consistent with the global-to-local model. Lupker summarizes the picture as follows:

> When a letter is presented, an observer initially perceives a large array of perceptual data. Over time, a clearer view of the stimulus emerges as the perceptual system brings the letter into focus. Thus, global information about the letter is available quite early in processing, while the letter's more local aspects become available only after relatively extensive perceptual processing. (1979, p. 303)

As is the case with other problem areas we have considered, the research and theory in this area are relatively recent, and the controversy will remain for some time to come. Lupker's study illustrates the nature of the problem, the research methodology, and the kinds of results that can be used to test hypotheses concerning letter perception.

Grapheme-to-phoneme correspondence

We shall now examine the relation between spelling and sound, or what is sometimes referred to technically as grapheme-to-phoneme correspondence. This aspect of reading is familiar to most of us from discussions of the irregularity of English spelling rules and the difficulties that this creates for children who are learning to read. We shall summarize two general points. First, written languages certainly do vary in the complexity of the rules that relate spelling to sound. At one extreme there is Finnish, which many linguists consider to have the most regular letter-sound correspondence of any language, approaching the regularity of the International Phonetic Alphabet. At the other extreme, English is quite irregular, with many letters and groups of letters being pronounced in different ways in different words (for example, a in *cap* and *cape;* e in *met, mete,* and *merge;* ow in *fowl* and *snow;* and so on). Conversely, the same sound may be represented in different ways (for example, [k] in *cat* and *kit,* [s] in *prince* and *rinse*). Such variation in spelling-to-sound correspondence would be extremely important if reading

were entirely a phonetic matter in which the reader translated writing directly into sound. Such phonetic reading is approximated when an adult attempts to read a totally unfamiliar language aloud, using the letter-to-sound correspondences of that language. The difficulties are legend when English is the foreign language.

However—and this is our second point—native-language reading is quite another matter. Children who are beginning to read can speak reasonably well, which means that they know the rules of pronunciation, have a considerable vocabulary, and so on. They will use this knowledge as they attempt to read, rather than relying on letter-to-sound correspondences alone. In brief, they read for *meaning,* and pronunciation comes as a result of determining the representations of meaningful units in their "internal lexicon." This is the implication of an approach that Noam Chomsky and Halle (1968) proposed in regard to English spelling. Carole Chomsky (1970) wrote a clear account of their views, with particular reference to reading. Chomsky and Halle showed by linguistic analyses that the spelling-to-sound correspondence of English is much closer than is ordinarily assumed, provided that one considers the deep structure of the language. Thus, the spellings of words correspond more closely to the abstract, underlying representations of the sound system of English than they do to the surface structures of spoken words. The relation between the regularities in deep structure and the variants in surface structure can be captured by the rules of the phonological component of a transformational generative grammar of English (cf. chapter 3). Such rules would specify, for example, that words undergo pronunciation shifts when suffixes are added to them: [eɪ] becomes [æ] in the pairs *nation-national, nature-natural, sane-sanity,* and so on. Speakers of English recognize that these word pairs are phonetic variants of the same word. It would be convenient to have this fact reflected in the lexicon of English grammar by postulating just one spelling for the sound unit (the vowel /a/ in our examples) together with rules that state how the pronunciation changes in different word forms.

One implication of this account is that reading goes on at different levels. A child initially might respond primarily on the basis of letter-to-sound correspondences and gradually shift to lexical interpretations as "phonological competence" increases and there is more familiarity with the underlying regularities in spelling. For the mature reader, English spelling may in fact be a highly efficient way of representing the spoken language. Chomsky and Halle made an important contribution by suggesting this general possibility, regardless of the ultimate value of transformational generative grammar as a way of expressing the idea in theory.

Syntactic effects in reading

The foregoing discussion leads naturally to a consideration of the role of complex structural variables in reading, the final topic in this section. Lexical influences on the pronunciation of particular letters are one example. Here we consider the effect of the syntax of entire sentences on the efficiency of "mechanical" reading. The problem can be posed with reference to the situation in which our minds wander as we read a children's story aloud to a child. Is such "mindless" reading nonetheless sensitive to the grammar of the text? That this might be the case is suggested by the informal observation that such reading preserves normal

pause and stress patterns, rather than being performed in a steady monotone. This could mean that the repeated reading of the same text has made habitual the entire response pattern. According to this S-R interpretation, the naturalness of automatic reading should be reduced when the text is new or even nonsensical. The sparse research relevant to the problem suggests, however, that grammatical sensitivity is retained even for unfamiliar text.

Kolers (1970) has used geometrically transformed text to study the above problem. He presented his subjects with pages of normal text or pages on which the printed lines were transformed in some way. For example, the lines might be rotated in the plane of the page, inverted, or presented as mirror reflections. Subjects read the text aloud, and their sensitivity to grammar was revealed particularly by the errors that they made. Not surprisingly, fewer words were misread in normal than in transformed sentences, but the nature of the errors was similar over transformations. For example, most errors were substitutions of words from the same part of speech as the printed word: nouns were substituted for nouns, verbs for verbs, and so on. Conversely, nouns were almost never replaced by pronouns, nor were pronouns, conjunctions, or articles replaced by nouns. Thus the substitution errors were selective in that they had a syntactic similarity to what was printed. Moreover, grammatical relations tended to be preserved in that most errors were grammatically acceptable with respect to the preceding words in the text. Finally, the errors were systematically related to the grammatical structure of clauses. The most errors were in the part of an independent clause that pertains to verbs, suggesting that it is more difficult to perceive the relations a printed sentence expresses than it is to perceive the things being related. Those and other findings reviewed by Kolers show that grammar plays a potent role in reading.

It is difficult, of course, to conclude that these effects occur at the level of automatic rather than meaningful reading or that they are due to visual structure or grammatical variables rather than to semantic ones. In brief, it is as difficult to separate the effects of meaning from those of structural factors in reading as it is in comprehension and memory tasks (chapters 7 and 8). Rather than pursue that issue further, we shall move directly to the central problem in the psychology of reading, namely, reading for meaning.

Reading for Comprehension

The common-sense way of stating the present problem is in terms of "getting the meaning" from text. Although certainly acceptable in everyday communication, such a statement is imprecise and misleading as a psychological description. It implies that the print itself *contains* something called meaning and that the reader learns to *extract* it. It is nothing of the kind. Instead, the reader learns to *respond* to text in ways that we call meaningful. Speech itself is one kind of response, when we read aloud or pronounce the words covertly to ourselves. This is not the only kind of response, however, and it is even questionable whether pronunciation is necessary for textual understanding. Nonverbal actions, emotions, and images are among the main outcomes of meaningful reading. They are components or expressions of our knowledge of the world, and when we have learned to read, written symbols can evoke the component responses. A reader constructs meaning

from text, just as a listener constructs meaning from speech. The problem at this level is simply one aspect of the overall problem of understanding language, as discussed in chapter 7.

To deal with the problem we must consider ways of measuring meaningful reading, the variables that affect it, and theoretical interpretations of such effects. Much relevant information has already been covered in earlier chapters. We shall remind you of that information and then go on to present additional information. Word recognition as measured by duration thresholds and reaction times (chapter 6) is important because the subject's task in such experiments is to identify a meaningful word. The essential variables included such word attributes as frequency, meaningfulness, affective value, and concreteness. We also considered context effects on visual recognition thresholds, word-nonword decisions, and backward masking. These and other effects of written stimuli should be understood as relevant to the problem of reading. We now shall discuss two response measures that have been applied specifically to the study of reading, namely, eye movements and the eye-voice span.

Eye movements

Modern studies of eye movements use a photographic technique in which a beam of light is reflected off the cornea onto moving picture film. By superimposing the stimulus material onto the film, we can determine the location, duration, and sequence of fixation points as well as the direction of eye movements during reading. This technique has revealed a number of reliable facts. A basic one is that reading is accompanied by *saccadic* eye movements. These consist of a series of pauses of varying duration, with a rapid movement from one fixation point to the next. Saccades contrast with smooth pursuit movements that occur when the eyes are following a moving object. The jerky nature of eye movements in reading is interesting in that it is not obvious to the reader.

The effects of several other variables have been reviewed by Tinker (1958, 1965; see also Just & Carpenter, 1980). In general, much more time is spent in fixation pauses than in movements, about 94 percent as compared to 6 percent on the average. Pause duration is particularly relevant to meaningful reading because it varies with the difficulty of the text. For example, average pause duration is longer for difficult prose than for easy prose. Thus, like the pauses that occur during subject-controlled, word-by-word processing of visual or auditory passages (chapter 7) and during speech production (chapter 9), reading pauses evidently are thinking pauses.

Eye movements are also sensitive to grammatical structure (Gibson & Levin, 1975, pp. 372-375). Adults read active sentences more smoothly than simple passive sentences. That is, they generally show fewer and briefer forward fixations and regressions (returning to an earlier point in the sentence) in active sentences. This general effect is reversed in the area of the *by* phrase that introduces the agent of action in passives, in which the regressions are infrequent and brief. Readers also make more and longer regressive fixations in agent-deleted passives (*The boy was hit by the school*) than in full passives (*The boy was hit by the car*). This is consistent with other data in suggesting that the former are linguistically and psychologically more complex than the latter (cf. chapter 8).

Eye-voice span

Another common measurement technique in reading research is the eye-voice span. This is the distance, usually measured in words, that the eyes are ahead of the voice when one is reading aloud. The eyes are normally ahead of the voice because the reader must have advance information about the sentence in order to read with natural intonation. The phenomenon can be informally demonstrated by having someone read a page of text aloud, covering the page at some point, and asking the person to report as much of the coming text as possible. This is achieved under more controlled conditions in the laboratory by turning off the light or covering the lens of the projector that presents the reading material. Another method is to record the voice and eye movements at the same time so that the two can be correlated.

The eye-voice span, like eye movements, is affected by the difficulty and grammatical structure of the material being read (Gibson & Levin, 1975, p. 361). The more difficult the text is, the shorter the eye-voice span; and the more grammatically structured the text is, the longer the span. For example, both children and adults show a much longer span when they read sentences than when they read an unstructured list of words. Span also varies with the syntactic structure of sentences. Active and passive sentences have been found to differ in sequential dependencies, so that the latter part of the sentence is more constrained and more predictable in passives than in actives. This difference shows up as an increase in the eye-voice span for passive sentences, beginning in the region of the verb that precedes the *by* phrase (Levin & Kaplan, 1968). Consider the sentence *The cute chubby boy was slowly being wheeled by the maid along the lane to the country store.* When the light is turned off at different points during reading, the eye-voice span increases after *being.* There is no comparable increase in active sentences like *The brash tall man was certainly being loud at the meeting of the new group on the main campus,* apparently because the verb and object are relatively independent of the subject. The effects of grammatical structure have been similarly demonstrated in other experiments, but our example illustrates this particular approach to the study of variables that affect reading. The studies have been primarily concerned with syntactic rather than semantic variables, but authors such as Gibson and Levin assume that the grammatical structure permits the reader to identify the meaningful units of the sentence.

From print to meaning

The discussion up to this point has taken for granted the processes in going from written stimuli to meaningful responses. What is the nature of these processes? Two general views continue to be debated. One view is that the reader goes directly from print to meaning. The other is that meaning is reached only indirectly, through the arousal of a phonemic code. That is, writing must activate the speech system before it can be understood. Within the latter hypothesis there are specific alternatives, such as the behavioral interpretation that speech motor reactions are actually present (one subvocalizes while reading) and the cognitive view that the phonemic stage need not include covert speaking. Note that these theoretical alternatives are similar to those discussed in the context of the motor theory of speech perception (chapter 6).

The issue would be closed if it could be shown that subvocalization is always associated with silent reading, or at least correlated with level of comprehension during reading. What are the facts? We all know that we sometimes "talk to ourselves" when we are reading silently. This subvocalization might be accompanied by obvious movements of the lips and tongue, or it might spill over into whispered speech. Even when it cannot be seen or heard, the inner speech can still be detected by electromyographic (EMG) recordings of the subtle voltage changes that accompany speech muscle activity, which are picked up by electrodes attached to the tongue, lips, chin, or laryngeal area.

A number of EMG studies have shown that the degree of subvocalization correlates with indices of comprehension. For example, subvocalization increases as the reading material becomes more difficult to understand (for example, Hardyck & Petrinovich, 1970) or as the reading is made more difficult by distracting the subject in some way (McGuigan & Rodier, 1968). However, it does not follow from such results that subvocalization is necessary for understanding. Individuals vary greatly in the degree to which they subvocalize, and these differences need not be related to reading proficiency. In fact, some individuals with reading problems show high levels of subvocalization, and attempts have been made to *reduce* the level in the hope of improving their reading skills. Such reduction has been achieved, for example, by feedback training in which EMG signals from the speech muscles are converted into sounds that the subject hears over earphones. Using such a procedure, Hardyck, Petrinovich, and Ellsworth (1966) instructed college students to read so that there would be no sound. All subjects did so after one training session. Hardyck and Petrinovich (1970), however, found that reading comprehension for difficult material suffered when subvocal activity was reduced by feedback training. This was taken as evidence that reading comprehension is mediated by the speech motor system.

The evidence, however, is not conclusive in regard to the motor theory. Gibson and Levin (1975) appropriately ask why speech muscles become active only when people read difficult material. What mechanism mediates comprehension during reading of easy text, when the speech muscles are inactive? Apparently *detectable* subvocal activity does not inevitably accompany reading. It depends on the nature of the text, the reader's skill, and the reader's task.

Proponents of the phonemic recoding theory can nonetheless argue that the speech system is activated during reading, if only at the cortical level where it cannot be picked up by EMG electrodes. We must, therefore, rely on other kinds of evidence to test the hypothesis and the alternative view that meaning can be aroused directly by written stimuli. A few representative studies will illustrate the methods, results, and theoretical interpretations in the problem area. Rubenstein, Lewis, and Rubenstein (1971) presented their subjects with English words or nonwords, some of which followed English orthography and phonology—that is, they looked like English words and sounded like them when pronounced. The subjects' task was to decide as quickly as possible whether or not the presented stimulus was an English word. The subjects took longer to decide that the stimulus was a nonword when it was phonologically "legal" (like English) than when it was not. Moreover, homophonic nonsense words like *brane* (which sounds like *brain*) required more time than nonhomophonic but legal nonwords. Finally, word decision latencies were longer for real word homophones like *yoke* and *yolk* than for real word nonhomo-

phones. They concluded, therefore, that visually presented words are read by recoding them into a phonemic form and then comparing that form with its internal lexical representation.

Other experiments using homophones and based on a similar logic have led to a different conclusion. For example, Baron and Thurston (1973) found that information about pronunciation (sound) did not influence the results in word-nonword recognition. On the basis of such results, Baron (1973) concluded that meaning can be derived directly from visual analysis of text without mediation by a phonemic code. Frederiksen and Kroll (1976) reported a series of experiments in which they showed subjects words and pronounceable nonwords that varied in length, syllabic structure, and frequency. The subjects were required either to name the stimulus or to decide whether it was a word or a nonword. The analysis of response latencies permitted the authors to conclude that phonemic recoding is not a prerequisite for lexical retrieval during reading. Instead, lexical access can be performed on the basis of visual information—that is, print rather than sound.

The issue has not been resolved by these studies. Mewhort and Beal (1977) used words and pseudowords in a series of experiments designed to test a scanning model of word identification. Their results suggested that a string of characters is converted into a verbal-temporal representation by a "sequential scan operator," which ordinarily operates on the syllable as a unit. Meaning is presumably determined by the verbal-temporal representation rather than by visual representations.

Given the empirical inconsistencies, perhaps the appropriate conclusion is that a text can be read for meaning either *directly* by visual processing of the printed words or *indirectly* by a phonemic code, depending on the precise conditions of the reading task and on individual differences among readers. Such a conclusion was suggested by Hawkins, Reicher, Rogers, and Peterson (1976) in regard to performance in a tachistoscopic recognition experiment in which subjects had to decide which of two words had been presented. Phonetic information was used when it distinguished between the alternatives (for example, *sold* versus *cold*), but visual, or perhaps even semantic, information could be used when phonetic information did not permit a choice (for example, between *sent* and *cent*). Other factors, such as memory demands, are presumably relevant as well, but their implications are only beginning to be explored. We shall leave the topic with the conclusion that meaning probably can be attained from text by different processes.

Imagery in reading comprehension

What is the nature of the meaning that the reader constructs from text? Presumably it consists of any of the processes and reactions—emotions, verbal associations, images—that were discussed earlier (chapter 7) in relation to comprehension generally. We shall consider only imagery here because it has a long history in the literature on reading and because the arguments for and against imagery apply also to the other classes of associative reactions. The role of imagery in reading was discussed in a classical work by Huey (1908). He argued essentially that, in reading for meaning, sentences arouse images and feelings. Like other psychologists of the day, however, Huey was unable to resolve the impasse created for the image theory by the difficulty of imaging to words like *the, and, but,* or relational words like *under* and *upon,* so he abandoned the problem. Another argument that

is often raised even today is that skilled reading is so rapid that there is simply no time for images to be aroused for each meaningful word.

With regard to the problem of imaging to articles, prepositions, and the like, Bugelski (1971) argued that Huey gave up too soon. There is no problem accepting the idea that images can occur to such words provided that we recognize that they do not normally appear alone. One cannot visualize to the word *in,* but one can visualize relationships between objects brought together by that word—a car in a garage, for example. "When subject and predicate are taken together, in short, when there is a sentence, meaning emerges, and it emerges as a matter of tapping prior experience in terms of imagery and feeling" (p. 319).

The problem raised by reading speed can be similarly answered. Reading rates vary greatly among individuals, but we can take five English words per second as the average rate for American university students (Gibson & Levin, 1975, p. 164). Reaction time studies also show great variability in the latency of image arousal to words, particularly as a function of word class (see chapter 5). Paivio (1971b) suggested about .6 seconds as the true latency for concrete nouns. Thus, even if all the words in a page of text were concrete nouns, one could generate images only at a rate of less than two words per second, far lower than the reading rate. However, if the unit of meaningful reading is larger than the word—perhaps a phrase or sentence—then image arousal does become a possibility, at least for concrete sentences. We construct images in response to concrete words as we read, not one image per word but a sequence of images for groups of words. Further, even if it takes some time to form an image, the time to alter the image to incorporate later information might be rapid indeed.

This reasoning is essentially what Paivio and Begg (1971) proposed in regard to imagery and comprehension reaction times to visually presented concrete and abstract sentences. In one experiment, image latencies were actually faster on the average than comprehension latencies to concrete sentences. This was interpreted to mean that the subject had constructed an image before the entire sentence had been read. Under comprehension instructions, however, the entire sentence had to be read in order to make sure that it was fully understood. The study was summarized in chapter 7, which also included other evidence that imagery processes play a role in reading. Recall, for example, that Brooks (1967) found that verbal tasks presumed to use imagery were disrupted more by reading than by listening. Thus, sentences that describe spatial relations were remembered more poorly when they were read than when they were heard. In the present context, such findings imply that visual imagery or some similar process is used in comprehension and memory for sentences and that the visual demands of reading interfere to some degree with that process.

Having presented the case for the role of imagery in reading for meaning, we hasten to add once again that imagery cannot carry the entire explanatory burden. Such concepts as verbal-associative reactions, schematic world knowledge, and levels of comprehension are as relevant here as in speech comprehension. From a dual-coding viewpoint, reading employs both verbal and nonverbal symbolic systems. Written symbols must first activate visual long-term memory representations in the verbal system. Ordinarily this would be followed by arousal of auditory-motor representations (logogens) corresponding to meaningful spoken words. This stage is equivalent to the phonemic stage discussed above and represents a first level of meaning, that is, verbal representational meaning (cf. chapter 5). Deeper levels of

reading comprehension would arouse imagery (referential meaning) and verbal associations (associative meaning), as well as general emotional and covert motor reactions. We say that the higher levels of meaning are *ordinarily* mediated by a phonemic stage because we do not exclude the possibility that images, emotions, and so on might be directly activated by written language.

Learning and Remembering through Reading

The main questions we shall consider here are whether there is anything special about learning and remembering verbal material through reading as compared to listening, and what characteristics of text might influence performance. Modality differences obviously would be expected if presentation favored one mode or the other. This can easily happen under normal circumstances because text endures whereas speech is fleeting. Thus reading provides more opportunity for rehearsal than does listening. Memory studies comparing the two modes have generally attempted to control for such effects by equating study time in some way. This is easier with lists of words and sentences than it is with longer passages, but it is nonetheless important for the researcher to be aware of the problem and to deal with it in some way.

There is much literature on modality differences in the free recall of words. The most consistent effect observed is related to the position of items in the list and to the order in which they are recalled. After some experience with the free-recall task, subjects tend to recall the most recently presented items first. In other words, they first report some of the items from the end of the input list and then the items listed earlier. The former are called *recency* items (or items from the recency position) because the delay between presentation and recall is brief. Items coming early in the list (usually recalled later) are sometimes called *primacy* items. These positions are associated with a characteristic U-shaped recall curve, with recall being high for recency and primacy positions and low for items from the middle of the list. These basic facts are relevant here because modality differences are most striking for recency items: recall is better when such items are presented auditorily than when they are presented visually. This difference is usually attributed to the nature of short-term memory for verbal material. Such memory is assumed to have auditory-motor properties, equivalent to the phonemic code discussed earlier. This code is reached more directly when the verbal input is auditory than when it is visual, hence the recency effect.

The implication of the modality research is that one is likely to remember what one has just heard better than what one has just read, but that difference may vanish for information received earlier. This inference is drawn from experiments with lists of unrelated words. Does it generalize to sentences and longer passages? The evidence is rather scarce, but what there is suggests that visual presentation exceeds auditory presentation in memory for the verbatim form of the sentences. Begg (1971) reasoned that syntactic changes are more important to meaning in written material than in speech, in which gestures and intonation assume some of the functions of syntax in writing. Consistent with this view, subjects were more accurate in distinguishing between verbatim repetitions of earlier presented sentences and paraphrases of those sentences when the sentences were read rather than heard. More recently, Flagg and Reynolds (1977) compared visual and audi-

tory presentation of sentences in a memory task and confirmed Begg's finding of better memory for syntax. In neither study was there any difference in memory for meaning, however. Thus the general picture seems to be that reading produces somewhat better memory for surface details of sentences than does listening, perhaps because such surface details are more meaningful in writing than in speech (cf. Olson, 1977).

Another question concerns the characteristics of text that might affect learning and memory. Most research has been on the content of textual material. These studies have generally not included comparisons with the same material presented auditorily, so we cannot be sure that the findings pertain only to reading. Nonetheless, we mention some of the more salient contributions to the problem. Several researchers have attempted to develop indices of the general readability of text. For example, Flesch (1948, 1949) developed a readability index based on a count of various types of words occurring in the text—personal pronouns, concrete as compared to abstract words, and so on. Rubenstein and Aborn (1958) related the Flesch count and one developed by Dale and Chall (1948) to the amount learned from two-hundred-word passages by college students. Verbatim recall per minute of study time was the learning score. The results showed that the two measures of readability were highly correlated (.91) and that each measure correlated substantially (.61 and .75) with the amount remembered.

Smith, Rothkopf, and Koether (1970, summarized in Rothkopf, 1972) measured various aspects of readability, including the Flesch count, for ten fifteen-hundred-word passages. The passages had been written by ten different authors but were similar in content. Subjects read each of the passages, and then learning was evaluated by short-answer questions and a free-recall test. The Flesch measure correlated only .28 and .30 with the two measures of learning. Other stylistic features such as sentence length, word length, and number of technical terms also correlated modestly with one learning measure or the other. The best predictor was a measure of the number of incidental or irrelevant facts contained in the text, which correlated -.59 and -.71 with the learning scores. Thus "sticking to the point" seems to be more important than various stylistic features of text when it comes to memorable writing (see also Reder & Anderson, 1980).

Not surprisingly, grammatical and semantic organization are related to the ease of learning from text. Coleman (1965a), for example, found that active sentences were easier to learn than their passive counterparts, and nonembedded sentences were easier than embedded ones. The organization of sentences within paragraphs or longer passages is also important. For example, a doctoral thesis study by Kircher (cited in Gibson & Levin, 1975, pp. 419-420) showed that college students recalled more sentences when they were presented in passages in which they formed an organized, meaningful structure than when the same sentences were scattered among different passages. The related sentences were also clustered together during recall of the organized passages but not the mixed ones. These and other similar findings illustrate the effects of organizational factors considered in chapter 8. Chunking, integration, or unitization were the key explanatory concepts in that context, and they are equally applicable here. Any factor that helps the reader to organize information into meaningful chunks will promote learning from text.

The structural organization of the material is important. So too is the seman-

tic content, in particular the imagery value or concreteness of the text. The lesson for the writer who wants to teach in print is to organize the material carefully and to supply concrete examples whenever possible. The lesson for the reader who wants to learn is to look for the organization that has been provided and, if this does not seem satisfactory, to reorganize the content to suit his or her own purposes, relating each idea unit to at least one concrete example or conceptual peg.

The preceding discussion was on linguistic structure and content of text. The printed page also has a visual structure that can be varied in many ways, such as the general layout of the page, kind of type, use of capitals and italics, use of color, and so on. A glance at the front page and the advertising layouts of a newspaper or the typographical style of any textbook will reveal some of this variety. What effect, if any, do such typographical features have on learning? Hershberger and Terry (1965) studied the problem using three typographical formats. One contained no special typographical cues. A second was a simple typographical cuing condition in which the essential content was printed in red to distinguish it from the nonessential content, which was printed in black. The third contained complex typographical cuing that combined underlining, capitals versus lowercase, and color of type in various ways intended to distinguish five categories of textual importance. The dependent variable was the amount learned by eighth-grade students from conventional and programmed texts.

The results showed little effect of typography. The group with no typographical cuing performed at least as well as the one that received the complex cues. Colored type resulted in superior performance only on the core content, and even this gain was not large relative to normal text. These results suggest that enrichment of the visual structure of text has little effect.

Individual Differences in Reading Skills

Everyone knows that people differ greatly in their ability to read. In particular, some children find it unusually difficult to learn to read, and others seem to learn with little effort. There is much psychological literature on such problems, and we can do no more than touch on some of the highlights. We shall examine characteristics of the skilled reader on the one hand and reading problems on the other.

Skilled reading

Jackson and McClelland (1979) carried out an extensive study of differences in cognitive ability between fast and average readers. The subjects were university students selected on the basis of tests of effective reading speed. The tests used passages of text which the students read as fast as possible, with the understanding that afterwards they would be tested for comprehension. The fast readers selected on the basis of the test read the material faster and understood it better than the average readers. Both groups were then tested on a number of reaction-time tasks designed to determine the speed of encoding visual information at several different levels. In addition, they were given tests of sensory functions, verbal and quantitative reasoning ability, short-term auditory memory span, and ability to comprehend spoken text.

The reaction-time tasks were patterned after the same-different matching tasks developed by Posner and his colleagues (for example, Posner, Boies, Eichelman, & Taylor, 1969). The logic and general procedure are the same as those described in chapter 7 in relation to information-processing approaches to comprehension. Jackson and McClelland presented two stimulus elements simultaneously, and their subjects were required to indicate as quickly as possible whether the two were the same or different. In one version of the task, the stimuli were simple patterns. In another version, the stimuli were letters, and the participants were required to respond "same" if the letters were either physically identical (for example, AA) or identical in name (Aa); otherwise, "different." In a third version, the stimuli were words, and subjects responded "same" if the words were synonymous (ABRUPT-SUDDEN). In another case, the "same" response depended on sound similarity (BARE-BEAR). Thus the tasks were intended to tap different levels of processing including the formation of visual letter codes, letter-identity coding, semantic coding, and verbal (acoustic or articulatory) coding. The results showed that the fast readers had faster reaction times than average readers on all of these tasks.

The results for the other tasks will be briefly summarized. The two groups did not differ on the simple sensory tasks (for example, thresholds for letter identification), but the faster readers performed more accurately in verbal and quantitative reasoning, short-term auditory memory, and listening comprehension.

Correlations were also computed among all of the tests, and a procedure called a stepwise multiple-regression analysis was used to determine which variables were the best predictors of effective reading speed. These analyses indicated that listening comprehension was the single most powerful predictor, followed by the letter-matching reaction-time task. Thus fast readers have high ability in comprehending spoken material, and they can quickly reach the long-term memory codes for visually presented letters.

The relation between listening comprehension and effective reading speed cannot be interpreted as reflecting specific processes. It suggests rather that some general verbal ability is required in processing language material, regardless of modality. The letter-processing data, on the other hand, point to a rather specific decoding skill using small units of text. Other studies suggest that skilled readers also excel in their ability to process larger chunks of text. For example, eye-movement studies show that fast readers generally make fewer fixations and briefer pauses per line of text than slower readers (Gibson & Levin, 1975, chap. 10). Thus, fast readers seem to be able to process more text per fixation. This suggestion was directly supported in a study by Gilbert (1959): fast readers reported more of the content from briefly presented sentences (approximating a single fixation) than slow readers did.

What processes might account for the skilled reader's ability to process large chunks of text? Associative and grammatical skills are important in that fast readers are better than slower readers at predicting words on the basis of contextual information. For example, in one of several experiments reported by Perfetti, Goldman, and Hogaboam (1979), skilled and less skilled readers were required to predict words that would be exposed on a screen. The crucial condition was a story context in which the subjects heard or read sentences, and their task was to predict deleted words before they were exposed. Skilled readers made more correct predic-

tions than unskilled readers did. However, this difference in contextual ability did not explain all the differences in reading speed, since other experiments in the study showed that the latency of identifying the exposed words was reduced by the story context (as compared to no context), at least as much among the less skilled readers as among the skilled ones. Perfetti and his colleagues suggest that the contextual ability of the skilled reader may show up in more demanding tasks, requiring that entire phrases or sentences be read.

These studies suggest that skilled reading requires a high level of ability to extract information from text during each fixation. This ability seems to operate on units of different size, ranging from letters to phrases and sentences. This is more of a description of the correlates of reading skill than it is a causal explanation, however, since we know very little about the factors responsible for the development of the component skills.

Do we nonetheless know enough about those skills to be able to teach the average reader to improve his or her effective reading speed? Numerous speed-reading courses make such a claim in their advertising. The procedures emphasized in these courses generally concentrate on the two features of skilled reading discussed above, one related to eye movements and the other to chunking. First, the skilled reader makes fewer fixations and regressions and tends to pause more briefly during each fixation than the less skilled reader does. Second, the skilled reader seems to take in more information at a glance. A well-known course, the Evelyn Wood Dynamic Reading Program, translates these two characteristics into the following basic techniques (described by Carver, 1971, and cited in Gibson & Levin, 1975, p. 542): (a) read down pages instead of across them, (b) read in whole concepts and ideas rather than one word at a time, and (c) use the hand as a guiding pacer.

Reading down the page implies that the reader looks at the center of each line and moves down without regressing, under the guidance of the hand that precedes the eye movements. It is claimed that this training procedure will eventually triple the student's reading speed without loss of comprehension. The reader in effect learns to see and understand entire lines at each fixation. Evaluation of such claims depends on how one interprets them. Gibson and Levin (1975, pp. 542–549) review the relevant evidence. First, a single fixation could take in a span of ten letters at most, not an entire line. Second, it is impossible for the eyes to move quickly enough to permit the reader to see fifteen hundred words per minute (the reading rate claimed for a group of highly skilled speed readers). Third, studies of the eye-movement patterns of graduates of the Reading Dynamics course and of other high-speed readers show that the fixations do not progress vertically down the page. Instead, they are similar to those that have been observed during skimming or scanning activities. The patterns are sometimes very unusual, one speed reader following a pattern that resembled a square, crossing both pages of an open book, but without any fixations in the lower third of the page. Another subject's eye movements showed a zigzag pattern down the page. Finally, and most important, the high reading rates and eye-movement patterns cannot be and are not achieved with full comprehension. Readers cannot get any information from those parts of the page that they do not see, so comprehension will be limited to inferences drawn from the words fixated during scanning. Research studies of graduates of speed-reading courses and control subjects show that the former do indeed

read faster in terms of material covered in a given time period. However, the faster reading is not done with increased comprehension; instead, it is usually associated with a loss of detailed information.

Gibson and Levin (1975, p. 548) conclude their discussion of effective reading by emphasizing flexibility of reading style as being of the greatest importance. Rapid skimming or scanning is useful on many occasions, such as during an initial overview with the idea of deciding what should be reread more carefully. Slower reading is necessary when one is trying to understand and remember difficult ideas written in compact prose. Skilled readers are able to modify their rate according to their purpose and the difficulty of the text. It is not clear yet how to achieve such skills, but emphasis on speed alone is not the answer.

Dyslexia

Here we glance at the negative side of reading skills, namely, the problem of dyslexia. The term refers generally to reading difficulties that cannot be attributed to disorders such as severe brain injury, mental retardation, or emotional problems. In other words, dyslexic children are slow in learning to read, although they are otherwise normal. It is important to understand at the outset that there is considerable disagreement in the literature over the definition of dyslexia because reading problems do not fall into neat categories as do medical syndromes, nor do they have a single, easily identified cause. Instead, dyslexia covers a variety of specific problems that result from different causes.

Reading difficulties are diagnosed by standard reading tests. A child has a reading problem if reading performance falls below the average for children at the same grade level. Such children are especially likely to be labeled dyslexic if their reading difficulty is accompanied by specific cognitive or perceptual-motor problems. The most frequently mentioned correlates include reversals of letters and words, faulty serial ordering, deficient intersensory integration, difficulties in sound segmentation, and poor perceptual-motor coordination.

Each of the above problems has been viewed by some researchers as a possible cause of dyslexia, but firm evidence for most of them is sparse. Gibson and Levin (1975) summarize the findings and the arguments. One idea is that dyslexia is particularly associated with a tendency to reverse letters, letters within words, and words. Thus, *bog* may be read as *dog, saw* as *was,* and so on. Shankweiler and Liberman (1972) studied such errors among a large number of second- and third-grade children. Reversals generally accounted for only a small proportion of the total number of errors in reading word lists, even among poor readers. Moreover, individual children were not consistently high or low on such errors on different occasions. This lack of reliability, and evidence that both normal and poor readers make reversals, suggest that dyslexia is not due to persistent tendencies to reverse letters or words.

Although letter reversals are visual-spatial confusions (b and d, for example), reversals of letters within words or words within larger units could be a deficit in the temporal ordering of linguistic units: one reads things in the wrong order. This has been suggested as a possible basis of dyslexia because dyslexic children have been found to have relatively low scores on such sequencing tasks as immediate memory span. Moreover, the deficit is quite general in that S. Corkin (cited in

Gibson & Levin, 1975, p. 498) found that dyslexic children scored lower than normal readers both on a task in which they had to remember the serial positions of cubes as they were tapped by the experimenter, and on an auditory digit span test. Thus the deficit cuts across symbolic (verbal versus nonverbal) and sensory modalities.

It has also been proposed that dyslexics have special difficulty in sound segmentation, that is, in distinguishing phonemes or other linguistic units. If true, this could make it difficult for them to learn the relationships between sound and print. However, dyslexics are generally unimpaired in their spoken language, which means that they must be able to discriminate linguistic units adequately in listening and speaking.

Intermodal integration refers to the process of matching visual to auditory input. Such integration may be a component of reading skill, which requires one to be able to match print and sounds. A relation to dyslexia is suggested by the finding that good readers surpassed poor readers on a task that required them to deal simultaneously with verbal and nonverbal visual material, but not on a task using only visual nonverbal material (Vellutino, Harding, Phillips, & Steger, 1975; Vellutino, Steger, Harding, & Phillips, 1975). The verbal-nonverbal task required learning associations between bisyllabic nonsense words and pairs of new geometric designs. Examples are shown in Figure 14-5. This training was followed by a transfer test in which the component syllables of the words and the two parts of the designs were re-paired, as shown in the right-hand panel of Figure 14-5. We mention these details in order to emphasize what seems to us to be an important point: the nonsense words were presented both visually and orally. Thus the task is not an example of pure sensory integration. Instead, it is best viewed as one employing verbal-nonverbal integration. In terms of dual-coding theory, it requires the subject to learn referential relations between new words and geometric patterns and to infer new referential relations in the transfer test. We are not suggesting that the development of referential meaning is uniquely related to reading skill. The point is that sensory integration was confounded with symbolic integration in the cited study. It would be interesting to disentangle the alternatives by combining sensory (auditory versus visual) and symbolic (verbal versus nonverbal) modalities in all possible ways with good and poor readers.

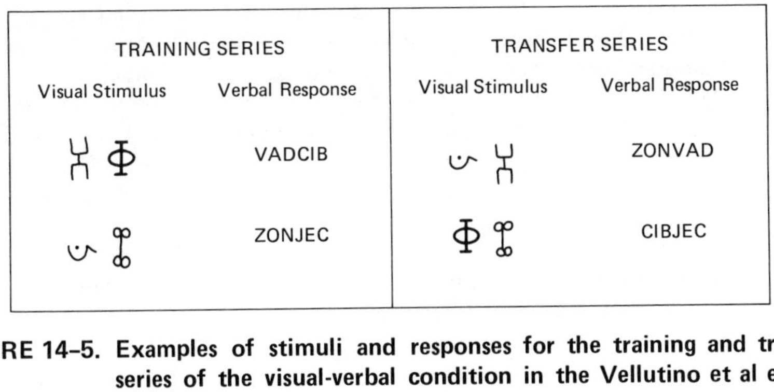

FIGURE 14-5. Examples of stimuli and responses for the training and transfer series of the visual-verbal condition in the Vellutino et al experiment. Based on Vellutino, Harding, et al (1975).

Finally, it has been proposed that dyslexia is associated with problems of perceptual and motor coordination. This appears to stem from the observation that children with perceptual-motor problems sometimes also have reading problems. However, there are striking exceptions, such as people with cerebral palsy who are expert readers. Moreover, dyslexic children and normal readers have been found to be equivalent on a variety of perceptual-motor skills (Nielsen & Ringe, 1969). Thus it appears unlikely that such skills are systematically related to reading ability.

We are left with the conclusion that among the various correlates investigated, only sequential ordering problems seem to be consistently correlated with dyslexia. This is in accord with the importance of sequential organization to language behavior generally (cf. chapter 4).

There are a number of causal explanations of dyslexia. We shall review these briefly. One explanation states that dyslexic children have been experientially deprived in some way relevant to language development generally or to reading in particular. The communicative relationship between mother and child may be so poor that the stimulation necessary for normal language acquisition is absent. Children's motivation to engage in language-related tasks would be lowered if, for example, they are spoken to rarely or only angrily. General cultural and educational deprivation as a result of poverty can lead to reading problems along with a host of other difficulties. The homes of culturally deprived children may lack books, the schools they attend may be inferior, and so on.

Other explanations attribute dyslexia to organic causes. One such explanation is minimal brain dysfunction (which is not to be confused with severe brain damage or mental retardation). The idea is that the dyslexic child may have some minor irregularity in brain functioning caused by some early injury, illness, or biochemical imbalance. These may show up in the form of perceptual-motor problems, abnormalities in EEG (the EEG is explained in chapter 15), and so on. The evidence suggests that some cases of dyslexia can be attributed to minimal brain dysfunction, but Gibson and Levin (1975, p. 491) conclude that the percentage is very small. An extensive study by Owen, Adams, Forrest, Stolz, and Fisher (1971), for example, showed that only 4 of 304 dyslexic children in their sample could be definitely diagnosed as neurologically impaired.

Another organic explanation is that dyslexia is caused by some genetic (hereditary) factor that affects the skills necessary for reading. Studies of twins have provided some support for this hypothesis: when one twin has a reading disability, the other is highly likely to have a similar problem. The probability of nonidentical (fraternal) twins having similar reading disorders is much lower. Other studies similarly show that dyslexia tends to run in families. The interested reader can find detailed reviews in Lenneberg (1967) and Gibson and Levin (1975). We point out only that hereditary factors seem to be present in some cases of dyslexia, but the evidence does not warrant the conclusion that all dyslexias are genetically determined.

We conclude that dyslexia is a complex phenomenon, both behaviorally and causally. It manifests itself in various specific symptoms and correlates, and it can be caused by experiential and/or organic deficits. The prevention and correction of the problem will depend on a much fuller scientific understanding of the phenomenon and its causes than is now available.

Reading Ideograms and Gestures

Thus far we have dealt mainly with the problems and processes associated with reading alphabetic writing. Here we consider possible differences in the way that iconic and ideographic symbol systems are read. We examine the problem with particular reference to Chinese ideographic (or logographic) writing and the iconic gestures used in sign language. The comparisons are of special interest because they have implications for a dual-coding approach to reading.

We pointed out earlier that Chinese characters include pictographic or iconic representations for some objects. However, they also include ideographic representations of abstract concepts like love and peace. Ideograms nonetheless differ from alphabetic writing in that they stand for concepts rather than sounds, and the ideographic patterns are generally more complex than are letters. Thus ideographic writing is more picturelike than phonographic writing. One implication is that ideograms, like pictures and pictograms, are likely to be encoded relatively directly for meaning, whereas alphabetic writing is usually encoded phonemically before meaning is determined (see the earlier discussion of phonemic coding). Note that this parallels the dual-coding notion that concrete meaning is represented in a non-verbal symbolic system, which is more directly reached by pictures than by words.

Another general implication is the contrast between synchronous and sequential processing. Recall from chapter 4 that synchronous processing refers to simultaneous (parallel) processing of complex information, so that different components are grasped and remembered at once. Sequential processing refers to the successive processing of the components of a series. Synchronous processing is characteristic of visual perception and imagery, and sequential processing is characteristic of language behavior. The point here is that the reading of ideograms may require relatively more synchronous processing than does the reading of phonographic symbols, at least at the *symbolic* level. We emphasize symbolic because synchronous processing at the *perceptual* level must be present in all reading. The earlier reference to a visual span of seven or so letters makes the point clear—the average reader sees that many letters at each fixation. The difference comes in at the level of *meaningful* information. In alphabetic writing, the visual system grasps seven letters, which might amount to only one word. That word might be highly meaningful, or it might not. Ideographic symbols, being idea units, should permit the reader to grasp more meaningful information at each glance.

The two points considered thus far are related in that taken together, they imply more direct access to larger amounts of meaningful information per glance in ideographic than in phonographic writing. A third point is implicit in the discussion: to the extent that the first two points are true, different mechanisms must operate in the two kinds of reading.

The theoretical ideas lead to predictions. An obvious one is that the reading rate should be faster for ideographic than for phonographic writing. This follows from the idea of more direct access to more meaningful information for the former. The little evidence available on the problem is contradictory. An early study by Shen (1927) showed that Chinese students read Chinese writing at about the same rate as American students read English. The estimates were six Chinese "words" per second as compared to five English words per second. More recently, Sakamoto and

Makita (1973, cited in Gibson & Levin, 1975, p. 164) described reading rates and eye-movement data for Japanese college students reading sentences of identical meaning when they were written entirely in *hiragana* (a syllabary script) and when they were written in a combination of *hiragana* and *kanji* (an ideographic script). The reading of the all-*hiragana* sentences took twice as long as the *hiragana-kanji* combination. Furthermore, the *hiragana* sentences required a shorter perceptual span, more frequent fixations, longer fixation pauses, and more regressive eye movements than the combined syllabic-ideographic sentences. In view of such contrasting findings, we must await further evidence before we can be confident about any theoretical interpretation.

The theoretical distinctions also have implications for memory. For example, if ideograms resemble pictures in their functional properties, they should be more memorable than phonographic symbols of comparable meaning. Park and Arbuckle (1977) investigated this possibility among others and interpreted their results in relation to dual-coding theory. Their experiments used Korean subjects who were presented with words written in the two writing systems used in Korea, one alphabetic and the other ideographic. The word concepts were based on forty concrete and forty abstract nouns selected from the Paivio, Yuille, and Madigan (1968) norms. Different experiments used different memory tasks. The results were only partly like those obtained by others in comparable picture-word memory experiments. Words presented in ideographic script were remembered better than words presented in alphabetic script in recognition memory and free-recall tasks, but not in paired-associates or serial learning. These results differ from picture-word comparisons in that pictures are usually remembered better than words in all of these tasks.

The other theoretically interesting results were with the concreteness variable. Concrete words were remembered better than abstract words in all tasks except recognition memory. These results are generally like those obtained in prior studies. The absence of a difference in the case of recognition is a departure from the usual pattern, although even there the overall trends were in the appropriate direction. Park and Arbuckle were also especially interested in possible interactions between concreteness and type of script. Their interpretation of the dual-coding hypothesis suggested that if ideograms are like pictures, then abstract nouns written in ideographic script should be remembered better than abstract norms written alphabetically. The effect of script should be smaller for concrete nouns because they already have easy access to the imaginal code. In brief, type of script should have more effect on abstract than on concrete words. But this did not turn out to be the case, since there was no interaction of concreteness and type of script in any of the experiments.

Park and Arbuckle suggest that the independent effects of script and concreteness cannot be easily explained in terms of a common imagery code. Instead, more than one factor seems to be involved. They considered several alternatives, including the possibility of two image codes, one consisting of a symbolic imaginal code for ideograms and the other an iconic imaginal code for referents of concrete nouns. For our purposes, we leave the problem with the general observation that type of script does have an effect on performance in some memory tasks and that in those instances, ideograms behave like pictures.

The suggested processing differences between ideographic and phonetic

writing have also been considered in relation to reading disorders. Rozin, Poritsky, and Sotsky (1971) took a group of second-grade children who had difficulty learning to read English and taught them to read Chinese logographs. The material consisted of thirty characters combined in various ways to form sentences that could be read in English. The children had a series of tutoring sessions on the Chinese material and also on normal English. The children learned to read the Chinese characters over periods ranging from 2.5 to 5.5 hours of tutoring. By contrast, they made little progress in reading English print. The authors suggest that the success with Chinese can be attributed to the novelty of Chinese orthography and to the fact that Chinese characters convert to speech at the level of words rather than phonemes. The interpretation is consistent with the hypothesis that meaning can be determined more directly from Chinese ideograms than from phonetic writing. We should add that the study has been criticized on methodological grounds and that strong generalizations may not be warranted at this time (the interested reader can pursue the controversy in *Science,* 1971, *173*, 190-191). Nonetheless, the possibilities are intriguing.

Japanese researchers (for example, Sasanuma, 1974; Yamadori & Ikumura, 1975) have also found that aphasia (speech loss resulting from brain injury; see chapter 15 for a fuller description) can have different effects on the patient's ability to read ideographic and phonetic scripts. The effect depends on the locus of the injury, with damage to some areas affecting the reading of ideographic characters and to others, syllabary script. The authors' hypothesis is that ideographic characters are read directly for meaning but that syllabary script requires phonetic mediation.

Reading problems are also encountered by people with sensory deficits, including especially the blind and the deaf. The blind must either listen to others read or rely on the sense of touch to profit from written language. The written code developed for the blind is called Braille, which consists of patterns of raised dots that the blind learn to discriminate by touch. The dot patterns correspond to ordinary written language in much the same way that Morse code corresponds to the alphabet. The reading problems of the blind are related directly to differences between the visual and tactile sensory systems. For example, reading rate is generally slower for Braille than for print. Reading for meaning may also differ in subtle ways related to the sensory deficit. For example, Paivio and Okovita (1971) found evidence that the meaning of concrete nouns for the blind is related to auditory but not visual imagery. Such problems have not been extensively explored as yet, especially as they relate to reading, so we shall not pursue them here. More research effort has been directed at inventing devices that would transform visual print into patterns of touch on the surface of the skin, so that the blind might learn to read by scanning printed messages and decoding the resulting tactile patterns. These developments are psychologically interesting because they raise questions about the discriminative capacity of the sense of touch. Many researchers (for example, Craig, 1976, 1977) are currently investigating such problems, and future books on the psychology of language will undoubtedly reflect their findings.

The reading problems of the blind have an entirely different psychological basis than those of the deaf. The singularly striking fact is that individuals who are born deaf or become deaf in infancy have difficulty learning to read even though reading is a visual activity. The problem is instead related to a more general language deficit. The fact is that the majority of persons who are born deaf do not acquire

normal language competence (see Furth, 1966). Why should this be so? Apparently it is due to the auditory nature of speech input, to which the deaf have no access. Normal language skills, including reading, depend on that auditory substrate, hence the emphasis on the role of subvocalization and phonemic coding in the psychological study of reading. The reading problems of the deaf attest to the importance of such coding. It was once a fairly common view that the problem may even be more general, that the language deficit is accompanied by and perhaps causes a general intellectual deficit. However, experiments using nonverbal procedures have shown that deaf adolescents and adults can be quite comparable and even superior to hearing subjects (for example, Furth, 1966; Vernon, 1967). Thus the cognitive deficits of the deaf are specific to tasks that depend on language development.

The statement refers specifically to "normal" languages, such as English. What about sign language, which the deaf are able to learn and use? Can it compensate for the lack of an auditory-motor language system in tasks such as reading? The answer appears to be yes. Vernon and Koh (1970) found that deaf children who are signed to from infancy because their parents also are deaf could read better than deaf children whose parents could hear and did not know sign language. The early development of another system of communication apparently helped the deaf children to process written language, despite differences in the processes underlying the two kinds of language.

What exactly is the nature of language processing in the deaf? Various kinds of evidence suggest that it is based on gestural-visual mechanisms of some kind, at least among deaf signers. Recall that sign languages such as Ameslan use iconic symbols and signs for letters of the alphabet. When deaf signers learn verbal material, they can use iconic signing and finger spelling to mediate recall. For example, Odom, Blanton, and McIntyre (1970) found that deaf (but not hearing) subjects learned more words in a verbal-learning task when the words had sign equivalents than when they did not. Conlin and Paivio (1975) studied the same problem using words that had been rated on both visual imagery and signability (a measure of the ease with which a word can be represented as a gestural sign). Pairs of words were presented in printed English, so that they had to be read. The results showed better learning of high-imagery than of low-imagery pairs by both deaf and hearing subjects. However, only the deaf showed a positive effect of word signability. Both groups also reported using visual imagery to learn pairs, but the deaf were again unique in that they reported considerable use of gestural signs to help them remember the pairs, particularly when they consisted of words easy to sign.

This brief review suggests that the deaf can use a gestural-visual code, perhaps along with an articulatory one, even when they are reading alphabetic script. Perhaps researchers and educators will be able to take advantage of that capacity to develop more efficient approaches to teaching the deaf to read. Such procedures would be a part of a general aim designed to develop "bicodal" individuals with two communicational systems that parallel the two languages of bilinguals. The interested reader can find a full treatment of such possibilities in Klima and Bellugi (1979).

Summary

In this chapter, we have presented an overview of problems and questions concerning visual language in general and reading in particular. Although most of us are especially familiar with alphabetic writing, many other means of expressing

ideas in visual form have developed around the world, and even a superficial consideration of these different systems raises many questions about psychological processes. People using any system must learn to discriminate linguistic signals from nonlinguistic signals in the same modality. Although children are quite good at such discrimination even before they can read, it is not clear whether such discrimination is accomplished by accumulating features of visual language or by narrowing down the discrimination from a general to a local level. The central concern in any analysis of reading is comprehension of what has been read. In this context, researchers have studied eye movements, eye-voice span, and imagery processes as they are used in transferring from print to meaning, with or without an intervening process of phonemic translation. Other research has concerned the importance of reading to learning and remembering information. One area of great practical concern centers on skilled readers on the one hand, on poor readers on the other, and on parallel distinctions within other symbolic modalities, like Braille and Ameslan.

language
and the brain

15

A momentous discovery was made in 1861 by the French surgeon Paul Broca. He performed an autopsy on the brain of a patient who had lost his speech without being otherwise impaired. Broca found a lesion, or damaged area, in the patient's left hemisphere (in the third frontal convolution) which apparently caused the speech loss. This observation had a great impact on the development of neurology and neuropsychology. It was the first clear evidence for the localization of speech function in a region of the left cerebral hemisphere. It led to further discoveries of functional deficits traced to brain lesions and to the development of other techniques that would provide evidence for the role of the brain in language and cognition. However, the original generalization from Broca's observation remains correct today only in broad terms. It is true for most people that the neural mechanisms used to generate speech are located in the temporal and frontal regions of the left hemisphere, although not only in Broca's area. Other language functions are located elsewhere, including the right hemisphere.

These observations are important for practical as well as theoretical reasons. The identification of specific language and other cognitive functions with particular regions of the brain may help in the choice of treatment and may permit a surgeon to avoid damaging crucial functions during brain operations. Understanding the relation between the brain and language is theoretically interesting in its own right, but the information can also be used to choose between different cognitive theories. The fact that some functions go together in that they are subserved by the same hemisphere or by the same region within one hemisphere limits the range of possible theories of language structure and function, and the relation between language and other cognitive phenomena.

Our review will selectively examine certain facts and theoretical issues relevant to our earlier discussions. For example, the neuropsychological evidence bears on the behavioral approach to language insofar as it implicates motor centers of the brain. The evidence may also permit us to choose between different cognitive theories, such as dual coding as compared to single-code theories of the propositional type. More generally, the facts are relevant to the biological, evolutionary origins of language. Before addressing such issues, we shall present an overview of the different sources of evidence concerning brain function.

Sources of Evidence Concerning Brain Function

Brain function must be inferred from data on behavior in relation to brain anatomy and physiology. The inferences are based on dysfunctions resulting from localized brain lesions, surgical separation of the two cerebral hemispheres, and effects of certain drugs. They are also based on the effects of electrical stimulation of the cortex during brain surgery, lateralized presentation of stimuli to the ears or eyes, measurement of the electrical activity of the brain at the surface of the skull, and a recently developed brain-scanning procedure. The following are brief descriptions of each approach and the kinds of conclusions that result from the approaches.

Focal brain lesions

Focal brain lesions provided the earliest clues to brain function, and they are still an important source of evidence. The damage may result from accidents, gunshot wounds, blockage of cerebral arteries by blood clots, poisoning, surgical operations for brain tumors and epilepsy, and so on. Any of these may produce a language disorder of some kind, depending on the locus and extent of the damage. *Aphasia,* the loss of the ability to speak, generally is caused by damage to the left hemisphere. A distinction has commonly been drawn between expressive and receptive aphasia. Expressive aphasia is a deficit in the ability to speak, and it has generally been identified with lesions of the anterior (forward) part of the left hemisphere, including Broca's area and other regions of the frontal lobe. Receptive aphasia refers to disturbances of perception and comprehension, associated with lesions farther back, in the so-called posterior speech zone or *Wernicke's area,* after the neurologist who first reported such disturbances shortly after Broca's discovery. Thus the traditional contrast is between expressive, motor, or Broca's aphasia on the one hand and sensory, receptive, or Wernicke's aphasia on the other. These areas are shown in Figure 15-1, along with the locations of lesions typically associated with the two classes of deficits. Although the classical distinction is still useful in broad terms, most evidence does not justify such a sharp distinction, and there has been a tendency to shift to other kinds of classifications, the most pertinent of which are described in later sections. As we shall see, it remains generally true that the primary source of language disorders is damage to the left hemisphere rather than to the right hemisphere, whereas disturbances in various nonverbal skills result primarily from damage to the right hemisphere.

Cerebral commissurotomy

A cerebral commissurotomy is the surgical separation of the right and left hemispheres. The surgery has been done on a small number of patients as a last-resort treatment for severe epileptic convulsions that could not be controlled by medication. The procedure has provided a unique opportunity for the psychological study of the functions of each hemisphere. Such work was initiated by Roger Sperry and his colleagues (see Gazzaniga, 1970; Sperry, 1973). To appreciate the dramatic effect of the surgical procedure, it is necessary to understand the nature of the neural connections between the cerebral hemispheres and peripheral sense organs and muscles. The left hemisphere processes information primarily from the right hand and entirely from the right visual field, and the right hemisphere does

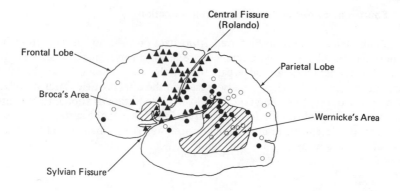

FIGURE 15-1. **Left hemisphere speech areas and locations of traumatic lesions associated with aphasic symptoms. The left middle cerebral artery runs along the Sylvian fissure and branches through the entire lateral face of the hemisphere. This artery is most often implicated in strokes caused by a clot or rupture of the vessel, which results in an insufficient blood supply to areas served by the artery. Lesion locations based on Lenneberg (1967, Figure 2-22a).**

the reverse. The nature of the visual connections is shown in Figure 15-2, which also illustrates the surgical division. The corpus callosum and other major fiber systems that connect the two hemispheres are severed by the surgery, so that each hemisphere receives information only from the contralateral (opposite) visual field and mainly from the contralateral hand.

Our interest is with psychological tests in which verbal or nonverbal material is presented to only one or the other visual field by a tachistoscope, or in which objects are presented to the right or left hand, and so on. Such tests provide "a striking confirmation of hemispheric lateralization with respect to language in general." The disconnected left hemisphere "does essentially all the talking, reading, writing, and mathematical calculations in these right-handed subjects [whereas the] right hemisphere . . . remains essentially mute, alexic, agraphic, and unable to carry out calculations beyond simple additions to sums under 20" (Sperry, 1973, p. 212). The right hemisphere, on the other hand, excels on tests of spatial aptitude. Again, we leave the details and the qualifications of these generalizations to later sections, except for the general point that the two hemispheres do seem to have different abilities to deal with language.

Stimulation of the cortex

Brain surgery for the treatment of epilepsy and other dysfunctions is carried out under local anesthesia so that the patients remain conscious and can describe their experiences during mild electrical stimulation of specific cortical areas. The procedure is used to localize the area responsible for the epileptic seizures. At the

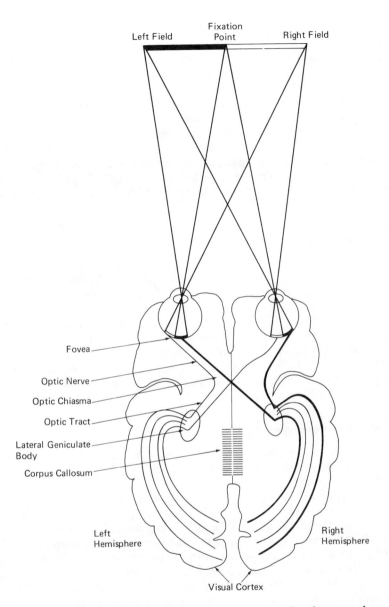

FIGURE 15-2. Classical view of the visual pathways showing complete crossing of the pathways so that all of the visual field to the left of the fixation point stimulates the right visual cortex whereas the right visual field stimulates the left visual cortex. The corpus callosum, which normally connects the two hemispheres, is schematized as being surgically divided.

same time, it reveals the behavioral functions of different areas. Much of this work was done by the late Dr. Wilder Penfield, a Canadian neurosurgeon, and he and a colleague (Penfield & Roberts, 1959) reported the results for language in particular. One interesting finding is that stimulation produces some incoherent vowel sounds but no coherent speech. However, stimulation of certain areas *interferes* with speech when, for example, the patient is naming a series of objects or counting. The general result is that stimulation of the left hemisphere, more often than stimulation of the right hemisphere, produces "hesitations, slurring, repetition, and distortion of speech; confusion of numbers while counting, inability to name with retained ability to speak; misnaming with or without evidence of perseverations, difficulty in reading, and difficulty in writing" (Penfield & Roberts, 1959, p. 136). Thus we have further confirmations of the lateralization of language functions.

Sodium amytal test

J. A. Wada developed the sodium amytal test, in which sodium amytal is injected into the carotid artery on one side of the neck. The sedative drug interferes for a few minutes with the functioning of the cerebral hemisphere on the injected side. If speech is disturbed, we can infer that speech is represented in that hemisphere. This information is clinically useful in diagnosis and as a potential guide in brain surgery. The information about lateralization of function is also important to the research psychologist: when used in conjunction with experimental tasks, it strengthens inferences about more specific language functions. At this point we note only that the amytal test also indicates that it is the left hemisphere that is dominant for speech in most people.

Lateralized presentation of stimuli

The lateralized presentation of stimuli was introduced by Doreen Kimura (1961) as a purely behavioral approach to the study of the different functions of the cerebral hemispheres. She capitalized on the behavioral implications of the crossed neuroanatomical arrangement already discussed. Specifically, the auditory system is predominantly crossed, so that the right ear has stronger neural connections with the left than with the right hemisphere. Kimura reasoned that since the left hemisphere is usually specialized for speech, speech sounds presented to the right ear should have readier access to the speech perception systems in the left hemisphere than would sounds presented to the left ear. She confirmed this using a dichotic listening task, introduced earlier by D. E. Broadbent (1958), in which a series of spoken digits is presented simultaneously to each ear through earphones, and subjects are asked to report as many as they can. The result was that both normal subjects and preoperative patients reported the digits more accurately for the right than for the left ear, as predicted, provided that their speech was represented in the left hemisphere as independently determined by the sodium amytal test. The reverse results were expected and were in fact obtained with patients who were known to have speech represented in the right hemisphere. Finally, Kimura confirmed the prediction that nonverbal material (melodies) would be recognized more accurately by the left ear by subjects with speech represented

in the left hemisphere, indicating some specialization of the right hemisphere for nonspeech sounds.

Kimura suggested that there should be a similar functional asymmetry for the visual recognition of verbal stimuli flashed to the right or left visual half-fields (that is, to one side or the other of a fixation point). Because of the crossed neural systems, stimuli presented to each hemified project impulses to the visual receiving area in the opposite side of the brain. Accordingly, verbal material presented to the right field should excite the left (speech-dominant) hemisphere first and be more accurately perceived than material presented to the left field. This has been confirmed in numerous studies using letters of the alphabet and printed words. Conversely, nonverbal stimuli tend not to show the same asymmetry, or they show the opposite effect. As in the dichotic listening task, specific experimental conditions are needed to reveal the functional asymmetries. For example, the presentation must be brief enough so that the subjects do not have time to shift their focus. Note that the auditory effect is obtained with simultaneous presentation to the two ears, but the visual asymmetries can occur with successive presentation to one field or the other. Asymmetries are also found when material is presented simultaneously to both fields, but in this case input to the left field, whether verbal or not, tends to be reported first and more accurately than right-field input. This effect results from left-to-right scanning, which was originally attributed to reading habits. That interpretation is now questionable because the same results have been observed among Israelis, who read from right to left (Ghent-Braine, 1968).

Various questions have arisen in connection with the research on lateralized stimulus presentation. One concerns the role of memory in the dichotic listening task—are the results attributable to an early perceptual stage as opposed to memory processes? Others concern various qualifications of the general verbal-nonverbal asymmetries summarized in this section. These will be discussed in later sections.

Evoked potentials

Evoked potentials recorded from the brain provide yet another promising, though problematic, approach to the study of brain function in relation to language. The electrical activity of the brain can be picked up by means of scalp electrodes and then recorded in visual form as an electroencephalogram (EEG). Continuous brain activity takes a waveform that varies with the level of wakefulness or arousal of the subject. The effects of specific stimuli are generally overshadowed by this background activity, but the voltage change produced by a stimulus can be revealed as a wavelike response by a technique that averages the effects of the same task performed repeatedly on the same class of stimuli, such as numbers or letters. Other influences on the EEG are more random and are accordingly averaged out, whereas the evoked potentials in the repeated task build up until they stand out from the background.

The typical procedure in language studies is to compare the evoked potentials in both hemispheres as the subject performs verbal and nonverbal tasks. For example, Wood, Goff, and Day (1971) required their subjects to indicate, on each of a series of trials, whether a given auditory stimulus was /ba/ or /da/. A nonlinguistic task in the same study required the subjects to decide whether a given syllable (for example, /ba/) was high or low in pitch. Evoked potentials from the

left hemisphere that occurred just before the subject pressed an appropriate key differed for the linguistic and nonlinguistic tasks. The linguistic-nonlinguistic difference was not significant for recordings from the right hemisphere. As we shall see later, comparable results have been obtained for production tasks. We should note, however, that EEG data are particularly sensitive to artifactual influences (Gevins, Zeitlin, Doyle, Yingling, Schaffer, Callaway, & Yaeger, 1979), and it may be premature to draw strong inferences from them in regard to linguistic-nonlinguistic differences in hemispheric specialization.

The measurement of regional changes in cortical blood flow

The measurement of regional changes in cortical blood flow is carried out by a photographic scanning procedure and is another recent approach to the study of brain function that may provide new information as the technology matures. The technique was developed in the early 1960s by Lassen, Ingvar, and Skinhoj (1978). It is based on the fact that cerebral metabolism and blood flow increase in regions of the cerebral cortex activated during the performance of specific tasks. Lassen and his colleagues measured the regional changes in blood flow using radioactive isotopes. Xenon 133 (a radioactive isotope of the inert gas xenon) is dissolved in a sterile saline solution, and a small volume is injected into one of the main arteries of the brain. The passage of the isotope through many brain regions is followed for one minute by a gamma-ray camera with a battery of 254 "scintillation detectors," each of which scans approximately one square centimeter of brain surface. The information is picked up and processed by a computer and is displayed graphically on a color-television monitor. The information is color coded so that the mean blood-flow rate is green, rates up to 20 percent below the mean appear as various shades of blue, and rates up to 20 percent above the mean are shades of red. The procedure was used routinely with patients undergoing brain x-ray procedures that made it possible to add the scanning procedure without further inconvenience or harm to the patient.

Lassen and his colleagues measured the changes in blood flow during a variety of tasks ranging from presenting simple visual, auditory, and tactile stimuli to more complex ones presenting verbal stimuli with overt or covert verbalization on the part of the patient. A surprising observation was that verbalization activated the same general regions in both sides of the brain, including the region corresponding to Broca's area. However, the blood-flow pattern was more differentiated and showed more activity in the left hemisphere than in the right. Listening to spoken words resulted in the greatest activity in the auditory cortex and in the adjacent Wernicke's area, which, as we noted earlier, has been traditionally identified with the understanding of speech, on the basis of effects of lesions.

Lassen, Ingvar, and Skinhoj view the blood-flow technique as a rather crude approach to cortical mapping, but more refined and powerful techniques are being developed. This approach may become increasingly important as a source of information about the functioning of the brain in linguistic and nonlinguistic tasks.

We turn next to a more detailed consideration of brain function in various tasks, beginning with perception. In each case, the emphasis is on language tasks, but as before, the interpretations hinge on comparisons with the effects of nonlinguistic tasks as well.

Brain Function in Language Perception

Chapter 6 stressed the difficulty of distinguishing perception from comprehension and memory and the resultant tendency among some theorists to view perceptual information processing as a series of stages that include memory. We shall limit our discussion in this section to processes present at a relatively early stage of perception, as inferred from tasks that minimize memory load.

The evidence generally suggests that perceptual processing of both auditory and visual linguistic stimuli is hemispherically asymmetrical, but the situation is more equivocal for nonlinguistic stimuli, at least when these are visual (for example, pictures). Much of the evidence comes from studies of dichotic listening and visual hemifield presentation. As stated earlier, Kimura's (1961) research showed that spoken digits presented simultaneously to each ear were recognized more accurately in the right ear by subjects known to have speech represented in the left hemisphere, and vice versa for subjects with right-hemisphere speech representation.

Kimura (1967) interpreted the auditory difference in perceptual terms, based on the relative strength of contralateral and ipsilateral (same side) pathways from the ear to the auditory cortex. Specifically, she suggested that the strong contralateral pathways from the right ear to the left hemisphere occlude (shut out) the weaker ipsilateral impulses. However, it is also possible that the effect is due to memory rather than to perceptual processes. A short-term memory interpretation is reasonable because typically the dichotic listening task successively presents three pairs of stimuli. Because of this memory load and time interval, the subjects could forget some items before they are asked to report them. The ear asymmetry might reflect different rates of forgetting by the two hemispheres.

There have been various attempts to resolve the issue. Much of the evidence suggests that the ear asymmetry in the dichotic task is due to perceptual mechanisms. For example, O'Neill (1971) dichotically presented subjects with pairs of meaningful words, varying the number of pairs and the delay between the presentation of a single pair and the subject's report. He found right-ear superiority even under conditions of minimal memory load, with one pair and a short delay. Thus, it is clear that the ear asymmetry occurs at a relatively early stage of processing.

The dichotic listening task has also yielded information about the size of the minimal linguistic unit in speech perception. Recall from our discussion in chapter 6 that the syllable rather than the phoneme appears to be the smallest perceptual unit. One kind of supporting evidence is that right-ear superiority has been found for the perception of syllables but not isolated vowels (Studdert-Kennedy & Shankweiler, 1970). Kimura and King (reported in Kimura, 1973) cut up a tape recording of natural speech into short segments of various lengths. They found that the briefest duration that yielded a right-ear superiority was about two hundred milliseconds, which is about the duration of an average spoken syllable. Thus it appears that the left hemisphere is specialized for perceiving spoken syllables.

By contrast, left-ear superiority has been obtained in the perception of certain kinds of nonspeech sounds. Milner (1962) found that lesions in the right temporal lobe specifically impaired the perception of melodies. Kimura (1964) consequently expected and found that normal subjects in a dichotic listening task could recognize melodies presented to the left ear better than those presented to

the right ear. King and Kimura (1972) also found significant, though weak, left-ear superiority in dichotic perception of such vocal nonspeech sounds as laughing, crying, coughing, and sighing. The hemispheric asymmetry in the perception of linguistic and nonlinguistic sounds is supported also by the evoked-potential research described earlier (for example, Wood et al., 1971). Thus the available evidence suggests that verbal and nonverbal vocal stimuli are processed by different hemispheres.

In regard to visual stimuli, the evidence generally shows that linguistic symbols such as letters and words are recognized better when flashed tachistoscopically to the right visual field than when presented to the left field. This happens with words even when they are displayed vertically, thereby controlling somewhat for left-to-right scanning habits that might favor perception of the initial letters of words presented to the right of the fixation point. Since stimuli presented to the right field first stimulate the left hemisphere, the observation suggests that the left hemisphere is specialized also for perceptual processing of visual linguistic stimuli. This interpretation is strengthened by the contrasting results that have been obtained in certain nonverbal tasks. Kimura (1973) described several experiments in which left-field (hence right hemisphere) superiority was obtained for the location of a point in two-dimensional space, and in depth perception (Durnford & Kimura, 1971).

The results have been less clear for simple recognition of visual stimuli such as pictures of familiar objects and geometrical forms. Generally, normal subjects recognize such stimuli equally well in either visual field. Split-brain patients show similar results when a stimulus is flashed to one or the other field and they then are required to select the correct pattern from a group of five stimuli displayed on cards before them (Gazzaniga, 1970, pp. 94–96). They can do so with great accuracy by pointing with the hand corresponding to the field of presentation (for example, right field—right hand), thus indicating that both hemispheres can process such stimuli perceptually. This also occurred with visual-tactile tests in which pictures of objects (orange, ball, spoon, and the like) were flashed to either field and the subjects were required to match them by feeling a series of objects placed out of view and picking out the correct one. The right hand could do so accurately when visual presentation had been to the right field and the left hemisphere accordingly processed both input and test stimuli. Conversely, the left hand was able to identify objects that had been flashed in the left field. Performance remained at a chance level when the visual and tactile stimuli were processed by different hemispheres, as in right visual field–left-hand matches. Moreover, as stated earlier, verbal identification, or naming, was possible only with visual stimuli presented to the right field or with tactile stimuli to the right hand.

These findings are interesting because they indicate that both hemispheres must "contain" neural representations corresponding to perceptual objects; otherwise recognition would not be possible. Moreover, the fact that pictures, geometric forms, and so on presented to the right visual field can be named by the split-brain patients must mean that the left hemisphere contains neural connections between the verbal and nonverbal representations. These conclusions also are consistent with the observation that localized lesions in the left hemisphere can be associated with difficulty in naming objects (see further below).

The above conclusions are qualified by other findings. Bryden and Rainey

(1963) found no visual field difference in the recognition of geometric forms but did find right-field superiority for pictures of familiar objects and for letters. They suggested that right-field superiority increases with stimulus familiarity and its verbal relatedness, so that pictures and letters showed right-field superiority because they were familiar and easily named. Paivio and Ernest (1971) found, however, that the pattern of results depended upon certain presentation conditions and the subjects' imagery ability. The subjects were given blocks of trials with each type of material. Overall, right-field superiority was obtained for all types of material, consistent with a model suggested by Kinsbourne (1970), according to which a subject's attention could be biased to one or the other side of the fixation point, depending on whether verbal or nonverbal material was expected. Since the subjects in the Paivio and Ernest experiment were exposed to three types of materials in the blocks of trials, any differential expectancies would have been confounded when all the trials were included in the analysis. However, different groups had received letters, pictures, or forms as their first list, so that they presumably had maintained an expectancy for only one type of material until the end of the first list. Accordingly, the data were analyzed separately for the first trial block, along with the separation of the subjects into high and low scorers on an imagery test battery.

The results of the analysis are shown in Figure 15-3. It can be seen that the field effect was obtained only for letters, which were recognized more accurately in the right field. The only significant effect for the pictures was that correct recognition scores were much better for high-imagery than for low-imagery subjects. Finally, the geometric forms yielded a significant interaction of visual field and imagery, so that high imagers showed a slight left-field superiority and low imagers showed a substantial right-field superiority; another way to view this result is that high-imagery subjects were greatly superior to low-imagery subjects when forms

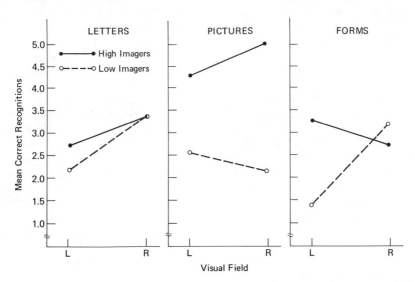

FIGURE 15-3. Recognition accuracy scores as a function of imagery ability, stimulus attribute, and visual field. From Paivio and Ernest (1971).

were presented to the left field, but not when they were presented to the right field.

These results confirm the general right-field (left hemisphere) advantage for letters and reveal that the processing of pictures and forms is qualified by the person's ability to manipulate spatial information. Those with high ability generally excelled in the identification of nonverbal but not verbal material, and their superiority was specific to the left visual field in the case of geometric forms, which may be regarded as the least verbal of the stimuli in that it takes longer to name geometric forms than either letters or pictures.

Many other factors influence field effects and hemispheric differences in perceptual recognition, but we shall consider only one more example. Bryden and Allard (1976) found that the effects depended upon typeface. Most typefaces showed the usual right-field superiority for letter identification, but some showed left-field superiority. The latter was the case particularly for scriptlike material. The authors concluded that visual field differences cannot be explained in terms of verbal response requirements. They suggest instead that the initial processing is carried out more efficiently by the right hemisphere and that the field effects depend on how much of this early visual processing is required. Block letters require little early processing, so the right-hemisphere contribution does not show up. Script requires more early processing, and so the right hemisphere dominates. An observation reported by Sperry (1973, p. 217) seems to be relevant to this analysis. The split-brain patients showed dominance of the right over the left hemisphere in perception of words written in cursive script, provided that the task required only a direct visual matching of the word pattern. The left hemisphere became dominant, however, when the task required the subject to take account of the meaning of the word.

The results considered up to this point reveal generally that perceptual processing of language-related material is more efficient in the hemisphere (usually the left) that is also specialized for speech. More interesting psycholinguistically is the possibility that the perceptual differences may be qualified by the semantic and grammatical characteristics of the verbal material itself. Grammatical classes and concreteness level of words are two variables that have received considerable attention.

Gazzaniga (1970, pp. 119-122) reported that two split-brain patients were capable of perceiving and comprehending words presented visually to the "silent" right hemisphere, but more so for some classes of words than others. The subjects were allowed to view the words first; then a test stimulus was flashed to one visual field or the other, and they were required to point to the word (or picture) that best matched the flashed stimulus. The subjects were able to read letters, numbers, and short words in the left field (right hemisphere). Gazzaniga reports that performance was best for "noun-object words" such as knife, pen, and orange. Performance was second best for adjectives and poorest for verbs. It is not clear from the report, however, whether these differences occurred at an early perceptual stage or at a later (comprehension) stage of processing, since the tests generally required the subjects to respond in a way that indicated that they understood the meaning of the items. Moreover, it would be inappropriate to generalize too freely from a sample of two unusual subjects.

Other investigators have used lateralized presentation to study the effects of

the imagery value (concreteness) of words. This interest came from the powerful effect of this variable on memory performance in particular and from the evidence that concrete words have a more direct association with nonverbal representations than do abstract words—essentially the dual-coding hypothesis discussed in chapter 5. Given the additional neuropsychological evidence that the right hemisphere is specialized for processing spatial information and that both hemispheres apparently have cognitive representations corresponding to concrete objects, it seemed conceivable that the concrete nouns that describe spatial information and name objects might be represented in both hemispheres, whereas abstract nouns might not. It turns out that the perceptual evidence is quite equivocal, with some studies yielding the predicted difference and others showing no difference.

Ellis and Sheperd (1974) and Hines (1977) obtained right-field superiority in visual recognition of abstract words but not concrete words. Day (1977) similarly found greater lateral asymmetry for abstract than for concrete words in a reaction-time task that required subjects to decide whether a letter array was a word or a nonword. In contrast, a number of studies have failed to find differential asymmetries with either auditory or visual stimuli. Borkowski, Spreen, and Stutz (1965) and O'Neill (1971) found an equivalent right-ear superiority in dichotic recognition of concrete and abstract nouns. Two unpublished experiments by Paivio and O'Neill similarly yielded equivalent right-field superiority in visual recognition of the two classes of words. The above studies differed in various procedural details, and no resolution of the inconsistencies is possible without systematic research on the effects of these procedural differences.

Considered as a whole, the perceptual studies have yielded interesting results in regard to hemispheric differences in the perceptual representation and processing of linguistic and nonlinguistic material. There still are uncertainties as to the degree to which the nonspeech hemisphere can carry out the perceptual processing of language, and vice versa for nonlinguistic material. Moreover, the unique contribution to our psychological understanding of language is limited to a few examples, such as the support for the syllable as the minimal perceptual unit. The gains are greater from studies of memory, to which we now shall turn.

Verbal and Nonverbal Memory and the Brain

The contrasting verbal and nonverbal functions of the two hemispheres are revealed most clearly in memory tasks. The evidence comes largely from studies of the effects of unilateral lesions, particularly those induced during operations on epileptic patients. Much of the work has been done by Brenda Milner and her colleagues at the Montreal Neurological Institute, McGill University (for example, see Milner, 1971, 1973). The severest effects result from the removal of the anterior temporal lobe, including parts of the hippocampus (a structure inside the temporal lobe, which is particularly crucial to memory). It is important to note that the effects summarized below are generally *memory specific;* that is, they have been obtained without similar selective loss in the ability to perceive verbal or nonverbal material, or in the ability to understand or produce speech.

It has been found that removal of the temporal lobe in the left (speech dominant) hemisphere selectively impairs learning and memory for verbal material. The effect holds for tasks ranging from memory for prose passages to lists of words,

whether heard or read. For example, in one experiment (Milner, 1967, pp. 126–127), left-temporal patients showed a sharp drop in both visual and auditory verbal recall from a preoperative to a postoperative test. A comparable group of patients whose right temporal lobes had been removed showed no such loss. Moreover, the post-operative scores of the left-temporal groups were significantly lower than those of the right. Conversely, removal of the right temporal lobe impaired memory for non-verbal material, such as faces, melodies, nonsense patterns, or places, whereas left-temporal lesions did not. The reciprocal material-specific deficits were most directly demonstrated in experiments by Corsi (1972, cited in Milner, 1973) using comparable verbal and nonverbal tasks. One was a verbal short-term memory task described by Peterson and Peterson (1959), in which the subject had to recall three consonants, such as FRL, after a brief retention interval that varied from zero to eighteen seconds. The interval was filled by a counting-backward task designed to prevent rehearsal. Performance typically declines over the retention interval, as it did in Corsi's experiment. The important finding in this case was that patients with left-temporal lesions performed more poorly than right-temporal patients or normal controls. The latter two groups did not differ significantly. The results are shown in Figure 15-4, averaged over all retention intervals. Another important point is that the memory deficit among left-temporal patients was directly proportional to the amount of hippocampus destroyed during the lobectomy.

The comparable nonverbal task required the patient to recall the visual loca-tion of a circle on an eight-inch line after a time interval ranging from zero to twenty-four seconds. After the delay, subjects tried to reproduce the position of the circle on an unmarked line. Responses were scored according to location errors, shown in Figure 15-5. Note that the right-temporal patients had the highest error scores and that the left-temporal patients and normals did not differ. Further analysis showed that the error scores among the right-temporals rose with increases in the amount of hippocampal destruction, particularly at the longest retention interval. These results are exactly the opposite of those observed for verbal material.

The double disassociation between material-specific memory functions of the two hemispheres has been recently extended to the frontal lobes, but the effects are present for quite a different memory task, namely, determining the temporal order of events. Corsi (described in Milner, 1973) showed some patients a deck of cards, each containing a pair of words. The subjects read the words aloud as they worked through the deck. Periodically, a test card appeared on which the two words had a question mark between them, and the subject then had to indicate which of the two words had been read more recently. Subjects with damage to the left temporal lobes were unimpaired in this task, but both frontal-lobe groups showed a deficit. More important, the deficit was greater for those with lesions in the left frontal lobe than for those with lesions in the right frontal lobe. Other patients received a nonverbal form of the test, in which the stimuli were reproductions of abstract paintings. Now, patients with right frontal lobe lesions performed very poorly, at about a chance level, whereas neither the left-frontal group nor the right-temporal group was significantly impaired.

An additional condition in the experiment showed that the contrasting frontal-lobe deficits were specific to memory for the temporal order of events. Some test pairs in the task consisted of an old item paired with a new item that had not previously been in the list. The task in those cases was simply recognition

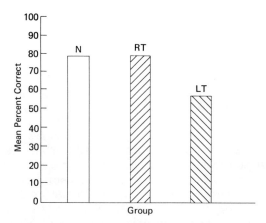

FIGURE 15-4. Mean recall of three consonants in the Peterson task, averaged over different retention intervals, for normal subjects (N) and those with right (RT) or left (LT) temporal lobectomies. Data from Corsi (1972) as reported by Milner (1973).

memory for the *items,* not their order. The results paralleled previous ones in that now the temporal-lobe groups showed the material-specific memory deficits, and the frontal-lobe groups did not.

Our review thus far establishes the reliability and generality of the verbal-nonverbal memory distinction associated with the left and right hemispheres, along with evidence for a further front-back differentiation within each hemisphere. The general pattern is for the left side of the brain to be the more important for processing linguistic material, with the right side the more important for nonverbal material. Within the hemispheres, as we move forward, we find localization of perception and comprehension, then production, and then temporal discriminations in the frontal areas. Although this classification is oversimplified, it does organize quite a bit of evidence from standard episodic memory tasks. Next we shall consider

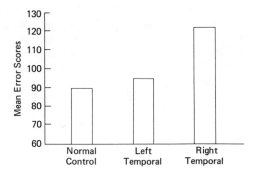

FIGURE 15-5. Corsi's results for the spatial memory task under interpolated activity conditions, showing impairment after right but not left temporal lobectomy. After Milner (1973).

some attempts to demonstrate hemispheric differences as a function of type of verbal material and instructions.

Effects of word concreteness and imagery instructions

Some researchers have investigated the possibility, already described in connection with perceptual studies, that the two hemispheres might differ with respect to processing concrete and abstract language. In this case, our interest centers on memory effects. Marilyn Jones (1974) reported an extensive study of the problem. Her subjects included patients with either the right or the left temporal lobe removed, two amnesic patients with damage to both temporal lobes (including the hippocampus), and normal control subjects. All groups learned three lists of ten paired associates composed of seven pairs of concrete words and three pairs of abstract words. The first list was presented without any special instructions; the second included imagery instructions along with interactive pictures of the referents of the concrete words; and the third required the subjects to generate their own images of the concrete pairs. A group of normal subjects learned all three lists without pictures or imagery instructions, as a control for simple practice effects. All groups had three alternating study-test trials on each list and then a retention test two hours later.

Jones did not report statistical analyses of the concrete-abstract differences in recall, but examination of her data indicates that proportionate recall was much lower for abstract than for concrete pairs under all conditions. Moreover, the differences appear to be about the same for all groups of subjects. Comparisons of groups and conditions within each word type revealed the following: as usual, the subjects with the left temporal lobe removed were generally inferior to the right temporals and normal subjects, who performed at about the same level. Pictures and imagery instructions greatly helped immediate and delayed recall of concrete pairs for all groups, except the amnesics. Thus, even the patients with left temporal lobe damage were able to improve their verbal memory performance by using imagery. Moreover, the *right-temporal* patients benefited as much as normal subjects did from the use of imagery, although they usually resorted to verbal labeling to remember nonverbal material.

Jones's observations have been confirmed by other studies. Patten (1972) observed that four patients with lesions of the dominant hemisphere were able to improve their verbal memory performance after training in the use of imagery. An unpublished study carried out by Mishkin and Fedio at the National Institute of Mental Health, Bethesda, Maryland, to which one of the present authors (Paivio) served as adviser, independently used conditions similar to those used by Jones. The subjects were patients whose left or right temporal lobes had been removed some years earlier. They were tested on two tasks, one requiring paired-associates learning of concrete and abstract pairs; the other, free recall of concrete words with or without the use of imagery. As in Jones's study, both temporal lobe groups showed comparably higher paired-associates recall for concrete than for abstract pairs, and both benefited equally from imagery in free recall.

These results are theoretically and practically interesting because of the positive effects of imagery variables among all patient groups. They are also disconcerting, however, in that the imagery effects were unqualified by the locus of

damage, which is at odds with the contrasting capacities of the two hemispheres in regard to memory for verbal and nonverbal material. Confirmation of the same pattern in repeated studies would force us to conclude that the mnemonic imagery generated from words as stimuli cannot be equated with the memory processes brought into play by nonverbal stimuli. Fortunately, these inconsistencies were partly resolved through subsequent studies by Marilyn Jones (now publishing as Jones-Gotman) and Brenda Milner. Jones-Gotman and Milner (1978) tested a group of right temporal lobectomy patients on two paired-associates learning tasks. One used a long list of sixty concrete-word pairs learned under instructions to use visual imagery as a mediator. The other used a shorter list of ten abstract-word pairs learned under instructions to link the pairs by sentences (the abstract list was short because of the difficulty of learning such pairs). The results showed that the right temporal patients performed more poorly than a matched normal control group with the imagery-linked concrete pairs, but the two groups performed equally well with the sentence-linked abstract pairs. Thus, for the first time we have a demonstration of a specific *imagery* memory deficit associated with damage to the right temporal lobe.

A similar selective effect was obtained by Jones-Gotman (1979) using an incidental free-recall task in which patients with temporal lobectomies and normal controls were required to visualize the referents of concrete or abstract words or to pronounce the words. Subsequent recall scores were higher under imagery than under pronunciation conditions for all groups. The right-temporal group did not differ from the control group under the imagery condition when recall was tested immediately, but they were significantly inferior to the normals on a delayed recall test two hours later.

Why did the last two studies reveal an imagery-memory deficit among right temporals, whereas the earlier studies did not? The answer apparently lies in the different memory demands of the various experiments. The earlier ones used relatively short lists and immediate recall tests. Apparently these were not demanding enough to reveal image-specific memory problems. The deficits showed up, however, with a long list of imagery-mediated paired associates and with a delayed free-recall test that permitted images to be forgotten.

We describe these results in some detail because they bear on important theoretical and practical issues. Note, first of all, that all groups were able to generate mental images for words when instructed to do so. This was true even for the two amnesic patients tested by Jones (1974), who were apparently able to generate and describe their images, although they were unable to remember them from trial to trial. The right temporal patients also forgot or confused their images, given a sufficient delay or a long recall list. It is reasonable to conclude from these observations that the imagery-*encoding* processes cannot be equated with the temporal lobes; but imagery *memory* is particularly associated with the right temporal lobe. The situation appears to be somewhat comparable to the one we described earlier for material-specific memory losses: although both hemispheres are able to identify nonverbal material such as pictures, the right temporal lobe dominates in memory for such material.

A second aspect of the results is that all groups benefited from imagery instructions. This is particularly important for patients with left temporal lobe damage, for whom verbal memory is a particular problem. Although this group

remained inferior to right temporals under all experimental conditions, they none-theless showed comparable improvement in verbal recall under the imagery conditions. Thus the left-temporal subjects dramatically improved their verbal memory by using mediating imagery. The practical implication of this observation is obvious, but how is it to be explained theoretically?

The simplest explanation relates the effect to comprehension and production mechanisms, to be discussed in a later section. Suffice it to note at this point that the left- and right-temporal patients alike are able to understand and produce speech. Understanding is evidenced in part by the ability to point to a pictorial referent of a concrete word or, as in Jones-Gotman's experiments, to visualize the referent. Conversely, meaningful production is demonstrated by the ability to name objects or pictures—or images. All of this is consistent with dual coding in that it implicates relatively intact referential connections between verbal and nonverbal representations in long-term memory. However, it leaves us with considerable uncertainty about the nature of the reciprocal material-specific, verbal and non-verbal memory deficits known to be associated with damage to only one temporal lobe. The simplest view is that those represent deficiencies in episodic memory functions that are presumably carried out by mechanisms located in hippocampal structures. Subjects with damage to those mechanisms have difficulty remembering material that was presented in the task but can compensate by being able to establish a connection with information in the intact hemisphere—a connection that provides an additional retrieval route during test trials. Suggestions of this kind must remain tentative until more research on the problem is available.

Thus far we have considered the mnemonic functions of the cerebral hemispheres only in the light of the negative effects of unilateral brain damage. The evidence from other sources is relatively sparse and unsystematic by comparison, perhaps because of the difficulty of presenting complex material or lists of material to only one of two intact hemispheres. This can be done with split-brain subjects using tactile material, and some recent work has used contact lenses that restrict visual input to either the left or the right visual field. The available results are rather ambiguous with respect to hemispheric specialization in memory for verbal and nonverbal material (Zaidel, 1977), and we will not discuss them here. The other source is lateralized presentation to normal subjects. As indicated earlier, dichotic listening tasks in which several words or musical patterns are presented to each ear show different ear advantages according to the type of material used. Although short-term memory is involved, the ear asymmetry seems to be attributable to perceptual rather than to memory mechanisms in those studies.

However, McFarland, McFarland, Bain, and Ashton (1978) did obtain an asymmetrical effect using a recognition-memory procedure with concrete and abstract words. They presented a series of words to one ear while simultaneously presenting different kinds of interfering stimuli to the other ear. Each word occurred twice in the list, separated by an average of fifteen intervening words. The subject responded to each word by saying whether it was "old" (that is, it was a repeated word) or "new." The interesting results were found when the competing material was a spoken prose passage. There were more errors with abstract words when they were presented to the left ear than when they were presented to the right ear, suggesting left-hemisphere superiority in memory for abstract words. Also, there was a nonsignificant trend in the opposite direction for concrete words,

suggesting that such words aroused images in the right hemisphere, thereby compensating for the interfering effect of speech competition. The authors concluded that these findings are consistent with a dual-coding interpretation that incorporates the idea of differential lateralization of verbal-semantic and imagery processes. Although it is not entirely clear in this case whether the asymmetries reflect memory as opposed to perceptual processes, the results and the interpretation generally agree with those of Jones-Gotman and Milner.

Finally, Seamon and Gazzaniga (1973) used a short-term, sequential memory task in which subjects were presented with a series of words, followed by a single "probe" stimulus which may or may not have been in the preceding series. The subjects' task was to indicate whether or not the stimulus had been in the set. One important feature of the experiment was the use of different instructions, one requiring subjects to rehearse; the other, to generate relational images for each set of words. Another feature was that the probes were presented to one or the other visual field. The results showed that left-field (right hemisphere) probes produced faster decisions under the imagery instructions, but only when pictures were used as probes. Conversely, picture probes to the left hemisphere resulted in faster decisions under the rehearsal instructions. These findings, too, seem consistent with the effects of temporal lobectomy under demanding memory conditions in that they implicate the right hemisphere in imagery-mediated verbal memory. Nonetheless, a confident interpretation must await further evidence (see Kelly & Orton, 1979).

All of the preceding studies have used episodic memory tasks. We comment, finally, on hemispheric differentiation in semantic memory tasks, which require subjects to make decisions on the basis of their long-term knowledge.

Wilkins and Moscovitch (1978) studied the problem using patients who had had their left or right temporal lobe removed, as well as a normal control group. One task required the subjects to classify a series of common objects as larger or smaller than a chair. Some objects were presented as words and some as line drawings. Note that this task is like the size-comparison problem described in chapter 11. The task was included because of the earlier evidence that the performance is mediated by a nonverbal analogue system, for which the right hemisphere may be specialized. Another task required the subjects to classify objects as living or manufactured, a decision that was thought to require verbal processing. The results showed that in the larger-smaller classification task, semantic memory was not impaired among either patient group. However, patients with left-temporal removals were impaired in the living-manufactured classification relative to the right-temporal and normal subjects. The authors suggest that "removal of the anterior left temporal lobe leads to a disruption of semantic systems that involve verbal or lexical representations, but leaves intact those systems that involve visual or analogue representations" (p. 77). This interpretation also accommodated another finding from their study, namely, that the left-temporal group also showed a deficit in naming objects. Thus, left temporal lobe lesions apparently impair both semantic memory and episodic memory performance, when verbal representations are used. Wilkins and Moscovitch suggest, too, that the disruption may be smaller in semantic than in episodic memory.

Warrington (1975) presented an analysis of three patients with object agnosia in terms of semantic memory impairment. Agnosia ("not knowing") is a deficit in recognizing or identifying the meaning of common objects or their names. The

patients had diffuse cerebral lesions, so the localization of agnosia was not known, but other evidence suggests the left posterior region as a likely site. Warrington administered a variety of tests which showed that the patients were particularly impaired in their ability to identify superordinate categories and, to a lesser degree, subordinate properties of animals and objects presented as either pictures or words. For example, they made many errors when asked to indicate whether a given animal was foreign, bigger than a cat, or which of two names corresponded to it. Weight and name were poorly identified in the case of objects. These problems could not be attributed to impairment of visual form perception or expressive speech. Warrington concluded, therefore, that the agnosia included damage to the semantic storage systems, which she interpreted as encompassing "knowledge of objects, words, facts, concepts, etc., and the relationship between them" (p. 652). Moreover, she proposed that such knowledge included "two semantic memory hierarchies, . . . one primarily visual [nonverbal] and the other primarily verbal" (p. 656). The statement obviously represents a kind of dual-coding position in regard to semantic memory as inferred from the agnosic syndrome.

We shall conclude this section by discussing one study in which lateralized visual presentation was used to investigate the semantic memory functions of the two hemispheres. Various studies have found a reaction-time advantage favoring the left visual field (right hemisphere) in tasks using numbers (for example, Cohen, 1975). Such tasks are not purely semantic, however, since the visual transformation is performed on the presented figure itself. Moreover, the studies generally have not compared verbal and nonverbal tasks performed with the same stimuli.

Beebe (1978) achieved such verbal and nonverbal comparability using numbers as stimuli. Pairs of numbers (3-2, 2-4, 9-11, and so on) were flashed tachisto-scopically so that the first number of a pair appeared at central fixation and the second appeared either to the right or left of center. The subjects performed three tasks. One, based on a prior study (Paivio, 1978a), required the subject to think of the numbers as clock times with the minute hand always at :00 and to indicate by pressing one of two keys whether the angle formed by the minute and hour hand in the second (lateralized) time was smaller or larger than in the first time. Thus, for the pair 2-5, the angle corresponding to five o'clock is larger than for two o'clock. This task is semantic in that it requires the subject to respond on the basis of knowledge of analogue clocks, and its performance uses visual imagery (Paivio, 1978a).

Two other tasks were performed with such pairs. One used a logical algorithm to arrive at the same answer as in the clock task. If the first number is smaller than six, then the true numerical difference determines the response. Thus the correct answer for 2-5 is "larger." When the first number is larger than six, however, the relationship is reversed. For example, 7-10 is correctly answered "smaller." (Note that in the corresponding clock task, the angle formed by the two hands is smaller for ten o'clock than for seven o'clock.) The second (verbal) task required the subject simply to decide whether the names of the two numbers began with the same or different letters. Note that both of these tasks depend on the use of verbal knowledge, or verbal semantic memory.

The results were that the analogue clock-comparison task was performed faster with left-field than with right-field presentations of the second number, whereas the reverse was true for the two verbal symbolic tasks, particularly the one with the computational algorithm. Thus the laterality data suggest right-hemisphere

superiority in the performance of nonverbal semantic memory tasks and left-hemisphere superiority in verbal semantic memory tasks. We thus have evidence from both neurological and laterality studies for semantic memory processes in both hemispheres and for the involvement of temporal as well as more posterior cortical regions. The right-left distinction is at least partly correlated with a verbal-nonverbal distinction, but not completely so. The latter qualification is further strengthened by studies of comprehension and production, which we shall examine next.

Comprehension and Production

Much of the neuropsychological information about language comprehension and production has come from studies of aphasia. The classical picture of aphasic symptoms included an important distinction between receptive and expressive disorders, corresponding essentially to difficulties related to comprehension and production. Receptive disorders were identified particularly with the posterior speech (Wernicke's) area. Expressive disorders were associated with anterior structures, including Broca's area. The distinction no longer seems as clear as it once did, but it retains a rough validity. Summarizing the data from many studies, Figure 15-1 shows the lesioned areas found to be associated with sensory (receptive) symptoms and motor (expressive) symptoms. Although there is some overlap, the front-back distinction is generally apparent.

The qualified front-back distinction is also supported by other techniques. The radioactive isotope procedure for measuring blood-flow changes associated with cortical activity (Lassen et al., 1978) revealed strong localized activity in the auditory cortex in the temporal lobe and in the adjacent Wernicke's area when the subject was listening to speech. Speaking aloud also resulted in increased blood flow in the auditory cortex (presumably because subjects hear themselves speak) and in addition activated somatosensory and motor areas, including those subserving the face, tongue, and mouth, as well as Broca's area. However, internal speech in the form of counting from one to twenty "in one's head" was associated with activity of the supplementary motor area of the frontal lobe but not of Broca's or Wernicke's speech areas. These results should be interpreted cautiously because of the crude nature of the procedure. Nonetheless, the data agree with those from studies of aphasia in that they implicate distinct but overlapping posterior and anterior cortical areas in comprehension and production.

The left-right functional distinction between the hemispheres has also been qualified by recent observations. The classical picture of one hemisphere being dominant for speech is supported by all sources of evidence with respect to speech production. In particular, studies of aphasia and the verbal performance of split-brain subjects indicate that speech output is controlled by the left hemisphere in most people. This does not mean, however, that the other hemisphere is inactive. Lassen and his colleagues observed increased blood flow in the same areas of both hemispheres during speech, with the difference that the increases in certain areas of the cortex were more clearly differentiated in the left than in the right hemisphere. They concluded, therefore, that the right hemisphere "makes some contribution (albeit a nonessential one) to the final synthesis and mobilization of speech"

(1978, p. 70). The term "nonessential" alludes to the fact that destruction of the relevant parts of the right hemisphere usually has no effect on speech.

Behavioral evidence suggests, however, that both hemispheres contribute functionally to linguistic comprehension. We have already noted that split-brain subjects are able, with their left hands, to pick out or point to the objects corresponding to the names that have been flashed in the left visual field. Thus the "silent" right hemisphere must be able to comprehend the referential meanings of those words. The right hemisphere also seems to have a "surprisingly rich aural lexicon" (Zaidel, 1977; Searleman, 1977). For example, Levy (1970) devised procedures that revealed right-hemisphere comprehension of verbs and spoken commands. Rather than requiring split-brain subjects to perform a named act with their left hands—a procedure previously shown to be unsuccessful—Levy asked them to pick out an object associated with the verb, such as a toy chair in response to *sit*. This they were able to do. Dichotic listening studies carried out with the same patients (for example, Milner, Taylor, & Sperry, 1968) showed that their left hands could carry out commands directed to the left ear. Zaidel has even obtained evidence for right-hemisphere auditory comprehension of phrases and sentences, although left-hemisphere lateralization is stronger at this level than at the word level. Thus we have a gradation of functional asymmetry, with speech production the most completely lateralized to the left hemisphere, word reading (with understanding) less lateralized, and auditory comprehension the least strongly lateralized at the word level (but more so at the syntactic level). Nonetheless, the left hemisphere remains more or less dominant in all of the linguistic tasks.

The support for right-hemisphere language functions comes largely from studies of split-brain patients. How well do the generalizations hold for normal individuals? Perhaps the commissurectomized patients have simply developed bilateral language representation because the epileptic seizures that originally led to the surgical operation had produced cerebral damage. If so, careful testing of normals might reveal less right-hemisphere language ability than suggested by the results with clinical samples. Moscovitch (1973) evaluated this possibility by a reaction-time technique in which normal subjects heard a series of binaurally presented letters, which they were to memorize. The series was followed immediately by a single probe letter presented visually to either the left or the right field. The subject responded as quickly as possible with the fingers of the left hand to indicate whether or not the probe letter had been part of the memory set. Moscovitch's reasoning was as follows: The left-hand response is initiated by the right hemisphere. Therefore, if the right hemisphere can process the verbal stimuli, the response should be faster when the probe letter is flashed to the left visual field from where it would first reach the right hemisphere. Letters flashed to the right field must first be processed by the left hemisphere and then "sent" across the corpus callosum to the right hemisphere which then initiates the left-hand finger press. However, if the right hemisphere cannot process the stimuli, stimuli presented to the right field would be faster because those presented to the left must cross the corpus callosum twice—that is, from the right hemisphere to the left for linguistic processing, then back to the right for the left-hand response.

The results were generally in accord with the second possibility. Left-field (right hemisphere) probes were faster than right-field probes only when the memory set contained a single letter. Moscovitch concluded, therefore, that the right hemi-

sphere was simply using a visual ("template") match to determine whether the probe letter was in the memory set. Note, however, that this could not be a direct *perceptual* match, since the memory set was presented auditorily. Thus the left hemisphere must have activated a visual letter representation from long-term memory information in the right hemisphere. To that extent at least, the right hemisphere could be said to have linguistic representation.

Moscovitch proposed a *functional localization model* which assumes that the right-hemisphere linguistic ability of normals is equal to that of split-brain and aphasic subjects. According to the model, the observed differences result from differences in the inhibitory role of the left hemisphere. That hemisphere normally inhibits or suppresses linguistic processing in the right hemisphere by inhibitory impulses across the corpus callosum. These inhibitory influences are reduced when the corpus callosum is sectioned, so the right hemisphere is freed to perform its linguistic functions. This model is currently favored by a number of researchers because it accounts for various findings, including those stemming from studies with aphasics (see Searleman, 1977). The relevant point for our purposes is that the model preserves the idea that the right hemisphere can play a role in language comprehension, although not to the same degree as the left.

We shall turn now to a more detailed discussion of the role of both hemispheres in language comprehension and production, but with particular attention to left-hemisphere functions. Moreover, we emphasize possible distinctions in the processing of words as compared to larger language units and of semantic as compared to syntactic information. The inferences are based primarily on studies of aphasics. It should be recognized at the outset that taken as a whole, the literature on the area presents a picture of bewildering complexity as to the neurological facts, their relation to behavior, and the descriptive terminology that has arisen. Although we touch on some of the fine distinctions and complexities, our brief account is necessarily selective and simplified. We concentrate, at the word level, on the meaningful use of words in production and comprehension; at the level of larger units, on the problems in understanding or producing grammatical sequences of various sizes.

Word comprehension and production

Defects in the use of names are a classical problem in the study of aphasia. They may be difficulties in producing or understanding names of common objects or their properties; moreover, the difficulties can vary according to the sensory modality of the object or the verbal stimuli. The tasks used to identify production deficits typically ask the patient to name objects or pictures, patches of color, and so on. Comprehension is assessed by presenting names of such stimuli and requiring the patient to point to the corresponding object or color in a set of stimuli. The tests may reveal deficits only in comprehension or only in production, but often both comprehension and production are impaired to some degree.

Note that the tasks implicate a connection between words and their referents, or referential meaning, which makes a dual-coding analysis particularly appropriate. In dual-coding terms, any particular naming deficit could represent damage to the neural representation corresponding to words, to referent objects, or to the connections between them (the last representing one kind of *disconnection syndrome;*

cf. Geschwind, 1965). It is difficult in practice to point to one as the source of the impairment, although the possibilities can be narrowed down by judicious testing. Thus, if the patient can point to named objects but cannot name them, the locus of the problem presumably is the motor aspects of the verbal system or the connections between that system and nonverbal representations. The latter would be the more likely interpretation if name responses can be elicited by verbal cues, such as asking the person to repeat spoken words, respond associatively to words, describe properties of named objects, and so on.

The following case study illustrates how one goes about making a diagnostic interpretation of a naming deficit: Geschwind and Fusillo (1966) described a color-naming defect also associated with pure alexia (inability to read). They summarized the color-naming results as follows: "The patient failed to name seen colors correctly and could not select a color from a group when given its name; in other words, he showed an isolated difficulty in uttering or comprehending the names of seen colors" (p. 145). Other tests ruled out difficulties related to color perception, object-color association, and long-term verbal memory for object colors. For example, the patient was able to match colors by hue, to match seen colors to uncolored pictures of objects (for example, a yellow crayon to a banana), and to give orally the names of colors corresponding to named objects and vice versa. Thus the syndrome specifically reflected "an inability to match seen colors to their spoken names" (p. 146).

The patient died, and a postmortem revealed destructive lesions in the left visual cortex, the splenium of the corpus callosum, and other areas served by the left posterior cerebral artery. The neuropsychological interpretation that followed from the observations was that the visual information was cut off from the speech area in the left hemisphere. The visual functions of the left hemisphere were eliminated by the destruction of the left visual cortex, and the intact right visual cortex lost its commissural connections to the speech area in the left hemisphere. Thus the patient could neither read nor match colors to their names. Colors could be matched with pictures of objects by the right hemisphere, and verbal memory for color names was retained by the intact verbal representational system of the left hemisphere.

How is it, then, that the patient was able to name objects, but not colors? Geschwind and Fusillo suggested that the discrepancy might be attributed to the role of tactile associations. Object naming might be preserved because an object can arouse tactile associations farther forward in the right hemisphere, which could then cross the callosum over its intact portions anterior to the splenium. Colors lack tactile associations, so that color information could not reach the speech area by this indirect route.

We cannot generalize from one case, particularly since the one described by Geschwind and Fusillo is unique even in the limited area of color-name agnosia. However, the specific idea that names can be retrieved by alternative routes based on different sense modalities appears to have considerable generality, since it receives support from other studies of naming impairment. Gardner (1973, cited in Caramazza & Berndt, 1978) had anterior and posterior aphasics name pictures of "operative" (easily manipulated) and "figurative" (not easily manipulated) objects. The operative items were easier to name, which Gardner attributed to the arousal of associations in several sensory modalities. Figurative items suffered because they

were limited to the visual modality. Goodglass, Barton, and Kaplan (1968, cited in Caramazza & Berndt, 1978) found that patients were equally able to name objects on the basis of visual, tactile, olfactory, or auditory cues. Caramazza and Berndt also cite research by North (1971) which showed that the various sensory modalities of an object contributed additively to the probability of correct object naming by aphasics.

Caramazza and Berndt interpreted such findings as suggesting that the naming difficulties indicated disruption in the retrieval of concepts that mediate between the level of sensory stimulation and the production of the word. They make no specific assumption about the nature of the conceptual representation itself other than to suggest that it could consist of sets of features, propositions, or a mental image. Whatever the representation, the implication is that the referential connection between concept and naming response may be intact, but the pathways between sensory information and the conceptual representation are not. This interpretation differs from the dual-coding idea that referential connections between verbal and nonverbal representations may be disrupted. Both views are theoretically possible, but they are difficult to tease apart empirically.

Broca's and Wernicke's aphasics appear to differ somewhat in the nature of their naming difficulties. Goodglass, Klein, Carey, and Jones (1966) studied the comprehension and naming ability of both types of patients, as well as amnesics, using stimuli from several semantic categories, including letters, objects, numbers, colors, body parts, and actions. The name-production tests required the subjects to name the items, and the comprehension tests required them to point to items named by the examiner. The traditional contrast between expressive and receptive symptoms was not supported by the overall results, but the two types of aphasics did differ in the pattern of difficulties they showed in all semantic categories. The most striking specific finding was that the Wernicke's aphasics were characterized by a combination of relatively low scores on object naming and high scores on letter naming. The Broca's aphasics reversed this finding to some degree, so that the constrast between the two groups was clearest on these items. With respect to comprehension, object names were relatively easy to understand, but letters were the most difficult for both groups. A simplified interpretation is that object representations are located in posterior regions whose connections with anterior verbal production systems were most cut off by posterior damage among the Wernicke aphasics, whereas letter representations, the most "verbal" among the stimuli used, are located in more anterior regions that were most disrupted among the Broca's aphasics.

The preceding discussion has been on name comprehension and production, particularly as inferred from naming or pointing responses to objects or their properties. Studies have also considered the frequency with which different classes of words occur in the spontaneous speech of aphasics or as elicited by a word-association test. Howes (1967) showed that Broca's (anterior) and Wernicke's (posterior) aphasics differed in the characteristics of their spontaneous speech and word associations. The proportion of function words (conjunctions, prepositions, etc.) and pronouns showed a decrease in the speech of severe Broca's but not Wernicke's aphasics relative to their distribution among normals. Thus, Broca's aphasics appear to speak in a telegraphic style. On the word-association test, Broca's aphasics gave essentially the same associations as normals did, but Wernicke's apha-

sics gave associations that were quite eccentric. Wepman, Bock, Jones, and van Pelt (1956) compared the spontaneous speech of an anomic aphasic (usually associated with posterior damage) and a normal subject. The aphasic's speech was especially deficient in low-frequency words. The nouns that were retained were very general words such as "thing" and "people," but more specific nouns were lacking. This was generally true also for verbs and adjectives in that very general and common verbs ("do," "go," "look") and adjectives ("good," "wonderful," "nice") were used excessively, but more specific words were omitted. The authors speculated that the patient had lost voluntary control of informative words and had retained automatic use of overlearned words and word combinations.

These results suggest that patients with posterior damage suffer particularly in their ability to deal with concrete, picturable words in spontaneous speech and word-association tests, just as they do in naming tasks. Anterior patients, on the other hand, seem to be deficient in dealing with words that have a linking or sequencing function in sentences. The former could be interpreted as a problem of referential interconnections and the latter, intraverbal interconnections including those usually described by grammatical rules. However, the area is complex and has problems with the different word attributes, including especially frequency, concreteness, and associative meaningfulness, making interpretation difficult. The data also lead naturally to considerations of the associative or semantic structure of the aphasic's verbal system or "internal lexicon," as well as his or her grammatical behavior. We shall briefly examine each topic.

Verbal associative and semantic structure

The naming and word-association research with aphasics has revealed that such individuals generally produce erroneous responses (for example, substituting *pen* for *pencil*) that are strikingly similar to the word-association norms for normal speakers (see Rinnert & Whitaker, 1973). Caramazza and Berndt (1978) accordingly suggested that the word associations of aphasics could be used as a basis for making inferences about semantic structure. One relevant experiment (Goodglass & Baker, 1976) required aphasics and nonaphasic control subjects to squeeze a bulb whenever one of a series of spoken words reminded them of a simultaneously presented target picture. The words included the name of the pictured item and a variety of associations to the item—superordinates, coordinates, functional associates (the name of an action associated with the word), and functional context (the name of a situation or context in which the item could be found). Analysis of reaction times and error rates yielded the following results of interest: All groups recognized the names of the pictures equally well. Anterior aphasics and controls were comparable in reacting to superordinates, descriptive attributes, and functional context words as the most clearly related associates of the target pictures. Posterior aphasics had great difficulty recognizing functional contexts and functional associates as related to the target. Since the latter group had had difficulty producing names for the pictures in a previous test, although they could recognize the names of the objects, Goodglass and Baker suggested that the ability to produce a name depends on arousing various kinds of information associated with the name, and when the posterior speech zone is damaged, it is the associative (or semantic) structure that is disrupted.

Another relevant study (Whitehouse, Caramazza, & Zurif; cited in Caramazza & Berndt, 1978, pp. 906-907) had anterior and posterior aphasics name a series of pictures that were variations of a modal *cup*, so that some looked more or less like *bowls* and others like *glasses*. The functional context was also varied by depicting a coffeepot pouring coffee, a cereal box pouring cereal, or ice water pouring into the container, so as to provide cup, bowl, and glass contexts. The question was whether the two types of aphasics would differ in their ability to categorize the containers on the basis of perceptual and contextual information. The results showed that the anterior aphasics, like normal speakers, named the clear (prototypical) examples of each type of container consistently and the borderline ones inconsistently, indicating that they were sensitive to the fuzzy boundaries between categories. The posterior aphasics either named all items inconsistently or based their name selection on one feature, such as the presence or absence of a handle. The anterior group was similarly sensitive to the contextual information in that they appropriately changed the name with shifts in context, whereas the posterior aphasics failed to make appropriate use of the context.

The authors concluded from the results that the semantic information associated with the words *cup, bowl,* and *glass* was not well structured in the posterior aphasics. That is, their naming difficulty seemed to be attributable to their inability to differentiate among members of the semantic category, food containers, rather than to their failure to activate an intact word representation per se.

Comprehension data derived from semantic classification tasks are also consistent with the hypothesis. For example, Zurif, Caramazza, Meyerson, and Galvin (1974; cited in Caramazza & Berndt, 1978, pp. 908-909) had aphasics and normal controls choose from a group of three words the two that were most similar in meaning. The words were concrete nouns that varied on several semantic features, especially ±Human (for example, *shark, trout, dog; mother, cook, knight*). The patients' similarity judgments were analyzed to determine the structural relationships that they had imposed on the stimuli. The major finding was that controls and anterior aphasics clustered the human and animal items separately, whereas posterior aphasics did not clearly differentiate the two categories, although they had been able to recognize definitions of the nouns on a pretest.

The semantic clusters produced by anterior aphasics and normals differed in one interesting respect. Within the animal category, the control patients combined items by species, discriminating among fish, reptiles, and mammals. By contrast, the anterior aphasics primarily differentiated animals in terms of ferocity, so that one major cluster consisted of *shark, crocodile,* and *tiger,* and another consisted of *trout* and *turtle.* Thus the normal controls used more abstract, technical semantic features when judging similarities and differences, and the patients with anterior neurological damage apparently based their judgments more on concrete, perceptual characteristics. Caramazza and Berndt accordingly suggested that anterior aphasics are relatively restricted in their range of conceptual integration.

Verbal concepts in anterior aphasia appear to be more tightly tied to affective and situational data . . . the normal adult has a number of levels at which he can organize his lexicon—some referentially practical, others linguistically practical—whereas the aphasic primarily retains those features of words that relate to perceived or imagined environmental situations. (1978, p. 909)

The various studies of word production and comprehension have yielded a rather mixed assortment of findings, which nonetheless retain some general consistency with the classical distinction between Broca's (anterior, motor, expressive) aphasia on the one hand and Wernicke's (posterior, sensory, receptive) aphasia on the other. Anterior aphasics appear to retain the ability to process language in terms of its concrete meaning (that is, its relation to perceptual objects and events) while suffering disruption at a more abstract, intraverbal level. Conversely, posterior aphasics are more likely to retain intraverbal habits but show disruption in their processing of the concrete, perceptual attributes of language. In the extreme, the latter problem may be a loss of the referential connection between a specific perceptual attribute (for example, color) or an entire concept and its name. More often, there seems to be a disruption of the relationships among attributes. However, there are many exceptions to such generalizations, and data are lacking with respect to many issues relevant to contemporary theories of language and cognition.

Grammatical behavior and aphasia

We shall discuss next the effect of brain damage on the grammatical (syntactic) aspects of language use. The traditional term for an extreme form of breakdown in syntactic relations is agrammatism. It is characterized by laborious speech consisting of disconnected content words and short stereotypical phrases, often described as telegraphic speech. Function words (articles, relational words, and so on) are most often omitted and confused with each other. The following is a patient's reply to an interviewer who asked what brought him back to the hospital, and is a sample of agrammatic speech as described by Goodglass (1968):

> Yes . . . ah . . . Monday . . . ah . . . Dad and Peter Hogan, and Dad . . . ah . . .
> Hospital . . . and ah . . . Wednesday . . . Wednesday, nine o'clock and ah
> Thursday . . . ten o'clock ah doctors . . . two . . . two . . . an doctors and
> . . . teeth . . . yah. And a doctor . . . an girl . . . and gums, and I. (p. 178)

Some students of aphasia have considered agrammatism as a distinct form of aphasia, but others see it as an aspect or correlate of motor aphasia. We have already described such agrammatical correlates in connection with our discussion of production problems in anterior aphasics. A distinction has also been drawn between agrammatism and *paragrammatism* (or sensory agrammatism, sometimes called "fluent aphasia"), which is also characterized by grammatical errors but seemingly contains less syntactic disruption than does agrammatism. What is especially salient in paragrammatism is the inappropriate choice of content words such as nouns, so that the speech seems to be informationally empty. Moreover, paragrammatism has been traditionally associated with temporal lobe rather than frontal lobe lesions. These distinctions are based on clinical observations, and they are not as clear as the descriptions suggest when examined in the light of experimental studies that include comparisons of various types of aphasics and nonaphasic controls. Nonetheless, certain consistencies have emerged from the observations.

Goodglass (1968) studied the grammatical behavior of several different patient groups, including agrammatic and paragrammatic ("fluent") aphasics. The tasks were patterned after those used with children to determine their ability to produce various syntactic morphemes (see chapter 10). Possessives and plurals are

particularly interesting because they all use the same allophones /s, z, ɨz/ and are therefore indistinguishable phonologically. Goodglass found, as he had in earlier research, that the different types of aphasics showed the same order of difficulty among the morphemes. Plurals were generally easier than possessives and the verbal tense marker /s/. In addition, however, paragrammatic aphasics had more difficulty producing the more complex allomorphs /ɨz/ and /ɨd/ than their simpler counterparts, /z,d/, whereas the reverse was true for agrammatic aphasics. The paragrammatic pattern is typical of children as well, but the agrammatic problem is not. Thus, syntactic behavior was selectively impaired by anterior brain damage among the agrammatic aphasics. Other studies by Goodglass and his colleagues (cited by Caramazza & Berndt, 1978, p. 913) have demonstrated that agrammatism is associated with selective impairment of the ability to use transformational rules.

The preceding studies were done with production tasks. Caramazza and Zurif (1976; cited in Caramazza & Berndt, 1978) used a sentence-picture matching task to evaluate the comprehension capacities of anterior and posterior aphasics. Sentences were read to the patients, and they were asked to choose from two pictures the one that depicted the proposition described by the sentence. The sentences were center embedded so as to be either reversible or nonreversible if one ignored syntactic constraints. Under such conditions, a reversible sentence such as *The lion the tiger is chasing is fat* could be interpreted in various ways (the tiger is chasing a fat lion, the lion is chasing a fat tiger, and so forth). However, lexical selection restrictions on nonreversible sentences such as *The bicycle that the boy is holding is broken* permit only one reading (the boy is holding a broken bicycle). The picture pairs were constructed so that in some contrasts the correct picture could be chosen on the basis of lexical information alone. In other contrasts, a correct choice was possible only if the patient used the correct syntax of the sentence.

The agrammatic (anterior) aphasics showed a clear effect of contrast type, responding correctly about 90 percent of the time on the lexical contrasts and 70 percent of the time on the syntactic contrasts. The paragrammatic patients showed no consistent pattern but were inferior to the agrammatics in overall performance. With respect to the reversible-nonreversible variable, agrammatic patients were 90 percent accurate on nonreversible sentences but performed only at the chance level on reversible sentences. The paragrammatic patients were unaffected by this manipulation of sentence syntax. Thus the agrammatic patients were impaired in sentence comprehension just as they were in production, and the disruption seemed to occur at the level of syntactic processing.

These and other studies suggest that damage to the anterior speech region selectively affects the aphasics' ability to process grammatical information. The agrammatic patients can produce, comprehend, and remember content words, indicating that semantic processing is intact. They are unable to cope adequately with grammatical morphemes and function words, indicating that syntactic processing has been impaired. By contrast, damage to the posterior speech zone is more appropriately characterized as impaired semantic processing, with apparently no damage to syntactic processing. Note that these generalizations cut across the comprehension-production contrast: the relative syntactic impairment of the anterior aphasic applies to both comprehension and production, as does the relative semantic impairment of the posterior aphasic. This psycholinguistic conceptualization of aphasic problems contrasts similarly with the traditional distinctions between

sensory and motor, or receptive and expressive aphasia. The descriptive distinction between fluent and nonfluent aphasia, however, remains compatible with the more theoretical psycholinguistic distinction between syntactic and semantic disorders.

This concludes our review of the research findings concerning brain function and those aspects of language behavior that have occupied us through this book. We finally shall summarize the general theoretical implications of the evidence presented. What has been revealed, clarified, or challenged by the neuropsychological studies of language and nonlinguistic functions?

Summary and Implications

The neuropsychological data are especially relevant to the verbal-nonverbal representational distinction. Certain verbal and nonverbal functions are differentiated by hemisphere. Speech production is most clearly lateralized, so that the left hemisphere is the "speaking" brain, whereas the right is silent. Situation-specific (episodic) memory shows a double dissociation by material, so that memory for verbal stimuli is "stronger" in the left hemisphere for most people, but nonverbal memory is stronger in the right. There is also some support for hemispheric functional distinctions for verbal and nonverbal material in perceptual and semantic memory tasks. Theoretically, such data seem more consistent with a dual-coding approach to language and cognition than with single-code theories, since it is difficult to see how the anatomical-functional distinctions are compatible with the idea that verbal and nonverbal information are handled by a single (propositional or other) conceptual system. The picture is not that clear, however. John Anderson, for example, argues as follows:

> These studies on hemispheric specialization really provide very little evidence on the form of information representation. One could propose that all information has a propositional form, but that propositions encoding visual information are stored in the right hemisphere and propositions encoding verbal in the left. Another possibility . . . is that rather than having the data differentially stored, one could have procedures differentially stored. That is, procedures for performing verbal tasks would be in the left hemisphere and procedures for spatial tasks in the right hemisphere. Both types of procedures could take the propositional information as their data. (1978, pp. 271–272)

Anderson's statement would have to be modified to draw the distinction between verbal and nonverbal (rather than visual) information, since the nonverbal functional superiority of the right hemisphere in certain tasks is not specific to the visual modality. Nonetheless, the same statement could be made—verbal and nonverbal propositions (or procedures) are handled by different hemispheres. Such an argument is irrefutable, since it amounts to redefining the dual-coding distinction by adjectival modification: *verbal* propositions versus *nonverbal* (or visual) propositions. Such a position is formally equivalent to a dual-coding one. It is possible to marshal arguments against the value of such a compromise, but that would lead us into areas that are irrelevant to the psychology of language. We conclude that the neuropsychological data seem to demand some kind of strong dual-coding or dual-processing interpretation.

The data are important also to the distinction between comprehension and production. Some theories imply that comprehension and production use the same processes or mechanisms. This is the case if the motor theory of speech perception is extended to speech comprehension. The implication is that production and understanding are mediated by the same speech motor system. Behavioral approaches that emphasize covert speech responses during thinking, as in Skinner's verbal operant approach (see Winokur, 1976, p. 146) and McGuigan's (1978) behavioral-psychophysiological approach to cognition, contain a similar assumption. Noam Chomsky's transformational generative grammar has also been interpreted to imply that the same deep structures and transformations are used in the production and comprehension of speech—consider, for example, the transformational decoding hypothesis discussed in chapter 7. The neuropsychological data seem not to be compatible with rigid forms of such theories. Although speech is clearly lateralized in the dominant (usually left) hemisphere, the nondominant (right) hemisphere has considerable "competence" with respect to the comprehension of language. Moreover, although the distinction is less clear than once assumed, anterior and posterior portions of the dominant hemisphere seem to be differentially involved in production and comprehension. The reasonable conclusion is that production and comprehension of language are mediated to a significant (nontrivial) degree by different neurophysiological systems. This does not exclude the likely possibility that a common (perhaps speech motor) system is normally used in both functions as well (cf. Kimura, in press).

The evidence also bears on the distinction between syntax and semantics. Caramazza and Berndt (1978) in particular conclude that the two aspects of language processing are subserved by different regions of the brain. Syntactic functions are mediated by anterior structures of the left hemisphere, semantic functions by posterior regions of that hemisphere and also by the right hemisphere. The conclusion parallels the one regarding comprehension and production, with the difference that Caramazza and Berndt find evidence that syntactic production and comprehension both are affected in anterior aphasia.

The above examples most clearly illustrate the contribution that neuropsychological data can make in resolving general theoretical issues and assumptions associated with language behavior. Conversely, they illustrate the guiding role of psychological theories in analyzing neuropsychological data. The verbal-nonverbal distinction, which is the essence of dual-coding theory, leads one to look for differences in how the brain processes different materials. Conversely, single-code models suggest that one might find common systems for handling different materials provided that the semantic processing is the same. Behavioral theorists should (and do) look for evidence that motor systems are used in different language tasks, such as comprehension and production. Word-association theorists should look for evidence that associative networks or fields are selectively affected by lesions in particular areas. And so on. Our review has shown the operation of such guiding ideas, and the interested reader can find other examples in the literature on language and the brain.

references

AARONSON, D., & SCARBOROUGH, H. S. Performance theories for sentence coding: Some quantitative evidence. *Journal of Experimental Psychology: Human Perception and Performance.* 1976, *2*, 56–70.

ALLPORT, F. H. *Social psychology.* Boston: Houghton Mifflin, 1924.

ALLPORT, F. H. *Theories of perception and the concept of structure.* New York: John Wiley, 1955.

ALLPORT, G. W., VERNON, P. E., & LINDZEY, G. *Study of values* (2nd ed.). Boston: Houghton Mifflin, 1951.

ANDERSON, C. C. The psychology of the metaphor. *Journal of Genetic Psychology,* 1964, *105*, 53–73.

ANDERSON, J. R. *Language, memory, and thought.* Hillsdale, N.J.: Erlbaum, 1976.

ANDERSON, J. R. Arguments concerning representations for mental imagery. *Psychological Review,* 1978, *85*, 249–277.

ANDERSON, J. R., & BOWER, G. H. Recognition and retrieval processes in free recall. *Psychological Review,* 1972, *79*, 97–123.

ANDERSON, J. R. & BOWER, G. H. *Human associative memory.* Washington, D.C.: Winston, 1973.

ANDERSON, R. C. Schema-directed processes in language comprehension. In A. Lesgold, J. Pellegrino, S. Fokkima, & R. Glaser (Eds.), *Cognitive psychology and instruction.* New York, Plenum, 1978.

ANDERSON, R. C., GOETZ, E. T., PICHERT, J. W., & HALFF, H. M. Two faces of the conceptual peg hypothesis. *Journal of Experimental Psychology: Human Learning and Memory,* 1977, *3*, 142–149.

ANDERSON, R. C., & HIDDE, J. L. Imagery and sentence learning. *Journal of Educational Psychology,* 1971, *62*, 526–530.

ANDERSON, R. C., & McGAW, B. On the representation of the meanings of general terms. *Journal of Experimental Psychology,* 1973, *101*, 301–306.

ANDERSON, R. C. & ORTONY, A. On putting apples into bottles—a problem in polysemy. *Cognitive Psychology,* 1975, *7*, 167–180.

ANGLIN, J. M. *Word, object, and conceptual development.* New York: W. W. Norton & Co., Inc., 1977.

ANTTILA, R. *An introduction to historical and comparative linguistics.* London: Macmillan, 1972.

ARCHER, L. A. Blissymbolics–a nonverbal communication system. *Journal of Speech and Hearing Disorders*, 1977, *42*, 568–579.

ARNHEIM, R. *Visual thinking.* Berkeley & Los Angeles: University of California Press, 1969.

ASCH, S. E. The metaphor: A psychological inquiry. In R. Tagiuri & L. Petrullo (Eds.), *Person perception and interpersonal behavior.* Stanford, Calif.: Stanford University Press, 1958.

ASHER, J. J. The total physical response approach to second language learning. *Modern Language Journal*, 1969, *53*, 3–17.

ASHER, J. J., & PRICE, B. S. The learning strategy of the total physical response: Some age differences. *Child Development*, 1967, *38*, 1219–1227.

ATKINSON, R. C. Mnemotechnics in second-language learning. *American Psychologist*, 1975, *30*, 821–828.

ATKINSON, R. C., & RAUGH, M. R. An application of the mnemonic keyword method to the acquisition of a Russian vocabulary. *Journal of Experimental Psychology: Human Learning and Memory*, 1975, *1*, 126–133.

BAARS, B. J., & MOTLEY, M. T. Spoonerisms as sequencer conflicts: Evidence from artificially elicited errors. *American Journal of Psychology*, 1976, *89*, 467–484.

BAIRD, R. On the role of chance in Imitation-Comprehension-Production test results. *Journal of Verbal Learning and Verbal Behavior*, 1972, *11*, 474–477.

BANKS, W. P. Encoding and processing of symbolic information in comparative judgments. In G. H. Bower (Ed.), *Psychology of learning and motivation* (Vol. 11). New York: Academic Press, 1977.

BANKS, W. P., & FLORA, J. Semantic and perceptual processes in symbolic comparisons. *Journal of Experimental Psychology: Human Perception and Performance*, 1977, *3*, 278–290.

BARIK, H. C., & SWAIN, M. English-French bilingual education in the early grades: The Elgin Study. *Modern Language Journal*, 1974, *58*, 392–403.

BARIK, H. C., & SWAIN, M. A longitudinal study of bilingual and cognitive development. *International Journal of Psychology*, 1976, *11*, 251–263.

BARIK, H. C., & SWAIN, M. Evaluation of a French immersion program: Ottawa study through grade 5. *Canadian Journal of Behavioral Science*, 1978, *10*, 192–201.

BARON, J. Phonemic stage not necessary for reading. *Quarterly Journal of Experimental Psychology*, 1973, *25*, 241–246.

BARON, J., & THURSTON, I. An analysis of the word-superiority effect. *Cognitive Psychology*, 1973, *4*, 207–228.

BARTLETT, F. C. *Remembering.* Cambridge: Cambridge University Press, 1932.

BATTIG, W. F., & MONTAGUE, W. E. Category norms for verbal items in 56 categories: A replication and extension of the Connecticut category norms. *Journal of Experimental Psychology, Monograph Supplement*, 1969, *80*(3, Pt. 2).

BEEBE, J. G. *Lateralization of imaginal and symbolic thinking.* Unpublished master's thesis, University of Western Ontario, 1978.

BEGG, I. Recognition memory for sentence meaning and wording. *Journal of Verbal Learning and Verbal Behavior*, 1971, *10*, 114–119.

BEGG, I. Recall of meaningful phrases. *Journal of Verbal Learning and Verbal Behavior*, 1972, *11*, 431–439.

BEGG, I. Imagery and integration in the recall of words. *Canadian Journal of Psychology*, 1973, *27*, 159–167.

BEGG, I. Acquisition and transfer of meaningful function by meaningless sounds. *Canadian Journal of Psychology*, 1976, *30*, 178–186.

BEGG, I. Imagery and organization in memory: Instructional effects. *Memory and Cognition*, 1978, *6*, 174–183.

BEGG, I., & CLARK, J. M. Contextual imagery in meaning and memory. *Memory and Cognition*, 1975, *3*, 117–122.

BEGG, I., & PAIVIO, A. Concreteness and imagery in sentence meaning. *Journal of Verbal Learning and Verbal Behavior,* 1969, *8,* 821–827.

BEGG, I., UPFOLD, D., & WILTON, T. D. Imagery in verbal communication. *Journal of Mental Imagery,* 1978, *2,* 165–186.

BEGG, I., & YOUNG, B. J. An organizational analysis of the form-class effect. *Journal of Experimental Child Psychology,* 1977, *22,* 503–519.

BERLIN, B., & KAY, P. *Basic color terms: Their universality and evolution.* Berkeley & Los Angeles: University of California Press, 1969.

BERLYNE, D. E. *Conflict, arousal, and curiosity.* New York: McGraw-Hill, 1960.

BEVER, T. G. The cognitive basis for linguistic structures. In J. R. Hayes (Ed.), *Cognition and the development of language.* New York: John Wiley, 1970.

BEVER, T. G., LACKNER, J. R., & KIRK, R. The underlying structures of sentences are the primary units of immediate speech processing. *Perception and Psychophysics,* 1969, *5,* 225–231.

BIERWISCH, M. Semantics. In J. Lyons (Ed.), *New horizons in linguistics.* Harmondsworth, U. K.: Pelican, 1970.

BILLOW, R. M. A cognitive-developmental study of metaphor comprehension. *Developmental Psychology,* 1975, *11,* 415–423.

BILLOW, R. M. Metaphor: A review of the psychological literature. *Psychological Bulletin,* 1977, *84,* 81–92.

BLACK, H. C. *Black's law dictionary.* St. Paul: West Publishing, 1951.

BLACK, J. B., TURNER, T. J., & BOWER, G. H. Point of view in narrative comprehension, memory, and production. *Journal of Verbal Learning and Verbal Behavior,* 1979, *18,* 187–198.

BLACK, M. Metaphor. In M. Black, *Models and metaphors.* Ithaca, N.Y.: Cornell University Press, 1962.

BLACK, M. More about metaphor. In A. Ortony (Ed.), *Metaphor and thought.* Cambridge: Cambridge University Press, 1979.

BLISS, C. K. *Semantography–Blissymbolics* (2nd ed.). Sydney, Australia: Semantography, 1965.

BLOOM, L. M. *Language development.* Cambridge, Mass.: M.I.T. Press, 1970.

BLOOM, L. M. *One word at a time: The use of single-word utterances before syntax.* The Hague: Mouton, 1973.

BLOOMFIELD, L. *Language.* New York: Henry Holt, 1933.

BLUMENTHAL, A. Promoted recall of sentences. *Journal of Verbal Learning and Verbal Behavior,* 1967, *6,* 203–206.

BLUMENTHAL, A., & BOAKES, R. Prompted recall of sentences. *Journal of Verbal Learning and Verbal Behavior,* 1967, *6,* 674–676.

BOAKES, R. A., & LODWICK, B. Short term retention of sentences. *Quarterly Journal of Experimental Psychology,* 1971, *23,* 399–409.

BOLINGER, D. The atomization of meaning. *Language,* 1965, *41,* 555–573.

BOOMER, D. Hesitation and grammatical encoding. *Language and Speech,* 1965, *8,* 148–158.

BORKOWSKI, J. G., SPREEN, O., & STUTZ, J. Z. Ear preference and abstractness in dichotic listening. *Psychonomic Science,* 1965, *3,* 547–548.

BOUSFIELD, W. A. The problem of meaning in verbal behavior. In C. N. Cofer (Ed.), *Verbal learning and verbal behavior.* New York: McGraw-Hill, 1961.

BOUSFIELD, W. A., WHITMARSH, G. A., & BERKOWITZ, H. Partial response identities in associative clustering. *Journal of General Psychology,* 1960, *63,* 233–238.

BOWER, G. H. Imagery as a relational organizer in associative learning. *Journal of Verbal Learning and Verbal Behavior,* 1970, *9,* 529–533.

BOWER, G. H., & BLACK, J. B. *Action schemata in story comprehension and memory.* Paper

presented at the meeting of the American Psychological Association, San Francisco, 1977.

BOWER, G. H., & GLASS, A. L. Structural units and the redintegrative power of picture fragments. *Journal of Experimental Psychology: Human Learning and Memory,* 1976, *2,* 456–466.

BOWER, T. G. R. The visual world of infants. *Scientific American,* 1966, *215,* 80–92.

BOWERMAN, M. *Early syntactic development: A cross-linguistic study with special reference to Finnish.* Cambridge: Cambridge University Press, 1973.

BRAINE, M. D. S. On learning the grammatical order of words. *Psychological Review,* 1963, *70,* 323–348.

BRAINE, M. D. S. Learning the positions of words relative to a marker element. *Journal of Experimental Psychology,* 1966, *72,* 532–540.

BRAINE, M. D. S. On two types of models of the internalization of grammars. In D. I. Slobin (Ed.), *The ontogenesis of grammar.* New York: Academic Press, 1971.

BRANSFORD, J. D., & FRANKS, J. J. The abstraction of linguistic ideas. *Cognitive Psychology,* 1971, *2,* 331–350.

BRANSFORD, J. D., & McCARRELL, N. S. A sketch of a cognitive approach to comprehension: Some thoughts about understanding and what it means to comprehend. In W. B. Weimer & D. S. Palermo (Eds.), *Cognition and the symbolic processes.* Hillsdale, N. J.: Erlbaum, 1974.

BREGMAN, A. S., & STRASBERG, R. Memory for the syntactic form of sentences. *Journal of Verbal Learning and Verbal Behavior,* 1968, *7,* 396–403.

BRENNER, M., FELDSTEIN, S., & JAFFE, J. The contribution of statistical uncertainty and test anxiety to speech disruption. *Journal of Verbal Learning and Verbal Behavior,* 1965, *4,* 300–305.

BREWER, W. Memory for ideas: Synonym substitution. *Memory and Cognition,* 1975, *3,* 458–464.

BROADBENT, D. E. *Perception and communication.* London: Pergamon Press, 1958.

BROADBENT, D. E. Word-frequency effect and response bias. *Psychological Review,* 1967, *74,* 1–15.

BROCA, P. Remarques sur le siège de la faculté du langage articulé, suivies d'une observation d'aphémie (perte de la parole). *Bulletin de la Société Anatomique de Paris* (2nd series), 1861, *6,* 330–357.

BROOKS, L. R. The suppression of visualization in reading. *Quarterly Journal of Experimental Psychology,* 1967, *19,* 289–299.

BROOKS, L. R. Spatial and verbal components in the act of recall. *Canadian Journal of Psychology,* 1968, *22,* 349–368.

BROWN, R. W. *Words and things.* Glencoe, Ill.: Free Press, 1958.

BROWN, R. W. *Psycholinguistics.* New York: Free Press, 1970.

BROWN, R. W. *A first language: The early stages.* Cambridge, Mass.: Harvard University Press, 1973.

BROWN, R. W. Reference—In memorial tribute to Eric Lenneberg. *Cognition,* 1976, *4,* 125–153.

BROWN, R. W. In reply to Peter Schonbach. *Cognition,* 1977, *5,* 185–187.

BROWN, R. W., CAZDEN, C., & BELLUGI, U. The child's grammar from I to III. In J. P. Hill (Ed.), *The 1967 Minnesota Symposium on Child Psychology.* Minneapolis: University of Minnesota Press, 1968.

BROWN, R. W., & LENNEBERG, E. H. A study in language and cognition. *Journal of Abnormal and Social Psychology,* 1954, *49,* 454–462.

BRUNER, J. S. Neural mechanisms in perception. *Psychological Review,* 1957, *64,* 340–358.

BRYDEN, M. P., & ALLARD, F. Visual hemifield differences depend on typeface. *Brain and Language,* 1976, *3,* 191–200.

BRYDEN, M. P., & RAINEY, C. A. Left-right differences in tachistoscopic recognition. *Journal of Experimental Psychology, 1963, 66,* 568–571.

BUGELSKI, B. R. *The psychology of learning applied to teaching.* Indianapolis: Bobbs-Merrill, 1971.

BUGELSKI, B. R. Imagery and verbal behavior. *Journal of Mental Imagery, 1977, 1,* 39–52.

BYRNE, B. Item concreteness vs. spatial organization as predictors of visual imagery. *Memory and Cognition, 1974, 2,* 53–59.

CARAMAZZA, A., & BERNDT, R. S. Semantic and syntactic processes in aphasia: A review of the literature. *Psychological Bulletin, 1978, 85,* 898–918.

CARROLL, J. B. Introduction. In B. L. Whorf, *Language, thought, and reality.* Cambridge, Mass.: M.I.T. Press, 1956.

CARROLL, J. B. *Language and thought.* Englewood Cliffs, N.J.: Prentice-Hall, Inc., 1964.

CARROLL, J. B. The contributions of psychological theory and educational research to the teaching of foreign languages. *Modern Language Journal, 1965, 49,* 273–281.

CARROLL, J. B. Aptitude in second language learning. *Proceedings of the Fifth Symposium of the Canadian Association of Applied Linguistics, 1974,* 8–23.

CARROLL, J. B., & SAPON, S. M. *Modern language aptitude test, Form A.* New York: The Psychological Corporation, 1959.

CARVER, R. P. *Sense and nonsense in speed reading.* Silver Spring, Md.: Revrac, 1971.

CHAFE, W. L. *Meaning and the structure of language.* Chicago: University of Chicago Press, 1970.

CHAPIN, P. G., SMITH, T. S., & ABRAHAMSON, A. A. Two factors in perceptual segmentation of speech. *Journal of Verbal Learning and Verbal Behavior, 1972, 11,* 164–173.

CHASE, W. G., & CLARK, H. H. Mental operations in the comparison of sentences and pictures. In L. Gregg (Ed.), *Cognition in learning and memory.* New York: John Wiley, 1972.

CHOMSKY, C. *The acquisition of syntax in children from 5 to 10.* Cambridge, Mass.: M.I.T. Press, 1969.

CHOMSKY, C. Reading, writing, and phonology. *Harvard Educational Review, 1970, 40,* 287–309.

CHOMSKY, N. *Syntactic structures.* The Hague: Mouton, 1957.

CHOMSKY, N. Review of *Verbal behavior* by B. F. Skinner. *Language, 1959, 35,* 26–58.

CHOMSKY, N. *Aspects of the theory of syntax.* Cambridge, Mass.: M.I.T. Press, 1965.

CHOMSKY, N. *Reflections on language.* New York: Pantheon, 1975.

CHOMSKY, N., & HALLE, M. *The sound pattern of English.* New York: Harper & Row, Pub., 1968.

CLARK, E. V. First language acquisition. In J. Morton & J. C. Marshall (Eds.), *Psycholinguistics: Developmental and pathological.* Ithaca, N.Y.: Cornell University Press, 1977.

CLARK, H. H. Some structural properties of simple active and passive sentences. *Journal of Verbal Learning and Verbal Behavior, 1965, 4,* 365–370.

CLARK, H. H. Linguistic processes in deductive reasoning. *Psychological Review, 1969, 76,* 387–404.

CLARK, H. H. On the evidence concerning J. Huttenlocher and E. T. Higgins' theory of reasoning: A second reply. *Psychological Review, 1972, 79,* 428–431.

CLARK, H. H. *Semantics and comprehension.* The Hague: Mouton, 1976.

CLARK, J. M. *Synonymity and concreteness effects on free recall and free association: Implications for a theory of semantic memory.* Unpublished doctoral dissertation, University of Western Ontario, 1978.

CLÉMENT, R. *Motivational characteristics of francophones learning English.* Quebec: International Center for Research on Bilingualism, Laval University, 1977.

COFER, C. N. Conditions for the use of verbal associations. *Psychological Bulletin, 1967, 68,* 1–12.

COHEN, A. D. The Culver City Spanish immersion project: The first two years. *Modern Language Journal,* 1974, *58,* 95–103.

COHEN, G. Hemispheric differences in the effects of cueing. *Journal of Experimental Psychology: Human Perception and Performance,* 1975, *1,* 366–373.

COLEMAN, E. B. Learning of prose written in four grammatical transformations. *Journal of Applied Psychology,* 1965, *49,* 332–341. (a)

COLEMAN, E. B. Responses to a scale of grammaticalness. *Journal of Verbal Learning and Verbal Behavior,* 1965, *4,* 521–527. (b)

COLLINS, A. M., & LOFTUS, E. F. A spreading-activation theory of semantic processing. *Psychological Review,* 1975, *82,* 407–428.

COLLINS, A. M., & QUILLIAN, M. R. Retrieval time from semantic memory. *Journal of Verbal Learning and Verbal Behavior,* 1969, *8,* 240–247.

CONLIN, D., & PAIVIO, A. The associative learning of the deaf: The effects of word imagery and signability. *Memory and Cognition,* 1975, *3,* 335–340.

COOK, V. J. The comparison of language development in native children and foreign adults. *International Review of Applied Linguistics in Language Teaching,* 1973, *11,* 13–28.

COOK, V. J. Cognitive processes in second language learning. *International Review of Applied Linguistics in Language Teaching,* 1977, *15,* 1–20.

CRAIG, J. C. Vibrotactile letter recognition: The effects of a masking stimulus. *Perception and Psychophysics,* 1976, *20,* 317–326.

CRAIG, J. C. Vibrotactile letter perception: Extraordinary observers. *Science,* 1977, *196,* 450–452.

CRAIK, F. I. M., & LOCKHART, R. S. Levels of processing: A framework for memory research. *Journal of Verbal Learning and Verbal Behavior,* 1972, *11,* 671–684.

CUMMINS, J. The cognitive development of children in immersion programs. *Canadian Modern Language Review,* 1978, *34,* 855–883.

CUTTING, J. E., & EIMAS, P. D. Phonetic feature analyzers and the processing of speech in English. In J. F. Kavanagh & J. E. Cutting (Eds.), *The role of speech in language.* Cambridge, Mass.: M.I.T. Press, 1975.

CUTTING, J. E., & ROSNER, B. S. Categories and boundaries in speech and music. *Perception and Psychophysics,* 1974, *16,* 564–570.

DALE, E., & CHALL, J. S. A formula for predicting readability. *Educational Research Bulletin,* Ohio State University, 1948, *27,* 11–20; 37–54.

DALE, P. S. *Language development: Structure and function* (2nd ed.). New York: Holt, Rinehart & Winston, 1976.

DALRYMPLE-ALFORD, E. C. Interlingual interference in a color naming task. *Psychonomic Science,* 1968, *10,* 215–216.

DALRYMPLE-ALFORD, E. C., & AAMIRY, A. Speed of responding to mixed language signals. *Psychonomic Science,* 1967, *9,* 535–536.

D'ANGLEJAN, A. Language learning in and out of classrooms. In J. Richards (Ed.), *Understanding second and foreign language learning.* Rowley, Mass.: Newbury House, 1978.

D'ANGLEJAN, A., & TUCKER, G. R. Acquisition of complex English structures by adult learners. *Language Learning,* 1975, *25,* 281–296.

DANKS, J. H. Grammaticalness and meaningfulness in the comprehension of sentences. *Journal of Verbal Learning and Verbal Behavior,* 1969, *8,* 687–696.

DANKS, J. H. Producing ideas and sentences. In S. Rosenberg (Ed.), *Sentence production: Development in research and theory.* Hillsdale, N.J.: Erlbaum, 1977.

DANKS, J. H., & GLUCKSBERG, S. Psychological scaling of adjective orders. *Journal of Verbal Learning and Verbal Behavior,* 1971, *10,* 63–67.

DANKS, J. H., & SORCE, P. A. Imagery and deep structure in the prompted recall of passive sentences. *Journal of Verbal Learning and Verbal Behavior,* 1973, *12,* 114–117.

DASHIELL, J. F. Affective value distances as a determinant of esthetic judgment times. *American Journal of Psychology,* 1937, *50,* 57–67.

DAY, J. Right-hemisphere language processing in normal right-handers. *Journal of Experimental Psychology: Human Perception and Performance,* 1977, *3,* 518–528.

DEESE, J. From the isolated verbal unit to connected discourse. In C. N. Cofer (Ed.), *Verbal learning and verbal behavior.* New York: McGraw-Hill, 1961.

DEESE, J. On the structure of associative meaning. *Psychological Review,* 1962, *69,* 161–175.

DEESE, J. *The structure of associations in language and thought.* Baltimore: Johns Hopkins Press, 1965.

DeSOTO, C., LONDON, M., & HANDEL, S. Social reasoning and spatial paralogic. *Journal of Personality and Social Psychology,* 1965, *2,* 513–521.

DESROCHERS, A. *Effects of an imagery mnemonic on the acquisition and retention of French article-noun pairs.* Unpublished doctoral dissertation, University of Western Ontario, 1980.

DE VILLIERS, J. G., & DE VILLIERS, P. A. Development of the use of word order in comprehension. *Journal of Psycholinguistic Research,* 1973, *2,* 331–341.

DILLER, K. C. "Compound" and "coordinate" bilingualism: A conceptual artifact. *Word,* 1970, *26,* 254–261.

DINNEEN, F. P. *An introduction to general linguistics.* New York: Holt, Rinehart & Winston, 1967.

DiVESTA, F. J. *Language, learning, and cognitive processes.* Monterey, Calif.: Brooks/Cole, 1974.

DiVESTA, F. J., & WALLS, R. T. Factor analysis of the semantic attributes of 487 words and some relationships to the conceptual behavior of fifth-grade children. *Journal of Educational Psychology Monograph,* 1970, *61*(6, Pt. 2).

DIXON, P. W., & OAKES, W. T. Effect of intertrial activity on the relationship between awareness and verbal operant conditioning. *Journal of Experimental Psychology,* 1965, *69,* 152–157.

DORNIC, S. *Information processing and bilingualism* (Tech. Rep. 510). Stockholm: University of Stockholm, Department of Psychology, 1977.

DUNCAN, S., Jr., & FISKE, D. W. *Face to face interaction: Research, methods and theory.* Hillsdale, N. J.: Erlbaum, 1977.

DUNNE, M. M. The effect of syntactic structure on learning. *Journal of Verbal Learning and Verbal Behavior,* 1968, *7,* 458–463.

DURNFORD, M., & KIMURA, D. Right hemisphere specialization for depth perception reflected in visual field differences. *Nature,* 1971, *231,* 394–395.

EBBINGHAUS, H. *Memory: a contribution to experimental psychology.* Ruger and Bussenius, trans. New York: Dover, 1964. (Originally published, 1885.)

EDWARDS, D. Sensory-motor intelligence and semantic relations in early child grammar. *Cognition,* 1973, *2,* 395–434.

EIMAS, P. D., SIQUELAND, E. R., JUSCZYK, P., & VIGORITO, J. Speech perception in infants. *Science,* 1971, *171,* 303–306.

ELLIS, H. D., & SHEPERD, J. W. Recognition of abstract and concrete words presented in left and right visual fields. *Journal of Experimental Psychology,* 1974, *103,* 1035–1036.

EPSTEIN, W. The influence of syntactic structure on learning. *American Journal of Psychology* 1961, *74,* 80–85.

EPSTEIN, W. A further study of the influence of syntactical structure on learning. *American Journal of Psychology,* 1962, *75,* 121–126.

EPSTEIN, W., ROCK, I., & ZUCKERMAN, C. B. Meaning and familiarity in associative learning. *Psychological Monographs,* 1960, *74* (4, Whole No. 491).

ERDELYI, M. H. A new look at the new look: Perceptual defense and vigilance. *Psychological Review,* 1974, *81,* 1–25.

ERIKSEN, C. W. Unconscious processes. In M. R. Jones (Ed.), *Nebraska Symposium on Motivation.* Lincoln: University of Nebraska Press, 1958.

ERNEST, C. H. Imagery ability and cognition: A critical review. *Journal of Mental Imagery,* 1977, *1,* 181–216.

ERVIN, S. M. Changes with age in the verbal determinants of word-association. *American Journal of Psychology*, 1961, *74*, 361-372.

ERVIN-TRIPP, S. M. Structure and process in language acquisition. *Monograph Series on Languages and Linguistics*, 1970, *23*, 313-344.

ERVIN-TRIPP, S. M. Is second language learning like the first? *TESOL Quarterly*, 1974, *8*, 111-127.

ESPER, E. A. *Mentalism and objectivism in linguistics*. New York: American Elsevier, 1968.

ESPY, W. R. *The game of words*. New York: Bramhall House, 1971.

FELDMAR, A. *Syntactic structure and speech decoding: The judgment of sequence in auditory events*. Unpublished master's thesis, University of Western Ontario, 1969.

FERNALD, C. D. Control of grammar in imitation, comprehension, and production. *Journal of Verbal Learning and Verbal Behavior*, 1972, *11*, 606-613.

FILLENBAUM, S., & RAPOPORT, A. *Structures in the subjective lexicon*. New York: Academic Press, 1971.

FILLMORE, C. J. The case for case. In E. Bach & R. T. Harms (Eds.), *Universals in linguistic theory*. New York: Holt, Rinehart & Winston, 1968.

FILLMORE, C. J. Types of lexical information. In D. D. Steinberg & L. A. Jakobovitz (Eds.), *Semantics: An interdisciplinary reader in philosophy, linguistics, and psychology*. Cambridge: Cambridge University Press, 1971.

FISHMAN, J. A. A systematization of the Whorfian hypothesis. *Behavioral Science*, 1960, *5*, 323-339.

FISHMAN, J. A., & COOPER, R. L. Alternative measures of bilingualism. *Journal of Verbal Learning and Verbal Behavior*, 1969, *2*, 276-282.

FLAGG, P. W., & REYNOLDS, A. G. Modality of presentation and blocking in sentence recognition memory. *Memory and Cognition*, 1977, *5*, 111-115.

FLESCH, R. F. A new readability yardstick. *Journal of Applied Psychology*, 1948, *32*, 221-232.

FLESCH, R. F. *The art of readable writing*. New York: Harper, 1949.

FODOR, J. A. Could meaning be an r_m? *Journal of Verbal Learning and Verbal Behavior*, 1965, *4*, 73-81.

FODOR, J. A. Tom Swift and his procedural grandmother. *Cognition*, 1978, *6*, 229-247.

FODOR, J. A. In reply to Philip Johnson-Laird. *Cognition*, 1979, *7*, 93-95.

FODOR, J. A., & BEVER, T. G. The psychological reality of linguistic segments. *Journal of Verbal Learning and Verbal Behavior*, 1965, *4*, 414-420.

FORSTER, K. I. Visual perception of rapidly presented word sequences of varying complexity. *Perception and Psychophysics*, 1970, *8*, 215-221.

FORSTER, K. I., & RYDER, L. A. Perceiving the structure and meaning of sentences. *Journal of Verbal Learning and Verbal Behavior*, 1971, *10*, 285-296.

FOSS, D. J. Some effects of ambiguity upon sentence comprehension. *Journal of Verbal Learning and Verbal Behavior*, 1970, *9*, 699-706.

FOSS, D. J., & HAKES, D. T. *Psycholinguistics*. Englewood Cliffs, N.J.: Prentice-Hall, 1978.

FOSS, D. J. & HARWOOD, D. Memory for sentences: Implications for human associative memory. *Journal of Verbal Learning and Verbal Behavior*, 1975, *14*, 1-16.

FOSS, D. J., & LYNCH, R. H., Jr. Decision processes during sentence comprehension: Effects of surface structure on decision times. *Perception and Psychophysics*, 1969, *5*, 145-148.

FOTH, D. L. Mnemonic technique effectiveness as a function of word abstractness and mediation instructions. *Journal of Verbal Learning and Verbal Behavior*, 1973, *12*, 239-245.

FRAISSE, P. Latency of different verbal responses to the same stimulus. *The Quarterly Journal of Experimental Psychology*, 1967, *19*, 353-355.

FRAISSE, P. Motor and verbal reaction times to words and drawings. *Psychonomic Science*, 1968, *12*, 235-236.

FRANKS, J. J., & BRANSFORD, J. D. The acquisition of abstract ideas. *Journal of Verbal Learning and Verbal Behavior,* 1972, *11,* 311–315.

FRASER, C., BELLUGI, U., & BROWN, R. W. Control of grammar in imitation, comprehension and production. *Journal of Verbal Learning and Verbal Behavior,* 1963, *2,* 121–135.

FREDERIKSEN, J. R., & KROLL, J. F. Spelling and sound: Approaches to the internal lexicon. *Journal of Experimental Psychology: Human Perception and Performance,* 1976, *2,* 361–379.

FRINCKE, G. Word characteristics, associative-relatedness, and the free-recall of nouns. *Journal of Verbal Learning and Verbal Behavior,* 1968, *7,* 366–372.

FROMKIN, V. A. The non-anomalous nature of anomalous utterances. *Language,* 1971, *47,* 27–52.

FROMKIN, V. A. *Speech errors as linguistic evidence.* The Hague: Mouton, 1973.

FURTH, H. G. *Thinking without language: Psychological implications of deafness.* Glencoe, Ill.: Free Press, 1966.

GALTON, F. *Inquiries into human faculty and its development* (2nd ed.). London: J. M. Dent & Sons, 1907. (Originally published, 1883.)

GARDNER, R. C., & GARDNER, B. T. Teaching sign language to a chimpanzee. *Science,* 1969, *165,* 664–672.

GARDNER, R. C., & LAMBERT, W. E. Motivational variables in second-language learning. *Canadian Journal of Psychology,* 1959, *13,* 266–272.

GARDNER, R. C., & LAMBERT, W. E. *Attitudes and motivation in second-language learning.* Rowley, Mass.: Newbury House, 1972.

GARRETT, M. F. The analysis of sentence production. In G. H. Bower (Ed.), *Psychology of learning and motivation* (Vol. 9). New York: Academic Press, 1975.

GARRETT, M. F. Syntactic processes in sentence production. In R. J. Wales & E. Walker (Eds.), *New approaches to language mechanisms.* Amsterdam: North Holland, 1976.

GARSKOF, B. E., & HOUSTON, J. P. Measurement of verbal relatedness: An idiographic approach. *Psychological Review,* 1963, *70,* 277–288.

GAZZANIGA, M. S. *The bisected brain.* New York: Appleton-Century-Crofts, 1970.

GELB, I. J. *A study of writing.* Chicago: University of Chicago Press, 1952.

GEORGE, H. V. *Common errors in language learning: Insights from English.* Rowley, Mass.: Newbury House, 1972.

GESCHWIND, N. Disconnexion syndrome in animals and man. *Brain,* 1965, *88,* 237–294; 585–644.

GESCHWIND, N., & FUSILLO, M. Color-naming defects in association with alexia. *Archives of Neurology,* 1966, *15,* 137–146.

GEVINS, A. S., ZEITLIN, G. M., DOYLE, J. C., YINGLING, C. D., SCHAFFER, R. E., CALLAWAY, E., & YAEGER, C. L. Electroencephalogram correlates of higher cortical functions. *Science,* 1979, *203,* 665–668.

GHENT-BRAINE, L. Asymmetries of pattern perception observed in Israelis. *Neuropsychologia,* 1968, *6,* 73–88.

GIBSON, E. J. *Principles of perceptual learning and development.* New York: Appleton-Century-Crofts, 1969.

GIBSON, E. J., BISHOP, C. H., SCHIFF, W., & SMITH, J. Comparison of meaningfulness and pronunciability as grouping principles in the perception and retention of verbal material. *Journal of Experimental Psychology,* 1964, *67,* 173–182.

GIBSON, E. J., & LEVIN, H. *The psychology of reading.* Cambridge, Mass.: M.I.T. Press, 1975.

GILBERT, L. Speed of processing visual stimuli and its relation to reading. *Journal of Educational Psychology,* 1959, *55,* 8–14.

GLANZER, M., & CLARK, W. H. The verbal loop hypothesis: Binary numbers. *Journal of Verbal Learning and Verbal Behavior,* 1963, *2,* 301–309.

GLAZE, J. A. The association value of nonsense syllables. *Journal of Genetic Psychology*, 1928, *35*, 255-267.

GLUCKSBERG, S., & DANKS, J. H. Grammatical structure and recall: A function of the space in immediate memory or of recall delay? *Perception and Psychophysics*, 1969, *6*, 113-117.

GLUCKSBERG, S., TRABASSO, T., & WALD, J. Linguistic structures and mental operations. *Cognitive Psychology*, 1973, *5*, 338-370.

GLUSHKO, R. J., & COOPER, L. A. Spatial comprehension and comparison processes in verification tasks. *Cognitive Psychology*, 1978, *10*, 391-421.

GOLDIAMOND, I., & HAWKINS, W. F. Vixierversuch: The log relationship between word-frequency and recognition obtained in the absence of stimulus words. *Journal of Experimental Psychology*, 1958, *56*, 457-463.

GOLDMAN-EISLER, F. Speech production and the predictability of words in context. *Quarterly Journal of Experimental Psychology*, 1958, *10*, 96-106.

GOLDMAN-EISLER, F. Hesitation and information in speech. In C. Cherry (Ed.), *Information theory*. London: Butterworths, 1961.

GOODGLASS, H. Studies on the grammar of aphasics. In S. Rosenberg & J. Koplin (Eds.), *Developments in applied psycholinguistic research*. New York: Macmillan, 1968.

GOODGLASS, H., & BAKER, E. Semantic field, naming, and auditory comprehension in aphasia. *Brain and Language*, 1976, *3*, 359-374.

GOODGLASS, H., KLEIN, B., CAREY, P., & JONES, K. J. Specific semantic word categories in aphasia. *Cortex*, 1966, *2*, 74-89.

GOUGH, P. B. Grammatical transformations and speed of understanding. *Journal of Verbal Learning and Verbal Behavior*, 1965, *4*, 107-111.

GOUGH, P. B. The verification of sentences: The effects of delay of evidence and sentence length. *Journal of Verbal Learning and Verbal Behavior*, 1966, *5*, 492-496.

GOULD, J. L. Honey bee recruitment: The dance-language controversy. *Science*, 1975, *189*, 685-693.

GREENSPOON, J. The reinforcing effect of two spoken sounds on the frequency of two responses. *American Journal of Psychology*, 1955, *68*, 409-416.

GUESS, D., SAILOR, W., RUTHERFORD, G., & BAER, D. M. An experimental analysis of linguistic development: The productive use of the plural morpheme. *Journal of Applied Behavior Analysis*, 1968, *1*, 297-306.

GUILFORD, J. P. *The nature of human intelligence*. New York: McGraw-Hill, 1967.

HABER, R. N. Nature of the effect of set on perception. *Psychological Review*, 1966, *73*, 335-351.

HALLIDAY, M. A. K. *Explorations in the functions of language*. London: Edward Arnold, 1973.

HAMERS, J. F., & LAMBERT, W. E. Bilingual interdependencies in auditory perception. *Journal of Verbal Learning and Verbal Behavior*, 1972, *11*, 303-310.

HARDYCK, C. D., & PETRINOVICH, L. F. Subvocal speech and comprehension level as a function of the difficulty level of reading material. *Journal of Verbal Learning and Verbal Behavior*, 1970, *9*, 647-652.

HARDYCK, C. D., PETRINOVICH, L. F., & ELLSWORTH, D. W. Feedback of speech muscle activity during silent reading: Rapid extinction. *Science*, 1966, *154*, 1467-1468.

HARE, R. D. Cognitive factors in transfer of meaning. *Psychological Reports*, 1964, *15*, 199-206.

HARRIS, C. S., & HABER, R. N. Selective attention and coding in visual perception. *Journal of Experimental Psychology*, 1963, *65*, 328-333.

HARRIS, J., & MONACO, G. E. Psychology of pragmatic implications: Information processing between the lines. *Journal of Experimental Psychology: General*, 1978, *107*, 1-22.

HARWOOD, D. L., & VERBRUGGE, R. R. *Metaphor and the asymmetry of similarity*. Paper

presented at the meeting of the American Psychological Association, San Francisco, 1977.

HAWKINS, H. L., REICHER, G. M., ROGERS, M., & PETERSON, L. Flexible coding in word recognition. *Journal of Experimental Psychology: Human Perception and Performance,* 1976, *2,* 380–385.

HAYES-ROTH, B., & HAYES-ROTH, F. The prominence of lexical information in memory representations of meaning. *Journal of Verbal Learning and Verbal Behavior,* 1977, *16,* 119–136.

HEALY, A. F., & LEVITT, A. G. The relative accessibility of semantic and deep-structure syntactic concepts. *Memory and Cognition,* 1978, *6,* 518–526.

HEBB, D. O. *The organization of behavior.* New York: John Wiley, 1949.

HEBB, D. O., LAMBERT, W. E., & TUCKER, G. R. Language, thought and experience. *Modern Language Journal,* 1971, *55,* 212–222.

HEBB, D. O., & THOMPSON, W. R. The social significance of animal studies. In G. Lindzey (Ed.), *Handbook of social psychology* (Vol. 1). Cambridge, Mass.: Addison-Wesley, 1954.

HERSHBERGER, W. A., & TERRY, D. F. Typographical cuing in conventional and programmed texts. *Journal of Applied Psychology,* 1965, *49,* 55–60.

HINES, D. Differences in tachistoscopic recognition between abstract and concrete words as a function of visual half-field and frequency. *Cortex,* 1977, *13,* 66–73.

HJELMSLEV, L. [*Prolegomena to a theory of language*]. (F.J. Whitfield, trans.). Madison: University of Wisconsin Press, 1961.

HOCKETT, C. F. The problem of universals in language. In J. H. Greenberg (Ed.), *Universals of language.* Cambridge, Mass.: M.I.T. Press, 1963.

HOLYOAK, K. J., GLASS, A. L., & MAH, W. A. Morphological structure and semantic retrieval. *Journal of Verbal Learning and Verbal Behavior,* 1976, *15,* 235–247.

HOLYOAK, K. J., & WALKER, J. H. Subjective magnitude information in semantic orderings. *Journal of Verbal Learning and Verbal Behavior,* 1976, *15,* 287–299.

HOLZ, W. C., & AZRIN, N. H. Conditioning human verbal behavior. In W. K. Honig (Ed.), *Operant behavior: Areas of research and application.* Englewood Cliffs, N. J.: Prentice-Hall, 1966.

HONECK, R. P., RIECHMANN, P., & HOFFMAN, R. R. Semantic memory for metaphor: The conceptual base hypothesis. *Memory and Cognition,* 1975, *3,* 409–415.

HOWES, D. On the relation between the intelligibility and frequency of occurrence of English words. *Journal of the Acoustical Society of America,* 1957, *29,* 296–305.

HOWES, D. H. Some experimental investigations of language in aphasia. In K. Salzinger & S. Salzinger (Eds.), *Research in verbal behavior and some neuro-psychological implications.* New York: Academic Press, 1967.

HUEY, E. B. *The psychology and pedagogy of reading.* Cambridge, Mass.: M.I.T. Press, 1968. (Originally published, 1908.)

HULL, C. L. The meaningfulness of 320 selected nonsense syllables. *American Journal of Psychology,* 1933, *45,* 730–734.

HULL, C. L. *Principles of behavior.* New York: Appleton-Century-Crofts, 1943.

HUNT, E. Mechanics of verbal ability. *Psychological Review,* 1978, *85,* 109–130.

HUTTENLOCHER, J. Constructing spatial images: A strategy in reasoning. *Psychological Review,* 1968, *75,* 550-560.

HUTTENLOCHER, J., & HIGGINS, E. T. On reasoning, congruence, and other matters. *Psychological Review,* 1972, *79,* 420–427.

JACKSON, M. D., & McCLELLAND, J. L. Processing determinants of reading speed. *Journal of Experimental Psychology: General,* 1979, *108,* 151–181.

JACOBSON, J. Z. Effects of association upon masking and reading latency. *Canadian Journal of Psychology,* 1973, *27,* 58–69.

JAKOBSON, R., FANT, G. M., & HALLE, M. *Preliminaries to speech analysis.* Cambridge, Mass.: M.I.T. Press, 1951.

JAMES, C. T. Theme and imagery in the recall of active and passive sentences. *Journal of Verbal Learning and Verbal Behavior,* 1972, *11,* 451–454.

JAMES, C. T., THOMPSON, J. G., & BALDWIN, J. M. The reconstructive process in sentence memory. *Journal of Verbal Learning and Verbal Behavior,* 1973, *12,* 51–63.

JENKINS, J. J. Mediation theory and grammatical behavior. In S. Rosenberg (Ed.), *Directions in psycholinguistics.* New York: Macmillan, 1965.

JENKINS, J. J., & PALERMO, D. S. Mediation processes and the acquisition of linguistic structures. In U. Bellugi & R. W. Brown (Eds.), *The acquisition of language. Monographs of the Society for Research in Child Development,* 1964, *29*(1), 141–169.

JENKINS, J. J., & RUSSELL, W. A. Associative clustering during recall. *Journal of Abnormal and Social Psychology,* 1952, *47,* 818–821.

JOHNSON, M. G. A cognitive-feature model of compound free associations. *Psychological Review,* 1970, *77,* 282–293.

JOHNSON, M. G. *The abstraction of meaning from complex pictures.* Paper presented at the meeting of the Psychonomic Society, Washington, D.C., 1977.

JOHNSON, M. K., BRANSFORD, J. D., NYBERG, S. F., & CLEARY, J. J. Comprehension factors in interpreting memory for abstract and concrete sentences. *Journal of Verbal Learning and Verbal Behavior,* 1972, *11,* 451–454.

JOHNSON, N. F. The psychological reality of phrase-structure rules. *Journal of Verbal Learning and Verbal Behavior,* 1965, *4,* 469–475.

JOHNSON, N. F. Sequential verbal behavior. In T. R. Dixon & D. L. Horton (Eds.), *Verbal behavior and general behavior theory.* Englewood-Cliffs, N.J.: Prentice-Hall, 1968.

JOHNSON, R. C. Latency and association value as predictors of rate of verbal learning. *Journal of Verbal Learning and Verbal Behavior,* 1964, *3,* 77–78.

JOHNSON, R. C., THOMSON, C. W., & FRINCKE, G. Word values, word frequency, and visual duration thresholds. *Psychological Review,* 1960, *67,* 332–342.

JOHNSON-LAIRD, P. N. The three-term series problems. *Cognition,* 1972, *1,* 57–82.

JOHNSON-LAIRD, P. N. Procedural semantics. *Cognition,* 1977, *5,* 189–214.

JOHNSON-LAIRD, P. N. What's wrong with Grandma's guide to procedural semantics: A reply to Jerry Fodor. *Cognition,* 1978, *6,* 249–261.

JONES, M. K. Imagery as a mnemonic aid after left temporal lobectomy: Contrast between material-specific and generalized memory disorders. *Neuropsychologia,* 1974, *12,* 21–30.

JONES-GOTMAN, M. Incidental learning of image-mediated or pronounced words after right temporal lobectomy. *Cortex,* 1979, *15,* 187–197.

JONES-GOTMAN, M., & MILNER, B. Right temporal lobe contribution to image-mediated memory. *Neuropsychologia,* 1978, *16,* 61–71.

JUST, M. A., & CARPENTER, P. A. A theory of reading: From eye fixations to comprehension. *Psychological Review,* 1980, *87,* 329–354.

KATZ, A. N. Differences in the saliency of sensory features elicited by words. *Canadian Journal of Psychology,* 1978, *32,* 156–179.

KATZ, A. N., & PAIVIO, A. Imagery variables in concept indentification. *Journal of Verbal Learning and Verbal Behavior,* 1975, *14,* 284–293.

KATZ, J. J. Mentalism in linguistics. *Language,* 1964, *40,* 124–137.

KATZ, J. J., & FODOR, J. A. The structure of a semantic theory. *Language,* 1963, *39,* 170–210.

KATZ, J. J., & POSTAL, P. M. *An integrated theory of linguistic description.* Cambridge, Mass.: M.I.T. Press, 1964.

KELLOGG, G. S., & HOWE, M. J. A. Using words and pictures in foreign language learning. *Alberta Journal of Educational Research,* 1971, *17,* 89–94.

KELLY, L. G. *Twenty-five centuries of language teaching.* Rowley, Mass.: Newbury House, 1969.

KELLY, R. P., & ORTON, K. D. Dichotic perception of word-pairs with mixed image values. *Neuropsychologia,* 1979, *17,* 363–371.

KENNEDY, J. M. *Pictorial metaphor: A theory of movement indicators in static pictures.*

Paper presented at the Information through Pictures Symposium, Swarthmore College, Swarthmore, Pa., 1976.

KENT, G. H., & ROSANOFF, K. A study of association in insanity. *American Journal of Insanity*, 1910, *67*, 37-96; 317-390.

KERST, S. M., & HOWARD, J. H., Jr. Mental comparisons for ordered information on abstract and concrete dimensions. *Memory and Cognition*, 1977, *5*, 227-234.

KESS, J. F., & HOPPE, R. A. On psycholinguistic experiments in ambiguity. *Lingua*, 1978, *45*, 125-140.

KESS, J. F., & HOPPE, R. A. Directions in ambiguity theory and research. In G. Prudeaux (Ed.), *Perspectives in experimental linguistics*. Amsterdam: John Benjamins, 1979.

KIMURA, D. Cerebral dominance and the perception of verbal stimuli. *Canadian Journal of Psychology*, 1961, *15*, 166-171.

KIMURA, D. Left-right differences in the perception of melodies. *Quarterly Journal of Experimental Psychology*, 1964, *16*, 355-358.

KIMURA, D. Functional asymmetry of the brain in dichotic listening. *Cortex*, 1967, *3*, 163-178.

KIMURA, D. The asymmetry of the human brain. *Scientific American*, 1973, *228*, 70-78.

KIMURA, D. Neuromotor mechanisms in the evolution of human communication. In H. D. Steklis & M. J. Raleigh (Eds.), *Neurobiology of social communication in primates: An evolutionary perspective*. New York: Academic Press, in press.

KING, F. L., & KIMURA, D. Left-ear superiority in dichotic perception of vocal nonverbal sounds. *Canadian Journal of Psychology*, 1972, *26*, 111-116.

KINSBOURNE, M. The cerebral basis of lateral asymmetries in attention. *Acta Psychologica*, 1970, *33*, 193-201.

KINTSCH, W. Notes on the structure of semantic memory. In E. Tulving & W. Donaldson (Eds.), *Organization of memory*. New York: Academic Press, 1972.

KINTSCH, W. *The representation of meaning in memory*. New York: John Wiley, 1974.

KINTSCH, W., & VAN DIJK, T. Toward a model of text comprehension and production. *Psychological Review*, 1978, *85*, 363-394.

KISS, G. R. Grammatical word classes: A learning process and its simulation. In G. H. Bower (Ed.), *The psychology of learning and motivation* (Vol. 7). New York: Academic Press, 1973.

KISS, G. R. An associative thesaurus of English: Structural analysis of a large relevance network. In A. Kennedy & A. Wilkes (Eds.), *Studies in long-term memory*. New York: John Wiley, 1975.

KLEE, H., & EYSENCK, M. W. Comprehension of abstract and concrete sentences. *Journal of Verbal Learning and Verbal Behavior*, 1973, *12*, 522-529.

KLIMA, E., & BELLUGI, U. *The signs of language*. Cambridge, Mass.: Harvard University Press, 1979.

KOEN, F. An intra-verbal explication of the nature of metaphor. *Journal of Verbal Learning and Verbal Behavior*, 1965, *4*, 129-133.

KOLERS, P. A. Interlingual word associations. *Journal of Verbal Learning and Verbal Behavior*. 1963, *2*, 291-300.

KOLERS, P. A. Bilingualism and bicodalism. *Language and Speech*, 1965, *8*, 122-126.

KOLERS, P. A. Interlingual faciliation of short-term memory. *Journal of Verbal Learning and Verbal Behavior*, 1966, *5*, 314-319. (a)

KOLERS, P. A. Reading and talking bilingually. *American Journal of Psychology*, 1966, *79*, 357-376. (b)

KOLERS, P. A. Three stages of reading. In H. Levin & J. P. Williams (Eds.), *Basic studies in reading*. New York: Basic Books, 1970.

KONEČNI, V. J., & SLAMECKA, N. J. Awareness in verbal nonoperant conditioning: An approach through dichotic listening. *Journal of Experimental Psychology*, 1972, *94*, 248-254.

KRUEGER, W. C. F. The relative difficulty of nonsense syllables. *Journal of Experimental Psychology,* 1934, *17,* 145–153.

KUIPER, N. A., & PAIVIO, A. Incidental recognition memory for concrete and abstract sentences equated for comprehensibility. *Bulletin of the Psychonomic Society,* 1977, *9,* 247–249.

KUSYSZYN, I., & PAIVIO, A. Transition probability, word order, and noun abstractness in the learning of adjective-noun paired associates. *Journal of Experimental Psychology,* 1966, *71,* 800–805.

KUUSINEN, J., & SALIN, E. Children's learning of unfamiliar phonological sequences. *Perceptual and Motor Skills,* 1971, *33,* 559–562.

LACHMAN, R., & DOOLING, D. J. Connected discourse and random strings: Effects of number of inputs on recognition and recall. *Journal of Experimental Psychology,* 1968, *77,* 517–522.

LAFFAL, J. Response faults in word association as a function of response entropy. *Journal of Abnormal and Social Psychology,* 1955, *50,* 265–270.

LAFFAL, J. *Pathological and normal language.* New York: Atherton Press, 1965.

LAKOFF, R. On generative semantics. In D. D. Steinberg & L. A. Jacobovits (Eds.), *Semantics.* Cambridge, U. K.: Cambridge University Press, 1971.

LAMB, S. M. *Outline of stratificational grammar.* Washington, D.C.: Georgetown University Press, 1966.

LAMBERT, W. E. Measurement of the linguistic dominance of bilinguals. *Journal of Abnormal and Social Psychology,* 1955, *50,* 197–200.

LAMBERT, W. E. Psychological studies of the interdependencies of the bilingual's two languages. In J. Puhvel (Ed.), *Substance and structure of language.* Berkeley and Los Angeles: University of California Press, 1969.

LAMBERT, W. E. The language laboratory: Other alternatives? In L. J. Chatagnier & G. Taggart (Eds.), *Language laboratory learning: New directions,* Montreal: Aquila, 1971.

LAMBERT, W. E. The effects of bilingualism on the individual: Cognitive and sociocultural consequences. In P. Hornby (Ed.), *Bilingualism: Psychological, social and educational implications.* New York: Academic Press, 1977.

LAMBERT, W. E., HAVELKA, J. & CROSBY, C. The influence of language acquisition contexts on bilingualism. *Journal of Abnormal and Social Psychology,* 1958, *56,* 239–244.

LAMBERT, W. E., HAVELKA, J. & GARDNER, R. C. Linguistic manifestations of bilingualism. *Journal of Personality,* 1959, *72,* 77–82.

LAMBERT, W. E., IGNATOW, M., & KRAUTHAMER, M. Bilingual organization in free recall. *Journal of Verbal Learning and Verbal Behavior,* 1968, *7,* 207–214.

LAMBERT, W. E., & MOORE, N. Word association responses: Comparison of American and French monolinguals with Canadian monolinguals and bilinguals. *Journal of Personality and Social Psychology,* 1966, *3,* 313–320.

LAMBERT, W. E., & PAIVIO, A. The influence of noun-adjective order on learning. *Canadian Journal of Psychology,* 1956, *10,* 9–12.

LAMBERT, W. E., & TUCKER, G. R. *Bilingual education of children: The St. Lambert experiment.* Rowley, Mass.: Newbury House, 1972.

LANDAUER, T. K., & STREETER, L. A. Structural differences between common and rare words: Failure of equivalence assumptions for theories of word recognition. *Journal of Verbal Learning and Verbal Behavior,* 1973, *12,* 119–131.

LANGER, S. K. *Philosophy in a new key.* New York: NAL, Mentor Books, 1948. (Originally published, 1942.)

LANTZ, D. L., & STEFFLRE, V. Language and cognition revisited. *Journal of Abnormal and Social Psychology,* 1964, *69,* 472–481.

LASSEN, N. A., INGVAR, D. H., & SKINHOJ, E. Brain function and blood flow. *Scientific American,* 1978, *239*(4), 62–71.

LAVINE, L. O. *The development of perception of writing in pre-reading children: A cross-cultural study.* Unpublished doctoral dissertation, Cornell University, 1972.

LAY, C. H., & PAIVIO, A. The effects of task difficulty and anxiety on hesitations in speech. *Canadian Journal of Behavioural Science.* 1969, *1,* 25–37.

LAZARUS, R., & McCLEARY, R. Autonomic discrimination without awareness: An experiment on subception. *Psychological Review,* 1951, *58,* 113–122.

LENNEBERG, E. H. *Biological foundations of language.* New York: John Wiley, 1967.

LENNEBERG, E. H., & ROBERTS, J. M. *The language of experience.* Bloomington: Indiana University Press, 1956.

LEVELT, W. J. M. *Formal grammars in linguistics and psycholinguistics: Psycholinguistic applications* (Vol. 3). The Hague: Mouton, 1974.

LEVELT, W. J. M., VAN GENT, J. A. W. M., HAANS, A. F. J., & MEIJERS, A. J. A. Grammaticality, paraphrase and imagery. In S. Greenbaum (Ed.), *Acceptability in language.* The Hague: Mouton, 1977.

LEVIN, H., & KAPLAN, E. L. Eye-voice span (EVS) within active and passive sentences. *Language and Speech,* 1968, *11,* 251–258.

LEVY, J. Information processing and higher psychological functions in the disconnected hemispheres of human commissurotomy patients (Doctoral dissertation, California Institute of Technology, 1970). *Dissertation Abstracts International,* 1970, *31B,* 1542. (University Microfilms No. 70–14, 844.)

LEVY, J. Psychobiological implications of bilateral asymmetries. In J. Dimond & J. G. Beaumont (Eds.), *Hemisphere function in the human brain.* New York: John Wiley, 1974.

LIBERMAN, A. M. Some results of research on speech perception. *Journal of the Acoustical Society of America,* 1957, *29,* 117–123.

LIBERMAN, A. M., COOPER, F. S., SHANKWEILER, D. P., & STUDDERT-KENNEDY, M. Perception of the speech code. *Psychological Review,* 1967, *74,* 431–461.

LOFTUS, E. F., & ZANNI, G. Eyewitness testimony: The influence of the wording of a question. *Bulletin of the Psychonomic Society,* 1975, *5,* 86–88.

LOHR, J. M. Concurrent conditioning of evaluative meaning and imagery. *British Journal of Psychology,* 1976, *67,* 353–358.

LORAYNE, H. *How to develop a super-power memory.* New York: NAL, Signet Books, 1974.

LOVELL, K., & DIXON, E. M. The growth of the control of grammar in imitation, comprehension, and production. *Journal of Child Psychology and Psychiatry,* 1967, *8,* 31–39.

LUPKER, S. J. On the nature of perceptual information during letter perception. *Perception and Psychophysics,* 1979, *25,* 303–312.

LURIA, A. R. *The role of speech in the regulation of normal and abnormal behavior.* New York: Liverright, 1961.

LYONS, J. *Introduction to theoretical linguistics.* London: Cambridge University Press, 1968.

MacCORQUODALE, K. On Chomsky's review of Skinner's *Verbal behavior. Journal of the Experimental Analysis of Behavior,* 1970, *13,* 83–99.

MacKAY, D. G. Spoonerisms: The structure of errors in the serial order of speech. *Neuropsychologia,* 1970, *8,* 323–350.

MACKEY, W. F. Bilingual interference: Its analysis and measurement. *Journal of Communication,* 1965, *15,* 239–249.

MACLAY, H., & OSGOOD, C. E. Hesitation phenomena in spontaneous English speech. *Word,* 1959, *15,* 19–44.

MACMILLAN, N. A., KAPLAN, H. L., & CREELMAN, C. D. The psychophysics of categorical perception. *Psychology Review,* 1977, *84,* 452–471.

MACNAMARA, J. (Ed.), Problems of bilingualism. *Journal of Social Issues,* 1967, *33,* 1–137.

MACNAMARA, J. How can one measure the extent of a person's bilingual proficiency? In L. G. Kelly (Ed.), *Description and measurement of bilingualism.* Toronto: University of Toronto Press, 1969.

MACNAMARA, J. Cognitive basis of language learning in infants. *Psychological Review*, 1972, 79, 1-13.

MACNAMARA, J. Nurseries, streets, and classrooms. *Modern Language Journal*, 1973, 57, 250-254.

MACNAMARA, J., & KUSHNIR, S. L. Linguistic independence of bilinguals: Input switch. *Journal of Verbal Learning and Verbal Behavior*, 1971, 10, 480-487.

MacNEILAGE, P. F. & MacNEILAGE, L. A. Central processes controlling speech production during sleep and waking. In F. J. McGuigan & R. A. Schoonover (Eds.), *The psychophysiology of thinking*. New York: Academic Press, 1973.

MÄGISTE, E. *Recall of concrete and abstract sentences in bilinguals* (Tech. Rep. 514). Stockholm: University of Stockholm, Department of Psychology, 1977.

MAHL, G. F., & SCHULZE, G. Psychological research in the extralinguistic area. In T. A. Sebeok A. S. Hayes, & M. C. Bateson (Eds.), *Approaches to semiotics*. London: Mouton, 1964.

MALGADY, R. G., & JOHNSON, M. G. Modifiers in metaphors: Effects of constituent phrase similarity on the interpretation of figurative sentences. *Journal of Psycholinguistic Research*, 1976, 5, 43-52.

MANDLER, G. Associative frequency and associative prepotency as measures of response to nonsense syllables. *American Journal of Psychology*, 1956, 68, 662-665.

MARCHAND, H. *The categories and types of present day English word-formation: A synchronic-diachronic approach* (2nd ed.). Munich : Beck, 1969.

MARKS, L. E., & MILLER, G. A. The role of semantic and syntactic constraints in the memorization of English sentences. *Journal of Verbal Learning and Verbal Behavior*, 1964, 3, 1-5.

MARLER, P. On the origin of speech from animal sounds. In J. F. Kavanagh & J. E. Cutting (Eds.). *The role of speech in language*. Cambridge, Mass.: M.I.T. Press, 1975.

MARSCHARK, M. *Prose processing: A chronometric study of the effects of imageability*. Unpublished doctoral dissertation, University of Western Ontario, 1978.

MARSCHARK, M. The syntax and semantics of comprehension. In G. Prideaux (Ed.), *Perspectives in experimental linguistics*. Amsterdam: John Benjamins, 1979.

MARSCHARK, M., & PAIVIO, A. Integrative processing of concrete and abstract sentences. *Journal of Verbal Learning and Verbal Behavior*, 1977, 16, 217-231.

MARSHALL, G. R., & COFER, C. N. Associative indices as measures of word relatedness: A summary and comparison of ten methods. *Journal of Verbal Learning and Verbal Behavior*, 1963, 1, 408-421.

MARTIN, J. E. Semantic determinants of preferred adjective order. *Journal of Verbal Learning and Verbal Behavior*, 1969, 8, 697-704.

MARTIN, J. G. Hesitations in the speaker's production and listener's reproduction of utterances. *Journal of Verbal Learning and Verbal Behavior*, 1967, 6, 903-909.

MASSARO, D. W. Preperceptual images, processing time, and perceptual units in speech perception. In D. W. Massaro (Ed.), *Understanding language*. New York: Academic Press, 1975.

MATTHEWS, W. A. Transformational complexity and short-term recall. *Language and Speech*, 1968, 11, 120-128.

McCARTHY, D. Language development in children. In L. Carmichael (Ed.), *Manual of child psychology*, (2nd ed.). New York: John Wiley, 1954.

McCAWLEY, J. D. The role of semantics in a grammar. In E. Bach & R. T. Harms (Eds.), *Universals in linguistic theory*. New York: Holt, Rinehart & Winston, 1968.

McCAWLEY, J. D. Interpretive semantics meets Frankenstein. *Foundations of Language*, 1971, 7, 285-296.

McCORMACK, P. D. Recognition memory: How complex a retrieval system? *Canadian Journal of Psychology*, 1972, 26, 19-41.

McCORMACK, P. D. Language as an attribute of memory. *Canadian Journal of Psychology*, 1976, 30, 238-248.

McCORMACK, P. D. Bilingual linguistic memory: The independence-interdependence issue

revisited. In P. Hornby (Ed.), *Bilingualism: Psychological, social and educational implications.* New York: Academic Press, 1977.

McFARLAND, K., McFARLAND, M. L., BAIN, J. D., & ASHTON, R. Ear differences of abstract and concrete word recognition. *Neuropsychologia,* 1978, *16,* 555–561.

McGUIGAN, F. J. *Cognitive psychophysiology: Principles of covert behavior.* Englewood Cliffs, N. J.: Prentice-Hall, Inc., 1978.

McGUIGAN, F. J., & RODIER, W. I. Effects of auditory stimulation on covert oral behavior during silent reading. *Journal of Experimental Psychology,* 1968, *76,* 649–655.

McLAUGHLIN, B. Second-language learning in children. *Psychological Bulletin,* 1977, *84,* 438–459.

McLAUGHLIN, B. *Second-language acquisition in childhood.* Hillsdale, N.J.: Erlbaum, 1978.

McNAUGHTON, S. Mr. Symbol Man. *Pot Pourri-National Film Board Newsletter,* February 1975.

McNEILL, D. *The acquisition of language: The study of developmental psycholinguistics.* New York: Harper & Row, Pub., 1970.

McNEILL, D. *The conceptual basis of language.* Hillsdale, N.J.: Erlbaum, 1979.

MEHLER, J. Some effects of grammatical transformations on the recall of English sentences. *Journal of Verbal Learning and Verbal Behavior,* 1963, *2,* 346–351.

MEWHORT, D. J. K., & BEAL, A. L. Mechanisms of word identification. *Journal of Experimental Psychology: Human Perception and Performance,* 1977, *3,* 629–640.

MEYER, D. E., SCHVANEVELDT, R. W., & RUDDY, M. G. Loci of contextual effects on visual word recognition. In P. M. A. Rabbit & S. Dornic (Eds.), *Attention and Performance V.* London: Academic Press, 1975.

MILLER, G. A. The magical number seven, plus or minus two. *Psychological Review,* 1956, *63,* 81–97.

MILLER, G. A. Some psychological studies of grammar. *American Psychologist,* 1962, *17,* 748–762.

MILLER, G. A. Psycholinguistic approaches to the study of communication. In D. L. Arm (Ed.), *Journeys in science.* Albuquerque : University of New Mexico Press, 1967.

MILLER, G. A. A psychological method to investigate verbal concepts. *Journal of Mathematical Psychology,* 1969, *6,* 169–191.

MILLER, G. A., BRUNER, J. S., & POSTMAN, L. Familiarity of letter sequences and tachistoscopic identification. *Journal of Genetic Psychology,* 1954, *50,* 129–139.

MILLER, G. A., HEISE, G. A., & LICHTEN, W. The intelligibility of speech as a function of the context of the test materials. *Journal of Experimental Psychology,* 1951, *41,* 329–335.

MILLER, G. A., & ISARD, S. Some perceptual consequences of linguistic rules. *Journal of Verbal Learning and Verbal Behavior,* 1963, *2,* 217–228.

MILLER, G. A., & McNEILL, D. Psycholinguistics. In G. Lindzey & E. Aronson (Eds.), *The handbook of social psychology* (Vol. 3). Reading, Mass. : Addison-Wesley, 1969.

MILLER, G. A., & NORMAN, D. *Research on the use of formal languages in the behavioral sciences* (Semiannual Tech. Rep.). Department of Defense, Advanced Research Projects Agency, 1964. [Also see Miller, G. A., Project Grammarama. In G. A. Miller (Ed.) *The psychology of communication.* New York : Basic Books, 1967.]

MILLER, G. A., & SELFRIDGE, J. A. Verbal context and the recall of meaningful material. *American Journal of Psychology,* 1950, *63,* 176–187.

MILNER, B. Laterality effects in audition. In V. B. Mountcastle (Ed.), *Interhemispheric relations and cerebral dominance.* Baltimore : Johns Hopkins Press, 1962.

MILNER, B. Brain mechanisms suggested by studies of temporal lobes. In F. L. Darley (Ed.), *Brain mechanisms underlying speech and language.* New York : Grune & Stratton, 1967.

MILNER, B. Interhemispheric differences in the localization of psychological processes in man. *British Medical Bulletin,* 1971, *27,* 272–277.

MILNER, B. Hemispheric specialization : Scope and limits. In F. O. Schmitt & F. G. Worden (Eds.), *The neurosciences: Third study program.* Cambridge, Mass : M.I.T. Press, 1973.

MILNER, B., TAYLOR, L., & SPERRY, R. W. Lateralized suppression of dichotically presented digits after commissural section in man. *Science,* 1968, *161,* 184–186.

MINSKY, M. A framework for representing knowledge. In P. Winston (Ed.), *The psychology of computer vision.* New York: McGraw-Hill, 1975.

MISTLER-LACHMAN, J. L. Queer sentences, ambiguity, and levels of processing. *Memory and Cognition,* 1975, *3,* 395–400.

MITTERAND, H. *Les mots français* (5th ed.). Paris: Presses universitaires de France, 1976.

MITTERER, J. O. *There are two kinds of poor reader.* Unpublished doctoral dissertation, Mc-Master University, 1980.

MOESER, S. D., & BREGMAN, A. S. The role of reference in the acquisition of a miniature artificial language. *Journal of Verbal Learning and Verbal Behavior,* 1972, *11,* 759–769.

MOESER, S. D., & BREGMAN, A. S. Imagery and language acquisition. *Journal of Verbal Learning and Verbal Behavior,* 1973, *12,* 91–98.

MONTAGUE, R. Universal grammar. *Theoria,* 1970, *36,* 373–398.

MOORE, T. V. The temporal relations of meaning and imagery. *Psychological Review,* 1915, *22,* 177–225.

MORRIS, C. *Foundations of the theory of signs.* Chicago: University of Chicago Press, 1938.

MORRIS, V. A., RANKINE, F. C., & REBER, A. S. Sentence comprehension, grammatical transformations and response availability. *Journal of Verbal Learning and Verbal Behavior,* 1968, *7,* 1113–1115.

MORTON, J. Interaction of information in word recognition. *Psychological Review,* 1969, *76,* 165–178.

MORTON, J., & LONG, J. Effects of word transition probability in phoneme identification. *Journal of Verbal Learning and Verbal Behavior,* 1976, *15,* 43–51.

MOSCOVITCH, M. Language and the cerebral hemispheres: Reaction time studies and their implications for models of cerebral dominance. In P. Pliner, L. Krames, & T. Alloway (Eds.), *Communication and affect; Language and thought.* New York: Academic Press, 1973.

MOWRER, O. H. *Learning theory and the symbolic processes.* New York: John Wiley, 1960.

MOYER, R. S. Comparing objects in memory: Evidence suggesting an internal psychophysics. *Perception and Psychophysics,* 1973, *13,* 180–184.

MOYER, R. S., & BAYER, R. H. Mental comparison and the symbolic distance effect. *Cognitive Psychology,* 1976, *8,* 228–246.

MOYER, R. S., & DUMAIS, S. T. Mental comparison. In G. H. Bower (Ed.), *The psychology of learning and motivation* (Vol. 12). New York: Academic Press, 1978.

NEISSER, U. *Cognitive psychology.* New York: Appleton-Century-Crofts, 1967.

NELSON, K. Concept, word, and sentence: Interrelations in acquisition and development. *Psychological Review,* 1974, *81,* 267–285.

NELSON, K. The syntagmatic-paradigmatic shift revisited: A review of research and theory. *Psychological Bulletin,* 1977, *84,* 93–116.

NEUFELD, G. G. Towards a theory of language learning ability. *Language Learning,* in press.

NEWMAN, J. E., & DELL, G. S. The phonological nature of phoneme monitoring: A critique of some ambiguity studies. *Journal of Verbal Learning and Verbal Behavior,* 1978, *17,* 359–374.

NIELSEN, H. H., & RINGE, K. Visuo-perceptive and visuo-motor performance of children with reading disabilities. *Scandinavian Journal of Psychology,* 1969, *10,* 225–231.

NIGHTINGALE, R. F. G. *A comparison of the keyword method and verbal mediation of the keyword method in the acquisition of a small Finnish vocabulary.* Unpublished honours bachelor's thesis, University of Western Ontario, 1976.

NOBLE, C. E. An analysis of meaning. *Psychological Review,* 1952, *59,* 421–430.

NORMAN, D. A., & RUMELHART, D. E. *Explorations in cognition.* San Francisco: W. H. Freeman & Company Publishers, 1975.

NORTH, B. *Effects of stimulus redundancy in naming disorders in aphasia.* Unpublished doctoral dissertation, Boston University, 1971.

NOTT, R., & LAMBERT, W. E. *Organization of memory in bilinguals.* Paper presented at the meeting of the Eastern Psychological Association, Washington, D. C., 1968.

ODEN, G. C. A fuzzy logical model of letter identification. *Journal of Experimental Psychology: Human Perception and Performance, 1979, 5,* 336-352.

ODOM, P. B., BLANTON, R. L., & McINTYRE, C. K. Coding medium and word recall by deaf and hearing subjects. *Journal of Speech and Hearing Research,* 1970, *13,* 54-59.

OLSON, D. R. Language and thought: Aspects of a cognitive theory of semantics. *Psychological Review,* 1970, *77,* 257-273.

OLSON, D. R. From utterance to text: The bias of language in speech and writing. *Harvard Educational Review,* 1977, *47*(3), 257-281.

OLSON, D. R., & FILBY, N. On comprehension of active and passive sentences. *Cognitive Psychology,* 1972, *3,* 361-381.

OLSON, L. L., & SAMUELS, S. J. The relationship between age and accuracy of foreign language pronunciation. *Journal of Educational Research,* 1973, *66,* 263-368.

O'NEILL, B. J. *Word attributes in dichotic recognition and memory.* Unpublished doctoral dissertation, University of Western Ontario, 1971.

O'NEILL, B. J., & PAIVIO, A. Semantic constraints in encoding judgments and free recall of concrete and abstract sentences. *Canadian Journal of Psychology,* 1978, *32,* 3-18.

O'ROURKE, T. J. *A basic vocabulary: American sign language for parents and children.* Silver Springs, Md.: T. J. Publishers, 1978.

ORTONY, A. Why metaphors are necessary and not just nice. *Educational Theory,* 1975, *25,* 45-53.

ORTONY, A. Beyond literal similarity. *Psychological Review,* 1979, *86,* 161-180.

OSGOOD, C. E. *Method and theory in experimental psychology.* New York: Oxford University Press, 1953.

OSGOOD, C. E. Comments on Professor Bousfield's paper. In C. N. Cofer (Ed.), *Verbal learning and verbal behavior.* New York: McGraw-Hill, 1961.

OSGOOD, C. E. Language universals and psycholinguistics. In J. H. Greenberg (Ed.), *Universals in language.* Cambridge, Mass.: M.I.T. Press, 1963.

OSGOOD, C. E. Where do sentences come from? In D. D. Steinberg & L. A. Jakobovits (Eds.), *Semantics.* Cambridge: Cambridge University Press, 1971.

OSGOOD, C. E. The discussion of Dr. Paivio's paper. In F. J. McGuigan & R. A. Schoonover (Eds.), *The psychophysiology of thinking.* New York: Academic Press, 1973.

OSGOOD, C. E., & BOCK, J. K. Salience and sentencing: Some production principles. In S. Rosenberg (Ed.), *Sentence production: Development in research and theory.* Hillsdale, N.J.: Erlbaum, 1975.

OSGOOD, C. E., & HOOSAIN, R. Salience of the word as a unit in the perception of language. *Perception and Psychophysics,* 1974, *15,* 168-192.

OSGOOD, C. E., & LURIA, Z. A blind analysis of a case of multiple personality using the semantic differential. *Journal of Abnormal and Social Psychology,* 1954, *49,* 579-591.

OSGOOD, C. E., LURIA, Z., JEANS, R. F., & SMITH, S. W. The three faces of Evelyn: A case report. *Journal of Abnormal Psychology,* 1976, *85,* 247-286.

OSGOOD, C. E. & McGUIGAN, F. J. Psychophysiological correlates of meaning: Essences or tracers? In F. J. McGuigan & R. A. Schoonover (Eds.), *The psychophysiology of thinking.* New York: Academic Press, 1973.

OSGOOD, C. E., SUCI, G. J., & TANNENBAUM, P. H. *The measurement of meaning.* Urbana: University of Illinois Press, 1957.

OSGOOD, C. E., & TANNENBAUM, P. H. The principle of congruity in the prediction of attitude change. *Psychological Review,* 1955, *62,* 42-55.

OWEN, F. W., ADAMS, P. A., FORREST, T., STOLZ, L. M., & FISHER, S. Learning disorders in children: Sibling studies. *Monographs of the Society for Research in Child Development,* 1971, *36,* (4, Serial No. 144).

OWENS, J., DAFOE, J., & BOWER, G. H. *Taking a point of view. Character identification and attributional processes in story comprehension and memory.* Paper presented at the Meeting of the American Psychological Association, San Francisco, 1977.

PAAP, K. R. Theories of speech perception. In D. W. Massaro (Ed.), *Understanding language.* New York: Academic Press, 1975.

PAIVIO, A. Learning of adjective noun paired-associates as a function of adjective-noun word order and noun abstractness. *Canadian Journal of Psychology,* 1963, *17,* 370-379.

PAIVIO, A. Generalization of verbally conditioned meaning from symbol to referent. *Canadian Journal of Psychology,* 1964, *18,* 146-155.

PAIVIO, A. Latency of verbal associations and imagery to noun stimuli as a function of abstractness and generality. *Canadian Journal of Psychology,* 1966, *20,* 378-387.

PAIVIO, A. A factor-analytic study of word attributes and verbal learning. *Journal of Verbal Learning and Verbal Behavior,* 1968, *7,* 41-49.

PAIVIO, A. Mental imagery in associative learning and memory. *Psychological Review,* 1969, *76,* 241-263.

PAIVIO, A. Imagery and deep structure in the recall of English nominalizations. *Journal of Verbal Learning and Verbal Behavior,* 1971, *10,* 1-12. (a)

PAIVIO, A. *Imagery and verbal processes.* New York: Holt, Rinehart & Winston, 1971. (b) (Reprinted by Lawrence Erlbaum Associates, Hillsdale, N.J., 1979.)

PAIVIO, A. Coding distinctions and repetition effects in memory. In G. H. Bower (Ed.), *The psychology of learning and motivation* (Vol. 9). New York: Academic Press, 1975. (a)

PAIVIO, A. Imagery and synchronic thinking. *Canadian Psychological Review,* 1975, *16,* 147-163. (b)

PAIVIO, A. Perceptual comparisons through the mind's eye. *Memory and Cognition,* 1975, *3,* 635-647. (c)

PAIVIO, A. Comparisons of mental clocks. *Journal of Experimental Psychology: Human Perception and Performance,* 1978, *4,* 61-71. (a)

PAIVIO, A. Mental comparisons involving abstract attributes. *Memory and Cognition,* 1978, *6,* 199-208. (b)

PAIVIO, A. On exploring visual knowledge. In B. S. Randhawa & W. E. Coffman (Eds.), *Visual learning, thinking, and communication.* New York: Academic Press, 1978. (c)

PAIVIO, A. Psychological processes in the comprehension of metaphor. In A. Ortony (Ed.), *Metaphor and thought.* Cambridge: Cambridge University Press, 1979.

PAIVIO, A., & BEGG, I. Imagery and comprehension latencies as a function of sentence concreteness and structure. *Perception and Psychophysics,* 1971, *10,* 408-412.

PAIVIO, A., & BEGG, I. Pictures and words in visual search. *Memory and Cognition,* 1974, *2,* 515-521.

PAIVIO, A., & CSAPO, K. Concrete-image and verbal memory codes. *Journal of Experimental Psychology,* 1969, *80,* 279-285.

PAIVIO, A., & CSAPO, K. Picture superiority in free recall: Imagery or dual coding? *Cognitive Psychology,* 1973, *5,* 176-206.

PAIVIO, A., & DESROCHERS, A. Effects of an imagery mnemonic on second language recall and comprehension. *Canadian Journal of Psychology,* 1979, *33,* 17-28.

PAIVIO, A., & ERNEST, C. Imagery ability and visual perception of verbal and nonverbal stimuli. *Perception and Psychophysics,* 1971, *10,* 429-432.

PAIVIO, A., & OKOVITA, H. W. Word imagery modalities and associative learning in blind and sighted subjects. *Journal of Verbal Learning and Verbal Behavior,* 1971, *10,* 506-510.

PAIVIO, A., & O'NEILL, B. J. Visual recognition thresholds and dimensions of word meaning. *Perception and Psychophysics,* 1970, *8,* 273-275.

PAIVIO, A., & STEEVES, R. The relations between personal values and the imagery and meaningfulness of value words. *Perceptual and Motor Skills,* 1967, *24,* 357-358.

PAIVIO, A., & YUILLE, J. C. Changes in associative strategies and paired-associate learning over trials as a function of word imagery and type of learning set. *Journal of Experimental Psychology,* 1969, *79,* 458-463.

PAIVIO, A., YUILLE, J. C., & MADIGAN, S. A. Concreteness, imagery and meaningfulness values for 925 nouns. *Journal of Experimental Psychology Monograph Supplement,* 1968, *76*(1, Pt. 2).

PALERMO, D. S. Developmental aspects of speech perception: Problems for a motor theory. In J. F. Kavanagh & J. E. Cutting (Eds.), *The role of speech in language.* Cambridge, Mass.: M.I.T. Press, 1975.

PALERMO, D. S., & JENKINS, J. J. *Word association norms: Grade school through college.* Minneapolis: University of Minnesota Press, 1964.

PARK, S., & ARBUCKLE, T. Y. Ideograms versus alphabets: Effects of script on memory in "biscriptual" Korean subjects. *Journal of Experimental Psychology: Human Learning and Memory,* 1977, *3,* 631–642.

PARTEE, B. H. Montague grammar and transformational grammar. *Linguistic Inquiry,* 1975, *6,* 203–300.

PARTEE, B. H. (Ed.). *Montague grammar.* New York: Academic Press, 1976.

PARTEE, B. H. John is easy to please. In A. Zampolli (Ed.), *Linguistic structures processing.* Amsterdam: North Holland, 1977.

PATTEN, B. M. The ancient art of memory. *Archives of Neurology,* 1972, *26,* 25–31.

PATTERSON, F. Conversations with a gorilla. *National Geographic,* 1978, *154,* 438–465.

PEAL, E., & LAMBERT, W. E. The relation of bilingualism to intelligence. *Psychological Monographs,* 1962, *76,* Whole No. 546.

PENFIELD, W., & ROBERTS, L. *Speech and brain-mechanism.* Princeton, N.J.: Princeton University Press, 1959.

PERFETTI, C. A., GOLDMAN, S. R., & HOGABOAM, T. W. Reading skill and the identification of words in discourse context. *Memory and Cognition,* 1979, *7,* 273–282.

PETERSON, L. R., & PETERSON, M. J. Short-term retention of individual items. *Journal of Experimental Psychology,* 1959, *58,* 193–198.

PEZDEK, K., & ROYER, J. M. The role of comprehension in learning concrete and abstract sentences. *Journal of Verbal Learning and Verbal Behavior,* 1974, *13,* 551–558.

PHILIPCHALK, R. P. *The development of imaginal meaning in verbal stimuli.* Unpublished doctoral dissertation, University of Western Ontario, 1971.

PHILIPCHALK, R. P. Thematicity, abstractness, and the long-term recall of connected discourse. *Psychonomic Science,* 1972, *27,* 361–362.

PIAGET, J. *La formation du symbole.* Neuchâtel, Switzerland: Delachaux et Niestle, 1949.

PINKER, S. Formal models of language learning. *Cognition,* 1979, *7,* 217–284.

PISONI, D. B. Identification and discrimination of the relative onset time of two-component tones: Implications for voicing perception in stops. *Journal of the Acoustical Society of America,* 1977, *61,* 1352–1361.

POLLIO, H. R., & BURNS, B. C. The anomaly of anomaly. *Journal of Psycholinguistic Research,* 1977, *6,* 247–260.

POLLIO, H. R., RICHARDS, S., & LUCAS, R. Temporal properties of category recall. *Journal of Verbal Learning and Verbal Behavior,* 1969, *8,* 529–536.

POMPI, K. F., & LACHMAN, R. Surrogate processes in the short-term retention of connected discourse. *Journal of Experimental Psychology,* 1967, *75,* 143–150.

POSNER, M. I., BOIES, S., EICHELMAN, W., & TAYLOR, R. Retention of visual and name codes of single letters. *Journal of Experimental Psychology Monographs,* 1969, *79* (1, Pt. 2).

POSNER, M. I., & KEELE, S. W. On the genesis of abstract ideas. *Journal of Experimental Psychology,* 1968, *77,* 353–363.

POSTMAN, L., BRUNER, J. S., & McGINNIES, E. Personal values as selective factors in perception. *Journal of Abnormal and Social Psychology,* 1948, *43,* 142–154.

POTTER, M. C. Mundane symbolism: The relations among objects, names and ideas. In N. R. Smith & M. B. Franklin (Eds.), *Symbolic functioning in childhood.* Hillsdale, N.J.: Erlbaum, 1979.

POTTER, M. C., VALIAN, V. V., & FAULCONER, B. A. Representation of a sentence and its

pragmatic implications: Verbal, imagistic, or abstract? *Journal of Verbal Learning and Verbal Behavior,* 1977, *16,* 1–12.

PREMACK, D. Language in chimpanzee? *Science,* 1971, *172,* 808–822.

PRENTICE, J. L. Intraverbal associations in sentence behavior. *Psychonomic Science,* 1968, *10,* 213–214.

PRESSLEY, M. Children's use of the keyword method to learn simple Spanish vocabulary words. *Journal of Educational Psychology,* 1977, *69,* 465–472.

PRESSLEY, M., LEVIN, J. R., HALL, J. W., MILLER, G. E., & BERRY, J. K. The keyword method and foreign word acquisition. *Journal of Experimental Psychology: Human Learning and Memory,* 1980, *6,* 163–173.

PRESTON, M. S., & LAMBERT, W. E. Interlingual interference in a bilingual version of the Stroop color-word task. *Journal of Verbal Learning and Verbal Behavior,* 1969, *2,* 295–301.

Principles of the International Phonetic Association. London: International Phonetic Association, 1949.

PYLYSHYN, Z. W., & FELDMAR, A. Grammatical category as mediator. *Psychonomic Science,* 1968, *13,* 115–116.

QUILLIAN, M. R. Semantic memory. In M. Minsky (Ed.), *Semantic information processing.* Cambridge, Mass.: M.I.T. Press, 1968.

REBER, A. S., & ANDERSON, J. R. The perception of clicks in linguistic and nonlinguistic messages. *Perception and Psychophysics,* 1970, *8,* 81–89.

REDER, L. M., & ANDERSON, J. R. A comparison of texts and their summaries: Memorial consequences. *Journal of Verbal Learning and Verbal Behavior,* 1980, *19,* 121–134.

REESE, H. W. *The perception of stimulus relations: Discrimination learning and transposition.* New York: Academic Press, 1968.

REICH, P. A. A relational network model of language behavior (Doctoral dissertation, University of Michigan, 1970). *Dissertation Abstracts International,* 1971, *31B,* 7578. (University Microfilms No. 71–15, 279.)

REYNOLDS, A., & PAIVIO, A. Cognitive and emotional determinants of speech. *Canadian Journal of Psychology,* 1968, *22,* 164–175.

RHEINGOLD, H. L., GEWIRTZ, J. L., & ROSS, H. W. Social conditioning of vocalizations. *Journal of Comparative and Physiological Psychology,* 1959, *52,* 68–73.

RICHARDS, I. A. *The philosophy of rhetoric.* London: Oxford University Press, 1936.

RICHARDS, J. C. Error analysis and second-language strategies. *Language Sciences,* 1971, *17,* 12–22.

RICHARDS, J. C. Word lists: Problems and prospects. *Regional English Language Center Journal,* 1974, *2,* 69–84.

RICHARDS, M. M. Ordering preferences for congruent and incongruent English adjectives in attributive and predictive contexts. *Journal of Verbal Learning and Verbal Behavior,* 1977, *4,* 489–504.

RICHARDSON, J. T. E. Imagery, concreteness, and lexical complexity. *Quarterly Journal of Experimental Psychology,* 1975, *27,* 211–223.

RINNERT, C., & WHITAKER, H. A. Semantic confusions by aphasic patients. *Cortex,* 1973, *9,* 56–81.

ROBINSON, W. P. *Language and social behavior.* London: Penguin, 1972.

ROCHESTER, S. R., & GILL, J. Production of complex sentences in monologues and dialogues. *Journal of Verbal Learning and Verbal Behavior,* 1973, *12,* 203–210.

ROHRMAN, N. L. The role of syntactic structure in the recall of English nominalizations. *Journal of Verbal Learning and Verbal Behavior,* 1968, *7,* 904–912.

ROHWER, W. D., Jr. Elaboration and learning in childhood and adolescence. In H. W. Reese (Ed.), *Advances in child development and behavior* (Vol. 8). New York: Academic Press, 1973.

ROMNEY, A. K., & D'ANDRADE, R. G. (Eds.). Cognitive aspects of English kinship terms. *Transcultural Studies in Cognition, American Anthropologist Special Issue,* 1964, *66,* (3, Pt. 2).

ROSCH, E. Cognitive reference points. *Cognitive Psychology*, 1975, *7*, 532–547. (a)

ROSCH, E. Cognitive representations of semantic categories. *Journal of Experimental Psychology: General*, 1975, *104*, 192–233. (b)

ROSCH, E. Universals and cultural specifics in human categorization. In R. W. Bristin, R. Bochner, & W. J. Lonner (Eds.), *Cross-cultural perspectives on learning*. New York: John Wiley, 1975. (c)

ROSCH, E., MERVIS, C. B., GRAY, W., JOHNSTON, D., & BOYES-BRAEM, P. Basic objects in natural categories. *Cognitive Psychology*, 1976, *8*, 382–439.

ROSE, R. G., ROSE, P. R., KING, N., & PEREZ, A. Bilingual memory for related and unrelated sentences. *Journal of Experimental Psychology: Human Learning and Memory*, 1975, *1*, 599–606.

ROSENBERG, S. Recall of sentences as a function of syntactic and associative habit. *Journal of Verbal Learning and Verbal Behavior*, 1966, *5*, 392–396.

ROSENBERG, S. The relation between association and syntax in sentence production. *Studies in Language and Behavior, Progress Report V*. Ann Arbor: University of Michigan Center for Research on Language and Language Behavior, 1967.

ROSENBERG, S. Association and phrase structure in sentence recall. *Journal of Verbal Learning and Verbal Behavior*, 1968, *7*, 1077–1081.

ROSENBERG, S. The recall of verbal material accompanying semantically well-integrated and semantically poorly-integrated sentences. *Journal of Verbal Learning and Verbal Behavior*, 1969, *8*, 732–736.

ROSENBERG, S. *Semantics and imagery in sentence recall*. Paper presented at the meeting of the Psychonomic Society, Washington, D. C., 1977.

ROSENBERG, S., & JARVELLA, R. Semantic integration and sentence perception. *Journal of Verbal Learning and Verbal Behavior*, 1970, *9*, 548–553.

ROSENBERG, S., & KOEN, M. J. Norms of sequential associative dependencies in active declarative sentences. In J. C. Catford (Ed.), *Studies in Language and Language Behavior, Supplement to Progress Report VI*. Ann Arbor: University of Michigan Center for Research on Language and Language Behavior, 1968.

ROSENFELD, J. B. *Information processing: Encoding and decoding*. Unpublished doctoral dissertation, Indiana University, 1967.

ROSS, J. R. Parallels in phonological and semantactic organization. In J. F. Kavanagh & J. E. Cutting (Eds.), *The role of speech in language*. Cambridge, Mass.: M.I.T. Press, 1975.

ROTHKOPF, E. Z. Structural text features and the control of processes in learning from written materials. In J. B. Carroll & R. O. Freedle (Eds.), *Language comprehension and the acquisition of knowledge*. Washington, D.C.: Winston, 1972.

ROUSE, R. O., & VERINIS, J. S. The effect of associative connections on the recognition of flashed words. *Journal of Verbal Learning and Verbal Behavior*, 1962, *1*, 300–303.

ROWE, E. J., & PAIVIO, A. Imagery and repetition instructions in verbal discrimination and incidental paired-associate learning. *Journal of Verbal Learning and Verbal Behavior*, 1971, *10*, 668–672.

ROZIN, P., PORITSKY, S., & SOTSKY, R. American children with reading problems can easily learn to read English represented by Chinese characters. *Science*, 1971, *171*, 1264–1267.

RUBENSTEIN, H., & ABORN, M. Learning, prediction, and readability. *Journal of Applied Psychology*, 1958, *42*, 28–32.

RUBENSTEIN, H., LEWIS, S. S., & RUBENSTEIN, M. A. Evidence for phonemic recoding in visual word recognition. *Journal of Verbal Learning and Verbal Behavior*, 1971, *10*, 645–657.

RUMBAUGH, D. M. (Ed.), *Language learning by a chimpanzee*. New York: Academic Press, 1976.

RUMELHART, D. E., LINDSAY, P. H., & NORMAN, D. A. A process model for long-term memory. In E. Tulving & W. Donaldson (Eds.), *Organization of memory*. New York: Academic Press, 1972.

RUMELHART, D. E., & SIPLE, P. Process of recognizing tachistoscopically presented words. *Psychological Review*, 1974, *81*, 99–118.

RUSSELL, W. A., & STORMS, L. H. Implicit verbal chaining in paired-associate learning. *Journal of Experimental Psychology*, 1955, *49*, 287–293.

SACHS, J. S. Recognition memory for syntactic and semantic aspects of connected discourse. *Perception and Psychophysics*, 1967, *2*, 437–442.

SAEGERT, J., HAMAYAN, E., & AHMAR, H. Memory for language of input in polyglots. *Journal of Experimental Psychology: Human Learning and Memory*, 1975, *1*, 607–613.

SAEGERT, J., & YOUNG, R. K. Translation errors for abstract and concrete responses in a bilingual paired-associate task. *Bulletin of the Psychonomic Society*, 1975, *6*, 429. (abstract)

SALZINGER, K., PORTNOY, S., & FELDMAN, R. S. The effect of order of approximation to the statistical structure of English on the emission of verbal responses. *Journal of Experimental Psychology*, 1962, *64*, 52–57.

SAPIR, E. *Language: An introduction to the study of speech.* New York: Harcourt, Brace & World, 1949.

SASANUMA, S. Kanji versus kana processing in alexia with transient agraphia: A case report. *Cortex*, 1974, *10*, 89–97.

SAUSSURE, F. De. *[Course in general linguistics]* (C. Bally & A. Sechehaye, Eds. and W. Baskin, trans.). Glasgow, Scotland: Fontana, 1974.

SAVIN, H. B. & PERCHONOCK, E. Grammatical structure and the immediate recall of English sentences. *Journal of Verbal Learning and Verbal Behavior*, 1965, *4*, 348–353.

SCHANK, R. C. Conceptual dependency: A theory of natural language understanding. *Cognitive Psychology*, 1972, *3*, 552–631.

SCHANK, R. C., & ABELSON, R. P. Scripts, plans and knowledge. In *Advance Papers of the Fourth International Joint Conference on Artificial Intelligence*. Tbilisi, USSR, 1975.

SCHONBACH, P. In defense of Roger Brown against himself. *Cognition*, 1977, *5*, 181–183.

SCHWELLER, K. G., BREWER, W. F., & DAHL, D. A. Memory for illocutionary forces and perlocutionary effects of utterances. *Journal of Verbal Learning and Verbal Behavior*, 1976, *15*, 325–337.

SEAMON, J. G., & GAZZANIGA, M. S. Coding strategies and cerebral laterality effects. *Cognitive Psychology*, 1972, *3*, 552–631.

SEARLEMAN, A. A review of right hemisphere linguistic capabilities. *Psychological Bulletin*, 1977, *84*, 503–528.

SEGAL, A. U. *Encoding and retrieval differences in verbal and nonverbal processing.* Unpublished doctoral dissertation, University of Western Ontario, 1976.

SEYMOUR, P. H. A model for reading, naming and comparison. *British Journal of Psychology*, 1973, *64*, 35–49. (a)

SEYMOUR, P. H. Rule identity classification of name and shape stimuli. *Acta Psychologica*, 1973, *37*, 131–138. (b)

SHAFTO, M. Space for case. *Journal of Verbal Learning and Verbal Behavior*, 1973, *12*, 551–562.

SHANKWEILER, O., & LIBERMAN, I. Y. Misreading: A search for causes. In J. F. Kavanagh & I. G. Mattingly (Eds.), *Language by ear and by eye.* Cambridge, Mass.: M.I.T. Press, 1972.

SHANNON, C. E., & WEAVER, W. *The mathematical theory of communication.* Urbana: University of Illinois Press, 1949.

SHEFFIELD, F. D. Theoretical considerations in the learning of complex sequential tasks from demonstration and practice. In A. A. Lumsdaine (Ed.), *Student response in programmed instruction.* Washington, D.C.: National Academy of Sciences–National Research Council, 1961. (NAS-NRS Publication No. 943)

SHEN, E. An analysis of eye movements in the reading of Chinese. *Journal of Experimental Psychology*, 1927, *10*, 158–183.

SHUGAR, G., & GEPNER-WIECKO, K. Effects of language structure on associative responses

to word equivalents in two languages: A cross-linguistic comparison of word associations in Polish and English. *Polish Psychological Bulletin,* 1971, *2,* 99–105.

SIEGEL, W., SIEGEL, J. A., HARRIS, G., & SOPO, R. *Categorical perception of pitch by musicians with relative and absolute pitch.* London, Ont.: University of Western Ontario, Department of Psychology, Research Bulletin No. 305, 1974.

SIEGMAN, A., & POPE, B. Effects of question specificity and anxiety–producing messages on verbal fluency in the initial interview. *Journal of Personality and Social Psychology,* 1965, *2,* 522–530.

SILVERMAN, F. H. *Communication for the speechless.* Englewood Cliffs, N.J.: Prentice-Hall, Inc., 1980.

SINCLAIR-De ZWART, H. Language acquisition and cognitive development. In T. E. Moore (Ed.), *Cognitive development and the acquisition of language.* New York: Academic Press, 1973.

SINGER, G. Enjoying vocabulary learning in junior high: The keyword method. *Canadian Modern Language Review,* 1978, *34,* 80.

SINGH, S., BROKAW, S. P., & BLACK, J. W. Effects of delayed sidetone, noise, and syntactic structure on the level and duration of speech. *Journal of Verbal Learning and Verbal Behavior,* 1967, *6,* 629–633.

SKEHAN, P. *The relation of visual imagery to true-false judgment of simple sentences.* Unpublished master's thesis, University of Western Ontario, 1970.

SKINNER, B. F. The verbal summator as a method for the study of latent speech. *Journal of Psychology,* 1936, *2,* 71–107.

SKINNER, B. F. *Verbal behavior.* New York: Appleton-Century-Crofts, 1957.

SLOBIN, D. I. The acquisition of Russian as a native language. In F. H. Smith & G. A. Miller (Eds.), *The genesis of language: A psycholinguistic approach.* Cambridge, Mass.: M.I.T. Press, 1966. (a)

SLOBIN, D. I. Grammatical transformations and sentence comprehension in childhood and adulthood. *Journal of Verbal Learning and Verbal Behavior,* 1966, *5,* 219–227. (b)

SLOBIN, D. I. Recall of full and truncated passive sentences in connected discourse. *Journal of Verbal Learning and Verbal Behavior,* 1968, *7,* 876–881.

SMITH, M. E. ROTHKOPF, E. Z., & KOETHER, M. *The evaluation of instructional text: Relating properties of free recall protocols to text properties.* Paper presented at the meeting of the American Educational Research Association, Washington, D.C., 1970.

SMYTHE, P. C., STENNETT, R. G., & GARDNER, R. C. The best age for foreign-language training: Issues, opinions, and facts. *Canadian Modern Language Review,* 1975, *32,* 10–23.

SNODGRASS, J. G., BURNS, P. M., & PIRONE, G. V. Pictures and words in space and time: In search of the elusive interaction. *Journal of Experimental Psychology: General,* 1978, *2,* 206–230.

SOLOMON, R. L., & POSTMAN, L. Frequency of usage as a determinant of recognition thresholds for words. *Journal of Experimental Psychology,* 1952, *43,* 195–201.

SPERRY, R. W. Lateralization of function in the surgically separated hemispheres. In F. J. McGuigan & R. Schoonover (Eds.), *The psychophysiology of thinking.* New York: Academic Press, 1973.

SPIELBERGER, C. D., & LEVIN, S. M. What is learned in verbal conditioning? *Journal of Verbal Learning and Verbal Behavior,* 1962, *1,* 125–132.

SPURGEON, C. F. E. *Shakespeare's imagery and what it tells us.* New York: Cambridge University Press, 1935.

STAATS, A. W. Verbal habit families, concepts, and the operant conditioning of word classes. *Psychological Review,* 1961, *68,* 190–204.

STAATS, A. W. *Learning, language, and cognition.* New York: Holt, Rinehart & Winston, 1968.

STAATS, A. W., & STAATS, C. K. Meaning and *m*: Correlated but separate. *Psychological Review,* 1959, *66,* 136–144.

STAATS, A. W., STAATS, C. K., & CRAWFORD, H. L. First-order conditioning of meaning and the parallel conditioning of GSR. *Journal of General Psychology*, 1962, *67*, 159–167.

STAATS, A. W., STAATS, C. K., & HEARD, W. G. *Denotative meaning established by classical conditioning* (Tech. Rep. 13). Tempe: Arizona State University, 1959. (a)

STAATS, A. W., STAATS, C. K., & HEARD, W. G. Language conditioning of meaning to meaning using a semantic generalization paradigm. *Journal of Experimental Psychology*, 1959, *57*, 187–192. (b)

STAATS, C. K., & STAATS, A. W. Meaning established by classical conditioning. *Journal of Experimental Psychology*, 1957, *54*, 74–80.

STEFFLRE, V., VALES, C. V., & MORLEY, L. Language and cognition in Yucatan: A cross-cultural replication. *Journal of Personality and Social Psychology*, 1966, *4*, 112–115.

STEVENS, K. N. The quantal nature of speech: Evidence from articulatory-acoustic data. In E. E. David, Jr. & P. B. Denes (Eds.), *Human communication: A unified view*. New York: McGraw-Hill, 1972.

STUDDERT-KENNEDY, M. The perception of speech. In T. A. Sebeok (Ed.), *Current trends in linguistics* (Vol. 12). The Hague: Mouton, 1974.

STUDDERT-KENNEDY, M. From continuous signal to discrete message. In J. F. Kavanagh & J. E. Cutting (Eds.), *The role of speech in language*. Cambridge, Mass.: M.I.T. Press, 1975.

STUDDERT-KENNEDY, M., & SHANKWEILER, O. Hemispheric specialization for speech perception. *Journal of the Acoustical Society of America*, 1970, *48*, 579–594.

STURTEVANT, E. H. *Linguistic change: An introduction to the historical study of language*. Chicago: University of Chicago Press, 1961. (Originally published, 1917.)

SVARTVIC, J. *On voice in the English verb*. The Hague: Mouton, 1966.

TANNENBAUM, P. H., WILLIAMS, F., & HILLIER, C. Word predictability in the environments of hesitation. *Journal of Verbal Learning and Verbal Behavior*, 1965, *4*, 134–140.

TAYLOR, I. How are words from two languages organized in bilinguals' memory? *Canadian Journal of Psychology*, 1971, *25*, 228–240.

TAYLOR, I. *Introduction to psycholinguistics*. New York: Holt, Rinehart & Winston, 1976.

TEJIRIAN, E. Syntactic and semantic structures in the recall of orders of approximation to English. *Journal of Verbal Learning and Verbal Behavior*, 1968, *7*, 1010–1015.

TERRACE, H. S., PETITTO, L. A., SANDERS, R. J., & BEVER, T. G. Can an ape create a sentence? *Science*, 1979, *206*, 891–902.

THIGPEN, C. H., & CLECKLEY, H. A. A case of multiple personality. *Journal of Abnormal and Social Psychology*, 1954, *49*, 135–151.

THORNDIKE, E. L., & LORGE, I. *The teacher's word book of 30,000 words*. New York: Columbia Teachers College, Bureau of Publications, 1944.

THUMB, A., & MARBE, K. *Experimentelle Untersuchungen über die psychologischen Grundlagen der sprachlichen Analogiebildung*. Leipzig: W. Engelmann, 1901.

TINKER, M. A. Recent studies of eye-movements in reading. *Psychological Bulletin*, 1958, *55*, 215–231.

TINKER, M. A. *Bases for effective reading*. Minneapolis: University of Minnesota Press, 1965.

TOLMAN, E. C. More concerning the temporal relations of meaning and imagery. *Psychological Review*, 1917, *24*, 114–138.

TRIER, J. Das sprachliche Feld. *Neue Jahrbucher für Wissenschaft und Jugendbildung*, 1934, *10*, 428–449. (Cited in Ullmann, 1962.)

TULVING, E. Episodic and semantic memory. In E. Tulving & W. Donaldson (Eds.), *Organization of memory*. New York: Academic Press, 1972.

TULVING, E., & GOLD, C. Stimulus information and contextual information as determinants of tachistoscopic recognition of words. *Journal of Experimental Psychology*, 1963, *66*, 319–327.

TULVING, E., & PATKAU, J. E. Concurrent effects of contextual constraint and word fre-

quency on immediate recall and learning of verbal material. *Canadian Journal of Psychology*, 1962, *16*, 83–95.

TURBAYNE, C. M. *The myth of metaphor.* Columbia: University of South Carolina Press, 1971.

TVERSKY, A. Features of similarity. *Psychological Review*, 1977, *84*, 327–352.

TVERSKY, B. Breadth of pictorial and verbal codes in memory. *Bulletin of the Psychonomic Society*, 1974, *4*, 65–68.

TVERSKY, B. Pictorial and verbal encoding in a short-term memory task. *Perception and Psychophysics*, 1969, *6*, 225–233.

ULLMANN, S. *Semantics: An introduction to the science of meaning.* Oxford, U.K.: Blackwell & Mott, 1962.

UNDERWOOD, B. J. The language repertoire and some problems in verbal learning. In S. Rosenberg (Ed.), *Directions in psycholinguistics.* New York: Macmillan, 1965.

UNDERWOOD, B. J., & RICHARDSON, J. Some verbal materials for the study of concept formation. *Psychological Bulletin*, 1956, *53*, 84–95.

VELLUTINO, F. R., HARDING, C. J., PHILLIPS, F., & STEGER, J. A. Differential transfer in poor and normal readers. *Journal of Genetic Psychology*, 1975, *126*, 3–18.

VELLUTINO, F. R., STEGER, J. A., HARDING, C. J., & PHILLIPS, F. Verbal vs nonverbal paired-associates learning in poor and normal readers. *Neuropsychologia*, 1975, *13*, 75–82.

VERBRUGGE, R. R., & McCARRELL, N. S. Metaphoric comprehension: Studies in reminding and resembling. *Cognitive Psychology*, 1977, *9*, 494–533.

VERNON, M. Relationships of language to the thinking process. *Archives of General Psychiatry*, 1967, *16*, 325–333.

VERNON, M., & KOH, S. D. Early manual communication and deaf children's achievements. *American Annals of the Deaf*, 1970, *115*, 527–535.

Voix et images de France. Paris: Didier, 1958.

Von FRISCH, K. [*The dance language and orientation of bees*] (C. E. Chadwick, trans.). Cambridge, Mass.: Belknap Press, 1967.

WAKEFIELD, J. A., BRADLEY, P. E., LEE YOM, B. H., & DOUGHTIE, E. B. Language switching and constituent structure. *Language and Speech*, 1975, *18*, 14–19.

WALLACE, A. F. C., & ATKINS, J. The meaning of kinship terms. *American Anthropologist*, 1960, *62*, 58–80.

WALSH, L. *Read Japanese today.* Rutland, Vt.: Charles E. Tuttle, 1969.

WANNER, E. *On remembering, forgetting, and understanding sentences.* The Hague: Mouton, 1974.

WARDHAUGH, R. *Introduction to linguistics.* New York: McGraw-Hill, 1972.

WARRINGTON, E. K. The selective impairment of semantic memory. *Quarterly Journal of Experimental Psychology*, 1975, *27*, 1–23.

WASON, P. C. The contexts of plausible denial. *Journal of Verbal Learning and Verbal Behavior*, 1965, *4*, 7–11.

WATSON, J. B. Psychology as the behaviorist views it. *Psychological Review*, 1913, *20*, 158–177.

WATSON, J. B. *Behaviorism.* Chicago: University of Chicago Press, 1930.

WEBBER, N. E. Pictures and words as stimuli in learning foreign language responses. *Journal of Psychology*, 1978, *98*, 57–63.

WEINREICH, U. Explorations in semantic theory. In T. Sebeok (Ed.), *Current trends in linguistics 3.* The Hague: Mouton, 1966.

WEINREICH, U. Explorations in semantic theory. In D. D. Steinberg & L. A. Jakobovits (Eds.), *Semantics: An interdisciplinary reader in philosophy, linguistics, and psychology.* New York: Cambridge University Press, 1971.

WEPMAN, J. A., BOCK, R. D., JONES, L. V., & VanPELT, D. Psycholinguistic study of apha-

sia: A revision of the question of anomia. *Journal of Speech and Hearing Disorders,* 1956, *21,* 468–477.

WERNER, H., & KAPLAN, B. *Symbol formation: An organismic-developmental approach to the psychology of language and the expression of thought.* New York: John Wiley, 1963.

WEXLER, K., & ROMNEY, A. K. *Some cognitive implications derived from multidimensional scaling.* Paper presented at the Mathematics Social Science Board Advanced Research Seminar, Irvine, Calif., 1969.

WHORF, B. L. *Language, thought, and reality.* Cambridge, Mass.: M.I.T. Press, 1956.

WICKENS, D. D. Characteristics of word encoding. In A. Melton & E. Martin (Eds.), *Coding processes in human memory.* Washington, D.C.: Winston, 1972.

WILKINS, A., & MOSCOVITCH, M. Selective impairment of semantic memory after temporal lobectomy. *Neuropsychologica,* 1978, *16,* 73–79.

WILLERMAN, B., & MELVIN, B. Reservations about the keyword mnemonic. *Canadian Modern Language Review,* 1979, *35,* 443–453.

WIMER, C., & LAMBERT, W. E. The differential effects of word and object stimuli on the learning of paired associates. *Journal of Experimental Psychology,* 1959, *57,* 31–36.

WINOGRAD, E., COHEN, C., & BARRESI, J. Memory for concrete and abstract words in bilingual speakers. *Memory and Cognition,* 1976, *4,* 323–329.

WINOKUR, S. *A primer of verbal behavior: An operant view.* Englewood Cliffs, N.J.: Prentice-Hall, Inc., 1976.

WITMER, L. R. The association value of three-place consonant syllables. *Journal of Genetic Psychology,* 1935, *47,* 337–359.

WOLLEN, K. A., WEBER, A., & LOWRY, D. Bizarreness versus interaction of mental images as determinants of learning. *Cognitive Psychology,* 1972, *3,* 518–523.

WOOD, C. C., GOFF, W. R., & DAY, R. S. Auditory evoked potentials during speech perception. *Science,* 1971, *173,* 1248–1251.

WOODWORTH, R. S. *Experimental psychology.* New York: Henry Holt, 1938.

WOODWORTH, R. S., & SCHLOSBERG, H. *Experimental psychology.* New York: Henry Holt, 1954.

WORTHINGTON, A. G. Differential rates of dark adaptation to "taboo" and "neutral" stimuli. *Canadian Journal of Psychology,* 1964, *18,* 257–268.

YAMADORI, A., & IKUMURA, G. Central (or conduction) aphasia in a Japanese patient. *Cortex,* 1975, *11,* 73–82.

YNGVE, V. A model and an hypothesis for language structure. *Proceedings of the American Philosophical Society,* 1960, *104,* 444–466.

YUILLE, J. C., & PAIVIO, A. Abstractness and recall of connected discourse. *Journal of Experimental Psychology,* 1969, *82,* 467–471.

ZAIDEL, E. Concepts of cerebral dominance in the split brain: Lexical organization in the right hemisphere. In P. Buser & A. Rougel-Buser (Eds.), *Cerebral correlates of conscious experience.* Amsterdam: Elsevier, 1977.

ZAJONC, R. B. Response suppression in perceptual defense. *Journal of Experimental Psychology,* 1962, *64,* 206–214.

ZAJONC. R. B. Attitudinal effects of mere exposure. *Journal of Personality and Social Psychology Monograph Supplement,* 1968, *9,* 1–27.

ZIMMERMAN, B. J., & ROSENTHAL, T. L. Observational learning of rule-governed behavior by children. *Psychological Bulletin,* 1974, *81,* 29–42.

ZIPF, G. K. *The psycho-biology of language,* Boston: Houghton-Mifflin, 1935.

ZIPF, G. K. The meaning-frequency relationship of words. *Journal of General Psychology,* 1945, *33,* 251–256.

Grateful acknowledgement is made to the following sources for permission to reproduce tables and figures:

Table 5-2: J. Deese, "On the structure of associative meaning," *Psychological Review* (1962), 69: 161–75, © 1962 by the American Psychological Association. Reprinted by permission.

Figure 5-10: D. R. Olson, "Language and thought: aspects of a cognitive theory of semantics", *Psychological Review* (1970), 77: 257–73, © 1970 by the American Psychological Association. Reprinted by permission.

Figure 6-1: Based on Figure 3, "Some results of research on speech perception" by A. M. Liberman. *Journal of the Acoustical Society of America*, 1957, *29*, 117–23.

Figure 6-2: Adapted from J. Morton, "Interaction of information in word recognition," *Psychological Review* (1969), 76: 165–78, © 1969 by the American Psychological Association. Reprinted by permission.

Figure 6-3: Adapted from J. Morton, "Interaction of information in word recognition", *Psychological Review* (1969), 76: 165–78, © 1969 by the American Psychological Association. Reprinted by permission.

Figure 6-4: After Miller, Bruner, and Postman, "Familiarity of letter sequences and tachistoscopic identification." *Journal of Genetic Psychology*, 1954, *50*, 129–39.

Figure 6-8: From G. A. Miller and S. Isard, "Some perceptual consequences of linguistic rules." *Journal of Verbal Learning and Verbal Behavior*, 1963, *2*, 217–28.

Table 7-1: G. A. Miller, "Some psychological studies of grammar," *American Psychologist* (1962), 17: 748–62, © 1962 by the American Psychological Association. Reprinted by permission.

Table 7-2: From P. B. Gough, "Grammatical transformations and speed of understanding." *Journal of Verbal Learning and Verbal Behavior*, 1965, *4*, 107–11.

Table 7-3: From P. C. Wason, "The contexts of plausible denial." *Journal of Verbal Learning and Verbal Behavior*, 1965, *4*, 7–11.

Table 8-1: I. Kusyszyn and A. Paivio, "Transition probability, word order, and noun abstractness in the learning of adjective-noun paired associates," *Journal of Experimental Psychology* (1966), 71: 800–805, © 1966 by the American Psychological Association. Reprinted by permission.

Figure 8-2: From N. F. Johnson, "The psychological reality of phase-structure rules." *Journal of Verbal Learning and Verbal Behavior*, 1965, *4*, 469–75.

Figure 10-1: H. L. Rheingold, J. L. Gewirtz, and H. W. Ross, "Social conditions of vocalizations in the infant," *Journal of Comparative & Physiological Psychology* (1959), 52: 68–73, © 1969 by the American Psychological Association. Reprinted by permission.

Figure 10-2: G. R. Kiss, "Grammatical word classes: a learning process and its simulation", in G. H. Bower (Ed), *The psychology of learning and motivation*, Vol. 7, Academic Press, 1973.

Figure 10-3: S. D. Moeser and A. S. Bregman, "Imagery and language acquisition," *Journal of Verbal Learning and Verbal Behavior* (1973), 21: 91–98.

Table 10-1: Reprinted with permission of Macmillan Publishing Co., Inc. from Roger W. Brown, *Psycholinguistics.* Copyright © 1970 by The Free Press, a division of Macmillan Publishing Co., Inc.

Table 10-2: From Fraser, Bellugi, and Brown, "Control of Grammar in comprehension and production." *Journal of Verbal Learning and Verbal Behavior*, 1963, *2*, 121–35.

Figure 13-1: Adapted from R. C. Atkinson and M. R. Rough, "Application of the mnemonic keyword method to the acquisition of a Russian vocabulary," *Journal of Experimental Psychology: Human Learning and Memory* (1975), 1: 126–33, © 1975 by The American Psychological Association. Reprinted by permission.

Figure 13-2: A. Paivio and A. Desrochers, "Effects of an imagery mnemonic of second language recall and comprehension, *Canadian Journal of Psychology* (1979), 33: 17–28, copyright © 1979 by the Canadian Psychological Association. Reprinted by permission.

Table 13-1 and 13-2: A. Paivio and A. Desrochers, "Effects of an imagery mnemonic of second language recall and comprehension, *Canadian Journal of Psychology* (1979), 33: 17–28, copyright © 1979, Canadian Psychological Association. Reprinted by permission.

Figure 14-2: Blissymbolics © used herein. Blissymbolics Communication Institute 1980. Toronto, Canada. Ⓑ indicates a symbol which differs from the C. K. Bliss version either in symbol form or accompanying wording or a new BCI symbol authorized in the absence of requested comment from C. K. Bliss.

Figure 14-4: Reprinted from Eleanor Gibson and Harry Levin, *The Psychology of Reading*, by permission of the MIT Press, Cambridge, Mass.

Figures 15-4 and 15-5: Reprinted from Schmitt and Worden, eds., *The Neurosciences: Third Study Program* by permission of MIT Press, Cambridge, Mass.

index